VOLUME 2

PROPERTY RIGHTS AND

ECONOMIC BEHAVIOR

THE COLLECTED WORKS OF
Armen A. Alchian

VOLUME 2

PROPERTY RIGHTS AND

ECONOMIC BEHAVIOR

EDITED AND WITH AN INTRODUCTION

BY DANIEL K. BENJAMIN

LIBERTY FUND

Indianapolis

This book is published by Liberty Fund, Inc.,
a foundation established to encourage study of the
ideal of a society of free and responsible individuals.

The cuneiform inscription that serves as our logo and
as the design motif for our endpapers is the earliest-known
written appearance of the word "freedom" (*amagi*), or "liberty."
It is taken from a clay document written about 2300 B.C.
in the Sumerian city-state of Lagash.

10 09 08 07 06 C 5 4 3 2 1

10 09 08 07 06 P 5 4 3 2 1

Library of Congress Cataloging-in-Publication Data
Alchian, Armen Albert, 1914–
Property rights and economic behavior / Armen A. Alchian ; edited and with an introduction by
Daniel K. Benjamin.
p. cm. — (The collected works of Armen A. Alchian ; v. 2)
Includes bibliographical references and index.
ISBN-13: 978-0-86597-634-4 (alk. paper)
ISBN-10: 0-86597-634-1 (alk. paper)
ISBN-13: 978-0-86597-635-1 (pbk. : alk. paper)
ISBN-10: 0-86597-635-X (pbk. : alk. paper)
1. Property. 2. Right of property. 3. Law and economics. 4. Economics.
I. Benjamin, Daniel K. II. Title.
HB701.A377 2006
306.3'2—dc22   2005044683

LIBERTY FUND, INC.
8335 Allison Pointe Trail, Suite 300
Indianapolis, Indiana 46250-1684

CONTENTS

INTRODUCTION

This is the second of two volumes that bring together Armen Alchian's collected works. Alchian is generally regarded as being (along with Ronald Coase and Harold Demsetz) one of the founders of the economic study of property rights. The papers in this volume make it clear that this reputation is fully justified. Alchian's *Wall Street Journal* editorial "Of Golf, Capitalism and Socialism" is set as a preface for this volume in part because I did not want it to get lost among the hundreds of other pages. But I have given it a prominent placement also because it captures so much of Alchian's style and personality, his irreverence and wit—and, especially, his love of golf. Remove the byline, and everyone who knows Alchian would nonetheless know that he had authored it.[1]

The initial paper in this volume, "Some Economics of Property," contains some material that is duplicated in published papers also included in this volume. Indeed, the discussion in this paper on the importance of the transferability of rights shows up in two other papers in the first section of this volume. Despite Alchian's lucid analysis of this issue, a remarkable number of people still miss the point: the freedom to acquire and dispose of property rights plays a fundamental role in ensuring that assets reach and remain in their highest valued uses. This fact alone warranted a bit of repetition here.

There were two other reasons for including this unpublished initial paper. First, it was written at a time when there literally was no other economic literature on this topic. Alchian and William Meckling began talking about some of these issues during the 1950s at RAND, where both were consultants in the economics department. They were trying to induce people in the engineering department at RAND to do some work with the economics group, but the engineers felt that they would not receive in their "home" department proper credit for their efforts. Alchian and Meckling struggled with various schemes that RAND might implement for awarding "points" for work done outside one's home department. But they soon realized that unless these points could be exchanged for goods that were valuable to other people, they were funda-

---

1. Armen A. Alchian, "Of Golf, Capitalism and Socialism," *Wall Street Journal*, July 13, 1977, sec. A.

mentally worthless. At about the same time, Alchian stumbled upon *History of English Law Before the Time of Edward I*, which traces the history of the original common law development of property rights. Alchian dropped the effort to implement a point scheme at RAND, but he became intrigued with the economics of property rights. This paper on the subject shows him struggling with issues that today either are taken for granted as settled or have been swept under the rug because they are simply too difficult to solve—at least for now.[2]

A second reason for including this paper is that, unadorned by the "cleanup" that accompanies papers before publication, it vividly illustrates Alchian's approach to problems, a method of attack well characterized by Susan Woodward, his coauthor on several occasions. As she put it at the 2001 Conference of the International Society for New Institutional Economics: "[T]he Alchian approach is 'Oh, here's an idea. Let's walk around the idea and see what it looks like from all of its sides. Let's tip it over and see what's under it and what kind of noise it makes when you turn it over. Let's light a fire under it and just see what happens. Drop it ten stories.'"[3] This approach, which is perhaps the dominating feature of personal discourse on economics with Alchian, is often hidden by the polish of his published papers.

Alchian is also characterized by a remarkable openness to new ideas and a willingness to learn from errors—whether they are his or someone else's. This may be nowhere more evident than in his work on the theory of the firm. In the paper with Harold Demsetz, "Production, Information Costs, and Economic Organization," the firm is seen as a means of taking advantage of teamwork, or synergy, as some might call it: Two people are individually incapable of lifting a heavy box, but together they can move it easily. If it is difficult for each to discern whether the other is doing his "fair share" in the lifting, it may be in their joint interest to hire someone to monitor their behavior and to punish anyone who does not perform as agreed. To ensure that the monitor does his job, he is assigned the rights to any output left over after the lifters are paid. The three individuals become a "firm," with an owner and two employees.[4]

2. Armen A. Alchian, "Some Economics of Property," RAND Corporation, P-2316, May 26, 1961; Sir Frederick Pollock and Frederic William Maitland, *History of English Law Before the Time of Edward I* (London: Smith Elder, 1903).

3. *ISNIE Newsletter* 3 (Fall 2001): 14.

4. Armen A. Alchian and Harold Demsetz, "Production, Information Costs, and Economic Organization," *American Economic Review* 62 (December 1972): 777–95.

Within a few years, Alchian realized that there were important examples of firms that existed for yet another reason. When an economic agent makes a highly specific investment in a joint venture with another individual or firm, an investment that may not cheaply be withdrawn, the agent is subject to what is called the "holdup" problem: The other party to the contract may refuse to continue to perform his obligations unless payments are renegotiated to favor him. As explained in "Vertical Integration, Appropriable Rents, and the Competitive Contracting Process," this risk can be avoided if the agent owns all the dependent resources under the umbrella of what we call the firm.[5]

Alchian's thinking continued to evolve. The result was a pair of papers with Woodward, which integrated the approaches taken in the earlier papers to produce a much more unified view not only of the firm, but of the entire panoply of contracting arrangements seen in the marketplace. These papers also brought coherence to several previously chaotic strands of the economics literature, and many of the other papers in this section can be seen as applications of the unified framework at which Alchian arrived.[6]

Some of Alchian's earliest work on property rights took economic analysis outside of the traditional profit-maximizing firm, namely, government agencies and nonprofit organizations. The first of his papers in this area was his justly famous article on tenure, which presented a radical view of an institution near and dear to the heart of most academics.[7] Alchian's argument is that tenure has nothing to do with protecting academic freedom *per se*, and everything to do with the fact that universities are nonprofit organizations subsidized by noncustomer income sources. In a world of for-profit education, the market would protect professors from the decisions of academic administrators who might otherwise purge them for espousing unpopular ideas; tenure would be unnecessary and counterproductive. The timing and revolutionary nature of this view explains why I chose to include the short piece that imme-

---

5. Benjamin Klein, Kenneth Crawford, and Armen A. Alchian, "Vertical Integration, Appropriable Rents, and the Competitive Contracting Process," *Journal of Law and Economics* 21 (October 1978): 297–326.

6. Armen A. Alchian and Susan Woodward, "Reflections on the Theory of the Firm," *Journal of Institutional and Theoretical Economics* 143 (March 1987): 110–36; "The Firm Is Dead; Long Live the Firm: A Review Article of Oliver Williamson's *The Economic Institutions of Capitalism*," *Journal of Economic Literature* 26 (March 1988): 65–79.

7. "Private Property and the Relative Cost of Tenure," in *The Public Stake in Union Power*, ed. P. D. Bradley (Charlottesville: University of Virginia Press, 1959), 350–71.

diately follows.[8] Although "Economics of Tenure" is drawn essentially verbatim from the "Relative Cost of Tenure," it was published—unsigned—in the UCLA Daily Bruin student newspaper in 1963, not long before Angela Davis joined (and was then fired from) the UCLA philosophy faculty, and not long before an attempt was made to bomb the offices of the UCLA economics department. I make no claim that "Economics of Tenure" had any causal link to these events; still, I believe the article is worth preserving, given the historical context of its appearance.

I think it is fair to say that until Alchian's seminal work on government and nonprofit organizations, the standard treatment of government was to assume that its goal was to maximize some sort of "social welfare function"—to do the right thing for the right reasons. Nonprofit organizations were either modeled analogously or simply ignored. Alchian revolutionized this literature by starting with the recognition that all decisions are made by individuals, even those decisions transmitted by committees or expressed in legislative votes. He noted that the wealth-maximization objective attributed to conventional business firms was explicitly suppressed for government agencies and nonprofit organizations, but that individual decision making could not be. Hence he analyzed the actions of these entities as being the result of the constrained choices of the individuals who populated them. What made the analysis so powerful, however, was that Alchian saw how to make the utility-maximization hypothesis operational in this setting: The crucial element was to discern how and when the constraints faced by government and nonprofit organization decision-makers changed and then to use basic economic principles to deduce the implied changes in their choices. It is a methodology that continues to dominate the literature today.

Daniel K. Benjamin
Clemson University
2005

8. "Economics of Tenure," UCLA Daily Bruin, April 4, 1963, 5–8.

OF GOLF, CAPITALISM AND SOCIALISM

A puzzle has been solved. Despite their intense interest in sports, no golf courses exist in the Socialist-Communist bloc. Why is golf solely in capitalist societies? Because it is not merely a sport. It is an activity, a lifestyle, a behavior, a manifestation of the essential human spirit. Golf's ethic, principles, rules and procedures of play are totally capitalistic. They are antithetical to socialism. Golf requires self-reliance, independence, responsibility, integrity and trust. No extenuation is granted misfortune, mistake or incompetence. No second chance. Like life, it is often unfair and unjust, with uninsurable risks. More than any other sport, golf exploits the whole capitalist spirit.

A golfer is his own creator, his own destroyer. He plays his own ball. It is a contest against Nature, by, and yet against, himself. No scapegoat can be found—no socializing of skill or consequences. No opponent's or partner's skill or clumsiness affects his performance. Tennis has an opponent on whom one can rely for aid or error. Football, with many partners and many opponents, is more socialistic.

Randomness of fortunes in golf, as in life and investment, defies specification, calculation or insurance. Rolling into a divot mark, getting a bad bounce or lie in a bunker is part of the game. The game even has a name for this unfairness—"rub of the green." Like illness or disaster it is to be borne without relief. The unfairness of golf is like that of capitalism. Some risks and hazards are foreseeable. Bunkers, trees, lakes and wind cunningly offer a rewarding or disastrous gamble or test resistance to temptation. A golfer plays his own style and reaps his own rewards—or consequences. Whatever causes misfortune makes no difference. He alone bears the consequences. No socializing of disaster or success.

No second chances. Every stroke counts in golf. In other activities, second and even third chances are given. Two serves in tennis, two free throws to make one in basketball, three strikes in baseball, four downs in football. No later act

Reprinted, by permission of the author, from *Wall Street Journal*, July 13, 1977, sec. A.

or good fortune will cancel earlier misfortunes. But later misfortune will cancel earlier good performance.

Honor and integrity are always at stake. A golfer monitors himself with no possibility for a stroke to be uncounted. Any temptation to dishonesty is thwarted by the impossibility of lying to one's self successfully. You live with what you do, not with what you may say you did. No umpire calls errors; no umpire judges performance. The game is purely objective. A stroke was taken or it wasn't; the ball is out of bounds or it isn't; on the green or it isn't; in the cup or it isn't.

How elegantly one performs is irrelevant. No A's for effort—only for results. Only the number of strokes counts, not how you did it. Results—not intentions, or procedure—count. How thoroughly capitalistic.

The game is unreliable. Disaster strikes in the midst of good performance. Confidence is shaken. Was it luck? Deterioration in ability? What change could be made, if any? As in capitalistic society, those persisting questions are answered privately with responsibility for consequences yours alone. The reward for good performance—whether by real skill or good luck—is insecure. If due to increased skill, a new reference base is established, and elusive improvement remains the goal. To do better—always better—is the goal. How powerfully capitalistic and antisocialist.

Antisocialist, but not antisocial. More, it is individualist and civilized. A golfer is courteous to other golfers. He does not distract others from their best play. He does not gain—and more important—does not lose by success, or failure, of others.

Golf is conservative. Rules change slowly; some never. Ancient and honorable customs must enhance survival values if they have withstood the test of time.

The socialist spirit, so pervasive in other areas, has tried to invade golf. Handicaps are proposed to equalize results. But a true golfer shuns handicap play. At best it is to him only an index—a prestige—of ability. Efforts to make competition more equal or "fair" are diseases that would have killed a less capitalistic game. The socialists have also sought to reduce the penalties for misadventure—the two-stroke penalty for a ball out of bounds or lost. A two-stroke penalty for a ball lost because of poor eyesight or because of weeds was deemed unfair. But not by the true golfer who understands the reasons. The game withstood that attempt and the conventional penalty has been restored.

Match play was introduced to permit partners or opponents to save one from himself. But the true golfer plays for his own score. What his playing companions do is of no interest, either during or after play.

Even in the beginning of golf we have evidence. Who but the self-reliant individualist Scots, the progenitors of Adam Smith, could create a game so congenial to the capitalist society and mentality. And at this end of history, who have become the most recent and avid devotees of golf? The Japanese and nationalist Chinese. Is more evidence required to demonstrate that golf is the spirit of capitalism?

Looking into the dim future, if golf is ever to enter in the rifts of the Socialist bloc, surely it will be where the latent, but suppressed, capitalistic spirit is strongest—in the valleys of Soviet Armenia. Actually, seven courses exist in Czechoslovakia, holdovers from pre–World War II society with 1,000 members—only 160 per course. Is it surprising the Czechs are the most troublesome people now behind the curtain?

1

THE ECONOMIC THEORY
OF PROPERTY RIGHTS

SOME ECONOMICS OF PROPERTY

CHAPTER 1. PROPERTY AND THE PURSUIT OF UTILITY

1.1. Introduction

Economics developed, in part, from attempts to interpret individual behavior in coordinated group action in terms of social consequences. The self-interest—or more generally, the utility-maximizing—postulate succeeded in implying for a free-enterprise private property economy correlated cooperative action among individuals with conflicting interests—i.e., without harmonious ends. The conflict of interest only superficially appeared as a harmony of ends, because individuals were induced by greater satisfaction of individual desires to cooperate in a mutually beneficial manner. At the same time, some institutional arrangements do not seem to have successfully appealed to private interests as a method of achieving some *organizational* goal. The relation between appeal to private interests and the organizational goals seems to have been left undeveloped. Thus Schumpeter reminds us that "the social meaning or function of parliamentary activity is no doubt to turn out legislation and, in part administrative measures. But in order to understand how democratic politics serve this social end, we must start from the competitive struggle for power and office and realize that the social function is fulfilled, as it were, incidentally— in the same sense as production is incidental to making profits."[1] In the same vein, Anthony Downs writes:

> Because every government is run by men, and because all men must be privately motivated to carry out their social functions, the structural relation between the function of government and the motives of those who run it is a crucial determinant of its behavior . . . Though explicit theories of government behavior are rare in economics, the remarks of several normative theorists reveal a common supposition that government's proper function is the maximization of social welfare. However, these theorists do not

Reprinted from RAND Corp., P-2316, May 26, 1961.

1. Joseph A. Schumpeter, *Capitalism, Socialism, and Democracy* (New York: Harper & Brothers, 1950), 282.

explain how the men who run governments are motivated to carry out this function. Thus they fail to apply the self-interest axiom to governments, although it is the foundation of analysis concerning private economic agents.[2]

Without much effort one can sense the possible applicability of the above argument to corporations, state-owned businesses, public schools, non-profit corporations, monopolies, fraternal clubs, governments, labor unions, and even the family.[3]

If it is true that the rewards-costs systems vary among these institutions, with economic theory one ought to be able to derive these differences as implied forms of behavior. Since the basic methodology in economic analysis in deriving implications is the individual's maximizing of his utility subject to constraints, and since it is assumed that the people operating in these various areas are basically similar in certain fundamental attributes of their utility or preference patterns, one must look to the nature of constraints for a differentiating factor. And it appears that the constraints do differ in the form of property rights that constrain the individual's realm of choice. The basic issue studied in this paper is first the nature and specification of these constraints on one's behavior. This will enable us to apply utility theory—the same theory that is applied to ordinary consumer goods and consumer behavior—to a wider class of behavior. The very same assumptions will be used as in ordinary consumer choice theory, but the commodities will be changed. Instead of bread, butter, meat, eggs, and champagne, we shall incorporate any or all desirable attributes or entities (e.g., prestige, friends, comforts). And, as hinted, a more general form of constraint than the usual budget restriction will be used. But first, to avoid misunderstanding, we briefly outline what we mean by utility maximization.

1.2. Meaning of Utility Maximizing

To say that a person is a utility maximizer is an esoteric way to say that he is a chooser or preferrer. As we shall see, nothing whatever is implied about welfare or "utilitarianism" or selfishness or greediness or sole concentration on "money." Nor is he assumed to be fully informed about the actual conse-

2. Anthony Downs, *An Economic Theory of Democracy* (New York: Harper & Brothers, 1957), 290, 293.

3. In fact, Adam Smith's *Wealth of Nations* is essentially a long discussion of the different kinds of individual behavior induced by the different rewards-costs systems of various

quences of the choice. He may be elegantly misinformed and bitterly disappointed with the consequences. Nevertheless he makes a choice on the basis of what *he* thinks the possible outcomes might be; i.e., he expresses preferences. Even so general an assumption as this has refutable implications. For one thing, it implies that a person will not always be willing to let others have the right to make choices for him.

Much more content can be obtained if the entities affecting one's utility (involved in any choice) can be classed as "desired" or "undesired." Once this is done it can be asserted that if a person is presented with a new possibility containing more of at least one of the desirable entities and the same of everything else, then he will choose the new over the old. This is, of course, merely the standard postulate in standard consumer theory wherein it is asserted that more is preferred to less—a consequence of the empirical assumption that all the entities considered *can* be categorized as "desired" or "undesired."

The next postulate is that entities in the desired set—and momentarily we assume that any entity referred to will be in the desired set—are substitutable. This means that for a *reduction* (not necessarily elimination) of any one of them, there is a set of incremental amounts of *some* others that will offset the reduced utility. This substitution postulate is the keystone of the economic theory of consumption and production. And with it is derived the classic demand proposition that the demand for *any* superior good (and for some, though not necessarily all inferior goods) is a negative function of its price.[4]

1.3. Self-Interest

We digress momentarily into side issues involving both substance and semantics. By self-interest we mean *precisely* no more and no less than utility-maximizing behavior. Objections are sometimes made to the utility-maximizing or self-interest postulate: Self-interest may be all right for some people and for some consumers' goods, but in general it is too restrictive to be widely applicable. The existence of charitable or philanthropic behavior refutes

---

kinds of institutions. His preference for one of these was so pointed that the general approach of his book is often overlooked. Furthermore, he did not present a systematic or theoretic structure for his analysis—even though he used economic theory.

4. The authors are prepared to go further and assume empirically that the demand for each and every good is a negative function of its price—at least until they are presented contradictory evidence. A superior good is one that is more demanded as wealth or income increases.

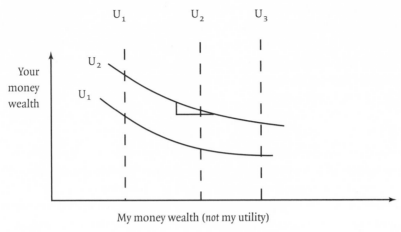

FIGURE 1.

self-interest. But this objection is wrong. The utility-maximization postulate means simply that the person chooses according to what he thinks will be the best result—where what is also included in his utility (or preference) scale are other people's situations (or utilities) as he judges them. "Self-interest" does not reject charity and philanthropy. Nor does it assume that any person will reduce his utility to help someone else. That would be inconsistent with utility maximizing. Instead of regarding my utility as substitutable with yours, my utility can be assumed to increase with increments in those entities that increase your utility, as I judge it. In other words, I am "better off" when you, too, are "better off."

Various possibilities can be shown by the indifference or utility curves in Figure 1.

Along the horizontal scale is measured the level of my money wealth, and along the vertical, your money wealth. My utility isoquants (or preference level) as functions of both your wealth and my wealth might be vertical dotted lines, with high levels of utility to the right. This would mean that my utility is not dependent on the level of your money wealth (and hence your utility as I judge it). But suppose my utility increased when yours did (as I judge yours). My utility isoquants would be negatively sloped, as indicated by the solid lines; I would be willing to give up some wealth in order to increase your wealth (and hence your utility). For example, if the slope of the isoquant were −1, I would be willing to give up a dollar if you were to get it. If the slope were −10.00, I would just be willing to pay $1.00 if somehow that would enable you to receive an increment of $10.00. All three possibilities portray a "selfish" person—a utility maximizer. If one defined a selfish person only as one who is not at all interested in other people's utility or situations, then only the vertical-dotted-line person is selfish. But he could be defined as a person whose utility isoquant's slope is steeper (less) than −1.00 (say, −10.00). Selfishness can be defined in several sensible ways—none of which violates the utility-maximizing postulate, and some of which are consistent with charity and profound interest in other people's situations.[5] All are consistent with the choice being made by oneself, rather than by someone else. A person is selfish in the sense that he wants to make the choices. (We prefer to call this "utility maximizing" rather than "self-interest," although we admit no logical basis for the choice.) Any person may, in considering his utility, take into account benefit to others, and in considering the costs, he may, if he wants, take into account not only his costs but those possibly imposed on others (smoke example). He is perfectly free to be humanitarian, charitable, socially conscious, or "whatever you choose to call it." But as long as he prefers to make his decisions, he is a utility maximizer. And this does not imply "truth by definition," as we shall see by ending our digression and returning to the essential proposition that the lower the cost, the greater the amount of the activity.

As a case in point, Becker has analyzed the incident of "discrimination" among employees and employers with respect to their non-monetary quality (color, race, personality, religion, etc.).[6] Treating people as utility maximizers enables one to consider not only the monetary productivities (on which attention would be focused if they were treated as wealth maximizers) but also the non-monetary productivities (as in consumers' goods, friendship, prestige, etc.). Just as in his consumption decisions, a man will in his business consider both non-monetary and monetary productivities. Becker shows that the relative hiring rates of employees, who are heavily endowed with non-monetary sources of utility, should exceed at equal money wage rates what they would have been if only monetary aspects are considered. The greater the non-monetary productivity, the greater the amount employed.

The addition of non-monetary attributes to the monetary productivities also requires replacing the profit-maximizing by the utility-maximizing crite-

---

5. See, for more elaboration of philanthropy under "selfishness," Gary Becker's The Economics of Philanthropy (unpublished).

6. Gary S. Becker, The Economics of Discrimination (Chicago: University of Chicago Press, 1956).

rion. A person may grow orchids or breed Thoroughbreds, and with fore-knowledge lose money every year, if the non-monetary factors increase utility more than the money loss reduces it—exactly as when he plays golf instead of "working." Why deny that a businessman will sacrifice any gain in money wealth for a gain in leisure, relaxation, health, life, or peace? A businessman is a utility maximizer if at least one of the components in his utility function con-sists of something other than salable private property. If he is allowed to vary any such component of his utility function—e.g., leisure, wife's attitude, tran-quility—as a possible alternative to an increase in property, he cannot be a profit maximizer. For as soon as any source of utility other than "property" is admitted into the controllable components of his utility function, and as soon as these affect any choice, utility maximization replaces wealth maximization. If, and only if, the choice among entities or actions involves nothing whatever except monetary or income-producing attributes, then a wealth-seeking or -maximizing postulate is *equivalent* to the utility-maximizing postulate.[7]

Consider the inevitable objection: How can business behavior directed toward increasing private property be handled under utility maximizing? Is it not a standard postulate that unless firms make profits (increase their private property) they will go out of business? Therefore, does not profit seeking over-ride all other conditions by sheer fact of its being a survival condition? The re-sponse was given long ago by various economists (e.g., Knight): business firms may, on the average, be wealth losers.

Businessmen may exist even though the expectation is negative. And it is not merely that the variance around the expectation is large enough to attract "gamblers" rather than insurer types; instead businessmen may be those people for whom there is love of gambling and risk-taking, for whom the game of business is as much a joy as playing poker or betting on the horse races. Some poker players make positive gains, but it does not follow that these play-ers must be those for whom playing poker is "work" in the sense of utility re-duction. Similarly the existence of positive profits in business does not prove that it is a compensation necessary to offset the "work" aspects. It may be the

7. The kinds of choices open involve (1) exchange of one form of income-producing private property for another (business activity), or (2) exchange of one form of non-monetary entity for monetary property (consumer behavior), or (3) exchange of one form of non-monetary entity for another non-monetary entity (social activity). All of these in-volve utility maximizing. The first one only *appears* not to, because it is assumed that the entities exchanged have no non-monetary attributes of any utility relevance whatsoever.

prize in an enjoyable game—a game that would be played even if losses were certain. But *the greater the losses, or the less the profits, the lower the survival rate.* This is the principle that substitutes for the "all or none" discrete principle that says survival is sure if profits are positive, and doomed if profits are negative, or that profits are necessary for survival. The distinction between business and hobbies or consumption, for example, is blurred—not by confusion, but by recognition of the common principle of behavior: "the higher the cost, the less the activity."

1.4. Nature of Constraints

This is all conventional enough when the costs or constraints within which a person is operating or choosing are defined in terms of exchanges of private property. The direct exchange costs are borne by him, and the boundary of available choices is well defined. But different forms of property rights change the costs that are borne by him, and his choice will be different. It will be different not because different kinds of people exist under other forms of property rights or exchange institutions, but rather because of the different costs of alternative choices open to the person. One need consider only tax deductible expenses, cost-plus-fixed-fee contracts, and dining out as a guest, examples of how the true "total" costs are not borne by the chooser, to see how one's choice is biased (toward the more expensive)—simply because in these cases the cost to him of expensive items is reduced relative to that of less expensive items. Similarly, use of public property and political choices are affected by the reduced cost imposed on the individual, as we shall see later.

In general, the constraint is not simply a *private* property constraint. We have access to public parks, roads, buildings; our use of them enters our utility functions. What constrains our use of these publicly owned entities? Almost all of us, as employees, have varying degrees of control over resources "owned" by other people. Every employee uses equipment owned by his employer. From some of these he gets non-monetary products (or more or less utility). For example, as your cook, I will shop for food, but since the alternative uses to which I may put your money are severely limited, if not eliminated, I shall be tempted to buy highly processed, easy-to-prepare foods (at Green Stamp–issuing stores?) because in that way my utility is increased, and the cost of my increments of utility are not borne by me to the extent they would be if the money spent were my private property.

What is the exact nature of the constraint on a person spending money in privately owned for-profit business, in non-profit corporations, in corporations, in public utilities, in government- or state-owned institutions? More broadly, not only particular institutions within which one is operating should be worth analyzing from this point of view, but, in addition, particular entities may be classified according to the kind of property rights attachable to them. For example, the property rights assignable to land, wood, oil, and water and public roads are quite different. Insofar as different degrees of property rights imply different accessibility of the benefits and responsibility for the costs, different use patterns and manners of behavior should be expected for land, oil, wood, water, and streets (e.g., traffic etiquette). Property rights in children, wives, wives' "property," office space, etc., are highly varied. Precisely wherein do the imposed constraints differ and correspondingly induce variations in the operating decisions of the individuals concerned? Wherein do the constraints induce behavior in conformity with the formal stated objectives of the organizations, and wherein do they induce diversionary behavior? Or in familiar terms, how are private and "social" costs affected by different forms of property rights? For example, the discrepancy between private and social costs so often described as "externalities" and identified with the "private" property marketplace is *also* present in the publicly owned or political market, an implication that seems to be ignored by those who argue that government-ownership markets should replace private-ownership markets whenever important "externalities" exist in private property!

All this can be generalized by asking: What are the constraints that apply to various entities and to the various forms of property rights? How do variations in property rights affect the cost and reward systems of those who operate under them? Can one derive implications about a correlation of behavior with forms of property rights? Apparently so, because Downs, in applying the utility-maximization principle to politics, derived important testable implications, and Smith alleged and exemplified many. That they have not yet been formally tested does not detract from their importance. But on reading Downs or Smith, one will look in vain for a *measure* of the constraint that is the logical counterpart to the private wealth constraint in "mainline" economic theory. How did they circumvent this? After all, one can't even have an interesting behavior problem if everything is available.

The solution is quite simple. It involves making a distinction between the *level* or "quantity" of the constraint and the *kind* of constraint. In economics, as narrowly construed, the constraint is giving up some privately owned goods to get others. Exchange rates are costs. But "giving up" means that one's property rights in the entity are reduced. To sell a car or to have property rights in it reduced or eliminated is the same thing. To each possible entity, then, we specify a kind of set of "rights." Without specifying a measure of the total of such rights (however defined and however measured), we simply postulate that there is some total which limits each person. And we then direct attention to the marginal-exchange conditions among these rights (the counterpart to prices or costs). Even without the *specified* (but nevertheless existing) *level* of restriction on his rights, we can ask how a person's choices will respond to *changes* in the marginal-exchange ratios among these rights, whatever they may be. In conventional economics we ask how a person will vary his purchase rates of various commodities in response to changes in their money prices, costs, or exchange ratios without knowing what his level of wealth is—we assume merely that there is some limit.[8]

There is no necessity to specify a specific *measure* of the limit of the constraining power. It is adequate—for some problems—to specify under what conditions the exchange ratios of utility-affecting entities, or rights in them, change. Then with an application of the fundamental theorem—the lower the cost, the more will be taken of any desirable entity or activity—a wider realm of action should be analyzable by economic theory, which is a branch of a theory of choice.[9]

CHAPTER 2. PROPERTY

2.1. Conflicts of Interests

In a world with more than one person, conflicts of interests about the use of scarce resources are inevitable. The use, possession, and even loss of scarce resources involve consequences for people. Some of these consequences are desired and some are not. Who will determine them and who will bear them? The

---

8. Similarly in political theory Downs postulated that there was a limit that constrained a person's realm of choices or actions in the political arena, and he asked how the responses in terms of various kinds of political entities (votes, lobbying, subsidies, taxes, appointments, promises) vary in response to changes in costs of such entities.

9. How does economics differ from sociology, anthropology, or political science? It doesn't, insofar as the underlying theory is concerned. All use the utility-maximizing theory, the substitution principle, and the law of demand. But economics, narrowly construed, concentrates on those exchanges involving money on one side of the exchange. Their relationship is like that of physics and chemistry; both use the same principles and postulates. But each concentrates on a different set of manifestations.

inescapable problem to which some solution must be reached is how to resolve these conflicts of interests. A discouraging part of this problem is that there may be no criterion of a "best" solution. We can think of a "way" of resolving the conflicts of interests (and conflict of interests does not necessarily mean physical violence) as being an assignment to particular individuals of the "authority" to select any of the "authorized" uses with its resultant consequences. We shall call this a system of property rights.

The rules for resolving conflicts of interests include etiquette, custom, and laws, in addition to property rights. Etiquette applies not only to what is narrowly construed as social behavior but also to our use of property. The kinds of clothes we wear is an example. Similarly, the rules of property enter into our social behavior. Our present interest is in property rights, although many of the rules of etiquette actually are designed to emulate or produce behavior that would be observed if certain kinds of private property rights were enforceable. Whatever the system of rights may be called, competition is involved; for competition is merely the effort to improve one's position.

Property and ownership rights are rights that will be enforced for one person against other people by the state police power. The force of social opprobrium through custom or rules of etiquette in producing certain viable forms of behavior is not a source of protection of property as we use the term here— regardless of how coercive spontaneous social pressures may be for certain individuals and regardless of borderline cases. For example, the Fifth Amendment gives a person specific legal rights that will be enforced by the state against itself. But this does not mean that the force of social opprobrium is supposed to be eliminated. Property rights are those the state will protect for me against a specific class of actions of other people—not from all actions designed to influence my behavior. Exactly what should be enforced by the state and what left to spontaneous pressures are constantly under adjustment. The attempt to determine this is, of course, the arena of much debate, thought, and conflict.

2.2. Types of Consequences

Suppose that I am declared to be the person authorized to select the use of some iron bars; i.e., I am the "owner." What uses am I permitted to select? I can't convert the iron to gold because that is impossible. My "ownership" authority to use the iron bars is an authority against other people, not "nature." It is a protected right to select without having to get any further permission from any one else. And yet, since that "authority" is enforced by the state or government against all other people, I cannot say that I could use the thing without having to get any authority or permission at all. What I get in the property right, which is enforced by the government, is the authorization to select from a specified set of uses, as against such choosing by someone else.

The authorized uses are those whose consequences are somehow deemed acceptable. (To say they are acceptable does not mean they are necessarily desirable.) Suppose that for the iron bars, among the uses from which I am authorized to select is the construction of iron window grating. I may even be allowed to sell this grating to other people. One of the consequences is that some other person who owns some window glass finds the demand for window glass decreasing as people use iron grating instead, and therefore the price at which he can sell his glass goes down. His wealth is decreased consequent to my proper, authorized use of the iron; as a result, he is worse off. So far as he is concerned, the reduction of his wealth *via* the price or value effect may be just as bad as if I had broken some of his glass with my iron bars.

We have, so far, two types of consequences here: one is a value effect, and the other (usually a prohibited one) is a physical one, e.g., breaking his glass. The fact is that the former is often among the authorized consequences while the latter is not. (We will not try, at the present moment, to explain why, other than to suggest that prohibition of the former would produce results that are extremely destructive of progress and of what is usually meant by human freedom.) The value consequences can be beneficial as well as harmful to other people. I might have invented a new iron window frame, with the result that the price of window glass went up in response to increased demand. Or I might have used the iron bars for a fence between our property, which you may regard as a desirable physical change in your situation. The consequences can be good or bad, value or physical.

But the consequences to my selected use from the authorized set might have neither value nor physical effect on what you "own." For example, I may use the iron bars to build up my muscular strength. If you happen to be a "life-arranger" for other people, and if you are depressed even by the *knowledge* that I am doing things that you think I shouldn't do purely because of their effects on me and no one else, this "informational" effect on you may be as unpleasant for you as a loss of some of your own wealth. After all, we all are affected not only by our quantity of wealth but also by our friends, our prestige, and our *knowledge* of the behavior and welfare of other people.

2.2.1. Informational Costs and Benefits

Often the non-owner informational consequences are not even considered to be undesirable. If my behavior arouses your envy or covetousness, that is so much the worse for you, and since such reactions by you are not "proper," these are excluded from the realm of pertinent or influential costs insofar as the owner is concerned. Of course, everyone need not agree with that judgment. But if the members of any society somehow make that kind of judgment the dominant one, then by that simple fact those non-owner consequences are excluded from the realm of consequences that ought not be imposed on or provided to other people. "Thou shalt not steal, nor covet thy neighbor's goods. You ought to emulate his success, etc." If those are the cultural mores, then obviously certain kinds of consequences are deemed perfectly acceptable and ought not to be prohibited by property laws.

What is called improper and unethical varies from society to society and from time to time and from person to person. Socially accepted attitudes toward homosexuality, obscene literature, and religious beliefs continue to vary. What the right attitude ought to be cannot be always discerned by investigating existing property rights. But often knowledge of what is included in property rights will tell one what the prevailing attitudes are, for they are reflected in the scope of property rights in the community.

Information benefits are familiar and need no elaboration here.

2.2.2. Physical Effect Costs and Benefits

Suppose I burn some leaves and that in the process the smoke and residual elements carried aloft by the hot air are blown onto your land. I am making you bear some consequences of the use of "my" property. I dump ashes on your property, and perhaps the smoke blocks your view, smells bad, and chokes you. You might think there was something wrong with "private" property rights. The source of the difficulty lies in the restrictions or allocation of property rights—whether they are called private or not.

1. People might be allowed to burn leaves, but at the same time they might be prohibited under any circumstances from dumping ashes on other people's property.
2. Or they might be allowed to burn leaves and dump the smoke and ashes against other people's wishes.
3. Or the law might prohibit all burning of leaves.
4. Or the law might permit burning of leaves and "dumping of smoke" on

other people's property only if each other person consents willingly to the dumping of ashes on his property—in return for a payment sufficient to obtain his consent.

Which of the four is preferable? The answer is momentarily unimportant. What is important here is that the so-called smoke nuisance case is one affecting the physical attributes of other people's property. This can be prohibited, permitted at the discretion of each other person, or permitted despite the preference of each other person. Actually, in our society we find the first and third of these alternatives being adopted, probably because the second is too expensive to enforce.[10] In some communities a fee is charged for the right to burn, the implication being that this fee which is paid to the public treasury is an indirect payment to the community that more than compensates it for the physical consequence imposed on other people.

Another point of this example is that it is not the comparison or evaluation of rights of different *people* that is involved but the comparison of *kinds of rights*. It is not an interpersonal comparison. In fact, it is *intrapersonal*. Is the advantage of a right to burn leaves greater for each person than the right to that same person to keep his property free of smoke and ashes dumped on him by everyone else who burns trash? If the community were made of people with weak noses and strong throats, probably burning would be permitted, whereas if people had strong noses and weak throats it would be prohibited. If each person could individually decide whether he was willing to permit smoke and smells in return for an adequate compensation, the question could be solved in each instance on a voluntary exchange basis—which does not make that solution necessarily ideal.

2.2.3. Value Costs and Benefits
Value, or pecuniary, costs are easy to impose on other people. When undersold, when a new product is offered that attracts away customers, or when better services are offered in new locations, other people may find the value of their property rights falling. Examples are obvious enough. Some may involve value gains. Such an example is the case where I invent a more efficient orange juice freezing mechanism, thereby increasing the demand for oranges to the benefit of orange growers. Or if demand for some product increases, the price

10. We venture to suggest that the first and the third alternatives both violate what most people mean by "private" property, although whether we are right or wrong in this conjecture is not as important as the attempt to clarify the situation.

may rise in order to ration out the demand to the benefit of producers. Also, increased demand results in higher prices, and these are certainly consequences of importance for other people who must now pay higher prices and buy less. The effect of a higher price of something one buys is equivalent to physical loss, e.g., fire or theft.

Three types of consequences to the use of property are evident—(a) physical attribute changes, (b) exchange value changes, and (c) informational changes. These consequences may raise or lower the utility of the other people—those not making the particular choice of use (and consequence).[11]

From the point of view of the owner, the same classification of effects of his decisions is helpful.

1. He can choose to change the physical form—either by using it up himself or by changing it (converting iron bars to window frames, for example).
2. He can exchange it for some other property. In this case, what he is exchanging can be thought of either as the thing owned or as the property or ownership rights. It makes no difference in substance which way one views this. If I trade my pencil for your book, we may exchange the items, but we also are exchanging the choice and control rights over the item—usually symbolized and made effective by transferring the physical object or by transferring a statement to the effect that such exchange of rights has occurred, even though the physical object is not moved from person to person.
3. If he simply looks at a painting, he gets a satisfaction. Call this a "contemplative" use, involving no physical destruction or "using up." Thus possessing a pile of wood gives satisfaction even before its burning as a source of heat.

11. Customarily, the value cost or effect on a non-owner has been called a "pecuniary external diseconomy." We have divided what is customarily called technological external diseconomy into two categories, physical and informational costs of the non-owner. The names chosen are not important, but the finer distinction between physical and informational knowledge as subdivisions of "technological" effects is, we believe, worth making. Remember, we might break someone's glass or block his view (light is physical radiation to his property) or reduce the value of his glass or, without even changing the physical attributes or value, the knowledge by him of our behavior may give him such dissatisfaction that he suffers a reduction in utility. (We do not want to argue at this point the case for including the view in the physical attribute category.)

The distinction between use and consequence is one that is more of words than of substance. From this point of view the use of property is the consequence. The "owner" can choose any except a stated set of prohibited uses—or consequences—for himself. He may change its physical form, hold it for contemplation or appreciation of enjoyment as he sees fit, or exchange it (or, as we have just seen, the rights to its use). As we shall see, sometimes a person is told that his rights include choice of use—but not the right to exchange something for something else. Or he may have the right to buy and sell (exchange) but not the right to change the physical form of the item. What he buys and sells (exchanges) are property rights in various things or services.

From the "owner's" point of view—e.g., from the point of view of the person authorized to select from sanctioned uses—the distinction that is most relevant is between the right to exchange and the right to use it in any other sanctioned way. In the latter use, the utility of his selected decision may depend upon changes in a property's physical form or even its destruction (as in consumption) or upon its effects on other things he owns. For example, if I own a paintbrush, painting my house may change the house more than it changes the brush. Furthermore, whether the use involves a change in the physical attribute of something or involves "merely" a change in the state of one's knowledge or information is not crucial for our purposes.

Any choice of the "owner" can change his utility by affecting the physical attributes of what he owns. This may in turn affect the exchange value of the item.

The exchange value of any item "owned" by a person depends not only upon what it is and in what physical condition it is but upon the permissible, or authorized, uses and consequences from which an "owner" may choose. In other words, the exchange value to some owner reflects, in part, the property rights authorized for him in that item. For example, if I had a car and was told I could exchange (transfer ownership) to any other male but not to a female, or if automobiles could be driven legally for only five years and then had to be junked, the exchange value of "my" auto would be different from what it would be if such "restrictions" were not placed on it—regardless of its physical condition. Or if the law stated that my car could be lubricated or repaired only by males between 24 and 25 years who were trained in an authorized school, the value of my car would be affected (whatever its physical condition), as contrasted with the situation in which no such constraints were imposed.

The point is that the structure of property rights affects exchange values; i.e., the set of authorized uses of any item has an effect on its exchange value.

This assertion, which we have not yet derived from our analysis, seems so obvious that at the moment it probably can be made without dispute.

2.3. "Choices" of Nature—or Acts of God

So far we have written as if all consequences were the result of some person's choice. What well may be an even more important source of consequences is nature—often called an act of God. Earthquakes, fires, floods, lightning, and freezes can produce consequences as bad as though someone had used devilish powers of destruction. If an earthquake destroys a mine, oil well, or building, who bears the loss? The loss was not the result of any choice by the "owner." Why should he be the person stuck with the consequences? It wasn't his "fault." But clearly fault is neither a sufficient nor even necessary basis for assigning consequences. Even though no one was at fault, in the sense of deliberately or even accidentally causing the damage, some person or group of persons *must* bear the consequences, simply because there are fewer resources. No amount of wishful thinking, wailing, scapegoating, or hard work will change that fact. Even if there were some foresight, this would still be true. When a future first becomes "seen," or anticipated, then—at that moment—the value of existing goods will change in reflection of the foreseen change. The destruction of a building by an earthquake, or of some crop by a pest, or of some house by a fire reduces the value of the item when knowledge of the event is obtained, whether in foresight or in retrospect. Fortunate events will increase the value. The gain in value is called profit; the decrease in value is called a loss. Usually the "owner" bears these effects. This does not mean that the "owner" *should* bear these gains or losses. In some way, society may say that he should not and that, instead, everyone should bear the consequences of events that are beyond the control of any person. But whatever it says, the loss or gain must be borne by someone. The question is, "who"?

Who, in fact, does depend in part upon the property laws. In a private property system—as it is commonly conceived—the person designated as the "owner" is authorized to make a choice from a range of available choices, but he is also made responsible for bearing "owner" consequences caused by nature—in the things "owned." Non-owners are free of that responsibility, but they are stuck with "non-owner consequences." Why should consequences of unavoidable natural events be borne as though consequences of deliberate or negligent choices? Probably because it is difficult to separate true acts of God from those occurrences that are dependent upon human action and also because any incentive to avoid or reduce the effects of acts of God (e.g., lightning rods, earthquake-resistant construction) will be adversely affected. In any event, for present purposes it is sufficient to note that some consequences that must be borne are derived from a larger class of initiators or selectors than man himself.

2.4. Owner Versus Non-owner Rights

This approach to the analysis of "property" suggests that property rights should be viewed as rights of the owner to select from non-prohibited uses and consequences. The consequences can be classified according to whether they fall on the "owner" or on other people. In the latter case they are called "non-owner," or "external," consequences, and in the former they are called owner consequences. If the consequences are desirable, they are called benefits; if undesirable, they are called costs. The particular association of (a) "thing," (b) person, and (c) sanctioned set of possible choices (uses and consequences) provides the specification or statement of what the property rights are.

The property rights may be so stated that the "non-owner" or "external" effects are severely limited or are more generally permitted. This statement of what a person may not do to other people or their property is merely the complement of what he may do. Whether those people should be called the "owners" who determine the range of the sanctioned set of choices or who are protected from certain use consequences, or whether those who are allowed to make the particular choices from the sanctioned set of uses should be called the owners, is answered by the fact that the latter are called owners in our everyday legal language. The "non-owners" are protected in certain rights just as the "owners" are protected in the complementary rights. This protection of non-owners arises from the prohibition of certain choices of use and consequences. It is not a question of whose rights are paramount. It is a question of *what* rights does each person have with respect to what uses (consequences) of what things. Nor is it a question of defining property rights so that all the consequences fall to the owner. This would be impractical.

To repeat the preceding idea somewhat more bluntly: if the property laws prohibit me from using things in ways that affect your welfare, then in a sense *you* are able to exercise, through the law, control over my decisions as to what use will be made of the thing of which I was called the "owner." Who shall be called the owner? I or the rest of society? Isn't everyone an owner in some sense or other insofar as his interests are influenced in affecting the use to some degree by laws passed (in a democracy)?

We shall, nevertheless, use the word "owner" to mean the person or persons to whom the state assigns (and will protect by law and police power) authority to choose uses (of what he is said to own) with respect to certain consequences. This authority assigned to him is against other people to select from these permitted uses and consequences. All other consequences are prohibited, and should he violate this restriction, the people on whom he has imposed the forbidden consequences can expect the state to use its police power to force the violators to compensate them.

For example, we often think of *private* property rights as an authorization (right) to use what is said to be private property in any way we like so long as no one else is affected with any of the consequences. Unfortunately, the presence of a single "life-arranger" will deny this possibility, for the "life-arranger" can say he bears the consequences (informational) of your "irrational" (to him) behavior. You may correctly reply that this is absurd because this amounts to trying to let everyone be a dictator—a manifest impossibility. The fact remains that almost all actions are certain to have some consequences for other people, consequences sometimes called *external* effects, *social* costs, or *non-owner* consequences.

It has been convenient to name those rights assigned to an owner as his property rights. Your right to use what you own but not to physically damage my goods means that I have property rights in my goods. Thus property rights in my goods are, in effect, expressions of non-owner rights in the goods you own. You can't hit me with your iron bar, because either the non-owner rights over that iron bar prohibit such use—or because my self is my property, and my ownership rights would be violated by your action.

We have now come full circle. We can interpret non-owner rights as nothing more nor less than other-owner rights in their goods and things. Our external or non-owner effects are really effects on other people's property. If these effects are consequences over which they are presumed, by the content of property law, to have rights of choice, then the external effects are illegal, for they weren't at the volition of the owner.

From the point of view of one person, there are owner and non-owner rights. From a group observer's point of view, there are only owner rights—if everything is owned. In each instance, the question is What rights shall be assigned to the owner? So long as these owner rights are applicable to each and every person who may be the owner, and are not dependent upon who the owner is, only owner rights need be specified. Equality before the law provides a mutual, symmetrical interpersonal relationship between owner and non-owner rights—much like an object and its mirror reflection.

We earlier spoke of owner and non-owner consequences, because we started with an individual approach. Now, with a society or group approach, we see that the distinction is a misleading one if carried too far. We hope we have carried it only far enough to justify the current conclusion that only owner rights need be specified. This is true *if* everything of relevance or interest or value is owned, and if everyone is equal under the law of property. If some things of value are not owned, this means that no rights in them are reserved to *some* owner. In that case, everyone can and will try to use the item. Although we shall analyze this later, we momentarily note that this is exemplified by roads, water, airspace, and the radio frequency spectrum. The consequent congestion, confusion, and "irrational" use of these resources is predictable by economic theory. We also note that some of these are public property—which, as we shall see later, is in some important respects essentially unowned.[12]

2.4.1. *Partitioning of Rights to Owners*

Our discussion started with a classification of rights by the value, use, and informational consequences as produced and borne by owners or non-owners. We now expand briefly on the question of what those rights may be, aside from the right to transfer the ownership. Does an owner of a piece of land have a right to the land free of animals owned by other people? Or must the landowner fence the property to keep off other people's animals? Or if there is water running through his land in a creek, does he have rights to take water out of the creek and use it as he sees fit with no water going to the next man's land? Questions such as these have caused much conflict in man's history, and the courts have, through the centuries, varied the rights attached to ownership of the land. At one time the landowner had to fence the land to keep out other people's animals. More recently English-American law has granted the landowner the "right" to his land free of other people's animals. In other words, now the animal owners must fence their animals in, instead of the landowner fencing them out. In some western parts of the United States domestic animals can walk on roads, and road users are responsible for not harming the animals. In some other areas, the animal owner is responsible for keeping animals off the road, and if accidents occur the animal owner is liable for damages.

---

12. One last interpolative forewarning. It is not sufficient for a "satisfactory" system of ownership merely to have rights to choices of uses or consequences assigned to someone. The particular group of rights assigned to the owner of some entity—with other rights implicitly assigned to owners of other things—is crucial.

In modern city society, rights of owners of dogs and cats are paramount over land ownership rights. A landowner must fence dogs and cats out, for it is legal for dogs and cats to run over and deface the landowner's land. We are reminded of the leaf-burning example given earlier. Also we leave it to the courts to explain why cows don't have the same privileges as dogs and cats. We also leave it to future legal historians to tell whether over the centuries there is a general convergence toward "fencing out" or "fencing in." The fact that for the past 1,000 years in Western Europe the trend of rights has been toward "fencing in" does not offer much reason to believe that there is something superior about this right to "fence in" over the right to "fence out." Nor is the best rights arrangement something we can judge from generally acceptable *a priori* normative standards. Can we believe that a historical evolutionary process of survival by selection of the "fittest" types of rights assignments is operating?

Although at first sight it would appear to reasonable men that "fencing in" was superior to fencing out, and therefore that we should take hope from the apparent convergence toward that property interpretation, the history of water rights provides a less "heartening" prognosis to those people who may think that socialism, or government ownership and control of resources, is undesirable.

Many physical attributes or entities are difficult to perceive as physical ownable things. Two of the most difficult are "light" and "sound." A view is a physical attribute because light waves are. And of light there are three classes to consider: (a) natural (sun and moon) light directly incident on the earth, (b) reflected natural light from other parts of the earth, and (c) man-made light. Since light rays move, the question of whom they belong to is particularly difficult. Furthermore, should light rays be treated as separate physical entities (from land or people on which they fall) and, hence, as separate pieces of property? Or should the light be identified with or regarded as part of the land or person it hits? Typically it has been associated with the land. But we shall defer this question to much later for a more detailed analysis. For the moment, we want to deal with the kind of problem of partitioning of rights that is provoked.

If these natural light rays have long been first incident on another piece of land, can a neighbor proceed to capture them—putting the other in the shade? The answer is one of convenience. In effect, it is like trying to establish rights in long-standing historically recurrent events. In other words, when does incident light become a physical attribute of the land to which it is incident? When it in fact hits, or when it first leaves the sun destined to be incident on the land, were it not for the action of other people who may block it?

Similarly with reflected natural light. Of which piece of land, if any, shall it be considered a physical attribute? The one from which it is reflected or the one to which it is reflected? If the answer is the piece from which it is reflected, then the view available to the second land is not a part of the "property" of the second piece of land. If the answer is the second—the one to which the light is reflected—then the view is part of the ownership of the second piece of land.

The same question can be put—not by asking who owns the reflected rays—but by asking, "who owns the right to determine how they will be reflected?" For once they are reflected, they pass out of control and ownership.

Our property laws have left this partitioning indeterminate. Each time someone feels that his view has been or is going to be changed for the worse (either by blocking incident or reflected light rays), he must go to court and get a decision as to what his ownership rights are. Zoning ordinances and heights of fences, buildings, and signs are specifications of property rights. But they are different from normal property rights in that the zoning ordinances are so readily changeable rather than exchangeable. People get or lose these rights not by exchange, but by passage of laws. For this reason, disputes over such laws are equivalent to disputes about expropriation of property.

The same problems arise with sound waves. These problems in both artificial light and sound arise probably because of the natural nature of most of our light and the long-standing uncontrolled reflection of it. For artificial light and sound, the problems arise because of the exceptionally high cost of controlling the light and sound so that they will not pass to other people's property. The high cost of fencing such light and sound reminds us of the laws of trespass of animals in days when fencing material must have been very costly. He who wanted no animals was obliged to fence them out. Now the animal owner must fence them in. Again zoning laws or special ordinances are set up to control emission of such light and sound; we allow the emitter to dump some of it on other people, but not "too much" in some cases—with "some" and "too much" being subject to specification in each instance, depending in part upon costs of controlling it.

Another notorious area of conflict is electromagnetic radiation. The characteristic common to light, sound, and radio is the *moving* attribute. All of these things have a "natural" fact of movement. They cross land and even bump across people. The idea of capturing these things and holding them destroys the concept itself. They are results of movements—of pressure waves, for example. Should someone have property rights in such a wave, or should the person whose air the sound wave passes through be presumed to be the owner?

So long as our natural senses were incapable of detecting certain wave fronts passing over our land or bodies, the whole problem was fanciful. But with detection techniques, the question arises as to how the rights to a wave front will be partitioned: to initiator, to receiver, or to him through whose space it passes? Should radiation rights be attached to land—as a measure and definition of space? Or should ownership of land include ownership (of what rights?) in the space perpendicular to it? How far? Or should land ownership not include the phenomena occurring in the space above it, e.g., electromagnetic radiation, light, and sound. Should radiation rights be defined in terms of certain frequencies without regard to where they are transmitted, or should they be defined in terms of where radiation occurs, but without regard to frequency? Or should both be used to define property rights in radiation? What kind of thing shall be declared as the radiation right that is "owned"? Should it be defined in terms of place, time, and frequency, or should it be in terms of only some subset of these characteristics? And whatever may be the physical or definitional characteristics, what about the transferability of the ownership?[13]

The mere asking of these questions brings to mind the principle that in many (but not all) situations it is better to have *a* rule than no rule at all. A rule can, of course, be a law, a social custom of etiquette, a tradition, or a moral doctrine. To leave things to private caprice or uncontrolled private force is not always a satisfactory state of affairs. A rule, any rule, is sometimes conservative of time, effort, and dispute. Driving on the right of the road is a rule (law), yet it could as well be the left side that ruled. Worse would have been no general rule at all. Yet for walking on the sidewalk, it is not the case that a parallel rule is preferred to private caprice or social custom and etiquette. And so, in the case

---

13. Quite similar is the case of water. Although water can be captured and stored, it shares the characteristics of moving across land and space. Rivers of water and clouds have been passing so long that one would have thought the property rights in water would have by now passed through a long evolutionary process of selection with convergence to a "good" kind of property or ownership system in water. But this seems in fact not to have happened. And for this reason we have doubts that there is a relatively fixed environment in which a most-fit concept could be selected from the varieties of tested property rights.

If paternalism and dictatorship characterize the "socially approved" form of society, one would expect water to be declared a public property, whereas if a more individualistic society were the "socially" approved type, private property rights in water, even as distinct from the land along which it flows, would be expected to become selected by the judicial process.

of electromagnetic radiation as well as some other things, a rule (whether of law or custom) may be better than no rule at all. The rule may not be completely "just," but it may be the most tolerable rule available, with recognition and resigned acceptance of the injustice it provokes. One of the important questions then is to determine whether the situation is one in which several alternative rules are equally good or whether it is the case that alternative rules or laws can be ranked in preference. What we want to suggest is that although we may have the criterion of "preference," economic theory is useful in deriving the implications of various partitionings of property and divisions of ownership. Just how useful it is or can be is of course the major point of this whole study.

2.5. Freedom Versus Coercion

As we have seen, property rights of the owner could be defined so severely that he imposes no consequences on other people as a result of his choice of actions. So severe a restriction would of necessity reduce the range of choices he had open to him—a restriction of the law. On the other hand, if property rights were defined so that an "owner" could make choices that imposed considerable consequences on other people, the actual or effective range of actions open to him would be reduced not so much by the property law itself as by the individual actions of other people who do things with their property that involve undesirable consequences for him. Thus if it were illegal to do anything that caused anyone else any undesirable consequences, there is little we could legally do in this world. Even an attempt to sell my labor service or a new invention could mean a loss of income to someone else. Obviously, a severely restricted set of non-owner, or external, consequences would restrict the owner's range of action. On the other hand, a loosely restricted set of non-owner or external consequences would mean that a person would be affected by other people's choices. Whether this second extreme of loose property rights with many external consequences or the first extreme of tight property rights gives more freedom or privacy of action is an unanswerable question. What does seem clear is that a movement toward either extreme is toward less "freedom of action." The second extreme is akin to anarchy, while the first is akin to either a dictatorship or a paternalist state.

It is possible to "quantify" this distinction by putting at the left extreme the case of property rights so defined that no external consequences are permissible—not even informational, value, or physical. As we move along to the right we might find more informational consequences being authorized and then, moving farther, some value effects being authorized. All the while, physical effects are being denied legality. Continuing to move along the scale to the right, we come to where even some physical effects are authorized; finally, at the right extreme, all effects are authorized (not made illegal). At this extreme we have reached what is akin to anarchy.

Such a scale is defective because it is not the case that *all* external informational effects are authorized (legalized) before any external value effects are legalized, nor that *all* external value effects are legalized before any external physical effects are legalized. Instead our laws authorize some of each. In the United States, typically—and this will be discussed at some length later—not many external informational effects are prohibited (i.e., many *are* legal), and many external value effects are legal, but not many external physical effects are legal. Typically it seems that a private property system is one in which external informational and value effects are broadly legalized, while external physical effects are generally illegal.

It is impossible to tell which extreme—permitting an owner to impose many consequences on others or not permitting him to impose consequences on other people—is more conducive to greater "freedom" or "privacy of action." At the former extreme the individual actions of other people impose all sorts of objectionable consequences and thus invade one's privacy or "freedom." At the latter, the legal choices (one's privacy or "freedom") are constrained by the laws which are the joint group decisions of society. Private property is at neither extreme. It is not at the former one, because privacy—however one interprets it—will certainly be negated by the individual actions of other people. The other extreme involves invasion of privacy by laws. The quest for the viable medium is a most fruitful source of conflict and enmity.

Often the rules we follow are the rules that we think are merely sensible ways to behave. Yet the fact that we don't behave some other way cannot usefully be explained by saying that it was simply a matter of non-coercive choice. All choice involves a weighing of gains and costs. Costs can be defined as the elements of coercion effective on us as reducers of welfare or utility. We emphasize, therefore, that talk of more- or less-coercive (or competitive) methods is often (usually?) misdirected. The question is one of more- or less-preferred methods of coercion (or competition)—with the judgment of preference being based in part upon the results—as reflected in viability of various personality traits, productive efficiency, cultural consequences, etc. (And we don't pretend to know whose judgment is crucial!)

This matter of freedom or coercion, we think, deserves enormous stress. Sometimes it is argued that the *private* property rights involve no coercion. But of course they do. Every society is composed, by definition, of people with conflicting interests. The question is, what system of coercion is desired? Or what kinds of competition will be tolerated? It is no answer to say that no coercion or no competition is wanted. That doesn't evade the problem. It merely ignores it. And yet discussions persist about which system is less coercive. We repeat, the issue is to determine what kind of coercion or competition is most acceptable. And this requires an answer to the question, What are the economic, cultural, moral, and personality consequences or kinds of behavior that are rewarded, made viable, or penalized under various systems of coercion, i.e., systems of property rights? The classic Adam Smithian extreme position is *not* normatively neutral or tolerant of all moral codes. The attempt of the Pareto welfare economic logicians to build a "non-normative" (at least in interpersonal relations) justification for private property under pure competition appears to be responsible for the mischievous belief that the classic *laissez-faire* positions are non-normative.

CHAPTER 3. PUBLIC AND PRIVATE PROPERTY

3.1. What about Legal Terms and Concepts?

Perhaps some surprise is provoked by the preceding discussion because, first, no reference has been made to usual legal distinctions—e.g., rights *in rem* and *in personam*, corporeal and non-corporeal property, real and personal property, *choses* in action, possessary interests, contracts, and equity—and, second, because as yet no distinction has been made among proprietorships, partnerships, and corporate and public property. As for the first, it happens that for present purposes—i.e., to find what aspects or variations of property rights have implications for behavior *that can be derived from economic theory*—none of these seems to be pertinent.

However, the distinction between individual and joint proprietorship and corporations and public property is relevant for our present purposes. Since economic theory is essentially a theory of constrained selections, one must discern the basis for the selection of one kind of behavior rather than another before knowing what choices will predominate in any given environment or circumstances. Obviously, if the consequences of some choice are made more favorable for the chooser (benefits increase or costs decrease), that choice will be observed more frequently.[14]

Therefore it seems natural and inevitable that property rights should be viewed by economic theory as a method of allocating among people the costs and benefits arising from the attempts of individuals to wrest wealth from nature and to resolve the inevitable interpersonal conflicts of interests.[15]

That one should use the theory or postulates of one field of endeavor (economics) to understand another (law) is not as unusual as it may, at first, seem. Modern physics and chemistry both use atomic theory. If, therefore, economists examine property rights or laws by means of economic theory, no offense nor presumption or superiority of economics over jurisprudence is implied, any more than the introduction of atomic chemistry into physics (or was it physics into chemistry?) carried such implications.

As we have seen, property rights of an owner can be defined by the set of uses and consequences among which the "owner" is allowed to choose, some of the consequences being imposed on him and some on other people. Unfortunately, there is no traditional or well-defined system for categorizing various sets of these rights so that each category differs from another in some significant way and is identified with some well-established name. At first thought one might have suspected that "private" property would be the name of a well-recognized partitioning of rights, but this is not the case. However, some partitioning of rights can be suggested as being characteristic of "private" property.

"Private" property items seem to be those that are "owned" by some person with the right to use them in any way so long as he does not impose the obviously physical consequences on other people's "private" property (although informational and value consequences are permissible). If someone is not authorized to sell something he "owns" at a lower price because it would affect

14. It makes no difference whether the individuals making the choices do so with rational analysis in the light of full information or whether they make choices rationally but in great ignorance (i.e., uncertainty) or whether they act haphazardly. Imitation and repetition of successful or more satisfactory acts (called trial and error) will provide predictable results for the rational but uncertain actor. For the non-calculating actors, the laws of survival of the fittest will provide a selection process with the selection being determined by economic viability (i.e., wealth and population).

15. It doesn't make any difference whether one thinks of the property rights as being rights to uses of things and persons or as rights and obligations for the benefits and costs resulting therefrom. These both mean the same thing.

the prices of other people's goods, or if someone is prohibited from offering for sale a new product because it would affect the salability of other products (e.g., restriction on margarine to protect butter), should this be considered a denial of "private" property rights? As usually defined, we believe the answer is yes.

In the suggested partitioning of rights in private property, we have included the right to thrust value and informational consequences on other people. For example, although one cannot affect another person's physical property, he can affect its sale value. Just why this is sanctioned is another question.

Certainly, private property does not mean that the owner can use his private property in any way he likes so long as no one else is affected. If anyone wants to define private property in that way, he is entitled to do so, but he will find the term being used "legally" to cover a much wider set of permissible uses.

It might be said that the partitioning of rights under private property is constantly changing. We would prefer to think as if there were some set of rights which were declared to be the set of rights that was denoted by the term "private property." Then the state, through the legislature or courts, would be deciding daily whether the state should enforce "private" property rights in certain items or, if not, exactly what sets of rights they were sanctioning. This alternative way of looking at the problem would require many names for the different rubrics, partitionings, or groupings of rights—each grouping being given some differentiating name. Under this scheme, we would have various sets of property rights with one being called property "type 1," another being called property "type 2," another property "type 3," etc. And with no great effort we could discern groupings that would cry for the designation of property type 1.113—indicating that all sorts of variations in the groupings of rights are conceivable.

A clean-cut analytic scheme is empirically extremely messy. It would require advance contemplation of all the possible combinations of rights structures—much as if the courts had to state in advance exactly what rights a person had in each potential future situation. The courts have refused to act in this way—they couldn't if they wanted to—instead, they await each situation that arises and then try to decide whether or not that selected use and imposed consequence is to be legalized.

We note that the present status of the law was not rationally thought out in advance from some *a priori* postulates or principles. Instead, a long evolutionary process finds us now at the stage where, for a large class of goods, private property includes the right to choose uses even though there are significant value consequences for other people's property—but not physical consequences. In courts and legislatures, every day new legislation is proposed to change the rights, so as to change the scope of authorized value consequences. Minimum wage rates, farm support programs, licensing, and price controls are examples of restrictions of the authorized range of value consequences. Many special restrictions on physical consequences are explicitly spelled out, probably because we do not normally recognize them as physical. Smoke, smell, sound, and radiation are all physical effects and can therefore affect the physical state of other people's "private" property. Since we do not normally think of them as physical, probably because of their atomic or subatomic nature, these special restrictions are often thought of as "special" cases, when in fact they are equivalent to the restriction on breaking someone's glass windows. The evolution of the structure of property rights may someday see such physical effects as belonging obviously to the prescribed effects, but for the present it is in general not obviously simply a case of physical consequences.

The accumulating experience and history of various kinds of rights encompassed in "property rights" at one time or another suggest that there has been an evolutionary process of development. If one were to select some set of rights and call them "private" property, he could have four different possible motivations. First, he may try to act scientifically, with the intent of deriving implications about behavior under this set of property rights as contrasted to another set. Second, a descriptive reason, he may think that he has a formulation of the property right that is dominant in his society. Third, a normative rationale could reflect his preferences. He might consider that kind of property rights system as one under which he would like to live. Fourth, on an evolutionary basis, he may think this is the system toward which the selective process is operating.[16] At the present time we accept the first and second reasons, although we have to admit an interest in the last two, as well.

3.2. Sharing Ownership

At this point there is a temptation to start classifying various partitionings of property rights (to choose among uses and bearing of consequences) into various kinds of property rights—private, public, bailments, easements,

16. Although it seems to be true that there has been a gradual rise of property rights for individuals as against a hierarchical ordering of rights, it is presumptuous to interpret this observed rise as an inexorable trend that will dominate evanescent aberrations toward paternalist property rights.

leases, licenses, franchises, inheritances, etc. This temptation is easy to avoid, because the task is so difficult. Another temptation is to list the various ways in which property rights of owners—ownership rights, as they are called here-after—whatever they may be, can be subdivided or shared among people as joint owners. For example, in a partnership, a single owner (a proprietor) can, by mutual agreement, share ownership rights with more than one person. Or corporations can be created as a means of sharing property rights of owners among voluntary sharers. Or public property may amount to everyone being an owner—although, as we shall see, this is not the real difference between public and private ownership.

The preceding paragraph suggests that there may be two independent aspects: property and ownership. One is the set of property rights that belong to a person. The other is the way in which the property rights are exercised, e.g., the sharing or subdividing of this ownership right among many joint owners. At first sight it appears as though the first is a classification of partitioning rights with those of the "owner" called property rights, and the other is the sharing or division of these property rights pro rata among several joint owners, e.g., as in a partnership agreement.

A lease of property or a rental agreement divides or shares the ownership right so that the renter gets the right to make certain decisions about the use of the item owned by the "owner"—decisions that are normally made by the owner. Normally the right of the renter to decide, say, where the furniture will be placed or when it will be sat on is not thought of as an ownership right, because they are so frequently allocated to the renter and because the ultimate value consequence rests on the "owner." However, our main point here is that the rights that belong to the owner can be partitioned, divided, and reallocated on a temporary or permanent basis so that the "ownership" rights are divided among two or more persons. This kind of division is not necessarily a cross-sectional division, with each owner now having equal parts of all the owner-ship rights. Instead it is a selective partitioning, with all of some of the sub-rights staying with the "owner" and all of some other rights being transferred temporarily at least to the "renter." Even though this is called a rental or leasing agreement, it does contain transfers of some of the rights that are included in ownership. The fact that these partitionings of owner rights are temporary makes it easy to decide who is the "owner," in the conventional sense.

The ability of individuals to enter into mutually agreeable contractual arrangements for the purpose of sharing or dividing the ownership rights they possess is evident from the tremendous variety of such arrangements. Corporations, partnerships, non-profit corporations, licenses, bailments, non-voting common stock, rentals, trusts, easements, agencies, franchises, employee-employer relationships, marriages, and adoptions are examples.

Should we be surprised that the state refuses to enforce some voluntary subdivision of legitimate property rights of an owner? Presumably the "undesirable" effects of such divisions or transfers justify the refusal to sanction the ownership division. For example, at one time the state refused to enforce property rights of a corporation—even though all the members of the corporation entered it voluntarily. And the state still insists on special request, which if approved, commits the state to enforce property rights for the corporation. Will it recognize any voluntary redivision of ownership rights among individuals as property rights to be enforced by the state? For example, could I transfer to you some of my property except for the right to sell or exchange the item to someone else, which I retain for myself? Or could I agree to transfer to someone else the right to sell something I own but, in the interim, keep the right to use it? Thus I might transfer to a "trustee" the right to determine what things I shall own, but whatever I have I can, otherwise, use as I like. These may sound like silly proposals, but the issue is their possibility, not their desirability. Or can I share property rights with another person, whereby each of us becomes an owner and can use what is owned as if it were each person's alone, each person having great faith in the other person's judiciousness? Or can I delegate to you authority (revocable at my will) to make decisions as to how certain of my property will be used, so if you decide to sell the property or change its form, I bear the consequences?

Could I agree with two other persons to be joint owners of some property with the owner consequences to be allocated one-third to each and with all decisions, on a one person–one vote basis, requiring a majority, except that the one-third allocation of consequences and decision right (or voting right) cannot be changed? If such agreements are made, will the state agree to recognize them and enforce the ownership rights of such a corporate entity? Some ownership agreements among owners for division of the property rights may be so complicated or of such a character that the government, for some reason or other, will refuse to enforce the property rights of such an entity.

Note that in all of these cases, I am not proposing to do something that the law prohibits me and you from doing. We are only transferring or dividing up property rights each of us already owns. The question is only whether the proposed redivision will be enforced by the state.

We ought not to be surprised if we find that in the relatively short history of man, he has already devised, tested, discarded, and retained an enormous variety of allocations and sharing of property rights. The history of the law of property reveals an overwhelming and literally incomprehensible variety.[17]

The variety of property and ownership rights is a testimony to man's ingenuity. But if one asked what the difference was between two of them, say public and private ownership, he would find the answer not so easy. In one sense it is adequate to say that the public is the owner as contrasted with a private group. But that is not very helpful if one is interested in discovering what difference it makes for the way things get done under each form. To be quite specific, compare a privately owned golf course with a publicly owned course (or auditorium, bus service, water service, garbage collection, airport, school, or spaghetti factory). There are differences in the way they are operated; at least anyone who has ever compared them will think so. Why do these differences occur? Are the objectives different? Is it because the kinds of people who operate one are different from those who operate the other? Is it because of the form of ownership?

It is not dishonest to admit that we believe (on the basis of something more than casual observation) that behavior under each institution is different, not because the objectives sought by organizations under each form are different, but, instead, because, even with the same explicit organization goals, the costs-rewards systems impinging on the employees and the "owners" of the organization are different. And we suspect that these differences are implied by economic theory if the trouble is taken to apply the theory. Further, preliminary speculation suggests, e.g., that the difference between a corporation with 1,000 equal owners and a state-owned entity with 1,000 public owners is quite significant—because the 1,000 individuals are furthering their own individual interests in each entity under two different systems of property rights; i.e., the rewards-costs schedules differ.

---

17. For example, Frederick Pollock and Frederic Maitland, *The History of English Law Before the Time of Edward I*, 2nd ed. (Cambridge, 1952); Roscoe Pound, *An Introduction to the Philosophy of Law* (New Haven: Yale University Press, 1921); William Blackstone, *Commentaries on the Laws of England*, 1765–1769; C. Reinhold Noyes, *The Institution of Property* (New York: Longmans, Green & Co., 1936); Glanville Williams, *Liability for Animals* (Cambridge: Cambridge University Press, 1939).

3.2.1. *Transferability*

Let's take the extremes of private and public ownership. Can there be identified some crucial differences between these two? For example, if ownership rights in proprietorships, partnerships, and corporations can be regarded as *private*, how do they differ from *public* ownership? How do private and public ownership rights differ? To sharpen the issue, consider a small-town theater owned by 1,000 corporate shareholders and an auditorium owned by the town's 1,000 residents as public property. This eliminates the question of sharing and of differences in the number of joint owners. Every function conducted at one building could just as well be held at the other. The city auditorium is operated to make money, not to subsidize some group (we shall assume here), and so is the private theater.

The pricing policy of the publicly and privately owned theaters could be identical, so the allocation of theater services among the members of the community was the same. In fact, often the precise purpose of public ownership is to get a different use of theaters than would be found with privately owned theaters. The owners of a privately owned theater could attend either theater as customers, and similarly so could the owners of a publicly owned theater.

The public auditorium and the private theater both serve the public. It is not the case that the former is designed to provide a public service and the latter not. The privately owned theater will survive only if it can provide services that the public wants at the price asked. It is a source of public service even though its purpose, from the owner's point of view, is to make money. It makes money by providing a service to the public. In the case of the privately owned theater, public service is a means toward private gain. But what about the publicly owned auditorium? Is its purpose public service or to make money for the public owners? Suppose its purpose *is* public service. This does not *require* that its means of action be any different than if its purpose were profits to the owners—public or private. And in both cases—the auditorium and the theater— the managers and employees are induced to take their jobs only because the salary enhances their own profit or well-being. They take the jobs not because they want to provide a public service or profit for the owners, but, instead, because they want to make a living for themselves. Even those residents who "own" the auditorium and voted for it did so because they felt it would make their own situations preferable, not because they wanted the auditorium to benefit someone else as a charity device.

In the public-ownership case, the stated objective of the enterprise may be to provide a public service as an end when viewed from the point of view of the abstract concept of a "public auditorium," but when viewed from the point of view of the people involved—not from inanimate conceptualization—the end is the same in both cases: individual benefit, with the institution serving as the means. But there are differences, and our proposition is that the differences between public and private ownership arise from *the inability of a public owner to sell his share of public ownership.* This is what makes public ownership a more appropriate medium for achieving the consequences for which it is often used—e.g., defense and policing. But let us be clear about this. We are not asserting that there are no other differences, nor is it claimed that this inability to sell has not been noticed before. Instead we are making an assertion about the unique *importance* of this difference in the ownership rights.

We aren't begging the issue by assuming away one general difference—the profit-making incentive or criterion. Both public and private property can seek profits. The desire to avoid or suppress the profit-making incentive is, however, often the reason society resorts to public ownership. But what we want to discover is why this resort to public ownership does so effectively accomplish this suppression. The objectives cannot merely be announced to the managers or operators or owners with any expectation that the announcement or exhortation will be either sufficient or even necessary to achieve the objective. Since our general postulate is that people—as individuals—seek to increase their utility and that wealth is a source of utility, we cannot expect people to change their goals or desires. Instead, we rely upon changes in the rewards-costs structure to explain differences in the way they seek to increase their utility or satisfy their desires.[18] And we shall try to show that the many differences that do exist between behavior in publicly and privately owned institutions are caused by or can occur only in the presence of this ownership difference—viz., the presence or the absence of the right to sell a share of ownership to someone else.

The difference can be put somewhat less euphemistically. Public ownership *must* be borne by all members of the public, and no member can divest himself of that ownership. Ownership of public property is not voluntary; it is compulsory as long as one is a member of the public. To call something "compulsory" usually is a good start toward condemning it.

A person must move from one town to another to change his ownership in public property. In that sense it is not compulsory, because it is not compulsory that one live in a particular community. But so long as one does live in any com-

---

18. Friends of Adam Smith will recognize this as the major postulate of his *Wealth of Nations,* a postulate which seems to have served economists well when not forgotten.

munity with public property he is a public owner and cannot divest himself of public ownership; but he can sell and shift private property ownership rights without also having to leave the community.[19]

3.3. Some Implications of Transferability

To see what difference is made by the right to transfer ownership, suppose public ownership could be sold. It would be possible for me to sell to someone else my ownership rights in the publicly owned water or bus or garbage or parks or school system. To separate out the fact that public ventures are usually run without the intent of making a profit, let us suppose that the water or bus system had been instructed to be as profitable as it could. Even though this may be a purely imaginative case (does anyone know of a publicly owned venture being operated with the intent of maximizing profit?), we shall suppose this to be the case. While the venture is publicly owned, the public owners have incentives to see that it is run "efficiently." But now that its ownership has become salable, with profits or losses accruing to the owners, will incentives be any different?

The answer is suggested by two implications of the specialization of "ownership," which is similar to the familiar specialization of other kinds of skills or activities. The two derivative implications are: (1) concentration of rewards and costs more directly on each person responsible for them and (2) comparative advantage effects of specialized applications of (a) knowledge in control and of (b) risk bearing.

3.3.1. Degree of Dependency

The concentration of rewards and costs means simply that each person's wealth is more dependent upon his own activities than upon those of other people. This is brought about as follows: the more he concentrates his wealth holding in particular resources, the more will his wealth respond to his own ac-

19. It is tempting to emphasize the possibility, under public ownership, of someone joining the community and thereby acquiring a share of public ownership without payment to any of the existing owners. This dilution of a person's share of ownership is presumably absent in private ownership. In fact, a community could cut off immigration, but public ownership would continue even if this dilution effect were an important problem. Furthermore, many corporations issue new shares without preemptive rights to former owners. Presumably this is done only when the receiver of the new shares pays the corporation something of at least equivalent value. And it is a safe assumption that the management deems the quid pro quo to have been worthwhile so far as present purposes are concerned. Still, it is sufficient that even if dilution of public ownership were eliminated

tivities in those areas. Consider the following example: Suppose there are 100 people in a community, with 10 separate enterprises. Suppose that each person, by devoting 1/10 of his time to some one enterprise as an owner, could produce a saving or gain of $1,000. Since the individual is a 1/100 part owner he will acquire $10. Suppose, further, that he does this for the 10 different enterprises, in each of which he owns 1/100 part. His total wealth gain will be $100, with the rest of the product, $9,900, going to the 99 other people. If the 99 other people act in the same way, he will get from their activities an increase of wealth of $990,000/100 = $9,900, which gives him a total of $10,000. This is exactly equal to his product, most of which was spread over the other owners.

However, if everyone each owns 1/10 part of one enterprise (which means that ownership has been reshuffled from pro rata equal shares in all enterprises to a concentration in fewer enterprises by each person, although with the same total number of enterprises), the individual will now be assumed to devote his whole time during one year to the one enterprise, so he again produces $10,000. (We assume that his productivity is proportional to the number of hours of work and that it is the same for everyone. Other assumptions will change the arithmetic but will not destroy the main principle being elaborated.) Of this he gets $1,000. The remainder, $9,000, goes to the owners of the other 9/10 share. Like them, he too receives portions of the other owners' products, and if all are assumed to be exactly alike, then he gets from the 9 other joint owners of his enterprise $9,000, for a total of $10,000—precisely the same as in the preceding example. The difference is that now $1,000 of this is dependent upon his own activities whereas formerly only $100 was. Or, more pertinently, the amount dependent upon the activities of other people is reduced from $9,900 to $9,000.

If we go to the extreme where the 10 enterprises are divided into 100, with each person as the sole owner, then all $10,000 of his year's wealth increase will depend upon his own activities. The first of these three examples corresponds to public ownership, the second to corporate joint private ownership, and the third to sole proprietorship.

If public ownership rights were made salable, they would in effect become private ownership rights, and there would be a movement toward concentra-

---

by restriction of entry, the inability to sell one's share of public ownership remains a potent factor in the costs-rewards system impinging on all members of the public and on the employees and administrators of the publicly owned institution.

tion of ownership of the type in the second example, at least. Why? In the second case, the wealth a person can get is more dependent upon his own activities than in the first case. Many people may prefer to let the situation stay as in Example 1, hoping to collect a major portion of their wealth gain from other people's activities. If this were the case, the total wealth gain would decrease since everyone would have incentive to "goof off." But it suffices that there be at least one person who prefers to make himself less dependent upon other people's activities than in Example 1 and who prefers at least some more wealth to some more leisure. He will then be prepared to buy some ownership rights and pay a higher price for them than they are worth to some other people. That he values them more highly is precisely another way of saying that he values independence more than they do, or that he prefers more wealth to less wealth— even if it requires some work by him.

3.3.2. *Comparative Advantage in Ownership: Control*

The preceding example required no differences among people with respect to their abilities, knowledge, or attitude toward risk. But if people differ in any of these respects, as we are sure they in fact do, then it can be shown that specialization of effort in various tasks—including that of *owning* a business— will increase their wealth. This demonstration is simply the logical theorem of gains from comparative advantage, which we shall not explain here.

Usually the illustrations of comparative advantage are based on labor productivities with no reference to "ownership" productivities. But people differ in their talents as owners. Owners bear the risk of value changes; they decide how much to produce and by what means, how much to invest, and who shall be employed as laborers and managers. The different skills of different people as owners make pertinent the principle of comparative advantage through specialization in ownership. If ownership rights are transferable, then specialization of ownership is possible with the attendant gains from differential degrees of ownership ability. Ownership ability includes attitude toward risk bearing, knowledge of different people's productive abilities, foresight, and, of course, judgment. These talents differ among people according to the particular industry, type of product, or productive resource one is considering. People will concentrate their ownership in those areas in which they believe they have a comparative advantage if they want to increase their wealth. Some people will own the bus lines; others will own the golf course. The fact that people differ in their abilities in management and degrees of knowledge of various technologies and fields of endeavour means that the old principle of comparative advantage usually reflected in specialization is at work. Just as specialization in typing, music, or various types of labor is more productive, so is specialization in ownership more productive. Some people specialize in electronics industry knowledge, some in airlines, some in dairies, some in automotives, etc. Public ownership practically eliminates such specialization among owners, though not among employees in the publicly owned venture. Private property owners can specialize in knowledge about electronics, devoting much of their effort and study to learning which electronic devices show promise, which are now most efficient in various uses, which should be produced in larger numbers, where investment should take place, what kinds of research and development to finance, etc.

It is not necessary that owners understand the law of comparative advantage any more than parents must understand the laws of genetics. The law of comparative advantage is a way of explaining why the offers by various people in their attempt to acquire ownership of certain resources will be different. It attributes the differences not merely to disagreement about what something is "really" worth, but, instead, to differential ownership productivities.

A person who is very knowledgeable about woodworking and cabinet or furniture building would have an advantage as an owner of a furniture company. He would, by being a stockholder, not necessarily make the company any better, but he would choose the better company—as judged by his knowledge—as one in which to own shares. The relative rise in the price of such companies enables the existing owners to issue new shares, borrow money more readily, and retain control. In this way the differences in knowledge enable people to specialize in the application of that knowledge to the management and operation of the company—albeit sometimes by indirect lines. Again this does not mean that this is done as effectively as in a proprietorship; instead the comparison is with public ownership (no transferability of ownership) and its greater difficulty in exploiting differences in knowledge.

3.3.3. Comparative Advantage in Ownership: Risk Bearing

A second aspect of ownership specialization is the risk-bearing function. People's attitudes toward risk differ. If various ventures or resources represent different prospects of values, then exchange of ownership will enable a reallocation of risks among people, leading to greater utility in the same sense that exchange of goods does. This risk-bearing difference reflects not only attitudes toward risk but beliefs about the prospects of future values of the assets whose ownership can be transferred. Differences in knowledge can be used not only in an effort to be more productive but also as a means for distinguishing different risk situations. For example, I may be the top administrator of the Carnation Milk Company, but I may choose to hold stocks in some electronic company because I prefer the risk pattern provided by that stock to that provided by ownership in Carnation. In this way a person can separate the productivity of knowledge and effort in what he owns from the risk bearing. He can, if he wants, combine them by holding stock in a company in which he is active. This possibility of separating the *control* (effective administration or operation of the company—an activity which rewards comparative superiority in ability and knowledge) from *risk bearing* is, of course, regarded as an advantage by those who act as employed managers or administrators and by those who choose to act as corporate stock owners without also bothering to exercise their vote or worry about control.

Not all of the owners have to think of themselves as owners who are going to exercise their voting rights so effectively as to exert an influence on management. Most of the owners may go along simply because they believe the prospects for profits and losses are sufficiently promising relative to other assets they could own. If eventualities are losses, the owners' only alternative is to sell out. To whom? To other buyers who, because of the reduced profit prospects, will offer only a lower price. This price must be low enough to make the new prospects for profits and losses favorable enough to induce someone to own the resources. These non-active owners perform a very important function in that they provide the willingness to bear some of the value consequences at least. So long as scarce resources *exist*, these value changes will occur. The changes in value simply mean that they are less valuable to society as a whole; the question left is which particular members are to bear the reduced value. Someone has to bear them. Their existence cannot be dreamed away.

Private owners make the value risk-bearing voluntary. But the effect on the utilization of the resources reflects the majority voting, or a controlling group who become owners, not merely to passively bear risks or bet on the management but, instead, to affect the management and convert any inefficiency into larger profits, higher property values, and, hence, capital gains as profits to the "active" owners of private property.

Often it is said that joint ownership in the modern corporation has separated ownership and control. What this means is that risk bearing and management are separate. This is correct in that each owner does not have the kind of control he would as the sole owner. But it is a long logical leap to decrying this. It can be a good thing. Further specialization in risk bearing and in management or decision making about particular uses of resources is now possible. Complete separation does not exist for every joint owner, for to the extent that some owners are inactive or indifferent to alternative choices or management problems, other stockholders (joint owners) will be more influential. In effect, the "passive" owners are betting on the "active" owners. "Betting" in the sense that they are prepared to pay other people for any losses produced by these "activists" and, in turn, to collect the winnings if any. In the absence of any right to buy and sell voluntarily, everyone would have to be betting on the activists (the case of public property). The right to sell concentrates this betting in these who are prepared to pay the most (or demand the least) for the right to do so. And it concentrates the control or management in those who believe they are relatively most able at that task—and these beliefs can be tested with the less able being eliminated more surely in private ownership than in public because (1) the evidence of poor management and the opportunity to capture wealth gains by eliminating it is revealed to outsiders by the lower selling price of the ownership rights, (2) the specialization of ownership in the sense of risk bearing from decision making, and (3) the possibility of concentrating one's wealth in certain areas permits greater correlation of personal interest and effort with wealth holdings.

But it may be objected that if it is the concentration of ownership that counts, progressive taxation wherein some people bear more than other people do of the potential gains or losses via a tax bill will have the same effect. Those who pay more taxes will be more alert than those who pay small taxes. But the difficulty with this line of objection is that the gains from any improvement of behavior in some particular branch of the public activity is disbursed over the whole government budget. This is equivalent to our first example in the earlier discussion of the effect of wealth concentration—where each person owned stock in all corporations. Concentration of ownership among people is not what we want; ownership must be concentrated in certain ventures. People must concentrate their wealth holding of particular things and not own a cross-section of the whole stock of private goods. Such a failure of concentration of individual ownership on certain items would occur if the public ownership were to be salable but where the ownership being sold is always a cross-section of all public property rather than separable parts.

We infer from the preceding discussion the theorem *Under public ownership the costs of any decision or choice are less fully thrust upon the selector than under private property.* In other words, the cost-benefit incentives system is changed toward lower costs. The converse of this implication is that the gains to any owner resulting from any cost-saving action are less fully effective. These do not mean that the true costs are reduced. The looser correlation between the costs borne by any chooser and the costs of the particular choices he makes is what is implied; part of the costs are thrust upon other people. Similarly, the capturable gains to the owners of their actions are reduced.

They are *less* fully borne than they would be if the same action were taken in a private property institution, with a similar number of owners.[20] From this theorem one would expect that public agencies would, in order to offset or counterbalance this reduced cost bearing, impose special extra costs or constraints on public employees or agents. If a public agent were to refuse the lowest bid on some public construction contract, he would be fired, *and* a jail sentence would be imposed. In a private firm, the agent would merely be fired. Also, public agents who are authorized to spend public funds should be more severely constrained with extra restrictions precisely because the costs of their actions are less effectively thrust upon them. And, of course, these extra constraints do exist. And these extra constraints may be so severe that the public agent acts even more cautiously than a private agent. But because of these extra constraints—or because of the "costs" of them—the public arrangement becomes a higher cost (in the sense of less efficient) than private property agencies.

For example, and as we shall show in more detail later, civil service, nepotism restrictions, tenure, single-salary structures for public school teachers, sealed bids, and line-item budget controls, to name a few, are some of the devices used.

But it is not easy—indeed, it is impossible—in many instances to impose extra subsidiary costs as offsets. How would one impose full costs upon a city manager who decided to have a garbage collection system (that turned out to be a big money-loser) more than the city would tolerate? By not re-electing him. But this cost is less than that borne by the private owner who decides to open a garbage collection system. He loses his job and the sunk costs. Similarly, how do we make a voter bear the costs of bad judgment in his votes? Are the prospects of costs that may be imposed on a voter equivalent to the costs-prospects that will be laid on a private owner (with share rights) voting in a private corporation? Not according to the theorem derived from our analysis. How would you propose to institute a system of extra costs so that each voter is

20. In other words, this difference between public and private ownership does not flow from differences in numbers of owners.

under the same constraints as under private property—on the not always acceptable assumption that you wanted to make them equally effective? I should, I suppose, avow at random intervals that all this is not a condemnation of public ownership any more than certain "deficiencies" of marriage, the human eye, the upright position of the human being, or smoking are to be regarded as condemnations of marriage, eyes, walking on two feet, or smoking. The "lesser" evils in some institution—and they exist in all—are borne for the greater good in some of them. We are not arguing that private property even in its purest form is perfect in the cost-bearing sense. No standard of perfection is available. All of our statements have been comparative in degrees of cost bearing.

The converse of this "apologia" is that others should not speak of the imperfections of the marketplace either. Nor should they assume that in those instances where the marketplace is inferior in certain respects to, say, public ownership or government control, we should switch from the market to the government.[21] The presence of one kind of relative deficiency does not simply justify a switch to another agency which has other kinds of deficiencies. We can't have either agency without also having all its attributes. We repeat that this neither justifies nor condemns more private or more public ownership, more market- or more government-directed activity. All this may help form such decisions, but it is only part of the story.

3.4. We Summarize

The main implication of the effects of specialization of ownership is that with private property the costs-rewards incentive system impinging on each person is more directly related to his own actions than in public ownership. Putting it suggestively, a person bears more of the costs and the gains of his actions or decisions in private property than in public property. Of all the value, use, and informational consequences created by some choice of use of resources, a greater amount of them are imposed on the responsible or initiative "owners" than under public ownership. In saying this we mean that whatever may have been the partitioning or structuring of rights or ranges of choices open to the nominal "owners," with the sanctioned consequences for non-owners and owners, a greater part of the "owner" consequences are identified

---

21. We are mindful that rabbits have greater skin-healing power (even for some equally large [100 cm²] sizes of skin injury) than do human beings. Should we deduce that rabbits should be used as soldiers?

with the initiating owners. Why? Precisely because the owners are no longer the entire society. The "owners" of resources can be concentrated by resources with the owner consequences also being concentrated on those "owners." Since "private property ownership" bears more surely and less diffusely the "owner" consequences private owners will have more incentive (greater rewards or costs) for making decisions or for controlling managers or employees more carefully.

Under private property—with whatever the ownership rights may be—the connection between choices and consequences is more directly imposed on the responsible owners than under public ownership. A larger part of the "owner" costs and gains is more dependent upon each joint owner's actions than under public ownership. It is from this difference in the costs-rewards system between public and private ownership that economic theory derives differences in implied behavior for the two systems.

As we suggested earlier, public and private ownership are used for different purposes, and in some cases just *because* of these different behavioral implications. If public ownership in some government activity were converted to private property, the success in achieving the government objectives would be seriously deterred. If the city and national parks, or golf courses owned by cities were converted to private property, they would no longer be operated as subsidies for certain groups. If the fire and police department ownership rights were converted to private property rights, vast changes would occur in their operation. And the same goes for the postal system, the garbage collection system, the bus lines, the street cleaning system, the federal mortgage insurance companies, and the army, navy, and air force. Because we do not want these changes to occur, these activities are conducted as public-ownership ventures rather than as privately owned ventures. And because the effects of greater dependence of benefits and costs on one's own actions are *not* wanted, resort is made to government activity—which is not to say that government activity is therefore good or bad. The extent to which "society" reduces risks that must be individually borne and instead has them borne by society at large—thus reducing the correlation between choice of action and consequences for people as individuals—determines the extent of public property. How much the extent of this depends upon a kind of *choice* to socialize certain risks and how much reflects the voting and decision-making *process* are questions we need not try to answer here.

CHAPTER 4. NOT-FOR-PROFIT AND PUBLIC UTILITY FIRMS

4.1. Not-for-Profit Organizations and Objectives

We continue our examination of forms of ownership, whatever may be the entity owned. Later, much later, we shall try to discern why property rights vary among various entities, e.g., water, radiation, oil, land, labor, gold. However, here we confine ourselves to the ownership rights, regardless of the entity owned. Two species of ownership—not-for-profit and limited profit—have existed for a long time. They have been used for religious, charitable, educational, and fraternal organizations, to name a few. What constitutes the essential feature of the not-for-profit organization? We believe it is the inability of the owners to convert value changes—or profits—of the organization into their personal wealth by direct payment of dividends in money out of the organization. Suppose a non-profit organization owned land and discovered oil on the land. Even though the intent was not to make a profit, the profit was in fact made. The not-for-profit organization has unintentionally and legally obtained a profit. What now can be done with it? Under the law, the profits must be spent in the pursuit of the objective of the organization—the organization's nominal or stated goals. The profits presumably cannot be spent by the individual owners for their own, non-organizational goals. Thus, the characteristic of a not-for-profit institution is that the profits, if made, must be devoted to the stated goals sought to be achieved through the organization rather than devoted to the private goals of the owners. This can be expressed briefly by saying that profits cannot be distributed legally to the owners in forms explicitly intended to enable them to pursue independently their private, non-organization oriented goals. "Independently" means independent of the attempt to achieve the organization's goals.

To explain why we introduce "independently": The profits can be spent for more luxurious office furnishing, which will certainly help achieve the private goals of the office occupant, but this achievement is obtained only in conjunction with, dependent upon, or incident to furthering the objective of the organization. Any disbursal of funds which is not in pursuit of the stated objective—no matter how much it may satisfy privately the goals of the individual—is illegal. The question of just what ratio must exist between achievement of organizational goals and "incidental" achievement of private goals, as a sort of complementary result, is of course most interesting. Would the law tolerate the expenditure of $100 in a way in which the goals of the organization were achieved to the extent of, say, $5 while the complementary effect in private goal attainment cost the remaining $95?

At first thought one would wonder why anyone would ever propose a non-profit organization as a means of accomplishing some objective. He could always use a profit-making institution for the same objective and simply continue to devote all the profits to accomplishment of the institution's objective. Why should he tie his own hands? He organized the institution voluntarily. Why, then, make the "not-for-personal-profit" constraint? Suppose he should want to change his mind? He couldn't take the profits out. And that, of course, is precisely why the not-for-profit form is used, not because he wants to protect himself from his own change of mind but to protect those from whom he seeks to obtain funds via his organization. His customers and other joint owners may cooperate with him because they seek also to further the goals for which the organization is intended. They want protection against his change of mind or intent—hence, the "not-for-profit" specification in the sense that the owners cannot use the funds as they could in ordinary privately owned organizations. This suggests that none of the wealth of the organization shall be considered to be privately owned profit in the usual sense of the term.

Another important reason for non-profit status is that the tax laws provide tax exemption in the presumption that the activities or the objectives (education, religion, charity, research, fraternizing) being sought by non-profit organizations are more to be encouraged than other kinds of activities or objectives.

Whatever the variations on the theme, "not-for-profit" connotes ownership in which all receipts must be spent in furtherance of the specified organizational objectives, objectives not identical with those of the "owners" as individuals. This contrasts with an ordinary for-profit business in which owners can use the receipts for their own individual interests. It is not necessary that either the employees or the customers share in any way whatsoever the desire to accomplish the goals of the organization. Customers will buy because the price is best; employees will work to help the organization achieve its ends only because the wages are sufficiently great to enable them to further their own interests better in this organization than elsewhere. Nor can the owners be excluded from this category. The owners need not be assumed to make any sacrifices. Although they earn no take-home profits, they can pay themselves sufficiently large salaries as directors or top "employees" to induce them to take themselves away from other activities.

The only thing that prevents the owners from using salaries as masking devices with which to take out profits is that the salaries must in some sense be reasonable—and if profits of an exceptional nature are somehow earned, they cannot legally be used to pay salaries that are obviously inconsistent with similar types of employee salaries elsewhere. Of course, as a matter of fact, the profits can always be invested by the company indirectly in safe securities, thus ensuring the "owners" of more secure or longer-lived salaries. Increased security of longer-lived salaries is equivalent to higher salary. Therefore, the profits can, in fact, and to a suitable extent, be extracted from the non-profit organization by this indirect means, if the "owners" so desire. Admittedly this device for extraction is not as efficient nor as cheap as the direct taking of profits out of the company.

An explanation for growth of this form of ownership lies in its tax-exempt status. The higher costs or greater inefficiency with which profits are extracted from a non-profit organization is more than compensated for by the lower tax bill. This, of course, means that other taxpayers in general are covering the cost of this inefficiency. However, even without the tax-exempt status, the not-for-profit organization would survive in the area of charity. And it would survive there precisely because the owners intend to make a contribution to charity of the amount of profits. In that one case, the charitable intent offsets the desire to take profits out of the company for personal use. Of course, even if the enterprise were for-profit the presumption is that the profits could go to charity by a charitable act of giving by the owners. The apparently identical results in the "not-for-profit" and the "for-profit" institutions would eliminate the not-for-profit arrangement *except* for its tax advantage and except for one other important feature. Usually, charitable organizations obtain funds by soliciting gifts, and potential donors are not likely to give if the solicitor can change his mind and divert the profits to his own use. Hence the act of binding the owners to give all the profits to charity is accomplished by the not-for-profit form of organization. It acts as a binder of faith with the donors of funds to the charity-intended organization.

In all other-intentioned firms, the owners do not have this intent of charity. They will be motivated more by their personal interests in disposing of the profits and in operating the non-profit firm. But since they face legal obstacles to taking funds out of the firm for their personal use, they will be under incentive to spend the money within the firm in connection with its avowed purposes but also in such a manner as to further their own private interests as well. The first reaction to this thought is that the same is true for a privately owned for-profit firm. Why would the owner when spending money in the for-profit business not also spend it in such a manner as to further his own private interests at the same time? Shouldn't behavior be the same in either case? The answer is no.

Although it is true that the money spent in the firm will also reflect some regard for the private interests of the owner, say for consumption activities, the owner *can* take out whatever amount he wants and leave in the firm whatever amount he wants. But in the not-for-profit case, the owner cannot do this. He is more constrained. He has to keep more in the firm than he would if he had as free a hand to transfer funds. In economic jargon, the schedule of marginal gain of another dollar kept in the firm can be the same for both firms. But in fact we will find the not-for-profit owner farther down that schedule where the marginal gains are smaller, in fact smaller than the marginal gains of utility to the for-profit owner who can take out dollars for personal uses. (Our resort to this jargon is more than a resort to jargon; it shows that the implied difference in behavior is in fact implied by the basic economic theorems of substitution and of demand.) What this means is that costs of personal-purpose expenditures in *the firm* in conjunction with business activities are higher in the for-profit firm than in the not-for-profit firm. "Costs" refer to the forsaken outside-the-firm personal expenditures. In the for-profit firm, a dollar spent in the firm to obtain some personal source of satisfaction in addition to the profits sought means one dollar less spent "at home." In the not-for-profit firm, a dollar spent in the firm could not be spent at home, because of the legal constraint on its withdrawal from the firm. Therefore the alternatives sacrificed are less than a dollar spent outside the not-for-profit firm. In other words, the cost of personally oriented activity carried on within the firm is lower in a not-for-profit firm than in a for-profit firm. Since the cost is lower for in-firm activity in the not-for-profit firm, the implication is that more of it will be found in the for-profit firm.

The preceding analysis, which may seem like a roundabout way to say what is obvious, is designed to show that this implication is contained in economic theory, given the premise about the legal conditions and constraints imposed on a not-for-profit firm as compared with those on a for-profit firm. Even if it is logically valid as an implication of economic theory, it still remains to show that this implication is empirically true.

Although we shall discuss these types of activities in more detail later, we mention one now. Discrimination in choosing employees by reason of race, creed, sex, beauty, or age will be more pronounced in not-for-profit firms than in business firms. The reason is that the kind of employees one works with is a non-pecuniary product or source of personal utility. Therefore the owner is willing to pay higher wages in order to get the kind of employees he personally likes. Why? Because the cost of doing so is cheaper in a not-for-profit firm. If the owner of a for-profit firm paid lower wages and was less concerned with the non-pecuniary productivity or attributes of the employees and more with the pecuniary productivity, he could have earned more profits and taken them home. This is, of course, merely an application of our general statement that the personally borne costs of such money profit–forsaking activity is lower in the not-for-profit firm than in the for-profit firm. The profit-sacrificing activity costs the not-for-profit owners less take-home profit. Hence the owners of such firms resort more to these cost-increasing activities that provide a greater non-pecuniary source of satisfaction.

At first thought, there may seem to be a counterargument to this line of reasoning. This counterargument is supposed to reflect the fact that in a for-profit business there is less legal constraint on what the owner can do with the business proceeds than in the not-for-profit firm; the law more severely constrains expenditure patterns of *money* within the not-for-profit firm. Therefore it might be argued that the absence of this constraint would permit more personal-activity expenditures in the for-profit firm than in the not-for-profit firm. If the owner wanted to make his office into a "second home," he could do so in the for-profit firm, but not in the not-for-profit firm, for that would be a clear violation of the authorized actions of a not-for-profit firm.

But the error in this counterargument is that even in a not-for-profit firm, the owner can make his office a second home *if* he spends his *own* money for the "home." There is nothing to stop him from using his own money to pay for the costs of that kind of "consumption" activity *at* the office—even in the not-for-profit case. Therefore if any person likes more consumptive activity in his business, he can personally pay for it in the not-for-profit exactly as he does in the for-profit case—out of what would have been his take-home profits. It's not the cost of putting money *into* such business's associated consumption or personally motivated activity. It's the differential cost of getting the money *out* of the business and into private or consumption motivated activity that produces the implied form of behavior. A *higher* cost of getting money *out* (nearly impossible) is the converse of a *lower* cost of using it *in* the business to pay for personal activity.

4.2. Profit-Regulated Public Utilities

Economically equivalent to the not-for-profit firm is a public utility that is earning profits at the maximum permissible rate. Public utilities are, in principle, supposed to be limited in the extent to which they can earn profits. Assuming that an investment base can be identified, the permissible profits are limited to some percentage of that amount, say 6%. If a public utility is earning the legal maximum rate, then any further profits would appear to be pointless from the point of view of the owners, since they could not capture them. The result, in principle, would be that the service prices would be cut to consumers until the increased output taken at the lower prices raised costs until the profits were reduced to their legal maximum.

Now this would do the owners little good. Instead, if they could have included in the costs the costs of activities that are primarily of benefit to the owners, then the owners could, in fact, capture some of the profits. They would have captured the profits, not as take-home dividends, but instead as business-paid, fringe-benefit types of personal gain. For example, if the costs of medical insurance or vacations or company cars used for domestic uses could be put into business costs, these higher costs would make profits look smaller, but the owners are really getting the profits spent for their benefit. In other words, costs and expenditures are cunningly devised so as to include activities of benefit to some of the owners. Just how this can be done is something we shall discuss in more detail later. But the crucial idea here is that it will be advantageous to the owners to include in business costs the costs of personal activities that would be carried on outside of the business if profits could be extracted. The incentive to all this comes from the possibility of reducing profits by increasing the costs in ways that benefit the owners. This circumvents, crudely and inefficiently—and only partially, to be sure—the profit limitation.

The derivation of this implication from economic theory is simple enough. The cost of getting the profit out of the public utility is practically infinite—meaning it is impossible. The costs of using the excess profits in the business are, then, zero. Therefore, all the excess profits will be used in the business and insofar as possible in ways that, although connected with the service function of the public utility, redound to the benefit of the owners. Again, the lower the cost of business expenditures as a means of obtaining personal gratification or utility, the more that will occur.

All this applies only to the public utility that is already at or near the profit ceiling. If the utility was losing money, there would be no extra incentive for this kind of business-connected personal gain, for the increase in profits available by avoiding this kind of activity could be taken out of the business as direct dividends, just as in an unregulated for-profit firm.

If it is objected that the public-utility regulatory agency is in principle supposed to thwart this kind of subterfuge or incentive, the response is simple.

People do what is in their self-interest to do, not necessarily what they are exhorted to do. The regulatory commission is made up of individuals who, although told they must regulate, will themselves consider the costs imposed on them by their regulatory activity. How much does a regulator get for his extra regulatory activity? Does he get rewarded in any sense commensurate with what he saves the public *via* more efficient public regulatory activity? That reward is little better, if at all, than the reward for doing an unobtrusive job that causes him neither ulcers nor loss of his job. The simple fact is that the *incentives* of the regulatory commission *members* are not in tune with the stated objectives of the commission as a regulatory body. This does not mean that the commissioners are two-faced, hypocritical opportunists without integrity, nor that the law is badly written or enforced. Quite the contrary. They and the law enforcers are honest, intelligent, moral, conscientious, hard-working individuals. But the system of rewards that impinges on each member does not make it worth his while to embark on a crusade to ferret out all cost-fattening activity, though he might, if he is intending to run for political office and seeks to use this as a publicity device and if he is willing to face up to the reaction of the public-utility directors. Even with this political incentive, the power of the regulatory agency to detect legal cost padding is below that of the owner of an unregulated for-profit business. The net effect is that the regulatory agency is—compared with the owners of an unregulated for-profit business—less efficient as an expense, cost, or management-efficiency control agency.

This does not say that a public utility or a not-for-profit institution will be operated less efficiently than a for-profit institution. That depends upon the kinds of competition to which it is exposed. Both may be inherently extremely efficient. But what the implications do say is that it will not be the case that the not-for-profit firms and full-profit-earning public utilities display the same general types of behavior as for-profit firms. The former will be involved in larger business expenditures that yield satisfaction of a consumption or nonpecuniary type of product to the owners.

All these implications derived from the theory remain to be verified empirically. But we defer a discussion of how these implications can be converted into statements about *observable* kinds of differential behavior to a later section.

SOME ECONOMICS OF PROPERTY RIGHTS

1. Scarcity, Competition, and Property

In *every* society, conflicts of interest among the members of that society must be resolved. The process by which that resolution (not elimination!) occurs is known as competition. Since, by definition, there is no way to eliminate competition, the relevant question is, What kind of competition shall be used in the resolution of the conflicts of interest? In more dramatic words designed to arouse emotional interest, What forms of discrimination among the members of that society shall be employed in deciding to what extent each person is able to achieve various levels of his goals? Discrimination, competition, and scarcity are three inseparable concepts.

2. Constraints

That list of concepts can be expanded—scarcity, competition, discrimination, constraints, property. In other words, constraints exist that prevent our individually achieving a level of want fulfillment beyond which none of us wants more. In still other words, these constraints, even though imposed by nature, include also the constraints imposed by other people who because they achieve certain levels of want fulfillment leave other people with lower levels. (I do not mean that *all* activities that enable one person to have a greater level of goal fulfillment will also necessarily mean less for someone else; we know that some forms of exchange permit joint increases. But we also know that cooperative action is possible, and also that competitive action is also present.) If we concentrate attention on constraints and classes of permissible action we find ourselves studying the *property* aspect of behavior.

Reprinted, by permission of the author, from Armen A. Alchian, *Economic Forces at Work* (Indianapolis: Liberty Fund, 1977), 127–49. This article was previously published in *Il Politico* 30, no. 4 (1965): 816–29, and is reprinted by permission.

Preparation of this paper was facilitated by a grant from the Lilly Endowment of Indianapolis, Indiana, to the University of California, Los Angeles, for a study of various forms of property rights.

Economists are, I think, too prone to examine exchange as a cooperative act whereby the buyer and seller each act in an effort to reach a more desired position. Yet I find it more interesting (now that I understand the cooperative aspect of exchange) to examine the competitive, or property, aspect of exchange. The act of exchange is a means whereby the buyer is able to compete against other claimants for the goods being obtained from the seller. The kinds of offers, forms of competition, and behavior that the members of society can employ in an endeavor to get more of the goods that would otherwise go to other people are brought more into the focus of attention. More directly, the forms and kinds of property rights sanctioned in a society define or identify the kinds of competition, discrimination, or behavior characteristic of that society.

Yet if we look at the "fields" of economics, say as presented by the American Economic Association's classification of areas of interest or specialization, we find no mention of the word "property." Either we can infer that the profession is so obviously aware of the pervasiveness of the effects of various forms of property rights that property rights cannot sensibly be regarded as merely a subfield; or else we can infer that economists have forgotten about the possibility of subjective, rigorous, systematic, coherent analysis of the various forms of property rights. My conviction is that the latter inference is the more valid one. As evidence I cite that the only systematic analysis of choice among "goods" postulates utility maximization subject to a budget or *wealth* constraint, wherein the constraint is almost invariably a *private* property type of wealth constraint.

3. Property Rights

If, in what follows, I talk as if the property rights were enforced by formal state police power, let me here emphasize that such an interpretation, regardless of what I may later say, is gross error. It seems to be a fact that individuals will not stand by idly while some other person's property is stolen. It seems to be a fact that *private* property rights are rights not merely because the state formally makes them so but because individuals want such rights to be enforced, at least for a vast, overwhelming majority of people. And yet if I recognize the number of socialist states, I must admit to some confusion (I appeal for edification).

The rights of individuals to the use of resources (i.e., property rights) in any society are to be construed as supported by the force of etiquette, social custom, ostracism, and formal legally enacted laws supported by the state's power of violence or punishment. Many of the constraints on the use of what we call private property involve the force of etiquette and social ostracism. The level of noise, the kind of clothes we wear, our intrusion on other people's privacy are restricted not merely by laws backed by the police force, but by social acceptance, reciprocity, and voluntary social ostracism for violators of accepted codes of conduct. The use of arabic numbers rather than roman, of certain types of clothing or styles of speech and address; printing from left to right and top to bottom, rather than the reverse; or keeping our garden up with Jones's are all subject to the force of social opprobrium. No laws require such behavior. Yet each of us (or nearly every one of us) will punish in one way or another those who violate these rules. Surely it is not the important rules that are left to the formal state power of enactment and compulsion. Obviously there is heated dispute as to which forms of behavior should be "enforced" by social voluntary ostracism and which by formal state police action.

By a system of property rights I mean a method of assigning to particular individuals the "authority" to select, for specific goods, any use from a nonprohibited class of uses. As suggested in the preceding remarks, the concepts of "authority" and of "nonprohibited" rely on some concept of enforcement or inducement to respect the assignment and scope of prohibited choice. A property right for me means some protection against other people's choosing against my will one of the uses of resources, said to be "mine."

Often the idea or scope of *private* property rights is expressed as an assignment of exclusive authority to some individual to choose any use of the goods deemed to be his private property. In other words the "owners," who are assigned the right to make the choice, have an unrestricted right to the choice of use of specified goods. Notice that we did not add "so long as the rights of other people are similarly respected." That clause is redundant in strict logic. Private property owners can use their goods in any way they choose. If some of these chosen uses involve the use or destruction of other people's private property, it follows that the private property system is being violated, for this use has denied to other people the control of use over the goods classed as private property. To say I have private property rights is to say that no one else has the right to make the choice of use of that good (contained in the class of private property). This means that if I select a use for the goods said to be my private property, the selection must not affect the physical attributes of your goods. If I own some iron, I can make window frames or fence posts out of it, but if I shove a piece of iron through "your" glass window, I shall be denying you the right of choice of the physical attributes of your private property. However, if I convert the iron to a special kind of good that other people are willing to buy instead of buying what you are selling, you may find that the reduced exchange value of your goods imposes a greater loss of exchange power (wealth) than if I had simply broken your window.

Although private property rights protect private property from physical changes chosen by other people, no immunity is implied for the exchange value of one's property. Nor does it imply that my use of my goods, which may not in any way affect your goods, cannot be a use that you find objectionable on moral or emotional grounds. If I use my resources to make lewd pictures for my own use or for exchange with other people, you may find your "utility" much affected. You may be more upset, annoyed, distressed, or hurt by my action than if I had broken your window or stolen some of your wealth.

Private property, as I understand it, does not imply that a person may use his property in any way he sees fit so long as no one else is "hurt." Instead, it seems to mean the right to use goods (or to transfer that right) in any way the owner wishes so long as the physical attributes or uses of all other people's private property is unaffected. And that leaves plenty of room for disturbance and alienation of affections of other people. If I open a restaurant near yours and win away business by my superior service, you are as hurt as if I had burned part of your building. If I open a restaurant and pour smells and smoke over your neighboring land, then I have changed the physical attributes of your property; I have violated your private property rights—incidentally, a form of violation very common in most societies.

But if the right for me to open a business was denied, this could, if it also was part of a system in which your rights to enter into various businesses were similarly restricted, be considered by you to be an undesirable restriction and one that did you more harm than would be encountered by you in a less restrictive environment.

In sum, it is only the choice over physical attributes that is constrained to owners, not the value-in-exchange effects nor the psychological, emotional effects that you may suffer in the knowledge that I am behaving in what you consider improper ways (short of changing the physical attributes of your property).

4. Partitioning of Property Rights

Whether or not the preceding suggested definition is useful, we examine another issue. What are the effects of various partitionings of use rights? By this I refer to the fact that several people may each possess at the same time some portion of the rights to use the land. A may possess the right to grow wheat on it. B may possess the right to walk across it. C may possess the right to dump ashes and smoke on it. D may possess the right to fly an airplane over it. E may have the right to subject it to vibrations consequent to the use of some neighboring equipment. And each of these rights may be transferable. In sum, private property rights to various partitioned uses of the land are "owned" by different persons.[1]

A lease or rental agreement partitions the rights so that the renter gets the right to make decisions about particular uses of the item by the "owner." Normally the rights of the renter to decide where the furniture will be placed and when it will be sat on, etc., are not thought of as ownership rights, because they are so frequently allocated to the renter and because the ultimate value consequence rests on the "owner." However, our main point here is that the rights can be partitioned, divided, and reallocated on a temporary—or even on a permanent—basis so that the "ownership" rights are partitioned among two or more persons. This kind of division is not necessarily a cross-sectional division, with each owner now having equal parts of all the ownership rights. Instead it is a selective partitioning, with all of some of the subrights staying with the "owner" and all of some other rights being transferred temporarily at least to the "renter." Even though this is called a rental or leasing agreement, it does contain transfers of some of the rights that are included in ownership. The fact that these partitionings of owner rights are temporary makes it easy to decide who is the "owner" in the conventional sense.

The partitioning of various types of rights to use, has been explored by Ronald Coase.[2] He notes that what are commonly called nuisances and torts apply to just such situations in which rights are partitioned and the exercise of one owner's rights involves distress or nuisance for the owners of other rights. For example, if a railroad spreads sparks and ignites fires in wheatfields near the tracks, the wheat grower can pay the railroad not to spread sparks (if the law gives the railroad the right to spread such sparks). On the other hand, if the right to decide about such land use is reserved to the farmer, the railroad could pay him for the right to drop sparks on the land (and save costs of spark

---

1. A different form of interpersonal sharing of rights is that in which all rights are possessed in common and jointly by the group, but the decision as to any use must be reached by the group. Rights to each different kind of use are not separated and possessed by different people. Instead the rights are commonly owned; and the problem is in devising or specifying some choice process which will "declare" the decision of the "group" of joint owners.

2. "The Problem of Social Costs," *Journal of Law and Economics* (1960): 1–5.

screens, etc.). If there were no costs of *negotiating* such exchanges of rights and policing them, the initial partitioning of rights would not affect the way resources are used. (Of course, wealth would be redistributed in accord with the initial assignment of the partitioned rights.)

But when we recognize that transaction costs do exist, it seems clear that the partitioned rights will be reaggregated into more convenient clusters of rights. If so, there should be an evolutionary force toward survival of larger clusters of certain types of rights in the sanctioned concept of property rights. But I am at a loss to formulate this more precisely, meaningfully, and fruitfully. Except for rare studies like those of Glanville Williams on the development of the laws of trespass and the two-volume work of Pollack and Maitland on the development of law (and property rights) in the 12th through 14th centuries, I suspect our main alternative is to initiate studies of our own.[3] For example, a study of the property rights in Ireland during the past 300 years and of water law in the United States may (and I believe, will) enable us to discover more rigorous formulation of the laws of development of property law.

5. Sharing Property Rights

At this point there is a temptation to start classifying various partitioning of property rights—private, public, bailments, easements, leases, licenses, franchises, inheritances, etc. This temptation is easy to avoid, because the task is so difficult. Another temptation is to list the various ways in which property rights of owners—ownership rights, as they are called hereafter—whatever they may be, can be shared among people as joint owners or as a partnership. Or corporations can be created as a means of sharing property rights of owners among voluntary sharers. Or public property may amount to everyone having a share—although, as we shall see, I think this is not the crucial difference between public and private ownership.

The ability of individuals to enter into a mutually agreeable sharing of the rights they possess is evident from the tremendous variety of such arrangements, e.g., corporations, partnerships, nonprofit corporations, licenses, bailments, nonvoting common stock, trusts, agencies, employee-employer relationships, and marriages.

Should we be surprised that the government refuses to enforce some volun-

---

3. Frederick Pollock and Frederic Maitland, *The History of English Law Before the Time of Edward I*, 2nd ed. (Cambridge, 1952); Glanville Williams, *Liability for Animals* (Cambridge: Cambridge University Press, 1939).

tary proposed sharing of legitimate property rights among owners? Presumably the "undesirable" effects justify the refusal to sanction some of the ownership sharing. For example, at one time the state refused to enforce corporate ownership—even though all the members of the corporation entered voluntarily. Will it enforce every voluntary sharing and partitioning of ownership rights among individuals?

The variety of joint sharing of property and ownership rights is a testimony to man's ingenuity. But if one asked what the difference was between any two of them, say public and private ownership, he would find the answer not so easy. In one sense it is adequate to say that the public is the owner as contrasted with a private group. But that is not very helpful if one is interested in discovering what difference it makes for behavior and use of resources. Compare a privately owned golf course with a publicly owned course (or auditorium, bus service, water service, garbage collection, airport, school, or spaghetti factory). There are differences in the way they are operated; at least anyone who has ever compared them will think so. Why do these differences occur? Are the objectives different? Is it because the kinds of people who operate one are different from those who operate the other? Is it because of the form of ownership?

I believe (on the basis of something more than casual observation) that behavior under each institution is different, not because the objectives sought by organizations under each form are different, but, instead, because even with the same explicit organization goals, the costs-rewards systems impinging on the employees and the "owners" of the organization are different. And I suspect that these differences are implied by economic theory, if the trouble is taken to apply the theory. Further, preliminary speculation suggests, e.g., that the difference between a privately owned corporation with 1,000 owners and a state-owned entity in a democracy with 1,000 citizens is quite significant, because the 1,000 individuals are furthering their own individual interests in each entity under two different systems of property rights; i.e., the rewards-costs schedules differ.

6. Private and Public Ownership

How do private and public ownership rights differ? To sharpen the issue, consider a small-town theater owned by 1,000 corporate shareholders (each with one share) and an auditorium owned by the 1,000 residents as public property. This eliminates the difference of sharing and differences in the number of joint "owners." Every activity conducted at one building could, in prin-

SOME ECONOMICS OF PROPERTY RIGHTS 59

ciple, just as well be held at the other building. Assume also that the city auditorium is operated to make money, not to subsidize some group, and so is the
private theater.

The public auditorium and the private theater both serve the public. It is not
the case that the former is designed to provide a public service and the latter
not. The privately owned theater will survive only if it can provide services that
the public wants at the price asked. It is a source of public service, even though
its purpose from the owners' point of view is to make money. But what about
the publicly owned auditorium? Is its end that of public service or to make
money for the public owners? Suppose its end is public service. This does not
require that its means of action be any different than if its ends were profits to
the owners—public or private. Furthermore, assume in both cases the managers and employees were induced to take their jobs only because the salary enhances their own wealth or well-being. They take the jobs not because they
want to provide a public service or wealth for the owners, but, instead, because
they want a better living for themselves. We can assume that those resident citizens who "own" the auditorium and voted for it did so because each felt it
would make his own situation preferable—not because he wanted to benefit
someone else as a charity device.

But there are differences, and we conjecture the proposition that the differences between public and private ownership arise from *the inability of a public
owner to sell his share of public ownership* (and the ability to acquire a share without
a purchase of the right). But let us be clear about this. We are not yet asserting
that there are no other differences, nor that this difference has not been noticed
before. Instead we are emphasizing the *unique* importance of this difference in
the ownership rights.

We are not begging the issue by assuming away one general difference—the
profit incentive or criterion. Both public and private property can seek profits.
The desire to avoid or suppress the effects of the profit-making incentive is,
however, often the reason society resorts to public ownership. However, the
objectives sought by public ownership cannot merely be announced to the
managers or operators with expectation that exhortation will be either
sufficient or necessary to achieve the objective. Since our general postulate is
that people, as individuals, seek to increase their utility and that wealth is a
source of utility, we cannot expect people to change their goals or desires.
Instead, we rely upon changes in the rewards-costs structure to redirect their
activities as they seek to increase their utility or level of satisfaction of their

desires.[4] And we shall try to show that many differences that do exist between behavior in public and privately owned institutions reflect this ownership difference—viz., the presence or the absence of the right to sell a share of ownership to someone else.

The difference can be put somewhat less euphemistically. Public ownership *must* be borne by all members of the public, and no member can divest himself of that ownership. Ownership of public property is not voluntary; it is compulsory as long as one is a member of the public. To call something "compulsory" usually is a good start toward condemning it.

A person must move from one town to another to change his ownership in public property. In one sense it is not compulsory, because it is not compulsory that one lives in a particular community. But so long as one does live in any community with public property he is a public owner and cannot divest himself of public ownership; but he can sell and shift private property ownership rights without also having to leave the community.

It is tempting to emphasize the possibility, under public ownership, of someone joining the community and thereby acquiring a share of public ownership without payment to any of the existing owners. This dilution of a person's share of ownership is presumably absent in private ownership. In fact, a community could cut off immigration, but public ownership would continue even if this dilution effect were an important problem. Furthermore, many corporations issue new shares without preemptive rights to former owners. Presumably this is done only when the receiver of the new shares pays the corporation something of at least equivalent value. And it is a safe assumption that the management deems the *quid pro quo* to have been worthwhile so far as present purposes are concerned. Still, it is sufficient that even if dilution of public ownership were eliminated by restriction of entry, the inability to sell one's share of public ownership remains a potent factor in the costs-rewards system impinging on all members of the public and on the employees and administrators of the publicly owned institution.

7. Some Implications of Transferability

To see what difference is made by the right to transfer ownership shares, suppose public ownership could be sold. It would be possible for me to sell to someone else my share in the publicly owned water or bus or garbage or parks

---

4. Friends of Adam Smith will recognize this as the major postulate of his *Wealth of Nations*, a postulate which seems to have served economists well when not forgotten.

or school system. To separate out the fact that public ventures are usually run without the intent of making a profit, let us suppose that the water or bus system had been instructed to be as profitable as it could. Now that its ownership has become salable, with capitalized profits or losses accruing to the owners, will incentives be any different?

The answer is suggested by two implications of the specialization of "ownership," which is similar to the familiar specialization of other kinds of skills or activities. The two derivative implications are: (1) concentration of rewards and costs *more* directly on each person responsible for them and (2) comparative advantage effects of specialized applications of (a) knowledge in control and of (b) risk bearing.

Degree of Dependency

The greater concentration of rewards and costs means simply that each person's wealth is more dependent upon his own activities. This is brought about as follows: the more he concentrates his wealth holding in particular resources, the more will his wealth respond to his own activities in those areas. Consider the following example: Suppose there are 100 people in a community, with 10 separate enterprises. Suppose that each person, by devoting one-tenth of his time to some one enterprise as an owner, could produce a saving or gain of $1,000. Since the individual is a 1/100 part owner he will acquire $10. Suppose, further, that he does this for each of the 10 different enterprises, in each of which he owns 1/100 part. His total wealth gain will be $100, with the rest of the product, $9,900, going to the 99 other people. If the 99 other people act in the same way, he will get from their activities an increase of wealth of $990,000/100 = $9,900, which gives him a total of $10,000. This is exactly equal to his product, most of which was spread over the other owners.

However, if everyone each owns one-tenth part of *one* enterprise only (which means that ownership has been reshuffled from pro rata equal shares in all enterprises to a concentration in one enterprise by each person, although with the same total number of enterprises), the individual will now be assumed to devote his whole time during one year to the one enterprise, so he again produces $10,000. (We assume that his productivity is proportional to the number of hours of work and that it is the same for everyone. Other assumptions will change the arithmetic but will not destroy the main principle being elaborated.) Of this he gets $1,000. The remainder, $9,000, goes to the owners of the other 9/10 share. Like them, he too receives portions of the other owners' products, and if all are assumed to be exactly alike, then he gets from the 9 other joint owners of his enterprise $9,000, for a total of $10,000—precisely the same as in the preceding example. The difference is that now $1,000 of this is dependent upon his own activities whereas formerly only $100 was. Or, more pertinently, the amount dependent upon the activities of other people is reduced from $9,900 to $9,000.

If we go to the extreme where the 10 enterprises are divided into 100, with each person as the sole owner of one enterprise, then all $10,000 of his year's wealth increase will depend upon his own activities. The first of these three examples corresponds to public ownership, the second to corporate joint private ownership, and the third to sole proprietorship.

If public ownership rights were made salable, they would in effect become private ownership rights, and there would be a movement toward concentration of ownership of the type in the second example, at least. Why? In the second case, the wealth a person can get is more dependent upon his own activities than in the first case. Many people may prefer to let the situation stay as in example 1, hoping to collect a major portion of their wealth gain from other people's activities. If this were the case, the total wealth gain would decrease since everyone would have less incentive to work. But it suffices that there be at least one person who prefers to make himself less dependent upon other people's activities than in example 1 and who prefers at least some more wealth to some more leisure. He will then be prepared to buy up some ownership rights and pay a higher price for them than they are worth to some other people. That he values them more highly is precisely another way of saying that he values independence more than they do, or that he prefers more wealth to less wealth—even if it requires some work by him.

Comparative Advantage in Ownership: Control

The preceding example did not involve interpersonal differences of abilities, knowledge, or attitude toward risk. But if people differ in any of these respects, as they in fact do, it can be shown that specialization in various tasks—including that of owning a business—will increase wealth. This demonstration is simply the logical theorem of gains from comparative advantage, which we shall not explain here.

Usually the illustrations of comparative advantage are based on "labor" productivities with no reference to "ownership" productivities. But people differ in their talents as owners. Owners bear the risk of value changes, make the decisions of how much to produce, how much to invest, and how it shall be produced and who shall be employed as laborers and managers. Ownership ability includes attitude toward risk bearing, knowledge of different people's productive abilities, foresight, and, of course, "judgment." These talents differ among people according to the particular industry, type of product, or productive resource one is considering. The differences in skills of people as owners make pertinent the principle of comparative advantage through specialization in ownership. If ownership rights are transferable, then specialization of ownership will yield gains. People will concentrate their ownership in those areas in which they believe they have a comparative advantage if they want to increase their wealth. Just as specialization in typing, music, or various types of labor is more productive, so is specialization in ownership. Some people specialize in electronics industry knowledge, some in airlines, some in dairies, some in retailing, etc. Private property owners can specialize in knowledge about electronics, devoting much of their effort and study to learning which electronic devices show promise, which are now most efficient in various uses, which should be produced in larger numbers, where investment should take place, what kinds of research and development to finance, etc. But public ownership practically eliminates possibilities of specialization among owners—though not among employees in the publicly owned venture.

A person who is very knowledgeable about woodworking and cabinet or furniture building would have an advantage as an owner of a furniture company. He would, by being a stockholder, not necessarily make the company any better, but instead he would choose the better company—as judged by his knowledge—as one in which to own shares. The relative rise in the price of such companies enables the existing owners to issue new shares, borrow money more readily, and retain control. In this way the differences in knowledge enable people to specialize in the application of that knowledge to the management and operation of the company—albeit sometimes by indirect lines.

Comparative Advantage in Ownership: Risk Bearing

A second aspect of ownership specialization is risk bearing. People's attitudes toward risk differ. If various ventures or resources represent different prospects of values, then exchange of ownership will enable a reallocation of risks among people, leading to greater utility in the same sense that exchange of goods does. This risk-bearing difference reflects not only attitudes toward risk but beliefs about the prospects of future values of the assets whose ownership can be transferred. Differences in "knowledge" can be used not only in an effort to be more productive but also as a means for distinguishing different risk situations. For example, I may be the top administrator of the Carnation Milk Company, but I may choose to hold stocks in some electronic company because I prefer the risk pattern provided by that stock to that provided by ownership in Carnation. In this way a person can separate the productivity of knowledge and effort in what he owns from the risk bearing. He can, if he wants, combine them by holding stock in a company in which he is active. This possibility of separating the *control* (effective administration or operation of the company—an activity which rewards comparative superiority in ability and knowledge) from *risk bearing* is, of course, regarded as an advantage by those who act as employed managers or administrators and by those who choose to act as corporate stock owners without also bothering to exercise their vote or worry about control. Yet, it is often criticized as undesirable.

Not all of the owners have to think of themselves as owners who are going to exercise their voting rights so effectively as to exert an influence on management. Most of the owners may go along simply because they believe the prospects for profits and losses are sufficiently promising relative to other assets they could own. If losses eventuate, the owners' only alternative is to sell out. To whom? To other buyers who, because of the reduced profit prospects, will offer only a lower price. These "nonactive" owners perform a very important function in that they provide the willingness to bear some of the value consequences at least. So long as scarce resources *exist*, value changes will occur. The question left is, then, which particular members are to bear the reduced value. Someone has to bear them. Those changes cannot be eliminated.

Often it is said that joint ownership in the modern corporation has separated ownership and control. What this means is that risk bearing and management are more separate. This is correct in that each owner does not have the kind of control he would as the sole owner. But it is a long logical leap to decrying this. It can be a good thing. Specialization in risk bearing and in management or decision making about particular uses of resources is now possible. Complete separation does not exist for every joint owner, for to the extent that some share owners are inactive or indifferent to alternative choices or management problems, other stockholders (joint owners) will be more influential. In effect, the "passive" owners are betting on the decisions of "active" owners; "betting" in the sense that they are prepared to pay other people for any losses produced by these "activists" and, in turn, to collect the profits, if any. In the absence of any right to buy and sell shared ownership rights voluntarily, everyone would have to bet on the activists as a group (the case of public property). The right to sell concentrates this betting on these who are prepared to pay the most (or demand the least) for the right to do so. And it concentrates the control or management with those who believe they are relatively most able at that task—and these beliefs can be tested with the less able being eliminated more surely in private ownership than in public because (1) the evidence of poor management and the opportunity to capture wealth gains by eliminating it is revealed to outsiders by the lower selling price of the ownership rights, (2) the specialization of ownership functions is facilitated, and (3) the possibility of concentrating one's wealth in certain areas permits greater correlation of personal interest and effort in line with wealth holdings.

We conjecture from the preceding discussion the theorem *Under public ownership the costs of any decision or choice are less fully thrust upon the selector than under private property.* In other words, the cost-benefit incentives system is changed toward lower costs. The converse of this implication is that the gains to any owner resulting from any cost-saving action are less fully effective. These do not mean that the true costs are reduced. The looser correlation between the costs borne by any chooser and the costs of the particular choices he makes is what is implied. Similarly, the capturable gains to the owners of their actions are reduced.

They are *less* fully borne than they would be if the same action were taken in a private property institution, with a similar number of owners.[5] From this theorem one would expect that public agencies would, in order to offset or counterbalance this reduced cost bearing, impose special extra costs or constraints on public employees or agents. Public agents who are authorized to spend public funds should be more severely constrained with extra restrictions precisely because the costs of their actions are less effectively thrust upon them. And, of course, these extra constraints do exist. Because of these extra constraints—or because of the "costs" of them—the public arrangement becomes a higher cost (in the sense of "less efficient") than that for private property agencies.

For example, civil service, nepotism restrictions, tenure, single-salary structures for public school teachers, sealed bids, and "line-item" budget controls, to name a few, are some of the costly devices used.

But it is not easy—indeed impossible—in many instances to impose "corrective" costs as offsets. How would one impose full costs upon a city manager who decided to have a garbage collection system (that turned out to be a big money loser) that the city would tolerate? By not reelecting him. But this cost is

---

5. In other words, this difference between public and private ownership does not flow from differences in numbers of owners.

less than that borne by the private owner who decides (erroneously) to start a garbage collection system. He loses his job *and* the sunk costs. Similarly, how do we make a voter bear the costs of bad judgment in his votes? Are the prospects of costs that may be imposed on a voter equivalent to the costs-prospects that will be laid on a private owner (with share rights) voting in a private corporation? Not according to the theorem derived from our analysis.

I should, I suppose, avow at random intervals that all this is not a condemnation of public ownership any more than certain "deficiencies" of marriage, the human eye, the upright position of the human being, or smoking are to be regarded as condemnations of marriage, eyes, walking on two feet, or smoking. The "lesser" evils in some institutions—and they exist in all—are borne for the greater good in some of them. We are not arguing that private property even in its purest form is perfect in the cost-bearing sense. No standard of perfection is available. All of our statements have been comparative in degrees of cost bearing.

The converse of this "apologia" is that one should not speak of the imperfections of the marketplace either. Nor should one assume in those instances where the marketplace is inferior in certain respects to, say, public ownership or government control, that we ought to switch from the private property market to the government. The presence of one kind of relative deficiency does not justify a switch to another agency which has other kinds of deficiencies.

8. We Summarize

As we suggested earlier, public and private ownership are used for different purposes, and in some cases *because* of these different behavioral implications. If public ownership in some government activity were converted to private property, the method of achieving the government objectives would be changed. If city and national parks, or golf courses owned by cities were converted to private property, they would no longer be operated as subsidies for certain groups. If the fire and police department rights were converted to private property rights, vast changes would occur in their operation. And the same goes for the postal system, the garbage collection system, the bus lines, streets, the federal mortgage insurance companies, and the army, the navy, and the air force. When "we" do not want (whatever that means) these changes to occur, these activities are conducted via public ownership instead of privately. And if the effects of greater dependence of benefits and costs on one's own actions are not wanted, resort is made to government activity, which is not to say that government activity is therefore good or bad. The extent to which "society" reduces risks that must be individually borne and instead has them borne by society at large—thus reducing the correlation between choice of action and consequences for people as individuals—determines the extent of public property. How much this depends upon a *choice* to socialize certain risks and how much reflects the voting and decision-making *process* are questions I cannot answer.

PRICING AND SOCIETY

How should prices be determined? Should prices be set by decree or by open-market competitive forces? Should collusive action by sellers or buyers be encouraged? Should price discrimination be allowed? These questions, if pressed far enough, lead to broader questions. What *competitive behaviour* should allocate scarce resources among competing claimants and uses? *Who* should have what? And for what purpose? What are the consequences of determining prices in various ways? What conditions must exist if prices are to be determined in this or that way? Put this way the questions ask how society should be ordered and what each person should be allowed to do.

A sociologist might put it in a more general form: What are the cultural, political and economic consequences of various processes of allocating goods, and what are the institutional conditions that must prevail if that allocation or process is to be realised?

Insofar as you can get some answers to these questions, you can judge what kind of society you prefer. Would your choice be influenced by knowledge that public employees are often less helpful to the public they serve than is the employee of a "selfish" private employer? That public, government (or non-profit) employers are more discriminatory in their employment policies than private property employers? That public services are more likely to be underpriced than are privately provided services? Would your preferred process depend upon the particular goods and the people involved? Would you want the same system to apply to drugs, books and shoes? For everyone, children, aged, literate, more informed? Do you prefer that the young shall not be able to buy alcohol? That licensed doctors can buy morphine, while unlicensed doctors cannot? That Frenchmen and Englishmen have less competitive clash of ideas and options via television and radio than do Americans? That minority groups are less likely to get jobs in public utilities and in strong unions? That doctors prohibit advertising and open competition for their services? That universities and schools

Occasional Paper 17 (London: Institute of Economic Affairs, 1967). Reprinted by permission of the Institute of Economic Affairs.

assign students to schools nearest their residence, whereas people who eat out are not so assigned to restaurants?

The list could easily be lengthened; but it is more important to understand why those phenomena occur. All are results of the pricing system used; but the ability to use particular pricing tactics depends upon the property system.

Pricing and Property

Let me emphasise the fundamental proposition that every question of pricing is a question of property rights. We could have asked: What system of property rights shall be used? The existing system of property rights establishes the system of price determination for the exchange or allocation of scarce resources. Many apparently diverse questions come down to the same element—the structure of property rights over scarce resources. In essence, economics is the study of property rights. Without scarce resources property rights are pointless. The allocation of scarce resources in a society is the assignment of rights to uses of resources. So the question of economics, or of how prices should be determined, is the question of how property rights should be defined and exchanged, and on what terms.

I cannot present a theory of all the implications of various forms of property rights as a means of deriving the implications of various ways of determining prices, that is, of rationing scarce goods among competing users. But a general outline of the standard elements, with some examples, can be attempted. Economic theory (which is a theory of society) postulates that behaviour conforms to the hypothesis that every person has goals or goods that are substitutes for one another. Eating, physical comfort, sex, honour, intellectual interchange and marketable wealth are some of the goods. Each person is limited to some feasible set—the set composed of all the achievable combinations for him. Typically in standard economic theory, the boundary of the feasible set is defined by one's marketable *private* property and market prices. Even mathematical economics, which is supposed to provide rigour and *generality*, has restricted itself to this special case.

Private Goods and Voluntary Exchange

Goods controlled as private property are more likely to be exchanged (allocated) via markets and money prices than goods not so controlled. The reason is simple. With private property, two persons may exchange rights to goods on whatever terms they mutually accept. The exchange of one good for other marketable goods, or for friendship, or for charity, or for whatever other service one wishes to contemplate is unrestricted. It is unrestricted in the sense that any person who prefers some other mixture or form of payment for the goods he sells can offer to ask for it. A seller can sell to a pretty woman rather than an ordinary woman if he prefers. He can accomplish that mixture by accepting a lower price from "beauties" in order to deal more with them. Or as a buyer he can pay higher wages or prices and get a choice of other characteristics in his employees, or pay higher prices and get better quality. He can discriminate more fully. Prices will reflect the variations in preferences and quality of goods.

This point bears repetition. In the open market, property rights can be privately reshuffled and exchanged for whatever kind of mixture of other rights or goods any two people can agree to. Any mixture of components or goods can be suggested as the components of price. No one has to sell for money only; he can sell for very little money and ask the buyers not to smoke or not to drink or to dress well, or to perform little dances, or to do any of a large variety of other things.[1] The buyer has his own trade-off values among units of the various goods or activities. So does the seller. If the two parties can agree on some mixture of services or rights to be made available to one party in exchange for some mixture from the other, we have a sale. Typically one party transfers money and the other some non-money good, commodity or service. But there is nothing to prevent someone from asking for less money and a bigger smile, or a pledge not to smoke; the more "side" conditions asked, the lower the money price available. With private property, the open market provides each person the broadest opportunities to find exchanges on the best terms possible. The person who wants pleasant employers who will also provide a more relaxed atmosphere can accept a lower money salary. That is why more pleasant working conditions are associated with lower money wages, and riskier, less pleasant work with higher wages. Conversely a less desired employee can obtain a job by asking for a lower money wage.

The principle of "equalising differences" applies to all exchange, not merely to labour and wage markets. The lower one desired component, the larger must be the "equalising differential." The lower the monetary payment asked

---

1. An interesting example is the restaurant in the King's Road, Chelsea, which carries across its window the message: "Les seules conditions d'admission dans cet etablisse-ment sont que nos clients aient une certaine elegance et soient sympathiques. Le Patron mange ici." And to give emphasis to the point, should it be necessary, the door bears the legend: "Interdit aux paysans!"—ED.

by one seller, the more he will be able to get in non-monetary forms of equalising differentials.

A private property system seems to be dominated by formal marketable means of payment—money; but, as we have seen, pleasant working conditions and congenial colleagues often serve as payments in attracting employees (who are a form of good purchased by the employer). Private property does not result in the maximum possible monetary price as the rationing criterion. If it did, we would not see people of the same skills working for less pay in *better working conditions*. An open market seems to maximise the permissible range of feasible mixtures—the variety of behaviour from which one can choose—perhaps to one's regret. My tentative conclusion is that if you would increase the range or variety of mixtures of goods and exchange conditions—and a society is essentially a means of facilitating exchange of specialised services—then a private property system scores high(est?). I am further tempted to include in the concept of "freedom" the *range* of options—not the *size* of the particular basket selected. Freedom is not the only goal in my utility function. I trade some of it for more porridge, that is, for a larger-sized basket out of a narrower option. I trade options for more of a given good; why, otherwise, would I be employed at a state-owned and state-operated university?

Policing Exchange—The Costs of Information

But in speaking of private property I have talked as if there were no costs of obtaining information about exchange options, or of negotiating contracts and of policing their enforcement. If we lump together the costs of discerning exchange opportunities and communicating with potential exchangers, and of contracting and enforcement, we can see that these costs will, in some instances and for some goods, be so large as to preclude market exchange. For example, the cost of policing (supervising and administering) a parking lot and of negotiating payment by occupants may be higher than the cost of providing the parking space. At a zero price the parking lot may always be full, with rationing accomplished on the principle of "first-come, first-served." If one desires to accommodate those who feel the cost of making themselves the "first-come" is excessive relative to the value of the parking space, more space could be provided, or the parking lot could be policed and the spaces sold *via* market (i.e., money) exchange. If policing costs exceed the costs of providing enough space to accommodate the desired "second-comers," and if having space for the second-comers is worth the extra cost of more space, then more space will be created and provided "free" until the marginal cost of the land equals the marginal gain—which may or may not be sufficient to avoid rationing at even a zero price. Free (i.e., non-priced) parking space near large department stores in suburban areas where land is cheaper but not economically free is more common than in cities where land is more expensive; they are not priced because the cost of transactions *via* the market is higher relative to the land value in the suburban areas. So if one thinks private property should be or is associated with market-clearing prices, one must first reckon with the costs of private property systems.

Other resources than land—for example, water in rivers or underground basins, radio rights or rights to airspace—may all be allocated by a non-market pricing system because the costs of policing the market contract exceed the value of using a "superior" rationing system. If radio rights are worth £1, but if the costs of recording and negotiating a market sale exceed £1, it is cheaper to assign them in some other way. The exchange price (value to the highest claimant) must exceed the cost of negotiation and contract enforcement by at least the cost of production of the exchanged good.[2]

Pricing the Costs of Employee Agents

Transaction or contracting or enforcement costs are present also in an employee-employer relationship. An employee acts for the owner of the private property rights to the goods being allocated. The employee-agent is supposed to act as if he were the owner himself. If the proceeds accrue to the employer as his private property, the employer will take some care that the employee charges the market-clearing money price. However, the employee's preference is for a lower money price so that he could ration the goods on some non-monetary price criteria in such a fashion that more of the payment accrues to him. For example, at a lower price the employee can be more relaxed in making sales and less solicitous to potential customers; he can induce customers to be "nicer" and even to perform some of the functions of the employee. The customers, in order to enhance their competitive basis (which is no longer completely manifested *via* money prices), will offer other kinds of appeals pleasing to the employee. We have all learned this from our experience with price controls and government employees. However, the lower the costs to the employer of watching and policing the activity of the employee, the closer the market price will be to the market-clearing price.

2. What fraction of total product is devoted to policing property and contracts? Is 10 per cent too large an estimate (excluding national defence)?

The costs of policing the activity of employee-agents increases both with the number of employees and with the number of people among whom ownership is divided, as in a corporation. Thus I would expect to find more deviations from market-clearing money prices in a large firm than in a small one, and more deviation in a widely held corporate firm than in a proprietorship or closely held firm. Rules and regulations imposed on employees serve to prevent their straying from the path of maximising employer wealth. We all know that in some special or unusual circumstances it would be better for the employer if the employee did violate some inflexible rules. At such times, we, as customers or subordinate employees, are annoyed by the "red tape" that prevents managers from acting in a "sensible" way. We complain that if only we could talk to the owner he would make an exception to his "rule"—a rule derived from the conflict of interest between employee and employer. However, if authority to deviate is granted, deviations will also occur to further the employees' interest, to the detriment of the employer. There is, moreover, a common area of interest. I am not arguing that employees of private employers behave just like employees of governments or non-private employers. They do not, as we shall see later.

This implied kind of deviant behaviour by the employee in large enterprises is frequently characterised by the assertion that large corporations are less likely to adjust prices to clear the market than the small firm, that the small firm will adapt itself to customer desires more readily than the large firm. The same kind of consequence is evident in the behaviour of foremen and supervisors intermediary between owners and employees. The larger the costs of surveillance and enforcement of activities directed at maximising the owner's wealth, the more supervisors, foremen and managers will engage in favouritism or "arbitrary" employee promotion or firing practices. The subordinate employee feels the supervisor or manager is "taking advantage" of his situation in a larger corporation. But the analysis is incomplete. Competition among present or potential employees and among supervisors has the effect of reducing behaviour that departs from employer interests. New employees will offer to take the place of old employees who are inefficient in attending to the interests of the employer. With perfect competition among employees we would eliminate this effect—if "perfect competition" provides information as a free good.

But information is not free. Potential new employees do not all know what can be achieved. Circumstances are always changing; opportunities change. Insiders may know more than some outsiders. Which employee is acting inefficiently? Which employer's interests could in practice be better attended to by you? It does not suffice to say that "inefficiency" exists. To eliminate it the person who can do better must know where the "inefficiency" is—and that is costly to ascertain; and to the extent that it is costly, employees can act inefficiently, and competition among employees will not immediately eliminate it. However, "inefficiency" will be more acceptable where the employer himself is not the owner of the enterprise nor a manager-agent for some private owner.

Kinds of Property Rights and Rewards of Exchange

Not all non-money-market-clearing prices occur because of high information, policing and transaction costs relative to the marketable value of the rights. The exchange value of the rights may be biassed downward by the kind of property rights in them. If no one owns a peach tree, the value of the ripe peaches is not reflected in any marketable way that anyone can capture. People will pick the peaches before they are ripe, for fear that someone will beat them to the peach. If no one possesses the right to pick, the marketable value will not be as effective. Indeed, one dimension of the concept of private property is that it is relatively easier to convert or exchange private rights for marketable value. If goods are publicly owned it is not legally possible for one person to sell his rights to them to some other people. The rights are not marketable individually as is corporate stock ownership. This feature is, I think, the "crucial" distinction between private and public property.

I do not intend to suggest only a bipolar distinction between public and private property; rather I use the terms as the two ends to the spectrum ranges in the marketable transferability of the rights. In passing it is wise to remember that marketability implies *capitalisation* of future effects on to present values. Thus, long-range effects are thrust back on to the current owner of the marketable value of the goods. He will heed the long-run effects of current decisions more carefully than if the rights were not transferable. It is this feature which some people forget when they say that all a stockholder can do in a corporation is sell his stock if he does not like the way things are going—as if to say that doing so has no effect on the way things will be going. There exists a strong temptation to misconceive the power of a person with his relative share of voting strength. It is wrong to equate the political power and acts of a single person in a society of ten thousand voters with that of an owner of one share of stock out of ten thousand.

Diffused private property still retains one powerful difference. Rights may be capitalised and exchanged and may be consolidated into blocks, so that

some people have large interests. This ability to sell an attribute has two features; first is the capitalisation of future effects on present value—something
that is not feasible with public property. A larger span of value effects is imposed on each current rights holder and is more effective on current decisions.
Secondly, the ability to sell the rights enables some to specialise and exercise
more control in particular goods. For example, the specialisation gives incentives to buy up shares of corporations that are managed inefficiently, improve
them and capture the capitalised gains. There is a similar incentive for politicians to assemble voting blocks. However, this kind of "block vote" does not
possess the same elements of capitalisation and concentration of power. One
should avoid the mistake of thinking of a large, dispersed private property
business as being identical to an equally large[3] publicly owned enterprise. The
costs-incentive-reward system is different, as we have shown.

An implied observable difference in behaviour is that private firms will be
closer to market-clearing prices than will the publicly owned agency. Examples
are water, telephone, power and transportation services. "Shortages" will be
more chronic in publicly owned than in privately owned enterprises, with the
consequent change in the weights of competitive factors and behaviour involved in the rationing of the available services.

Suppose that, as citizens of the state, we prefer to see public goods used
where their value is highest. The costs to each of us of enforcing efficient behaviour are higher and the gains lower than in a private, equally large enterprise. The absence of (a) transferable marketable rights that can have exchange
values revealed, and (b) the possibility of concentrating one's rights in particular directions, so as to capture more capital value gains of improved marketable
value of the resources, imply a weaker force toward market-clearing money
prices for services rendered by publicly owned agencies.

Potential revenue is less realisable as personal income or wealth to the directors of non-private organisations. Non-realisation of potential wealth is
less costly to the directors; they do not bear so much of any sacrifice of potential wealth which is a consequence of their actions. Furthermore the directors
and their subordinates find it less costly to themselves, in terms of their personal wealth, to use whatever revenue they do get to cover business-connected
activities—which will occur in larger amounts. Departures from private property therefore induce two kinds of behaviour. One is to charge prices below

3. As measured by the number of owners.

market-clearing levels more frequently. The other is to let business costs increase to absorb revenues. Thus underpricing and excessive business-connected activities are implied. Examples of both effects are easy to cite.

Before illustrating them it is useful to recall that there is a *spectrum* of rights from private to public. In between there can be placed, for example, non-profit enterprises, public utilities with limited profits, profit-sharing co-operatives, and labour unions.

The protected public utility with a limited profit is an instructive case. Increments of wealth beyond the limit would accrue not to the stockholders but to the customer; if profits exceed the legal limit, prices would be cut to pass the benefit to the customer. "Stockholders" will not be willing to incur as much costs to ensure wealth-maximising behaviour in the public utility. Employees will have more scope for personal non-market sources of utility increments, for example, easy working conditions, prettier secretaries, more discrimination according to colour, sex and age, easier retirement and weaker discharge policies. Unions will find public utility managers more readily agreeable to wage rises.

It is safe to say, I believe, although I have not tested this hypothesis systematically, that the kinds of behaviour characterised by Berle and Means in their famous book on corporate behaviour[4] applied more to the limited-profit, public utility corporation than to the privately owned, unrestricted corporation, and even less to the corporation with few stockholders.

In this range we can fit also the not-for-profit corporation and the publicly operated agency that is *supposed* to dispose of its product via the market. In non-profit institutions there are no private "owners." There are trustees or stockholders, but they cannot sell the stock or declare dividends for stockholders. Costs are inflated to match receipts by paying larger salaries, by not firing incompetent people, by hiring more expensive, luxurious surroundings in terms of buildings, furnishings and people. Prices of services will be set too low to clear the market so that the operators can reap more benefits either directly from customers or indirectly by making management easier.

The mutually owned co-operatives are prime examples. They are active in the savings and loan business in the USA, yet relative to privately owned stock corporations they are tardy and sluggish. It is the stock-owned companies that are first to adjust interest rates to clear the market and which have lower costs.

---

4. A. A. Berle and G. C. Means, *The Modern Corporation and Private Property*, Macmillan, New York, 1933.

Between the diffused ownership of a corporation and the citizen-owned rights to public property there is the labour union or self-licensed profession, in which licences are awarded by the profession itself. In a union to which entry is limited, entry permission constitutes a rationing and allocation of a monopoly rent. As the entry controllers do not have private property rights in "entry" permits (and the monopoly rents), they have less reason to sell them in the market, since marketable payments would rebound to the financial benefit of the union. Union entry will be underpriced (in money terms), but the non-money payment price of entry will be higher. Furthermore, applicants queueing for admission will agree not to advertise or to perform special services to help incumbents (do charity work for doctors or do the lower-paying jobs) and agree not to be critical of their colleagues.[5] Negroes and other minority groups will find exclusion more common.

Where should we rank government agencies (like the New York Port Authority, the Tennessee Valley Authority, or the Federal Reserve system) that have their own sources of revenue but are publicly or governmentally owned? State or public universities, with which we are better acquainted, are better understood examples of the ability to avoid market-clearing prices. We note in passing that there is an alternative hypothesis—that state universities are employed in order to avoid market rationing of services, that is, to avoid full-cost tuition as the rationing criterion.

Resumé

Before exploring that example more fully, let me review the discussion. Setting prices is the setting of standards and the criterion for the allocation of rights to scarce resources. But this process is also the allocation of property rights. And it affects the kinds of competitive behaviour people manifest in their attempts to improve their utility. Setting prices is itself dependent upon the rights possessed by those who can transfer the rights. In sum, the structure of property rights affects the way prices are determined—fixing prices itself depends upon the rights possessed by those who can transfer the rights.

Some classification of the rights' structure has been attempted, and I have tried to show how rights affect the pricing system used. By implication they would then affect the behaviour of the people, as they compete for access to rights or to transfer of rights. To ask how prices should be determined is to ask what kinds of behaviour we want, or what kinds of property rights should be

5. D. S. Lees, *Economic Consequences of the Professions*, Research Monograph 2, IEA, 1966.

instituted, in order to get the preferred kinds of behaviour—a worthwhile inquiry if knowledge of such questions would indeed affect policy.

Pricing University Services

To make the analysis vivid, I shall discuss the allocation of educational services. I shall interpret events as implications of the preceding theory of property rights and behaviour.

A public university is typically financed from taxes, not from sales to students. Even in private schools a large portion of their proceeds comes from endowment or sources independent of market sales. What is the rationing system? More generally, what behaviour by students and faculty and administrators is fostered by that institutional arrangement?

A defence of low or zero tuition fees is that university education should not be rationed at market-clearing prices and should not be controlled by market sales. If I accept that defence, I then ask what institutional system will permit that desired rationing system. If I do not accept—as I do not—then our discussion is shifted from intent to effect. And since intentions are not sufficient to make behaviour viable, the issue is one of visible, not of intended or unintended, behaviour.

Universities are marked by zero or low tuition fees. (For emphasis I shall put things in extreme black and white terms and the reader can interpret them in comparative terms.) We use grades as conditions of entry and of continuance in school. We impose required courses with examinations. We have faculty control, academic freedom, tenure and acquiescent students. Students are severely restricted in their ability to transfer from course to course, to drop courses in mid-term and to repeat courses until they obtain passing grades. They are policed in the kinds of behaviour that will result in dismissal or inability to enter.

Compare that with a department store. Do the employees or managers so control or select customers? Of course not; and the reason is *not* that education is different (which it is) but that the ownership arrangement—and *only* that— is different. Such is the bed I am making for myself; now notice how comfortably I can lie in it. I (a member of the faculty) could survive with a market-clearing price. But students would insist on better treatment or else they would transfer their custom to a competitor—and competitors would exist at market-clearing prices. Intentionally or not, with foresight or not, we keep the fees low in order to accommodate less wealthy, more needy but deserving students.

Low fees enable us (the faculty) to select students according to non-money criteria. I select the better learners and smarter people who obviously "deserve" a higher education. How easy to swallow that self-serving contention!

The same reasoning could be applied elsewhere. Concerts should be free and financed by the state so that musicians can select the audience, admitting those who have the keenest ear and are best at making music themselves. Less discerning people can do other things. After all, there is no sense in wasting music on those less able to appreciate it.

If food were rationed at a zero price, chefs and dieticians who prepare the food could see that only the most deserving got the good food, while those who were less appreciative of food would get standard food without luxurious and expensive desserts.

External Benefits: Why Not Free Clothing?

Or if we are couturiers and dress makers, we will let only the most beautiful women have the best clothes. The average woman can wear her shapeless, less expensive dress. How wasteful to spend hundreds of pounds on a woman of hopeless figure, while there are women who, if beautifully dressed, would provide external benefits to the rest of society. Clearly, on the external-benefit count alone, clothing should be distributed as is education.

That the beautiful and shapeless alike should both have to pay for clothes would never cross our minds. After all, how could a poor beautiful girl pay? Certainly she could not borrow and pay out of later proceeds, for how could she earn more? Education could readily be financed by borrowing, but not beautiful clothes. After all, education is productive of income, beauty is not. We must provide zero-priced beautiful clothes for the prettiest women, while education can be sold at market-clearing price, with repayments out of later enhanced income. Couturiers have long advocated that the state finance dressmaking, with zero prices for clothing, so that they too can select their clients with the gracious socially beneficial care that we teachers employ. But not until the designers get tax-supported endowment subsidy, or non-profit dress design and manufacturing institutions, will they be able to serve society as well as we teachers do.

We tax-supported professors ration our entrants according to criteria that increase our utility and bring in less revenue to the institution, but *we* do it in order to increase the welfare of society. Once a student has arrived with a good scholastic and behaviour record, we give him grades, not simply to tell him how he is doing, but to see that he continues to act in ways to support our utility. Of course I would accept a student who offered to pay £100 for the privilege of staying in my class a second time after failing, were it not for my contract with the university which prohibits such behaviour. Yet my golf teacher, my Berlitz foreign-language teacher, my teachers of music, typing, shorthand, driving, dancing and electronic-computer programming are all willing to continue to teach me so long as I pay the admission price. They do not seem to care if I take only part-time schooling or get drunk periodically.

But we teachers at zero-tuition-fee schools are less tolerant. Tolerance would to us be a waste of resources. Once the student has been admitted, he is subjected to a battery of tests to satisfy some psychological research worker; he must stand in line for hours to register and pay his bills (can you imagine a department store always making you stand in line to buy and to pay your bills!); he must continue to behave in an exemplary manner; he must not belong to fraternities that discriminate among races. Can you imagine a private for-profit store engaging in such customer-excluding tactics and suffering the loss of monetary wealth?

The student who seeks advice about courses is ignored. Professors do not advertise their courses in the student newspaper as do the booksellers. Since teaching services are not rationed by market-clearing price, we can mistreat students more readily. For the lower is the tuition fee relative to costs of education or the value of it to the student, the less the faculty has to lose from its high-handed behaviour.

The land and facilities of the university are assigned internally on a non-price basis. Faculty offices, parking lots and use of classrooms are not rented. They are distributed so that those in charge of the allocation get more utility than if the market-clearing sales proceeds were collected and turned over to the university administration or added to the state or university budget. As faculty I could get space before my students. But under a market-rationing system I would have to pay for space I now get "free." The sales proceeds would give less benefit to any administrator than if he were a manager for a privately owned enterprise. Hence parking spaces are more frequently allocated not by pricing but by hierarchical status. Allocation of rights to use of university space is based on a hierarchical system reflecting the avoidance of trouble and acquisition of an easier life for the administration—more so than if it were privately owned or market oriented. So we practice the principle of rationing whereby the squeaky wheel gets the oil.

Free Speech and Free Resources

What means do students have to exert pressures on the administration? They can leave, but that would have small effect, with queues of new students already "too long." Taking their business elsewhere is not as effective as it would be in a marketplace. What they can do is to protest by *staying* and being obnoxious. If students protest by sit-ins, and by physically taking over the premises in the name of free speech, the faculty, conditioned to respond to the phrase "free speech" like Pavlov's dog to the bell, will lick its collective chops and rush to the students' aid rather than expel them. So long as students want space to "talk," we of the faculty mistakenly think they have a constitutional right to the space. So long as students identify their demands with free speech, our faculty colleagues will associate free speech with free resources. But free speech has nothing to do with free resources. We think the students should have the right to take whatever resources they wish—as if resources were free—in order to engage in "free speech." How easy it is to confuse "free" (in the sense of governmentally unrestricted rights to say what you want to a willing listener) with "economically free" resources in which to talk. Free speech (in the sense of unrestricted voluntary conversation) does not require "free goods." One can hire a hall.

Free speech does not involve use of public resources. Until the distinction is understood I fear we shall go on thinking we have given students free speech, when in truth we give them paternalism and economic goods, that is, qualified rights to use university facilities for certain purposes (such as conversation). They may use the space only so long as they do not express immoral ideas. But in a privately hired hall, obscene words are consistent with free speech—even though many people would regard that as "abuse" of free speech—thereby exposing the fallacy that free speech is something provided by access to non-private property. The public space is allocated and rationed at a zero price so long as it is used as the rationer thinks appropriate. With private property, the rationer's own standards can be excluded and resources made available for whatever views are agreeable to the two debaters.

So we find that rationing goods that are controlled by an agent not responsible to private owners implies less use of market-clearing prices and an increase in non-marketable types of goods; namely, an increase in the ability of the allocator to condition the behaviour of applicants, as with students. Furthermore, we increase the resort to public demonstrations on public property as a means of acquiring control over more of the non-market price-rationed goods. Such protests impose costs on the allocators (rather than monetary rewards), and as a condition of being relieved of such costs the claimants are given what they seek. This is known as the inalienable right to protest, though I confess I fail to see the difference between that principle and the man who sits in my house and prevents my using it until I let him have a room. There *appears* to be a difference because my house is typically sold or rented at a market-clearing monetary price, whereas public property is not. Hence in the latter case rationing devices include "first-come, first-served" and political pressures upon the agent. Pressures include a wide gamut of devices such as simple blockage of any use of the resources, now popularly known as "sit-ins," or public demonstrations blocking use of the streets for travel.

It is not surprising that a "first-come, first-served" method of protest is applied to public streets. Since street use is normally rationed at a zero money-price with first-come, first-served, we are accustomed to that system for streets. We often ask why people drive so rudely, when they behave so nicely in other places. The simple fact is that we ration space on the road in accordance with the first-come, first-served principle; so we see that kind of "rude" behaviour on streets.

That is how prices should be determined if you wish to encourage that kind of behaviour. And to get prices set that way, it is more viable to have the streets (or resources) publicly owned. One can look at the range of public services and find this principle of rationing widely used: public parks, public housing, water, telephones, courtroom services—to name but a few. In some instances, I find it to my personal advantage, especially if I happen to have the characteristics that increase my being "first come," or if I happen to be the allocator, as with university resources. So do not condemn me for my remarks.

Market and "Political" Skills

Private property reduces the scope of control by politicians and the wealth derived from political power. Viable behavioural traits depend upon the political system. In some countries it is skill at military tactics. In others it is personality appeal and oratorical ability. We cannot imagine Lincoln or Gladstone acquiring political power in a military junta. We cannot imagine some dictators acquiring power in a democratic election. Certainly some people are more skilled at political endeavours than at the market-oriented survival skills. In students of political science, of business administration or in engineering, you will see signs of developing differential skills. Small wonder then that politicians will be rewarded by public ownership. The man who enters political life to restrain the growth of public ownership, publicly operated agencies and services, will find that he must dismantle his major sources of power and wealth once he is in office. His survival chances in political office will diminish compared with those of another man taking the opposite position.

Conclusion

I have tried to show that:

1. the kind of pricing or rationing criteria used has a significant effect on behaviour—socially and culturally as well as economically;
2. the pricing or rationing system employed depends upon the system of property rights held by the allocators in the goods;
3. a valid theory of the relationship between kinds of property rights and rationing criteria and techniques and generated personal behaviour is not completely absent.

Economics is social science. If we apply it narrowly to private property and business administration, we conceal its enormous applicability to sociology, political science and jurisprudence.

THE PROPERTY RIGHTS PARADIGM

ARMEN A. ALCHIAN AND HAROLD DEMSETZ

Introduction

Economics textbooks invariably describe the important economic choices that all societies must make by the following three questions: What goods are to be produced? How are these goods to be produced? Who is to get what is produced? This way of stating social choice problems is misleading. Economic organizations necessarily do resolve these issues in one fashion or another, but even the most centralized societies do not and cannot *specify* the answers to these questions in advance and in detail. It is more useful and nearer to the truth to view a social system as relying on techniques, rules, or customs to resolve conflicts that arise in the use of scarce resources rather than imagining that societies specify the particular uses to which resources will be put.

Since the same resource cannot simultaneously be used to satisfy competing demands, conflicts of interest will be resolved one way or the other. The arrangements for doing this run the full gamut of human experience and include war, strikes, elections, religious authority, legal arbitration, exchange, and gambling. Each society employs a mix of such devices, and the difference between social organizations consists largely in the emphasis they give to particular methods for resolving the social problems associated with resource scarcity.

Capitalism relies heavily on markets and private property rights to resolve conflicts over the use of scarce resources. These fundamental characteristics of an idealized capitalistic system have been taken for granted by most mainstream economists even though the discipline of economics developed contemporaneously with Western-style capitalism. It is unfortunate that the study of the underpinnings of capitalism has been left by default to its critics on the left.

From *Journal of Economic History* 33 (March 1973): 16–27. Reprinted by permission of Cambridge University Press.

Grateful acknowledgement for aid is made to the E. Lilly Endowment Inc. grant to the Economics Department, U.C.L.A. for research on behavioral effects of different property rights.

But recent years have witnessed increasing attention to the subject of property rights and to the beginning of a somewhat different approach to the analysis of social problems that find their source in scarcity. Three questions are suggested by this growing literature: (1) What is the structure of property rights in a society at some point of time? (2) What consequences for social interaction flow from a particular structure of property rights? and (3) How has this property right structure come into being? Economic historians can contribute very much to overcoming our ignorance about the answers to these questions, and our purpose here is to facilitate historical research on these problems by clarifying somewhat the content of these questions.

The Structure of Rights

In common speech, we frequently speak of someone owning this land, that house, or these bonds. This conversational style undoubtedly is economical from the viewpoint of quick communication, but it masks the variety and complexity of the ownership relationship. What is owned are *rights* to *use* resources, including one's body and mind, and these rights are always circumscribed, often by the prohibition of certain actions. To "own land" usually means to have the right to till (or not to till) the soil, to mine the soil, to *offer* those rights for sale, etc., but not to have the right to throw soil at a passerby, to use it to change the course of a stream, or to *force* someone to buy it. What are owned are socially recognized rights of action.

The strength with which rights are owned can be defined by the extent to which an owner's decision about how a resource will be used actually determines the use. If the probability is "1" that an owner's choice of how a particular right should be exercised actually dominates the decision process that governs actual use, then that owner can be said to own absolutely the particular right under consideration. For example, a person may have an absolute right to pick apples off a tree but not to prune the tree.

The domain of demarcated uses of a resource can be partitioned among several people. More than one party can claim some ownership interest in the same resource. One party may own the right to till the land, while another, perhaps the state, may own an easement to traverse or otherwise use the land for specific purposes. It is not the resource itself which is owned; it is a bundle, or a portion, of rights to *use* a resource that is owned. In its original meaning, property referred solely to a right, title, or interest, and resources could not be identified as property any more than they could be identified as right, title, or interest.

Distinct from the partitioning of the domain of uses to which a resource may be put is the decision process that may be relied upon to determine that use: The exercise of a particular right may depend on a decision process in which many individuals share, such as in the use of majority voting. The right to vote may be exercised individually, but it is the pattern of votes by many individuals that determines the way in which a right to use a resource will be exercised.

There are two important questions that can be asked about the structure of property rights in a society. The first asks which property rights exist. There may exist a particular right of use in a society that did not exist earlier or that does not exist in other societies. For example, early in the history of radio, users of frequencies did not own the right to prevent members of the community from broadcasting on these same radio frequencies. Any person who wished to could broadcast on any frequency, and that is still true today for certain bands of radio frequencies. The right to offer heroin for sale on the open market does not exist in the United States although it may in other countries. The right to advocate particular political doctrines exists in greater degree in the United States than in Russia. (It should be noted that the right to advocate is a right to use resources, for no advocacy could take place without the *use* of a place and other facilities.)

The second question calls attention to the fact that the identity of right owners may vary. Perhaps the most important ownership distinction is between state (public) ownership and private ownership. An easement right may be owned by the state or by an individual. The right to deliver first-class mail is owned by the state, whereas the right to board troops without permission is not. Needless to say, the classification of social systems according to the degree of centralization of control is closely related to the degree to which property rights are owned exclusively by the state.

There is some ambiguity in the notion of state or private ownership of a resource, because the bundle of property rights associated with a resource is divisible. There can and does exist much confusion about whether a resource or "property" is state or privately owned. Some rights to some uses of the resource may be state owned and others privately owned. While it is true that the degree of private control is increased when additional rights of use become privately owned, it is somewhat arbitrary to pass judgment on when the conversion to private control can be said to change the ownership of the bundle of rights from public to private. The classification of owners can be carried beyond the important state and private dichotomy. Corporate, school, and church owners of property are also of interest. The structure of rights can have important consequences for the allocation of resources, some of which we now illustrate.

The Social Consequences of the Structure of Rights

The significance of which rights exist can be appreciated by contrasting situations in which there is and is not a right to exclude. We shall use the phrase "communal rights" to describe a bundle of rights which includes the right to use a scarce resource but fails to include the right of an "absentee owner" to exclude others from using the resource. Operationally this means that the use of a scarce resource is determined on a first-come, first-served basis and persists for as long as a person continues to use the resource. The use of a city sidewalk or a "public" road is communal, and the rights to till or hunt the land have been subjected to this form of ownership frequently. Often communal ownership is technically associated with state ownership, as in the case of public parks, wherein the state technically has the capability of excluding persons from using its property. If this right is exercised by the state frequently, as it is on military reservations, then the property right is more properly identified as state owned, but if the right to exclude is seldom exercised by the state, as in public parks or thoroughfares, then as a practical matter the users of the resource will treat it as communal. Communal rights mean that the working arrangement for the use of a resource is such that neither the state nor individual citizens can exclude others from using the resource except by prior and continuing use of the resource. The first driver to enter the public road has a right of use that continues for as long as he uses the road. A second driver can follow the first but cannot displace or exclude him.

The difficulty with a communal right is that it is not conducive to the accurate measurement of the cost that will be associated with any person's use of the resource. Persons who own communal rights will tend to exercise these rights in ways that ignore the full consequences of their actions. For example, one of the costs of hunting animals, if they are not superabundant, is the resulting depletion in the subsequent stock of animals. This cost will be taken into account only if it is in someone's interest to do so. This interest is provided if someone can lay claim to or benefit from the increase in the stock of animals that results from a curtailment in his hunting activities. Under a communal right system anyone who refrains from hunting does so not to his benefit but to the benefit of others who will continue to exercise their communal right to hunt. Each person, therefore, will tend to hunt the land too intensively and deplete the stock of animals too rapidly.

Often the exercise of communal rights forces persons to behave in ways that are thought to be immoral. In 1970, the newspapers carried stories of the barbaric and cruel annual slaughter of baby seals on the ice floes off Prince Edward Island in the Gulf of St. Lawrence. The Canadian government permitted no more than 50,000 animals to be taken, so hunters worked with speed to make their kills before the legal maximum was reached. They swarmed over ice floes and crushed the babies' skulls with heavy clubs. Government offices received many protests that the seals were inhumanely clubbed (by humans) and often skinned alive. The minister of fisheries warned the hunters of the strong pressure he was under to ban the hunt and that he would do so unless the killing methods were humane in 1970. Clearly, it is not the hunters who are to blame but the regulations governing seal hunting that impose a communal right to hunt on hunters until 50,000 baby seals have been taken. The first 50,000 animals are offered free on a first-come, first-served basis, a rationing system that is bound to encourage rapid hunting techniques and to make a condition for success the degree to which the hunter can be ruthless.

The problems posed by communal rights are abundantly clear when we analyze the causes of pollution. Since the state has invited its citizens to treat lakes and waterways as if they are free goods, that is, since the state generally has failed to exclude persons from exercising communal rights in the use of these resources, many of these resources have been overutilized to the point where pollution poses a severe threat to the productivity of the resource.

An attenuation in the bundle of rights that disallows exchange at market clearing prices will also alter the allocation of resources. The interests pursued by men are both varied and many. If a price ceiling or price floor prevents owners from catering to their desires for greater wealth, they will yield more to the pursuit of other goals. For example, effective rent control encourages owners of apartments to lease them to childless adults who are less likely to damage their living quarters. Effective rent control also prompts landlords to lease their apartments to persons possessing personal characteristics that landlords favor. In a Chicago newspaper, the percentage of apartment-for-rent advertisements specifying that the apartment was for rent only on a "restricted" basis or only if the renter purchased the furniture rose from a pre-war low of 10 percent to a wartime high of 90 percent during the period of World War II when rent control effectively created queues of prospective renters. Attenuations in the right to offer for sale or purchase at market clearing prices can be expected to give greater advantages to those who possess more appealing racial or personal attributes.

The reallocation of resources associated with the absence of a right to exclude and the inability to exchange at market clearing prices is attributable to the increase in the cost of transacting brought about by these modifications in the property right bundle. A price-fixing law raises the cost of allocating resources vis-à-vis the price mechanism and, therefore, forces transactors to place greater reliance on nonprice allocation methods. This is obvious; but not equally obvious is the role played by transaction cost when the right to exclude is absent.

Consider the problem of congestion during certain hours in the use of freeways. No one exercises the right to exclude drivers from using freeways during these hours. The right to drive on freeways is a communal right. But drivers who desire less congestion are not legally prohibited from paying others to use alternative routes during these hours. This right system, however, encourages drivers to let someone else pay persons to use alternative routes, since those who do not pay cannot be excluded from the use of the freeway under a communal right system. The communal right system raises transaction cost by creating a free rider problem. Moreover, even if some temporary reduction in congestion is purchased, there may be many persons not now using the freeway who are attracted to it by the temporary reduction in congestion. The supply of freeway space is very likely to create a demand for its use under the communal right system because these new users cannot be excluded. They also must be paid to return to alternative routes, and this burdens the allocation system with additional costly transactions. A right system that includes the right to exclude nonpayers, such as is possible with toll roads, eliminates both these sources of high transaction cost. Persons not now using the road can use it only if they value the route enough to pay the toll, and the owner of the toll road is not handicapped by the psychology of a freeloader.

The social consequences of the identity of right owners also can have allocative effects. At the more obvious level, government and private owners, respectively, will respond in greater degree to political and market incentives, and this can be expected to yield differing resource uses. But the effect on resource allocation of altering the identity of owners, all of whom are private owners, is not so obvious. As a first approximation, each and all private owners can be expected to respond to market incentives in the same way so that the particular identity of owners will not alter the uses to which resources are put. All private owners have strong incentives to use their property rights in the most valuable way. Under certain conditions, this approximation can be expected to be very good. The most important of these conditions is that the cost of transactions be negligible; in this case, it will be easy for those who can put resources to their most valuable uses to contact and negotiate with those persons presently owning the rights to these resources. If the cost of transactions is not negligible, then an alteration in the identity of right owners can have allocative effects because negotiations toward a unique utilization of resources may be inhibited by positive transaction costs.

The most important effect of alterations in institutional arrangements may well be the impact of such reorganizations on the cost of transacting. The enclosure movement, for example, may have significantly reduced the cost of carrying on transactions among those possessing rights of use, and this may have eased the task of putting resources to their most productive uses. Perhaps some new insights about the consequences of the enclosure movement can be obtained if the researcher focuses his attention on the cost of transacting.

The Development of Property Right Structures

Under a communal right system each person has the *private* right to the use of a resource once it is captured or taken, but only a communal right to the same resource before it is taken. This incongruity between ownership opportunities prompts men to convert their rights into the most valuable form; they will convert the resources owned under communal arrangements into resources owned privately; that is, they will hunt in order to establish private rights over the animals. The problem can be resolved either by converting the communal right to a private right, in which case there will be no overriding need to hunt the animals in order to establish a private claim, or by restraining through regulation the incentive to convert communal rights to private rights.

There is a basic instability in an arrangement which provides for communal rights over a resource when that resource takes one form, and for private rights when the resource takes another form. The private right form will displace the communal right form. In itself this has important consequences *only* if the conversion of communal ownership into private ownership is costly. Thus, if unbranded animals are held to be communal property while branded animals are private, there will be a rush to place brands on the animals. This would not be very costly, especially since branding would be desirable for identification purposes anyway. There would be no need to kill the animals in order to establish private rights, so these animals can be husbanded appropriately once the cost of branding is incurred. But a conversion process that requires that the animals be killed in order to establish private rights must incur the larger social cost of depleting the stock of animals.

If the social adjustment to the incongruity between communal and private rights is resolved in favor of eliminating the private right, then the immediate problem is replaced by another—the problem of providing incentives to work. Thus, if we suppose that the communal right to hunt is supplemented by the stipulation that killed animals belong to the community, in which all citizens can share according to custom, and do not belong exclusively to the hunter, then the incentive to hunt will be diminished. This may cure the overhunting problem by creating an underhunting problem in which the able-bodied wait for others to do the hunting, the results of which will be shared by all. In order to reduce the severity of the shirking problem that is thereby created, it is necessary for societies which fail to establish private rights to move ever closer to a social organization in which the behavior of individuals is directly regulated by the state or indirectly influenced by cultural indoctrination. The option to hunt or not to hunt cannot be left with the individual who, unable to claim the fruit of his effort, will tend to shirk. Instead, the state will find it increasingly necessary to *order* the hunt, to insist on participation in it, and to regulate more closely the sharing of the kill. Or, possibly, the community can invest in cultural indoctrination that leads to an increase in the willingness to hunt. This is in fact the course that events have taken among many primitive peoples. The animals they hunt are "free" to all on a first-come, first-served basis, but the kill must be shared according to detailed ritual procedures, and the question of participating in the hunt is not left open to individuals. The attempt to resolve scarcity-created problems by reducing the scope of private rights must inevitably result in a more centrally regulated or indoctrinated society. One need not go so far afield to find this process at work. Our public schools are offered on a "free" right-to-use basis. As good schools attract increasing numbers of students, the community either must expand its resource commitment to public schools, in order to offset what it views as overutilization, or must somehow regulate the flow of newcomers. Zoning restrictions and building codes frequently have been used to restrict the rate of immigration into such communities.

If private rights can be policed easily, it is practicable to resolve the problem by converting communal rights into private rights.[1] Contrary to some popular

---

1. Alternatively, of course, the communal right can be converted to a state right in which the state seeks to exclude, perhaps by adopting a price mechanism, the issue raised by state vs. private ownership as not so much one of what can be done but one of what will be done by state owners.

notions, it can be seen that *private* rights can be socially useful precisely because they encourage persons to take account of *social* costs. The identification of private rights with anti-social behavior is a doctrine as mischievous as it is popular.

The instability inherent in a communal right system will become especially acute when changes in technology or demands make the resource which is owned communally more valuable than it has been. Such changes are likely to bring with them harmful and beneficial effects which can be measured and taken account of only by incurring large transaction costs under the existing property right structure. In such situations, we expect to observe modifications in the structure of rights which allow persons to respond more fully and appropriately to these new costs and benefits. The coming of the fur trade to the New Continent had two consequences. The value of furs to the Indians increased and so did the scale of hunting activities. Before the coming of the fur trade, the Indians could tolerate a social arrangement that allowed free hunting, for the scale of hunting activities must have been too small to seriously deplete the stock of animals. But after the fur trade, it became necessary to economize on the scale of hunting. The control system adopted by the Indians in the northeastern part of the continent was to substitute private rights in land for free access to hunting lands. By owning the right to exclude others from their land, Indian families were provided with an incentive to inventory their animals. Under a free access arrangement, such inventories would have been depleted by other hunters. With private rights to hunt the land, these inventories could be maintained at levels more consistent with the growing market for furs.

Similarly, Professor North notes that twelfth-century England experienced a relative rise in the value of land which led to efforts to convert the existing right structure into one that allowed for exclusive ownership and transferability.[2] During the thirteenth century, England experienced the development of an extensive body of land law, the initiations of enclosure, and, finally, the right to alienate land, and there were similar experiences on the Continent.

The relaying of radio signals between nations in Europe provides an interesting example of the breadth of the property right adjustment that is likely to follow from an economically significant technological development. The telephone company in Holland decided in 1926 that it would use its facilities to

---

2. D. North and R. Thomas, "The Rise and Fall of the Manorial System: A Theoretical Model," *Journal of Economic History*, 31 (December 1971), pp. 777–803.

relay radio programs received from outside Holland to subscribers in Holland in return for the payment of subscription fees. However, many of the programs originating from such countries as England, France, and Germany were owned under copyright, and the copyright owners were not compensated by the Holland telephone company. The use of a resource that automatically became available to one country once it was produced in another posed unusual legal problems that led to heated controversy and to the Berne Convention in 1928. That conference gave to copyright owners the sole right to authorize any communication to the citizens of signatory countries, whether over wires or not, of the radio transmission of the copyright material. And by 1938, in the United States, the Federal Radio Commission appeared to regard the unauthorized relay of broadcast signals as illegal.

We have merely touched on a few cases of evolving structures of property rights to which some contemporary thought has been given. There exist very many property right phenomena that could benefit from thoughtful attention. Consider the problem of the capital structure of corporations. The well-known Modigliani-Miller theorem that the value of an enterprise is independent of its capital structure is a special application of the assumption that the cost of transacting is zero. Titles of various kinds are assigned to parts of an enterprise's wealth, and the value of these titles is no more nor less than the present value of the enterprise's wealth potential, at least so long as entitlements are well defined, partitionable, and transferable at zero cost. Further, they will be revised and exchanged in ways that maximize the utility of their owner subject only to the constraint imposed by the wealth potential of the enterprise.

But, in fact, these bundles of rights are not costlessly transferable or revisable, so a question remains as to what bundles of rights are most appropriate for an enterprise to issue initially. Bonds, common stocks, preferreds, convertibles, warrants? Given the cost of transacting and of revising these bundles of rights, are there any factors that would explain the initial mix? We conjecture that differences in *beliefs* by investors about the potential performance of the enterprise can account for differences in the initial mix. An enterprise that desires to maximize the sum it raises from the sale of ownership claims would find it desirable to offer different bundles of rights; a warrant, for example, to optimistic investors and a bond to pessimistic investors, given that markets do not function costlessly. If the market could produce these different bundles costlessly, there would be no need for the firm to be concerned with different financial instruments. For, then, financial intermediaries could supplement and convert any financial instrument issued by the firm into the mix of financial instruments preferred by optimistic and pessimistic investors who hold different expectations about the firm's prospects.

Although articles dealing with property rights and transaction costs are accumulating at a rapid pace, they tend to be primarily of the "speculative theory" variety. Only a handful of empirical studies have been concluded, a few of which are concerned with phenomena old enough to be historical. But economic historians have much more to contribute, and we hope that we have made some of you curious enough to examine the partial bibliography appended to this paper.

BIBLIOGRAPHICAL APPENDIX

1. A. A. Alchian. "Unemployment and the Cost of Information," *Western Economic Journal*, 7 (June 1969), pp. 109–28.
2. ———, "Some Economics of Property Rights," *Il Politico*, 30 (1965), pp. 816–29.
3. A. Alchian and H. Demsetz, "Production, Information Cost, and Economic Organization," *American Economic Review*, 62 (December 1972).
4. A. Bottomley, "The Effect of the Common Ownership of Land Upon Resources Allocation in Tripolitania," *Land Economics* (February 1963), pp. 91–95.
5. K. Brunner and A. Meltzer, "Some Further Investigations of Demand and Supply Functions for Money," *Journal of Finance*, 19 (May 1964, pt. 1), pp. 240–83.
6. S. Cheung, *The Theory of Share Tenancy* (Chicago: Univ. of Chicago, 1969).
7. R. H. Coase, "The Nature of the Firm," Reprinted in *AEA Readings in Price Theory*, Stigler and Boulding, eds., Irwin, 1952, pp. 331–51.
8. ———, "The Problem of Social Cost," *Journal of Law and Economics*, 3 (October 1960), pp. 1–40.
9. T. D. Crocker, "Externalities, Property Rights, and Transaction Costs," *Journal of Law and Economics*, 14 (October 1971), pp. 451–64.
10. H. Demsetz, "Toward a Theory of Property Rights," *AEA Papers and Proceedings*, May 1967, pp. 253–57.
11. ———, "When Does the Rule of Liability Matter?," *Journal of Legal Studies*, 1 (January 1972), pp. 13–28.
12. ———, "The Private Production of Public Goods," *Journal of Law and Economics*, 13 (October 1970), pp. 293–306.
13. ———, "The Cost of Transacting," *Quarterly Journal of Economics*, 82 (February 1968), pp. 33–53.

14. A. S. Devany, R. D. Eckert, C. J. Meyers, D. J. O'Hara, and R. C. Scott, "A Property System for Market Allocation of Electro-Magnetic Spectrum: A Legal-Economic-Engineering Study," *Stanford Law Review*, 30 (June 1969), pp. 1499–1561.

15. E. Furubotn and S. Pejovich, "Property Rights and the Behavior of the Firm in a Socialist State," *Zeitschrift für Nationalökonomie*, 30 (Winter 1970), pp. 431–54.

16. S. MacCauley, "Non-Contractual Relations in Business: A Preliminary Study," *American Sociological Review*, 28 (February 1963), pp. 55–67.

17. R. N. McKean, "Products Liability: Implications of Some Changing Property Rights," *Quarterly Journal of Economics*, 82 (November 1970), pp. 611–26.

18. D. North and R. Thomas, "The Rise and Fall of the Manorial System: A Theoretical Model," *Journal of Economic History*, 31 (December 1971), pp. 777–803.

19. S. Pejovich, "Liberman's Reforms and Property Rights in the Soviet Union," *Journal of Law and Economics*, 12 (September 1969), pp. 193–200.

20. ———, "The Firm, Monetary Policy and Property Rights in a Planned Economy," *Western Economic Journal*, 7 (September 1969), pp. 193–200.

21. S. Rottenberg, "Property in Work," *Industrial Labor Relations Review*, 2 (April 1962), pp. 402–5.

PROPERTY RIGHTS [1987]

Private Property Rights. A property right is a socially enforced right to select uses of an economic good. A private property right is one assigned to a specific person and is alienable in exchange for similar rights over other goods. Its strength is measured by its probability and costs of enforcement, which depend on the government, informal social actions and prevailing ethical and moral norms. In simpler terms, no one may legally use or affect the physical circumstances of goods to which you have private property rights without your approval or compensation. Under hypothetically perfect private property rights none of my actions with my resources may affect the physical attributes of any other person's private property. For example, your private property rights to your computer restrict my and everyone else's permissible behaviour with respect to your computer, and my private property rights restrict you and everyone else with respect to whatever I own. It is important to note that it is the physical use and condition of a good that are protected from the action of others, not its exchange value.

Private property rights are assignments of rights to choose among inescapably incompatible uses. They are not contrived or imposed restrictions on the feasible uses, but assignments of exclusive rights to choose among such uses. To restrict me from growing corn on my land would be an imposed, or contrived, restriction denying some rights without transferring them to others. To deny me the right to grow corn on my land would restrict my feasible uses without enlarging anyone else's feasible physical uses. Contrived or unnecessary restrictions are not the basis of private property rights. Also, because those restrictions typically are imposed against only some people, those who are not so restrained obtain a "legal monopoly" in the activity from which others are unnecessarily restricted.

Under private property rights any mutually agreed contractual terms are permissible, though not all are necessarily supported by governmental en-

Reprinted from *New Palgrave Dictionary of Economics*, ed. John Eatwell, Murray Milgate, and Peter Newman (London: Macmillan Press Limited, 1987), by permission of Palgrave Macmillan.

forcement. To the extent that some contractual agreements are prohibited, private property rights are denied. For example, it may be considered illegal to agree to work for over 10 hours a day, regardless of how high a salary may be offered. Or it may be illegal to sell at a price above some politically selected limit. These restrictions reduce the strength of private property, market exchange and contracts as means of coordinating production and consumption and resolving conflicts of interest.

Economic Theory and Private Property Rights. A successful analytic formulation of private property rights has resulted in an explanation of the method of directing and coordinating uses of economic resources in a private property system (i.e., a capitalistic or a "free enterprise" system). That analysis relies on convex preferences and two constraints: a production possibility and a private property exchange constraint, expressible biblically as "Thou Shall Not Steal," or mathematically as the conservation of the exchange values of one's good.

For the decentralized coordination of productive specialization to work well, according to the well-known principles of comparative advantage, in a society with diffused knowledge, people must have secure, alienable private property rights in productive resources and products tradeable at mutually agreeable prices at low costs of negotiating reliable contractual transactions. That system's ability to coordinate diffused information results in increased availability of more highly valued goods as well as of those becoming less costly to produce. The amount of rights to goods one is willing to trade, and in which private property rights are held, is the measure of value; and that is not equivalent to an equal quantity of goods not held as private property (for example, government property). It probably would not be disputed that stronger private property rights are more valuable than weaker rights; that is, a seller of a good would insist on larger amounts of a good with weaker private property rights than if private property rights to the goods were stronger.

Firms, Firm-Specific Resources and the Structure of Property Rights. Though private property rights are extremely important in enabling greater realization of the gains from specialization in production, the partitionability, separability and alienability of private property rights enables the organization of cooperative joint productive activity in the modern corporate firm. This less formally recognized, but nevertheless important, process of cooperative production relies heavily on partitioning and specialization in the components of private property rights. Yet, this method is often misinterpreted as unduly restrictive and debilitating to the effectiveness and social accept-ability of private property rights. To see the error, an understanding of the nature of the firm is necessary, especially in its corporation form, which ac-counts for an enormous portion of economic production. The "firm," usu-ally treated as an output-generating "black box," is a contractually related collection of resources of various cooperating owners. Its distinctive source of enhanced productivity is "team" productivity, wherein the product is not a sum of separable outputs each of which is attributable to specific cooper-ating inputs, but instead is a non-decomposable, non-attributable value produced by the group. Thus, for something produced jointly by several sep-arately owned resources, it is not possible to identify or define how much of the final output value each resource could be said to produce separately. Instead, a marginal product value for each input is definable and measur-able.

Whereas specialized production under comparative advantage and trade is directed in a decentralized process by market price and spot exchanges, productivity in the team, called the firm, relies on long-term, constraining contracts among owners who have invested in resources specialized to the group of inputs in that firm. In particular, some of the inputs are specialized to the team in that once they enter the firm their alternative (salvage) values become much lower than in the firm. They are called "firm-specific." In the firm, firm-specific inputs tend to be owned in common, or else contracts among separate owners of the various inter-specific resources restrict their future options to those beneficial to that group of owners as a whole rather than to any individual. These contractual restrictions are designed to re-strain opportunism and "moral hazard" by individual owners, each seeking a portion of each other's firm-specific, expropriable composite quasi-rent. Taking only extremes for expository brevity, the other "general" resources would lose no value if shifted elsewhere. A firm, then, is a group of firm-specific and some general inputs bound by constraining contracts, produc-ing a non-decomposable end-product value. As a result, the activities and operation of the team will be most intensively controlled and monitored by the firm-specific input owners, who gain or lose the most from the success or failure of the "firm." In fact, they are typically considered the "owners" or "employers" or "bosses" of the firm, though in reality the firm is a cooper-ating collection of resources owned by different people.

Firm-specific resources can be non-human. Professional firms—law, ar-chitecture, medical—are composed of teams of people who would be less valuable elsewhere in other groups. They hire non-human general capital, such as building and equipment. The contract, which defines "hiring," depends on the specificity and generality, not on human or non-human attributes nor on who is richer. Incidentally, "industrial democracy" arrangements are rare, because the owners of more general resources have less interest in the firm than those of specific resources.

The Corporation and Specialization in Private Property Rights. In a corporation the resources owned by the stockholders are those the values of which are specific to the firm. The complexities in specialization in exercise of the components of property rights and the associated contractual restraints have led some people to believe that the corporation tends to insulate (i.e., "separate") decisions of use from the bearing of the consequences (i.e., control from ownership) and thereby has undermined the capacity of a private property system to allocate resources to higher market value uses. For example, it has been argued that diffused stock ownership has so separated management and control of resources from "ownership" that managers are able to act without sufficient regard to market values and the interests of the diffused stockholders. Adam Smith was among the first to propound that belief. Whatever the empirical validity, the logical analysis underlying those charges rests on misperceptions of the structure of private property rights in the corporation and the nature of the competitive markets for control and ownership which tend to restrain such managers. What individual managers seek and what those who survive are able successfully to do in the presence of competition for control are very different things.

An advantage of the corporation is its pooling of sufficient wealth in firm-specific resources for large-scale operations. Pooling is enabled if shares of ownership are alienable private property, thereby permitting individuals to eliminate dependence of their time path of consumption on the temporal pattern of return from firm-specific investments. Alienability is enabled if the shares have limited liability, which frees each stockholder from dependence on the amount of wealth of every other stockholder. The resultant ability to tolerate anonymity, that is, disinterest in exactly who are the other shareholders, enables better market alienability.

When voluntary separability of decision authority over firm-specific resources from their market value consequences is added to alienability, the ability to specialize in managerial decisions and talent (control) without also having to bear the risk of all the value consequences, enables achievement of beneficial specialization in production and coordination of cooperative productivity. Specialization is not necessarily something that is confined to the production of different end products; it applies equally to different productive inputs or talents. Voluntary partitionability and alienability of the component rights enable advantageous specialization (sometimes called "separation") in (a) exercise of rights to make decisions about uses of resources and of (b) bearing the consequent market or exchange values. The former is sometimes called "control" and the latter, "ownership." Separability enables the achievement of the gains from specialization in selecting and monitoring uses, evaluating the results and bearing the risk of consequent future usefulness and value. Because different uses have different prospective probability distributions of outcomes, and because outcomes are differentially sensitive to monitoring the prior decisions, separability and alienability of the component rights permit gains from specialization in holding and exercising the partitionable rights.

Thus, the modern corporation relies on limited liability to enhance alienability and on partitionability of components of private property rights in order to achieve gains from large-scale specialization in directing productive team activity and talents. Rather than destroying or undermining the effectiveness of private property rights, the alleged "separation" enables effective, productive "specialization" in exercising private property rights as methods of control and coordination.

Government Property Rights. It might be presumed that government property rights in a democracy are similar to corporate property with diffused stockholdings and that they should yield similar results. The analogy would be apt if each voting citizen had a share of votes equivalent to one's share of the wealth in the community, and if a person could shift wealth among governments, as one can among different corporations. If, for example, one could buy and sell land (as assets capturing essentially most of the value of whatever the government does in that particular state) in several different governments and could vote in each in proportion to the value of that "land," then government property would be closer to private property in its effects. But it is difficult to take that possibility seriously. The nature of government, public or communal property rights surely depends on the kind of government. Because these rights are so vaguely and indefinitely defined, attempts to deduce formally the consequences of resource allocation and behaviour under each have been hampered.

Non-existent Property Rights. Not all resources are satisfactorily controlled by private property rights. Air, water, electromagnetic radiation, noises and

PROPERTY RIGHTS [1987] 101

views are some examples. Water under my land flows to yours. Sounds and light from my land impinge on yours. Other forms of control are then designed, for example, political or social group decisions and actions, though these other forms are sometimes employed for ideological or political purposes, even where private property rights already exist.

If these other forms permit open, free entry with every user sharing equally and obtaining the average return, use will be excessive. Extra uses will be made with an increased realized total value that is less than the cost added; that is, the social product value is not maximized. This occurs because the marginal yield is less than the average to each user, to which each user responds. So, use occurs to the point where the average yield is brought down to marginal cost, with the consequence that the marginal yield is less than the marginal cost—often exampled as excessive congestion on a public road or public park, or over-fishing of communal, free-access fishing areas. The classic "communal property" implication that apples on the public apple tree are never allowed to ripen is an extreme example of the proposition that property rights, other than private, reduce conformity of resource uses to market-revealed values. Alternatively, if communal property rights mean that incumbent users can block more users, the resource will be under-utilized as incumbents maximize their individual yield, which is the average, not the marginal. This results in fewer users. Though more users or uses would lower the average value to the incumbents and hence dissuade a higher rate of use, the addition to the total group value (of the extra use) exceeds the extra costs. Examples are public, low-tuition colleges that restrict entry to maximize the "quality" of those who are educated—that is, to maximize the average yield of those admitted. Some labour unions (e.g., teamsters) are examples of similar situations.

A mistaken inference commonly suggested by the example of fishermen who over-fish unowned lakes is that independent sellers with open access to customers will "over-congest" in product variety and advertising to catch customers, with unheeded costs borne by other sellers. If, for example, Pall Mall cigarettes attract some customers from Camel, the loss to Camel is the reduced value of Camel-specific resources, not its lost sales revenue. General resources will be released from making Camels for use elsewhere with no social loss. But Camel-specific resources fall in value by the extent to which Pall Mall's product is better or cheaper. Camel's loss is more than offset by the sum of Pall Mall's increased net income plus the transfer gain to customers from lower prices or better quality. The loss to Camel is not

from new entry itself, but from its incorrect forecasts of its earlier investment value. It is presumed here that mistaken forecasts should not be protected by prohibiting the unexpected future improvements. This differs
from the over-fishing case in that consumers, in contrast to fish, have property rights in what they pay and what they buy. If each fish had a separate
owner or owned itself, none would allow it to be caught unless paid enough,
and over-fishing would not occur. One owner of all the fish is unnecessary;
it suffices that each fish (or potential customer) be owned by someone who
can refuse to buy. (Of course, unless the lake were owned, the lake surface
might be over-congested with too many fishermen, each fishing to a lesser
area, even if the fish were owned.)

Ownership of tradeable rights by customers is the feature that is missing
in the over-fishing, over-congestion case. Because rights to (or "of") the
fish or whales need not be bought, over-fishing does not imply over-
customering, where customers own rights to what the competing sellers are
seeking. Otherwise, customers could be caught like fish, wherein sellers
would be competing both to (1) establish property rights over the customers
and to (2) possess those rights. Costly redundant competition for initial establishment of rights could be avoided simply by establishing customers'
rights to themselves, as is in fact done. If the preceding seems fanciful,
replace "fish" with people and the lake surface with streets on which taxi
drivers cruise for customers. Excessive costs will be incurred in competition
for use of unowned, valuable resources, in this case, the streets.

Mutual Property Rights. "Mutual" forms of organization are used apparently
in order to sustain the maximum average per member or to reserve for the
incumbent members any greater group value from more members. Mutual
private property, a form that has barely been analysed, does not permit
anonymous alienability of interests in what are otherwise private property
rights. A "mutual" member can transfer his interest to other people only
upon permission of the other mutually owning members or their agents.
Fraternal, social and country clubs are examples. These activities have not
typically been viably organized and their services sold, as, for example, in
restaurants and health and exercise gymnasia. The intragroup-specific resources are themselves the members (erstwhile customers) who interact
and create their social utility. More members affect each incumbent's realized utility in two ways: by social compatibility and by congestion. An outside, separate owner interested in the maximum value of the organization,

but not the maximum average per member, could threaten to sell more memberships, which, although enabling a larger total social value with more members, would reduce the average value to the existing members. This is an example of the earlier analysed difference between maximizing the average yield per input rather than the total yield by admitting more members, who, while better off than if not admitted, nevertheless would reduce the average value to the incumbent members. In addition, the ability of newcomers to compensate incumbents for any loss in the individual (average) value to incumbent members is restrained if the membership fee were to go instead to an outside owner of the club. To the extent that a pecuniary compensation, via an initiation fee, were paid to an outside owner and exceeded the reduction in their average individual and total group utility, newcomers would be admitted, and the outside owner would gain, but incumbent members would lose their composite quasi-rent of their interpersonal sociability. (It is not yet well understood why, aside from tax reasons, the mutual form occurs in savings and loans and insurance firms.)

Torts, Conditional and Unassigned Property Rights. Private property rights may exist in principle but, quite sensibly, not be blindly and uncompromisingly enforced against all possible "usurpers." For example, situations arise in which someone's presumed private property rights do not exclude an "invader's" use. Accidental or emergency use of some other person's private property without prior permission constitutes an example, sometimes called a "tort." Another possibility is that the property rights are so ill-defined that whether a right has been usurped or already belonged to the alleged "usurper" is unclear. For example, my newly planted tree may block the view from your land. But did you have a right to look across my land? If the rights to views (or light rays) were clearly defined and assigned, we could negotiate a price for preserving the view or for my putting up a tree, depending upon which was more valuable to the both of us and with payment going to whoever proved to have the rights. Or while sailing on a lake, to escape a sudden storm and save my boat and life, I use your dock without your prior permission. Did I violate any of your rights, or did your rights not include the right to exclude users in my predicament? If such emergency action is deemed appropriate, then rights to use of the dock are not all yours, as you may have thought. Whereas in the tree-and-view case, a prior negotiation might have avoided a "tort" (except that initially we did not agree about who had what rights), in the emergency use of the dock, prior negotiation was unfeasible. If prior negotiation is uneconomic, rights to that emergency use "should" and will exist if that use is the most valuable use of the resource under the postulated circumstances. And compensation may or may not be required to the putative "owner." The principle underlying such a legal principle seems straightforward and consistent with principles of efficient economic behaviour. It suffices for present purposes merely to call attention to this aspect of economic efficiency underlying the law.

PROPERTY RIGHTS [1993]

One of the most fundamental requirements of a capitalist economic system—and one of the most misunderstood concepts—is a strong system of property rights. For decades social critics in the United States and throughout the Western world have complained that "property" rights too often take precedence over "human" rights, with the result that people are treated unequally and have unequal opportunities. Inequality exists in any society. But the purported conflict between property rights and human rights is a mirage—property rights are human rights.

The definition, allocation, and protection of property rights is one of the most complex and difficult sets of issues that any society has to resolve, but it is one that must be resolved in some fashion. For the most part social critics of "property" rights do not want to abolish those rights. Rather, they want to transfer them from private ownership to government ownership. Some transfers to public ownership (or control, which is similar) make an economy more effective. Others make it less effective. The worst outcome by far occurs when property rights really are abolished (see Tragedy of the Commons, The).

A property right is the exclusive authority to determine how a resource is used, whether that resource is owned by government or by individuals. Society approves the uses selected by the holder of the property right with governmental-administered force and with social ostracism. If the resource is owned by the government, the agent who determines its use has to operate under a set of rules determined, in the United States, by Congress or by executive agencies it has charged with that role.

Private property rights have two other attributes in addition to determining the use of a resource. One is the exclusive right to the services of the resource. Thus, for example, the owner of an apartment with complete property rights to the apartment has the right to determine whether to rent it out and, if so, which tenant to rent to; to live in it himself; or to use it in any other peaceful way. That is the right to determine the use. If the owner rents out the apartment, he also

Reprinted from *The Fortune Encyclopedia of Economics*, ed. David R. Henderson (New York: Warner Books, 1993), 69–73, by permission of David R. Henderson.

has the right to all the rental income from the property. That is the right to the services of the resources (the rent).

Finally, a private property right includes the right to delegate, rent, or sell any portion of the rights by exchange or gift at whatever price the owner determines (provided someone is willing to pay that price). If I am not allowed to buy some rights from you and you therefore are not allowed to sell rights to me, private property rights are reduced. Thus, the three basic elements of private property are (1) exclusivity of rights to the choice of use of a resource, (2) exclusivity of rights to the services of a resource, and (3) rights to exchange the resource at mutually agreeable terms.

The U.S. Supreme Court has vacillated about this third aspect of property rights. But no matter what words the justices use to rationalize recent decisions, the fact is that such limitations as price controls and restrictions on the right to sell at mutually agreeable terms are reductions of private property rights. Many economists (myself included) believe that most such restrictions on property rights are detrimental to society. Here are some of the reasons why.

Under a private property system the market values of property reflect the preferences and demands of the rest of society. No matter who the owner is, the use of the resource is influenced by what the rest of the public thinks is the most valuable use. The reason is that an owner who chooses some other use must forsake that highest-valued use—and the price that others would pay him for the resource or for the use of it. This creates an interesting paradox: although property is called "private," private decisions are based on public, or social, evaluation.

The fundamental purpose of property rights, and their fundamental accomplishment, is that they eliminate destructive competition for control of economic resources. Well-defined and well-protected property rights replace competition by violence with competition by peaceful means.

The extent and degree of private property rights fundamentally affect the ways people compete for control of resources. With more complete private property rights, market exchange values become more influential. The personal status and personal attributes of people competing for a resource matter less because their influence can be offset by adjusting the price. In other words, more complete property rights make discrimination more costly. Consider the case of a black woman who wants to rent an apartment from a white landlord. She is better able to do so when the landlord has the right to set the rent at whatever level he wants. Even if the landlord would prefer a white tenant, the black woman can offset her disadvantage by offering a higher rent. A landlord who takes the white tenant at a lower rent anyway pays for discriminating.

But if the government imposes rent controls that keep the rent below the free-market level, the price that the landlord pays to discriminate falls, possibly to zero. The rent control does not magically reduce the demand for apartments. Instead, it reduces every potential tenant's ability to compete by offering more money. The landlord, now unable to receive the full money price, will discriminate in favor of tenants whose personal characteristics—such as age, sex, ethnicity, and religion—he favors. Now the black woman seeking an apartment cannot offset the disadvantage of her skin color by offering to pay a higher rent.

Competition for apartments is not eliminated by rent controls. What changes is the "coinage" of competition. The restriction on private property rights reduces competition based on monetary exchanges for goods and services and increases competition based on personal characteristics. More generally, weakening private property rights increases the role of personal characteristics in inducing sellers to discriminate among competing buyers and buyers to discriminate among sellers.

The two extremes in weakened private property rights are socialism and "commonly owned" resources. Under socialism, government agents—those whom the government assigns—exercise control over resources. The rights of these agents to make decisions about the property they control are highly restricted. People who think they can put the resources to more valuable uses cannot do so by purchasing the rights, because the rights are not for sale at any price. Because socialist managers do not gain when the values of the resources they manage increase, and do not lose when the values fall, they have little incentive to heed changes in market-revealed values. The uses of resources are therefore more influenced by the personal characteristics and features of the officials who control them. Consider, in this case, the socialist manager of a collective farm. By working every night for one week, he could make 1 million rubles of additional profit for the farm by arranging to transport the farm's wheat to Moscow before it rots. But if neither the manager nor those who work on the farm are entitled to keep even a portion of this additional profit, the manager is more likely than the manager of a capitalist farm to go home early and let the crops rot.

Similarly, common ownership of resources—whether in what was formerly the Soviet Union or in the United States—gives no one a strong incentive to preserve the resource. A fishery that no one owns, for example, will be overfished. The reason is that a fisherman who throws back small fish to wait until they grow is unlikely to get any benefit from his waiting. Instead, some other fisherman will catch the fish. The same holds true for other common resources, whether they be herds of buffalo, oil in the ground, or clean air. All will be overused.

Indeed, a main reason for the spectacular failure of recent economic reforms in the Soviet Union is that resources were shifted from ownership by government to de facto common ownership. How? By making the Soviet government's revenues de facto into a common resource. Harvard economist Jeffrey Sachs, who advised the Soviet government, has pointed out that when Soviet managers of socialist enterprises were allowed to open their own businesses but still were left as managers of the government's businesses, they siphoned out the profits of the government's business into their private corporations. Thousands of managers doing this caused a large budget deficit for the Soviet government. In this case the resource that no manager had an incentive to conserve was the Soviet government's revenues. Similarly, improperly set premiums for U.S. deposit insurance give banks and S&Ls an incentive to make excessively risky loans and to treat the deposit insurance fund as a "common" resource.

Private property rights to a resource need not be held by a single person. They can be shared, with each person sharing in a specified fraction of the market value while decisions about uses are made in whatever process the sharing group deems desirable. A major example of such shared property rights is the corporation. In a limited-liability corporation, shares are specified, and the rights to decide how to use the corporation's resources are delegated to its management. Each shareholder has the unrestrained right to sell his or her share. Limited liability insulates each shareholder's wealth from the liabilities of other shareholders and thereby facilitates anonymous sale and purchase of shares.

In other types of enterprises, especially where each member's wealth will become uniquely dependent on each other member's behavior, property rights in the group endeavour are usually salable only if existing members approve of the buyer. This is typical for what are often called joint ventures, "mutuals," and partnerships.

While more-complete property rights are preferable to less-complete rights, any system of property rights entails considerable complexity and many issues that are difficult to resolve. If I operate a factory that emits smoke, foul smells, or airborne acids over your land, am I using your land without your permission? This is difficult to answer.

The cost of establishing private property rights—so that I could pay you a mutually agreeable price to pollute your air—may be too expensive. Air, underground water, and electromagnetic radiations, for example, are expensive to monitor and control. Therefore, a person does not effectively have enforceable private property rights to the quality and condition of some parcel of air. The inability to cost-effectively monitor and police uses of your resources means "your" property rights over "your" land are not as extensive and strong as they are over some other resources, such as furniture, shoes, or automobiles. When private property rights are unavailable or too costly to establish and enforce, substitute means of control are sought. Government authority, expressed by government agents, is one very common such means; hence the creation of environmental laws.

Depending upon circumstances certain actions may be considered invasions of privacy, trespass, or torts. If I seek refuge and safety for my boat at your dock during a sudden severe storm on a lake, have I invaded "your" property rights, or do your rights not include the right to prevent that use? The complexities and varieties of circumstances render impossible a bright-line definition of a person's set of property rights with respect to resources.

Similarly, the set of resources over which property rights may be held is not well defined and demarcated. Ideas, melodies, and procedures, for example, are almost costless to replicate explicitly (near-zero cost of production) and implicitly (no forsaken other uses of the inputs). As a result, they typically are not protected as private property except for a fixed term of years under a patent or copyright.

Private property rights are not absolute. The rule against the "dead hand" or the rule against perpetuities is an example. I cannot specify how resources that I own will be used in the indefinitely distant future. Under our legal system, I can only specify the use for a limited number of years after my death or the deaths of currently living people. I cannot insulate a resource's use from the influence of market values of all future generations. Society recognizes market prices as measures of the relative desirability of resource uses. Only to the extent that rights are salable are those values most fully revealed.

Accompanying and conflicting with the desire for secure private property rights for one's self is the desire to acquire more wealth by "taking" from others. This is done by military conquest and by forcible reallocation of rights to resources (also known as stealing). But such coercion is antithetical to—rather than characteristic of—a system of private property rights. Forcible reallocation means that the existing rights have not been adequately protected. Private property rights do not conflict with human rights. They are human rights. Private property rights are the rights of humans to use specified goods and to exchange them. Any restraint on private property rights shifts the balance of power from impersonal attributes toward personal attributes and toward behavior that political authorities approve. That is a fundamental reason for preference of a system of strong private property rights: private property rights protect individual liberty.

FURTHER READING

Alchian, Armen. "Some Economics of Property Rights." Il Politico 30 (1965): 816–29.

Alchian, Armen, and Harold Demsetz. "The Property Rights Paradigm." Journal of Economic History (1973): 16–27.

Demsetz, Harold. "When Does the Rule of Liability Matter?" Journal of Legal Studies 1 (January 1972): 13–28.

Siegan, B. Economic Liberties and the Constitution. 1980.

Interview with Jeffrey Sachs. Omni, June 1991: 98.

THE BISHOPS AND THE LAY COMMISSION
COMMENTS ON TWO LETTERS
ARMEN A. ALCHIAN AND WILLIAM H. MECKLING

Introduction

These two treatises are serious attempts by legitimate spokesmen for Catholicism to produce an economic policy prospectus for the United States. The Pastoral Letter is the product of a five-member ad hoc committee of the National Conference of Catholic Bishops chaired by the Reverend Rembert G. Weakland, Archbishop of Milwaukee. The Lay Letter is the product of a 30-member Lay Commission chaired by William Simon, former Secretary of the Treasury.

Policy Recommendations or "Goods"

What is least interesting about these two treatises is the policy recommendations they contain. Indeed, the critical reader will find it difficult even to find propositions specific enough to be labeled as policy recommendations. The recommendations for welfare reform made by the Bishops provide an example. Their eminences offer the following six "guidelines" for a "thorough" reform of "public assistance programs."

1. Public assistance programs should be adequately funded and provide recipients with decent support.
2. The United States should establish national eligibility standards and a national minimum benefit level for public assistance programs.
3. Public assistance programs should strengthen rather than weaken marriage and the family.
4. Public assistance programs should encourage rather than penalize gainful employment.
5. The design of public assistance programs should involve the participation of the recipient population and avoid or minimize stigma to clients.

Reprinted from *Economics, Theology, and the Social Order*, Center Symposia Series No. 18 (Rochester, N.Y.: Center for Research in Government Policy and Business, 1986), by permission of Bradley Policy Research Center of the William E. Simon Graduate School of Business Administration at the University of Rochester.

6. The administration of public assistance programs should show respect for clients.[1]

While it would be difficult to find fault with any of these as general objectives, only one of them, the second, is specific enough to provide any real direction in policymaking.

The moderation and vagueness which mark the guidelines above stand in sharp contrast to the discourse which serves as a rationale for them. A few statements from the Pastoral Letter on the subject of "poverty," "the poor," or "the marginalized" will illustrate the point.

1. Our fundamental norm in judging economic policies has been this: What will this approach or policy do to the poor and deprived members of the human community?[2]
2. The distribution of income and wealth in the U.S. is so inequitable that it violates the minimum standard of distributive justice.[3]
3. No one can claim the name Christian and at the same time acquiesce in the hunger and homelessness that exist around the world and in our own country.[4]
4. Increased economic participation for the marginalized takes priority over the preservation of privileged concentrations of power, wealth, and income.[5]

The contrast between these four statements and the preceding six policy guidelines characterizes both the Bishops' and the Lay Commission's monographs. Specific recommendations are conspicuous for their absence or moderation. Meanwhile, the reader is inundated by rhetoric intended to convey a definite point of view. Moreover, the two points of view are, in important respects, conflicting: in particular, the Lay Commission puts great reliance on markets and entrepreneurship to reduce the burdens of poverty and unemployment not only in the United States but worldwide, while the Bishops are much more prone to calling in the forces of law to impose "social justice."

What is most interesting in these two tracts is the articulation of these points of view. Our comments on that articulation fall into two categories:

1. Pastoral Letter, p. vi and pp. 76–78.
2. Ibid., p. i.
3. Ibid., p. v.
4. Ibid., p. 6.
5. Ibid., p. 35.

1. Catholic Social Teaching/Thought and the U.S. Economy
2. The Analysis

Catholic Social Teaching/Thought and the U.S. Economy

In an effort to win over their readers, the authors of both monographs appeal to authority: to "Catholic Social Teaching" as the Bishops put it, or to "Catholic Social Thought" in the words of the Lay Commission. Each tries to convince the Catholic constituency that the weight of Catholic authority is on its side. Thus, both monographs quote extensively from the Bible and from various declamations by officers of the Catholic Church (in particular, various Popes) and by church scholars.

Not very surprisingly, what these efforts demonstrate is that support can be found for almost any view somewhere in Catholic Social Teaching/Thought. Perhaps nowhere is this more apparent than in the treatment of property rights.

The Lay Commission is quite enthusiastic about private property. It states:

> One of the clearest limitations on the state is the principle of private property. Catholic social thought holds that the right to private property is a natural right, guaranteeing to conscience the means of self-expression, and holding the state in check. (This right which the Church itself exercises, also anchors the liberty of the Church.) The right to private property . . . is reflected in the ancient commandment: "Thou shalt not steal."[6]

The Ten Commandments are also cited by the Bishops in support of private property.[7] Moreover, the Bishops go on to quote John XXIII as follows:

> Experience and history testify that where political regimes do not allow to private individuals the possession also of productive goods, the exercise of human liberty is violated or completely destroyed in matters of primary importance.[8]

Elsewhere, however, they say that:

> the goods of this earth are common property and that men and women are summoned to faithful stewardship rather than to selfish appropriation or exploitation of what was destined for all. Cyprian writes in the middle of the

6. Lay Letter, p. 12.
7. Op. cit., p. 11.
8. Ibid., pp. 40–41.

third century that "whatever belongs to God belongs to all," and Ambrose states "God has ordered all things to be produced so that there should be food in common for all, and that the earth should be a common possession of all." Clement of Alexandria grounds the communality of possession not only in creation but in the Incarnation since "it is God himself who has brought our race to communion (*koinonia*) by sharing Himself, first of all, and by sending his Word to all alike and by making all things for all. Therefore everything is in common." Recent Church teaching, as voiced by John Paul II, while reaffirming the right to private property, clearly states that Christian tradition "has always understood this right within the broader context of the right common to all to use the goods of the whole creation."[9]

One theme echoed by both groups is that ownership is not "absolute," whatever that means. As the Bishops put it:

> whatever one's legal entitlement, no one can ever own these resources absolutely or use them without regard to others. . . . God is the only real owner: human beings are the trustees of the goods given them.[10]

As the Lay Commission put it:

> A word about the proper use of property is in order. The right is not absolute or abstract; it is based on a practical judgement about superior creativity of a system of private property. It is vindicated by a wise stewardship, which brings forth from property greater productivity than before. Moreover, those who own property have responsibilities to God, to their communities, and to all their fellow human beings. Thus, Thomas Aquinas once wrote that a human being "ought to possess external things not as his own but . . . so that . . . he is ready to communicate them to others in their need."
>
> . . . Owners are temporary stewards of a portion of the earth, and each one of us will one day give to the Creator an account of our stewardship, and especially of our practical assistance to the poor.[11]

---

9. Ibid., p. 12.

10. Ibid., p. 40. In a subtly deceptive way this statement confounds the normative and positive. It is a fact that no one, i.e., no government, can *absolutely* guarantee the rights of individuals. The extent to which such rights "ought to be" inviolable, however, is a different and purely normative question.

11. Op. cit., pp. 12–13.

Could anyone decide on the basis of this collection of statements whether the system of property rights extant in the United States today is more consistent with Catholic Social Teaching/Thought than that of the U.S.S.R. or vice versa? The truth is Catholic Social Teaching/Thought does not comprehend a coherent consistent view of property rights; and it would be surprising if it did. Catholic authorities and scholars and their Biblical forebears have been making pronouncements which have implications for property rights for 5,000 years under wildly disparate circumstances in every corner of the globe. Finding support for any position must by now be largely a matter of diligence in library search.

The work of the National Conference of Catholic Bishops' ad hoc committee and the Lay Commission both start from the same presumption: that there is a well-defined body of Catholic thought or, more accurately, set of values, which united with economic principles will yield an economic policy prospectus. The truth is there is no such well-defined body of Catholic thought, i.e., set of values, and it is quixotic to believe that there could be. If the history of the Catholic Church teaches us anything, it is that the Church as an organization has extraordinary survival characteristics both across nations and through time. The Catholic Church is nothing if not universal, i.e., catholic. It has been and is all things to all people. Can we reasonably expect such an organization to have a unified view on what constitutes justice, or what trade-off is appropriate between present and future poverty, or between freedom and distributive equality?[12] This lack of a coherent set of Catholic values, of course, says nothing about the quality of the analysis or the efficacy of the policy viewpoints contained in these monographs. What it does say is that the search for policy foundations in Catholic Social Teaching/Thought is on a par with the search for the Holy Grail.

The Analysis

Abortive attempts to find succor in Catholic Social Teaching/Thought aside, what can we say about the analysis that the authors of these two documents educe in support of their viewpoints? The Lay Letter deserves much higher marks on this dimension than the Bishops' Letter. For that reason our discussion will focus primarily on the analysis in the latter.

12. You may notice that this suggests the authors believe, contrary to Milton Friedman, that disagreements about policy do result from differences in values.

A. *The Garden of Eden Conception of Wealth Creation*

The primary concern of the Bishops is the poor. This is clear not only from the central role which subjects such as poverty and employment play in their discussion but from specific statements to that effect, e.g.,

1. The poor have a special claim on our concern . . .
2. *Our fundamental norm in judging economic policies has been this: What will this approach or policy do to the poor and deprived members of the human community?*
3. The justice of a community is measured by its treatment of the poor and the powerless . . .
4. There is a strong presumption against inequality of income or wealth as long as there are poor, hungry, and homeless people in our midst.
5. The fulfillment of the basic needs of the poor is of the highest priority.[13]

In order to alleviate the suffering of the poor, the Bishops clearly favor forced transfers of wealth. They commend private charity and voluntary action to assist the poor.

> all citizens have a duty to assist the poor through acts of charity and personal commitment . . . we ask all citizens to expand and intensify their personal involvement in helping to alleviate poverty.[14]

But they go on to add:

> But we are also fully aware of the limits of private charity and voluntary action. . . . The works of charity cannot and should not have to substitute for humane public policy. Society's responsibility to alleviate poverty must also be carried out through the government acting as the agent of the common good. Justice, therefore, requires that all members of society help to establish fair, humane, and effective policies to eradicate the root causes of poverty.[15]

Humane government policy includes:

maintaining a healthy government economy, removal of barriers to employment for women and minorities, removal of taxes on the poor, progres-

---

13. Ibid., pp. i–iii.
14. Ibid., p. 71.
15. Ibid., p. 71.

sivity in the tax system, government programs to foster self-help among the poor, higher quality education for poor children, improved child care services. These are in addition to the welfare system reforms listed earlier. (p. 3 above)

That, however, is only the domestic front. On the international front, the Bishops:

deplore recent retrenchments in U.S. policy with respect to international agencies such as the World Bank (particularly the International Development Association—the so-called soft loan window) and the International Monetary Fund. They are distressed that lending agencies require developing nations, as a condition of extending or renewing loans, to adopt economic policies which impact on the poor. They are unhappy with the U.S. refusal to ratify the Law of the Sea Treaty. They are disturbed that the U.S. is moving from multilateral aid to unilateral, and that the latter is largely taking the form of military aid. Finally, they want the U.S. to expand the amount of aid in the form of outright grants, and at the same time forgive many of the loans which are outstanding.[16]

The Bishops have the endorsement of the Lay Commission in calling out the police powers for the benefit of the needy. According to the latter:

we strongly support the social welfare systems which help the truly needy until they regain their self-reliance. And we recognize that because of age or disability or other necessity, some cannot be self-reliant. . . . The political system has many wholly legitimate and important economic roles, including care for the truly needy. . . . The young, the elderly, the disabled, those visited by sudden misfortune, and many others are permanently or for a time unable to work. In a good society, the moral system and the political system must come to the assistance of such persons.[17]

Except for a one-sentence genuflection to progressivity and a brief plea that the poor be relieved of taxes, the Bishops carefully avoid saying anything about how their program is to be implemented. There is no doubt about what they intend, however. They intend that it be implemented by exercise of the police powers. This confronts them with a moral dilemma. Using the police powers,

16. The recommendations of the Bishops in the international arena are more specific than anywhere else.

17. Op. cit., pp. 32–33.

i.e., physical coercion, to take resources from some individuals to benefit others is a fundamental violation of human rights—of human freedom. (And this is in addition to any adverse efficiency consequences the exercise of those powers is likely to produce.) How are they to morally rationalize this violation of freedom and human rights in the name of their version of justice?

The Bishops salve their consciences with the Garden of Eden conception of wealth creation.

> creation is a gift; men and women are to be faithful stewards in caring for the earth . . . the goods of this earth are common property and . . . men and women are summoned to faithful stewardship rather than to selfish appropriation or exploitation.[18]

> Misuse of the resources of the world or appropriation of them by a minority of the world's population betrays the gift of creation meant for all people. . . .[19]

> No one can ever own . . . resources absolutely. . . . God is the only real owner: human beings are the trustees of the goods given them. This applies first of all to the land and other natural resources. . . . The resources created by human industry and ingenuity are also held in trust . . . the right to own must bow to the higher principles of stewardship and the common use of the goods of creation. There is a "social mortgage" on private property which implies that "private property does not constitute for anyone an absolute or unconditioned right. No one is justified in keeping for his exclusive use what he does not need, when others lack necessities.". . . true stewardship may also sometimes demand that the right to own cede to public involvement in the planning or ownership of certain sectors of the economy.[20]

There is nothing immoral about using the police powers to transfer wealth—to take resources from some and use them to benefit others. After all, it is all a gift of God: no human sacrifice or effort is involved in wealth creation.

18. Ibid., p. 12.
19. Ibid., p. 15.
20. Ibid., pp. 40–41.

B. *On Rights*

The Bishops have much to say about rights.[21] Some of what they have to say has already been quoted above. In addition, however, they advocate a set of rights which they describe as "The Minimum Conditions for Life in Community."

They say:

> The nation must take up the task of framing a new consensus that *all persons have rights in the economic sphere and that society has a moral obligation to take the necessary steps to ensure that no one among us is hungry, homeless, unemployed, or otherwise denied what is necessary to live with dignity.*
>
> The experiment in political democracy carried out by America's founders did a great deal to ensure the protection of civil and political rights in our nation. The time has come for a similar experiment in economic democracy: the creation of an order that guarantees the minimum conditions of human dignity in the economic sphere for every person.[22]
>
> Everyone has a legitimate claim on economic benefits to at least the minimum level necessary for the social protection of human dignity. No one can be legitimately excluded or abandoned by the larger community in its activity. The economic minimum owed to every person by society is made explicit in the human rights standards affirmed in Church teaching. These rights have been most systemically outlined by Pope John XXIII in his encyclical *Peace on Earth*. It will be useful to recall them here.
>
> In the first place stand the rights to "food, clothing, shelter, rest, medical care." These express the absolute minimum for the protection of human life. In order to insure their protection, certain social guarantees are indispensable. These include "the right to security in case of sickness, inability

---

21. As is so common in rights discussions these days, the Bishops modify rights with the adjective "human," implying there are some rights which are not human. The purpose, of course, is to evoke a favorable emotional response to the particular rights being advocated. It is also worth noting in this context that a false distinction is often made between property rights and human rights; and the distinction is then used to argue that the latter take precedence over the former. Neither the Human Rights Organization nor the U.S. State Department includes property rights in its list of human rights. Indeed, our State Department has encouraged expropriation of land in Latin America. It is also common practice to characterize some rights as "civil": another classification more emotive than taxonomically useful.

22. Ibid., p. ii.

to work, widowhood, old age, unemployment, or in any other case in which one is deprived of the means of subsistence through no fault of one's own." Further, all persons have rights to "free initiative in the economic field and the right to work." They have the right to "working conditions in which physical health is not endangered," to "carry on economic activities according to the degree of responsibility of which one is capable," and to wages sufficient to guarantee one's family "a standard of living in keeping with human dignity."[23]

The Bishops simply ignore the rights which individuals already have in "the economic sphere." Somehow, the right to decide how physical objects will be used, including our persons, the right then to actually use those objects, the right to sell or otherwise transfer rights, etc., are neither human nor economic rights.

As a corollary, the Bishops are not conferring new rights: they are simply taking rights from some to confer benefits on others. Granting citizens the right to own[24] houses or factories in the U.S.S.R. constitutes a conferral of new rights. Requiring employers to provide health insurance is not a conferral of new rights. Employees always have the right to contract with employers to provide health benefits as a part of their compensation package. Enacting a statute which requires employers to provide health benefits destroys employees' rights in their persons. In contracting for the use of their services, they are coerced into accepting health benefits as part of their compensation.

Curiously, this distinction is implicit in the language used by the Bishops. At one point they say:

> if the economy is to function in a way that respects the dignity of persons, these qualities should be present: *it should enable persons to find a significant measure of self-realization in their labor; it should permit persons to fulfill their material needs through adequate remuneration; and it should make possible the enhancement of unity and solidarity within the family, the nation, and the world community.*[25]

One sentence later, however, "enable" and "permit" are replaced by "legitimate claim" as follows:

23. Ibid., pp. 27–28.
24. The meaning of "own" is an important and complex question, but for purposes of this discussion the popular notion of ownership is good enough.
25. Ibid., p. 27.

Everyone has a legitimate claim on economic benefits to at least the minimum level necessary for the social protection of human dignity.[26]

The words "enable" and "permit" are perfectly consistent with free labor markets in which each individual has the rights to his own person: each person has the right to choose his occupation, if any. He can choose unemployment, self-employment, or the sale of services in the marketplace. But he does not have a claim on economic benefits. He may acquire claims as a consequence of sale of his labor, but he has no such claims ab initio. The Bishops, on the other hand, intend to bestow economic benefits as a matter of law. In practice, what this means is restrictions on the rights individuals have in their persons. If employers are required to supply such benefits, individuals thereby lose part of their right to contract for the sale of their labor. If the benefits are supplied by government, individuals are taxed to pay for them.

The Bishops have company from the Lay Commission in confounding freedom with bestowal of benefits. The latter state:

Freedom from fear, freedom from want, freedom of expression, and freedom to worship—these are the four freedoms which are at the core of human development.[27]

The first two of these so-called freedoms are no doubt desirable states but have nothing to do with freedom. Freedom has to do with what people are *permitted* to do, to use the words of the Bishops, not what they *can* do. Freedom of expression and religion (insofar as they exist) *permit* individuals to say what they want and *permit* them to practice whatever religion they choose. Freedom from want is not something that can be achieved by simply permitting it. Freedom from want is a matter of what people *can* do; it is a matter, to use the Bishops' words again, of what claims individuals have on resources.

The issue of freedom aside, using the police powers to take rights from some in order to confer benefits on others also significantly affects economic performance, in particular, wealth creation and output. Both the supply of labor and the level of investment depend on *after-tax* returns, and labor productivity is not independent of the rewards to being productive. Moreover, job security or income security imposed on employers by law reduces rewards to labor productivity.

26. Ibid., p. 27.
27. Op. cit., p. 70.

Beyond efficiency effects like those mentioned above, confiscation and de-struction of rights have subtle consequences much less widely recognized.

Rights are not simply a matter of *what* individuals are entitled to do but also *how long* they will be entitled to do it. . . . If an individual possesses a right today, his behavior depends . . . on the likelihood that he will possess it at any given time in the future . . . frequent *expropriation* of rights drasti-cally affects the nature of those rights . . . the higher the rate at which rights are being confiscated and reassigned . . . the lower will be the estimate that people will place on the chances that their own rights are secure.

As people become aware that rights are becoming more tenuous . . . their behavior changes. They become increasingly sensitive to keeping their wealth in forms that are not easily appropriable through *confiscation* by the political sector, such as art work, precious metals, jewelry, and edu-cation. . . . they will also shift investments away from productive assets that have long lives, toward assets with short lives . . . instability in rights through its impact on investment makes us poorer in the aggregate than we would otherwise be.[28]

Nowhere, perhaps, is the problem of instability of rights more serious than in the so-called developing countries. Indeed, that is the reason for their lack of development. Neither inhabitants nor outsiders are disposed to invest in long-lived productive assets for domestic use. Instead, there is a pronounced dispo-sition to hold wealth in the form of portable, easily concealed objects and in claims on assets of foreign countries (Switzerland) where rights are more stable. Investors weigh both political history and current political affairs in forming their expectations. This is particularly evident in areas such as Latin America and, more recently, Africa, where political upheaval accompanied by expropriations of rights has been endemic. The "flights of capital" generated by the prospect of new regimes who threaten expropriation of rights—e.g., the socialists in France and the "People's Republic" in Hong Kong—provide other examples. In police states such as the U.S.S.R., it is difficult to convince managers that they will be rewarded handsomely for success. They know that rights are tenuous—that the state can and does take away what it has given and that there are no courts to which one can appeal.

28. *Human Rights and the Meaning of Freedom*, Michael C. Jensen and William H. Meck-ling, University of Rochester, Graduate School of Management, Rochester, N.Y. Revised, February 1985. pp. 23–24.

The Lay Commission notes the political instability problem as follows: "(We note, though, the moral dilemma of persons of virtue who would like to invest in their own country, yet find its political economy wracked by inflation, instability, and uncertainty)."[29] The Bishops, on the other hand, seem totally oblivious to the adverse welfare consequences of the rights expropriations inherent in their rhetoric.

c. *Job Creation, The Vertical Demand Curve for Labor, and Say's Law*

Both the Bishops and the Laymen make much of "job creation." The Bishops say:

> The most urgent priority for U.S. domestic economic policy is the creation of new jobs with adequate pay and decent working conditions. The prime goal must be to make it possible for everyone who is seeking a job to find employment which befits human dignity. . . . Current levels of unemployment are morally unjustified. . . . Efforts to generate employment: should be aimed specifically at bringing marginalized persons into the labor force; should produce goods and services needed by society; should be as economically efficient as possible; and should include both the private and public sectors.[30]

The Laymen point out that:

> In 1970, the total number of employed civilians in the U.S. was 78 million. In mid-1984, this number had climbed to 105 million. Such a record of job creation is unmatched by any other economy in the world, and is historically almost unprecedented. . . . Nonetheless the task of creating new jobs during the next decade is also formidable. As of mid-1984, the number of unemployed stands at approximately 8.5 million . . . by 1995 the numbers of new entrants into the labor force will probably continue to grow by another 5 million.[31]

> Jobs do not simply happen, as fruit grows on trees; they must be created. New ideas are crucial in this creation. New waves of entrepreneurs must

29. Op. cit., p. 66.

30. Op. cit., p. iv.

31. This statement doesn't make much sense. A footnote in the Lay Letter at this point states that the labor force should grow by 21 million workers between 1982 and 1995. Where the 5 million came from is a mystery to this writer.

learn to look alertly for unmet needs—for new products and new services—
and to invent new ways of meeting older needs.[32]

The Lay Commission adopts what is nowadays a very popular view of how
labor markets operate.[33] The number of jobs is bounded and independent of
the supply of labor. This concept of *job creation* denies the operation of elementary microeconomic principles in labor markets. It denies that higher levels of
employment can be achieved by moving down a labor demand curve. It suffers
from myopia; i.e., the creation of new (or the destruction of old) positions is
literally equated with additions to (or subtractions from) employment. No new
positions created have the effect of eliminating old positions; e.g., the introduction of new products never reduces the demand for old products. No destruction of old positions (as a result of foreign competition, for example) ever
results in the creation of new positions, e.g., expanded production of existing
products or services because labor costs fall.

In terms which have become somewhat unfashionable in macroeconomic
circles, the notion of job creation denies Say's Law. Surely, viewed in modern
macroeconomic terms, aggregate demand increases do accompany the ab-
sorption of new entrants into the workforce. The reason new entrants keep
finding employment is that aggregate demand increases with increases in employment. In that context, one could just as logically argue that new entrants
create their own jobs as to argue that the jobs are created by entrepreneurs.

It is one thing to argue that insufficiency of demand explains cyclical unemployment. It is another thing to argue that expansions in employment such as
those that have occurred recently in the United States are a result of job crea-

32. Op. cit., p. 68.

33. Job creation and what one would have to define as its converse, job destruction,
are of central interest to Industrial Policy buffs. A recently released study by the U.S. International Trade Commission concluded that the so-called voluntary limits on car imports had cost American buyers $17 billion over four years. However, it then went on
to assert that the quotas created 44,000 more jobs in the auto industry and additional
jobs in steel and other industries. An article in *Public Interest*, Number 65, Fall 1981, by
David L. Birch entitled "Who Creates Jobs?" states: "As a nation, we must create about 15
million new jobs in the 1980s to employ all of our expanding adult population. This is
less than the 19 million we created in the 1970's to absorb 'war babies' into the labor
force but it is still quite a large number . . . the government sector as a whole will produce
no more than one-quarter of the needed 15 million. The private sector will have to produce the rest."

tion, or to argue that assimilation of new entrants to the workforce during the next decade poses a formidable task of job creation.[34]

If we are truly interested in explaining the extraordinary recent growth in employment, we must look to factors affecting the supply of labor rather than the demand. Outside of the baby boom, increased labor market participation seems to have arisen from two sources: (1) an increase in the number of workers per household, and (2) an increase in the number of households. Two technological revolutions have played important roles in changing household behavior. First, modern consumer technology, from laundry equipment and wrinkle-free fabrics to microwave ovens and frozen foods, has dramatically reduced the returns to labor in the home at the margin relative to work for wages. Second, new birth control devices have led to smaller families and to more single-person household units.[35] Both of these latter developments have also reduced the returns to home labor relative to market labor.

Entrepreneurs are very useful members of society. They can and do raise labor productivity, thereby increasing the demand for labor. In part, this increase in productivity will be reflected in higher wages. In part, it will be reflected in increased employment, but only to the extent that the supply of labor permits, i.e., to the extent that it either induces individuals to market their labor rather than utilize it at home or induces them to give up some leisure. To the extent that entrepreneurs have created the new technology mentioned above, they can take further credit for enlarging employment, but again by shifting the labor supply to markets, not by "creating jobs" à la the Lay Commission Letter. Surely, however, the benefits which entrepreneurs confer on us largely take the form of higher real incomes, not increased employment. And that is as it should be. For most of us (golfers), at any rate, work is a means to an end, not an end in itself.

34. It is worth noting in this context that the number of persons who will be entering the workforce never seems to depend on earnings. It is some single absolute number.

35. In the long run this could cause a relative decrease in employment because of slower population growth.

SOME IMPLICATIONS OF RECOGNITION OF
PROPERTY RIGHT TRANSACTIONS COSTS

The list of fields of economics in the directory of the American Economic Association contains no references to transactions costs or to property, despite
much recent interest and research in that area. Probably the paper in *recent* times
that most stimulated progress was Coase's "The Problem of Social Costs."[1] It
demonstrated that, with costless exchange transactions and well-defined and
transferable property rights, resource uses—aside from wealth effects on relative consumption demands—are independent of initial rights assignments.
This statement signifies that transactions costs—the *costs* attendant to transferring entitlements or rights—destroy the classic standard theorems on market exchange efficiency. It indicates that many so-called market failures are failures of *existence* of markets or, more accurately, are results of obstacles (costs)
to transactions, agreements, contracts, or understandings about uses of resources. These costs arise because of difficulties of communication, information collation, contract stipulation, ambiguities of entitlements or rights that
might be traded. A host of activities are encompassed by the rubric "transactions costs."

Transactions

An oral tradition (a euphemism for a rubric of terminology, conjectures, and
plausible assertions) exists on the role of entitlement and transactions costs.
The conception of transactions remains sufficiently indefinite to permit
superficial reference to "transactions costs" as the key to any paradox, externality, public goods provision, etc.

The following activities seem to be worth noting in the transactions conception:

Reprinted from *Economics and Social Institutions*, ed. K. Brunner (Boston: Nijhoff, 1979),
233–54, by permission of Bradley Policy Research Center.

Presented at the First Annual Interlaken Seminar on Analysis and Ideology, Switzerland, June, 1974.

1. Ronald H. Coase, *Journal of Law and Economics* 3 (1960): 1–5.

1. *Search* over society for *who* has what rights. The cost of this search is reduced by specialists—as for nearly all activity. For land or houses, there are real estate agents and for stocks, stockbrokers. Employment agencies, Yellow Pages, and advertising convey information about *who* has what rights available for transfer.

2. The investigation of *what rights* each person has in each case. Title search firms identify rights holders and their entitlements. Automobile registration gives clearer evidence. Retail merchants provide assurance that goods are not stolen or of bad title, and we can't forget lawyers.

3. Technological *attributes* of goods. Investigation of physical attributes is sometimes sufficiently expensive to interdict transactions. Advertising or display of a good or of evidence about its characteristics is often provided by specialist "middlemen" who trade in the good. Indeed, this is a major function of merchants. Should we (a) include only the costs of conveying information about attributes of the goods or (b) take the state of knowledge as exogenous and include only the costs of providing risk-sharing provisions, guarantees, assurances, or remedies—if attributes are not as represented? For the moment, we include both and dub the first "attribute determination" and the second "risk sharing." Means for providing attribute information are diverse as well as specialized; examples are brand names, franchises, warranties, guarantees, commitments of wealth to a long-run venture (a means of self-imposed losses for bad performance, which thus serves to inform potential customers of the greater loss the seller will incur for unreliable performance), free trials, advertising of attributes, and governmentally imposed standards.

4. *Price search* and *price predictability.* The discovery of bid-and-offer prices is facilitated by essentially the same procedures as the search for rights holders. Centralized markets and quick public reporting of actual prices benefit those who create markets as well as the public. Stockbrokers specialize in "making" a predictable market for specific stocks. "Scalping" on the futures markets provides more price predictability. Specialists (retailers, wholesalers, brokers) who make a market or maintain inventories and contribute to price predictability thereby reduce costs of search and planning. Futures markets provide more predictability. If prices were revised instantly and unpredictably to constantly clear markets, their reduced predictability would make planning and optimizing more difficult and would induce more pretransaction search. For example, an architect can design a house more efficiently the more accurately he can predict the prices of alternative components at construction time. Predictability over time is of greater value where planning preparation costs are

more sensitive to haste, where larger inventories are held, or where adjustment costs in switching to other sellers are greater.

A geographical—or temporal—distribution of potential prices with a higher mean *but smaller variance* can be efficient. For example, resale price maintenance over a set of retailers is, in some cases, a price-search economizing device, which is more economical for people whose search time is valuable and for purchases of low value relative to search-time costs—where the gains from marginal search per unit time are therefore low. Constancy of prices, despite queues of random length and timing, provide price predictability at the expense of unpredictability of queue times. Clearly, it seems inappropriate to expect fluctuating, instantaneously market-clearing prices, for that would induce more costly search and adjustment than would a combination of both greater predictability and queuing, depending upon costs of search relative to costs of queuing and the gains from predictability. Long-term constant (though lower) wages with secure employment is a means of providing predictability to employees.

5. *Contract stipulation.* The complexity of contract stipulations depends on the rights being transferred, objective predictability and measurability of performance, and the contingencies for which advance provision is made. Many contingencies are met by ex post settlement in the way they would have been met if anticipated—using goodwill as a reward for mutually satisfactory settlements. Contract formation or stipulation includes specification of performance conditions and the allocation of risk resulting from the unpredictability of actual performance. These conditions are as significant as the price, since the price itself will depend upon those terms and conditions. (The activity referred to here is not that of *reaching agreement* on what to include in the conditions but that of making those conditions objectively testable, unambiguous, and measurable.)

If all contingencies could be stipulated unambiguously *and enforced costlessly*, then the quality attributes of any good could be left unknown to any or all parties, with payment being determined by actual subsequent performance. But "of course," since that stipulation and enforcement is not costless, the cost of discerning attributes of a good cannot be treated as unessential or unimportant. Some techniques for economizing on stipulative activity are the use of standard forms, or conventions, of explicit contract laws, and of agreements to submit to arbitration. Continued sales relations between the parties make satisfactory performance desirable to preserve the capital value of anticipated future sales. Undoubtedly, the vast majority of contracts contain incomplete specification of performance conditions, relying instead on the loss of goodwill wealth consequent to a termination of sales or purchases if performance deviates from the predicted performance.

Complex performance or a long-term performance will not necessarily be associated with long-term or complex contracts. If the performance, however complex, can be detected sequentially, payment can be provided sequentially in accord with performance. It is not so much the length of the activity to be agreed upon in a transaction as the costs of detecting the quality of continuing performance that seems to suggest the complex variety of detailed, contractual arrangements. For example, labor employment arrangements often contemplate a long-term relationship; yet no long-term contracts are formalized. Instead, the pay and termination conditions are *expressed* in short-term contracts, but the terms of pay and termination are those that would typify a long-term contract if such contracts were formalized. This view of employment contracts will go far to explain types of unemployment, layoffs, seniority, and relatively constant wages and pay patterns over time. One of the major efforts of this study proposal will be centered on employment transactions costs.[2]

6. *Contract performance.* Without monitors, controls, and ex post adjustments, incentives exist to shirk or neglect performance. Techniques for detecting or measuring performance and for providing payment in accord with performance will be varied and will be used only insofar as they are worth the costs. In some situations, failure to watch pay and performance will cause a loss of future contracts and impose a "goodwill" or "present value" loss on negligent parties. In other cases, a contractual system of rewards or payment procedures will be devised to monitor or facilitate mutual performance or appropriate revisions in subsequent exchange rates.

Some Categories of Property Rights

A transaction culminates in a rights or entitlements transfer. What is a "property right"? In the *rights* of a person to a resource we include the probability that his decision about demarcated uses of the resource will determine the use, in the sense that his decision dominates that of any other person. If my decisions about some use or condition of a car dominate those of all other per-

---

2. See D. Gordon, "The Neo-Classical Theory of Keynesian Unemployment," *Economic Inquiry* 12 (1974): 431–59.

sons—so that their decisions are ineffective in upsetting or attenuating my decisions—then I, rather than they, have a property right to the car. The decision
class of demarcated uses or actions or conditions appurtenant to that resource
identifies the *domain* of rights held in that resource, not the strength of the
right. If the probability is one—certainty—that my decision will dominate, I
have an "absolute" right with respect to the demarcated class of conditions or
uses to which the rights apply. For example, I may have an "absolute" right to
pick apples off a tree, but not to prune the tree. I may have an absolute right to
drive an automobile, but not to have it repainted some other color. The domain
or scope of demarcated uses or conditions of a good can be partitioned among
several people. Call this *use-domain partitioning.*

Distinct from the partitions of the domain of uses of an entity is the *decision
sharing* with other people with whom some rights over the same domain of uses
are jointly held. A shared *decision process* states the procedure whereby those persons shall identify a decision to which all are bound. Majority vote is but one example whereby several joint holders identify or achieve a decision (which is not
necessarily "agreement"). All engage in the *process* of selecting a decision even
though not all may have preferred the resultant decision. Sharing a decision
right with other people reduces the probability that any one sharer's preference
will determine the decision, but it does not reduce the probability of a reached
decision being effective. Though sharing of decision authority attenuates individual power to determine decisions with respect to some resource, that power
often is thereby spread over a wider set of resources, as when a larger group
shares a larger pooled set of assets.

In decision-shared rights we must consider the probability that one sharer's
preference among potential decisions will be the selected decision, as determined by the decision-process arrangement, not by the personality or persuasive powers of the individual, however strong those might be. We are here
referring not to what determines each individual's preference ordering of decisions but, instead, to what role his preference (however influenced) has in determining the group's selected decision.

Related, but different, is the consequence sharing of the resulting use or
saleable value of the resource. How these *consequences* are shared is not necessarily the same as for the *decision* sharing. One "vote" per head (or share of common stock) does not require that the consequences be shared equally per capita
(or per share).

If we were to try to categorize or differentiate property rights, we would, we conjecture, do so on the basis of a vector of characteristics including at least: (1) the domain of activities or uses over which a decision may be assigned, (2) the process of reaching a decision for a group of sharing rights holders, (3) the rules for assigning consequences to sharing members, and (4) the transferability of each of these elements (entitlements) to other people.

A right will be said to be broader, the broader its decision domain. The less a potential domain is partitioned to others, the broader the property right. Authority to decide who will be allowed to rent "my" house and at what price is more partitioned by fair-housing and rent-control and zoning laws, which transfer to political processes some decision authority. The wider the set of possible uses that are collected into one domain or set of uses, the broader the domain of the property right. But what makes it more private?

We seem to use also the degree of decision sharing (number of sharers in the decision process) as a criterion. A private property right can refer to the fact that one person holds the decision rights alone, rather than severally with others. Or *private* can identify the indefinitely large domain of uses that are collected into one parcel of rights, so we could set as a limiting form, *unlimited* indefinite domain of uses to be decided by *one* person. These *two* components— (a) *unlimited domain* and (b) *single*-person, unshared decision processes—seem to be characteristics of "private" property rights.

Ability to *transfer* (or alienate) decision authority to another is also an attribute characterizing private property rights. Another characteristic is *responsibility*, which means that the technological or exchange-value consequences of his decisions about his goods are to be borne by the decision maker. If the good changes value in use, or in exchange, the decision maker has that value of use or of exchange. No other person has to transfer some rights to him in order to compensate him for loss because of inappropriate decision, nor can others compel unilateral transfer of value from him. In sum, all persons are bound by the same class of rights in the goods in which they are said to possess rights. Thus, (1) indefiniteness of use domain, (2) nonsharing of decisions, (3) responsibility, and (4) transferability are elements heavily weighted in the *private* property conception.

If decisions are shared, the property could be corporate or partnership, although still characterized as "private" property. If the shares are not alienable, the term "private" property seems at odds with common usage.

Now let us contrast this rubric of private property with public property in order to identify some differences.

Public and Private Property

Compare a privately owned golf course with a publicly owned golf course (or auditorium, bus service, water service, garbage-collection service, airport, school, or even spaghetti factory). There are differences in their operation; at least anyone who has ever compared them will think so. Why do these differences occur?

Preliminary investigation suggests, for example, that the difference between a privately owned corporation with 1,000 owners and a state-owned entity in a democracy with 1,000 citizens is quite significant, because the 1,000 individuals are furthering their own individual interests in each entity under different systems of property rights. In economic jargon, "the opportunity sets differ." A desire to avoid, or suppress, the effects of the profit-making incentive is often a reason for resort to public property. The objectives sought via public property, however, cannot merely be announced to the managers or operators with the expectation that exhortation will be either sufficient or necessary to achieve the objective.

Public property entitlements and consequences must be borne by all members of the public; none can divest himself of any portion of that ownership. A person must move from one town to another to change his ownership in public property. But while one lives in any community with public property, he has rights in that community's property and cannot divest himself of that public entitlement; but, by definition, he can sell and shift private property rights without also having to leave the community.[3]

To see what difference is made by the right to transfer ownership shares, suppose public ownership could be sold. With capitalized profits or losses accruing to the owners, will incentives be any different?

An answer is suggested by two implications of the specialization of "ownership," which is similar to the familiar specialization of other kinds of skills

3. It is tempting to emphasize the possibility, under public ownership, of someone joining the community and thereby acquiring a share of public ownership without payment to any of the existing owners. This dilution of a person's share of ownership is presumably absent in private ownership. Of course, a community could close off immigration or require purchase of land, but public ownership would continue even if this dilution effect were important. Furthermore, many corporations issue new shares without preemptive rights to incumbents. Still, even if dilution of public ownership were eliminated by restriction of entry, the inability to sell one's share in public property rights remains a factor in the costs-rewards system impinging on all members of the public and on the employees and administrators of the governmental institution.

or activities. The two are: rewards and costs are *more* strongly imposed on each person responsible for them (1) via (*a*) concentration of rights and (*b*) capitalization of future effects into present sales value and (2) via comparative-advantage effects of (*a*) specialized knowledge in control and (*b*) specialized risk bearing.

Concentration

Greater concentration of rewards and costs means that a person's wealth is more dependent upon his activities. The more he concentrates his wealth holding in particular resources, the larger is his wealth response to his own activities in those areas. For example, suppose there are 100 people in a community, with ten separate enterprises; and suppose each person, holding a 1 percent interest in each, could, by devoting one-tenth of his attention to some one enterprise, produce a saving or gain of $1,000. Since the individual is a one-hundredth part owner, he will acquire $10. If he does this for each of the ten different enterprises, his total wealth gain will be $100, with the rest of the wealth increment, $9,900, going to the 99 other people. Of course, if the 99 other people act in the same way, he will get from their activities an increase of wealth of $990,000/100 = $9,900, which gives him a total of $10,000. This is exactly equal to his own marginal product, most of which was spread over the other owners.

Let us now suppose a more concentrated holding; each person owns a one-tenth part of *one* enterprise only (which means that ownership has been reshuffled from pro rata equal shares in all ten enterprises to a concentration in one enterprise by each person). He will now be assumed to devote all his attention to one enterprise, so he again produces $10,000. Of this he gets $1,000. The remaining $9,000 goes to the other owners. The difference is that now $1,000 is dependent upon his own activities whereas formerly only $10 was. Or, more pertinently, the amount dependent upon the activities of other people is reduced from $9,900 to $9,000.

If we go to the extreme where the ten enterprises are divided into 100, with each person as the sole owner of one enterprise, then all $10,000 of his year's wealth increase will be his to keep. The first of these three examples corresponds to "public property rights," the second to corporate joint private rights, and the third to sole proprietorship.

If public property rights were saleable, they would, in effect, become capitalizable private ownership rights, and there would be a movement toward concentration of ownership. Why? The wealth that a person can get or lose is more dependent upon his own activities. If, however, people prefer to collect a major portion of their wealth gain from other people's activities, the total wealth gain would decrease, since everyone would have less incentive to work. It suffices that there be at least one person who prefers to make himself less dependent upon other people's activities and who prefers at least some more wealth to some more leisure. He will then be prepared to buy up some property rights and pay a higher price for them than they are worth to some other people in their current forms of property.

Capitalization

Capitalization of values of future service into *present* exchange values of rights, and hence capitalization on the present wealth of rights owners, is more complete (i.e., less expensive to realize) for private than for public property rights. This means that, for making present decisions, foreseen future consequences are more fully heeded for private than for public property resources. The weaker impact on present values of marketable wealth reduces incentives to heed market values of both present and future consequences. One would therefore conjecture that privately owned resources will be used and priced differently from publicly owned insofar as these differences are differential responses to potential marketable values. Briefly, the wealth incentive is less strongly applicable for public property.

Comparative Advantage in Ownership: Control

The preceding example did not involve differences of abilities, knowledge, beliefs, or attitudes toward risk. But if people differ in any of these respects, specialization in various tasks—including owning—will increase wealth. This is simply an extension of the logical theorem of gains from comparative advantage, which we shall not explain here.

The usual discussion of comparative advantage ignores "ownership" productivities. But people differ in their talents as owners—as monitors and decision makers. Owners bear the risk of value changes and make the decisions about how much to produce, how much to invest, how it shall be produced, and who shall be employed as laborers and managers.[4] Ownership ability includes attitude toward risk bearing, knowledge of and monitoring of different people's productive performance, foresight, and, of course, decision "judg-

---

4. Armen A. Alchian and Harold Demsetz, "Production, Information Costs, and Economic Organization," *American Economic Review* 62 (1972): 777–93.

ment." These talents differ among people according to the particular industry, type of product, or productive resource associated with that industry. Differences in these skills make comparative advantage in property rights pertinent. If property rights are transferable, people will concentrate and use their property rights in those areas in which they believe they have a comparative advantage. Just as specialization in typing, music, or various types of labor is more productive, so is specialization in ownership. Some people specialize in electronics industry knowledge, some in airlines, some in dairies, some in retailing, etc. Private property owners can specialize in knowledge about electronics, devoting much of their effort and study to learning which electronic devices show promise, which are now most efficient in various uses, which should be produced in larger numbers, where investment should take place, what kinds of research and development to finance, etc. But public ownership reduces (by high transactions costs) specialization among owners—though not among employees in the publicly owned venture.

A person who is very knowledgeable about woodworking and cabinet or furniture building would have an advantage as an owner of a furniture company. He would, by being a stockholder, not necessarily make the company any better, but instead he would choose the better company—in terms of his knowledge—as one in which to own shares. The relative rise in the price of such companies enables the existing owners to issue new shares, borrow money more readily, and retain control. In this way the differences in knowledge enable people to specialize in the application of that knowledge to the management and operation of the company—albeit, sometimes by indirect lines.

Comparative Advantage in Ownership: Risk and Beliefs

A second aspect of ownership specialization is risk bearing. If various ventures or resources represent different prospects of values, then exchange of ownership will enable a wealth-increasing reallocation of rights among people, leading to greater utility in the same sense that exchange of goods does. In addition, people differ in beliefs about the prospects of future values of the assets whose ownership can be transferred. Differences in "knowledge" can be used not only in an effort to be more productive but also as a means for distinguishing different prospect situations. For example, I may be the top administrator of the Carnation Milk Company, but I may hold stocks in some electronics company because I prefer the risk pattern provided by that combination rather than by holding Carnation stock also. In this way a person can separate the productivity of knowledge and effort (received as salary) from the risk bearing. I can, if I want, combine them by holding stock in a company in which I am active. This possibility of separating the *control* (effective administration or operation of the company—an activity that rewards comparative superiority in ability and knowledge) from *risk* and *beliefs* is, of course, regarded as an advantage by those who act as employed managers or administrators and by those who choose to act as corporate stockowners without also bothering to exercise their vote or worry about control. Yet it is often criticized as undesirable.

Not all of the stockholders have to exercise voting rights effectively to exert an influence on management. Most stockholders may go along simply because they believe the prospects for profits and losses are sufficiently promising relative to other assets they could own. If losses eventuate, the owners' pertinent alternative is to sell out. To whom? To other buyers who, because of the reduced profit prospects, will offer only a lower price. These "nonactive" owners perform a function in that, at least, they provide the willingness to bear some of the value consequences. So long as scarce resources *exist*, value changes will occur. The question left is, then, who is to bear the reduced value; someone has to.

Often it is said that joint ownership in the modern corporation has separated ownership and control. What this means is that risk bearing and management are more independent. This is correct in the sense that each stockholder does not have the same kind of control as does a sole owner. But it is a long normative leap to decrying this. Specialization in risk bearing and in managerial decision making about uses of resources is now possible. Complete separation of the two does not exist for *every* joint stockholder, for to the extent that some share owners are inactive or indifferent to alternative choices or management problems, other stockholders (joint owners) will be more influential. In effect, the "passive" owners are betting on the decisions of "active" owners—"betting" in the sense that they are prepared to pay for any losses produced by these "activists" and, in turn, to collect some of the profits, if any. In the absence of any right to buy and sell shared rights, everyone would have to bet on the activists as a group (the case of public property). The right to sell concentrates this betting on those who are prepared to pay the most (or demand the least) for the right to do so. And it concentrates the control or management with those who believe they are relatively most able at that task—with the less able being eliminated more surely in private, transferable rights than in public because: (1) evidence of poor management and the opportunity to capture profits by eliminating it is revealed to outsiders by the lower selling price of the owner ship rights; (2) the specialization of ownership functions is facilitated; and (3) the possibility of concentrating one's wealth in certain areas permits greater correlation of personal interest and effort in line with wealth holdings.

We conjecture: *Under public community rights the consequences of any decision are less fully thrust upon the decision maker than under private property.* They are less fully borne than if the same action were taken in a private property institution, with a similar number of owners. One would expect that public agencies would, in order to offset or counterbalance this reduced cost bearing, impose special constraints on public employees or agents. Public agents who are authorized to spend public funds will be more severely constrained with extra restrictions because the costs of their actions are less effectively thrust upon them.

Some Suggested Analytical Interpretations

Transactions costs and their relationship to property rights suggest several ramifications that may merit some attention.

1. It is often said that someone who pollutes the air—or disturbs the peace and quiet—should not do so or should buy rights for doing so. Why? Because he is presumed not to own the resource being abused. The tacit assumption is that air is owned by nondrivers of autos, that rights to the use of land are owned by residers on the land and not by those who put noise or smoke on it. This is a sheer presumption about where rights "should" be assigned. Commentators have jumped to the conclusion that, because no one now is explicitly assigned those rights, the rights belong to those who have no reason to change the prior existing state of resources or that the rights should be assigned to political agents. If auto drivers owned the air, so people who wanted less smog or cleaner air had to buy the air rights (to cleaner air) from drivers, the results would be no different from the results if rights were initially assigned the opposite way—*absent transactions costs!* Since smoke and smog are produced in the act of increasing someone's utility, the reduction of clean air is no different from the reduction of my leisure when I work for the university rather than relaxing on the golf course, contemplating the path of my golf ball. So I contend that the university imposes pollution on me.

Clearly, the growing concern about various forms of "pollution" and environmental law—and even torts—indicates the value of developing an understanding of the factors contributing to "transactions costs" and of the institutions and means for adapting to or reducing them.

2. Because the world is not characterized by costlessly "well-defined" property rights and costless transactions activity, some resources appear to be used

wastefully or inappropriately. Apparently some desirable revisions of resource use are apparent (to observers) and, if brought about, would produce gains beyond the sacrificed values of current uses—if only the people could be made aware of and *responsive* to these potentialities, as could be done if the costs of reaching a contract and enforcing it were not so high. Coase illustrated ways in which these potential gains, if not achieved by voluntary contracts among the parties, were often achieved by judicial settlements or by direction of law. Jurists often enforce the highest-valued uses by assigning disputed entitlements or rights to the persons whose interest it was to use resources in that way (or whose interest it would have been to buy those use rights had the market been sufficiently well organized and rights sufficiently well defined to permit transferability).

An explicit conjecture is that over decades, judicial evolution is toward well-defined rights in the sense of making them more definite, secure, and cheaply transferable. The conjecture is that this would tend toward *private* property rights. But this conjecture remains to be evaluated.

3. The well-known Modigliani-Miller theorem that the value of an enterprise is independent of its form of financing is a special application of the Coase theorem; absent transactions costs, rights will be partitioned in their highest-valued ways and thereby have the highest values.[5] So long as entitlements are well defined, partitionable, and transferable, under the motive of enhanced wealth they will be revised and used in the maximum-valued ways—if transactions costs are absent. Their initial sale value will be capitalized to reflect those values.

In fact, of course, rights are not costlessly transferable or revisable. Therefore, what forms of rights are most appropriately issued initially by, say, a new corporation? Bonds, common stocks, preferreds, convertibles, warrants? Are there any factors that would explain the optimal initial mix, given transactions costs of subsequent revisions or transfers? We conjecture that differences in beliefs by investors about the potential performance of the enterprise can account for differences in appropriate initial mixes—given transactions costs that are not insignificant.

4. A remaining vestige of confusion about the meaning of the propositions about effects of transactions costs arises from "blackmail" or nuisance liability problems. Smith would threaten to impose larger damages on Jones at triv-

---

5. Franco Modigliani and Merton Miller, "The Cost of Capital, Corporation Finance and the Theory of Investment," *American Economic Review* 48 (1958): 268–97.

ial cost to Smith—say by cheaply creating smoke or by revealing secret, malign information about Jones. Similarly, the low cost of creating smoke to extract preventive payment from the threatened party was believed, erroneously, to upset the "costless" transactions analysis. What the blackmail or nuisance threats do, however, is simply reveal that rights to the land's condition are not held by the threatened party but are instead *distributed* among many other people, no *one* of whom can by agreement with the threatened party and the others exclude other parties from creating smoke. (From every other party, the rights would have to be purchased by one agent who could exercise or transfer exclusive authority.) There exists the problem of assembling all the dispersed entitlements from the various holders into one general exclusion right. Thus, if there were many neighbors of my land, each of whom had a nonexclusive entitlement to dump smoke on my land (i.e., could not prevent others from doing so), and if the sum of values to each person of dumping his smoke was less than the damage to me, it would pay me to buy and consolidate the rights from all the neighbors (the rest of the society).

If it be thought that each would have an incentive to hold out for the total value and thereby obstruct agreement, it should be recognized that this so-called blackmail is really "bargaining." Each party tries to obtain most of the value of the land use—whether by threatening to withhold agreement or, in so-called blackmail cases, by threatening to destroy potential use value by dumping smoke. But this really is only the classic bilateral monopoly bargaining problem, common in many other areas. It does not depend on the rights assignments; it instead reflects an obstacle to achieving an agreed-upon price. The parties are "bargaining" over the exchange rate for transfer of rights. With "pure" competition on both sides, the exchange rate would be uniquely determined by rivalry of alternative bidders and sellers. But otherwise, there is a *range* of mutually beneficial exchange prices. When threatening to quit while bargaining over my salary, I am imposing a bargaining cost and trying to obtain more of the transactions surplus. When I threaten not to accept an offer, I am "blackmailing" my employer (given that I would have accepted his initial offer if I knew for sure that there was no possibility of getting more from that employer). This so-called blackmail becomes merely the cost of bilateral monopoly-monopsony bargaining.

But there is another kind of problem that should not be confused with "the" blackmail problem. Suppose rights to privacy were deemed to exist and to be held by the person himself but were inadequately guarded by state legal action, with less than adequate compensation for invasion of privacy (even though the revealers were punished). Since state punishment does not guarantee complete deterrence, some whose privacy is threatened will add private action. Society may deem some of such private action *improper* because of its perverse effects of *inducing* activity designed to penetrate privacy. For example, suppose thieves could resell stolen goods to victims (at a price less than the owner's costs of going to the state for protection and recovery). Such private actions would undermine the punitive state-provided system of deterrence and protection. In a collusive agreement of protected people, although it pays individuals to break the agreement privately, it pays even more for the group not to. Lacking a theory of government and social norms, we can only call attention to the differences between the monopoly-monopsony bargaining case and this blackmail undermining of state-enforced deterrence. Do not confuse the two.

5. Another consequence of the entitlements–transactions costs analysis has been to aid the *formal* economic analysis of liability rules. Is the producer liable or is the consumer? The employer or the employee? The driver of this car or that car or neither? Unfortunately, the term *liability* is ambiguous. If the consumer is liable, does it mean that in the absence of contracts to the contrary he is presumed to bear the losses of contingent events? Does it mean that he cannot legally contract with a seller about the risks of consequences of future performance? If the former, it merely identifies a presumed contractual condition *in the absence of specific contract terms* to the contrary. It presumably is an approximation to terms that a majority of contracts would contain and thereby reduces contract stipulation costs.

If, on the other hand, *liability* means stipulation of conditions that *must* be included in any contract, does the imposed liability rule make a difference? In what effects? Other terms of the contract, as when employer liability for accidents is imposed, can be altered to reduce wages that compensated for self-insurance against accidents. What is changed is only the *system* of insurance for accidents. Employees now must purchase group insurance via lower wages, whereas formerly they could accept higher wages and *either* pay for group insurance *or* self-insure. To *impose* a mandatory contract stipulation in all employee-employer contracts is to impose prohibitively high transactions costs for some contract revisions. Employees must buy employer-administered group insurance. Only if transactions costs (*including* legal restrictions on rights transfers) are absent are *initial* assignments of liabilities irrelevant, for they can be renegotiated. With costs of renegotiation, initial rights allocation does alter the end result. In sum, since "bearing the liability" is merely another way to say something about who starts with what rights, the *rule* of liability is a negotiable, initial provision in a contract.

If (*a*) it is a negotiable, initial suggestion that will hold only in the absence of explicit provisions to the contrary, nothing is changed if there are no costs of making contracts. If (*b*) the specified liability is not negotiable and *must* be included in all *new* contracts, then other negotiable conditions will offset the imposed conditions so as to more closely, though not completely, achieve the results that would have been achieved in the absence of the imposed stipulations. If (*c*) new stipulations are imposed on *existing* contracts without any permissible revisions in the continuing contract, the rule of liability matters (at least) for the duration of the contract. With transactions costs present, as they always are, *imposed* rules of liabilities or rights make a difference in who takes what kind of, more, or less preventive or precautionary action.

6. Another major clarification consequent to the analysis of the costs of transfer of rights was that of "externalities," which are now explained or interpreted as consequences of poorly defined, poorly assured property rights, which implies high transactions costs. It became clear also that the Pigou tradition of "externalities" as something to be handled by taxes, subsidies, or government activity was inappropriate. It is neither obvious nor demonstrable that all government processes would induce a "better" allocation than had been achieved already. Furthermore, an alternative to *that* kind of governmental action is making the property rights better defined, transferable, and secure and easier to enforce at law. This second facet attracted significant empirical study beyond that being given to other political means of meeting the problem of "externalities." The implications for basic reinterpretation of the tort laws are wide ranging.

The concept of externalities is bankrupt because of its ambiguity. Buchanan and Stubblebine restructured the term *externalities* in such a way as to permit its graceful abandonment—via the route of adding adjectives, adverbs, and other modifiers to distinguish the various subconcepts and thereby exposing the many inconsistent meanings of *externality*.[6] In one sense, almost all human actions have externalities in that one person's acts affect other people. Sometimes only those acts that affect the technological production function of other people are called externalities—though Viner was considerate enough to call

6. James M. Buchanan and Wm. Craig Stubblebine, "Externality," *Economica* 29 (1962): 371–84.

these "technological external diseconomies"[7]—a conception that is well worth retaining. Sometimes *externalities* has been used to describe only unheeded effects on other people. Whatever the terminology, it is worth distinguishing the case in which someone else would benefit from my actions, but by less than the cost to me, from those cases in which the marginal effects on others have a value in excess of the value to me, but in which there are costs of communicating or negotiating an enforceable agreement between the interacting parties. In this case, it seems the issue is usefully describable, not as one of "externalities," but as one of communication, contracting, or property rights costs, all mingled in the term *transactions costs*.

7. The above suggests a new question: What institutional arrangements have evolved to reduce the costs of communicating information, of contracting, and of defining and enforcing property rights so as to induce potentially mutually beneficial resource uses and activity? (The question is *not*, What if, miraculously, all those costs were absent? This latter query is equivalent to asking for zero costs of steel, cloth, and food. We would be richer, obviously.)

We have analytically explored one facet of this pertinent question with a proposition that what is known as a firm is essentially a contractual arrangement for reducing the costs of detecting and monitoring (adjusting rewards appropriately) joint production performance. This explanation, though not inconsistent with the elements contained in the interpretations of Knight and Coase,[8] does provide refutable implications. It does so by moving beyond the idea that transactions costs are obstacles to the pure market economy's assigning every resource use via pairwise market contracting. Also, a definition of a firm is provided. And implications are derived about whom the control monitor is responsible to, who will receive the residual, the assets that will be owned by that firm's owner, the types of activities that will be more likely managed by partnerships, and some differences among profit-sharing, nonprofit, corporate, socialist, cooperative, and governmentally owned firms.

And of course, we need not emphasize the problems into which socialists have been led. The Czechoslovaks were moving toward a market system—as some Russians would like to do—but the Czechs faced up to the issue more

7. Jacob Viner, "Cost Curves and Supply Curves," *Zeitschrift für Nationalökonomie* 3 (1931): 23–46.

8. Frank H. Knight, "Fallacies in the Interpretation of Social Costs," *Quarterly Journal of Economics* 38 (1924): 524–606; Ronald H. Coase, "The Nature of the Firm," *Economica* 4 (1937): 368–405.

bluntly and with less political opposition and perceived that more private rights are necessary for a market pricing system to work as desired. Younger plant managers were pushing in that direction for efficiency incentives. Power would be transferred from the political authorities to individual businessmen. A continuation of that trend would weaken the socialist party control. That handwriting on the wall clearly predicted, and "justified," the Russian invasion. In Yugoslavia, property rights in resources are persistently being privatized—that is, removed from political agents. In every Communist country, there will develop a conflict between the new aspiring plant managers who see ways to improve operations and increase their wealth if only they could reap more of the harvests of their increased output. The necessity for rights to be transferable if the market is to be used is the dilemma the Russian economists are slowly discerning. The conflict between a potential rising entrepreneurial class and the political authorities is inevitable. And it is pathetic to observe Russian economists in their agonizing, awakening awareness of this dependence of an "efficient" market system on a system of transferable private property rights. They struggle to avoid the term *property rights*, just as they avoid the term *interest*; but they have accepted the latter under the name of *efficiency index*—which is, admittedly, a pretty good name. What will they call the private property rights in productive assets in Russia?

8. Another clarification stemming from a formal analysis of property rights and their transfer costs pertains to the public-good *analytic* concept. If heavy goods involved greater transactions costs than lighter goods, market forces would have less influence on the use of heavy goods; if animate services had higher transactions costs, they would be allocated less by individual exchange in private markets. For any goods with higher transactions costs, the same would follow. The implication is that a public-private goods *technological* distinction provides in itself *no implications whatsoever* about efficient or "appropriate means of disposition, production, or control of public and private goods." Literally, nothing makes the public-versus-private-good *technological* attribute an appropriate criterion for political or market control—despite articles by the "high" and "low" to that effect—unless that technological characteristic is merely a name for high transactions costs.

A technological characteristic is relevant if and only if it correlates with—and then only as a proxy for—transactions costs. Wild animals, airplane airspace, and underground oil and gas all have relatively high cost components in the transactions rubric, and that makes them more fit for group or nonmarket control. Some technologically public goods involve lower property rights and transactions costs than some private goods; the consequence should not be missed for analysis of procedures of control.

Many policies about problems of "free riders" or of reaching agreements about production and uses of public goods presume that government activities provide superior methods of overcoming these questions. As yet, no clear theory of government behavior has been established on the basis of which to derive such presumptions. The private sector does have much that serves to meet many so-called free riders and the problem of reaching agreements. Direct attention to transactions costs under various forms of property rights will avoid at least the technological fallacy.

9. Taking a lesson from the public goods–private goods misclassification, we can ask if there is any significance to the private *property*–public *property* distinction. Is there any reason to believe the incidence of the private-public good characteristic is correlated with transactions costs? We think so. And if it is correlated with transactions costs, we should expect to be able to derive contrasting implications about behavior and uses of resources under public and private property rights.

THE BENEFICIARIES OF CLEANER AIR

Thank you, public, for reducing smog—particularly my smog. I say thank you because you haven't made me pay the bill.

Lest you not perceive my benefits, let me detail some. The Los Angeles basin, where I live, now has less smog because of your efforts. As a result, land values have increased as more people from elsewhere moved to occupy Los Angeles land which now provides access to cleaner air. Land values in the formerly smoggiest areas have risen most, reflecting the better quality of the air. And they will rise even more if the smog is reduced more.

Of course, all Los Angeles residents, current and new, who *rent* land must pay higher rents and consequently have less to spend on other goods like food, clothing, entertainment, and medical services. These land-renting residents now have fewer material goods and services in order to have fresher air. Are they better off with cleaner air but less of other goods? No, not better nor healthier if you consider that they have given up income that could have been spent for medical attention or better food.

But I have certainly benefited. That's why I'm writing to thank you. I am a landowner in a formerly more smoggy area and am better off, since my land value has risen by much of the value of the cleaner air. I still am able to buy as much of other goods and services. My increased wealth is entirely devoted to consuming superior air quality, unless I move to a smaller plot of land.

But renters, people like most of those poor people in Watts, are unambiguously harmed. In fact, the rental value of land has risen even more than the fresher air is worth to residents who lived there during the smoggier times. That's because newcomers moving into the area place a higher value on cleansed air than do those already there. As a result, on average, the rise in land prices exceeds the value of the benefits of cleaner air to those people who were already residing in the smoggier areas.

Even more surprising effects should be acknowledged. Land in the peripheral, suburban developments far from the formerly smoggy city center loses value. People no longer value that suburban land so highly if they can now live

Reprinted, by permission of the author, from *Los Angeles Times* (1979), n.p.

nearer the center of the city and still have fresher air. But since I own land nearer the city center area, I encourage people to contribute to campaigns to clean the air in the smoggy areas.

You might believe those who benefit should pay for cleaning the air. You might think I should be taxed to subsidize catalytic converters and other engine-fouling devices on your car to increase the wealth of landowners like me in the smoggy areas. But you haven't, so I thank you. Keep up your good work.

Even if you were allowed to go around taxing the increased value of land, you would have insuperable ethical problems. Some people have owned their land for decades, so when the smog increased years ago, their land values suffered. Now when the smog is reduced, they could rightfully claim to be getting back what they earlier lost, so they shouldn't be taxed.

On the other hand, some like me who bought land after the smog had developed paid less because the land provided less-clean air at that time. Now that the land has better air, we are getting a gain created by the public's expensive use of air-cleaning devices.

So, before taxing away increases of land values we should know who purchased the land and when. Not a feasible task.

Let me speak for some other people who should thank you, too. Other unambiguous beneficiaries are those people not now residing in the L.A. smoggy area but who will move here when the air is cleaner. But the biggest set of unambiguous beneficiaries (besides owners like me) are those who remain elsewhere as renters (not as landowners), because rents elsewhere fall relative to what they would have been had the smog not been reduced in the Los Angeles basin.

Consider any other smoggy areas—New York, Chicago, or whatever—and the results are the same. Only if all areas are equally dense in population and in air quality and all are equally improved will the landowners' value not capture much, if not all, of the benefits of cleaner air. Indeed, you members of the public might find it cheaper to create cleaner air and benefits for me if you were to use remote, less valuable sites to generate power in order to have cleaner air in the smoggier areas.

While I have no superb proposals as to how to finance the smog-reduction activity, one thing is pretty clear. If we would create energy sources by some dirtying of the air in the other areas, such as the deserts of Arizona and Utah, where coal deposits are available, the total costs to society would be lower. And more reliance on land taxes, rather than less—reversing the Proposition 13 trend—would be appropriate.

But happily for me, some of you advocates of cleaner air seem not to understand or publicize these effects and are instead determined to clean the air in a manner more expensive and more effective in providing benefits to landowners of currently smoggier areas while making those least benefited pay the bill. You can see why some economic analysis is instructive in explaining why I thank you and wish you continued success.

2

THE THEORY OF THE FIRM

PRODUCTION, INFORMATION COSTS, AND ECONOMIC ORGANIZATION

ARMEN A. ALCHIAN AND HAROLD DEMSETZ

The mark of a capitalistic society is that resources are owned and allocated by such nongovernmental organizations as firms, households, and markets. Resource owners increase productivity through cooperative specialization, and this leads to the demand for economic organizations which facilitate cooperation. When a lumber mill employs a cabinetmaker, cooperation between specialists is achieved within a firm, and when a cabinetmaker purchases wood from a lumberman, the cooperation takes place across markets (or between firms). Two important problems face a theory of economic organization—to explain the conditions that determine whether the gains from specialization and cooperative production can better be obtained within an organization like the firm, or across markets, and to explain the structure of the organization.

It is common to see the firm characterized by the power to settle issues by fiat, by authority, or by disciplinary action superior to that available in the conventional market. This is delusion. The firm does not own all its inputs. It has no power of fiat, no authority, no disciplinary action any different in the slightest degree from ordinary market contracting between any two people. I can "punish" you only by withholding future business or by seeking redress in the courts for any failure to honor our exchange agreement. That is exactly all that any employer can do. He can fire or sue, just as I can fire my grocer by stopping purchases from him or sue him for delivering faulty products. What then is the content of the presumed power to manage and assign workers to various tasks? Exactly the same as one little consumer's power to manage and assign his grocer to various tasks. The single consumer can assign his grocer to the task of

Reprinted from Armen A. Alchian, *Economic Forces at Work* (Indianapolis: Liberty Fund, 1977), 73–110. This article was previously published in *American Economic Review* 62 (December 1972): 777–95, and is reprinted by permission of the American Economic Association.

Acknowledgment is made for financial aid from the E. Lilly Endowment, Inc., grant to UCLA for research in the behavioral effects of property rights.

obtaining whatever the customer can induce the grocer to provide at a price acceptable to both parties. That is precisely all that an employer can do to an employee. To speak of managing, directing, or assigning workers to various tasks is a deceptive way of noting that the employer continually is involved in renegotiation of contracts on terms that must be acceptable to both parties. Telling an employee to type this letter rather than to file that document is like my telling a grocer to sell me this brand of tuna rather than that brand of bread. I have no contract to continue to purchase from the grocer, and neither the employer nor the employee is bound by any contractual obligations to continue their relationship. Long-term contracts between employer and employee are not the essence of the organization we call a firm. My grocer can count on my returning day after day and purchasing his services and goods even with the prices not always marked on the goods—because I know what they are—and he adapts his activity to conform to my directions to him as to what I want each day . . . he is not my employee.

Wherein then is the relationship between a grocer and his employee different from that between a grocer and his customers? It is in a *team* use of inputs and a centralized position of some party in the contractual arrangements of *all* other inputs. It is the *centralized contractual agent in a team productive process*—not some superior authoritarian directive or disciplinary power. Exactly what is a team process and why does it induce the contractual form called the firm? These problems motivate the inquiry of this paper.

1. The Metering Problem

The economic organization through which input owners cooperate will make better use of their comparative advantages to the extent that it facilitates the payment of rewards in accord with productivity. If rewards were random, and without regard to productive effort, no incentive to productive effort would be provided by the organization; and if rewards were negatively correlated with productivity, the organization would be subject to sabotage. Two key demands are placed on an economic organization—metering input productivity and metering rewards.[1]

Metering problems sometimes can be resolved well through the exchange of products across competitive markets, because in many situations markets yield

1. *Meter* means to measure and also to apportion. One can meter (measure) output, and one can also meter (control) the output. We use the word to denote both; the context should indicate which.

a high correlation between rewards and productivity. If a farmer increases his output of wheat by ten percent at the prevailing market price, his receipts also increase by ten percent. This method of organizing economic activity meters the *output directly*, reveals the marginal product, and apportions the *rewards* to resource owners in accord with that direct measurement of their outputs. The success of this decentralized market exchange in promoting productive specialization requires that changes in market rewards fall on those responsible for changes in *output*.[2]

The classic relationship in economics that runs from marginal productivity to the distribution of income implicitly *assumes* the existence of an organization, be it the market or the firm, that allocates rewards to resources in accord with their productivity. The problem of economic organization, the economical means of metering productivity and rewards, is not confronted directly in the classical analysis of production and distribution. Instead, that analysis tends to assume sufficiently economic—or zero-cost—means, as if produc-

2. A producer's wealth would be reduced by the present capitalized value of the future income lost by loss of reputation. Reputation, i.e., credibility, is an asset, which is another way of saying that reliable information about expected performance is both a costly and a valuable good. For acts of God that interfere with contract performance, both parties have incentives to reach a settlement akin to that which would have been reached if such events had been covered by specific contingency clauses. The reason, again, is that a reputation for "honest" dealings—i.e., for actions similar to those that would probably have been reached had the contract provided this contingency—is wealth.

Almost every contract is open-ended in that many contingencies are uncovered. For example, if a fire delays production of a promised product by A to B, and if B contends that A has not fulfilled the contract, how is the dispute settled and what recompense, if any, does A grant to B? A person uninitiated in such questions may be surprised by the extent to which contracts permit either party to escape performance or to nullify the contract. In fact, it is hard to imagine any contract, which, when taken solely in terms of its stipulations, could not be evaded by one of the parties. Yet that is the ruling viable type of contract. Why? Undoubtedly the best discussion that we have seen on this question is by Stewart Macaulay.

There are means not only of detecting or preventing cheating but also for deciding how to allocate the losses or gains of unpredictable events or quality of items exchanged. Sales contracts contain warranties, guarantees, collateral, return privileges, and penalty clauses for specific nonperformance. These are means of assignment of *risks* of losses of cheating. A lower price without warranty—an "as is" purchase—places more of the risk on the buyer, while the seller buys insurance against losses of his "cheating." On the other hand, a warranty or return privilege or service contract places more risk on the seller, with insurance being bought by the buyer.

tivity automatically created its reward. We conjecture the direction of causation is the reverse—the specific system of rewarding which is relied upon stimulates a particular productivity response. If the economic organization meters poorly, with rewards and productivity only loosely correlated, then productivity will be smaller; but if the economic organization meters well, productivity will be greater. What makes metering difficult and hence induces means of economizing on metering costs?

II. Team Production

Two men jointly lift heavy cargo into trucks. Solely by observing the total weight loaded per day, it is impossible to determine each person's marginal productivity. With team production it is difficult, solely by observing total output, to either define or determine *each* individual's contribution to this output of the cooperating inputs. The output is yielded by a team, by definition, and it is not a *sum* of separable outputs of each of its members. Team production of Z involves at least two inputs, X_i and X_j, with $\partial^2 Z / \partial X_i \partial X_j \neq 0$.[3] The production function is *not* separable into two functions, each involving only inputs X_i or only inputs X_j. Consequently there is no *sum* of Z of two separable functions to treat as the Z of the team production function. (An example of a *separable* case is $Z = aX_i^2 + bX_j^2$ which is separable into $Z_i = aX_i^2$ and $Z_j = bX_j^2$, and $Z = Z_i + Z_j$. This is not team production.) There exist production techniques in which the Z obtained is greater than if X_i and X_j had produced separable Z. Team production will be used if it yields an output enough larger than the sum of separable production of Z to cover the costs of organizing and disciplining team members— the topics of this paper.[4]

Usual explanations of the gains from cooperative behavior rely on exchange and production in accord with the comparative advantage specialization principle with separable additive production. However, as suggested above, there is a source of gain from cooperative activity involving working as a *team*, wherein individual cooperating inputs do not yield identifiable, separate products which can be *summed* to measure the total output. For this cooperative produc-

---

3. The function is separable into additive functions if the cross partial derivative is zero, i.e., if $\partial^2 Z / \partial X_i \partial X_j = 0$.

4. With sufficient generality of notation and conception, this team production function could be formulated as a case of the generalized production function interpretation given by our colleague E. A. Thompson.

tive activity, here called "team" production, measuring marginal productivity and making payments in accord therewith is more expensive by an order of magnitude than for separable production functions.

Team production, to repeat, is production in which (1) several types of resources are used and (2) the product is not a sum of separable outputs of each cooperating resource. An additional factor creates a team organization problem—(3) not all resources used in team production belong to one person.

We do not inquire into why all the jointly used resources are not owned by one person but instead inquire into the types of organization, contracts, and informational and payment procedures used among owners of teamed inputs. With respect to the one-owner case, perhaps it is sufficient merely to note that (a) slavery is prohibited, (b) one might assume risk aversion as a reason for one person's not borrowing enough to purchase all the assets or sources of services rather than renting them, and (c) the purchase-resale spread may be so large that costs of short-term ownership exceed rental costs. Our problem is viewed basically as one of organization among different people, not of the physical goods or services, however much there must be selection and choice of combination of the latter.

How can the members of a team be rewarded and induced to work efficiently? In team production, marginal products of cooperative team members are not so directly and separably (i.e., cheaply) observable. What a team offers to the market can be taken as the marginal product of the team but not of the team members. The costs of metering or ascertaining the marginal products of the team's members are what call forth new organizations and procedures. Clues to each input's productivity can be secured by observing behavior of individual inputs. When lifting cargo into the truck, how rapidly does a man move to the next piece to be loaded, how many cigarette breaks does he take, does the item being lifted tilt downward toward his side?

If detecting such behavior were costless, neither party would have an incentive to shirk, because neither could impose the cost of his shirking on the other (if their cooperation was agreed to voluntarily). But since costs must be incurred to monitor each other, each input owner will have more incentive to shirk when he works as part of a team, than if his performance could be monitored easily or if he did not work on a team. If there is a net increase in productivity available by team production, net of the metering cost associated with disciplining the team, then team production will be relied upon rather than a multitude of bilateral exchange of separable individual outputs.

Both leisure and higher income enter a person's utility function.[5] Hence, each person should adjust his work and realized reward so as to equate the marginal rate of substitution between leisure and production of real output to his marginal rate of substitution in consumption. That is, he would adjust his rate of work to bring his demand prices of leisure and output to equality with their true costs. However, with detection, policing, monitoring, measuring, or metering costs, each person will be induced to take more leisure, because the effect of relaxing on *his realized* (reward) rate of substitution between output and leisure will be less than the effect on the *true* rate of substitution. His realized cost of leisure will fall more than the true cost of leisure, so he "buys" more leisure (i.e., more nonpecuniary reward).

If his relaxation cannot be detected perfectly at zero cost, part of its effects will be borne by others in the team, thus making *his* realized cost of relaxation less than the true total cost to the team. The difficulty of detecting such actions permits the private costs of his actions to be less than their full costs. Since each person responds to his private realizable rate of substitution (in production) rather than the true total (i.e., social) rate, and so long as there are costs for other people to detect his shift toward relaxation, it will not pay (them) to force him to readjust completely by making him realize the true cost. Only enough efforts will be made to equate the marginal gains of detection activity with the marginal costs of detection; and that implies a lower rate of productive effort and more shirking than in a costless monitoring, or measuring, world.

In a university, the faculty use office telephones, paper, and mail for personal uses beyond strict university productivity. The university administrators could stop such practices by identifying the responsible person in each case, but they can do so only at higher costs than administrators are willing to incur. The extra costs of identifying each party (rather than merely identifying the presence of such activity) would exceed the savings from diminished faculty "turpitudinal peccadilloes." So the faculty is allowed some degree of "privileges, perquisites, or fringe benefits." And the total of the pecuniary wages paid is lower because of this irreducible (at acceptable costs) degree of amenity-seizing activity. Pay is lower in pecuniary terms and higher in leisure, conveniences, and ease of work. But still every person would prefer to see detection made more effective (if it were somehow possible to monitor costlessly) so that

---

5. More precisely, "if anything other than pecuniary income enters his utility function." Leisure stands for all nonpecuniary income for simplicity of exposition.

he, as part of the now more effectively producing team, could thereby realize a higher pecuniary pay and less leisure. If everyone could, at zero cost, have his reward-realized rate brought to the true production-possibility real rate, all could achieve a more preferred position. But detection of the responsible parties is costly; that cost acts like a tax on work rewards.[6] Viable shirking is the result.

What forms of organizing team production will lower the cost of detecting "performance" (i.e., marginal productivity) and bring personally realized rates of substitution closer to true rates of substitution? Market competition, in principle, could monitor some team production. (It already *organizes* teams.) Input owners who are not team members can offer, in return for a smaller share of the team's rewards, to replace excessively (i.e., overpaid) shirking members. Market competition among potential team members would determine team membership and individual rewards. There would be no team leader, manager, organizer, owner, or employer. For such decentralized organizational control to work, outsiders, possibly after observing each team's total output, can speculate about their capabilities as team members, and, by a market competitive process, revised teams with greater productive ability will be formed and sustained. Incumbent members will be constrained by threats of replacement by outsiders offering services for lower reward shares or offering greater rewards to the other members of the team. Any team member who shirked in the expectation that the reduced output effect would not be attributed to him will be displaced if his activity is detected. Teams of productive inputs, like business units, would evolve in apparent spontaneity in the market—without any central organizing agent, team manager, or boss.

But completely effective control cannot be expected from individualized market competition for two reasons. First, for this competition to be completely effective, new challengers for team membership must know where, and to what extent, shirking is a serious problem, i.e., know they can increase net output as compared with the inputs they replace. To the extent that this is true

---

6. Do not assume that the sole result of the cost of detecting shirking is one form of payment (more leisure and less take-home money). With several members of the team, each has an incentive to cheat against the others by engaging in more than the average amount of such leisure if the employer cannot tell at zero cost which employee is taking more than average. As a result the total productivity of the team is lowered. Shirking-detection costs thus change the form of payment and also result in lower total rewards. Because the cross partial derivatives are positive, shirking reduces other people's marginal products.

it is probably possible for existing fellow team members to recognize the shirking. But, by definition, the detection of shirking by observing team output is costly for team production. Second, assume the presence of detection costs, and assume that in order to secure a place on the team a new input owner must accept a smaller share of rewards (or a promise to produce more). Then his incentive to shirk would still be at least as great as the incentives of the inputs replaced, because he still bears less than the entire reduction in team output for which he is responsible.

III. The Classical Firm

One method of reducing shirking is for someone to specialize as a monitor to check the input performance of team members.[7] But who will monitor the monitor? One constraint on the monitor is the aforesaid market competition offered by other monitors, but for reasons already given, that is not perfectly effective. Another constraint can be imposed on the monitor: give him title to the net earnings of the team, net of payments to other inputs. If owners of co-operating inputs agree with the monitor that he is to receive any residual product above prescribed amounts (hopefully, the marginal value products of the other inputs), the monitor will have an added incentive not to shirk as a monitor. Specialization in monitoring plus reliance on a residual claimant status will reduce shirking; but additional links are needed to forge the firm of classical economic theory. How will the residual claimant monitor the other inputs?

We use the term monitor to connote several activities in addition to its disciplinary connotation. It connotes measuring output performance, apportioning rewards, observing the input behavior of inputs as means of detecting or estimating their marginal productivity, and giving assignments or instructions in what to do and how to do it. (It also includes, as we shall show later, authority to terminate or revise contracts.) Perhaps the contrast between a football coach and team captain is helpful. The coach selects strategies and tactics and sends

---

7. What is meant by performance? Input energy, initiative, work attitude, perspiration, rate of exhaustion? Or output? It is the latter that is sought—the *effect* or output. But performance is nicely ambiguous, because it suggests both input and output. It is *nicely* ambiguous because, as we shall see, sometimes by inspecting a team member's input activity we can better judge his output effect, perhaps not with complete accuracy but better than by watching the output of the *team*. It is not always the case that watching input activity is the only or best means of detecting, measuring, or monitoring output effects of each team member, but in some cases it is a useful way. For the moment, the word *performance* glosses over these aspects and facilitates concentration on other issues.

in instructions about what plays to utilize. The captain is essentially an observer and reporter of the performance at close hand of the members. The latter is an inspector-steward, and the former a supervisor manager. For the present all these activities are included in the rubric "monitoring." All these tasks are, in principle, negotiable across markets, but we are presuming that such market measurement of marginal productivities and job reassignments are not so cheaply performed for team production. And in particular our analysis suggests that it is not so much the costs of spontaneously negotiating contracts in the markets among groups for team production as it is the detection of the performance of individual members of the team that calls for the organization noted here.

The specialist *who receives the residual rewards* will be the monitor of the members of the team (i.e., will manage the use of cooperative inputs). The monitor earns his residual through the reduction in shirking that he brings about, not only by the prices that he agrees to pay the owners of the inputs but also by observing and directing the actions or uses of these inputs. *Managing or examining the ways to which inputs are used in team production is a method of metering the marginal productivity of individual inputs to the team's output.*

To discipline team members and reduce shirking, the residual claimant must have power to revise the contract terms and incentives of *individual* members without having to terminate or alter every other input's contract. Hence, team members who seek to increase their productivity will assign to the monitor not only the residual claimant right but also the right to alter individual membership and performance on the team. Each team member, of course, can terminate his own membership (i.e., quit the team), but only the monitor may unilaterally terminate the membership of any of the other members without necessarily terminating the team itself or his association with the team; and he alone can expand or reduce membership, alter the mix of membership, or sell the right to be the residual claimant-monitor of the team. It is this entire bundle of rights—(1) to be a residual claimant; (2) to observe input behavior; (3) to be the central party common to all contracts with inputs; (4) to alter the membership of the team; and (5) to sell these rights—that defines the *ownership* (or the employer) of the *classical* (capitalist, free-enterprise) firm. The coalescing of these rights has arisen, our analysis asserts, because it resolves the shirking-information problem of team production better than does the noncentralized contractual arrangement.

The relationship of each team member to the *owner* of the firm (i.e., the party common to all input contracts *and* the residual claimant) is simply a "quid pro quo" contract. Each makes a purchase and sale. The employee "orders" the owner of the team to pay him money in the same sense that the employer directs the team member to perform certain acts. The employee can terminate the contract as readily as can the employer, and long-term contracts, therefore, are not an essential attribute of the firm. Nor are "authoritarian," "dictational," or "fiat" attributes relevant to the conception of the firm or its efficiency.

In summary, two necessary conditions exist for the emergence of the firm on the prior assumption that more than pecuniary wealth enters utility functions: (1) It is possible to increase productivity through team-oriented production, a production technique for which it is costly to directly measure the marginal outputs of the cooperating inputs. This makes it more difficult to restrict shirking through simple market exchange between cooperating inputs. (2) It is economical to estimate marginal productivity by observing or specifying input behavior. The simultaneous occurrence of both these preconditions leads to the contractual organization of inputs known as the *classical capitalist firm*, with (a) joint input production, (b) several input owners, and one party who (c) is common to all the contracts of the joint inputs, (d) has rights to renegotiate any input's contract independent of contracts with other input owners, (e) holds the residual claim, and (f) has the right to sell his central contractual residual status.[8]

Other Theories of the Firm

At this juncture, as an aside, we briefly place this theory of the firm in the contexts of those offered by Ronald Coase and Frank Knight.[9] Our view of the firm is not necessarily inconsistent with Coase's; we attempt to go further and identify refutable implications. Coase's penetrating insight is to make more of the fact that markets do not operate costlessly, and he relies on the cost of using markets to *form* contracts as his basic explanation for the existence of firms. We do not disagree with the proposition that, *ceteris paribus*, the higher is the cost of transacting across markets, the greater will be the comparative advantage of organizing resources within the firm; it is a difficult proposition to disagree with or to refute. We could with equal ease subscribe to a theory of the firm based on the cost of managing, for surely it is true that, *ceteris paribus*, the lower is the cost of managing, the greater will be the comparative advantage of or-

8. Removal of (b) converts a capitalist proprietary firm to a socialist firm.
9. Recognition must also be given to the seminal inquiries by Morris Silver and Richard Auster and by H. B. Malmgren.

ganizing resources within the firm. To move the theory forward, it is necessary to know what is meant by a firm and to explain the circumstances under which the cost of "managing" resources is low relative to the cost of allocating resources through market transaction. The conception of and rationale for the classical firm that we propose take a step down the path pointed out by Coase toward that goal. Consideration of team production, team organization, difficulty in metering outputs, and the problem of shirking are important to our explanation but, so far as we can ascertain, not to Coase's. Coase's analysis insofar as it had heretofore been developed would suggest open-ended contracts but does not appear to imply anything more—neither the residual claimant status nor the distinction between employee and subcontractor status (nor any of the implications indicated below). And it is not true that employees are generally employed on the basis of long-term contractual arrangements any more than on a series of short-term or indefinite-length contracts.

The importance of our proposed additional elements is revealed, for example, by the explanation of why the person to whom the control monitor is responsible receives the residual, and also by our later discussion of the implications about the corporation, partnerships, and profit sharing. These alternative forms for organization of the firm are difficult to resolve on the basis of market transaction costs only. Our exposition also suggests a definition of the classical firm—something crucial that was heretofore absent.

In addition, sometimes a technological development will lower the cost of market transactions while, at the same time, it expands the role of the firm. When the "putting out" system was used for weaving, inputs were organized largely through market negotiations. With the development of efficient central sources of power, it became economical to perform weaving in proximity to the power source and to engage in team production. The bringing in of weavers surely must have resulted in a reduction in the cost of negotiating (forming) contracts. Yet what we observe is the beginning of the factory system in which inputs are organized within a firm. Why? The weavers did not simply move to a common source of power that they could tap like an electric line, purchasing power while they used their own equipment. Now team production in the joint use of equipment became more important. The measurement of marginal productivity, which now involved interactions between workers, especially through their joint use of machines, became more difficult, though contract negotiating cost was reduced, while managing the *behavior* of inputs became easier because of the increased centralization of activity. The firm as an organization expanded even though the cost of transactions was reduced by the advent of centralized power. The same could be said for modern assembly lines. Hence the emergence of central power sources expanded the scope of productive activity in which the firm enjoyed a comparative advantage as an organizational form.

Some economists, following Knight, have identified the bearing of risks of wealth changes with the director or central employer without explaining why that is a viable arrangement. Presumably, the more risk-averse inputs become employees rather than owners of the classical firm. Risk averseness and uncertainty *with regard to the firm's fortunes* have little, if anything, to do with our explanation, although they help to explain why all resources in a team are not owned by one person. That is, the role of risk taken in the sense of absorbing the windfalls that buffet the firm because of unforeseen competition, technological change, or fluctuations in demand is not central to our theory, although it is true that imperfect knowledge and, therefore, risk, in *this* sense of risk, underlie the problem of monitoring team behavior. We deduce the system of paying the manager with a residual claim (the equity) from the desire to have efficient means to reduce shirking so as to make team production economical and not from the smaller aversion to the risks of enterprise in a dynamic economy. We conjecture that "distribution-of-risk" is not a valid rationale for the *existence* and organization of the *classical* firm.

Although we have emphasized team production as creating a costly metering task and have treated team production as an essential (necessary?) condition for the firm, would not other obstacles to cheap metering also call forth the same kind of contractual arrangement here denoted as a firm? For example, suppose a farmer produces wheat in an easily ascertained quantity but with subtle and difficult-to-detect quality variations determined by how the farmer grew the wheat. A vertical integration could allow a purchaser to control the farmer's behavior in order to more economically estimate productivity. But this is not a case of joint or team production unless "information" can be considered part of the product. (While a good case could be made for that broader conception of production, we shall ignore it here.) Instead of forming a firm, a buyer can contract to have his inspector on the site of production, just as home builders contract with architects to supervise building contracts; that arrangement is not a firm. Still, a firm might be organized in the production of many products wherein no team production or jointness of use of separately owned resources is involved.

This possibility rather clearly indicates a broader, or complementary, approach to that which we have chosen. (1) As we do in this paper, it can be argued that the firm is the particular policing device utilized when joint team production is present. If other sources of high policing costs arise, as in the wheat case just indicated, some other form of contractual arrangement will be used. Thus to each source of informational cost there may be a different type of policing and contractual arrangement. (2) On the other hand, one can say that where policing is difficult across markets, various forms of contractual arrangements are devised, but there is no reason for that known as the firm to be uniquely related to or even highly correlated with team production, as defined here. It might be used equally probably and viably for other sources of high policing cost. We have not intensively analyzed other sources, and we can only note that our current and readily revisable conjecture is that (1) is valid and has motivated us in our current endeavor. In any event, the test of the theory advanced here is to see whether the conditions we have identified are necessary for firms to have long-run viability rather than merely births with high infant mortality. Conglomerate firms or collections of separate production agencies into one owning organization can be interpreted as an investment trust or investment diversification device—probably along the lines that motivated Knight's interpretation. A holding company can be called a firm because of the common association of the word *firm* with any ownership unit that owns income sources. The term *firm* as commonly used is so turgid of meaning that we cannot hope to explain every entity to which the name is attached in common or even technical literature. Instead, we seek to identify and explain a particular contractual arrangement induced by the cost of information factors analyzed in this paper.

IV. Types of Firms

A. *Profit-Sharing Firms*

Explicit in our explanation of the capitalist firm is the assumption that the cost of *managing* the team's inputs by a central monitor, who disciplines himself because he is a residual claimant, is low relative to the cost of metering the marginal outputs of team members.

If we look within a firm to see who monitors—hires, fires, changes, promotes, and renegotiates—we should find him being a residual claimant or, at least, one whose pay or reward is more than any others correlated with fluctuations in the residual value of the firm. They more likely will have options or rights or bonuses than will inputs with other tasks.

An implicit "auxiliary" assumption of our explanation of the firm is that the cost of team production is increased if the residual claim is not held entirely by the central monitor. That is, we assume that if profit sharing had to be relied upon for all team members, losses from the resulting increase in central monitor shirking would exceed the output gains from the increased incentives of other team members not to shirk. If the optimal team size is only two owners of inputs, then an equal division of profits and losses between them will leave each with stronger incentives to reduce shirking than if the optimal team size is large, for in the latter case only a smaller percentage of the losses occasioned by the shirker will be borne by him. Incentives to shirk are positively related to the optimal size of the team under an equal profit-sharing scheme.[10]

The preceding does not imply that profit sharing is never viable. Profit sharing to encourage self-policing is more appropriate for small teams. And, indeed, where input owners are free to make whatever contractual arrangements suit them, as generally is true in capitalist economies, profit sharing seems largely limited to partnerships with a relatively small number of *active*[11] partners. Another advantage of such arrangements for smaller teams is that it permits more effective reciprocal monitoring among inputs. Monitoring need not be entirely specialized.

Profit sharing is more viable if small team size is associated with situations where the cost of specialized management of inputs is large relative to the increased productivity potential in team effort. We conjecture that the cost of managing team inputs increases if the productivity of a team member is difficult to correlate with his behavior. In "artistic" or "professional" work, watching a man's activities is not a good clue to what he is actually thinking or doing with his mind. While it is relatively easy to manage or direct the loading of trucks by a team of dock workers, where input activity is so highly related in an obvious way to output, it is more difficult to manage and direct a lawyer in the preparation and presentation of a case. Dock workers can be directed in detail without the monitor himself loading the truck, and assembly line workers can be monitored by varying the speed of the assembly line, but detailed direction in the preparation of a law case would require in much greater degree that the monitor prepare the case himself. As a result, artistic or professional inputs, such as lawyers, advertising specialists, and doctors, will be given rela-

10. While the degree to which residual claims are centralized will affect the size of the team, this will be only one of many factors that determine team size, so as an approximation, we can treat team size as exogenously determined. Under certain assumptions about the shape of the "typical" utility function, the incentive to avoid shirking with unequal profit sharing can be measured by the Herfindahl index.

11. The use of the word *active* will be clarified in our discussion of the corporation, which follows.

tively freer rein with regard to individual behavior. If the management of inputs is relatively costly—or ineffective, as it would seem to be in these cases—but, nonetheless, if team effort is more productive than separable production with exchange across markets, then there will develop a tendency to use profit-sharing schemes to provide incentives to avoid shirking.[12]

B. Socialist Firms

We have analyzed the classical proprietorship and the profit-sharing firms in the context of free association and choice of economic organization. Such organizations need not be the most viable when political constraints limit the forms of organization that can be chosen. It is one thing to have profit sharing when professional or artistic talents are used by small teams. But if political or tax or subsidy considerations induce profit-sharing techniques when these are not otherwise economically justified, then additional management techniques will be developed to help reduce the degree of shirking.

For example, most, if not all, firms in Yugoslavia are owned by the employees in the restricted sense that all share in the residual. This is true for large firms and for firms which employ nonartistic or nonprofessional workers as well. With a decay of political constraints, most of these firms could be expected to rely on paid wages rather than shares in the residual. This rests on our auxiliary assumption that general sharing in the residual results in losses from enhanced shirking by the monitor that exceed the gains from reduced shirking by residual-sharing employees. If this were not so, profit sharing with employees should have occurred more frequently in Western societies where such organizations are neither banned nor preferred politically. Where residual sharing by employees is politically imposed, as in Yugoslavia, we are led to expect that some management technique will arise to reduce the shirking by the central monitor, a technique that will not be found frequently in Western societies, since the monitor retains all (or much) of the residual in the West, and profit sharing is largely confined to small, professional-artistic team production situations. We do find in the larger-scale residual-sharing firms in Yugoslavia that there are employee committees that can recommend (to the state) the termination of a manager's contract (veto his continuance) with the enterprise. We

---

12. Some sharing contracts, like crop sharing, or rental payments based on gross sales in retail stores, come close to profit sharing. However, it is gross-output sharing rather than profit sharing. We are unable to specify the implications of the difference. We refer the reader to S. N. Cheung.

conjecture that the workers' committee is given the right to recommend the termination of the manager's contract precisely because the general sharing of the residual increases "excessively" the manager's incentive to shirk.[13]

c. The Corporation

All firms must initially acquire command over some resources. The corporation does so primarily by selling promises of future returns to those who (as creditors or owners) provide financial capital. In some situations resources can be acquired in advance from consumers by promises of future delivery (for example, advance sale of a proposed book). Or where the firm is a few artistic or professional persons, each can "chip in" with time and talent until the sale of services brings in revenues. For the most part, capital can be acquired more cheaply if many (risk-averse) investors contribute small portions to a large investment. The economies of raising large sums of equity capital in this way suggest that modifications in the relationships among corporate inputs are required to cope with the shirking problem that arises with profit sharing among large numbers of corporate stockholders. One modification is limited liability, especially for firms that are large relative to a stockholder's wealth. It serves to protect stockholders from large losses no matter how they are caused.

If every stock owner participated in each decision in a corporation, not only would large bureaucratic costs be incurred, but many would shirk the task of becoming well informed on the issue to be decided, since the losses associated with unexpectedly bad decisions will be borne in large part by the many other corporate shareholders. More effective control of corporate activity is achieved for most purposes by transferring decision authority to a smaller group whose main function is to negotiate with and manage (renegotiate with) the other inputs of the team. The corporate stockholders retain the authority to revise the membership of the management group and over major decisions that affect the structure of the corporation or its dissolution.

As a result, a new modification of partnerships is induced—the right to sale of corporate shares without approval of any other stockholders. Any share-

---

13. Incidentally, investment activity will be changed. The inability to capitalize the investment value as "take-home" private property *wealth* of the members of the firm means that the benefits of the investment must be taken as annual income by those who are employed at the time of the income. Investment will be confined more to those with shorter life and with higher rates or payoffs if the alternative of investing is paying out the firm's income to its employees to take home and use as private property. For a development of this proposition, see the papers by Eirik Furubotn and Svetozar Pejovich, and by Pejovich.

holder can remove his wealth from control by those with whom he has differences of opinion. Rather than try to control the decisions of the management, which is harder to do with many stockholders than with only a few, unrestricted salability provides a more acceptable escape to each stockholder from continued policies with which he disagrees.

Indeed, the policing of managerial shirking relies on across-market competition from new groups of would-be managers as well as competition from members within the firm who seek to displace existing management. In addition to competition from outside and inside managers, control is facilitated by the temporary congealing of share votes into voting blocs owned by one or a few contenders. Proxy battles or stock purchases concentrate the votes required to displace the existing management or modify managerial policies. But it is more than a change in policy that is sought by the newly formed financial interests, whether of new stockholders or not. It is the capitalization of expected future benefits into stock prices that concentrates on the innovators the wealth gains of their actions if they own large numbers of shares. Without capitalization of future benefits, there would be less incentive to incur the costs required to exert informed decisive influence on the corporation's policies and managing personnel. Temporarily, the structure of ownership is reformed, moving away from diffused ownership into decisive power blocs, and this is a transient resurgence of the classical firm, with power again concentrated in those who have title to the residual.

In assessing the significance of stockholders' power it is not the usual diffusion of voting power that is significant but instead the frequency with which voting congeals into decisive changes. Even a one-man-owned company may have a long term with just one manager—continuously being approved by the owner. Similarly a dispersed voting power corporation may be also characterized by a long-lived management. The question is the probability of replacement of the management if it behaves in ways not acceptable to a majority of the stockholders. The unrestricted salability of stock and the transfer of proxies enhance the probability of decisive action in the event current stockholders or any outsider believes that management is not doing a good job with the corporation. We are not comparing the corporate responsiveness to that of a single proprietorship; instead, we are indicating features of the corporate structure that are induced by the problem of delegated authority to manager-monitors.[14]

14. Instead of thinking of shareholders as joint *owners*, we can think of them as investors, like bondholders, except that the stockholders are more optimistic than bond-

D. *Mutual and Nonprofit Firms*

The benefits obtained by the new management are greater if the stock can be purchased and sold, because this enables *capitalization* of anticipated future improvements into present wealth of new managers who bought stock and created a larger capital by their management changes. But in nonprofit corporations, colleges, churches, country clubs, mutual savings banks, mutual insurance companies, and "co-ops," the future consequences of improved man-

------

holders about the enterprise prospects. Instead of buying bonds in the corporation, thus enjoying smaller risks, shareholders prefer to invest funds with a greater realizable return if the firm prospers as expected, but with smaller (possibly negative) returns if the firm performs in a manner closer to that expected by the more pessimistic investors. The pessimistic investors, in turn, regard only the bonds as likely to pay off.

If the entrepreneur-organizer is to raise capital on the best terms to him, it is to his advantage, as well as that of prospective investors, to recognize these differences in expectations. The residual claim on earnings enjoyed by shareholders does not serve the function of enhancing their efficiency as monitors in the general situation. The stockholders are "merely" the less risk-averse or the more optimistic members of the group that finances the firm. Being more optimistic than the average and seeing a higher mean value future return, they are willing to pay more for a certificate that allows them to realize gain on their expectations. One method of doing so is to buy claims to the distribution of returns that "they see," while bondholders, who are more pessimistic, purchase a claim to the distribution that they see as more likely to emerge. Stockholders are then comparable to warrant holders. They care not about the voting rights (usually not attached to warrants); they are in the same position insofar as voting rights are concerned as are bondholders. The only difference is in the probability distribution of rewards and the terms on which they can place their bets.

If we treat bondholders, preferred and convertible preferred stockholders, and common stockholders and warrant holders as simply different classes of investors—differing not only in their risk averseness but in their beliefs about the probability distribution of the firm's future earnings, why should stockholders be regarded as "owners" in any sense distinct from the other financial investors? The entrepreneur-organizer, who, let us assume, is the chief operating officer and sole repository of control of the corporation, does not find his authority residing in common stockholders (except in the case of a takeover). Does this type of control make any difference in the way the firm is conducted? Would it make any difference in the kinds of behavior that would be tolerated by competing managers and investors (and we here deliberately refrain from thinking of them as owner-stockholders in the traditional sense)?

Investment old-timers recall a significant incidence of nonvoting common stock, now prohibited in corporations whose stock is traded on listed exchanges. (Why prohibited?) The entrepreneur in those days could hold voting shares while investors held nonvoting shares, which in every other respect were identical. Nonvoting shareholders were simply

agement are not capitalized into present wealth of stockholders. (As if to make more difficult that competition by new would-be monitors, multiple shares of ownership in those enterprises cannot be bought by one person.) One should, therefore, find greater shirking in nonprofit, mutually owned enterprises. (This suggests that nonprofit enterprises are especially appropriate in realms of endeavor where more shirking is desired and where redirected uses of the enterprise in response to market-revealed values is less desired.)

E. *Partnerships*

Team production in artistic or professional intellectual skills will more likely be by partnerships than other types of team production. This amounts to market-organized team activity and to a nonemployer status. Self-monitoring

------

investors devoid of ownership connotations. The control and behavior of inside owners in such corporations has never, so far as we have ascertained, been carefully studied. For example, at the simplest level of interest, does the evidence indicate that nonvoting shareholders fared any worse because of not having voting rights? Did owners permit the nonvoting holders the normal return available to voting shareholders? Though evidence is prohibitively expensive to obtain, it is remarkable that voting and nonvoting shares sold for essentially identical prices, even during some proxy battles. However, our casual evidence deserves no more than interest-initiating weight.

One more point. The facade is deceptive. Instead of nonvoting shares, today we have warrants, convertible preferred stocks, all of which are solely or partly "equity" claims without voting rights, though they could be converted into voting shares.

In sum, is it the case that the stockholder-investor relationship is one emanating from the *division of ownership* among several people, or is it that the collection of investment funds from people of varying anticipations is the underlying factor? If the latter, why should any of them be thought of as the owners in whom voting rights, whatever they may signify or however exercisable, should reside in order to enhance efficiency? Why voting rights in any of the outside, participating investors?

Our initial perception of this possibly significant difference in interpretation was precipitated by Henry Manne. A reading of his paper makes it clear that it is hard to understand why an investor who wishes to back and "share" in the consequences of some new business should necessarily have to acquire voting power (i.e., power to change the manager-operator) in order to invest in the venture. In fact, we invest in some ventures in the hope that no other stockholders will be so "foolish" as to try to toss out the incumbent management. We want him to have the power to stay in office, and for the prospect of sharing in his fortunes we buy nonvoting common stock. Our willingness to invest is enhanced by the knowledge that we can act legally via fraud, embezzlement, and other laws to help assure that we outside investors will not be "milked" beyond our initial discounted anticipations.

partnerships, therefore, will be used rather than employer-employee contracts, and these organizations will be small to prevent an excessive dilution of efforts through shirking. Also, partnerships are more likely to occur among relatives or long-standing acquaintances, not necessarily because they share a common utility function, but also because each knows better the other's work characteristics and tendencies to shirk.

F. *Employee Unions*

Employee unions, whatever else they do, perform as monitors for employees. Employers monitor employees, and similarly, employees monitor an employer's performance. Are correct wages paid on time and in good currency? Usually, this is extremely easy to check. But some forms of employer performance are less easy to meter and are more subject to employer shirking. Fringe benefits often are in nonpecuniary contingent form; medical, hospital, and accident insurance, and retirement pensions are contingent payments or performances partly in kind by employers to employees. Each employee cannot judge the character of such payments as easily as money wages. Insurance is a contingent payment—what the employee will get upon the contingent event may come as a disappointment. If he could easily determine what other employees had gotten upon such contingent events he could judge more accurately the performance by the employer. He could "trust" the employer not to shirk in such fringe contingent payments, but he would prefer an effective and economic monitor of those payments. We see a specialist monitor—the union employees' agent—hired by them and monitoring those aspects of employer payment most difficult for the employees to monitor. Employees should be willing to employ a specialist monitor to administer such hard-to-detect employer performance, even though their monitor has incentives to use pension and retirement funds not entirely for the benefit of employees.

v. Team Spirit and Loyalty

Every team member would prefer a team in which no one, not even himself, shirked. Then the true marginal costs and values could be equated to achieve more preferred positions. If one could enhance a common interest in nonshirking in the guise of a team loyalty or team spirit, the team would be more efficient. In those sports where team activity is most clearly exemplified, the sense of loyalty and team spirit is most strongly urged. Obviously the team is better, with team spirit and loyalty, because of the reduced shirking—not because of some other feature inherent in loyalty or spirit as such.[15]

Corporations and business firms try to instill a spirit of loyalty. This should not be viewed simply as a device to increase profits by *overworking* or misleading the employees, nor as an adolescent urge for belonging. It promotes a closer approximation to the employees' potentially available true rates of sub-

---

15. *Sports leagues:* Professional sports contests among teams are typically conducted by a *league* of teams. We assume that sports consumers are interested not only in absolute sporting skill but also in skills *relative* to other teams. Being slightly better than opposing teams enables one to claim a major portion of the receipts; the inferior team does not release resources and reduce costs, since they were expected in the play of contest. Hence, absolute skill is developed beyond the equality of marginal investment in sporting skill, with its true social marginal value product. It follows there will be a tendency to overinvest in training athletes and developing teams. "Reverse shirking" arises, as budding players are induced to overpractice hyperactively relative to the social marginal value of their enhanced skills. To prevent overinvestment, the teams seek an agreement with each other to restrict practice, size of teams, and even pay of the team members (which reduces incentives of young people to overinvest in developing skills). Ideally, if all the contestant teams were owned by one owner, overinvestment in sports would be avoided, much as ownership of common fisheries or underground oil or water reserve would prevent overinvestment. This hyperactivity (to suggest the opposite of shirking) is controlled by the league of teams, wherein the league adopts a common set of constraints on each team's behavior. In effect, the teams are no longer really owned by the team owners but are supervised by them, much as the franchisers of some product. They are not full-fledged owners of their business, including the brand name, and cannot "do what they wish" as franchises. Comparable to the franchiser is the league commissioner or conference president, who seeks to restrain hyperactivity, as individual team supervisors compete with each other and cause external diseconomies. Such restraints are usually regarded as anticompetitive, antisocial, collusive-cartel devices to restrain free open competition and reduce players' salaries. However, the interpretation presented here is premised on an attempt to avoid hyperinvestment in team sports production. Of course, the team operators have an incentive, once the league is formed and restraints are placed on hyperinvestment activity, to go further and obtain the private benefits of monopoly restriction. To what extent overinvestment is replaced by monopoly restriction is not yet determinable; nor have we seen an empirical test of these two competing, but mutually consistent interpretations. (This interpretation of league-sports activity was proposed by Earl Thompson and formulated by Michael Canes.) Again, athletic teams clearly exemplify the specialization of monitoring with captains and coaches; a captain detects shirkers while the coach trains and selects strategies and tactics. Both functions may be centralized in one person.

stitution between production and leisure and enables each team member to achieve a more preferred situation. The difficulty, of course, is to create economically that team spirit and loyalty. It can be preached with an aura of moral code of conduct—a morality with literally the same basis as the Ten Commandments—to restrict our conduct toward what we would choose if we bore our full costs.

VI. Kinds of Inputs Owned by the Firm

To this point the discussion has examined why firms, as we have defined them, exist. That is, why is there an owner-employer who is the common party to contracts with other owners of inputs in team activity? The answer to that question should also indicate the kind of the jointly used resources likely to be owned by the central-owner-monitor and the kind likely to be hired from people who are not team owners. Can we identify characteristics or features of various inputs that lead to their being hired or to their being owned by the firm?

How can the residual-claimant, central-employer-owner demonstrate ability to pay the other hired inputs the promised amount in the event of a loss? He can pay in advance or he can commit wealth sufficient to cover negative residuals. The latter will take the form of machines, land, buildings, or raw materials committed to the firm. Commitments of labor-wealth (i.e., human wealth), given the property rights in people, are less feasible. These considerations suggest that residual claimants—owners of the firm—will be investors of resalable capital equipment in the firm. The goods or inputs more likely to be invested than rented, by the owners of the enterprise, will have higher resale values relative to the initial cost and will have longer expected use in a firm relative to the economic life of the good.

But beyond these factors are those developed above to explain the existence of the institution known as the firm—the costs of detecting output performance. When a durable resource is used it will have a marginal product and a depreciation. Its use requires payment to cover at least use-induced depreciation; unless that user cost is specifically detectable, payment for it will be demanded in accord with *expected* depreciation. And we can ascertain circumstances for each. An indestructible hammer with a readily detectable marginal product has zero user cost. But suppose the hammer were destructible and that careless (which is easier than careful) use is more abusive and causes greater depreciation of the hammer. Suppose, in addition, the abuse is easier to detect by observing the way it is used than by observing the hammer only after its use, or by measuring the output scored from a hammer by a laborer. If the hammer were rented and used in the absence of the owner, the depreciation would be greater than if the use were observed by the owner, and the user charged in accord with the imposed depreciation. (Careless use is more likely than careful use—if one does not pay for the greater depreciation.) An absentee owner would therefore ask for a higher rental price because of the higher *expected* user cost than if the item were used by the owner. The expectation is higher because of the greater difficulty of observing specific user cost by inspection of the hammer after use. Renting is therefore in this case more costly than owner use. This is the valid content of the misleading expressions about ownership being more economical than renting—ignoring all other factors that may work in the opposite direction, for example, tax provision, short-term occupancy, and capital risk avoidance.

Better examples are tools of the trade. Watch repairers, engineers, and carpenters tend to own their own tools, especially if they are portable. Trucks are more likely to be employee owned rather than other equally expensive team inputs because it is relatively cheap for the driver to police the care taken in using a truck. Policing the use of trucks by a nondriver owner is more likely to occur for trucks that are not specialized to one driver, for example, public transit busses.

The factor with which we are concerned here is one related to the costs of monitoring not only the gross product performance of an input but also the abuse or depreciation inflicted on the input in the course of its use. If depreciation or user cost is more cheaply detected when the owner can see its use than by only seeing the input before and after, there is a force toward owner use rather than renting. Resources whose user cost is harder to detect when used by someone else tend, on this count, to be owner-used. Absentee ownership, in the lay language, will be less likely. Assume momentarily that labor service cannot be performed in the absence of its owner. The labor owner can more cheaply monitor any abuse of himself than if somehow labor services could be provided without the labor owner observing its mode of use or knowing what was happening. Also his incentive to abuse himself is increased if he does not own himself.[16]

16. Professional athletes in baseball, football, and basketball, where athletes having sold their source of service to the team owners upon entering into sports activity, are owned by team owners. Here the team owners must monitor the athletes' physical condition and behavior to protect the team owners' wealth. The athlete has *less* (not, *no*) incentive to protect or enhance his athletic prowess since capital value changes have less impact on his own wealth and more on the team owners'. Thus, some athletes sign up for big ini-

The similarity between the preceding analysis and the question of absentee landlordism and of sharecropping arrangements is no accident. The same factors which explain the contractual arrangements known as a firm help to explain the incidence of tenancy, labor hiring, or sharecropping.[17]

VII. The Firm as a Specialized Market Institution for Collecting, Collating, and Selling Input Information

The firm serves as a highly specialized surrogate market. Any person contemplating a joint-input activity must search and detect the qualities of available joint inputs. He could contact an employment agency, but that agency in a small town would have little advantage over a large firm with many inputs. The employer, by virtue of monitoring many inputs, acquires special superior information about their productive talents. This aids his *directive* (i.e., market hiring) efficiency. He "sells" his information to employee-inputs as he aids them in ascertaining good input combinations for team activity. Those who work as employees or who rent services to him are using him to discern superior combinations of inputs. Not only does the director-employer "decide" what each input will produce, he also estimates which heterogeneous inputs will work together jointly more efficiently, and he does this in the context of a privately owned market for forming teams. The department store is a firm and is a supe-

---

tial bonuses (representing present capital value of future services). Future salaries are lower by the annuity value of the prepaid "bonus," and hence the athlete has less to lose by subsequent abuse of his athletic prowess. Any decline in his subsequent service value would in part be borne by the team owner who owns the players' future services. This does not say these losses of future salaries have no effect on preservation of athletic talent (we are not making a "sunk cost" error). Instead, we assert that the preservation is reduced, not eliminated, because the amount of loss of wealth suffered is smaller. The athlete will spend less to maintain or enhance his prowess thereafter. The effect of this revised incentive system is evidenced in comparison of the kinds of attention and care imposed on the athletes at the "expense of the team owner" in the case where athletes' future services are owned by the team owner with that where future labor service values are owned by the athlete himself. Why athletes' future athletic services are owned by the team owners rather than being hired is a question we should be able to answer. One presumption is cartelization and monopsony gains to team owners. Another is exactly the theory being expounded in this paper—costs of monitoring production of athletes; we know not on which to rely.

17. The analysis used by Cheung in explaining the prevalence of sharecropping and land tenancy arrangements is built squarely on the same factors—the costs of detecting output performance of jointly used inputs in team production and the costs of detecting user costs imposed on the various inputs if owner used or if rented.

rior private market. People who shop and work in one town can as well shop and work in a privately owned firm.

This marketing function is obscured in the theoretical literature by the assumption of homogeneous factors. Or it is tacitly left for individuals to do themselves via personal market search, much as if a person had to search without benefit of specialist retailers. Whether or not the firm arose because of this efficient information service, it gives the director-employer more knowledge about the productive talents of the team's inputs and a basis for superior decisions about efficient or profitable combinations of those heterogeneous resources.

In other words, opportunities for profitable team production by inputs already within the firm may be ascertained more economically and accurately than for resources outside the firm. Superior combinations of inputs can be more economically identified and formed from resources already used in the organization than by obtaining new resources (and knowledge of them) from the outside. Promotion and revision of employee assignments (contracts) will be preferred by a firm to the hiring of new inputs. To the extent that this occurs, there is reason to expect the firm to be able to operate as a conglomerate rather than persist in producing a single product. Efficient production with heterogeneous resources is a result not of having *better* resources but of *knowing more accurately* the relative productive performances of those resources. Poorer resources can be paid less in accord with their inferiority; greater accuracy of knowledge of the potential and actual productive actions of inputs rather than having high productivity resources makes a firm (or an assignment of inputs) profitable.[18]

---

18. According to our interpretation, the firm is a specialized surrogate for a market for team use of inputs; it provides superior (i.e., cheaper) collection and collation of knowledge about heterogeneous resources. The greater the set of inputs about which knowledge of performance is being collated within a firm, the greater are the present costs of the collation activity. Then, the larger the firm (market), the greater the attenuation of monitor control. To counter this force, the firm will be divisionalized in ways that economize on those costs—just as will the market be specialized. So far as we can ascertain, other theories of the reasons for firms have no such implications.

In Japan, employees by custom work nearly their entire lives with one firm, and the firm agrees to that expectation. Firms will tend to be large and conglomerate to enable a broader scope of input revision. Each firm is, in effect, a small economy engaging in "intranational and international" trade. Analogously, Americans expect to spend their whole lives in the United States, and the bigger the country, in terms of variety of resources, the

VIII. Summary

While ordinary contracts facilitate efficient specialization according to comparative advantage, a special class of contracts among a group of joint inputs to a team production process is commonly used for team production. Instead of multilateral contracts among all the joint inputs' owners, a central common party to a set of bilateral contracts facilitates efficient organization of the joint inputs in team production. The terms of the contracts form the basis of the entity called the firm—especially appropriate for organizing team production processes.

Team productive activity is that in which a union, or joint use, of inputs yields a larger output than the sum of the products of the separately used inputs. This team production requires—like all other production processes—an assessment of marginal productivities if efficient production is to be achieved. Nonseparability of the products of several differently owned joint inputs raises the cost of assessing the marginal productivities of those resources or services of each input owner. Monitoring or metering the productivities to match marginal productivities to costs of inputs and thereby to reduce shirking can be achieved more economically (than by across market bilateral negotiations among inputs) in a firm.

The essence of the classical firm is identified here as a contractual structure with: (1) joint input production; (2) several input owners; one party who (3) is common to all the contracts of the joint inputs, (4) has rights to renegotiate any input's contract independent of contracts with other input owners, (5) holds the residual claim, and (6) has the right to sell his central contractual residual status. The central agent is called the firm's owner and the employer. No authoritarian control is involved; the arrangement is simply a contractual structure subject to continuous renegotiation with the central agent. The contractual structure arises as a means of enhancing efficient organization of team production. In particular, the ability to detect shirking among owners of jointly used inputs in team production is enhanced (detection costs are reduced) by this arrangement, and the discipline (by revision of contracts) of input owners is made more economic.

---

easier it is to adjust to changing tastes and circumstances. Japan, with its lifetime employees, should be characterized more by large conglomerate firms. Presumably, at some size of the firm, specialized knowledge about inputs becomes as expensive to transmit across divisions of the firms as it does across markets to other firms.

Testable implications are suggested by the analysis of different types of organizations—nonprofit, proprietary for profit, unions, cooperatives, partnerships, and by the kinds of inputs that tend to be owned by the firm in contrast to those employed by the firm.

We conclude with a highly conjectural but possibly significant interpretation. As a consequence of the flow of information to the central party (employer), the firm takes on the characteristic of an efficient market, in that information about the productive characteristics of a large set of specific inputs is now more cheaply available. Better recombinations or new uses of resources can be more efficiently ascertained than by the conventional search through the general market. In this sense inputs compete with each other within and via a firm rather than solely across markets as conventionally conceived. Emphasis on interfirm competition obscures intrafirm competition among inputs. Conceiving competition as the *revelation and exchange* of knowledge or information about qualities, potential uses of different inputs in different potential applications indicate that the firm is a device for enhancing competition among sets of input resources as well as a device for more efficiently rewarding the inputs. In contrast to markets and cities, which can be viewed as publicly owned or non-owned marketplaces, the firm can be considered a privately owned market; if so, we would consider the firm and the ordinary market as competing types of markets, competition between private proprietary markets and public or communal markets. Could it be that the market suffers from the defects of communal property rights in organizing and influencing uses of valuable resources?

REFERENCES

M. Canes, "A Model of a Sports League," unpublished doctoral dissertation, UCLA, 1970.

S. N. Cheung, The Theory of Share Tenancy, Chicago, 1969.

R. H. Coase, "The Nature of the Firm," Economica 4 (November 1937): 386–405; reprinted in G. J. Stigler and K. Boulding, eds., Readings in Price Theory, Homewood, 1952, pp. 331–51.

E. Furubotn and S. Pejovich, "Property Rights and the Behavior of the Firm in a Socialist State," Zeitschrift für Nationalökonomie 30 (1970): 431–54.

F. H. Knight, Risk, Uncertainty and Profit, New York, 1965.

S. Macaulay, "Non-Contractual Relations in Business: A Preliminary Study," Amer. Sociological Rev. 28 (1968): 55–69.

H. B. Malmgren, "Information, Expectations and the Theory of the Firm," Quart. J. Econ. 75 (August 1961): 399–421.

H. Manne, "Our Two Corporation Systems: Law and Economics," *Virginia Law Rev.* 53, no. 2 (March 1967): 259–84.

S. Pejovich, "The Firm, Monetary Policy and Property Rights in a Planned Economy," *Western Econ. J.* 7 (September 1969): 193–200.

M. Silver and R. Auster, "Entrepreneurship, Profit, and the Limits on Firm Size," *J. Bus. Univ. Chicago* 42 (April 1969): 277–81.

E. A. Thompson, "Nonpecuniary Rewards and the Aggregate Production Function," *Rev. Econ. Statist.* 52 (November 1970): 395–404.

VERTICAL INTEGRATION, APPROPRIABLE RENTS, AND THE COMPETITIVE CONTRACTING PROCESS

BENJAMIN KLEIN, ROBERT G. CRAWFORD,

AND ARMEN A. ALCHIAN

More than forty years have passed since Coase's fundamental insight that transaction, coordination, and contracting costs must be considered explicitly in explaining the extent of vertical integration.[1] Starting from the truism that profit-maximizing firms will undertake those activities that they find cheaper to administer internally than to purchase in the market, Coase forced economists to begin looking for previously neglected constraints on the trading process that might efficiently lead to an intrafirm rather than an interfirm transaction. This paper attempts to add to this literature by exploring one particular cost of using the market system—the possibility of postcontractual opportunistic behavior.

Opportunistic behavior has been identified and discussed in the modern analysis of the organization of economic activity. Williamson, for example, has referred to effects on the contracting process of "*ex post* small numbers opportunism,"[2] and Teece has elaborated:

Reprinted from *Journal of Law and Economics* 21 (October 1978): 297–326, published by The University of Chicago. Copyright 1978 by the University of Chicago. All rights reserved.

We wish to acknowledge useful comments on previous drafts by Harold Demsetz, Stephen Friedberg, Victor Goldberg, Levis Kochin, Keith Leffler, Lynne Schneider, Earl Thompson, and participants at a seminar at the Center for the Study of American Business at Washington University and at Law and Economics Workshops at UCLA and the University of Chicago. Financial assistance was provided by a grant of the Lilly Endowment Inc. for the study of property rights and by the Foundation for Research in Economics and Education. The authors are solely responsible for the views expressed and for the remaining errors.

    1. R. H. Coase, "The Nature of the Firm," 4 *Economica* 386 (1937), reprinted in *Readings in Price Theory* 331 (George J. Stigler & Kenneth E. Boulding, eds., 1952).

    2. Oliver E. Williamson, *Markets and Hierarchies: Analysis and Antitrust Implications* 26–30 (1975).

Even when all of the relevant contingencies can be specified in a contract, contracts are still open to serious risks since they are not always honored. The 1970's are replete with examples of the risks associated with relying on contracts . . . [O]pen displays of opportunism are not infrequent and very often litigation turns out to be costly and ineffectual.[3]

The particular circumstance we emphasize as likely to produce a serious threat of this type of reneging on contracts is the presence of appropriable specialized quasi rents. After a specific investment is made and such quasi rents are created, the possibility of opportunistic behavior is very real. Following Coase's framework, this problem can be solved in two possible ways: vertical integration or contracts. The crucial assumption underlying the analysis of this paper is that, as assets become more specific and more appropriable quasi rents are created (and therefore the possible gains from opportunistic behavior increase), the costs of contracting will generally increase more than the costs of vertical integration. Hence, *ceteris paribus*, we are more likely to observe vertical integration.

I. Appropriable Quasi Rents of Specialized Assets

Assume an asset is owned by one individual and rented to another individual. The quasi-rent value of the asset is the excess of its value over its salvage value, that is, its value in its next best *use* to another renter. The potentially appropriable specialized portion of the quasi rent is that portion, if any, in excess of its value to the second highest-valuing *user*. If this seems like a distinction without a difference, consider the following example.

Imagine a printing press owned and operated by party A. Publisher B buys printing services from party A by leasing his press at a contracted rate of $5,500 per day. The amortized fixed cost of the printing press is $4,000 per day, and it has a current salvageable value of $1,000 (daily rental equivalent) if moved elsewhere. Operating costs are $1,500 and are paid by the printing press owner, who prints final printed pages for the publisher. Assume also that a second publisher C is willing to offer at most $3,500 for daily service. The current quasi rent on the installed machine is $3,000 (= $5,500 − $1,500 − $1,000), the revenue minus operating costs minus salvageable value. However, the daily quasi rent from publisher B relative to use of the machine for publisher C is only $2,000 (= $5,500 − $3,500). At $5,500 revenue daily from publisher B the

---

3. David J. Teece, *Vertical Integration and Divestiture in the U.S. Oil Industry* 31 (1976).

press owner would break even on his investment. If the publisher were then able to cut his offer for the press from $5,500 down to almost $3,500, he would still have the press service available to him. He would be appropriating $2,000 of the quasi rent from the press owner. The $2,000 difference between his prior agreed-to daily rental of $5,500 and the next best revenue available to the press once the machine is purchased and installed is less than the quasi rent and therefore is potentially appropriable. If no second party were available at the present site, the entire quasi rent would be subject to threat of appropriation by an unscrupulous or opportunistic publisher.

Our primary interest concerns the means whereby this risk can be reduced or avoided. In particular, vertical integration is examined as a means of economizing on the costs of avoiding risks of appropriation of quasi rents in specialized assets by opportunistic individuals. This advantage of joint ownership of such specialized assets, namely, economizing on contracting costs necessary to insure nonopportunistic behavior, must of course be weighed against the costs of administering a broader range of assets within the firm.[4]

An appropriable quasi rent is not a monopoly rent in the usual sense, that is, the increased value of an asset protected from market entry over the value it would have had in an open market. An appropriable quasi rent can occur with no market closure or restrictions placed on rival assets. Once installed, an asset may be so expensive to remove or so specialized to a particular user that if the price paid to the owner were somehow reduced the asset's services to that user would not be reduced. Thus, even if there were free and open competition for entry to the market, the specialization of the installed asset to a particular user (or more accurately the high costs of making it available to others) creates a quasi rent, but no "monopoly" rent. At the other extreme, an asset may be costlessly transferable to some other user at no reduction in value, while at the same time, entry of similar assets is restricted. In this case, monopoly rent would exist, but no quasi rent.

We can use monopoly terminology to refer to the phenomenon we are dis-

---

4. Vertical integration does not completely avoid contracting problems. The firm could usefully be thought of as a complex nonmarket contractual network where very similar forces are present. Frank Knight stressed the importance of this more than fifty years ago when he stated: "[T]he internal problems of the corporation, the protection of its various types of members and adherents against each other's predatory propensities, are quite as vital as the external problem of safeguarding the public interests against exploitation by the corporation as a unit." Frank H. Knight, *Risk, Uncertainty, and Profit* 254 (1964).

cussing as long as we recognize that we are not referring to the usual monopoly created by government restrictions on entry or referring to a single supplier or even highly concentrated supply. One of the fundamental premises of this paper is that monopoly power, better labeled "market power," is pervasive. Because of transaction and mobility costs, "market power" will exist in many situations not commonly called monopolies. There may be many potential suppliers of a particular asset to a particular user, but once the investment in the asset is made, the asset may be so specialized to a particular user that monopoly or monopsony market power, or both, is created.

A related motive for vertical integration that should not be confused with our main interest is the optimal output and pricing between two successive monopolists or bilateral monopolists (in the sense of marginal revenue less than price). A distortion arises because each sees a distorted marginal revenue or marginal cost.[5] While it is true that this successive monopoly distortion can be avoided by vertical integration, the results of the integration could, for that purpose alone, be achieved by a long-term or more detailed contract based on the true marginal revenue and marginal costs. Integrated ownership will sometimes be utilized to economize on such precontractual bargaining costs. However, we investigate a different reason for joint ownership of vertically related assets—the avoidance of postcontractual opportunistic behavior when specialized assets and appropriable quasi rents are present. One must clearly distinguish the transaction and information costs of reaching an agreement (discovering and heeding true costs and revenues and agreeing upon the division of profits) and the enforcement costs involved in assuring compliance with an agreement, especially one in which specialized assets are involved. It is this latter situation which we here explore as a motivation for intrafirm rather than interfirm transactions.

We maintain that if an asset has a substantial portion of quasi rent which is strongly dependent upon some other particular asset, both assets will tend to be owned by one party. For example, reconsider our printing press example. Knowing that the press would exist and be operated even if its owner got as

5. This matter of successive and bilateral monopoly has long been known and exposited in many places. See, for example, Robert Bork, "Vertical Integration and the Sherman Act: The Legal History of an Economic Misconception," 22 U. Chi. L. Rev. 157, 196 (1954); and the discussion in Fritz Machlup & Martha Taber, "Bilateral Monopoly, Successive Monopoly, and Vertical Integration," 27 Economica 101 (1960), where the problem is dated back to Cournot's statement in 1838.

little as $1,500, publisher B could seek excuses to renege on his initial contract to get the weekly rental down from $5,500 to close to $3,500 (the potential offer from publisher C, the next highest-valuing user at its present site). If publisher B could effectively announce he was not going to pay more than, say, $4,000 per week, the press owner would seem to be stuck. This unanticipated action would be opportunistic behavior (which by definition refers to unanticipated nonfulfillment of the contract) if the press owner had installed the press at a competitive rental price of $5,500 anticipating (possibly naively) good faith by the publisher. The publisher, for example, might plead that his newspaper business is depressed and that he will be unable to continue unless rental terms are revised.

Alternatively, and maybe more realistically, because the press owner may have bargaining power due to the large losses that he can easily impose on the publisher (if he has no other source of press services quickly available), the press owner might suddenly seek to get a higher rental price than $5,500 to capture some newly perceived increase in the publisher's profits. He could do this by alleging breakdowns or unusually high maintenance costs. This type of opportunistic behavior is difficult to prove and therefore litigate.

As we shall see, the costs of contractually specifying all important elements of quality varies considerably by type of asset. For some assets it may be essentially impossible to effectively specify all elements of quality, and therefore vertical integration is more likely. But even for those assets used in situations where all relevant quality dimensions can be unambiguously specified in a contract, the threat of production delay during litigation may be an effective bargaining device. A contract therefore may be clearly enforceable but still subject to postcontractual opportunistic behavior. For example, the threat by the press owner to break his contract by pulling out his press is credible even though illegal and possibly subject to injunctive action. This is because such an action, even in the very short run, can impose substantial costs on the newspaper publisher.[6]

---

6. While newspaper publishers generally own their own presses, book publishers generally do not. One possible reason book publishers are less integrated may be because a book is planned further ahead in time and can economically be released with less haste. Presses located in any area of the United States can be used. No press is specialized to one publisher, in part because speed in publication and distribution to readers is generally far less important for books than for newspapers, and therefore appropriable quasi rents are not created. Magazines and other periodicals can be considered somewhere between books and newspapers in terms of the importance of the time factor in distribution. In ad-

This more subtle form of opportunistic behavior is likely to result in a loss of efficiency and not just a wealth-distribution effect. For example, the publisher may decide, given this possibility, to hold or seek standby facilities otherwise not worthwhile. Even if transactors are risk neutral, the presence of possible opportunistic behavior will entail costs as real resources are devoted to the attempt to improve posttransaction bargaining positions in the event such opportunism occurs. In particular, less specific investments will be made to avoid being "locked in."[7] In addition, the increased uncertainty of quality and quantity leads to larger optimum inventories and other increased real costs of production.

This attention to appropriable specialized quasi rents is not novel. In addition to Williamson's[8] pathbreaking work in the area, Goldberg's[9] perceptive analysis of what he calls the "hold up" problem in the context of government regulation is what we are discussing in a somewhat different context. Goldberg indicates how some government regulation can usefully be considered a means of avoiding or reducing the threat of loss of quasi rent. (Goldberg treats this as the problem of providing protection for the "right to be served.") He also recognizes that this force underlies a host of other contractual and institutional arrangements such as stockpiling, insurance contracts, and vertical integration. Our analysis will similarly suggest a rationale for the existence of particu-

---

dition, because magazines are distributed nationally from at most a few plants, printing presses located in many different alternative areas are possible competitors for an existing press used at a particular location. Hence, a press owner has significantly less market power over the publisher of a magazine compared with a newspaper, and we find magazines generally printed in nonpublisher-owned plants. (See W. Eric Gustafson, "Periodicals and Books," in *Made in New York* 178, 190 [Max Hall, ed., 1959].) But while a magazine printing press may be a relatively less specific asset compared with a newspaper printing press, appropriable quasi rents may not be trivial (as possibly they are in the case of book printing). The magazine printing contract is therefore unlikely to be of a short-term one-transaction form but will be a long-term arrangement.

7. The relevance for private investments in underdeveloped, politically unstable, that is, "opportunistic," countries is painfully obvious. The importance for economic growth of predictable government behavior regarding the definition and enforcement of property rights has frequently been noted.

8. Oliver E. Williamson, "The Vertical Integration of Production: Market Failure Considerations," 61 *Am. Econ. Rev.* 112 (Papers & Proceedings, May 1971); and Oliver E. Williamson, *Markets and Hierarchies: Analysis and Antitrust Implications* (1975).

9. Victor P. Goldberg, "Regulation and Administered Contracts," 7 *Bell J. Econ. & Management Sci.* 426, 439–41 (1976).

lar institutions and the form of governmental intervention or contractual provisions as alternatives to vertical integration in a wide variety of cases.

II. Contractual Solutions

The primary alternative to vertical integration as a solution to the general
problem of opportunistic behavior is some form of economically enforceable
long-term contract. Clearly a short-term (for example, one-transaction, nonre-
peat sale) contract will not solve the problem. The relevant question then becomes when will vertical integration be observed as a solution and when will
the use of the market-contracting process occur. Some economists and lawyers
have defined this extremely difficult question away by calling a long-term contract a form of vertical integration.[10] Although there is clearly a continuum
here, we will attempt not to blur the distinction between a long-term rental
agreement and ownership. We assume the opportunistic behavior we are concentrating on can occur only with the former.[11]

For example, if opportunism occurs by the owner-lessor of an asset failing
to maintain it properly for the user-lessee and hence unexpectedly increasing
the effective rental price, legal remedies (proving contract violation) may be
very costly. On the other hand, if the user owned the asset, then the employee
who failed to maintain the asset properly could merely be fired.[12] If the employee could still effectively cheat the owner-user of the asset because of his

10. See, for example, Friedrich Kessler & Richard H. Stern, "Competition, Contract,
and Vertical Integration," 69 *Yale L.J.* 1 (1959).

11. It is commonly held that users of assets that can be damaged by careless use and
for which the damage is not easy to detect immediately are more likely to own rather than
rent the assets. However, these efficient maintenance considerations apply to short-term
contracts and are irrelevant if the length of the long-term rental contract coincides with
the economic life of the asset. Abstracting from tax considerations, the long-term contract remains less than completely equivalent to vertical integration only because of the
possibility of postcontractual opportunistic reneging. These opportunistic possibilities,
however, may also exist within the firm; see note 4 *supra.*

12. We are abstracting from any considerations of a firm's detection costs of determining proper maintenance. Ease of termination also analytically distinguishes between
a franchisor-franchisee arrangement and a vertically integrated arrangement with a
profit-sharing manager. If cheating occurs, it is generally cheaper to terminate an employee rather than a franchisee. (The law has been changing recently to make it more
difficult to terminate either type of laborer.) But the more limited job-tenure rights of an
employee compared with those of a franchisee reduce his incentive to invest in building
up future business, and the firm must trade off the benefits and costs of the alternative

specific ability to maintain the asset, then the problem is that vertical integration of a relevant asset, the employee's human capital, has not occurred. For the moment, however, we will concentrate solely on the question of long-term rental versus ownership of durable physical assets.[13]

Long-term contracts used as alternatives to vertical integration can be assumed to take two forms: (1) an explicitly stated contractual guarantee legally enforced by the government or some other outside institution, or (2) an implicit contractual guarantee enforced by the market mechanism of withdrawing future business if opportunistic behavior occurs. Explicit long-term contracts can, in principle, solve opportunistic problems, but, as suggested already, they are often very costly solutions. They entail costs of specifying possible contingencies and the policing and litigation costs of detecting violations and enforcing the contract in the courts.[14] Contractual provisions specifying compulsory arbitration or more directly imposing costs on the opportunistic party (for example, via bonding) are alternatives often employed to economize on litigation costs and to create flexibility without specifying every possible contingency and quality dimension of the transaction.

Since every contingency cannot be cheaply specified in a contract or even known and because legal redress is expensive, transactors will generally also rely on an implicit type of long-term contract that employs a market rather than legal enforcement mechanism, namely, the imposition of a capital loss by the withdrawal of expected future business. This goodwill market-enforcement mechanism undoubtedly is a major element of the contractual alternative to

---

arrangements. A profit-sharing manager with an explicit long-term employment contract would essentially be identical to a franchisee.

13. The problems involved with renting specific human capital are discussed below.

14. The recent Westinghouse case dealing with failure to fulfill uranium-supply contracts on grounds of "commercial impossibility" vividly illustrates these enforcement costs. Nearly three years after outright cancellation by Westinghouse of their contractual commitment, the lawsuits have not been adjudicated, and those firms that have settled with Westinghouse have accepted substantially less than the original contracts would have entitled them to. A recent article by Paul L. Joskow, "Commercial Impossibility, the Uranium Market, and the Westinghouse Case," 6 J. Legal Stud. 119 (1977), analyzes the Westinghouse decision to renege on the contract as anticipated risk sharing and therefore, using our definition, would not be opportunistic behavior. However, the publicity surrounding this case and the judicial progress to date are likely to make explicit long-term contracts a less feasible alternative to vertical integration in the situations we are analyzing.

vertical integration. Macaulay provides evidence that relatively informal, legally unenforceable contractual practices predominate in business relations and that reliance on explicit legal sanctions is extremely rare.[15] Instead, business firms are said to generally rely on effective extralegal market sanctions, such as the depreciation of an opportunistic firm's general goodwill because of the anticipated loss of future business, as a means of preventing nonfulfillment of contracts.

One way in which this market mechanism of contract enforcement may operate is by offering to the potential cheater a future "premium," more precisely, a price sufficiently greater than average variable (that is, avoidable) cost to assure a quasi-rent stream that will exceed the potential gain from cheating.[16] The present-discounted value of this future premium stream must be greater than any increase in wealth that could be obtained by the potential cheater if he, in fact, cheated and was terminated. The offer of such a long-term relationship with the potential cheater will eliminate systematic opportunistic behavior.[17]

15. Stewart Macaulay, "Non-Contractual Relations in Business: A Preliminary Study," 28 Am. Soc. Rev. 55 (Feb. 1963).

16. The following discussion of the market enforcement mechanism is based upon the analysis of competitive equilibrium under costly quality information developed in Benjamin Klein & Keith Leffler, "The Role of Price in Guaranteeing Quality," J. Pol. Econ. (forthcoming 1979), which formally extends and more completely applies the analysis in Benjamin Klein, "The Competitive Supply of Money," 6 J. Money, Credit, & Banking 423 (1974). It is similar to the analysis presented in Gary S. Becker & George J. Stigler, "Law Enforcement, Malfeasance, and Compensation of Enforcers," 3 J. Legal Stud. 1 (1974), of insuring against malfeasance by an employer. This market-enforcement mechanism is used in Benjamin Klein & Andrew McLaughlin, "Resale Price Maintenance, Exclusive Territories, and Franchise Termination: The Coors Case," (1978, unpublished manuscript), to explain franchising arrangements and particular contractual provisions such as resale price maintenance, exclusive territories, initial specific investments, and termination clauses.

17. Formally, this arrangement to guarantee nonopportunistic behavior unravels if there is a last period in the relationship. No matter how high the premium, cheating would occur at the start of the last period. If transactors are aware of this, no transaction relying on trust (that is, the expectation of another subsequent trial) will be made in the penultimate period, because it becomes the last period, and so on. If some large lump-sum, final-period payment such as a pension as part of the market-enforcement scheme, as outlined by Gary S. Becker & George J. Stigler, supra note 16, this last-period problem is obvious. One solution to this unrecognized last-period problem is the acceptance of some continuing third party (for example, escrow agents or government enforcers) to prevent reneg-

The larger the potential one-time "theft" by cheating (the longer and more costly to detect a violation, enforce the contract, switch suppliers, and so forth) and the shorter the expected continuing business relationship, the higher this premium will be in a nondeceiving equilibrium. This may therefore partially explain both the reliance by firms on long-term implicit contracts with particular suppliers and the existence of reciprocity agreements among firms. The premium can be paid in seemingly unrelated profitable reciprocal business. The threat of termination of this relationship mutually suppresses opportunistic behavior.[18]

The premium stream can be usefully thought of as insurance payments made by the firm to prevent cheating.[19] As long as both parties to the transaction make the same estimate of the potential short-run gain from cheating, the

---

ing on the implicit contracts against reneging we are outlining. Alternatively, the potential loss of value of indefinitely long-lived salable brand-name assets can serve as deterrents to cheating even where the contract between two parties has a last period. If one party's reputation for nonopportunistic dealings can be sold and used in later transactions in an infinite-time-horizon economy, the firm that cheats in the "last" period to any one buyer from the firm experiences a capital loss. This may partially explain the existence of conglomerates and their use of identifying (not product-descriptive) brand names.

18. Although it may not always be in one's narrow self-interest to punish the other party in such a reciprocal relationship since termination may impose a cost on both, it may be rational for one to adopt convincingly such a reaction function to optimally prevent cheating. R. L. Trivers, "The Evolution of Reciprocal Altruism," 46 Q. Rev. Bio. 35, 49 (March 1971), discusses similar mechanisms, such as "moralistic aggression," which he claims have been genetically selected to protect reciprocating altruists against cheaters. Similarly, throughout the discussion we implicitly assume that cheating individuals can cheat only once and thereafter earn the "competitive" rate of return. They may, however, be forced to earn less than the competitive wage if they are caught cheating, that is, take an extra capital loss (collusively, but rationally) imposed by other members of the group. This may explain why individuals may prefer to deal in business relations with their own group (for example, members of the same church or the same country club), where effective social sanctions can be imposed against opportunistic behavior. Reliance on such reciprocal business relationships and group enforcement mechanisms is more likely where governmental enforcement of contracts is weaker. Nathaniel H. Leff, "Industrial Organization and Entrepreneurship in the Developing Countries: The Economic Groups," 26 Econ. Dev. & Cultural Change 661 (1978), for example, documents the importance of such groups in less-developed countries. Industries supplying illegal products and services would likely be another example.

19. It is, of course, an insurance scheme that not only pools risks but also alters them.

quantity of this assurance that will be demanded and supplied will be such that no opportunistic behavior will be expected to occur.[20] If postcontractual reneging is anticipated to occur, either the correct premium will be paid to optimally prevent it or, if the premium necessary to eliminate reneging is too costly, the particular transaction will not be made.

We are not implicitly assuming here that contracts are enforced costlessly and cannot be broken, but rather that given our information-cost assumptions, parties to a contract know exactly when and how much a contract will be broken. An unanticipated broken contract, that is, opportunistic behavior, is therefore not possible in this particular equilibrium. In the context of this model, expected wealth maximization will yield some opportunistic behavior only if we introduce a stochastic element. This will alter the informational equilibrium state such that the potential cheater's estimate of the short-run gain from opportunistic behavior may be at times greater than the other firm's estimate. Hence, less than an optimal premium will be paid and opportunistic behavior will occur.

The firms collecting the premium payments necessary to assure fulfillment of contractual agreements in a costly information world may appear to be earning equilibrium "profits" although they are in a competitive market. That is, there may be many, possibly identical, firms available to supply the services of nonopportunistic performance of contractual obligations, yet the premium will not be competed away if transactors cannot costlessly guarantee contractual performance. The assurance services, by definition, will not be supplied unless the premium is paid and the mere payment of this premium produces the required services.

Any profits are competed away in equilibrium by competitive expenditures on fixed (sunk) assets, such as initial specific investments (for example, a sign) with low or zero salvage value if the firm cheats, necessary to enter and obtain this preferred position of collecting the premium stream.[21] These fixed (sunk) costs of supplying credibility of future performance are repaid or covered by future sales on which a premium is earned. In equilibrium, the premium

20. As opposed to the analysis of Michael R. Darby & Edi Karni, "Free Competition and the Optimal Amount of Fraud," 16 J. Law & Econ. 67 (1973), the equilibrium quantity of opportunistic behavior or "fraud" will be zero under our assumptions of symmetrical information.

21. A more complete analysis of market equilibrium by the use of specific capital in guaranteeing contract enforcement is developed in Benjamin Klein & Keith Leffler, supra note 16.

stream is then merely a normal rate of return on the "reputation," or "brand-name" capital, created by the firm by these initial expenditures. This brand-name capital, the value of which is highly specific to contract fulfillment by the firm, is analytically equivalent to a forfeitable collateral bond put up by the firm which is anticipated to face an opportunity to take advantage of appropriable quasi rents in specialized assets.

While these initial specific investments or collateral bonds are sometimes made as part of the normal (minimum-cost) production process and therefore at small additional cost, transaction costs and risk considerations do make them costly.[22] We can generally say that the larger the appropriable specialized quasi rents (and therefore the larger the potential short-run gain from oppor-

---

22. An interesting example of the efficient creation of such a specific collateral investment is provided in In re Tastee-Freeze International, 82 F.T.C. 1195 (1973). In this case the franchisor required the franchisee to purchase all the equipment to make soft ice cream except the final patented feeder mechanism, which they would only rent at the nominal price of one dollar per month. This, we believe, served the function of substantially reducing the salvage value of the equipment upon termination and therefore was part of the enforcement mechanism to prevent cheating (for example, intentionally failing to maintain quality) by franchisees. If the feeder were sold, the equipment plus the feeder would have a substantial resale value and would not serve the purpose of assuring contract compliance. Similarly, if the equipment were rented along with the feeder, the franchisee would not experience a capital loss if terminated. Since the assets of the franchisee are contractually made specific, a situation is created where the assets are now appropriable by an opportunistic franchisor. Generally, a franchisor will lose by terminating a franchisee without cause, since that will produce poor incentives on the remaining franchisees to maintain quality and will make it more difficult for the franchisor to sell franchises in the future. But what prevents the franchisor from an unanticipated simultaneous termination of all franchisees, especially after growth of a chain is "complete"? This is logically equivalent to the last-period problem discussed at note 17 supra and is restrained in part by its effects on the salable value of the brand name of the franchisor. While we do not know of any evidence of such systematic franchisor cheating, an analysis of this problem which merely asserts that franchisees voluntarily sign contracts with knowledge of these short-term termination provisions is certainly incomplete (see, for example, Paul H. Rubin, "The Theory of the Firm and the Structure of the Franchise Contract," 21 J. Law & Econ. 223 [1978]).

This example and much of this section of the paper is based upon a more complete theoretical and empirical analysis of actual contractual relationships developed for an ongoing study by Benjamin Klein of FTC litigation in the area of vertical-distribution arrangements.

tunistic behavior) and the larger the premium payments necessary to prevent contractual reneging, the more costly this implicit contractual solution will be. We can also expect the explicit contract costs to be positively related to the level of appropriable quasi rents since it will pay to use more resources (including legal services) to specify precisely more contingencies when potential opportunities for lucrative contractual reneging exist.

Although implicit and explicit contracting and policing costs are positively related to the extent of appropriable specialized quasi rents, it is reasonable to assume, on the other hand, that any internal coordination or other ownership costs are not systematically related to the extent of the appropriable specialized quasi rent of the physical asset owned. Hence we can reasonably expect the following general empirical regularity to be true: the lower the appropriable specialized quasi rents, the more likely that transactors will rely on a contractual relationship rather than on common ownership. And conversely, integration by common or joint ownership is more likely, the higher the appropriable specialized quasi rents of the assets involved.

III. Examples of Appropriable Specialized Quasi Rent

This section presents examples of specialized quasi rents where the potential for their appropriation serves as an important determinant of economic organization. A series of varied illustrations, some quite obvious and others rather subtle, will make the analysis more transparent and provide suggestive evidence for the relevance of the protection of appropriable quasi rents as an incentive to vertically integrate. It also suggests the direction of more systematic empirical work that obviously is required to assess the significance of this factor relative to other factors in particular cases. Where this force towards integration (that is, the economizing on contracting costs necessary to assure nonopportunistic behavior in the presence of appropriable quasi rents) does not appear to dominate, important insights regarding the determinants of particular contracting costs and contract provisions are thereby provided.[23]

---

23. It is important to recognize that not only will contracting and enforcement costs of constraining opportunistic behavior determine the form of the final economic arrangement adopted by the transacting parties, but they will also influence the firm's production function. That is, the level of specific investment—and therefore the size of the potentially appropriable quasi rent—is not an independent "technological" datum in each of these following cases, but is economically determined in part by transaction costs.

A. *Automobile Manufacturing*

An illustrative example is the ownership by automobile-producing companies of the giant presses used for stamping body parts. The design and engineering specifications of a new automobile, for example Mustang for Ford, create value in Ford auto production. The manufacture of dies for stamping parts in accordance with the above specifications gives a value to these dies specialized to Ford, which implies an appropriable quasi rent in those dies. Therefore, the die owner would not want to be separate from Ford. Since an independent die owner may likely have no comparable demanders other than Ford for its product and to elicit supply requires payment to cover only the small operating costs once the large sunk fixed cost of the specific investment in the dies is made, the incentive for Ford to opportunistically renegotiate a lower price at which it will accept body parts from the independent die owner may be large. Similarly, if there is a large cost to Ford from the production delay of obtaining an alternative supplier of the specific body parts, the independent die owner may be able to capture quasi rents by demanding a revised higher price for the parts. Since the opportunity to lose the specialized quasi rent of assets is a debilitating prospect, neither party would invest in such equipment. Joint ownership of designs and dies removes this incentive to attempt appropriation.[24]

In this context, it is interesting to study in some detail the vertical merger that occurred in 1926 of General Motors with Fisher Body. The original production process for automobiles consisted of individually constructed open, largely wooden, bodies. By 1919 the production process began to shift towards largely metal closed-body construction for which specific stamping machines became important. Therefore in 1919 General Motors entered a ten-year contractual agreement with Fisher Body for the supply of closed auto

24. The argument also applies to die inserts, which can be utilized to make slight modifications in original dies. The value of die inserts is largely an appropriable quasi rent, and so they will also be owned jointly with the designs and basic dies. Aside from the engineering design of the car, the engine blocks, the exterior shell (and possibly the crankshafts, camshafts, and gearing), no other part of the automobile would appear to possess specialized appropriable quasi rents and therefore necessarily be made exclusively by the automobile company. The integration of Ford into the manufacture of spark plugs—a part which seems to be easily standardizable among different autos—by their merger with Autolite therefore must be explained on other grounds. See Ford Motor Co. v. United States, 405 U.S. 562 (1972).

bodies.[25] In order to encourage Fisher Body to make the required specific investment, this contract had an exclusive-dealing clause whereby General Motors agreed to buy substantially all its closed bodies from Fisher. This exclusive-dealing arrangement significantly reduced the possibility of General Motors acting opportunistically by demanding a lower price for the bodies after Fisher made the specific investment in production capacity. Since exclusive-dealing contractual conditions are relatively cheap to effectively specify and enforce, General Motors's postcontractual threat to purchase bodies elsewhere was effectively eliminated.

But large opportunities were created by this exclusive-dealing clause for Fisher to take advantage of General Motors, namely to demand a monopoly price for the bodies. Therefore, the contract attempted to fix the price which Fisher could charge for the bodies supplied to General Motors. However, contractually setting in advance a "reasonable" price in the face of possible future changes in demand and production conditions is somewhat more difficult to effectively accomplish than merely "fixing" required suppliers. The price was set on a cost plus 17.6 per cent basis (where cost was defined exclusive of interest on invested capital). In addition, the contract included provisions that the price charged General Motors could not be greater than that charged other automobile manufacturers by Fisher for similar bodies nor greater than the average market price of similar bodies produced by companies other than Fisher and also included provisions for compulsory arbitration in the event of any disputes regarding price.

Unfortunately, however, these complex contractual pricing provisions did not work out in practice. The demand conditions facing General Motors and Fisher Body changed dramatically over the next few years. There was a large increase in the demand for automobiles and a significant shift away from open bodies to the closed body styles supplied by Fisher.[26] Meanwhile General

25. The manufacturing agreement between General Motors and Fisher Body can be found in the minutes of the Board of Directors of Fisher Body Corporation for November 7, 1919.

In addition to this long-term contract General Motors also purchased a 60 per cent interest in Fisher at this time. However, as demonstrated by future events, the Fisher brothers clearly seem to have maintained complete control of their company in spite of this purchase.

26. By 1924 more than 65 per cent of automobiles produced by General Motors were of the closed-body type. See *Sixteenth Annual Report of the General Motors Corporation*, year ended December 31, 1924.

Motors was very unhappy with the price it was being charged by its now very important supplier, Fisher. General Motors believed the price was too high because of a substantial increase in body output per unit of capital employed. This was an understandable development given the absence of a capital cost pass-through in the original contract.[27] In addition, Fisher refused to locate their body plants adjacent to General Motors assembly plants, a move General Motors claimed was necessary for production efficiency (but which required a large very specific and hence possibly appropriable investment on the part of Fisher).[28] By 1924, General Motors had found the Fisher contractual relationship intolerable and began negotiations for purchase of the remaining stock in Fisher Body, culminating in a final merger agreement in 1926.[29]

B. Petroleum Industry

Appropriable quasi rents exist in specialized assets of oil refineries, pipelines, and oil fields. This leads to common ownership to remove the incentive for individuals to attempt to capture the rents of assets owned by someone else.

Suppose several oil wells are located along a separately owned pipeline that leads to a cluster of independently owned refineries with no alternative crude supply at comparable cost. Once all the assets are in place (the wells drilled and the pipeline and refineries constructed), the oil-producing properties and the refineries are specialized to the pipeline. The portion of their value above the value to the best alternative user is an appropriable specialized quasi rent. The extent of the appropriable quasi rent is limited, in part, by the costs of entry to a

27. Deposition of Alfred P. Sloan, Jr., in *United States v. DuPont & Co.*, 366 U.S. 316 (1961), from complete set of briefs and trial records in custody of General Motors, 186–90 (April 28, 1952). Also see direct testimony of Alfred P. Sloan, Jr., in *United States v. DuPont & Co.*, vol. 5, trial transcript, 2908–14 (March 17, 1953). (The government was attempting to demonstrate in this case that General Motors vertically integrated in order to get Fisher to purchase its glass requirements from DuPont.)

28. Id. It is obvious that long-term exclusive-dealing contracts are necessary if such investments are to be made by nonvertically integrated firms. See In re Great Lakes Carbon Corp., 82 F.T.C. 1529 (1973), for an example of the government's failure to understand this. Great Lakes Carbon Corporation built plants highly specific to particular refineries to process petroleum coke (a by-product of the refining process) for these refineries and was prosecuted for requiring long-term exclusive-dealing contracts with refineries.

29. *United States v. DuPont & Co.*, vol. 1, defendants trial exhibits numbers GM-32, GM-33, GM-34.

potential parallel pipeline developer. Since pipelines between particular oil-producing properties and particular refineries are essentially natural monopolies, the existing pipeline owner may have a significant degree of market power.

These specialized producing and refining assets are therefore "hostage" to the pipeline owner. At the "gathering end" of the pipeline, the monopsonist pipeline could and would purchase all its oil at the same wellhead price regardless of the distance of the well from the refinery. This price could be as low as the marginal cost of getting oil out of the ground (or its reservation value for future use, if higher) and might not generate a return to the oil-well owner sufficient to recoup the initial investment of exploration and drilling. At the delivery-to-refinery end of the pipeline, the pipeline owner would be able to appropriate the "specialized-to-the-pipeline quasi rents" of the refineries. The pipeline owner could simply raise the price of crude oil at least to the price of alternative sources of supply to each refinery that are specialized to the pipeline. Given the prospects of such action, if the pipeline owner were an independent monopsonist facing the oil explorers and a monopolist to the refinery owners, everyone (explorers and refiners) would know in advance their vulnerability to rent extraction. Therefore oil-field owners and refinery owners would, through shared ownership in the pipeline, remove the possibility of subsequent rent extraction.[30]

30. Our argument is distinct from the traditional argument in the oil-business literature that vertical integration occurs to achieve "assurance" of supplies or of markets in the face of implicitly or explicitly assumed disequilibrium conditions. See, for example, P. H. Frankel, "Integration in the Oil Industry," 1 J. Indus. Econ. 201 (1953); Melvin G. de Chazeau & Alfred H. Kahn, Integration and Competition in the Petroleum Industry 102–4 (1959); and Michael E. Canes, "A Theory of the Vertical Integration of Oil Firms" (Oct. 1976, unpublished manuscript, Amer. Petroleum Inst.). Jerry G. Green, "Vertical Integration and Assurance of Markets" (Oct. 1974, Discussion Paper No. 383, Harvard Inst. of Econ. Research), similarly argues more formally that price inflexibility in an intermediate market which causes shortages and overproduction is an incentive for vertical integration.

It is also important to distinguish between this risk-reducing reason for joint ownership (that is, the reduction in the risk of appropriation of user-associated specialized quasi rents) and the possible risk reduction from joint ownership when there is negative correlation of changes in values of nonappropriable generalized quasi rents. Joint ownership of assets whose value fluctuations are negatively correlated so that gains in one are offset by losses in the other is said to provide a form of insurance against total value changes of the resources used in the manufacturing process. These changes are not the result of any postcontractual opportunistic behavior but of general economic forces outside the control of the immediate parties. For example, a refinery and an oil-producing

The problem would not be completely solved if just the oil field or the re-fineries (but not both) was commonly owned with the pipeline, since the local monopoly (or monopsony) would persist vis-à-vis the other. Prospectively, one would expect the common ownership to extend to all three stages. If several refineries (or oil fields) were to be served by one pipeline, all the refinery (or oil-field) owners would want to jointly own the pipeline. A common practice is a jointly owned company which "owns" the pipeline, with the shares by produc-ers and refiners in the pipeline company corresponding roughly to the respec-tive shares of oil to be transported.[31]

———

property fluctuate in value in opposite directions if a new oil field is discovered. The price of oil will fall, but the price of refined products will not fall until additional refineries can process larger amounts of oil into more refined products at essentially constant produc-tion costs. Then, some of the oil-field owner's losses in value of crude oil are gained by his refinery. This reduces the fluctuation in values caused by factors unrelated to the efficiency of oil-producing, refining, and distributing abilities.

However, diversification can also be achieved by methods other than vertical integra-tion. One way is for the investor to buy stocks in the separate unintegrated firms—in effect integrating their ownership by joint holding of common stocks. Although individual ac-tion may not always be as cheap or effective as action through intermediaries, financial in-termediaries are available such as mutual funds rather than direct diversification by inte-grated firms. One possible reason why negatively correlated assets could be worth more combined in a single firm is the reduction in the probability of bankruptcy and hence the probability of incurring bankruptcy costs (such as legal fees). An integrated firm with negatively correlated assets could increase its debt-to-equity ratio while keeping the prob-ability of bankruptcy constant and therefore decrease the taxes on equity without any additional risk. This may be one of the gains of many conglomerate mergers.

31. Jane Atwood & Paul Kobrin, "Integration and Joint Ventures in Pipelines" (Sept. 1977, Research Study No. 5, Am. Petroleum Inst.), find an extremely high positive corre-lation between a firm's crude production and its share of ownership in the pipeline. On the other hand, natural gas pipelines, although apparently economically similar in terms of potentially appropriable quasi rents, do not appear to be vertically integrated. Rather than joint-ownership arrangements with the gas producers, these pipelines are often in-dependently owned. The difference may be due to more effective FPC (and now the Fed-eral Energy Regulatory Commission) regulation (of the wellhead and city-gate gas prices and the implied pipeline tariff) compared with the direct Interstate Commerce Commis-sion regulation of oil pipelines as common carriers. Regulation of oil pipeline tariffs could, for example, be easily evaded by opportunistic decreases in the wellhead prices paid for oil. More complete government regulation of gas prices may effectively prevent op-portunistic behavior by the natural gas pipeline owners and thereby serve as an alternative to vertical integration. (See Victor P. Goldberg, *supra* note 9.) Edmund Kitch informs us

Consider other inputs in the production process. The oil tanker, for example, is specialized to crude-oil transportation. But since it is essentially equivalued by many alternative users, the appropriable quasi rent is near zero. So we would expect oil tankers not to be extensively owned by refiners or producers. Similarly, the assets used for refinery construction are not specialized to any single refiner or refinery, and they should also not be commonly owned with the refinery.

Preliminary examination of the development of the American petroleum industry in the nineteenth century reveals numerous examples that appear consistent with the hypothesis that as technological change leads to assets involved in production, transportation, refining, and marketing becoming more specialized to other specific assets, joint ownership became efficient as a means of preventing opportunistic behavior.

For example, Rockefeller recognized the importance of the pending technological change implied by the substitution of highly specific long-distance pipelines for the somewhat more general capital of the railroads as the efficient mode of transporting oil and took advantage of it. First, before long-distance pipelines were clearly economical, Rockefeller used his dominant oil-refining position to obtain a price reduction on oil he shipped by rail and also rebates from the railroads on oil shipped by competitive oil producers. We conjecture that Rockefeller obtained these price reductions by threatening to build a pipeline parallel to the railroad. He was therefore able to extract the appropriable quasi rents of the railroads. This explains why the rebates were solely a function of oil shipped and not related to nonoil products such as agricultural goods. It also explains why the discount and rebate to Rockefeller were often of the same magnitude. The payment should be a function of total demand for transporting oil.

The obvious question is why some small oil producer or even a non-oil-producing firm did not similarly threaten the railroads with building a pipeline early (before it was cheaper than rail transport) and demand a payment as a function of total oil shipped. The answer, we believe, is that only a dominant oil producer would have credible bargaining power with the railroads in this situation because only a dominant producer would be able to make such a highly specific investment. If a small producer or non-oil-producing firm made such an investment, it could easily be appropriated by the oil-producing

---

that the evidence does indicate a much greater degree of vertical integration of natural gas pipelines in the period before FPC regulation.

firms, especially with an alternative means of transportation available. It was therefore necessary for Rockefeller to gain a dominant oil-producing and refining position in order to make a credible threat to the railroads. Appropriating the quasi rents of the railroads by discounts and rebates not only effectively metered the demand for oil transportation but also made it easier for Rockefeller to gain a monopolistic position in the industry without being forced to buy out rivals at prices that would completely reflect future-discounted monopoly profits.[32]

c. Specific Human Capital

The previous analysis has dealt with examples of physical capital. When specific human capital is involved, the opportunism problem is often more complex and, because of laws prohibiting slavery, the solution is generally some form of explicit or implicit contract rather than vertical integration.

For example, consider the following concrete illustration from the agricultural industry. Suppose someone owns a peach orchard. The ripened peaches, ready for harvest, have a market value of about $400,000. So far costs of $300,000 have been paid, and the remaining harvesting and shipping costs will be $50,000 ($5,000 transport and $45,000 labor), leaving $50,000 as the com-

32. Although our preliminary investigation indicates that control of the transportation system and vertical integration of it with the oil fields and refineries were significant, there were many other factors in Rockefeller's success. For example, the unpredictability of the life of oil fields raised the risks of a substantial investment in an integrated pipeline transportation system from one field. That Rockefeller correctly or luckily surmised that the Bradford field in 1874 would be long-lived was surely a source of his success. Also his skill in discovering consumer-preferred retailing methods, achieving lower-cost refining, and correctly assessing the ability to refine sulphurous Ohio crude undoubtedly were additional factors. See, for example, Ralph W. Hidy & Muriel E. Hidy, *History of Standard Oil Company (New Jersey)*, vol. 1, *Pioneering in Big Business 1882–1911* (1955); Allan Nevins, *John D. Rockefeller: The Heroic Age of American Enterprise* (1940); and Harold F. Williamson & Arnold R. Daum, *The American Petroleum Industry* (1959).

This oil-pipeline analysis of appropriable specific capital may be applicable in many other situations. It should hold, for example, for ore mines and refineries which are specialized to each other. We predict that copper smelters specialized to a single mine will tend to be jointly owned, as will a cement quarry and its nearby smelter (mill). Railroad spur lines (and the land on which the track runs) from ore mines to smelters should likewise be owned by the mine-smelter owner. In addition, we would expect television program producers in an area with a single transmitter tower to be joint owners of the tower.

petitive return on the owner's capital. Assume the laborers become a union (one party to whom the crop is now specialized) and refuse to pick unless paid $390,000. That would leave $5,000 for transport and only $5,000 for the owner of the peach orchard, instead of the $350,000 necessary to cover incurred costs and the cost of capital. If the union had power to exclude other pickers, it could extract all the appropriable quasi rent of that year's crop specialized to that particular labor union's service. The union would be extracting not just the usual monopoly rents involved in raising wages, but also the short-run appropriable quasi rents of the farmer's specific assets represented by the ripened peaches. This gain to the union is a one-period return, because obviously the farmer will not make any additional specific investments in the future if he knows it will be appropriated by the union.

To reduce this risk of appropriation, the farmer may have a large clan family (or neighbors of similar farms) do his picking. Because of diseconomies of scale, however, this "cooperative" solution is not generally the lowest-cost arrangement, and some reliance on market contracting will be necessary. The individual farmer, for example, may want the labor union to put up a forfeitable bond to compensate him in the event the union under threat of strike asks for more wages at harvest time. Alternatively, but equivalently, the collateral put up by the union could be the value of the brand-name capital of the union, a value which will depreciate if its leaders engage in opportunistic behavior. The farmer would then make a continuing brand-name payment to the union (similar to the premium payment noted above) for this collateral.[33]

The market value of the union's reputation for reliability of contract observance is the present-discounted value of these brand-name payments, which will be greater than any short-run opportunistic gain to the union leaders that could be obtained by threats at harvest time. These payments which increase the cost to the union of opportunistic behavior would be substantial for a perishable product with a large appropriable quasi rent. It is therefore obvious why producers of highly perishable crops are so antagonistic to unionization of field labor. They would be especially hostile to unions without established rep-

---

33. If the premium is a payment to the union per unit time, then the arrangement is identical to a collateral-bond arrangement where the union collects the interest on the bond as long as no opportunistic behavior occurs. Because of possible legal difficulties of enforcing such an arrangement, however, the premium may be reflected in the price (that is, a higher wage).

utations regarding fulfillment of contract and with politically motivated (and possibly myopic) leaders.[34]

In addition to implicit (brand-name) contracts, opportunistic union behavior may be prevented by use of explicit contracts, often with some outside arbitration as an element of the contract-enforcement mechanism. Although it is difficult for an outsider to distinguish between opportunistic behavior and good-faith modifications of contract, impartial arbitration procedures may reduce the necessity of explicitly specifying possible contingencies and thereby reduce the rigidity of the explicit long-term contract.[35]

When the problem is reversed and quasi rents of firm-specific human capital of employees may be opportunistically appropriated by the firm, implicit and explicit long-term contracts are also used to prevent such behavior. Be-

---

34. It is interesting to note in this context that California grape farmers preferred the established Teamsters Union to the new, untried, and apparently more politically motivated field-workers union organized by Cesar Chavez.

Since unions are not "owned," union leaders will not have the proper incentive to maximize the union's value; they will tend more to maximize returns during their tenure. If, however, union leadership (ownership) were salable, the leaders would have the optimal incentive to invest in and conserve the union's brand-name capital. They therefore would not engage in opportunistic actions that may increase current revenue while decreasing the market value of the union. "Idealistic" union leaders that do not behave as if they own the union may, in fact, produce less wealth-maximizing action than would "corrupt" leaders, who act as if they personally own the union. Alternatively, the current members of the union may have control, not in the sense of having directly salable shares, but in the sense that the valuable union asset can be transferred to their children or relatives. If government regulations force union members to give away these rights to future rents (for example, by forcing them to admit minorities and eliminate nepotism), we can expect them to intentionally depreciate or not create the reputation capital of the union by opportunistic strikes. See Benjamin Klein, *supra* note 16, where similar problems with regard to the supply of money by non-privately-owned, non-wealth-maximizing firms are discussed.

35. An interesting legal case in this area is *Publishers' Ass'n v. Newspaper & Mail Del. Union*, 114 N.Y.S. 2d, 401 (1952). The union authorized and sanctioned a strike against the *New York Daily News*, although the collective bargaining agreement had "no-strike" and arbitration clauses. The *Daily News* took the union to arbitration, and the arbitrator found actual damages of $2,000 and punitive damages of $5,000 if the union again violated the contract. (The court, however, overturned the punitive damages for technical reasons.) See David E. Feller, "A General Theory of the Collective Bargaining Agreement," 61 *Calif. L. Rev.* 663 (1973), for a discussion of the flexibility obtained with arbitration provisions in labor contracts.

cause of economies of scale in monitoring and enforcing such contracts, unions may arise as a contract cost-reducing institution for employees with investments in specific human capital.[36]

In addition to narrow contract-monitoring economies of scale, a union creates a continuing long-term employment relationship that eliminates the last-period (or transient employee) contract-enforcement problem and also creates bargaining power (a credible strike threat) to more cheaply punish a firm that violates the contract. Even when the specific human-capital investment is made by the firm, a union of employees may similarly reduce the contract-enforcement costs of preventing individual-worker opportunism. There are likely to be economies of scale in supply credibility of contract fulfillment, including the long-term continuing relationship aspect of a union. The existence of a union not only makes it more costly for a firm to cheat an individual worker in his last period but also makes it more costly for an individual worker in his last period to cheat the firm, because the union has the incentive (for example, withholding pension rights) to prevent such an externality on the continuing workers. Therefore unions are more likely to exist when the opportunistic cheating problem is greater, namely, when there is more specific human capital present.[37]

The first Becker analysis of the specific human-capital problem[38] ignored opportunistic bargaining difficulties and implicitly assumed arbitrary contracting costs in particular situations to determine a solution. Becker initially assumed that the firm would cheat the employee if the employee made the specific investment. He then argued that the only reason the firm would not make the entire specific investment is because the quit rate of employees, which is a negative function of wages, would then be greater than optimal. Becker did not consider the completely reciprocal nature of the possibilities for cheating. The opportunistic behavior we are emphasizing suggests the possibility of the employee threatening to quit after the firm makes the specific in-

---

36. We should explicitly note that we are not considering unions as cartelizing devices, the usually analyzed motivation for their existence. This force is obviously present in many cases (for example, interstate trucking) but is distinct from our analysis.

37. When allowing for this "reverse" effect of employee-specific capital, and therefore higher wages, on the formation of unions, the usual positive effect of unions on wages appears to vanish. See, for example, O. Ashenfelter & G. Johnson, "Unionism, Relative Wages, and Labor Quality in U.S. Manufacturing Industries," 13 Int'l Econ. Rev. 488 (Oct. 1972); and Peter Schmidt & Robert P. Strauss, "The Effect of Unions on Earnings and Earnings on Unions: A Mixed Logit Approach," 17 Int'l Econ. Rev. 204 (Feb. 1976).

38. Gary S. Becker, Human Capital 18–29 (1964).

vestment unless the wage rate is readjusted upward. Becker's solution of a sharing of the costs and benefits of the specific investment via an initial lump-sum payment by the employee and a later higher-than-market wage does not eliminate the bilateral opportunistic bargaining problem, because the employer may later decrease the wage back to the competitive level (or the employee may demand a higher wage to appropriate the partial specific investment by the employer). If it is assumed that employers will not cheat or break contracts in this way, then the efficient solution would be to merely have the employee make the entire specific investment (and therefore have the optimal quit rate), because the employer can costlessly "guarantee" (by assumption) a higher wage reflecting the increased productivity of the firm. But, more generally, to obtain an equilibrium solution to the problem, the costs of creating credibility of contract fulfillment and the costs of enforcing contracts must be explicitly considered.

One of the costs of using an explicit contract which relies on governmental or other outside arbitration for enforcement—rather than on an implicit contract which relies on depreciation of the value of a firm's brand name (that is, the loss of future premium payments)—is the likely increase in rigidity. For example, the difficulty of specifying all contingencies in labor contracts and of adjusting to unanticipated conditions is likely to lead to wage rigidity. Because contractual changes tend to create suspicion regarding the purpose of the contract alteration and, in particular, raise the question of whether a firm is using the changed conditions as an opportunity to seize some of the specific quasi rents, long-term labor contracts may consist of rigid wages and layoff provisions. If in the face of declining demand, a firm must keep wages fixed and lay off workers rather than merely reduce wages, the incentive for it to opportunistically claim a false reduction in demand is substantially reduced.[39]

39. This argument is distinct from the recent argument for the existence of rigid long-term implicit labor contracts as a means of bearing risk. See, for example, D. F. Gordon, "A Neo-Classical Theory of Keynesian Unemployment," 12 *Econ. Inquiry* 431 (Dec. 1974); and Costas Azariadis, "Implicit Contracts and Underemployment Equilibria," 83 *J. Pol. Econ.* 1183 (1975). We should also note that although Masamori Hashimoto, "Wage Reduction, Unemployment, and Specific Human Capital," 13 *Econ. Inquiry* 485 (Dec. 1975), has correctly argued that cyclically flexible wages are more likely when specific human capital is present, because both workers and employers will want to minimize the likelihood of job separation and thereby protect future returns on the specific human-capital investment, he ignores the contrary effect of increased specific human capital increasing the potential for opportunistic cheating and therefore increasing wage rigidity. The net

The fear of opportunistic behavior leads to price (and often also output) rigidity in all kinds of long-term explicit contracts where specific capital is present. This, in turn, leads to the creation of institutions to encourage increased flexibility in the face of changing market conditions. For example, the prime-rate convention, an announced benchmark in terms of which interest rates of corporate bank loans are stated, may be partially rationalized as a cheap means by which the bank can convey information to borrowers that the bank is not opportunistically raising interest fees to a particular customer. A corporate client who has made a specific investment in the supply of information to the bank regarding its credit worthiness (including its financial record of transactions with the bank) creates some appropriable quasi rents. However, when the price of the loan is stated as, say, prime plus one per cent, unless the bank decides to cheat all customers simultaneously and thereby limit new business, an individual customer can clearly distinguish between general market movements in interest rates and any changes the bank decides to make in the particular customer's credit rating. "Price protection" clauses in contracts, where a price decrease to any customer is guaranteed to be given to all customers, may be explained on similar grounds.

These information-cost-reducing institutions, including the use of impartial arbitrators, are highly imperfect. Therefore contracts involving specific assets, even where a price is not explicitly fixed long term, will consequently involve some price rigidity. The macroeconomic implications of this observation (for example, the employment effects of aggregate nominal demand shocks) are obvious.[40] But the interaction of macroeconomic considerations and industrial organization may not be that obvious. In particular, an increase in the variance of price-level movements, which increases the expected costs to both

---

theoretical effect is indeterminate. One possible reason that high-ranking corporate executives with a great deal of specific human capital appear to have highly flexible wages is because of the large amount of information about the firm they possess and therefore the shorter lag in detecting opportunism.

40. The recent "rational-expectations" approach to business cycles, which relies on consumer and producer uncertainty regarding whether a particular demand shock is a relative or an aggregate shift (see, for example, Robert E. Lucas, Jr., "Some International Evidence on Output-Inflation Tradeoffs," 63 *Am. Econ. Rev.* 326 [1973]), implicitly assumes economic agents do not observe current movements of money supply and price level. A more realistic assumption is that economic agents are not "fooled," especially over long periods, about the nature of the shock but rather are bound, either explicitly or implicitly, by long-term contracts that have previously fixed prices.

parties of price rigidity and thereby increases the acceptable degree of price flexibility, also makes it easier for a firm to cheat by opportunistically raising its price. Increased price uncertainty is therefore likely to lead to increased vertical integration.

Where more trust is present and implicit rather than explicit contracts are used, contract prices including wages are likely to be more flexible. If the variance of the price level increases—which makes it more difficult to detect opportunistic behavior and therefore the short-run gains from such cheating—the equilibrium implicit contract will imply a larger premium stream. The interesting question is what are the economic determinants of the implicit relative to explicit contracting costs which will in turn determine the degree of price flexibility.

One determinant of implicit contracting costs is the anticipated growth of demand for the firm's product. The more rapidly demand is expected to grow, the more likely a firm will rely on an implicit contract with its customers. Creating trust is cheaper for firms facing rapid demand growth compared with firms with stable or declining demand, because the loss of future business by customer termination if the firm is found to be cheating implies a relatively larger cost. Therefore a smaller current premium payment is necessary to assure nonopportunistic behavior. Hence the higher the anticipated growth in demand for a firm, the lower the contracting cost of using implicit relative to explicit contracts and the more flexible prices and other contract terms set by the firm can be expected to be.[41]

The cost to a growing firm of cheating on laborers, for example, would be

41. A crucial determinant of economic organization is therefore the anticipated demand growth compared with the actual demand growth, or the demand growth anticipated at the time of contract and the demand growth actually experienced and therefore anticipated at some later time. For example, one possible reason for the recent movement by oil-refining companies towards vertically integrated retail-marketing operations may be the increased cost of controlling franchised dealers due to the large decrease in the anticipated growth of demand for gasoline in the period since the large OPEC-initiated price increase of crude oil. With demand growing slower than originally anticipated, the initial equilibrium "premium" earned by dealers will now be less than necessary to assure their noncheating behavior. The anticipated decrease in the total number of dealers (that is, the fact that future demand is anticipated to be zero for many dealers in the new equilibrium) will create last-period problems for particular locations that can be largely avoided by employee-operated outlets. See Benjamin Klein & Keith Leffler, *supra* note 16, for a more complete discussion of these issues.

higher in terms of the future increased wages (of increased employment) it would have to pay if it cheated. The penalty for not relying on the firm's brand name is then more effective. This may explain why firms such as International Business Machines appear to have highly flexible labor compensation arrangements that are, in fact, quite similar to Japanese wage payments, which consist of large, highly variable, biannual bonuses. Our analysis suggests that it is not because of different cultural values that Japanese labor relations rely on much trust, but because the high growth rate of future demand makes it relatively cheap for firms to behave in this way.[42]

D. *Leasing Inputs and Ownership of the Firm*

Examination of leasing companies should reveal that leases are less common (or too expensive) for assets with specialized quasi rents that could be appropriated by the lessee or lessor. Leasing does not occur in the obvious cases of elevators or the glass of windows in an office building where postinvestment bilaterally appropriable quasi rents are enormous, while the furniture in the building is often rented. In banks, the safe is owned by the bank, but computers (though not the memory discs) are sometimes rented.[43] Though this may seem like resorting to trivialities, the fact that such leasing arrangements are taken for granted merely corroborates the prior analysis.

The standard example of leasing arrangements occurs with transportation capital, such as the planes, trucks, or cars used by a firm. This capital is generally easily movable and not very specific. But leasing arrangements are far from universal, because some of this capital can be quite specific and quasi rents appropriated. For example, early American steam locomotives were specialized to operating conditions such as high speed, hill climbing, short hauls, heavy loads,

---

42. Walter Galenson & Konosuke Odaka, "The Japanese Labor Market," in *Asia's New Giant* 587 (Hugh Patrick & Henry Rosovsky, eds., 1976); and Koji Taira, *Economic Development and the Labor Market in Japan* (1970), both documented the fact that this highly flexible wage feature of Japanese labor contracts did not become widespread until the postwar period, a time of extremely rapid growth.

43. In addition to computers being less specific and hence possessing smaller appropriable quasi rents than elevators, firms (for example, IBM) that supply computers generally possess extremely valuable brand names per unit of current sales due to a large anticipated growth in demand. Since there are some quasi rents associated with the use of a computer by a bank that could possibly be appropriated by threat of immediate removal, we would expect that if rental contracts existed they would more likely be with highly credible firms with high anticipated demand growth.

sharp corners, as well as types of coal for fuel. Slight differences in engines created significant differences in operating costs. High specialization made it desirable for the rail companies to own locomotives (as well as the land on which water was available for steam). The advent of the more versatile, less specialized diesel locomotive enabled more leasing and equipment trust financing. Similarly, Swift, the meat packer and innovator of the refrigerator car for transporting slaughtered beef, owned the specialized refrigerator cars it used.[44]

On the other hand, some capital may be quite specific to other assets in a firm's productive process and yet leased rather than owned. These cases provide useful insights into the nature of the contracting costs underlying our analysis. For example, consider the fact that agricultural land, a highly specific asset, is not always owned but often is rented. Land rented for farming purposes is typically for annual crops, like vegetables, sugar beets, cotton, or wheat, while land used for tree crops, like nuts, dates, oranges, peaches, apricots, or grape vines—assets that are highly specialized to the land—is usually owned by the party who plants the trees or vines.[45] However, long-term rental arrangements even for these "specialized asset" crops are not entirely unknown.

It is instructive to recognize why land-rental contracts, rather than vertical integration, can often be used without leading to opportunistic behavior. The primary reason is because it is rather cheap to specify and monitor the relevant contract terms (the quality of the good being purchased) and to enforce this particular rental contract. In addition, the landowner generally cannot impose a cost on the farmer by pulling the asset out or reducing the quality of the asset during the litigation process. Note the contrast with labor rental, where it is essentially impossible to effectively specify and enforce quality elements (for example, all working conditions and the effort expended by workers) and where

44. The great bulk of all refrigerator cars is not owned by the railroads, but rather by shipper-users such as packers and dairy companies. See Robert S. Henry, *This Fascinating Railroad Business* 247 (1942).

45. While 25 per cent of vegetable and melon farms in California in 1974 were fully owned by the farm operator, 82 per cent of fruit and nut tree farms were fully owned, a significantly different ownership proportion at the 99 per cent confidence interval. Similarly, the ownership proportions of cash grain and cotton farms were 40 per cent and 39 per cent, respectively, both also significantly different at the 99 per cent confidence interval from the proportions of fruit and nut tree farm ownership. See 1 U.S. Dep't of Commerce, Bureau of the Census, *1974 Census of Agriculture, State and County Data*, pt. 5, at tab. 28. "Summary by Tenure of Farm Operator and Type of Organization," id., 1974, California, pp. 1-29 to 1-30.

the possibility of withdrawal by strike or lockout is real and costly. Therefore, we do observe firms making highly specific investments in, for example, trees or buildings on land they do not own but only rent long term.[46] This is because credible postcontractual opportunistic threats by the landowner are not possible. However, if the landowner can vary the quality of the land, for example, by controlling the irrigation system to the crops or the electricity supply to a building, then a significant possibility of postinvestment opportunistic behavior exists, and we would therefore expect vertical integration.[47]

One specific asset that is almost always owned by the firm is its trade-name or brand-name capital and, in particular, the logo it uses to communicate to consumers. If this asset were rented from a leasing company, the problems would be obvious. The firm would be extremely hesitant to make any investments to build up its goodwill, for example, by advertising or by successful performance, because such investments are highly specific to that "name." The quasi rents could be appropriated by the leasing company through increases in the rental fee for the trade name. Not only would the firm not invest in this specific asset, but there would be an incentive for the firm to depreciate a valuable rented brand name. Although these problems seem insurmountable, rental of the capital input of a firm's brand name is not entirely unknown. In fact, franchisors can be thought of as brand-name leasing companies. A franchisee is fundamentally a renter of the brand-name capital (and logo) owned by the franchisor. Because of the specific capital problems noted above, direct controls are placed on franchisee behavior. The rental payment is usually some form of profit-sharing arrangement and, although the franchisee is legally considered to be an independent firm, the situation is in reality much closer to vertical integration than to the standard contractual relationship of the independent market.

46. Rental terms may be related to sales of the firm using the land in order to share the risk of real-value changes and to reduce the risk of nominal land-value changes involved with a long-term contract.

47. Coase's example of a monopolist selling more of a durable good, say land, after initially selling a monopoly quantity at the monopoly price is analytically identical to the problem of postcontractual opportunistic behavior. Existing contractual relationships indicate, however, that the land case may be relatively easy to solve, because it may not be expensive to make a credible contract regarding the remaining land. But one of Coase's indicated solutions, the short-term rental rather than sale of the land, is unlikely because it would discourage specific (to land) investments by the renter (such as building a house, developing a farm, and so forth) for fear of appropriation. See R. H. Coase, "Durability and Monopoly," 15 J. Law & Econ. 143 (1972).

Finally, the analysis throws light on the important question of why the owners of a firm (the residual claimants) are generally also the major capitalists of the firm.[48] As we have seen, owners may rent the more generalized capital but will own the firm's specific capital. This observation has implications for recent discussions of "industrial democracy," which fail to recognize that although employees may own and manage a firm (say, through their union), they will also have to be capitalists and own the specific capital. It will generally be too costly, for example, for the worker-owners to rent a plant, because such a specific investment could be rather easily appropriated from its owners after it is constructed. Therefore it is unlikely to be built. A highly detailed contractual arrangement together with very large brand-name premium payments by the laborers would be necessary to assure nonopportunistic behavior. This is generally too expensive an alternative and explains why capitalists are usually the owners of a firm.[49]

E. *Social Institutions*

Much of the previous analysis has dealt with tangible capital. Contractual arrangements involving such assets are often cheaper than complete vertical integration, even when the assets are highly specific (for example, the land-rental case). As the discussion on human capital suggests, however, when the specific assets involved are intangible personal assets, the problems of contract enforcement become severe. In addition, when the number of individuals involved (or the extent of the specific capital) becomes very large, ownership arrangements often become extremely complex.

48. We are grateful to Earl Thompson for discerning this implication.

49. Armen A. Alchian & Harold Demsetz, "Production, Information Costs, and Economic Organization," 62 *Am. Econ. Rev.* 777 (1972), claim that if the owner of the firm also owns the firm's capital, it supplies evidence that he can pay for rented inputs, including labor. This appears to be incorrect, since the owner could supply credibility by using some of his assets completely unrelated to the production process, such as treasury bonds, for collateral. Michael C. Jensen & William H. Meckling, "On the Labor-Managed Firm and the Codetermination Movement" (Feb. 1977, unpublished manuscript), emphasize the costs of monitoring managerial performance and the maintenance of rented capital, and the problems of efficiently allocating risks in a pure-rental firm. They also note that it is "impossible" for a firm to rent all the productive capital assets, because many of them are intangible and therefore "it is impossible to repossess the asset if the firm refused to pay the rental fee" (*id.* at 20). This argument is similar to our analysis of opportunistic behavior. However, rather than asserting that such rentals are impossible, we would merely recognize the extremely high contracting costs generally present in such situations. More importantly, we claim that such an argument also extends to the rental of tangible specific capital.

For example, consider country clubs. Golf country clubs are social, as well as golfing, organizations. Sociability of a country club involves substantial activities away from the golf course: dinners, dances, parties, cards, games, and general social activities with friends who are members of the club. However, some golf courses are operated with very few social activities for the set of members and their families. The social clubs (usually called "country clubs") are mutually owned by the members, whereas golf courses with virtually no off-course social activity often are privately owned, with members paying daily golf fees without owning the golf course.

Mutual ownership is characteristic of the social country club because the specialized quasi rent of friendship is collected by each member whose friendship is specialized to the other members. The members' behavior towards one another constitutes an investment in forming valuable friendships, a congenial milieu, and rapport among the members. Each member has invested in creating that congenial milieu and atmosphere specialized to the other members. And its value could be stolen or destroyed by opportunistic behavior of a party authorized to admit new members.

To see how, suppose the club were owned by someone other than the members. Once the membership value is created by the interpersonal activities of the members, the owner of the club could then start to raise the fees for continuing members. Assuming some costs of the members moving away en masse and forming a new club, the owner could expropriate by higher fees some of the specialized quasi-rent value of the sociability created by the members' specialization to each other in their own group. Alternatively, the owner could threaten to break the implicit contract and destroy some of the sociability capital by selling admission to "undesirable" people who want to consort with the existing members.

Similarly, if the social country club were owned by the members as a corporation, with each member owning a share of stock salable without prior approval of existing members (as is the case for the business corporation), a single member could, by threatening to sell to an "undesirable" potential member, extract some value of congeniality from the current members as a payment for not selling.[50]

An extreme case of this general problem is a marriage. If each mate had a

---

50. The "free-rider" problems of bribing an opportunistic member to prevent sale to an "undesirable" member are obvious. This analysis could be applied to social clubs such as Elks, Masonic Order, and so forth.

transferable share salable to a third party, there would be far fewer marriages with highly specific investments in affection and children. If a relationship is not one of specialized interest (specialized to a particular other party) or if it required no investment by any member, then the marriage relationship would be more like a corporation. As it is one of highly specific investments, a marriage has historically been a mutually owned entity, with permission of both parties generally required for alteration of membership. Government arbitration of this relationship to prevent postinvestment opportunistic behavior by either party can contribute towards lower bargaining costs and investments of resources (recoverable dowries) by both parties to improve their respective postinvestment bargaining positions, and, most importantly, create confidence that opportunistic behavior will not be successful. The legislative movement to "no-fault" divorce suggests that modern marriages may have less specific assets than formerly.[51]

The importance of mobility costs when many individuals in a group must jointly decide to take action, as in the case of an opportunistic country-club owner, and the importance of government intervention are clearly reflected in the case of the money-supply industry.[52] The decision regarding what is used as the dominant money (medium of exchange) in society, like many other social agreements and customs, entails a large degree of rigidity on the individual level. A decision to change a social institution, in this case what is used as money, must involve a large subset of the population to be effective. Given this natural monopoly, the cost to an individual or a new entrant of attempting change may be prohibitively costly. Therefore, once a dominant money supplier is established, the potential wealth gain that can be realized through op-

51. Similarly, people whose work is highly specialized to each other will be partners (common ownership). For example, attorneys that have become highly specialized to their coattorneys will become partners, whereas new associates will at first be employees. A small team of performers (Laurel and Hardy, Sonny and Cher) who were highly specialized to each other would be "partners" (co-owners) rather than employee and employer. While it is still difficult to enforce such contracts and prevent postcontractual opportunistic behavior by either party, joint ownership creates an incentive for performance and specific investment not present in an easily terminable employer-employee contract that must rely solely on the personal brand-name reputation of contracting parties. Trust, including the reputation of certifying institutions such as theatrical agents, law schools, and so on, and the presence of social sanctions against opportunistic partners remain important.

52. The following discussion extends the analysis in Benjamin Klein, *supra* note 16.

portunistic behavior by the money issuer (that is, by unanticipated inflation) is enormous. The private implicit contractual solution would therefore entail an extremely high brand-name "premium" payment (seigniorage return) to guarantee that a wealth-maximizing, unregulated, private dominant money supplier will not cheat by increasing the money supply faster than anticipated. Because this premium payment and therefore the rental price of money will be so high, it is unlikely that a private, implicit contractual solution is the cheapest arrangement.[53] Traditional vertical integration would also be extremely costly in this case of a consumer asset used by so many individuals (in fact it is difficult to even understand exactly what it would mean). Some form of government intervention is obviously likely, either in the form of regulation by enforcing an explicit contractual guarantee, or in the form of outright nationalization. Government ownership of the monetary unit is actually close to what one may consider vertical integration on the part of consumers in this particular case.

iv. Concluding Comment

We should emphasize in conclusion that most business relationships are neither likely to be as simple as the standard textbook polar cases of vertical integration or market contract nor as easily explained as some of the above examples. When particular examples are examined in detail, business relationships are often structured in highly complex ways not represented either by a simple rental contract or by simple vertical integration. A timely example is the

---

53. The alternative cost of holding money will be significantly above the marginal cost of producing cash balances (where costs are defined exclusive of the costs necessary to guarantee nonopportunistic behavior), thereby leading to less than "the optimum" quantity of cash balances. See, for example, Milton Friedman, "The Optimum Quantity of Money," in *The Optimum Quantity of Money and Other Essays* 1 (1969), for the original statement of this supposed inefficiency.

An alternative solution analytically equivalent to the "premium" solution would be the putting up by the dominant money supplier of a large forfeitable collateral bond equal to the value of the possible short-run wealth gain from cheating. This bond would be held in part by each of the demanders of the firm's money in proportion to each particular individual's money holdings, and interest received on the bond by each individual would be paid to the firm if cheating did not occur. While this would not create any inefficiencies of price greater than marginal cost as implied by the premium solution, the transaction costs of enforcing such an arrangement among such a large and changing number of individuals would be extremely high. If the government acted as the consumers' agent, the solution would now be similar to a regulated industry, with the potential for opportunistic expropriation of the bond by the government.

ownership rights of common services supplied in condominium or "new-town" projects. One solution often adopted is joint ownership of common assets, similar to the joint ownership by petroleum producers and refiners of oil pipeline as noted above. In the condominium case, however, the number of shareowners is sometimes equal to hundreds or even thousands of individuals, and the resulting contractual arrangements are closer to a constitution for a local "government" than to the simple paradigm of a two-person market transaction. When governing costs are high, individuals have often opted for a long-term management contract (often with the builder of the housing project) for maintaining the common assets. The possible problems associated with the opportunistic appropriation by the manager of the quasi rents in specialized assets of the individual owners (including specific assets used to furnish each apartment such as carpeting and any specific "friendship capital" from association with other owner occupants) are obvious. The fact that there has been a great deal of litigation in this area is not surprising. The difficulty may be partially due to what appear to be significant economies of scale in supplying confidence concerning contract performance and diseconomies of scale in the actual production and management of housing. Some insurance or franchising arrangement may therefore evolve in this area.

There is a continuing search in this difficult area using market and governmental (regulatory, legislative, and judicial) processes to produce institutional and private contractual innovation that will lead to more economical contractual relations and ownership rights. We have little idea why one solution appears to have been efficient for one condominium project and another solution for another project. This merely indicates that as we move towards more complex ownership relationships the problem of efficiently structuring the economic relationship, either within the firm or via contracts, also becomes highly complex. Stating that the world is complicated is another way of admitting our ignorance. However, explicitly recognizing that contracting costs are not zero, as they are often implicitly assumed to be in economic analysis, and explicitly considering the determinants of these costs (such as the presence of appropriable quasi rents) are the first steps in explaining the large variety of contractual and ownership arrangements we observe in the real world.

More generally, we have seen that once we attempt to add empirical detail to Coase's fundamental insight that a systematic study of transaction costs is necessary to explain particular forms of economic organization, we find that his primary distinction between transactions made within a firm and transactions made in the marketplace may often be too simplistic. Many long-term contractual relationships (such as franchising) blur the line between the market and the firm. It may be more useful to merely examine the economic rationale for different types of particular contractual relationships in particular situations and consider the firm as a particular kind or set of interrelated contracts.[54] Firms are therefore, by definition, formed and revised in markets, and the conventional sharp distinction between markets and firms may have little general analytical importance. The pertinent economic question we are faced with is, What kinds of contracts are used for what kinds of activities, and why?

54. If we think of firms as collections of interrelated contracts rather than the collection of goods operative in the contracts, the question of who "owns" the firm (the set of contracts) appears somewhat nonsensical. It may be useful to think solely of a set of claimants to various portions of the value consequences of the contractual coalition, with no "owner" of the firm.

FIRST NEGOTIATION, FIRST REFUSAL RIGHTS

ARMEN A. ALCHIAN, BENJAMIN KLEIN,

AND EARL A. THOMPSON

Some contracts contain options to one of the parties wherein that party may at some future time select one of a set of options that the other party will have to perform. Some contracts are virtually entirely options, such as financial "puts" and "calls." In other cases, one party has the right to decide whether or not to renew an employment or rental contract at prespecified terms, or an option to have "first refusal" rights to preempt a third-party offer. In some cases one party has the "right of approval" of some action, e.g., to whom a sale of common stock or transfer of membership in a country club may be made. "First negotiation, first refusal" is an example of a compound option held by one party against the other. In these cases one of the parties has committed itself to the obligation to perform whichever of the alternative actions is selected or acceptable to the other party. People bind themselves or restrict their future actions only because they are paid enough to do so.

In what circumstances are such options or constraints useful? Aside from the puts and calls of the financial markets, which are easily explainable as bets on the price of the asset against which a put or call is sold, why are these constraints useful in labor contracts, for example? What is a general explanation? Why would a prospective buyer pay a prospective seller to promise to return to the first prospective buyer, when a rational seller would want to return and give a chance to bid again? However, as we shall see, this conception of "rational" is too narrow. The seller can engage in "opportunistic" behavior and rationally *refuse* to return.

Opportunistic behavior can be rational. It has been expounded by Williamson. Applications of the analysis to some practical situations have been indicated by Goldberg, and Klein, Crawford, and Alchian. Commitments as a means of avoiding the problem have been illustrated by Schelling. A more rig-

This previously unpublished, undated article appears here by permission of the author.

orous, general theory of commitment to overcome anticipated bargaining problems about future renewals or contract prices has been attempted by Thompson and Faith.[1]

1. Why First Refusal Rights?

First refusal rights are stipulated constraints on renewals of contracts. A party has the right of first refusal on the asset sale of another if he has an option to buy the asset at any price offered the seller by third parties. Assume one party, here called the "incumbent employer," is contemplating making an investment jointly specific to that employer and an employee. By "jointly specific" we mean the investment enhances the value of the team of the employer and employee above the sum of what their values would be if they subsequently are separated and used in their next best options.

Consider a simple example. "Incumbent employer" makes an investment of $4; as a result some employee becomes worth $20 to the employer, while the employee is worth only $15 elsewhere. The resulting investment value is *specific* to the investor-employer. Assume also that the contract binding the two expires before this difference disappears. (We'll explore later why the contract is not sufficiently long-lived.) At the time for renewal, the employer-investor wants to pay only $15 in order to protect his $5 investment value.

The key idea is that the employee could engage in an opportunistic tactic if he could *commit* himself to leave and work elsewhere unless paid more than $15.00, i.e., unless he is paid some of the quasi-rents of the specific asset financed by the investor. Suppose the employee could, for example, have irrevocably *committed* himself to accept an outside offer for $15.01 unless the incumbent employer offered, say, $19.50. If this irrevocable commitment were made prior to any countervailing blocking commitment by the incumbent employer, the incumbent employer would have no better option than to pay the $19.50. Since the employee has *committed* to going elsewhere unless he receives $19.50, the employer will certainly lose $4.50 of the $5.00 quasi-rent invest-

1. Oliver E. Williamson, *Markets and Hierarchies: Analysis and Antitrust Implications* (New York: Free Press, 1975); Victor P. Goldberg, "Regulation and Administered Contracts," *Bell Journal of Economics and Management Science* 7, no. 2 (1976): 426–48; Benjamin Klein, Robert G. Crawford, and Armen A. Alchian, "Vertical Integration, Appropriable Rents, and the Competitive Contracting Process," *Journal of Law and Economics* 21 (October 1978): 297–326; Thomas C. Schelling, *Micromotives and Macrobehavior* (New York: W. W. Norton, 1978); Earl A. Thompson and Roger Faith, "A Pure Theory of Strategic Behavior and Social Institutions," *American Economic Review* 71, no. 3 (1981): 366–80.

ment value if he refuses but will retain $0.50 if he agrees to pay $19.50 (and holds his loss to $4.50). The employee would have expropriated $4.50 of the $5.00 employer investment value. The employee would be willing, if necessary, to have incurred costs of up to $4.49 to make that preemptive commitment.

If the employer had to earlier devote any significant resources (up to $5.00) to blocking the possibility of the employee's commitment tactic, then his original investment would have been less valuable. (Since the employee is willing to devote up to $4.99 to making his commitment first [to $19.99], it does not seem likely that any less expensive commitment by the employer would be enough to beat out the employee.) And therefore without a low-cost prior commitment or action by the employer that blocks the employee's attempt to expropriate that investment value, the efficient investment by an employer would be dissuaded. Nor would the employee finance the initial investment himself without a similar shield against an employer's attempt to opportunistically extract the investment value from the employee. Potentially profitable investments would be precluded by these problems.

A first refusal right held by the investor (here, the employer) prevents an employee bargaining commitment, since the incumbent investor can always preempt the employee from any challenger and thereby prevent an effective employee commitment. The employer avoids the bargaining problems without a fight, and the efficient investment becomes profitable.

The initial contracts could not contain enforceable renewal prices that would eliminate the threat of opportunistic behavior if the following three conditions are present: (1) *Present uncertainty as to the performance and future value* of an investment (else it would be put into the contract), (2) the fact that at the future time the inputs will be *unique*—i.e., not objectively priced by virtually identical or proportionally priced substitutable inputs (else that future discoverable value could be used in the contract renewal), and (3) *specificity* between the assets as a result of the earlier investment (else there would be no expropriable quasi-rent). The combination of these three features creates a potential for (a) consuming resources in opportunistic bargaining and (b) expropriating wealth of an investor, or (c) dissuading such investments in the first place.

Though we initially assumed the contract between the two parties expired before the expropriable quasi-rent disappeared, we could have alluded to any situation with an expropriable quasi-rent. At any time during a contract, the party to whom the other's resources are specific could threaten to withhold adequate services, thereby destroying some of the asset's value, unless the specific asset investor agreed to share some of the quasi-rent with the expropriator. If the controllable services were clearly and cheaply identifiable in contractual form and enforceable, opportunistic behavior could contractually be controlled. But, as is very commonly the case with personal services, contractual provisions would be ineffective. Instead an alternative means, such as the refusal, negotiation, and approval clauses, may be helpful. Incidentally, if *both* parties to the arrangement provided each other with controllable specializing services that were not contractually specifiable, these clauses would be of no value, and instead possibly common ownership of both parties' services would be required—if possible.

ii. Why First Negotiations?

First negotiation, first refusal rights (FN/FR) limit the right to preempt only those third-party offers that are less favorable than the renewal price asked by the seller during renegotiation and refused, at that time, by the first party. (The appendix gives a typical FN/FR contractual clause.)

FN/FR clauses are almost universal in television network contracts, which are typically five-year licenses to exhibit a series of shows created by some producer. The contract provides that at the end of five years the network has FN/FR rights to subsequently produced episodes of the show. If the network rejects the producer's asking price, the producer may then look for other buyers of his program or services. If another buyer proposes an *acceptable* price *below* that asked of, and refused by, the network, the network has the right to match and preempt that offer. If the network exercises that right, the producer and the network have a new contract at the terms proposed by the third-party offerer. Another example is in tenant leases, where the tenant has FN/FR rights against the building owner when a lease expires.

Suppose it is anticipated that the seller's (employee's) services *may* become more valuable at some future date to a *different* buyer. For example, in the above case, the value of the employee to alternative employers may jump from $15 to $25 near the end of the five-year contract. In this case the employee would want to terminate the contract or not renew it. To avoid the bargaining costs of buying the old employer out of an excessively long contract, the initial contract is written to automatically expire at the end of five years.

First refusal rights at contract renewal time (absent first negotiation) are sufficient for the situation in which the employee's *alternative* value *stayed* at $15, even though his value with the employer who made the investment is $20. But in the case where the alternative wage increased to above $15, the employer could opportunistically use his first refusal rights to delay or hinder the employee's ability to respond to or attract competing offers, and reduce the employee's attractiveness to the new buyer to below $20. This is true if seeking new buyers or employers and getting them to make offers is not costless. The first refusal right held against the employee-seller would then be an albatross. However, with the *first negotiation* clause combined with the first refusal right, the employee is protected. The reason is that the employee and employer must first negotiate for renewal. In the event of nonagreement, the employee records his lowest refused asking price, and if he later acquires an offer above this refused asking price from a challenger, he may accept it, because the incumbent employer has *no* right of first refusal of such offers. The employer cannot sabotage a *superior* competing offer.

Absent FN/FR clauses, otherwise avoidable bargaining costs are a constraint on the willingness to make specific investments in the seller's resources. The clause provides gains to both parties. It avoids bargaining costs that would occur if the seller could make commitments that enabled him to acquire the quasi-rent from the buyer's specific investments in the seller. The seller, who forsakes his opportunity to engage in subsequent opportunist attempts to expropriate specific quasi-rents, is rewarded with a higher contractual pay, an increase payable from the savings of costs that would otherwise have been incurred in the battle of renegotiation or from the returns to specific investments that would otherwise have been precluded by the high bargaining cost.

III. Who Acquires First Negotiation, First Refusal Rights?

In general, the party making the specializing investment in the combination will be the party desiring FN/FR rights to protect the specific expropriable quasi-rent of his investment from expropriation by the other party. In the above TV and tenant examples, the buyers or employer (networks) or the tenant who made the specializing investment received the rights. Whoever finances the specializing investment will receive FN/FR rights.

The possibility of *both* parties making substantial "interspecific" investments somewhat complicates the situation. In this case FN/FR is still beneficial in that it serves to cheaply *define* the rights to the quasi-rents of specific investments and to preclude future bargaining. To induce specific investments by the parties, *given these protective rights*, then would require special incentive payments. Thus, in the examples above, the seller may be the natural person to undertake certain specific investments. Say the worker is the only party who can observe his private sacrifices at improving himself for his specific job. If the buyer (or employer) initially receives the revenue from such investment, he will seek to reward and induce specific investments by the employee. Thus we observe that network contracts with employee-producers have substantial explicit bonus and incentive-payment features to induce the producers to make specific investments. Similarly, we observe tenants who obtain first refusal rights to lease renewals often contributing substantially to the owner's investments in the rented building—investments of value to the franchisee but specific to the building.

Along the same lines, franchisees may make investments in resources that are specialized to the franchisor, so if the franchisee is terminated, the franchisor retains the quasi-rent of the investment made by the franchisee. That is, of course, the common fear of every franchisee who contemplates making investments specialized to the franchisor. Presumably franchisees are made of indefinite life, not requiring renewal, but terminable only for "good cause," i.e., not in order to engage in opportunistic behavior. But the possibility the franchisee wants to sell out must be contemplated. In that case, the franchisor wants to avoid a new franchisee who would free ride on the franchisor's value. First refusal rights protect the franchisor from undesired or uncongenial replacements and, contrary to "right of approval," will not subject the franchisee to the threat of opportunistic exploitation of any franchisor-specific quasi-rent investments made by the franchisee. Each party would ideally like to have rights to protect the quasi-rents of its investments.

If both parties are making investments it is awkward to give FN/FR rights to just one of the parties, and it is difficult (impossible?) to assign separate FN/FR rights to different investment values. For example, a network might make investments in enhancing the value of the series produced jointly with some writer and actor. At the same time, the writer and actor may make some investments that enhance the value of the coalition. In this case all the members invest in a coalition value that exceeds what each could get elsewhere. But since the investments were made by different people, the FN/FR rights should ideally be assigned to each party with respect to the renegotiation of the particular asset in which that party invested. This is not an easy task. In the network series case, the networks have found ways to encourage the writer-actors to make investments that are specific to the program. Substantial bonuses and incentive payments are made to the writer-actor as rewards to induce the investment. The bonus or incentive payments may be considered advance purchases by the network of the investment value. Similarly, we observe tenants making investments in a building, an investment of value to the building owner even if the tenant should leave. Some system of side payments or rent allowances must be used as adjuncts to induce that kind of investment that the building owner himself could not make as well as could the tenant.

IV. The Role of Commitment

We review by asking why a buyer would demand first refusal rights when any "rational" seller would return to him with any outside offer and allow him to match it. It is obvious now that that is too narrow a view of rational action. As we have seen, it is *rational* for an initially unfettered seller to attempt to obtain a price above his lowest supply price by committing himself to accepting from a third-party buyer a lower price than asked of the current trading partner unless the supplier's price asked of the current buyer is met. That commitment irrevocably limits his trading partner's options. It is rational to execute this behavior, because limiting one's options limits the trading partner's options to those more favorable to the committer. This is a rational individual strategy as long as it affects the strategies or options of his trading partner in a sufficiently desirable fashion.

The prevalence of FN/FR reveals the extent of opportunities for commitments in the bargaining process to protect expropriable quasi-rents. Avoiding the devotion of substantial resources to attempting expropriative commitments, and, probably more important, removing obstacles to the willingness to invest in creating "specific" wealth are the reasons for expropriation-avoiding clauses such as FN/FR. Both the use of resources to make commitments and also the discouragement of investments are called the "costs" of bargaining.

Summarizing, uncertainty about alternative future values (else the contract would not have to be renegotiated or renewed) with specificity of one input to the other (else there would be no expropriable quasi-rent) and uniqueness of the input (else easy substitutability would prevent any ability to expropriate the quasi-rent) all deter otherwise profitable investments. FN/FR clauses help to overcome those obstacles. To overcome the side problem of one of the inputs later being worth more elsewhere, that input can protect himself by conjoining the first negotiation clause to the first refusal clause.

V. Alternative Renewal Contracts

FN/FR is only one contractual arrangement that eliminates those bargaining costs that would otherwise occur in the above-mentioned situations, that is, (a) future values uncertain and (b) specific quasi-rents may be expropriable by "rational," i.e., "opportunistic," bargainers. The leasing of new automobiles is quite common without FN or FR clauses because of the relatively high likelihood of rapid subsequent resale or replacement by close substitutes. Similarly, in the leasing of new business equipment and commercial real estate or in the selling of part of the natural gas and oil reserves in a field to particular pipelines, renewal usually proceeds without the aid of FN or FR, because the availability of alternative sources of demand or supply guarantees the parties' option to renew at observed prices of obviously close available substitutes with low adjustment costs. For cars, business equipment, and commercial real estate, published indices of wholesale prices can be used to set renewal prices, and availability of substitutes at about the same costs eliminates the bargaining possibility. For oil and gas with *several* suppliers with resources specific to a single gathering pipeline system, the highest price paid by any pipeline in the area is a typical, publicly posted renewal price.

A common, posted price paid to *all* suppliers of gas or oil from one field to the gathering system in that field prevents opportunistic bargaining against any one particular supplier whose equipment is highly specific to the existing gathering system. To act opportunistically with respect to one supplier only would not be possible under a system of posted price, which requires that all suppliers be equally treated. Changing prices to *all* suppliers in a field with that intent would make the price less dependent on marketwide conditions and make the gatherer a less attractive party with whom to deal in the future. Posted prices in other industries are called "most favored nations" clauses. They protect any one party from opportunistic bargaining by the other party who deals with many parties. Yet such claims have been misinterpreted and condemned by the Federal Trade Commission agents as devices to ensure price-fixing—though how it achieves that has not been explained in the complaints.[2]

The Pre-renewal Adjustment of Existing Contract Prices

A related problem is the response of the contracting parties to changes occurring *within* the contract period in the *general* productivity (alternative user values) of the assets, i.e., changes in value that are the same with both existing and alternative users. An optimal response to such a general change does not entail a change in users, but it does require a price change in order to maintain efficient uses of resources. Here we should expect to find, and do indeed find, pre-renewal price revisions and adjustments. Entertainment producers regu-

2. E. I. *du Pont de Nemours & Co. v. FTC*, 729 F. 2d 128 (2d Cir. 1984).

larly revise contract prices when such *general*, alternative-use value variations occur, e.g., when union scales change.

Appendix

If the parties shall fail to agree, then immediately on the expiration of the Negotiating Period, (i) ABC will furnish to Contractor in writing the terms and conditions of at least one offer that ABC had made to Contractor, and (ii) Contractor shall furnish to ABC in writing the terms and conditions least favorable to Contractor that Contractor had offered to ABC with respect thereto. In that event, Contractor may, after the expiration of the Negotiating Period, make any agreement with respect thereto that shall not conflict with the terms of this Agreement; provided, however, that if during the period of one year following the expiration of the Negotiating Period, Contractor shall have the opportunity to make any such agreement with a third party on terms and conditions *less favorable to Contractor* than those referred to in subdivision (ii) of . . . this paragraph, then in any such instance Contractor shall promptly make a written offer to ABC that shall by its own terms be irrevocable for at least five (5) days (excluding Saturdays, Sundays and holidays) from the time of ABC's receipt thereof, to enter into such an agreement with ABC on the same terms and conditions as would be contained in such agreement with such third party.[3]

---

3. This appendix is reprinted from Richard L. Barovick, *Packaging for Television and Motion Pictures* (New York: Practising Law Institute, 1973), pp. 30–31, by permission of Richard L. Barovick. Emphasis added.

DECISION SHARING AND
EXPROPRIABLE SPECIFIC QUASI-RENTS
A THEORY OF *FIRST NATIONAL MAINTENANCE CORPORATION V. NLRB*

In First National Maintenance Corporation v. National Labor Relations Board,[1] the Supreme Court tried to resolve conflicting interpretations of the circuit courts[2] about the scope of an employer's duty (under the National Labor Relations Act, as amended[3]) to bargain in good faith "with respect to wages, hours, and other terms and conditions of employment." First National, a New York provider of commercial cleaning services, legally discontinued service to a customer, Greenpark Care Center, a nursing home in Brooklyn, because its costs were too high. First National had hired approximately 35 employees to render services exclusively to Greenpark. First National's employees are not transferred to other customers if a contract with a customer is terminated. The expenses of serving Greenpark exceeded the initially negotiated fee, so First National, as permitted under the contract, terminated services after negotiations to revise the fee had failed. In the meantime, the National Union of Hospital and Health Care Employees, Retail, Wholesale and Department Store Union, AFL-CIO (the union) successfully campaigned for recognition in an election among First National's Greenpark employees. Upon First National's notice to these employees that it was terminating service to Greenpark, and hence their employment status, the union agent requested a delay in termination "for the purpose of bargaining."[4] First National refused, contending that termination of the contract with Greenpark and the discharge of those employees was final.

Reprinted from *Supreme Court Economic Review* 1 (1982): 235–47; originally published by Macmillan. Copyright 1983 by the University of Chicago Press.

1. 452 U.S. 666 (1981).
2. See *infra* note 8.
3. 29 U.S.C. §§ 158(a)(5), 158(d) (1976).
4. 452 U.S. at 669.

The union claimed violation of the National Labor Relations Act sections 8(a)(1) and (5), which require a duty to bargain and negotiate in good faith with respect to wages, hours, and other terms and conditions of employment, with a certified employee representative. No union animus was charged. A National Labor Relations Board (NLRB) administrative law judge ruled for the union, saying in part,

> When an employer's work complement is represented by a union and he wishes to alter the hiring arrangements, be his reason lack of money or a mere desire to become richer, the law is no less clear that he must first talk to the union about it. . . . [S]omething might have been worked out to transfer these people. . . . [or to] have persuaded Greenpark to use these same employees to continue doing its maintenance work either as direct employees or as later hires by a replacement contractor.[5]

The NLRB adopted the administrative law judge's ruling and ordered First National to pay back-pay (from the date of discharge until agreement was reached) and to bargain with the union about the employment status of the employees servicing Greenpark. The NLRB also ordered First National to re-employ the discharged employees by discharging employees subsequently hired for other operations.

The Court of Appeals for the Second Circuit (with one judge dissenting) affirmed the NLRB order, arguing that section 8(d) of the Act creates a presumption for mandatory bargaining that is rebuttable if bargaining would be futile, if an emergency financial situation exists for the employer, or if the custom in the industry is not to bargain over such issues.[6] In short, the presumption in support of mandatory bargaining remains unless the employer can show "that the purpose of the statute would not be furthered by imposition of a duty to bargain."[7]

This appellate decision varied from those of some other circuit courts. In particular, as the Supreme Court noted,[8] in some circuits, duty to bargain did

5. 242 N.L.R.B. 462, 465 (1979).

6. NLRB v. First Nat'l Maintenance Corp., 627 F.2d 596, 601–602 (2d Cir. 1980).

7. Id. at 601.

8. The Supreme Court reviewed the circuit courts' holdings thus. The Second Circuit's view was as in NLRB v. First Nat'l Maintenance Corp., 627 F.2d 596 (2d Cir. 1980). The Sixth and Seventh Circuits agree with the Second. See Davis v. NLRB, 617 F.2d 1264, 1268–1270 (7th Cir. 1980) (change of full-service restaurant to self-service cafeteria held to be

not exist if management's decision involved complete closing rather than partial closing, or a "major commitment of capital investment," or a change in the scope or direction of the enterprise, or no union animus. Because of these variations among the circuits, as well as inconsistencies in NLRB rulings,[9] the Supreme Court granted *certiorari*.

The Court's majority, per Justice Blackmun, held that the decision to discharge employees hired solely for a particular customer was not included within the "terms of employment" and that the burden placed on an employer by requiring bargaining over shutting down a part of its business solely for economic reasons outweighs the benefits for labor-management relations and the

---

mandatory bargaining subject); NLRB v. *Production Molded Plastics, Inc.*, 604 F.2d 451, 453 (6th Cir. 1979) (plant closing held to require bargaining). In *Brockway Motor Trucks v. NLRB*, 582 F.2d 720, 731 (3d Cir. 1978), the Third Circuit agreed with the presumption of bargaining, but included a balancing of employer and employee interests as a way to rebut the presumption. See also *Equitable Gas Co. v. NLRB*, 637 F.2d 980, 982 (3d Cir. 1981) (subcontract not a mandatory subject of collective bargaining); *ABC TransNat'l Transp., Inc. v. NLRB*, 642 F.2d 675, 682 (3d Cir. 1981) (partial closing raises rebuttable presumption of mandatory bargaining); NLRB v. *Royal Plating & Polishing Co.*, 350 F.2d 191 (3d Cir. 1965) (partial closing). Other circuit courts do not require bargaining if capital investments or basic "operational changes" are included. See NLRB v. *Int'l Harvester Co.*, 618 F.2d 85, 87 (9th Cir. 1980); *Royal Typewriter Co. v. NLRB*, 533 F.2d 1030, 1039 (8th Cir. 1976); NLRB v. *Thompson Transp. Co.*, 406 F.2d 698, 703 (10th Cir. 1969); NLRB v. *Transmarine Navigation Corp.*, 380 F.2d 933, 939 (10th Cir. 1967); NLRB v. *Adams Dairy, Inc.*, 350 F.2d 108, 110–111 (8th Cir. 1965), *cert. denied*, 382 U.S. 1011 (1966); NLRB v. *Rapid Bindery, Inc.*, 293 F.2d 170, 172–176 (2d Cir. 1961). Still other circuit courts do not require bargaining unless there has been a partial closing involving an anti-union animus. See *Morrison Cafeterias Consol., Inc. v. NLRB*, 431 F.2d 254 (8th Cir. 1970); NLRB v. *Drapery Mfg. Co.*, 425 F.2d 1026 (8th Cir. 1970); NLRB v. *William J. Burns Int'l Detective Agency, Inc.*, 346 F.2d 897 (8th Cir. 1965). The Fifth Circuit finds a duty to bargain if partial closings are involved. See NLRB v. *Winn-Dixie Stores, Inc.*, 361 F.2d 512 (5th Cir.), *cert. denied*, 385 U.S. 935 (1966). For the Supreme Court's discernment in *First National* of the various conflicts among the circuits, see 452 U.S. at 672–674 & nn. 7–10.

9. The Court noted, 452 U.S. 666, 673 n.10 (1981), cases not requiring bargaining: *National Car Rental System, Inc.*, 252 N.L.R.B. 15 (1980) (employer's decision to terminate essentially economic); *Gen. Motors Corp.*, 191 N.L.R.B. 951 (1972), and *Summit Tooling Co.*, 195 N.L.R.B. 479 (1972) (decision to close a subsidiary takes respondent out of the business); and cases requiring bargaining: *Kingwood Mining Co.*, 210 N.L.R.B. 844 (1974), *aff'd sub nom. United Mine Workers v. NLRB*, 515 F.2d 1018 (D.C. Cir. 1975), and *Ozark Trailers, Inc.*, 161 N.L.R.B. 561 (1966) (closing down one of multiple plants).

collective bargaining process. Justices Brennan and Marshall, in dissent, argued, *inter alia*, that the NLRB, not the Supreme Court, should interpret the scope of employment terms subject to mandatory bargaining,[10] and furthermore, the majority weighing of the employer's burdens and the benefits to collective bargaining and labor-management relations fails to take the employees' interests into account.[11]

I argue here that the majority decision, though its rationale is not well articulated, is paradoxically consistent with the minority's appropriate, though ambiguously stated principle, and that it is the correct decision in the light of that principle. In particular, the minority's reference to the "interests of particular employees" could have been articulated more fully to reflect recent advances in understanding contractual relations.[12] Furthermore, the basic principle identified in these advances would provide reasonable criteria for the National Labor Relations Board or the courts to use in ascertaining the appropriateness of decision sharing. This essay explains that principle and applies it to the case.

I. Bargaining and Decision Sharing

The term-of-art meaning of conferring and bargaining is more than discussion and conferring in the exploration of possible acceptable initial contract terms—despite the Court's tendency at times to treat conferring and bargaining as no more than simple preliminary conversation.[13] The meaning is to "share in the decision process"—including revisions in terms and clauses of

10. 452 U.S. at 688, 691 (Brennan, J., dissenting).

11. *Id.* at 689–690.

12. See *infra* notes 15–16.

13. The Court in its decision quoted from an earlier important case: "Refusal to confer and negotiate has been one of the most prolific causes of strife. This is such an outstanding fact in the history of labor disturbances that it is a proper subject of judicial notice and requires no citation of instances." 452 U.S. at 674 n.11 (quoting *NLRB v. Jones & Laughlin Steel Corp.*, 301 U.S. 1, 42 [1937]). Furthermore,

> The [National Labor Relations] Act does not compel agreements between employers and employees. It does not compel any agreement whatever. It does not prevent the employer "from refusing to make a collective contract and hiring individuals on whatever terms" the employer "may by unilateral action determine. . . ." The theory of the Act is that free opportunity for negotiation with accredited representatives of employees is likely to promote industrial peace and may bring about the adjustments and agreements which the Act itself does not attempt to compel.

452 U.S. at 678 n.16 (quoting *NLRB v. Jones & Laughlin Steel Corp.*, 301 U.S. at 45 [1937]). The so-called outstanding fact is disputable. It was not simply a refusal to confer and negoti-

an existing contract. In other words, the question is, Does the employment contract contain explicit conditions that are now being revised without the approval of all affected parties? And if not, Should a court or administrative agency assume that such clauses would have been included by reasonably foresighted people if the contingencies that have developed could have been foreseen—and what would such clauses have stated? The Supreme Court asked whether typical *explicit, written* employment contracts contained clauses bearing on the dispute between the parties in the instant case. It found none that suggested that the employer was constrained in the kind of situation that provoked First National's decision.[14] The Court concluded that the evidence from such contracts was against the union's claim of mandatory bargaining.

A study of "typical" contracts, worthwhile as it may be in some cases, is not a reliable way to discern an implicit understanding about contingencies such as those under review, however. Many future contingencies are too difficult to predict or to verify if they do occur. Incomplete contracts seem to be the norm. What criterion could guide the Court in determining the implied restrictions that would be present if such unspecifiable future events should occur? More generally, what actions by the parties to a contract should be deemed inconsistent with the rational intent of reasonable people? Plainly, the notion of rational intent of reasonable people requires a theoretical approach with practical application to guide courts or agencies in this field of law.

------

ate that caused labor disturbances. Instead it was a refusal to be constrained to bargain with one exclusive representative of a supply of labor. The Court misquoted the law in referring to "representatives," whereas the law defines the duty to bargain as "the performance of the mutual obligation of the employer and the *representative* of the employees to meet at reasonable times and confer in good faith with respect to wages, hours, and other terms and conditions of employment. . . ." 29 U.S.C. § 158(d) (1976) (emphasis on singular added). Thus, it is a singular set of potential employees with whose representative the employer is to be confined in bargaining. Exclusive bargaining means that the employer cannot negotiate separately with competing potential employees. The constraint of exclusive representation—the demand that the employer bargain solely with a monopolist—arguably contributed as much (or more) to labor strife as did employer intransigence, not the requirement that there be some conferring and negotiating with employees or representatives, per se. Everyone confers and negotiates in every exchange and contract, because there is no other way to form exchanges and contracts.

14. 452 U.S. at 684.

II. Specific Quasi-Rents

A. *Theoretical Aspects*

The pertinent economic concepts and principles that can provide useful guidelines are formally, abstractly, and originally articulated in a general context by Oliver Williamson.[15] They have subsequently been further elaborated and applied by others.[16] To anticipate the discussion of concepts and principles, we state at the outset that the central phenomenon or economic concept involved is called "expropriable specific quasi-rent."[17] The problem that the concept describes is to find ways to induce investments in creating "expropriable specific quasi-rents" while at the same time avoiding their expropriation by opportunistic behavior.

When people make contracts, they anticipate that one of the contracting parties will perform an act or make an investment in some asset. The returns from that act or investment will depend on the actions of a particular other person—the other party to the contract. To illustrate, suppose that an employee *at his own expense* learns the details of his employer's business—knowledge that is worthless anyplace else. The employee thus makes an investment, the value of which depends on the subsequent actions of that particular, specific employer. The employee might take steps to prevent the employer from later reneging on the promises or overtures that induced the employee to finance the employer-specific investment. For example, before making the investment, the employee might obtain from the employer some commitment about the employer's future actions with respect to that investing employee. Obviously, the reason for contracts is to protect at least one of the parties (here, the employee) from opportunistic, self-seeking behavior by the other party (the employer), who might try to renege on the promise that induced the investment that has value specific to that other party only (the employer). Lest it be thought that this is a trivial matter, we note that the principal rationale for the employer-employee

15. O. Williamson, *Markets and Hierarchies: Analysis and Antitrust Implications* (1975).

16. Goetz and Scott, *Principles of Relational Contracts*, 67 Va. L. Rev. 1089 (1981); Goldberg, *Regulation and Administered Contracts*, 7 Bell J. Econ. & Mgt. Sci. 426 (1976); Klein, Crawford, and Alchian, *Vertical Integration, Appropriable Rents, and the Competitive Contracting Process*, 21 J. L. & Econ. 297 (1978).

17. Williamson initially called the concept a situation of opportunistic behavior involving "idiosyncratic assets," an "uncertain environment," "impacted information," and a "small number" of participants. Williamson, *supra* note 15.

status,[18] for the existence of firms,[19] and perhaps for many other kinds of economic organization[20] rests on this specificity of investment value.

To explain the contracting problem, we proceed by successive steps of classification. A *pure economic rent* is a payment received for the services of any resource, the payment for which is unnecessary for the resource's existence now and even in perpetuity. For example, the payment for a Picasso painting or a first edition of Adam Smith's *Wealth of Nations* is pure economic rent, meaning that the payment is unnecessary for the *permanent* existence of these objects. No matter how large the payment, these items will continue to exist, virtually forever.

Some other things, already produced at given costs, persist for shorter futures. They may sell or "rent" for more than the costs of keeping them in existence for this shorter future. If so, that excess over the existence cost is called a *quasi*-rent, because the excess persists *only* for the short time during which the resource would exist, payment or not. Though payment for the existing unit is unnecessary for *its* existence, anticipated payments in the future are necessary if new units are to replace it. More precisely, quasi-rent is any return to a resource above that necessary for its temporary existence. Obviously, the payment for the services of every existing durable good has an element of quasi-rent. A pencil, a piece of paper, a house, or an automobile, once produced, will earn some return that is quasi-rent, because the return is unnecessary for its existence during some sufficiently short time, but not forever.

A quasi-rent is *general* if the quasi-rent value of the resource does not depend on the actions of some particular, *specific* other person or resource. The market value of an automobile depends on no one person's demand for it if its value to all possible users is essentially the same. Its value is general. But its value would contain some *specific* quasi-rent if it has a higher value to some specific known person than to any other person. That value to a specific user in excess of its value to all other users is the *specific* quasi-rent.

18. Goetz and Scott, *supra* note 16.

19. Klein, Crawford, and Alchian, *supra* note 16. See also Alchian and Demsetz, *Production, Information Costs, and Economic Organization*, 62 Am. Econ. Rev. 777 (1972); Coase, *The Nature of the Firm*, 4 Econometrica 386 (1937); Jensen and Meckling, *Theory of the Firm: Managerial Behavior, Agency Costs and Ownership Structure*, 3 J. Fin. Econ. 305 (1976).

20. See, e.g., *infra*, Sec. III, Pt. B.

B. *Examples in Contracts Not Involving Labor*

A concrete arithmetic example proves helpful. Suppose that I own a printing press that serves your newspaper and that the value of the press is higher to you than to anyone else. Say it is worth $1000 a day to you, but only $600 to the next best placed user. Finally, suppose it costs only $100 to continue the press's operations, once it is made. The quasi-rent is $900, the excess paid over the amount required for its present services. The *specific* portion of the quasi-rent is $400, that is, $900 ($1000 − $100) minus $500 ($600 − $100). Your value is thus $400 higher than the value to the next highest valuing user.

The specific quasi-rent of an asset would be *expropriable* by you if you could somehow simply refuse to pay me more than $600. (If you offered me less than $600, I would sell the press's service to the next best placed user.) Expropriability requires that one be able to control the flow of his services (or payments) to the other party. It is not always possible to prevent expropriation by enforcing explicit contract terms that anticipate the expropriation's possibility. First, contracts cannot be sufficiently detailed and complete in all contingencies. Second, performance is not always easy to measure objectively. Third, legal enforcement and damages are not costlessly obtained. To ignore any of these three aspects of contract enforcement is to assume away a significant part of reality.

Inclusive ownership and integration as solutions. Consider other examples. I would not rent an elevator to you for your 40-story building, because I could do little if you threatened to terminate or reduce the rental payments. That is, I could not move the elevator at a feasible cost. Nor would I rent to a bank a safe embedded in concrete in its basement, since the bank's managers could say later that they cannot afford to pay the promised amount. Hence, banks own, rather than lease, their safe vaults and computer memory devices, and for similar reasons newspaper publishers usually own their printing presses rather than rent them from others. An oil refinery and a pipeline also might not be separately owned, since each could threaten to expropriate the value of the other's asset by withholding services or refusing to pay. Neither could remove the pipeline or refinery in the face of such a threat. The possibility of mutual retaliation does not avoid the subsequent bargaining problem. To avoid such "bilaterial monopoly" threats, the pipeline and refinery may be owned together, which is why the oil industry is so vertically integrated. End-to-end railroads, when each section was separately owned, motivated persistent fighting over the shares of the total revenue for freight traveling over more than one section. That is why many railroads were integrated end-to-end in the 19th century. Integration eliminates the expropriative threat. In all of these cases, opportunities for expropriation of specific quasi-rents would be present.

Dispersed contracting and regulation as solutions. Firms may also respond to these problems not by merging but by avoiding exclusive contracting for firm-specific services. For example, General Motors does not buy its unique body parts from a single outside supplier. But the exclusive-contracting problem might arise in other settings. A public utility that provides the only source of electric power to a city or factory could also extract the quasi-rents of all the electricity-using resources specific to it. One reason given for government regulation of utilities is not so much to prevent so-called monopoly pricing, as it is to prevent opportunistic expropriation of customers' specific quasi-rents.[21]

c. *Examples in Contracts Involving Labor*

A description of the specific quasi-rent problem using examples from labor suggests the very broad importance of the general situation and the principles governing the contractual relations thereby induced. It also moves us toward a discussion of *First National.* Thus, consider a theatrical producer who invests heavily in a story in which a particular actor will star. He will find that part of his investment value is expropriable to the extent that the story value is higher with that actor than with any other actor. Resources with values specific to another party can also arise by deliberate investment or by accident without prior investment. For example, Laurel did not create the comedy team of Laurel and Hardy by an investment that made his entertainment value specific to Hardy, although specific to Hardy it certainly was, and the same for Hardy. Each was specific to the other, or interspecific by virtue of personality. But both could not be owned by one person who could control each, to avoid any interpersonal threats to reduce the other's specific value unless paid part of it. However, no prior investment was involved, so neither could claim that the specific quasi-rent, which was expropriable or destroyable by the other, was "his," or the merited result of prior investment. Yet the two persons were in a (very difficult) situation characterized by interspecific quasi-rents, non-integrable ownership, and individual performance that is difficult to monitor and enforce against malingering.

More generally, without clear protections, I would not invest in personal skills that make me more valuable to you, my present employer, than to any

21. Goldberg, *supra* note 16.

other possible employer.[22] You could later refuse to pay me enough to cover my earlier investment costs, even though the investment has made me more valuable to you. If you could threaten to pay me only what I was worth elsewhere, I would lose the specific value of the investment; you would have expropriated it. As a precaution, I, the employee, would insist that you, the employer to whom that investment value will be specific, pay the costs of my specific (to your use) training. Then, although I will become more valuable to you, you will merely collect on your investment, not expropriate mine.

You might then want a commitment from me that after I am trained I will not threaten to leave your employ unless you give me some of that value. To avoid my opportunistic behavior, our contract might give you the "right of first refusal" to my services. An employer might also allow an employee to accumulate a right to a pension that he can collect only if he remains with that employer. The pension thus has a value that will disappear if the employee moves: the pension is specific to that employer. But the employee then faces the problem of avoiding expropriation of that value by the employer's opportunistic behavior (reducing the employee's pay or otherwise unfavorably adjusting his working conditions, because the employee is a "captive" of the pension arrangement). Similarly, while the pension system protects the employer-investor, it leaves the employee subject to losses if the fund is poorly managed. So the employee may seek means to oversee the pension fund's administration. In sum, anyone contemplating an investment that will have a value specific to a particular other person or firm will require some assurance that the other party will not dishonor the obligation to perform as anticipated and agreed to in the initial contract. The contract devices for insuring compliance are many.

Another employment example illustrates the principle's wide scope. A mine owner in an isolated area can insist that his employees come and buy land and houses in the area, or he can provide company housing. If the employees buy land and houses, they will own wealth specific to the mine owner's operations. His threat to shut down, if made believable, might induce them to accept reduced wages and working conditions as a price for not losing even more: the land value specific to that mine. So instead, to eliminate that threat, the mine owner owns the surrounding land and rents houses to abate his employees' fears about his own potential opportunistic behavior. This interpretation is in

22. This proposition assumes that any intrinsic satisfaction from investing in or adding to such employer-specific skills is not sufficient to overcome the investment's cost.

stark contrast with the more common belief that mine owners used company towns to extract higher rents.

I take a final labor example from an acquaintance's experience. An employee of Bell's Western Electric Laboratory, financed by Bell during his years of employment, developed skills useful only with Western Electric equipment. Later, he installed some Western Electric equipment in Pacific Telephone Company's offices. Pacific Telephone believed that if they could hire him, he would be worth more to them than his current salary, because Western Electric had already paid his training cost. By trying to hire this employee, Pacific Telephone (and the employee) would be trying to expropriate that quasi-rent value of the employee specific to Western Electric equipment. Should the law grant Western Electric the right to keep the employee bound to a long-term arrangement? One can argue that the employee understood his obligation all along and has no right to try to expropriate that investment value paid for by Western Electric. Or one can argue that Western Electric should have foreseen this possibility and paid the employee during the earlier investing years with a non-vested pension, mentioned earlier, which the employee would lose if he left.

III. Criteria for Decision Sharing

A. Economic Tests for Decision Sharing

A criterion for when and which employees should have a right to share in the contract alteration decision process is whether or not those employees have invested in creating specific, expropriable wealth that is hostage to another party's actions, and if so, how that situation arose. At issue here are attempts to alter the employment contract, or to exercise permitted discretion in ways that seem to the other party to be opportunistic or expropriative of its contractual rights, or to terminate unilaterally a contract of indefinite length.

The criteria as to whether some issue or activity that an employer contemplates is a proper subject of collective bargaining with the employee's agent are twofold. First, is there a future specific quasi-rent or premium in this job relative to the next best alternative? And if so, second, does the quasi-rent result from prior investment at the expense of the employee; that is, was it purchased at the employee's earlier cost?

Unless it is specifically contemplated in the contract, it is irrelevant whether or not the returns that the investor has received so far in the specific asset have recovered the investment cost and normal interest. No test of a proper profit or rate of return is available or necessary. If the employee who made the investment should find its high value persisting, then we cannot rationalize any attempt to expropriate it by arguing that it has already been paid for. Such arguments founder on the mythical concept of "fair profits." Similarly, if the firm to which the employee's asset is specific suffers a loss of business, then the quasi-rent itself will fall, because the asset's value to the firm has fallen. The employee has no promise that the value of his specific asset to that firm will remain high. All that is promised is that it will not be expropriated by opportunistic behavior. Any firm that runs up losses will make its employees worse off by the amount of the loss of specific quasi-rent, and the employee might have anticipated that possibility at the time he made his investment.

Neither the size of the employer's losses nor the returns to the employees' investments has any bearing on the issue of defining the matters that are subject to the duty to bargain and negotiate. The duty to bargain, in the sense of decision sharing, prevails in contract revisions. If previous contracts do not formally and explicitly cover the contested revision, then the courts or the NLRB can look to the circumstances that put the parties in their present situation— in particular, to the extent to which one party induced the other to make a firm- or employee-specific investment. If the employee who makes investments specific to an employer did so with some contractual agreement that imposes some constraints on the employer, then the employee has some decision-making rights over proposed changes in those terms. That would define the scope of "wages and terms of employment."

The courts[23] have referred to "substantial capital investments of the employer," or "inherent business decisions," or an employer's right to close down his business, or to transfer his business, or to make decisions that alter the basic nature of the enterprise. These may be ill-expressed gropings for the (employer's) specific investment value that is expropriable by the other party (employees). But these notions disregard similar specific investment values that employees might have made.

B. *Qualifications on Criteria*

The mere existence of specific investments is not sufficient for decision sharing. For example, suppose an employer, who has philanthropically paid a higher salary than any equivalently placed alternative employer decides to terminate the charity. Or equivalently, suppose that a grocery store is so favorably located for some customers that they have a net gain from that store, but the grocer closes down. The customers have a claim to enter into the closing deci-

---

23. *Supra* note 8.

sion only if the grocer induced them to make investments specific to his availability. And the employee may make a similar claim only if the employer induced him to make a specific investment on the basis of the assumption of long-continued largess.

c. Union Protection of Specific Quasi-Rents

Contract surveillance and evaluation of the other party's performance is not always easy. An employer's payment of wages in money is easily detectable, but monitoring the employer's performance becomes more troublesome for deferred payments (for example, future pensions) or payments in-kind (for example, insurance). An intermediary, such as a union agent, may perform the monitoring task. The union serves as a group action to enable each member more cheaply and accurately to detect and evaluate the employer's fulfillment of the promised future contractual activity. This monitoring is a useful agency function, similar to the escrow service provided to the buyer and seller of a house.[24]

Thus, one function of labor unions is to act as agents for employees in labor contract monitoring, disputes, and negotiations.[25] The union's monitoring would restrain an employer who tried to act opportunistically to reduce his performance below the contractual standards, or who called for contract revisions under the guise of changes in his business conditions that individual employees cannot easily detect, and which otherwise would have triggered acceptable alterations in the contractual terms, if the changes really had occurred. An employer could argue that business was poorer, and unless wages were cut he would have to reduce employment—a pretext that could be effective in expropriating any expropriable specific quasi-rents of employees. By collecting information more cheaply for all employees, and by threatening a concerted action of employees, the union could thwart the expropriation if, to the union

---

24. The monitoring function of unions with respect to the expropriable specific quasi-rent problem is far less controversial than are other purposes imputed to unions, such as balancing bargaining power between employers and employees. Such a balance makes little sense in the context of initial contract negotiations, although it makes more sense in the context of revising the terms of employment, which is often equivalent to protecting expropriable specific quasi-rents.

25. Freeman, *The Exit-Voice Tradeoff in the Labor Market: Unionism, Job Tenure, Quits and Separations*, Q. J. Econ. 643 (1980); R. Miller, F. Zeller, & G. Miller, *The Practice of Local Union Leadership* (1965); J. Reid, *Labor Unions in the American Economy: An Analytical Survey*, VPI&SU Center for Study of Public Choice Working Paper CE-80-9-5 (1980).

monitor, the evidence indicated that the employer's attempt was purely opportunistic.[26]

A union or employee agent may help to resolve disputes about contract interpretation and performance, just as other intermediary agents (for example, agents for athletes and artists, real estate agents, and escrow agents) increase reliability of performance and overcome personality conflicts in disputed contract performance. Union agents therefore appropriately monitor existing contractual terms under the obligatory bargaining clause of the National Labor Relations Act. This monitoring even extends beyond clauses concerning wages, hours, and other terms of employment, to include matters such as health insurance and parking spaces. Thus "wages, hours, and other terms of employment" is an inadequate denotation of the scope of a "duty to bargain." Employees could rightfully contend that the agent represents them in all matters explicitly in the contractual agreement as well as in those involving expropriable specific quasi-rents, all of which fall in the scope of, or in which there is, a duty to bargain.

IV. Application to *First National*

In the instant case, no allegation or evidence was introduced of any expropriable or specific employee investments the value of which depended on First National's actions. Nor was there evidence of a management ploy to reduce wages or otherwise to deprive employees of (non-existent) specific quasi-rents. The dismissed service employees appear to have had no significant wealth, however acquired, specific to First National, such as to warrant authority to share in First National's decision to terminate their jobs. The Court rendered a decision compatible with our analysis, although it also made some references to a theoretical balancing of the burden of bargaining on the employer and the benefits of bargaining to labor-management relations and the collective bargaining process.[27] The minority objected to this balancing, quite properly, I believe.[28]

Other ancillary features, such as whether the employer's proposed action involved a "substantial change in business," "large amounts of capital," or "basic

---

26. Perhaps the 1981–1982 negotiations to revise labor contracts with automobile firms is an example of union monitoring and determination that an opportunistic threat was absent.

27. 452 U.S. at 686.

28. Id. at 689–690 (Brennan, J., dissenting).

operations" are analytically useless and possibly misleading. For example, by threatening to close down, or change the basic nature of his business, or make a large capital investment in some other activity, an employer could threaten an employee's specific quasi-rent. The employee who has invested in developing skills or resources with values specific to his employer wants security against expropriation caused by the employer's discretionary action. If the loss occurs because the employer's business falters, which reduces the employee's specific value, then (unless the employee was assured or guaranteed against such non-opportunistic loss before making his investment) the employee's specific quasi-rent is reduced not by the employer's opportunistic behavior, but by his loss of business. Examining the contracts and the specific situation provides a better way to distinguish between employees' losses from opportunistic behavior and losses from business failure than does appealing to considerations such as "basic management" or "substantial change of operations." These considerations are irrelevant unless they serve as proxy indicators of expropriable specific quasi-rents. An employer who reneges on a contractual commitment that induced an employee to make an investment specific to the employer should not be able to escape his obligation by pleading any of these considerations.

The principle is clear enough. If an investment's expropriable specific quasi-rent was created in response to offers by the other party to whom the quasi-rent is specific, then decision sharing is appropriate. The way to make judgments about decision sharing is to examine the explicit or implicit contractual situation among the parties. Instead of trying to identify particular acts—a decision to close, or to move, or to paint the interior of a factory—one should conduct the analysis in terms of the presence of expropriable specific quasi-rents and how they came into being.[29] By this analysis, the Court in *First National* came to the correct conclusion but for inapposite reasons.

---

29. For that task, is the National Labor Relations Board better suited than the courts? The dissenters thought so. I make no pretense to know the answer. But interesting discussions of this issue for related administrative agencies are provided in H. Friendly, *Federal Jurisdiction: A General View* (1973) and in Posner, *The Behavior of Administrative Agencies*, 1 J. Legal Stud. 305 (1972) and references cited therein.

AMICUS CURIAE

MONSANTO COMPANY VS.

SPRAY-RITE CORPORATION

WESLEY J. LIEBELER, ARMEN A. ALCHIAN,

JEFFREY CONNOR, HAROLD DEMSETZ, MICHAEL GRANFIELD,

ROBERT L. JORDAN, AND STANLEY ORNSTEIN

Brief of Associates for Antitrust Analysis as Amicus Curiae in Support of Petitioner[1]

Interest of Amicus Curiae

Associates for Antitrust Analysis (AAA) is a group of faculty members from UCLA interested in the application of economic principles to government regulation in general and to antitrust law in particular. A list of members is attached as Appendix A. Financial support for this brief has been provided by the Center for the Study of Political Economy, Graduate School of Management, UCLA.[2] No support has been provided by either of the parties to this litigation.

The central issue in this case is whether government regulation of market processes will be expanded or contracted. The more particular question is whether the start which the Court made in GTE Sylvania[3] and in Broadcast Music[4] to base antitrust law on "demonstrable economic effect"[5] will proceed or be abandoned. AAA has an interest and an expertise in these issues. This brief addresses the economic issues in this case and the relationship between them and the relevant legal rules.

Brief for Monsanto Co. as *Amicus Curiae* supporting Petitioner, *Monsanto Co. vs. Spray-Rite Service Corp.*, 465 U.S. 752 (1984) (No. 82-914).

1. This brief is filed with the consent of the parties pursuant to Supreme Court Rule 36.2. The written consents have been filed with the Clerk of the Court.

2. The views expressed here are those of AAA and its members; they do not necessarily represent the view of the Regents of the University of California or UCLA.

3. *Continental T.V., Inc. v. GTE Sylvania Inc.*, 433 U.S. 36 (1977).

4. *Broadcast Music, Inc. v. Columbia Broadcasting System, Inc.*, 441 U.S. 1 (1979).

5. *Sylvania*, 433 U.S. at 59.

Summary of Argument

This case raises again one of the most troublesome issues in antitrust: What principles determine the scope of the *per se* rule and the rule of reason. A second question, what kind of inquiry is to be conducted under the rule of reason when it applies, does not arise in this case because plaintiff proceeded below only on a *per se* theory.

This Court has made it increasingly clear that the purpose of antitrust law is to help maximize consumer welfare, *i.e.,* to help increase the productivity of our predominantly free market economy. To serve this purpose, the *per se* rule can properly be applied only to restrictive transactions which do not have any significant capacity to create efficiency.

This standard for the scope of the *per se* rule is based on demonstrable economic effect, as required by *Sylvania.* It is different from the standard that was applied in the vast majority of cases decided before *Sylvania.* The traditional standard is based primarily on form. That standard provides that certain forms of arrangements—price fixing, group boycotts, and tie-ins—are illegal *per se.* The fact that some arrangements taking these forms can often produce significant efficiencies is irrelevant under the general statement of the rule. Legality depends on form rather than on effect.

A standard based on form, however, tends to come apart when it becomes clear that an arrangement which it makes illegal *per se* in fact creates significant efficiencies. Most courts are reluctant to strike down transactions that are obviously wealth producing. When confronted with an efficiency creating arrangement which the law holds to be illegal *per se,* many courts will try to find some way to avoid the rule.

This was true even before *Sylvania,* as the law of group boycotts, for example, makes clear.[6] This Court made broad statements that group boycotts were illegal *per se;* when lower courts confronted efficiency creating boycotts they often refused to apply the *per se* rule.[7] This has led to considerable confusion in that area of the law.

6. See W. Liebeler, *Antitrust Advisor* §1.32 (2d ed. Supp. 1982).

7. The court in *Cullum Electric & Mechanical, Inc. v. Mechanical Contractors Assn.,* 436 F.Supp. 418 (D. S.C. 1976), *aff'd* 569 F.2d 821 (4th Cir. 1978), stated that "[d]espite the pronouncements of the Supreme Court, a multitude of lower courts have continued to evaluate alleged boycotts under a 'rule of reason' analysis rather than by the per se doctrine employed by the Supreme Court. . . . As one commentator has observed, 'the law in Washington, however, is quite different from the law in the rest of the country.'" 436 F.Supp. at 428.

Sylvania complicated the problem even more when, announcing that departures from the rule of reason were to be based on demonstrable economic effect, it applied the rule of reason to certain distribution arrangements because they created efficiency. Many of the Court's prior decisions had applied the *per se* rule on the basis of a predominantly formal standard to arrangements that were designed precisely to create efficiencies of the type approved in *Sylvania*.[8] While *Sylvania* thus undercut many earlier decisions, none of this was mentioned in *Sylvania* itself.[9]

Lower courts were thus faced with two conflicting lines of authority. One was based on earlier cases like *Klor's*[10] and *Sealy*,[11] for example, which formalistically applied the *per se* rule to efficiency creating arrangements. The other was based on *Sylvania*, which applied an economic analysis to uphold restrictions because they created efficiency. Lower courts could decide cases like the one under review pretty much as they desired, just by choosing to follow the earlier cases, which *Sylvania* had not explicitly rejected, or to follow *Sylvania*. The former is exactly what the court below did.

There is a conflict between *Sylvania* and earlier cases like *Klor's, General Motors*,[12] and *Sealy* which the Court must resolve before we can expect any consistency in the decisions below.

The foregoing explains why the law governing the scope of the *per se* rule and the rule of reason is as confused as it is. This confusion imposes significant costs on the economy. There is more litigation than need be and businessmen find it hard to plan their affairs to stay within the law. The condition of the law in this area as it now stands is highly unsatisfactory.

For these reasons the Court should take this opportunity to clarify the

---

8. The three principal cases are *Klor's, Inc. v. Broadway-Hale Stores, Inc.*, 359 U.S. 207 (1959); *United States v. General Motors Corp.*, 384 U.S. 127 (1966); and *United States v. Sealy, Inc.*, 388 U.S. 350 (1967). The arrangements in all three cases appear to have been aimed at free rider problems similar if not identical to those involved in *Sylvania*. See R. Bork, *The Antitrust Paradox* 332 (1978); Liebeler, *Book Review*, 66 Cal. L. Rev. 1317 (1979), at 1325; Liebeler, *Intrabrand "Cartels" Under GTE Sylvania*, 30 UCLA L. Rev. 1 (1982), at 31 (hereinafter cited as Liebeler, *Intrabrand "Cartels"*).

9. See Posner, *The Rule of Reason and the Economic Approach: Reflections on the Sylvania Decision*, 45 U. Chi. L. Rev. 1 (1977).

10. *Klor's, Inc. v. Broadway-Hale Stores, Inc.*, 359 U.S. 207 (1959).

11. *United States v. Sealy, Inc.*, 388 U.S. 350 (1967).

12. *United States v. General Motors Corp.*, 384 U.S. 127 (1966).

scope of the *per se* rule and the rule of reason. A general statement of the efficiency approach adopted in *Sylvania* and advanced in this brief would help the lower courts decide all kinds of cases brought under Section 1 of the Sherman Act. It would also help businessmen plan their affairs, and lawyers to advise them. Such a statement would continue the process begun in *Sylvania*; it could contribute significantly to the efficiency of both the legal and the market systems.

When it comes specifically to restricted distribution systems, lower courts have confronted two principal problems in their attempts to apply the economic approach adopted in *Sylvania*. The first, and the main point on which the court below erred, is the distinction between "price" and "nonprice" restrictions. This characterization issue is crucial because of *Sylvania's* holding that the *per se* rule continued to apply to "price" arrangements, while "nonprice" restrictions were to be governed by the rule of reason. While the distinction seems simple, the discussion below will show that it is quite intractable. There are only two principled ways to deal with the distinction. It could be formally abandoned, as suggested by the Solicitor General.[13] Under this approach, the rule of reason would be explicitly applied to all distribution restrictions. Another approach, urged in this brief, would apply the characterization process described in *Broadcast Music* to determine which distribution restrictions constitute "*per se* price fixing." The *per se* rule would be applied to those restrictions; the rule of reason would be applied to all others.

The second principal problem is the distinction between vertical and horizontal arrangements. This characterization issue, too, is important because it determines the scope of the *per se* rule. *Sylvania* placed horizontal transactions under the *per se* rule and vertical "nonprice" agreements under the rule of reason. Attempts to make this vertical/horizontal distinction have led lower courts into a veritable jungle of formalistic line drawing.[14] The *Sylvania* standard itself is faulty here. A distinction based on the source of the arrangement is formalistic itself; the source of an arrangement, even if it could be determined without endless circumlocution, has no necessary relationship to its price and output effects. If the vertical/horizontal distinction is to persist in this area of the law, it must be

13. See Brief for the United States as *Amicus Curiae* in Support of Petitioner, *Monsanto Company v. Spray-Rite Service Corporation*, at 19.

14. The clearest recognition of this is Judge Posner's opinion in *Valley Liquors, Inc. v. Renfield Importers, Ltd.*, 678 F.2d 742 (7th Cir. 1982).

based on something that bears some plausible relationship to economic effect.[15] A standard based on the source of an arrangement does not meet that test.

The court below applied the *per se* rule primarily because plaintiff alleged that its termination was part of a plan to fix resale prices.[16] If this is all it takes to turn a nonprice restriction into a price restriction, there is little left of *Sylvania*. For this reason the approach taken below cannot stand. Neither the cases nor the commentators, however, have yet articulated a principled way to distinguish between "price" and "nonprice" restrictions. The other briefs in this case have not dealt effectively with this problem either.[17] This brief will, accordingly, focus primarily on that problem.

Section I of the brief discusses the economic factors relevant to any inquiry under Section 1 of the Sherman Act. It briefly describes the nature of "consumer welfare," the maximization of which underlies modern antitrust policy. It shows that under the consumer welfare standard the *per se* rule is properly applied only to transactions with a significant potential to restrict output and which lack a significant efficiency creating potential. The rule of reason comes into play if both output restricting and efficiency creating effects are present. The rule of reason inquiry itself involves a balancing of these two effects. This section also describes certain proxies that help the courts identify those transactions that have either an efficiency creating or an output restricting potential.

Section II of the brief shows that the "price"/"nonprice" distinction which

---

15. It would be best to tie the definition of the two terms directly to the possible economic effects of an arrangement. Thus, Bork says: "The test is simply whether, assuming market power to exist, the agreement eliminating competition could lead to a restriction of output. If it could, the restriction is horizontal; if it could not, the restraint is vertical." Bork, *The Rule of Reason and the Per Se Concept: Price Fixing and Market Division*, 75 Yale L. J. 373 (1966), at 424 (hereinafter cited as Bork, *Rule of Reason*). One way to implement this insight is to equate vertical with intrabrand and horizontal with interbrand. See generally Liebeler, *Intrabrand "Cartels."*

16. In its discussion of the boycott issue, however, particularly in footnote 4, the court below suggests that the *per se* rule would apply even in the absence of resale price fixing. See Section III below.

17. The Brief for the United States as *Amicus Curiae* in this case suggests that the restrictions here should be regarded as "nonprice" because "Monsanto's marketing program on its face did not pertain to price." *Id.* at 15. This is basically a formalistic approach. Monsanto argues that the rule of reason should apply unless "non-price restrictions are designed or used to implement a scheme to control resale prices and prevent intrabrand price competition." Petitioner's Brief at 26. It is not clear how we distinguish such arrangements from those that "affect price or limit intrabrand price competition." *Id.* at 27.

Sylvania used to determine the scope of the *per se* rule is intractable as now articulated. The reason is that "nonprice" arrangements (governed by the rule of reason under *Sylvania*) adopted to alleviate free rider problems must affect price to accomplish that purpose; the *Socony-Vacuum* rule, however, makes all arrangements which have even an indirect effect on price illegal *per se*. This dilemma can be avoided by using the characterization process which the Court adopted in *Broadcast Music*. This section also deals with the current vitality of *Broadcast Music* despite its seeming limitation in *Maricopa*.[18] It is concluded that *Broadcast Music* provides the only principled way to determine the scope of the *per se* rule in this area of the law, short of overruling *Dr. Miles* and applying the rule of reason across the board.

Section III of the brief briefly discusses the alleged boycott which prevented plaintiff from obtaining additional supplies of Monsanto's products. It argues that the efficiency-based characterization approach adopted in *Broadcast Music* should be applied to group boycotts as well as to price fixing agreements. Section IV touches on the problem of concerted action, suggesting that the lack of a clear standard to determine the scope of the *per se* rule has prompted some courts simply to find the absence of concerted action when they believe that the substantive behavior involved should not be an antitrust violation. The final section of the brief argues that a distinction between contract integration and ownership integration is formalistic; if demonstrable economic effect is to determine the scope of the *per se* rule, the legality of contract integrations should be determined by the same standards that are applied to mergers or to integration by internal expansion.

Argument

I. *The Economic Determinants of the Scope of the Per Se Rule and the Rule of Reason and the Rule of Reason Inquiry*

The bedrock of market analysis is the voluntary exchange transaction. Two parties will enter such a transaction only if they both believe that they will benefit. The benefits which both parties gain from these transactions are called the gains from trade. Simply put, the purpose of an antitrust policy based on market considerations is to proscribe private arrangements that reduce the gains from trade available to the community as a whole.[19]

18. *Arizona v. Maricopa County Medical Society*, 102 S. Ct. 2466 (1982).

19. The discussion of economic principles is taken from Liebeler, *Intrabrand "Cartels"* at 13. Supporting authorities are cited at that place.

Private transactions can either increase or decrease the community's possible gains from trade. Transactions that increase those gains increase efficiency; those that decrease them reduce efficiency. From an antitrust standpoint, arrangements will generally not reduce efficiency unless they restrict output. Arrangements increase efficiency if they reduce the costs of productive marketing activity or produce more desirable products or services.

Some arrangements may have both output restricting and efficiency creating effects. The effect of such a transaction on net available gains from trade can only be determined by estimating the relative magnitude of those two opposing effects. If the gains from more efficient productive activity exceed the losses from a restriction of output, net gains from trade (consumer welfare or economic efficiency) will increase. Net gains from trade will decline if the opposite is true.

A voluntary exchange transaction, thus, can have three possible effects or combinations of effects that are relevant to Sherman Act analysis.[20] The sole probable effect of some transactions will be to restrict output. Those transactions should be illegal *per se*. They can only reduce the total available gains from trade, thereby reducing economic efficiency and consumer welfare.

The sole probable effect of other transactions will be to increase efficiency. These transactions should not be subjects of concern to antitrust. They can only increase the total available gains from trade, thereby increasing economic efficiency and consumer welfare. These transactions should always be legal as far as the antitrust laws are concerned.

Still other transactions will have both of the above effects. They will have the potential both to increase efficiency and to restrict output. The rule of reason should be applied to these transactions and the inquiry under it should focus on the transactions' probable net effect. If the gains from trade available from increased efficiency seem likely to outweigh the losses from the output restriction effect, the transaction should be upheld. It should be struck down if the balance between these two factors appears to shift the other way. This is simply an economic statement of the legal formulation that the rule of reason inquiry is to balance the procompetitive effects of a transaction against its anticompetitive effects.

---

20. This discussion is a verbal statement of the tradeoff model that Professor Williamson first developed to analyze the effects of horizontal mergers. See Williamson, *Economies as an Antitrust Defense: The Welfare Tradeoffs*, 58 Am. Econ. Rev. 18 (1968); R. Bork, *The Antitrust Paradox* 107 (1978); Liebeler, *Intrabrand "Cartels"* at 16.

The crucial point for purposes of this case is that the rule of reason applies to any transaction that has a significant efficiency creating potential. It should also be remembered that a rule of reason inquiry is necessary only if there is a reasonable probability that the transaction will restrict output. The *per se* rule applies only to naked restraints of trade, *i.e.*, those that lack a significant efficiency creating potential. It is not the form of the transaction that determines whether or not it is "naked." An arrangement is "naked," and therefore subject to the *per se* rule, only if it lacks an efficiency creating potential. A transaction should be legal without more if it does not have a significant output restricting potential; if both output restricting and efficiency creating effects are present the tradeoff analysis described above should be conducted under the rule of reason.

Since it is difficult to observe the effects of efficiency or market power directly, the law has developed a set of proxies to make the theoretical structure outlined above operational in a legal context. William Howard Taft formulated the classic proxy for efficiency creating potential in 1898 as part of the ancillary restrictions doctrine.[21] Taft's proxy required a contract with a main legitimate end which could be used to determine the scope of the permissible limitation on competition.[22] Professor (now Judge) Bork describes this proxy as "a contract integration (the coordination of other productive or distributive efforts of the parties)."[23] This Court recently described an efficiency creating arrangement for the blanket licensing of copyrights as an "integration of sales, monitoring, and enforcement against unauthorized copyright use."[24] The presence of this integration prompted the Court properly to refuse to apply the *per se* rule, even though the arrangement clearly involved horizontal price fixing.

The paradigm integration of productive facilities is the partnership. Mergers, too, are clearly within the pale. But once again, it is not the form which an integration takes that is important; economic effect is the paramount consideration. All arrangements between a supplier and its resellers, for example, involve an integration of productive facilities; their relationship is the economic equivalent of a partnership, embodying the efficiency-creating potential which Taft specifically recognized in his third example of an ancillary restraint in

---

21. *United States v. Addyston Pipe & Steel Co.*, 85 F. 271 (6th Cir. 1898), *aff'd in pertinent part*, 175 U.S. 211 (1899).

22. 85 F. at 282.

23. Bork, *Rule of Reason* at 474.

24. *Broadcast Music, Inc. v. Columbia Broadcasting System*, 441 U.S. 1 (1979) at 20.

Addyston Pipe & Steel.[25] This "partnership" nature of the relationship between a supplier and its resellers should be enough in itself to remove all arrangements between them from the *per se* rule. The Court accepted this at least partially in *Sylvania* when it recognized the free rider problem and held that nonprice distribution arrangements should be governed by the rule of reason. We shall see below that the inability to make a principled distinction between "nonprice" and "price" restrictions provides an additional reason to extend this efficiency analysis to all arrangements between a supplier and its resellers in a restricted distribution system.

11. *The Distinction Between "Price" and "Nonprice" Distribution Restrictions Is Intractable: The Scope of the Per Se Rule and the Rule of Reason as Applied to Such Restrictions Can Only Be Determined by an Efficiency Standard*

Under *Sylvania* the rule of reason is applied to "nonprice" distribution restrictions; the *per se* rule continues to govern "price" restrictions. While it made the distinction between these two types of arrangements crucial, *Sylvania* itself did not address the difference between them. It was presumably thought that the distinction would not be difficult to make. As subsequent lower court cases attempting to apply *Sylvania* have shown, however, that distinction is intractable.[26]

The difficulty arises because most "nonprice" distribution arrangements are designed to solve free rider problems. These problems typically arise when one dealer cuts prices below the level that covers the cost of providing point-of-sale services desired by the manufacturer. In this regard *Sylvania* said:

25. "Again, when two men became partners in a business, although their union might reduce competition, this effect was only an incident to the main purpose of a union of their capital, enterprise, and energy to carry on a successful business, and one useful to the community. Restrictions in the articles of partnership upon the business activity of the members with a view of securing their entire effort in the common enterprise, were, of course, only ancillary to the main end of the union, and were to be encouraged." 85 F. at 280.

26. Compare the decision below, for example, with *Bruce Drug, Inc. v. Hollister, Inc.*, 688 F.2d 853 (1st Cir. 1982), and *Davis-Watkins Co. v. Service Merchandise Co.*, 686 F.2d 1190 (6th Cir. 1982). In both of the latter two cases a termination and boycott after receiving complaints about price cutting were held not to be price related and, therefore, not subject to the *per se* rule. The decisions of the courts of appeals on this issue have been *ad hoc*; there is no principled basis on which the divergent decisions on the price/nonprice issue can be explained.

Vertical restrictions promote interbrand competition by allowing the manufacturer to achieve certain efficiencies in the distribution of his products. These "redeeming virtues" are implicit in every decision sustaining vertical restrictions under the rule of reason. Economists have identified a number of ways in which manufacturers can use such restrictions to compete more effectively against other manufacturers. . . . Established manufacturers can use them to induce retailers to engage in promotional activities or to provide service and repair facilities necessary to the efficient marketing of their products. Service and repair are vital for many products, such as automobiles and major household appliances. The availability and quality of such services affect a manufacturer's good will and the competitiveness of his product. Because of market imperfections such as the so-called "free rider" effect, these services might not be provided by retailers in a purely competitive situation, despite the fact that each retailer's benefit would be greater if all provided the services than if none did.[27]

The reason that these services might not be provided by retailers, of course, is that price cutting by one or more dealers who fail to provide such services will prevent other dealers from recovering the costs of providing them. If they cannot recover their costs, they will not continue to provide the services, at least not at the optimal level.

It becomes clear, therefore, that free rider problems cannot be solved unless would-be free riders can be prevented from cutting prices. The so-called "nonprice" arrangements to which *Sylvania* applied the rule of reason must be able to prevent or control price cutting before they can be effective. "Nonprice" arrangements, therefore, have powerful effects in terms of stabilizing prices.[28] Tyler Baker makes this point as follows:

Virtually all of the justifications for *Sylvania* assume an indirect effect on price. For example, the Court referred to "market imperfections such as the so-called 'free rider' effect" that might discourage retailers from providing

27. 433 U.S. at 54–55.
28. Both Petitioner and the United States as *Amicus Curiae* recognized the price effects of "nonprice" restrictions. See Petitioner's Brief at 26. The Solicitor General noted specifically that "many restrictions commonly regarded as nonprice vertical restrictions, including the location clause at issue in *Sylvania*, may have an upward effect on the resale price of the manufacturer's products." Brief for the United States as *Amicus Curiae* in Support of Petitioner at 16. Neither brief provides a satisfactory solution to the dilemma which they both recognize.

the appropriate level of services. The same discounters that provide the price competition favored by the enforcement agencies may also "free ride" on the efforts of the authorized dealers. A "free rider" takes advantage of a competitor's investment and charges a price lower than the competitor's, thereby preventing the competitor from recouping its investment. The elimination of free riders may encourage investment, but it also may raise prices. For this reason a rule condemning all vertical restrictions having an indirect effect on price is flatly inconsistent with *Sylvania*.[29]

The conflict that arises between the price effects of "nonprice" restrictions and the breadth of the traditional rule against price fixing can best be seen by quoting some recent language from a decision in the Fourth Circuit Court of Appeals discussing *Socony-Vacuum*:[30]

> [P]rice fixing is one of those practices that the Court has held to be illegal per se. . . . The Court stated [in *Socony*] "a combination formed for the purpose and with the effect of raising, depressing, fixing, pegging or stabilizing the price of a commodity in interstate or foreign commerce is illegal per se." To be guilty of price fixing, the conspirators do not have to adopt a rigid price, substantially less has been found to be price fixing. An activity can violate the per se rule even if its effect upon prices is indirect. . . . In essence, an interference with market forces freely setting the prices of goods is sufficient.[31]

The traditional expression of the *per se* rule devours "nonprice" restrictions once we recognize, as we must, that the purpose and effect of "nonprice" arrangements is to affect prices. *Sylvania* and *Socony* are at war with each other; either *Socony* must be tempered in some way or *Sylvania* must give way. While a futile formalistic accommodation between *Socony*'s flat prohibition of arrangements that affect prices and *Sylvania*'s mandate to apply the rule of reason to "nonprice" restrictions could be made, *Sylvania* requires that this problem be solved in terms of demonstrable economic effect.

That can be done by following the approach that the Court took in defining price fixing in *Broadcast Music*. There the Court refused to apply the *per se* rule to

29. Baker, *Interconnected Problems of Doctrine and Economics in the Section One Labyrinth: Is Sylvania A Way Out?* 67 Va. L. Rev. 1457 (1981) at 1467.

30. *United States v. Socony-Vacuum Oil Co., Inc.*, 310 U.S. 150 (1940).

31. *National Electrical Contractors Association, Inc. v. National Constructors Association*, 678 F.2d 492 (4th Cir. 1982) at 500.

blanket copyright licenses issued by BMI, even though those licenses eliminated competition between individual copyrighted works and necessarily fixed prices. The Court said:

> To the Court of Appeals and CBS, the blanket license involves "price fixing" in the literal sense: the composers and publishing houses have joined together into an organization that sets its price for the blanket license it sells. But this is not a question simply of determining whether two or more potential competitors have literally "fixed" a "price." As generally used in the antitrust field, "price fixing" is a shorthand way of describing certain categories of business behavior to which the *per se* rule has been held applicable. The Court of Appeals' literal approach does not alone establish that this particular practice is one of those types or that it is "plainly anticompetitive" and very likely without "redeeming virtue." Literalness is overly simplistic and often overbroad. When two partners set the price of their goods or services they are literally "price fixing," but they are not *per se* in violation of the Sherman Act. . . . Thus it is necessary to characterize the challenged conduct as falling within or without that category of behavior to which we apply the label "*per se* price fixing." That will often, but not always be a simple matter.[32]

In establishing a standard by which to "characterize the challenged conduct as falling within or without the category of behavior to which we apply the label '*per se* price fixing'" the Court wrote:

> More generally, in characterizing this conduct under the *per se* rule, our inquiry must focus on whether the effect, and here because it tends to show effect . . . the purpose of the practice is to threaten the proper operation of our predominantly free market economy—that is, whether the practice facially appears to be one that would always or almost always tend to restrict competition and decrease output, and in what portion of the market, or instead one designed to "increase economic efficiency and render markets more rather than less competitive." . . . The blanket license, as we see it, is not a "naked restraint of trade with no purpose except stifling of competition," . . . but rather accompanies the integration of sales, monitoring, and enforcement against unauthorized copyright use.[33]

32. 441 U.S. at 8–9.
33. Id. at 19–20.

This language nicely brings together many of the points made in Section I of this brief. Justice White's language looks to output and competition restriction and efficiency creation as the principal determinants of the scope of the *per se* rule. A "naked" restraint is recognized as one which does not accompany an integration of productive facilities, which is used as a proxy for efficiency creating potential. Under the *Broadcast Music* approach, any arrangement that is not a "naked restraint of trade," i.e., that has a significant efficiency creating potential, would fall outside the category of "*per se* price fixing."[34] Since there was an integration of productive facilities involved in Monsanto's distribution system, and since that integration had the potential to create significant efficiencies of the type contemplated in *Sylvania*, the *Broadcast Music* approach would apply the rule of reason in the present case.

There remains, however, the question of when the efficiency-based characterization process adopted in *Broadcast Music* comes into play and when the "literal" approach to characterizing *per se* price fixing is appropriate. *Broadcast Music* itself did not answer this question. The most obvious answer, of course, is that the efficiency-based process should apply to all price fixing cases and, indeed, to all other transactions challenged under Section 1 of the Sherman Act as well.

This would not be difficult. The basic question in each case after an output restricting potential appeared would be whether the arrangement was a naked restraint of trade, i.e., without any significant efficiency creating potential. In most cases this question could be answered by inspecting the limitation on competition to see if it accompanied and was ancillary to an integration of productive facilities.[35] Appearance of this proxy for efficiency creating potential would signal the courts to move to the rule of reason inquiry or, at the very least, to a preliminary inquiry on the ancillarity issue.

If it were not for *Maricopa*, there would not be any reason to suppose that the *Broadcast Music* approach should not apply to all alleged price fixing agreements. In *Maricopa*, however, insisting that the Court had never wavered from

34. The restriction on competition must, of course, also be ancillary to the efficiency creating integration, as it appears to be in this case.

35. An integration of productive facilities will serve as an adequate proxy for efficiency creating potential most of the time. There may be some cases, however, where the efficiency creating potential is more subtle; it may be present even in the absence of an integration of productive facilities as that term is commonly understood. See Liebeler, *Book Review*, 66 Cal. L. Rev. 1317 (1979) at 1328–33. Most of the time, however, and certainly in this case, the integration of productive facilities will be a satisfactory proxy for efficiency creating potential.

the position that price fixing was illegal *per se*, Justice Stevens applied a literal *per se* approach to a system for delivering health care services that clearly produced significant cost savings. Justice Stevens relied heavily on *Socony* for the proposition that *all* price fixing arrangements are *per se* violations of Section 1 of the Sherman Act even though they may have, as was assumed on certiorari in *Maricopa*, "saved patients and insurers millions of dollars."[36] This position made it impossible for the majority to articulate a principled explanation of the Court's unanimous conclusion in *Broadcast Music* that the *per se* rule did not apply to the price fixing involved in the blanket copyright licenses granted by BMI and ASCAP. The majority could only indicate that the arrangement in *Maricopa* was "fundamentally different" from those in *Broadcast Music*, a position that the dissent found unsatisfactory.

The nature of the problem was clearly stated in Justice Powell's dissent:

It is settled law that once an arrangement has been labeled as "price fixing" it is to be condemned *per se*. But it is equally well settled that this characterization is not to be applied as a talisman to every arrangement that involves a literal fixing of prices. Many lawful contracts, mergers, and partnerships fix prices. But our cases require a more discerning approach. The inquiry in an antitrust case is not simply one of "determining whether two or more potential competitors have literally 'fixed' a 'price.' . . . [Rather], it is necessary to characterize the challenged conduct as falling within or without that category of behavior to which we apply the label "*per se* price fixing." That will often but not always, be a simple matter. *Broadcast Music, Inc. v. Columbia Broadcasting System, Inc., supra*, at 9.

Before characterizing an arrangement as a *per se* price fixing agreement meriting condemnation, a court should determine whether it is a "naked restrain[t] of trade with no purpose except stifling of competition." *United States v. Topco Associates, Inc.*, 405 U.S. 596, 608 (1972), quoting *White Motor Co. v. United States*, 372 U.S. 253, 263 (1963). See also *Continental T.V., Inc. v. GTE Sylvania Inc.*, 433 U.S. 36, 49–50 (1977). Such a determination is necessary because "departure from the rule-of-reason standard must be based upon demonstrable economic effect rather than . . . upon formalistic line drawing." *Id.*, at 58–59. As part of this inquiry, *a court must determine whether the procompetitive economies that the arrangement purportedly makes possible are substantial and not realizable in the absence of such an agreement.*[37]

36. 102 S. Ct. at 2472.
37. *Id.* at 2482 (emphasis added).

The dissent concluded:

> As in *Broadcast Music*, the plaintiff here has not yet discharged its burden of proving that respondents have entered a plainly anticompetitive combination without a substantial and procompetitive efficiency justification. In my view, the district court therefore correctly refused to grant the State's motion for summary judgment. This critical and disputed issue of fact remains unresolved.[38]

In the present case it is quite clear that plaintiff could not show that Monsanto's restricted distribution system did not have a substantial and procompetitive efficiency creating capacity. Absent such a showing, the *Broadcast Music* characterization approach would lead to the conclusion that Monsanto's conduct could not have constituted "*per se* price fixing."

Broadcast Music and *Maricopa* have not indicated when the *per se* rule should be applied literally and when the efficiency-based characterization process adopted in *Broadcast Music* must be undertaken. *Broadcast Music* provided little guidance on this issue; *Maricopa* compounded the confusion by applying a literal *per se* rule to an arrangement that quite clearly should have received the kind of analysis used in *Broadcast Music*. Our question, of course, is what are the implications of all this for using the efficiency-based characterization process to determine the scope of the *per se* rule in the context of distribution restrictions.

From a legal standpoint, the dilemma posed by the "price"/"nonprice" distinction advanced in *Sylvania* is a much more difficult problem than was involved either in *Broadcast Music* or in *Maricopa*. The arrangements in those cases either explicitly fixed prices (*Maricopa*) or were such that price fixing was a necessary effect of the arrangement (*Broadcast Music*). In either of those cases, therefore, the Court could have applied the literal *per se* rule without being out of line with the main body of traditional price fixing doctrine. No matter what one might think of such results from an economic perspective, the legal tools were at hand to decide those cases in a way that would not have been absurd when judged only by the standards of traditional legal doctrine.

This is not the case when it comes to dealing with the distinction between "price" and "nonprice" restrictions. As indicated above, it is simply impossible to make this distinction in a principled way by using a formalistic (legal) or literal approach. "Nonprice" restrictions clearly have the purpose and effect of reducing or eliminating price cutting by putative free riders; they thereby oper-

38. Id. at 2485.

ate at least to stabilize prices. Under traditional doctrine any agreement with such a purpose and effect, whether vertical or horizontal, is a *per se* illegal price fixing agreement. If *Socony* is applied without qualification, as it was in *Maricopa*, the category of "nonprice" restrictions becomes an empty set.

This is not acceptable. *Sylvania* holds that there are such things as "nonprice" distribution arrangements. But the distinction between "price" and "nonprice" arrangements is impossible to make on the basis of traditional legal doctrine. The only way out of this dilemma—to find some principled way to qualify and limit *Socony*—is to maintain the efficiency-based characterization approach adopted in *Broadcast Music*. We need not discuss the general scope of *Broadcast Music* or discuss the correctness of *Maricopa* to reach this conclusion and decide this case. Necessity alone dictates applying *Broadcast Music* to the dilemma created by the distinction between "price" and "nonprice" distribution agreements.

Once this is done, the efficiency creating capacity of Monsanto's restricted distribution system makes the *per se* rule inapplicable. It becomes clear that the decision below must be reversed.

III. *The Broadcast Music Approach Should Also Be Applied to the Alleged Boycott: Since It Also Had Significant Capacity to Create Efficiency It Must Also Be Governed by the Rule of Reason*

The court below upheld a jury instruction that group boycotts were illegal *per se* and that it should find that Monsanto violated Section 1 of the Sherman Act if it found that Monsanto agreed with some of its distributors to terminate plaintiff's distributorship or limit plaintiff's access to Monsanto products. Monsanto argued that only horizontal boycotts were *per se* illegal and that vertically imposed boycotts were subject to the rule of reason. The court held, on the basis of *Klor's* and *General Motors*, that an agreement between Monsanto and some of its distributors to terminate plaintiff was *per se* illegal even if it was not part of a scheme to fix retail prices.[39]

The decision below is faulty even granting the continuing vitality of *Klor's* and *General Motors*. The court simply misstated the facts of *Klor's*;[40] *General Motors*

39. 684 F.2d at 1235–36.

40. The court below said that "[i]n *Klor's*, a manufacturer and several retail stores agreed to boycott a retail store that competed with some of the boycotters." *Id.* at 1236. *Klor's* actually involved an agreement between one retail store (Broadway-Hale) and several manufacturers under which the manufacturers agreed not to supply Klor's with certain items sold by The Broadway.

was based on a horizontal agreement between the resellers, a factor not involved in the present case. For these reasons alone, the court below must be reversed on its boycott holding.

But this holding must also be reversed for all the reasons set forth in Section II above. The efficiency-based characterization process adopted in *Broadcast Music* is just as relevant to determining the scope of the *per se* rule as applied to group boycotts as it is to price fixing agreements. This approach has in fact been applied to group boycotts in an extremely able opinion by Judge Goldberg in the Fifth Circuit.[41] In dealing with a claim that certain restrictions on admission to a multiple listing service were *per se* illegal, he wrote:

> In light of the potency of the *per se* rule, however, the Supreme Court has recently reemphasized that the invocation of this conversation stopper must be limited to those situations which fairly fall within its rationale.[42]

After citing and discussing *Broadcast Music* and *Sylvania*, Judge Goldberg concluded:

> These and other recent cases make it clear that the legal characterization of a class of restraints requires "a judgment about [its] competitive significance" and that, in formulating that judgment, courts must pay heed to relevant "economic conceptions." . . . [43]

Since a multiple listing service carries with it a significant efficiency creating potential, the Fifth Circuit refused to apply the *per se* rule to the membership restrictions which that listing service had adopted. The efficiency creating capacity of restricted distribution systems strongly suggests that the same result should be reached here.

This conclusion is also supported by the fact that *Sylvania* sharply undercut the precedential value of *Klor's* and *General Motors*, the principal cases on which the court below relied in applying the *per se* rule to the alleged boycott in this case. The restrictions on competition in both of those cases seem to have been adopted to alleviate free rider problems similar to those involved in *Sylvania*. Indeed, it would not be going too far to conclude that *Sylvania* clearly even if implicitly overruled both of those cases, each of which has been sharply

---

41. *United States v. Realty Multi-List, Inc.*, 629 F.2d 1351 (5th Cir. 1980). See W. Liebeler, *Antitrust Advisor* §1.32 (2d ed. Supp. 1982).

42. 629 F.2d at 1363.

43. Ibid.

criticized.[44] It is respectfully suggested that the Court take this opportunity to clarify the relationship between *Sylvania* and these earlier cases, affirming and extending the *Sylvania* approach.

For all of these reasons, the court below should be reversed on its group boycott holding.

IV. *The Problem of Concerted Action*

This brief does not discuss in detail the question whether complaints to a supplier by one reseller about another reseller's price cutting followed by the latter's termination is sufficient evidence to go to the jury on the issue of concerted action. It does, however, suggest that so much emphasis has been placed on this issue because the courts have not been able to develop coherent standards for applying the *per se* rule and the rule of reason or for applying the rule of reason itself once concerted action is found. It appears that a refusal to find concerted action many times represents a judgment that the substantive behavior involved should not be treated as an antitrust violation.[45]

The rigidities of the *per se* rule require safety valves for its avoidance in those cases where its application seems inappropriate. One of those safety valves, as we have seen, is the process of characterization: If all price fixing agreements are *per se* illegal, the courts will refuse to characterize useful price fixing arrangements as price fixing arrangements. Another safety valve appears in connection with the question of concerted action. If joint action that seems useful would constitute a *per se* violation, many courts will refuse to find joint action. The difficulties of predicting the outcomes of cases under such circumstances are plain; a legal regime like this is inefficient.

These safety valves from the pressures of the *per se* rule would not be necessary if we had a principled way to determine when the *per se* rule applied and when a transaction was governed by the rule of reason. The efficiency-based characterization process of *Broadcast Music* provides a principled way to deal

44. See *Products Liability Insurance Agency, Inc. v. Crum & Forster Insurance Co.*, 682 F.2d 660 (7th Cir. 1982); Liebeler, *Book Review*, 66 Cal. L. Rev. 1317 (1979) at 1325; Liebeler, *Intrabrand "Cartels"* at 30; Posner, *The Rule of Reason and the Economic Approach: Reflections on the Sylvania Decision*, 45 U. Chi. L. Rev. 1 (1977) at 19–20.

45. There is a tendency to fall back on *United States v. Colgate & Co.*, 250 U.S. 300 (1919), whenever the going gets tough in this area of the law. This tendency for *Colgate* "to distort the analysis in other, apparently unrelated, areas of antitrust law" has been remarked in Baker, *Interconnected Problems of Doctrine and Economics in the Section One Labyrinth: Is Sylvania a Way Out?*, 67 Va. L. Rev. 1457 (1981) at 1471.

with this problem. Its adoption would help to solve the largely formalistic problems raised by the concerted action issue.

v. *A Distinction Between Contract Integration and Ownership Integration Is Formalistic Line Drawing: If Monsanto Could Legally Own and Operate Its Own Resale Outlets, It Should Legally Be Able to Make Contracts With Its Resellers That Would Replicate the Economic Incidents of Ownership*

Sylvania held that the scope of the *per se* rule and the rule of reason should be determined by demonstrable economic effect, not by formalistic line drawing. That decision necessarily calls into question the double standard that has long applied more rigorous tests of legality to contract arrangements than to ownership arrangements. Why, for example, should the *per se* rule ever be applied to a contract between a supplier and its resellers determining the manner in which the resellers should handle the supplier's product, when it would never be applied to a merger between those parties or to the supplier's expansion into reselling by means of internal growth? There is no satisfactory answer to this question in terms of demonstrable economic effect. The distinction is based on the formal differences between contract integration and ownership integration or on concern for the "freedom of traders," a concern that is not based on market considerations and which was explicitly rejected in *Sylvania*. After *Sylvania*, the same standards should be applied to contractual arrangements between a supplier and its resellers as would be applied to the acquisition of those resellers by the supplier, or to the supplier's integration into the resale level by means of expansion by growth. Under that standard the *per se* rule could not be applied in the present case, or indeed, in any other case involving restricted distribution arrangements.

This point was recently made by Judge Gee in an opinion of the Fifth Circuit Court of Appeals.[46] In upholding certain restrictions which Liquid Carbonic Corp. had placed by contract on its resellers, Judge Gee wrote:

> The final reason why we find the presumed reduction in intrabrand competition insufficient to constitute injury to competition is that, given the apparent nature of the market and Liquid's relative place in it, Liquid most probably could have chosen, consistent with the antitrust laws, to do all of its own distributing in the New Orleans area, either by cancelling its distributors and expanding internally or by simply acquiring the distributors

---

46. *Red Diamond Supply, Inc. v. Liquid Carbonic Corp.*, 637 F.2d 1001 (5th Cir. 1981).

themselves. If Liquid had thus vertically integrated into distribution, it clearly could have instructed its employees to abide by territorial and customer restrictions. And since Liquid could have accomplished these ends by either internal expansion or merger, either of which would have had an even greater impact on intrabrand competition, we fail to see why it would have been unreasonable for Liquid to accomplish the same ends by contract.[47]

This conclusion is consistent with the economic analysis of the scope of the *per se* rule and the rule of reason set forth above. It provides still another reason why the judgment below should be reversed.

Conclusion

The Court should reverse the judgment of the court below. That can be done most consistently both with the prior decisions of this Court and with the principles of demonstrable economic effect by applying the efficiency-based characterization process adopted in *Broadcast Music* to the problem of determining the scope of the *per se* rule and the rule of reason in restricted distribution cases. The same approach should be applied to the boycott issue, as discussed above.

Dated: June 20, 1983.
   Respectfully submitted,
   Wesley J. Liebeler,
   (Counsel of Record),
   UCLA Law School,
   Attorney for Amicus Curiae

---

47. *Id.* at 1006.

REMINISCENCES OF ERRORS
A TRIBUTE IN HONOR OF DEAN WILLIAM H. MECKLING ON HIS RETIREMENT

Happily we are gathered to honor Bill Meckling, who I am sure is honored by our presence. But not as impressed and honored had we all assembled at the Oak Hill Country Club earlier today—instead of this evening—to be a large gallery cheering Bill's golfing competence (and mine, of course) in a round of golf—ooohing and ahhing every stroke through eighteen holes, the faculty sharing duty as Bill's caddy. That would have been longer remembered and more widely noted. Alas, I was told, he doesn't yet deserve that much respect. So here we are, in a second best world.

To most of you Bill Meckling's departure as your dean is lugubrious; to me it is pleasant. It releases Bill from administrative and personnel trivialities, to the glory of golf with perhaps some writing, unless precluded by duties as antique finisher for his dear wife Becky's antique business—in which, you will note, she has permitted him no role as administrator or manager. And that is no error on her part. So that is not an error about which I shall talk, if I conform to the title of my talk.

Which reminds me, long ago it was my pleasure to introduce Bill to an audience as follows, "I present to you William Meckling, a most unusual man—one who has never managed a business, who has no advanced degree, and who has never been on a university staff as a teacher or administrator, but who, nevertheless, has just been appointed dean of the Graduate School of Management of the University of Rochester."

Now, you'd think that the university president who made that appointment must have been pretty dumb and that that is one of the errors about which I am going to reminisce, unless you know that person was Allen Wallis. And then you would begin to suspect that is precisely why Bill was appointed. Allen knew

Working Paper No. MERC 83-16 (Rochester, N.Y., University of Rochester Managerial Economics Research Center, June 1983), reprinted by permission of the William E. Simon Graduate School of Business Administration at the University of Rochester.

what the requirements are *not*, and what they *are*. He knew that required was an utter intolerance and impatience of incompetence. Bill certainly has displayed that trait, even intolerance in his own incompetence. I have seen, more often than I recall with happiness, his own spectacular occasional incompetence at golf, accompanied simultaneously by an explosion of wrath, expletives, and golf clubs flying across the fairway. But within minutes he is calm, collected, and forgiving, and naively insisting he has found what was wrong and will not make that kind of bad swing again. And he has always been correct in that promise—at least until the next hole. However, in others, intellectual incompetence, once displayed, is not forgiven for a long, long time—indeed, if ever—as some of those who are not here could testify.

But without that trait how else could he have searched, experimented, culled, retained, and formed this school of management, which, in my carefully considered opinion expressed several times to students and parents, is now the best school of management. You who have survived that screening—with screaming, I am sure—are the evidence for that proposition and for the wisdom of Allen Wallis's departure from the conventional in selecting Bill as dean.

Though this occasion is for Bill, I owe credit to Allen for bringing us together. In about 1938 or so Allen taught at Stanford, and I was one of his— I think it was four—students in his statistics course. Allen taught me a lot of statistics. Incidentally, if some of you people in finance had had that kind of course, a lot of the mumbo jumbo in the early capital-asset-pricing literature would have been avoided, and progress would have been a lot faster.

Though Allen was teaching statistics in the classroom, he was also teaching economics by his asides, random remarks, and observations about what the rest of the faculty was teaching. When he said something about statistics, I had learned to think hard and long to be sure I understood. So when he said something about economics, especially something contrary to what I was learning in the economics classes, I thought about that too. And when he asked if I had read Adam Smith—and I had not—I decided I had better read it if I wanted to pass the doctoral examination in statistics. He even had the nerve to give the back of his hand to Keynes' General Theory, which we were learning. And that's when my error rate began to decline.

But what has this to do with Bill? Years later, in the Fall of 1946 to be exact, when I had just joined UCLA, I got a phone call from Allen, who at the moment was consulting with the Douglas Aircraft Company, the sponsor-administrator of a new venture called the RAND Corporation. He asked if I could see him that evening, but I had a social engagement, and I couldn't graciously break it. Allen

then said, "Well later, maybe tomorrow." The next morning I phoned the Douglas Company and was told Allen had just flown out to Florida on one of their
new experimental planes—I think it was the DC-6. Even then he was flying
wherever he could.

A few weeks later I was invited to work with RAND, an opportunity arising
from Allen's suggestion to John Williams, then in charge of the nonexistent social science division. There is no doubt that except for my association with
RAND I would probably have later moved to Berkeley, a fate worse than death.
But now to the point: a few years later, Reuben Kessel showed up, and we became very close friends. Recognizing a good thing when he saw one, he then
was instrumental in inducing Bill to join RAND.

I remember my first "getting to know" meeting with Bill at Reuben's apartment on Sunset Boulevard. What Reuben and I said—plus probably the high
salary—attracted Bill to RAND, where we became and have remained close
friends for about thirty years. Now that must be very impressive to you on the
faculty here. How could anyone long remain a close friend of Bill? Well, it
hasn't been easy. But I knew how. You see, among my close friends I can count
people like Stephen Enke, Reuben Kessel, and Karl Brunner. Now if I could remain close friends with the likes of them, surely I could with Bill. The reason
is, I believe, that my genetic makeup is heavily loaded with tolerance and com-
passion, acquired from my famous Middle Eastern ancestors, like Saladin the
Great and Genghis Khan. And Bill surely has inherited his lovable traits from
his Middle European ancestors, like Frederick of Prussia and Attila the Hun.
We have well-matched genes.

However, the point is that it was Allen Wallis's influence that got me to
RAND and thence Bill. So, Allen, again my thanks to you.

But despite their help and influence, I have made some errors because of
imperfect competence in economic analysis. And I would like to confess and
ask for your forgiveness.

One is an error, or what I now believe is an error, in a paper I co-authored a
decade ago with Harold Demsetz on the "firm." My co-author doesn't know I'm
doing this. He might not even approve. So, I must say he is not responsible for
the initial error and not responsible if I am wrong now. So Harold, wherever
you are or are going, forgive me for selling out. It's tough being a co-author with
someone who is so indecisive as me. I hope you have better luck with your new
co-author, George Stigler, but don't count on it.

In that paper we—hereafter I shall say I to avoid implicating my co-author—
argued that a firm was a coalition of resource owners who had contracted to

jointly produce a salable product with the intention of each member becoming better off than in any other productive coalition. It was asserted that the performance of resources jointly used, but not jointly owned, by three or more owners could not be costlessly measured—sometimes described by the term "impacted information"—so that some method of monitoring—or "measurement" as some people now like to call it—would be used to reduce the losses from shirking—or what some people call "opportunistic" behavior. You should begin to think of Oliver Williamson's work at this point, for aside from our elaboration of his terms—"small numbers," "impacted information," "opportunism," and "idiosyncracies"—we added little except improved exposition, illustrations, and applications of his formal and opaquely exposited ideas.

In that article emphasis was on teamwork, monitoring to detect shirking, attention to who did the monitoring under what reward system, and on the revision of the coalition in response to the monitored performance. We stated that everyone had an incentive to reduce other people's shirking and that the monitor was rewarded with a residual as an inducement to good monitoring. I want now to suggest an improvement, i.e., admit an error. In a later article with Klein and Crawford on vertical integration, resource specificity, and expropriable quasi-rents, I recognized the necessity of a correction.

Whereas in the earlier article we claimed the monitor is offered a residual in order to induce good monitoring, my present belief is that the bearer of the coalition's unavoidable residual or loss potential will most want good monitoring. The bearer of that risk needs good monitoring; it is not that risk is imposed in order to induce good monitoring. I wish the earlier article had asked, Who most wants good monitoring? Who loses the most from poor monitoring, poor measurement, excessive opportunistic behavior, shirking, etc.? But those questions were not asked.

I won't here elaborate on what contingent or uncertain events the risk refers to. Suffice it to say it refers to the natural risk of environmental events, the uncertainty of outcomes of decisions, and the "certainty" about the self-interested behavior of one's fellow members in the coalition—or what are often called agency costs, moral hazard, and adverse selection.

There is another conjecture. Yoram Barzel conjectures that the person whose services are most difficult to monitor will be the risk-bearer because that makes him monitor himself. So we have three conjectures: (1) Risk bearing is imposed in order to induce good monitoring; (2) monitoring is most desired by, and performed by, the risk-bearer or his agent; and (3) those who are most difficult to monitor will bear the risk as a self-monitoring inducement. The first is, I think, mistaken. The third is also mistaken, or perhaps, I should say, is less significant, while the second—risk-bearers want good monitoring—is, I think, more potent, especially when tied to the fact of differential interresource specificity within a coalition.

Earlier I had thought excessively in terms of a team of resources and subadditivity of the production function rather than about differences in interspecificity of resources that imply special contractual relations. I now assert without empirical validation that the feature which is critical is that the several resources assembled into the coalition would have different costs or prospects of losses of mobility *after* dealing with the coalition, or different salvage value losses, which differences imply special contractual relations such as those that characterize what is called a "firm."

In other words, resources' specificity to a coalition is central to the analysis of the coalition. In forming a coalition, some members will make investments the subsequent value of which outside the coalition will be less than the value in the coalition and also less than its costs. If its value elsewhere is lower than its value in the coalition, it is called specific to the coalition. Resources in the coalition worth as much elsewhere are nonspecific, or general. If the coalition fails, the general resources lose no future income, but those specific to the coalition will lose the excess of the investment cost over the salvage value. The portion of investment cost that is nonsalvageable with other coalitions is the coalition specific quasi-rent, i.e., to the other resources with which it is associated. The resource to which it is specific may try to expropriate the quasi-rent specific to it.

For example, if I invest $1 that would be worth $1.15 when used with your resource, but worth only $.60 with any other, then $.40 is my resource's specific quasi-rent. The extra $.15 is profit, which might also be expropriable along with the $.40 under a threat to terminate your joint activity with me. Two features are involved: (1) specificity of quasi-rent of one resource to another owned by a different person, plus (2) the second's ability to control its flow of service. This concept is not new. *What I assert is that without specificity the entity we typically call a firm would not have evolved.* It is the owner of these specific, or interdependent, resources who has the greatest incentive to assure success of the coalition, whereas owners of completely general resources have no interest in the coalition's success. They could always do as well elsewhere.

I didn't appreciate the applicability and implications of that simple distinction to the rationale of the firm—though I had long known the distinction, of course—until working on the Klein, Crawford paper on vertical integration—a name for ownership of productive resources used in a generally recognized sequence of productive stages. In that paper, an incentive to vertical integration or joint ownership was attributed to the interspecificity of resources, which, once assembled into a productive sequence, became specific to the coalition. They would be worth less—let us say "nothing," to be dramatic—if removed from the coalition to which it had become "specific"—or "idiosyncratic," in Williamson's words. This opens the door to opportunistic expropriation of a resource's specific quasi-rent. Obviously the contractual arrangements and system of payments to each resource will depend, in part at least, on the anticipated degree of specificity to the coalition.

This suggests that in applying economic analysis to the composition and activity within the "firm," we should think in terms not only of labor (rentals of current services) or capital (purchases of future services) and of different supply responses to prices but also of effects of *ex post* coalitional specificity. Already we recognize the difference between general and specific assets, but I believe we have not yet applied that to organizational activity in general. As a result, the folklore of "industrial organization or antitrust" is virtually bankrupt, and the consequences for the validity of legal principles and laws that have been adopted are embarrassing.

Try to imagine a coalition of completely general resources, each of whom will be worth as much elsewhere as in this coalition. How would they contract for their services? Would they use a simple spot exchange? Not if the coalition operates as a team with superadditive nonseparable products. But it would involve payments according to revealed marginal productivities or alternatives. Competition among members to form unblocked coalitions would assure that no member obtained less than is known to be available outside this coalition. Potential coalitions would assure each person of an earning at least as large in other potential coalitions.

It *would* be the firm or team in the earlier, now partially obsolete, Alchian-Demsetz paper—a group performing team activity (now usually called subadditivity) with a monitor-measurer who was tacitly assumed to also be the director and risk-bearer.

By the way, what I mean by a "coalition" is any set of owners of resources with contracts among themselves *restricting* their own allowable choices among *future* alternatives. They *restrict their future* options with respect to each other. A series of spot contracts, like buying groceries from a store, does not restrict one's future options. However, a long-term contract—the name for one that does restrict future options—creates a coalition among the contracting members. So a *coalition* is here defined to be a set of resource owners constrained by long-term contracts. One reason for a binding contract that binds a second party is to induce a "first party" to make a preliminary investment in a resource which will become specific to a "second party," who restrains his future options so as to reduce the prospect of opportunistic behavior that would expropriate the first party's specific resource value. If the invested resources were not specific to the other resources, contractual restraints would be far less significant, if not zero. Spot renting or purchases of services would prevail. This is all obvious and well known, but it seems to have not received the weight it deserves in analyses of the "firm."

You can now see why I would like to erase the following assertion in the 1972 article on the firm: ". . . Long-term contracts between employer and employee are not the essence of the organization we call a firm," a statement I now believe to be dead wrong. The long-term contract in the context of Williamson's "idiosyncracies, small numbers, bounded rationality and opportunism" is surely his way of pointing attention to effects of expropriable quasi-rents.

The range of contractual or relational restraints is matched by the range of types of nonsalvageable specific investments. A buyer may merely "suggest" he will be a customer and induce a seller's trivial investment in buyer-specific service facilities in anticipation of the buyer's future business. Another buyer may have to make commitments in order to induce more extensive nonsalvageable specific investments by the supplier. Indefinite promises, expectations, and commitments will be formed in a variety of relationships among the parties and will take the form of long-term contracts, price protection, reciprocity, exchanges, hostages, price limitations, union representation, seniority, layoffs rather than wage renegotiation, and even government regulation. And, of course, common ownership of the interspecific resources, often called vertical integration, is most common, though it can take the horizontal form of joint ventures. But the terms "horizontal" and "vertical" are deceptive identifiers. In some cases the supplier is restrained to act as customers would like and expect, even when customers have made no explicit promise of future purchases and would lose if the supplier were to shut down (and provide no future repair services). The supplying firm acts this way when it has nonsalvageable specialized investment of value to customers, and the value of this specialized investment to the supplying firm can be maintained only if the firm acts reliably.

(Perhaps we can denote a firm in terms of the following features: measurability of performance of components in team production and the opportunity for expropriation of quasi-rents of interspecific resources. So we say, a firm is a (1) coalition of interspecific resources, some of which are owned in common, (2) and some of which are compensated according to some criteria other than separably additive outputs and other than by directly measured marginal productivity (3) of salable products.)

The implications of the recognition (I do not call it an interpretation) of the critical role of coalitional specificity in the conception of the firm are enormous. The people who are typically said to own a firm (how can one own a coalition?) turn out to be the owners of the resources whose values are specific to that coalition's activities. They are most interested in its adequate monitoring and direction and obtain the control of its monitoring, direction, activities, and future membership. They are mostly the people called the stockholders in a corporation. Indeed that is all the stockholders own—the resources specific to that coalition. They will typically rent the general resources, such as common labor.

Labor in a coalition will not always be general. Some will be specific to the coalition and will therefore initially demand some contractual control or share of authority in decisions. To the extent labor invests at its own cost in talent specific to a particular "firm" or coalition, the more will it initially demand decision authority. And to the extent any labor is paid more than it could earn elsewhere—a situation resulting possibly from monopoly power or tenure or any wage system in which later pay is larger than later marginal product—to that extent it will seek, possibly *ex post*, decision authority. The difficulty is for an outside observer to ascertain whether the labor in some firm has that kind of claim or is trying to expropriate wealth of other resources specific to the coalition.

The implications for the general interpretation I pass over; they are obvious, even if denied by "corporate democracy" advocates.

Another error into which I have been led by thinking of cooperation among independent firms or agents is that of the effects of unions in restricting new entrants. I now realize that union restriction of entry can prevent wasteful, excessive amounts of labor, even capital, in their occupations. When I assert it, as I just have, you may think I am not recounting, but making new errors. I am simply stating that the form of joint activity had misled me, much as federal judges are misled by the form of contractual relations, for example, as when they naively ask whether some joint venture is horizontal or vertical in order to cast judgment on its propriety. I have been constrained by a similar mind-set.

If any group acted through a union to restrict entry, as with taxis in New York, it must have been monopolizing.

But when it was brought to my attention that Texas shrimp fishermen were unionizing to keep out Vietnamese entrants in the shrimp fishing areas of Texas, and that they were doing so to avoid overfishing or overinvestment in efforts to capture rights to a common resource owned by no one, I realized that the union was establishing a system of surrogate private property rights *and* at the same time was assigning those rights to its own members. The critically important factor was the establishing of a system of enforceable property rights in shrimp breeding beds. The assignment of those newly enforced rights to union members was irrelevant as an economic criterion of propriety, and furthermore, none of this should be confused with monopoly restrictions, which might or might not also be present. Establishing rights prevents overentry which would have brought the average product down to the marginal opportunity value of new resources, thereby reducing the value of economic output, as does the absence of property rights in apples on the apple tree in the public park.

The union was performing a socially valuable service, though the members were only trying to improve their own circumstances. If they also acted to restrict entry to obtain monopoly rents, that does not deny that they were also acting to preserve true economic rents of the scarce, natural, unowned resource.

Similarly, taxis are limited in New York City. But how do I know that does not prevent overusage of unpriced streets? If the streets were rented to users, then the number of cabs might be even less. The value of the medallions might contain some of the street value as well as some monopoly rent value.

I want to be clear in indicating that the error I refer to is not that I had mistakenly thought the cabs and unions were acting in an unnecessarily restrictive monopolistic way, but that I had tended to think that a coalition of independent agents in the sense of a union or politically active group was somehow different from that of a group that has become a "firm." I therefore now regard the concept of a "firm" as vacuous and without analytical use. So I would go further than Ronald Coase and speak of the "irrelevance" of the "firm."

I now call to your attention a confusion of terminology, or a sort of error, with significant legal implications, one to which I hope I do not again in the future fall victim. Bill and I compete and cooperate when playing golf. We cooperate in making a contest, and we compete in trying to win. Cooperation means action to increase the wealth capable of being portioned among the cooperators, who are also competing in trying to enlarge their obtained portion of the larger total. We should refrain from thinking of competition and cooperation as mutually exclusive. Though this is a matter of words, consider the following. The law typically permits actions if the cooperative venture is deemed to be "within a firm" and considers the members to be cooperating in achieving their goals.

Yet cooperation across boundaries of firms is likely to be ruled illegal, on the belief that "firms" must only compete, not ever cooperate—for that would be monopolistic, anticompetitive, and similar emotive words which I hope you will eschew. But why is cooperation across so-called independent coalitions or firms less desirable than within them? If competition is desired, does that mean cooperation is not desired among firms? Or that competition does not occur within firms? That seems to be the premise of a substantial portion of the antitrust law, which thinks of a firm as a monolithic entity, like a black box or a single person, a conception suggested by people who say things like "the firm does this" or "the corporation does that."

The firm is not an individual entity with a single objective. It does not have goals in the sense individuals do. Some say the objective is to maximize the wealth of the stockholders, but that is valid *only under a particular contractual arrangement*. The individual interests may all be dependent on a common achieved value, but that does not make the coalition an entity with that goal. Instead each member has his own objectives which, under some appropriate contractual liaisons with other people, just happen to all be achieved under that contractual arrangement by a maximization of the total.

That does not warrant thinking of the coalition as an entity, for as we know, with slight changes in specificity to a coalition or with slight nonenforceability of the contracts, the objectives of each member no longer are best achieved by a mutual convergence on one surrogate objective—the maximum value of the stockholders' wealth. Other people besides the stockholders may acquire specificity in the coalition, and that leads to divergences among the members. Only if all the specific resources are held in common by one set of people, with no others held by a different set of people, does the maximization of the stockholders' interest clearly lead to maximizing the interests of each and all members. For example, trouble arises as soon as some laborers become specific, or as soon as some of the coalition-specific assets are claimed by bondholders (instead of all by stockholders). Competition and divergence of objectives develop within the coalition.

It is fallacious and misleading to think primarily of "cooperation within a firm" and "competition across independent firms." Cooperation, like competition, is not bound by the boundaries of a coalition or firm. Those boundaries are poor criteria for "legitimate, proper, ethical, legal" actions. To use the words "independence of firms" as a criterion of competitive versus collusive boundaries is to use an empty terminology.

Instead one should ask, What is the purpose and consequences of this or that type of cooperation or competition? not artful questions like, Is it one firm or independent firms? or Is it a group of independent firms that are acting jointly?

This exposes another error I used to commit. I thought baseball players, the stars especially, were exploited by a cartel of team owners under the reserve clauses. In the same vein, in a suit involving the National Football League, the Oakland Raiders, and the City of Los Angeles, the judge declared that the issue depends on whether the National Football League is "one firm" or a group of colluding "independent" entities. That is the kind of pitiful naivete economists have foisted on the law by careless terminology and conceptualizing. I no longer believe Major League Baseball is best characterized as a cartel nor that the star athletes were underpaid when they were not free agents under the reserve clause.

However, I am here only indicating the analytical deficiency that led to my possible misinterpretation. I will not here outline the alternative interpretation in which I now place more credence, though the empirical evidence with which to test that interpretation has not been systematically investigated.

All this may seem just a matter of semantics, but some of you are trying to be successful researchers seeking new understanding. But most of us are teachers, middlemen purveyors of that better understanding. The words we use can make a big difference. Especially impressive to me is the difference it makes in teaching. For example, now my student lawyers and jurists, when they run across terms like "anticompetitive," hesitate and act not reflexively but reflectively.

Since no other errors have I committed, or will here acknowledge, I end by thanking you, and I am sure you join me in wishing Bill, on the second nine of the great golf course at the Country Club of Perfect Life and Liberty, good health, low scores, and loving grandchildren as caddies.

SPECIFICITY, SPECIALIZATION, AND COALITIONS

Several flaws in the interpretation of "firms" have obscured understanding of evolving organizations. Among these are (1) a failure to recognize that what is called a firm is a special set of contracts among owners of resources used in the coalition; (2) a failure to see that a capitalistic firm involves ownership in common of the coalition-specific resources; (3) a failure to recognize specialization in components of the rubric of private property rights; (4) a failure to recognize incentives to renege on promises; (5) the failure to recognize monitoring by competition with the managerial and capital markets; (6) the erroneous belief that salable private property stockholder rights (common stock) in the large corporations are (or should be) identical to political voting rights; (7) preoccupation with firms rather than individuals as competitors; (8) the failure to recognize that competition and cooperation occur in the contractual forms of organizing and coordinating economic incentives. The significance of some of these will be indicated after some concepts are defined.

Private Property

By the exercise of property rights I mean (a) determination of use, (b) bearing of the market value, and (c) exchangeability of rights to (a) and (b). When all these rights to each resource are effectively held by identifiable, specific persons, the society is controlled by "private" property rights, i.e., capitalism.

The right to the marketable value does not mean the marketable value is independent of acts of other people—acts that do not affect any of the physical properties or characteristics of the good. You may write a better textbook and reduce the market value of mine, though my textbook is not changed in any physical or usable way. By definition, in a capitalist system the bearer of the exchange value of a good is the "owner." Risk of changing values is unavoidable. Someone will bear it.

All the components of property rights to a resource need not be held in common. It is possible to sell or delegate the rights to decide uses separately

Reprinted, by permission of the author, from *Zeitschrift für die gesamte Staatswissenschaft* (Journal of Institutional and Theoretical Economics) 140 (March 1984): 34–49.

from the rights and thereby obtain the gains of specialization, or separation, of use decision from control and ownership, where ownership is the right to the marketable value. The gains from specialization need no elaboration here.

Coalitions as Teams

Another source of gains is teamwork: a group of people can by "joint" action achieve more than the sum of their separate results, where the total is not the sum of separate amounts from each member. The action does not entail an exchange of identifiable products of one person to another person. The reward to each is a portion of the team's salable output value. (This sale value criterion is often used to distinguish a firm from other coalitions, such as the family.)

A coalition's achieved value can be affected by several stochastic events: the luck in assembling well-matched team members, the luck of the environment, and the contractual relations which affect incentives. We can think of the forming of a coalition as being a process of sampling among potential members of a team, the contractual relations, and the environment. The assembly of a profitable coalition is a stochastic, costly process. Successes must be expected to cover the cost of failures if search is to be induced. Uncertain imitability of successes protects successful coalitions and appears to result in larger profits—like "profits" on a winning lottery ticket. It follows that a successful firm is one that achieves a value exceeding that which its members could have earned elsewhere. The excess can reflect the simple fact of a successful search having a probability of less than 1.00.

Part of the value of a successful team is the value of having assembled a successful team—that is, the avoidance of future costs of *searching for* a successful team. Attempting to copy the successful performance of another firm requires search for and testing of performance of appropriate, well-matched inputs. It must be anticipated that future revenue will be sufficient to cover not only the subsequent operating costs but also the exploratory investments in detecting and creating a viable team. Therefore, though an existing successful firm may be making more than its continuing costs, in fact its investors may be only breaking even when the initial investment costs in discovery of that successful, well-matched team are included. That continuing excess of revenue over the remaining steady-state flow of wages and rents of the successful team is the value of an invisible asset—the successful assembly of a well-matched team.

Incidentally, if the employees of that successful team colluded effectively, they could expropriate the specific quasi-rent of the successful discovery and formation of a successful team. Also, this could explain attempts by some firms to buy other firms, rather than seek to create their own by a stochastic search and "internal growth," the cost of which should be expected to match the premium paid for the successful team.

A strong temptation, to which many succumb, is to regard the excess as a product individually attributable to the team members. For example, higher salaries obtained by star professional athletes when allowed to solicit offers from other teams are often regarded as evidence of the athletes' having been underpaid by a restrictive contract. But if the team organizer invested in search for such talents and in developing the talents, and if such talent would not otherwise have been noted, it is hard to say an athlete was "underpaid" or "exploited," or that preventing an athlete from soliciting or accepting such bids is improper. In any event, I am in no position to say what is "underpaid" or "improper," so I offer this as an unproven, incompletely formulated alternative to the usual view that athletes are victims of a bidding cartel. A germane issue is, What kind of contracts were formed in the endeavor to find, assess, organize, and direct that talent into a viable team? And, What contracts enhance that prospect?

As a terminological matter, I define members of a coalition to be cooperating in attempts to maximize the coalition value. They are competing, even while cooperating, when they act in ways designed to increase their individual shares of the group total, and some or all may end up with less than if none had so behaved. This has been posed in many different descriptive terms. For example, Williamson: "opportunism"; Barzel: "measurement problem"; Wilson: "moral hazard"; Stiglitz: "asymmetric information with uncertainty"; Alchian and Demsetz: "shirking and monitoring"; Klein and Leffler, and Telser: "self-enforcing contracts"; Klein, Crawford, and Alchian: "vertical integration"; Strotz: "time inconsistency"; Goldberg: "right to be served"; Coase: "the firm"; Jensen and Meckling: "agencies." But "in truth" it is simply a contract formation and enforcement problem. In some cases the danger is so slight as to be overlooked. In others it is so great that potential joint action is thwarted.

Resource Specificity

In forming a coalition, some members will make investments, the value of which elsewhere will be less than the value in the coalition (and also less than its costs). If its value in the coalition is higher than elsewhere, it is defined to be specific to the coalition. Some of the resources have values independent of the coalition. They will be able to earn just as much elsewhere. They are nonspecific to this coalition. If the coalition fails, they lose nothing. But resources that are specific to the coalition are those that will lose the excess of the investment cost over the salvage value.

Specificity to a "coalition" is not the same as specificity to a particular set of other resources. A set of commonly owned interspecific resources may be able to move away from a set of other resources (in the coalition) with no loss, and hence are not specific to the coalition, though the members of that particular subset are interdependent. An input with "specificity" is one whose value depends on—i.e., "is specific to"—the behavior of some other particular resource. The return on the investment cost that is nonsalvageable if the other resource to which it is specifically dependent disappears is called the specific quasi-rent. For example, if I invest in a machine, A, whose value depends on services rendered by some particular other resource or person, say B, then the loss of return on A's investment value if B's services are withdrawn is a nonsalvageable specific quasi-rent value of A specific to B.[1]

The specific quasi-rent is *expropriable* if the owner (or administrator) of the "specializing" resource can control its own effects on values of the resources specific to it.[2] For example, if a building is constructed on land owned by someone else who can do nothing to reduce the services rendered to the building, the building owner has no fear of opportunistic behavior by the landlord, though the landlord must be aware of the possibility that the building owner will refuse to pay the agreed rent. However, if the land contains a spring with water desired by the building owner, the landlord's possible threat to shut off the water is something the building owner should anticipate, especially if costs of contract enforcement or indemnities are high.[3]

1. Reciprocity-specific resources have values that depend on the presence and behavior of each other. (The degree of such dependence is here assumed to be all or nothing, in order to simplify exposition.) It is nonreciprocal if one depends on the presence of the other without reverse dependence. O. Williamson ("Credible Commitments: Using Hostages to Support Exchanges," *American Economic Review* 13 [1983]: 519–40) uses the term "dedicated" asset to refer to specificity to a particular user—a term I wish I had used first.

2. B. Klein, R. Crawford, and A. Alchian, "Vertical Integration, Appropriable Rents, and the Competitive Contracting Process," *Journal of Law and Economics* 21 (1978): 297–326.

3. A difference between a "quasi-rent" and what we will call a "bargain" may be pertinent. Any difference between the lowest and the next lowest price of supply to a buyer (setting aside the question of why a seller would give such favorable terms) is here called a

Anticipation of expropriability of quasi-rent will motivate *pre*-investment protective contractual arrangements. The owner of a resource whose value is alterable or affected by specific other people will have an interest in controlling or restricting their acts. If arrangements are made between the several resource owners to restrict or control the future actions, the several are said to be a coalition. Even if acts of one party can affect the value of another, if no arrangements are made to influence the future acts, the two are not in a coalition. Coalitions, as defined here, take many forms: marriages, business firms, cooperatives, franchises, to mention a few.

If an employee doesn't care at all whether the firm disappears, because the alternatives elsewhere are just as good—which is the way a customer may regard the presence of a grocery store—then in what useful sense is the employee any more regarded as a member of the coalition than a customer should be so regarded? None at all. What counts is the loss one experiences in the event one must leave the coalition—i.e., not be able to transact with the coalition. If someone's wealth (or utility) is dependent on the actions of the coalition, that person is a member of the coalition if protective arrangements have been mutually formed.

The Long-Term Contract

The proposition that long-term contracts are a necessary attribute of the coalition called a firm is prescient.[4] Spot contracts do not restrict responses to future developments by contractual provisions. A series of spot transactions is not a long-term contract. A long-term contract contractually restricts responses to future events. Long-term contracts induce investments by one party, the value of which will depend on the actions of the other party. We

---

"bargain." A new grocery store nearer some resident which provides better terms than the next best supplier gives the lucky resident a "bargain." Or an employee may be getting substantially higher pay than he could get from the next best employer—and not because of any investment made by the employee in improving his productivity to the employer. No prior investment is necessary for a "bargain" nor is any quasi-rent involved. Nevertheless, the "bargain" is specific to some supplier, without whom it would not be available. Incidentally, this bargain is not a "consumer surplus," which occurs even if all suppliers make identical offers with no resultant "bargain" to a buyer. And, of course, it is not a "quasi-rent," since no prior investment was made in any asset that yields that "bargain" for the beneficiary.

4. O. Williamson, *Markets and Hierarchies: Analysis and Antitrust Implications* (New York: Free Press, 1975).

would therefore expect to observe long-term contract restraints on one party to induce some dependent, expropriable, interspecific investment by the other. "Coadaptation" or behavior in conformity with implicit long-term contracts preserves and reflects reputability for not exploiting the "trust" of others. Thus, if a copper refiner supplies a fabricator who has made investments, the values of which depend on the expected behavior of the refiner, it is likely that the refiner will be expected to and will supply the fabricator with copper as if there were a formal long-term contract. (We leave aside the question of why explicit long-term contracts are not made.)

The range of promises and restraints accommodates the range of nonsalvageable, induced, coadapting investments. A buyer who merely "suggests" he will continue to buy may induce a seller's current investment in buyer-specific facilities. Indefinite promises, expectations, and commitments come in a variety of relationships: long-term contracts, price protection and stability, reciprocity, exchanges and hostages involving interspecific resources, loyal customer reputation, franchises, price limitations, advertising, exclusive dealing, job security, tenure, first refusal rights, union representation, and seniority are examples. Even if customers have made no implicit promises of future business, the seller may act responsibly and reliably to customers because the seller has made nonsalvageable specialized investments, the values of which can be maintained only if the coalition members perform as the public expects.[5]

In contrast, Alchian and Demsetz asserted that "neither the employee nor the employer is bound by any contractual obligations to continue their relationship. Long-term contracts between employer and employee are not the essence of the organization we call a firm." In the light of Williamson's analysis that assertion is incorrect. Williamson's remarkable discussion of the long-term contract in the context of "idiosyncracies, small numbers, bounded rationality and opportunism" is surely his way of calling attention to nonsalvageable investments with quasi-rent expropriation by opportunistic action of the other parties.[6] A long-lasting relationship without nonsalvageable investments specific to the other parties is not a representation of the contracts in a "firm." Typically, some parties must make some nonsalvageable, specialized

5. B. Klein and K. Leffler, "The Role of Market Forces in Assuring Contractual Performance," *Journal of Political Economy* 89 (1981): 615–41.

6. A. A. Alchian and H. Demsetz, "Production, Information Costs, and Economic Organization," *American Economic Review* 62 (December 1972): 775–95; Williamson, *Markets and Hierarchies*.

investment (e.g., location of residence, firm-specific learning by the employee, or some employer investment in employer-specific knowledge and techniques).

Earlier references to "teamwork" rested on the fact that aggregate output could be neither defined nor measured as the sum of outputs of individual members. This led to monitoring, i.e., detecting in some way the marginal product of each member. Team production makes measurability of *marginal* products difficult, but not impossible. Yet even without team production, the contribution of one person in any exchange may not be economically measurable in all pertinent characteristics. If one party can gain by shirking in its performance, this *means* the other party is "specific" to the shirker by the circumstances. This mode of expression emphasizes the specificity of one resource to another as a source of danger, but it obscures the significance of measurement of performance. On the other hand, if measurement of performance is emphasized, then the significance of expropriability of coalition, interspecific resource quasi-rents is obscured. Without substantial expropriable quasi-rents of specific resources, blatant, defiant cheating is less likely to be a serious problem.

One might therefore define the firm in terms of two features: the detectability of *input* performance *and* the expropriability of quasi-rents of interspecific resources. This leads to "A firm is a coalition of interspecific resources owned in common and some generalized inputs, whose owners are paid, because of difficulty of output measurability according to some criteria other than directly measured marginal productivity, and the coalition is intended to increase the wealth of the owners of the inputs by producing salable products." Ownership of interspecialized assets is a characteristic of a *capitalist* coalition—typically dubbed a firm. That "capitalist" firm would not exist if all resources were nonspecialized.[7] Whether or not that definition is accepted, the important question is what kind of contractual relations are institutionalized or used in what circumstances.

For example, in antitrust litigation the test of whether a group is a single entity (one firm) has been widely used and has been useful for some questions. But that ignores the variety of contractual structures that increase economic productivity and viability with consequent gains to consumers and producers. The family, the principal-agent relation, social clubs, holding companies, pro-

---

7. M. C. Jensen and W. Meckling, "Rights and Production Functions," *Journal of Business* 52 (1979): 469–506.

fessional sports leagues, cooperatives, groups of franchisees, not-for-profit foundations, NCAA, and the U.S. Golf Association are some examples of contractual coalitions. They may or may not be called "single entities" or "firms." It makes no difference. To attempt to ascertain effects by asking whether the arrangement is "one" firm is to blind oneself to the fact that the conception of a firm used in cartel theory *assumed* the member firms are simply "black-box" production functions and have *no* other motive than to restrict offerings to consumers in order to raise prices and make larger profits. As Williamson emphasizes, the conjoining of that assumption with the ignoring of internal governance relations among internally competing members within a "firm" obstructed understanding. That led to the view that all economic activity could be efficiently organized in the same way, viz., the standard classical organization called a "firm" (which appears to have *no* coalition-specific resources in it—if one relies on the literature). This suggests a reason the law—resting on that inadequate earlier economic analysis—has been characterized by an "inhospitality tradition" within antitrust. Fortunately that tradition is slowly being discarded as better economic analysis is achieved.

Labor Inputs

(i) People will seek to own the nonhuman resources to which they will be specific, especially if the other resource can control its services. If joint ownership is not feasible, the owners of the nonhuman resources will have to pay for the investment that creates the specificity. For example, a mine in a remote area will create, own, and offer houses at a rental to employees in order to reduce the dependence of an employee's wealth on the mine. Strategic threats to reduce the wages paid employees would be effective if the employees owned houses and land near (i.e., specific to) the isolated mine. The mine owner must invest in the resource (house), for otherwise more of the employee's wealth would be expropriably specific to this mine operator.

Studies of unemployment have begun to focus on layoffs as alternatives to wage changes or terminations. These suggest that it is not risk aversion but "moral hazard" or "opportunism" that is reduced by layoffs.

The point is that when demand really decreases, the employer reveals the decrease by cutting output. If without cutting output, he tried to reduce wages while alleging a demand reduction, how could belief in the alleged reduced demand be established? An employer can say, "Demand has decreased, and I will prove my honesty by cutting output. If I continued to produce after inducing you employees to cut wages, how could you know I was not deceiving you and trying to expropriate your form-specific quasi-rent? With layoffs, I tell you that you can offer to cut your wages if you like, but if you don't, I will also reduce output and will not replace you. If I threaten you with a layoff, I am also threatening myself with a loss of production. You can cut your wages if you like, and I will continue to produce, but if you don't, I, too, will stop production. My threats become more expensive for me." The employer is committed, by a policy of layoffs, to not continuing to produce with lower cost replacements— the kind of threatened action which could expropriate wealth from the employee.[8]

This suggests that in the field of labor relations and labor contracts there are many examples of ingenious contractual relations designed to reduce the moral hazard, or malincentives, arising from interspecificity of resources in a team. Severance pay, pensions, unions, and tenure rights apparently can so be interpreted, if I read correctly the burgeoning literature on employment contracts. The macroeconomic implications for output rather than price fluctuations are obvious, even if not yet fully explored.

Action by a cohort of interspecific laborers, possibly as a union, can protect labor specific to other resources. Expropriable quasi-rents of labor may be in pension and health benefit rights or in employee-invested skills specific of the firm. However, a *monopoly* union could expropriate the employer's quasi-rent of nonhuman resources specific to the kind of services provided by the union members. For example, monopoly unions could expropriate quasi-rent of agricultural capital by effectively threatening to strike at harvest time. Or monopoly unions can raise wages to extract the quasi-rent of resources specific to the services of a monopoly union by closure of access to substitutes. This two-edged function of unions: (a) "agency" to protect its expropriable quasi-rents and (b) its "monopoly strike-power" to expropriate the employer's quasi-rent, creates dispute about the "legitimate" roles of the union.

(ii) An interesting problem arises when *people* are interspecific as a team. How are interspecific *human* talents contractually organized, when not all members can be owned by some person? Some success in answering that has been

8. R. E. Hall and D. M. Lilien, "Efficient Wage Bargains under Uncertain Supply and Demand," *American Economic Review* 69 (1979): 868–79; J. Haltiwanger, "Asymmetric Information, Long Term Labor Contracts, Inefficient Job Separations" (working paper 276, UCLA Department of Economics, Los Angeles, 1982).

achieved for law firms and social country clubs[9] and conglomerates.[10] A team of interspecific people cannot be owned as private property, as slaves, and cannot guarantee performance as they can for machines. Instead teams of comedians, lawyers, athletes, or doctors whose services are highly dependent on the performance of a colleague will form partnerships or mutually owned organizations. Alternatively some forms of contracts such as first negotiation/first refusal, tenure, or group action among a group of resources specific to some "employer" can prevent opportunistic exploitation of some of the members of the group.

(iii) Generalized labor will be "casual," "transient," or independent contractors. Like customers, no *one* has significant effect on the salvageable value of any of the coalition's assets, even though the set of laborers or customers *as a set* would seriously affect the coalition value if they all refused to deal with the coalition.

Specificity and the Corporation

If some resources, when assembled into a team, become specific to that team's objective, how can the investment required for purchase of interspecific resources be assembled? Funds could be borrowed by an entrepreneur. But without full liability, a borrower's incentives are twisted, from maximizing the value of the coalition, toward maximizing the portion remaining after a potential default on bonds. (Of course, bond convenants are inserted to constrain the borrower's ability and incentive to act that way.)

While it is true that lenders will take this into account and demand a higher reward, it will be inferior to a system that would avoid this malincentive arising from the limited liability of the borrower. Why then is limited liability retained? The answer is not risk aversion. Liability is always limited to some degree. One cannot get more wealth than the borrower has. If it be argued that the borrower could be a consortium of people whose combined wealth is large enough to assure repayment (with liability not limited to an amount declared "invested" in the coalition by the consortium), consider the problem that would arise. How would any member later sell his interest to a newcomer? The problems in knowing who all the other members were—or were going to be—and what

9. A. Leibowitz and R. Tollison, "Free Riding, Shirking and Team Production in Legal Partnership," *Economic Inquiry* 18 (July 1980): 380–94; Klein, Crawford, and Alchian, "Vertical Integration."

10. O. Williamson, "The Modern Corporation: Origins, Evolution, Attributes," *Journal of Economic Literature* 19 (1981): 1537–68.

their wealth was, which would affect the newcomer's prospective liabilities, are overwhelming. But if liability were limited to the invested amount, sale of one's position in the consortium would be easier, and it could be done anonymously of the members. This facilitates the forming of consortiums to borrow and consortiums to operate a coalition involving extensive asset specificity. So-called limited liability facilitates resale and continuity. The French term "Société Anonyme" appears superior to the concept of "incorporated" or "limited" for easy transferability or liquidity—not risk avoidance.[11] Salability of rights enables continuity of a corporate venture beyond the departure of any one member. And this enables more complete capitalization of anticipated future results into current corporate stock values and managerial decisions.

Incidentally, the early English foreign-trading joint-stock companies initially were state-protected cartels during the mercantilist period.[12] Because salability of shares permitted continued existence despite membership changes, successful foreign-trade corporate cartels survived. The modern corporation, using the same organizational features, is, *in contrast, because of the absence of political restrictions on newcomers*, forced by competition to a different survival result—lower costs and improved products. The difference between the modern and the old mercantilist corporation flows from the absence of political restrictions on corporate competitors—not from changes in the corporate form or managerial and stockholder incentives.

The equity holder is the person owning the set of resources which are specific to the coalition. Those resources won't be rentable by the general resources in the coalition. They can be personal labor that for whatever reason have lower salvage values elsewhere—i.e., resources specific to the coalition. For example, people who are called employees in a firm are not the managers and risk bearers nor stockholders. The people who direct and manage a coalition are those who own the resources specific to the coalition, or they are responsible to them. Owners of those resources have the most of their coalition value to lose by failure of the coalition. They have a greater incentive to manage or be responsible for selecting and monitoring the management of the coalition. While stock-

11. H. Manne, "Our Two Corporation Systems," *Virginia Law Review* 53 (1967): 259; R. Meiners, J. Mofsky, and R. Tollison, "Piercing the Veil of Limited Liability," *Delaware Journal of Corporate Law*, vol. 25 (April 1979): 120–40; S. Woodward, "Unveiling the Economics of Limited Liability" (working paper, UCLA Department of Economics, Los Angeles, 1983).

12. R. Ekelund and R. D. Tollison, "Mercantilist Origins of the Corporation," *Bell Journal of Economics* 11 (1980): 715–20.

holders or managers bear risk, they do not bear that risk in order to be motivated. Instead that risk is inevitable, and those who bear it have the greater incentives to control and manage. At the same time, it is true that to induce interest in better management and control, some sharing of the value of the specific resources will be assigned or offered to managers because that induces behavior more highly correlated with the affected value of specific resources.

Specialization as Division of Labor in Management: Directing, Monitoring, Team Revising, and Risk Bearing

Confusion about "separation" and "specialization" of control (use decisions) and "ownership" (bearing risk of market value) reflects insufficient understanding of the principle of specialization of the partitionable components of private property rights. For example, that misunderstanding is manifest in assertions that middlemen increase costs to consumers by separating consumers and producers. In fact, middlemen, by specializing in communication, transport, product knowledge, etc., more effectively (i.e., at lower cost) correlate the interests and actions of consumers and producers. A consumer who grew wheat and ground it into flour could bake his bread in whatever form he was able. But when he permits specialists to intervene and perform these separate tasks, so that consumption is separated from production, the available variety of bread is greater and cheaper. Though some people believe producers decide what bread consumers eat, consumers determine which bread the baker can profitably continue to produce.

Similarly, specialization occurs for the elements of private property rights and thereby strengthens the power of a private property system. These component rights can sometimes be exercised separately by specialists more effectively than if all were held by one person who miraculously had all the specialized knowledge and talents of the several specialists.[13]

Management, Managerial Competition, and the Stock Market

Define management as "choosing" uses that affect the values of the specialized resources in the coalition. Of course, anyone can have a big effect by simply burning or bombing the resources. But let the *range* of selectable uses be specified for each person for each resource. Given the range of authorized op-

---

13. H. Manne, "Some Theoretical Aspects of Share Voting," *Columbia Law Review* 64 (1964): 1427; H. Manne, "Mergers and the Market for Corporate Control," *Journal of Political Economy* 73 (1965): 110–20; Manne, "Our Two Corporation Systems."

tional actions, there will be some probability distribution of value effects, called the "conditional" (or "constrained") value distribution, conditional on the range of selectable uses and the amount of monitoring of that person's behavior. Any person whose constrained, conditional distribution of effects on values of resources in the coalition is wider is more of a manager—no matter what particular tasks he performs. This defines a manager not by the types of actions but instead by the anticipated conditional probability distribution of effects on the values of specialized resources.

The common belief that in widely dispersed stock corporations managers are insufficiently responsive to owners' interests does not recognize the effects of competition among incumbent managers, between them and outside challengers, and the competition in the capital markets for control.[14] Management consists of self-interested persons seeking to displace others. Competition within the firm can be strong, because the personal qualities of each member may be more cheaply and reliably discerned within, than across, firms.

Managerial malfeasance can be reduced if managers anticipate their future salaries will be adjusted downward, in light of poor present or past performance, and be capitalized into a lower present value of the future stream of wages.[15] A source of information about present and past managerial performance is a change in a firm's common stock price, which reflects the changed value of the interspecialized resources, precisely the resources whose values managers are primarily influencing. The stock market thus serves as a signal not merely for "capital" investment but also for effects of, and rewards for, managerial performance. That signal can be more effective, the more widely the stock is dispersed. The extent of diffusion of stock ownership may be correlated with the size of the firm measured, say, by the number of people in the firm. Because larger firms usually have more levels of administration, their adaptability to new idiosyncratic circumstances and ability to coordinate information may be reduced by their more formal, restrictive standard operating procedures. Therefore *effectiveness* (but not extent) of task specialization may spuriously appear to be negatively correlated with stock diffusion when, in fact, effectiveness may be *increased* by stock diffusion.

14. Manne, "Mergers and the Market for Corporate Control"; E. Fama, "Agency Problems and the Theory of the Firm," *Journal of Political Economy* 88 (1980): 288–307.

15. Fama, "Agency Problems and the Theory of the Firm"; M. C. Jensen and W. Meckling, "Theory of the Firm: Managerial Behavior, Agency Costs and Capital Structure," *Journal of Financial Economics* 3 (1976): 305–60.

Effects of Types of Property Rights

Competition among managers helps disclose less valuable managers. But "valuable" to whom? The response to the information about values of specialized resources depends on whether the rights to those resources are held as cooperative, socialist, or private property rights.[16] In a socialist firm, the values of the specialized resources are less (if at all) capitalized into anyone's present salable wealth. In the cooperative or participatory democracy firm, the rights to specialized resources are claimed on some *nonsalable* basis by more of the *generalized* resource members. Since no one has salable rights to the specialized resources in socialist firms or cooperatives, members are interested in a shorter horizon—with less capitalization of future events, which affects the selection of investments.

The significance of salability is noticeable by comparing a large government agency like the Post Office or any state-owned enterprise—or nonprofit firm— with General Motors, with private property ownership. The rights of thousands of stockholders of a large corporation differ from those of the thousands of citizens of a city government. The process for selecting agents—voting— appears the same if one looks at the act of voting and the delegation of decisions. But I cannot sell my share of rights to the Tennessee Valley Authority, the Federal Reserve System, the Post Office, or the city golf course. With private property, I could decide whether or not to own rights to them.

If there were no salable right to vote for a manager or an agent to the Board of Directors, every stockholder would remain merely a residual claimant with little power over corporate resources. However, so long as some corporate shares have that voting right, and those shares can be bought, then stock markets can discipline managers to conform more to the interests of the stockholders. An ill-managed corporation can have its management displaced by the purchase of shares which are then voted. The gains of such acts appear to be realized by the risk in stock prices. The variety of ways capital markets permit

---

16. A. A. Alchian, "The Basis of Some Recent Advances in the Theory of Management of the Firm," *Journal of Industrial Economics* 14 (1965): 30–41; E. Furubotn and S. Pejovich, "Property Rights and the Behavior of the Firm in a Socialist State: The Example of Yugoslavia," *Zeitschrift für Nationalökonomie* 30 (1970): 431–54; M. Crain and R. D. Tollison, "On the Sufficient Conditions for Wealth Maximizing Conduct," *Kyklos* 31 (1978): 500–503.

displacement of poorer management appears to be corroborated by studies of stock-market tenders, takeovers, mergers, and "raids."[17]

The Role of the Board of Directors

With many stockholders, not all can be the chief executive officer nor the directors. Directors are agents believed more capable of detecting, assessing, and responding to information about managerial effects on the value of the specific resources. Directors need not *direct* managers; instead they should (do?) *detect* and *evaluate* managers' performance and may replace them. Common stock, preferred stock, debentures, notes, bonds, warrants, and options are claims to portions of the value of specialized resources. Their owners demand representation (as principals or by agents) by directors. And any persons or "employees" who have human capital specific and specialized to the firm will demand some control and monitoring *via* representation by directors or some other form of protection (e.g., long-term contracts of employment) from expropriation of their specialized investment's quasi-rent.[18]

Like any other agents, directors should anticipate post-performance rewards or punishments equal at least to any gains they might seek by excessively

17. M. Bradley, "Interfirm Tender Offers and the Market for Corporate Control," *Journal of Business* 53 (1980): 345–76; P. R. Dodd and R. Ruback, "Tender Offers and Stockholder Returns," *Journal of Financial Economics* 5 (1977): 351–74; Fama, "Agency Problems and the Theory of the Firm"; M. C. Jensen and R. S. Ruback, "The Market for Corporate Control," *Journal of Financial Economics* 11 (1983): 5–50; Manne, "Some Theoretical Aspects of Share Voting."

The Williams Act requires public disclosure of the tender's intentions. If the tenderer has knowledge of ways to improve the performance of the targeted firm, and if that must be disclosed before the shares can be acquired, then as a consequence of the Williams Act disclosure requirement, stock prices of the targeted firms would rise *more* upon disclosure of the tender's intentions than if the disclosure were not required. More precisely, more of the total rise would occur before the tender completion and less afterwards. Also the tenderer firm would experience a smaller rise, if any, in its own stock price after the Williams Act than before. This would imply the Williams Act reduced the rewards and incentives for managerial competition and enhanced the tenure of less able incumbent managers. It gave more of the potential improvement to the incumbent stockholders. The targeting management gets less of the gain they create in the acquired firm. These implications were corroborated by the Jerrold data.

18. V. Goldberg, "Toward an Expanded Economic Theory of Contract," *Journal of Economic Issues* 10 (1976): 45–61.

deviant behavior. If the directors are earning high salaries in other primary jobs, but fail as good agents, loss of reputability will affect their salaries in their primary jobs. They will tend to be people of extremely high reliability, reputability, and proven diligence with low probability of irresponsible actions.

Of course, everyone in the coalition would like to be a director, if they could, with impunity, divert the specialized asset value to their own welfare. The campaigns for "worker participation" or "industrial democracy" or codetermination on boards of directors appear to be attempts to control the wealth of stockholders' specialized assets in the coalition—a wealth-confiscation scheme. But no firm with that arrangement could profitably obtain new funds for specialized assets. Furthermore, *future* employees would have to pay incumbent employers for that right to control the specialized assets of stockholders. Control of specialized resources by generalized resource owners does not appear to be an economically viable arrangement for a voluntary coalition with specialized assets.[19]

Individuals in Competition

An implication of interpreting the firm as a nexus of contracts is that the "firm" loses some analytic significance as attention is focused more on competition among individuals, their particular resources, and types of contractual relationships. Thinking of firms as the fundamental actors conceals the *intra-firm* competition. New entrants into old firms can offer more options to consumers. Managers of firms may act as surrogate markets. Managers screen proposals for offerings by the firm. This screening may in some cases more cheaply estimate consumer response than actual experiment. But this is a conjecture. Take an extreme example of the principle. Only one newspaper in a town does not deny competition to serve readers. Among that paper's present

---

19. An example of the dangers of theorizing about the role of the board of directors without a clear theory of the nature of the capitalist firm is in M. A. Eisenberg ("Legal Models of Management Structure in the Modern Corporation: Officers, Directors, and Accountants," *California Law Review* 63 [March 1975]: 399n 2), though he gives one of the best discussions of the role of the board of directors. "The role of the board is to hold the executives accountable for adequate results *whether financial, social or both*, while the role of executives is to determine how to achieve such results" (emphasis supplied). However, in the capitalistic corporation the critical test is solely the effect on the market values of the interspecific resources (owned by stockholders) in the coalition, or whatever criteria the *owners of those* resources indicate should be used.

and potential staff a competitive struggle seeks to better satisfy readers' tastes for news and entertainment. How much difference does it make when people compete within an existing firm rather than via new small companies? Are new entrants more productive or tested more accurately or more cheaply under one procedure than under the other? Entry of "new firms" can be achieved by people moving from one firm to another, bringing resources and ideas either as an employee or as some other owner. Competition among people to own or manage those specialized resources (i.e., become part of the firm) changes the firm.

Even if the number and names of firms in an "industry" didn't change, that would tell nothing about the effectiveness of competition—for it tells nothing about the changing content and actions of any of the firms. There is little reason to contend that a few firms would not yield the same competitive results as many—so long as people are allowed to suggest admission in the expectation that it and the existing members will achieve better results. As a not entirely misleading analogy, one can imagine 10 cities in a country with people moving from city to city and altering the actions within a city without new cities being created or old ones disappearing. Every entry or departure changes the city, just as it is a change in the firm. It is not silly to consider the entry of a new stockholder to be the creation of a new firm. The usefulness of this approach of concentrating on people is indicated by the results of mergers and takeover bids.[20]

Organizational Competition

A principal lesson of this survey is that competition occurs in *forms of organizations and contracts*. For example, the extent of commonly owned assets (integration) of the corporate rather than partnership firms, of franchises rather than employee-operated branches, or of mutual membership rather than stock corporation types of firms—all these are features that are slighted by excessive attention to "numbers" of firms rather than to competition among and within types of contractual arrangements for furthering economic objectives. Which forms of contractual coalitions, and in which circumstances, enhance investment by avoiding agent-principal conflicts of specific asset quasi-rent expropriability? Which enhance correlation of reward with productivity? Which permit more effective displacement of inappropriate persons by more appropriate persons? Which induce better current responses to anticipated future consequences of proposed actions?

20. Jensen and Ruback, "The Market for Corporate Control."

ADDITIONAL REFERENCES

Alchian, A. A. "Property Rights, Specialization and the Firm." In *Corporate Enterprise in a New Environment*, edited by T. F. Weston and M. E. Grantfield, 11–36. New York, 1982.

Berle, A., and G. Means. *The Modern Corporation and Private Property*. New York, 1932.

Johnson, R. N., and G. D. Libecap. "Contracting Problems and Regulation: The Case of the Fishery." *American Economic Review* 72 (1982): 1005–22.

Lippman, S. A., and R. P. Rumelt. *Uncertain Imitability*. UCLA Working Paper. Los Angeles, 1980.

Reid, J. "Labor Unions in the American Economy: An Analytical Survey." Center for Study of Public Choice, CE80-9-5, Virginia Polytechnic Institute, 1980.

Watts, R. L. "Corporate Financial Statements, a Product of the Market and Political Processes." *Australian Journal of Management* 2 (1977): 53–75.

Williamson, O. "Transaction-Cost Economics: The Governance of Contractual Relations." *Journal of Law and Economics* 22 (1979): 233–61.

REFLECTIONS ON THE THEORY OF THE FIRM

ARMEN A. ALCHIAN AND SUSAN WOODWARD

1. Introduction

Gains from trade arise in markets where diverse agents specialize in productive activities at which they have a comparative advantage. Market prices direct their efforts.

But there are also gains from trade which arise as a result of cooperation not directed by market prices but by "management." Some of this cooperation undoubtedly involves specialization (the same source of gain as in markets), but much of it derives instead from a feature called "teamwork."[1] The chief distinction between economic activity outside the firm (i.e., across markets) vs. inside the firm (i.e., by teams) is that team participants do not make decisions regarding their activities on the basis of market prices, but rather give or seek and receive direction as to what to do.[2] Why this difference?

The answer, "high transaction costs," is merely the name for whatever it is that leads to the "firm." What are these "transaction costs"? Simply put, they are the costs of determining quality and negotiating price.

Determining quality is very cheap for some items. The value of a head of lettuce may be fairly certain after only casual observation. It could be potentially much more costly to ascertain the value of a drug or an automobile. The more expensive it is to determine quality before purchase, the more expensive it is for the market to work.

Negotiating price is also easy for some items. Generally speaking, the thicker the market, the fewer the possible values for price and the less room for negotiating. But when markets are thin and a gap arises between the lowest

Reprinted, by permission of the author, from *Zeitschrift für die gesamte Staatswissenschaft* (Journal of Institutional and Theoretical Economics) 143 (March 1987): 110–36.

1. A. A. Alchian and H. Demsetz, "Production, Information Costs, and Economic Organization," *American Economic Review* 62 (1972): 777–95.

2. R. H. Coase, "The Nature of the Firm," *Economica* 4 (1937): 386–405. Reprinted in George J. Stigler and Kenneth E. Boulding, eds., *Readings in Price Theory* (Homewood, Ill.: Irwin, 1952), 331–51.

price the seller will take and the highest price the buyer will pay, opportunities arise for buyer and seller to expend scarce resources negotiating price.

At some level of cost of either sort, simple spot exchanges will be abandoned and replaced by longer-lived arrangements which restrain the behavior of the transactors to assure each of getting and paying what was expected. Some of these agreements will be aspects of the constitutions and contracts that compose what we call the firm, and others will be constraints on the operations of markets. The understanding of these arrangements requires explicit consideration of information costs. The notion of market-directed gains from production via comparative advantage (i.e., production by lower cost producers) offers no insight into long-term contracts among the transactors.

Although the nature of teamwork and its relation to what we call a firm has been explored and found illuminating,[3] teamwork is not the essence of the firm.[4] Rather, the essence is the nexus of contracts restraining the behavior of the transactors.[5] But we have trouble imagining economic activity organized as "teamwork" that does not have the special relations among people and physical assets that we will argue give rise to the firm. We observe that in most cooperative production, people show up for work at the same place every day. In this paper we are more interested in why they show up at the same place every day (and related issues) than in why some workers are managers and some are managed. But the issues are not unrelated.

Consider that there are cooperative production efforts in which the relation between employer and employee is very short-lived. In most cities there are areas in which day laborers can be found and hired just for the day, usually for activities such as gardening and unskilled construction. Though these workers typically work for a given employer only for a day, many issues of firm organization are present. Are the tools used in the job owned by the employer or by the employees? Or possibly by a third party who rents them? Are they financed with any debt? Is the manager an employee of yet a larger firm or the owner and residual claimant of the activity? The economic forces that determine the an-

---

3. Alchian and Demsetz, "Production, Information Costs, and Economic Organization."

4. A. Alchian, "Specificity, Specialization, and Coalitions," *Zeitschrift für die gesamte Staatswissenschaft/Journal of Institutional and Theoretical Economics* 140 (1984): 34–39; O. Williamson, *The Economic Institutions of Capitalism* (New York, 1985).

5. See Alchian, "Specificity, Specialization, and Coalitions," and Williamson, *The Economic Institutions of Capitalism.*

swers to these questions are essentially the same as for firms with very long-lived teams.

Teamwork arises where information is costly. Restraining contracts and departures from continuous auction markets arise where information is costly. Teamwork seldom appears without a nexus of contracts, and a nexus of contracts seldom appears in the absence of teamwork. The aspect of teamwork that connects it to the nexus of contracts that we want to call the firm is that so much of the information involved in teamwork is long-lived.

Team production does not necessarily involve managers and managees. Some teams consist of a group of individuals who work together effectively but without a "leader," such as a law firm. Knowledge of one another's personal talents makes working together more productive than working with less well known associates. If the team members are not equally good at discerning one another's productivity, the team will have a manager and employees who follow the manager's instructions. Again, knowledge of one another makes them more productive. Within the team, there is specialization in information about the team, which may consist simply of the team members knowing one another better than outsiders know them, or of specialization on the part of a manager in assessing the talents and guiding the activities of the team members. In either case, because the information is durable, team members all have something to lose if any one is separated from the team.

Most team efforts involve the use of physical assets. Again, the people inside the team are likely to know more about these inanimate team members—the team's physical assets—than do outsiders. They are likely to know how well an asset has been treated and maintained and how much it has been worked. The differential cost of knowing about these assets—inside vs. outside the firm—will affect whether the firm owns, rents, or debt finances the physical assets it uses. We will explore the qualities that resources have that affect these cost differentials. In particular, we will address the following issues:

1. How and to what extent do the kinds and intended uses of certain combinations of resources determine the contractual arrangements for their use?
2. With which resources (if not owned by the users) does the user have long-term contracts and with which short-term contracts?
3. What protective arrangements have evolved—within firms and across markets—to restrain the resources from exploiting one another?
4. Which activities and related types of resources will motivate organiza-

tions that are large and have publicly traded equity claims and which will be small and privately held?

5. What characteristics of the jointly used resources determine the extent of debt rather than equity financing of the activity?

Within the firm, three basic problems must be solved. First, the firm must organize—determine the resources it will use, which tasks it will perform, and apportion the resulting value among the resources used. Second, the firm must monitor the performance of team resources to assure that each resource is delivering promised productivity. Third, the firm must control the potential for team members to renege on the original agreements for apportioning value by demanding a larger share of the firm's income. Economic activities using resources with different levels of monitoring costs and vulnerability to reneging by others will solve these problems in different ways. What we will focus on here is how these two features—monitoring costs and their resulting vulnerability to moral hazard, and vulnerability to holdup due to the presence of quasi-rents—together make assets "firm specific" and determine ownership, organization, financing, and some other features of firms and other institutions.

2. Preliminary Concepts: Firm, Composite Quasi-rent, Dependence and Holdup, Moral Hazard and Plasticity

2.1 Firm

The classic, paradigmatic private property firm we will initially characterize arbitrarily as an organization with (a) continuity of specialized mutual knowledge among several separately owned inputs, and (b) contracts among inputs for continuing services of resources used by the team. The owners of the "firm" will be the owners of the resources whose value depends on the performance of the team that makes up the firm. The owners, or equity holders, will (a) be common to all contracts with input owners, (b) possess the right to sell their contractual status, and (c) hold the claim to the residual value of the team.

2.2 Composite Quasi-rent

We first acknowledge the forgotten precedence of Alfred Marshall, who in his *Principles* identified "composite quasi-rent."[6] First, a quasi-rent is the excess above the return necessary to maintain a resource's current service flow. It is a recovery of sunk costs. Composite quasi-rent is that portion of the quasi-rent

---

6. A. Marshall, *Principles of Economics* (1890; 8th ed., New York, 1948).

which depends on continued association with some other specific resources and consequently is vulnerable to expropriation. Marshall's compelling example of such vulnerability was a steel mill that locates near a public utility and makes investments which depend on being able to buy power at some given price. Once the steel mill's investment is complete and the sunk costs are sunk, the utility can raise the price of power, and the steel mill will continue to operate, because marginal cost, even with the higher cost of power, still exceeds marginal revenue, even though the sunk costs are not being recovered.

Quasi-rent and profit are not the same. If a resource is profitable it will be getting a return that more than recovers sunk costs. However, neither a profit nor a recovery of sunk cost is necessary to induce the continuing services of an existing resource. Should quasi-rent be defined to include not only sunk costs but profits as well? We argue no, as the presence of quasi-rent (as we define it) and the presence of profit affect contractual arrangements differently. We concentrate, but not exclusively, on the protection of the recovery of sunk costs, though as will be obvious, the protective features may protect profits also.

Marshall recognized the danger of parties with sunk costs relying on those in a position to expropriate their quasi-rents. But Marshall assumed the threat was resolved by "doing what is right" or by "haggling." So far as we can ascertain he did not develop its importance for understanding the organization of the firm.

2.3 Dependence and Holdup

A resource is "dependent" when it would lose value if separated from the team (firm). A resource is "unique" when the other resources of the firm are dependent upon it; i.e., the remaining resources of the firm (members of the team) would lose value if it left. Dependence can take on two different aspects.

First, a resource may have made an investment useful only to the current team (i.e., specific to the team) upon joining the team and is now counting on the team to compensate it for both current effort and for sunk costs. If it leaves the team, it abandons its investment and does not recoup its sunk costs. But once the investment is made, the temptation is for the rest of the team to expropriate the quasi-rent—to refuse to pay the resource more than its highest value elsewhere—to "hold up" the dependent resource. In the legal literature, investments whose profitability depend on the behavior and continued use of resources of another are called "reliance" investments.

Second, a resource may be both dependent and depended upon. If a set of resources have all made non-recoverable or only partially recoverable investments in order to do the work they do together, they are mutually dependent. In the above example, departure of the resource that had made its investment may require the team to find another similar resource and induce it to make the same investment made by the first. If the team could lose by the departure of the resource, either because the search is costly or because it must agree to compensate the new resource for the investment, then the resource and the remainder of the team are mutually dependent. Only if for some reason the firm has been able to find a similar resource for which the investment is not necessary could the first resource be dependent but not unique. Mutual dependence does not require an investment made by any of the resources, only that they are more productive in this assembly than in any other use. Usually, dependence is reciprocal, which implies that dependent resources are unique, and vice versa, and that most specific capital is inter-specific capital.

Inside a firm, value is created by the collection of resources, and there is no market to clearly dictate what each should be paid. The "market" values—the opportunity costs or next best alternatives—of the resources sum to less than the value of their joint product. Hence the firm itself, not the market, must solve the problem of how to apportion the value created by the firm. This may require continuing and costly negotiation; one task of the firm is to minimize these costs.

It is usually true that after a team is formed, separation of the team members results in the loss of composite quasi-rent. Some sunk cost seems inevitable, because the information that makes the intra-firm relations valuable is durable. If a team fails, team-specific resource owners will lose. Their value depends heavily on the decisions of the administrative managers. It should be clear as daylight that the resources dependent on the team's fortunes and dependent on some of the other resources within the team would be very wary of vulnerability to expropriation by holdup.

The dependence we have in mind involves a continuous balancing of obligations among members. It is not like a series of short-term exchanges with deferred payment. Dependence in the sense of a creditor dependent on the firm to pay it does not characterize a firm. Such relations generally prevail outside the span of firms, and in fact we argue can only prevail when moral hazard and holdup potential are small. The critical feature is not creditor-type dependence, but instead the productive service flow dependence among inter-specific resources.

In most teams, some resources will be more vulnerable than others to holdup, depending on the degree to which they can threaten to alter the flow of services. For example, a landowner renting land as a site for a skyscraper is an owner of a resource that is "unique" to an immovable building. Though the land is unique to the building, the landowner cannot cheaply alter the services of the land as a means of extracting some of the quasi-rent of the building from the building owner. This unique resource is impotent. But the owner of the building could refuse to pay all of the promised rent, while nevertheless being secure in the knowledge that the landowner has no feasible alternative use of the land. The landowner's remedies by law limit the expropriation the building could extract, but the expense of the remedies limits the protection afforded the landowner through such remedies.

In this land/building example, the resources are mutually dependent (and mutually unique), but only one, the building owner, has a realistic opportunity to exploit the composite quasi-rent. The landowner appears to have more to fear from a holdup under a long-term lease than does the building owner. This is because the building owner can stop its service flow (payment of the rent) but the landowner cannot stop the service flow of the land. An owner of a unique resource will be more tempted to exploit the situation the larger the composite quasi-rent and the more it can control its own flow of services (fail to pay the rent or to show up for work). The more this temptation is likely and can be foreseen, the more will precautionary contractual terms be sought.

2.4 Moral Hazard and Plasticity

The notion of moral hazard can illuminate several aspects of the theory of the firm.[7] First, employee/employer relations,[8] second, debtor/creditor relations,[9] and third, the general problem of how owners and non-owners manage assets.

When the quality of an item is costly to detect, it will often pay to manufacture it in a firm rather than buy it in a market. Quality is controlled by supervising employees. But this gives rise to a different problem, the monitoring of employees. The tradeoff is between quality assurance in a market and quality and output control within a firm. When it is costly to monitor the effort of team

---

7. John M. Marshall, "Moral Hazard," *American Economic Review* 66 (December 1976): 880–90.

8. Alchian and Demsetz, "Production, Information Costs, and Economic Organization."

9. M. Jensen and W. Meckling, "Theory of the Firm: Managerial Behavior, Agency Costs, and Ownership Structure," *Journal of Financial Economics* 3 (1976): 305–60.

members, a single member can gain (relaxation, less exertion) by shirking in his performance. The individual who shirks reaps the entire benefit of the shirking himself, but the cost, which is undetectably all due to him, is borne by the entire team because average output, and consequently wages, are lower. The outcome with costly monitoring is inferior to what could be achieved if everyone's effort could be costlessly measured, no one shirked, and average product and wage were commensurately higher.

Another aspect of moral hazard arises when a firm is financed partially with debt, because the equity holders do not bear the full consequences of the decisions they make. Equity holders reap the benefits of good outcomes, but debt holders bear some of the costs of bad outcomes. Equity holders thus have an incentive to increase the riskiness of the firm's assets once they have borrowed. Debt holders know this, of course, and charge for the risk they anticipate bearing. Creditors are compensated for the risk they bear, but a moral hazard loss results. If it were possible for a contract to specify the behavior of equity holders, the equity holders would behave no differently with vs. without debt, and there would be no moral hazard loss.

When a team consists of both human and non-human assets, people can manage the assets with different degrees of care. It may be less trouble to manage the assets with less care. When will assets be managed in a profit-maximizing fashion? Either when it is easy to detect how the asset has been managed (monitoring costs are low), or when the asset managers are also owners and consequently bear the full cost and benefits of managing. Of course we may have different levels of monitoring costs from an assortment of different arrangements, e.g., from literally having owner and manager be the same party, from a party managing an asset owned by the firm for which the manager works, or from a party managing an asset rented from another firm. Since different costs are associated with different ownership arrangements due to the difficulty of controlling moral hazard, these costs will influence ownership of the asset.

The term "moral hazard" has been maligned for its moralistic connotations. Although we are not prepared to argue that shirking and ex post risk augmentation are immoral, we believe that the term correctly suggests that trustworthiness, reputation, and integrity are important in intra-firm and inter-firm relations, and that the cultivation of these "virtues" probably has social value. If everyone would simply agree to undertake a given standard of effort and abide by the promise, a more efficient outcome would result. The term "moral hazard" suggests that people cannot be counted on to do what they say they are going to do, and their failure to do so manifests itself in market organization. It also suggests that among the devices used to control such behavior are moralistic aggression and social opprobrium. But contracts and litigation may be cheaper.

The presence of moral hazard does not mean that transactions are regretted. Even though many markets bear moral hazard losses, all parties are better off making the transactions than they would have been without them. Workers produce and are paid their marginal products. Borrowers pay an interest rate which compensates the lender for risk. The moral hazard loss simply measures what could be gained if either the cost of monitoring behavior by the insurer/employer were zero, or if people could be counted on to do as they promise.

Some resources are susceptible to a wider range of morally hazardous uses than are others. Furthermore, in some cases it is more difficult for an observer/monitor to reliably and objectively establish the degree to which an agent's selections are biased toward the agent's interest. We call resources or investments "plastic" to indicate that there is a wide range of legitimate decisions within which the user may choose, or that an observer can less reliably monitor the choice. An administrator of more plastic resources is more able to covertly bias the expected outcomes toward the administrator's interest.

By plastic we do not simply mean risky. We argue, for example, that oil which has only to be pumped and sold is a highly implastic asset. The optimal rate at which to pump the oil depends only on the pattern of prices over time, and there is very little in the way of possibilities for exploiting an oil well either by increasing the riskiness of outcomes for its value or by changing its product into consumption. But an oil well is a risky asset in a world where the price of oil fluctuates.

We can illustrate the idea by a presumption that drug research company managers control decisions about resources that are relatively plastic: the initial options are wider and more difficult to "second guess" than for the resources used in, say, a steel mill. We conjecture as further illustrations that enterprises with "intellectual research and capital," e.g., fashion designers, professional service firms such as engineering, law, architecture, and computer software creation, are especially plastic and susceptible to moral hazard. In contrast, industries with less plastic resources are railroads, utility services, airlines, petroleum refining (but not exploration), and other activities involving much in the way of "hard" resources.

The quality of being plastic does not directly translate into the asset being subject to moral hazard. Cash, for example, is an asset of extreme plasticity, as it can be exchanged for almost anything, in particular both consumption and financial assets that are much more risky than cash, almost instantaneously. The implication is that managers, as agents of owners, handling large cash balances will be subjected to greater controls and review by principals. On the other hand, it is easy to record what happens to cash, and consequently the plasticity does not preclude the management of such an asset by an agent rather than a principal. The combination of plasticity plus high monitoring costs results in potential morally hazardous exploitation. An implastic asset simply does not need much monitoring.

The presence of teamwork in any economic activity indicates the costliness of information necessary to execute that activity. The information collected in undertaking the enterprise is very often durable. The durability and costliness of the information about the economic activity give rise to the possibility for moral hazard and for holdup, since the resources in the team have an interest in their relations being long-lived, yet what each resource is doing is not precisely known and exactly how much each ought to be paid is not objectively signaled by a market. These two problems give rise to the set of contractual relations we call the firm. We analyze them in the remainder of this paper.

3. Corporate Constitutions

3.1 Ownership Integration

Any resource that will become and remain dependent on the service of other members of a team will seek protection against expropriation. One form of protection is common ownership of the dependent and unique resources as one bundle, i.e., ownership integration.[10] Assets owned all together present nothing in the way of holdup, because their owners—residual claimants—collect the quasi-rent and profit from the entire set and are not concerned with allocating the produced value among the resources. Moreover, since the residual claimants are the owners, problems with moral hazard in the case of plastic assets are also solved by ownership integration. Thus, either vulnerability to holdup or plasticity and high monitoring costs, which result in vulnerability to moral hazard, will result in an asset used by a firm being owned by a firm. (Holdup vs. plasticity have very different implications for financing decisions, as we shall see later.)

---

10. B. Klein, R. G. Crawford, and A. A. Alchian, "Vertical Integration, Appropriable Rents, and the Competitive Contracting Process," *Journal of Law and Economics* 21 (1978): 297–326.

Another form of protection retains separate ownership but gives each of the interdependent resource owners some control and influence and also gives them a prespecified share of the team's residual value, net of non-contingent amounts (e.g., wages or rents) to the independent resources. Although sharing control and residual value is not equivalent to common ownership (since any could leave without permission of the other sharing members), it can, with adequate side restrictions concerning hostages in the event of a departure of a unique resource,[11] accommodate contractual sharing of net income among the interdependent resources.

3.2 Long-Term Contracts

Long-term, or what the law calls relational, contracts are essential to continuity of teamwork with dependent resources. A long-lasting series of spot exchanges, whether or not continuously balancing, differs from a long-term contract. The contract restrains future options and is not responsive to all possible later developments. One of the fixed or restrained terms is price, for if price were allowed to change or be renegotiated whenever either party proposed, no effective commitment would be present. Commitments to a price according to a prespecified arrangement that have met the agreement of both parties constrain the options and restrict future renegotiability, which is precisely the meaning of a long-term contract. Restrictive long-term contracts protect long-lived dependent resources, which rely on continuing service of a unique resource at a prespecified price. Without dependent and unique resources, there is no point to a constraining long-term contract.[12]

3.3 Firm Ownership

Owners of resources more heavily dependent on the team's product value will value the control of the direction and administration of the team more highly than will those whose alternatives are unaffected by the success or failure of the team. Those resource values most dependent on the performance of the team are called the "equity." It follows that the "equity" holders of the team will also be the directors, administrators, and managers (or their principals) of the team's activities and, by convention, are called the "owners of the firm."

11. O. Williamson, "Credible Commitments: Using Hostages to Support Exchange," *American Economic Review* 73 (1983): 519–40.

12. V. Goldberg, "Toward an Expanded Economic Theory of Contracts," *Journal of Economic Issues* 10 (1976): 45–61.

Owners of independent, non-firm-specific resources will not value the right of control as highly, because their wealth is not affected by the firm's fortunes. Competition in forming teams and choosing contractual arrangements will result in "firm-specific," dependent resources being the parties who place the highest value on the right to administer, while the "general" resources will, at the revealed costs of initially purchasing administration rights from firm-specific resource owners, choose instead non-administrative rights and pre-specified rewards. The party with the right to administer, i.e., the owner of the firm-specific resources and equity holder, will have contracts with all of the general inputs. The contract will include the right to renegotiate with any resource independent of the others and the right to sell the administration rights, i.e., the equity interest, the ownership of firm-specific, firm-dependent resources. This results in the existence of a category of resources called "employees" (the owners of the general resources), whose services are sold to the owners of the firm-dependent resources, though in fact no one owns the "firm" as an entity. The firm is an assemblage of resources under a contractual nexus, not all owned in common. We note in passing that employers are not employers because they are less risk averse than employees. The degree of interest (dependency) in the firm's fortunes dictates who does what.

It follows that the members of the Board of Directors will be the agents of the more team-specific resource owners, who primarily (but not exclusively) are the stockholders. All owners of resources who have agreed to make investments that are heavily firm-dependent will value and acquire some representation on the Board. Advocates of representation on corporate Boards of Directors by public, disinterested, or firm-independent resource owners are, possibly unwittingly, undermining the viability of efficient forms of production by making it easier for owners of independent resources to expropriate the composite quasi-rent of firm-dependent assets and by reducing initial willingness to invest in such assets.

In some firms, some "labor" may be highly dependent on the firm, while what is ordinarily thought of as "capital" (equipment, inventory, etc.) may be virtually general. A law firm or a medical clinic may be a well-matched team with strong interdependence among "separately owned" people, while all the equipment and premises are very cheaply transferable to other teams or uses. In that case one would expect the doctors or lawyers to be the manager-director-owner-residual claimants, with the general resource owners renting services to the group. It is in principle not a distinction between people and physical equipment (sometimes erroneously called "labor" and "capital") that is pertinent; rather it is the degree of dependence on the specific other resources and on the firm's product value. In fact, those who are typically called employees may in many cases have made investments highly specific to the firm. They too will seek some representation on the Board. In general, whoever has a value that has become firm specific will seek some form of control over the firm, as will be discussed in a subsequent section on labor unions.

Although a relatively clean separation has been made between (a) stockholders (as residual claimants), (b) creditors (as claimants prior to stockholders to specified dollar amounts), and (c) employees (the name for all those whose values are not dependent on, or specific to, the firm), in fact the participants in the firm do not fall purely into just one of these classes. Some employees may have made firm-specific investments. They may have developed skills or knowledge of more value here than in other firms; they may have purchased homes whose values depend on the firm's success; they may have accumulated rights to subsequent benefits, like pensions; or they may be receiving salaries that are compensation for underpayments in the past designed to elicit a long-term association with the firm. Also they may have high transfer or mobility costs to the next best work. Persons with such human or non-human types of firm-specific resources will demand some means of enforcing their contractual arrangements. They may seek representation on the Board of Directors, or at least some control with respect to certain decisions affecting the probability of the fulfillment of their implicit or explicit contractual, or "customary," arrangements.

The name "equity holder," which suggests someone who invested in firm-specific resources and has rights to any resulting values only if they exceed commitments to other parties, is inappropriate for those whose rights are like those described in the preceding paragraph. They have claims prior to those of residual claimants; they are "creditors" of the firm. The upshot is that resources with values that are firm-specific can be both those that are residual claimants and those that have prior explicit, non-residual claims. All will be willing to pay a price for (i.e., demand) some measure of control over some kinds of decisions about the firm's activity, depending on the degree of firm-dependent value. Whether that influence over decisions is made by having directors as agents or by other procedures, such as unions, insurers, bondholder committees initiating private suits, appeals to political authority, or regulation, will depend on the relative cost of each device.

Not to be forgotten are customers of the firm. A consumer who buys a product, the future performance of which depends on the firm's continued activity, will have purchased a firm-specific resource—much like Marshall's steel mill or a buyer of a computer or automobile for which future spare parts are valuable. An unusual example of customer reliance, social and country clubs, is analyzed later.

3.4 The Corporation

When firm-specific resources are long-lasting and are large in total value, they tend to be owned in common by many stockholders in a corporation, the dominant form of shared ownership. These organizations often have (a) persons in managerial positions who are not firm owners, (b) firm owners who play no managerial role, and (c) some debt financing. As a result of these features, possible conflicts of interest arise among the shareholders, between shareholders and managers, and between shareholders and creditors.

3.4.1 Tension Among Shareholders. The transferable share, limited liability corporation accommodates long-lived dependent teamwork but also gives firm owners flexibility. The advantage of transferable shares is evident: differences in individual desires for consumption over time can be indulged, and changes in individual preferences, wealth, and beliefs can be accommodated by revisions of individual portfolios without disturbing the productive decisions of the firm itself. Obviously, without transferable shares, the potential for shareholder conflicts over investment and dividend policy could kill the corporation.

The advantage of limited liability is not so obvious: alienability of the firm's shares depends on the presence of limited liability.[13] Imagine the contrary. If each shareholder had extended liability, the liability of each shareholder and the terms on which credit is extended to the firm would depend on the wealth of each shareholder. Shareholders and creditors both would want information about the shareholder's ability to meet firm commitments. All would want to restrict transferability in order to protect their own positions. Limiting liability transfers risks to the creditors (who are of course compensated for bearing it) and makes the identity of the individual shareholders irrelevant. It also eliminates any desire for less than fully transferable shares.

Because limiting liability transfers some risk from equity holders to creditors, and this risk is less effectively controlled by creditors than stockholders, there are some costs associated with limited liability, essentially the same in

---

13. S. Woodward, "The Economics of Limited Liability," *Zeitschrift für die gesamte Staatswissenschaft/Journal of Institutional and Theoretical Economics* 141 (1985): 601–11.

nature as the costs associated with debt, generally speaking, when the assets of shareholders are finite. But for the multi-shareholder firm, the costs are more than outweighed by the flexibility and fungibility that they buy. Although markets are not the prevailing institution for allocating the individual assets that compose the firm, the pool of assets and their associated value do exploit "market" economies of scale (the more identical [fungible] the claims, the cheaper the market operates) by being financed with transferable shares.

Another source of tension among shareholders has to do with who is minding the store. Diffusion of stock ownership is often thought to debilitate the corporation because individual stockholders have little incentive to monitor corporate activity. This reasoning confounds relative shares with absolute amounts of wealth. The absolute amount, not the percentage share, is pertinent in motivation. Whether a million-dollar investment is 100% of an enterprise or is only 5%, it is still a million dollars at stake. If any problem arises as a result of each shareholder having a small relative stake, it is likely to be the higher costs of influencing a decision made by many shareholders. But even in the largest companies the Boards of Directors are no larger than for much smaller companies. We see no logical implication from diffusing itself to reduced effectiveness of the Boards of Directors' monitoring of the activities of the corporations.

3.4.2 Tension Between Managers and Stockholders. Larger enterprises typically require extensive administrative organization. This potentially increases the principal-agent, moral-hazard problem. One way to help maintain a congruence of interests is to correlate the agent's (manager's) wealth with that of stockholders. Aside from the standard competitive process that adjusts managers' wages, managers can be granted options for future purchases of stock, or they can be, and often are, major stockholders in the firm.[14]

Another way managers can be compensated is by trading the firm's stock on inside information. If a corporation allows insiders to trade on any and all information, outsiders, aware that insiders are trading, and that when they buy or sell they may be buying from or selling to a better-informed party, would adjust accordingly what they were willing to pay for the stock, still earning a rate of return commensurate with the risk. Even if this is an inefficient way to compensate managers, the outside shareholders are not the losers. Instead the initial promoters would lose at the time of the initial offering because they get less for

14. H. Demsetz and K. Lehn, "The Structure of Corporate Ownership: Causes and Consequences," *Journal of Political Economy* 93 (1985): 1155–77.

the stock. Even if they remain insiders, they have not gained, as their inside trading gains are reflected in the lower price they get for the initial offering. Beyond this consideration, subsequent insider-managers would be getting explicit salaries that are lower than the salaries of non-trading insiders by the amount of the inside-manager's anticipated gains from trading on inside information.

If insiders gain by trading on inside information, they gain at the expense of outsiders. But we argued above that the outsiders earn competitive returns. There is no inconsistency. The outsiders who pay the managers for their services in firms with insider trading are those who choose the inopportune moment to sell when insiders are buying, or to buy when insiders are selling. In firms with no insider trading, managers get salaries directly out of revenues. If managers who trade on inside information get smaller salaries, this leaves a higher profit stream for stockholders, which on average offsets the losses to the outsiders who traded at the wrong moment. All this amounts to a method of payment of part of the salary of managers by a sort of random tax on the market value of the stock, levied on a randomly selected group of the stockholders—those who happened to be trading.

Another implication of the presence of trading insiders and competitive markets is that stockholders who rarely sell, but instead buy and hold, will get a higher than average yield on their holdings, but only in return for less liquidity. It predicts that in firms where there is a larger than average amount of insider trading, there should be a smaller than average amount of outsider trading, which appears to be the case.[15] It also suggests that in firms where insider trading is significant, the gross returns to the stock (insiders plus outsiders) will appear to be "too high" for the risk level. In fact, the outsiders are earning competitive returns, and the insiders superior returns, and the average exceeds what we would predict simply on the basis of risk. If small corporations have more insider trading, as appears to be true, their stocks should appear to have abnormally high returns, which also appears to be true. We believe that the "small firm" effect, identified in the literature on the asset pricing model as an anomaly, is the "insider trading" effect,[16] arising because of the predominance of concentrated ownership, and consequently trading by insiders, in smaller firms.

15. N. Seyhun, "Insiders' Profits, Costs of Trading, and Market Efficiency," *Journal of Financial Economics* (1986, forthcoming).
16. S. Woodward, "Insider Trading and the Small Firm Effect," working paper, 1986.

This argument that shareholders are on average not exploited by insider trading does not answer the question as to whether the best use of a manager's time is managing the firm's assets or his own portfolio. But we see no reason why market forces would not provide an efficient outcome if firms were left to decide for themselves whether or not managers should be allowed to trade on inside information.

A recent event which focused attention on a different kind of inequality among shareholders is a Delaware Chancery Court decision in *Unocal vs. Mesa* permitting Unocal directors to redistribute the firm's wealth among stockholders in a non-pro-rata per share fashion. Mesa had made a tender offer for Unocal and acquired a sizeable fraction of Unocal's stock. The tender offer was vigorously contested by Unocal. Unocal's Board of Directors in the end fought off the tender offer by an unusual means. Unocal made a tender offer for its own stock at an above-market price, but only to the shareholders *other than* Mesa. Mesa sued Unocal and lost.

Obviously, conflicts of interest arise within a Board of Directors whenever the members do not all represent anonymously alienable, fungible interests of principals, as for example stockholders who have no interest in the corporation other than their shared stock value. Even salaried managers have interests based on more than just the common stock value. This conflict among stockholders, who otherwise would have fungible, alienable interests in the firm-specific resources, creates difficulties. This is sensitively heeded in closely held corporations where managers and others whose interests in the corporation depend on more than just the stock value.

The Delaware Court did not merely refuse to second-guess a Board's "rational business judgment"; instead it permitted the Board to unilaterally alter the contract among the corporate Board's principals (the stockholders). The Court failed to heed the distinction between (a) the wealth redistribution or contract alteration among agents' principals, performed by the agent, not the principals, and (b) the right to choose among alternative actions intended to enhance the corporate wealth in which all the stockholders share (or thought they shared). The Unocal-Mesa issue was not one of a challenge to the wisdom or business judgment of the agents. Rather it was whether altering the contractual relationship among the principals and redistributing the corporate wealth among stockholders in ways other than permitted in the corporate charter fell within the conception of a "rational business purpose" and within the powers of the agents.

Since the initial draft of this paper, the United States Securities and Exchange Commission has ruled that discriminatory tender offers of the sort Unocal made are illegal. We believe that this is likely an efficient ruling, and had it not been made, the evolution of the firm would have gone in the direction of corporate charters that would have protected minority shareholders such as Mesa.

3.4.3 *Tension Between Creditors and Stockholders.* Corporations do not finance their entire operations solely with equity. Current liabilities for wages, purchase orders, and taxes are common forms of debt financing. Firms borrow from banks and issue bonds. Are potential shareholders less optimistic than current shareholders, who instead of paying for expensive equity from pessimistic shareholders offer creditors guarantees for debt financing? If so, the explanation for differing debt-equity ratios across firms should look to factors influencing the level of disagreement among shareholders. We have found little that is illuminating in the optimism-pessimism theory of corporate debt.

Another possibility is that the convention of treating interest paid on debt as a deductible expense of the corporation provides a powerful incentive to move income outside the firm in the form of interest to avoid paying corporate income tax on it. Against this force is the cost of creditor–equity holder conflicts and equity malincentives. Once indebted, the equity holders do not bear the full costs of losses on projects. Their incentive is to take bigger risks, because the bondholders bear part of the downside cost, but the equity holders get all of the upside gains. Bondholders are fully aware of this incentive, and design contracts between themselves and equity holders to control it. But the contracts are not perfect. Bondholders charge equity for the uncontrollable losses imposed on them. So in choosing debt financing, equity holders are trading off the moral hazard costs of debt against the tax advantages.

This view of debt would lead us to look to the degree of plasticity and monitoring costs of a firm's assets for an explanation of the debt-equity ratio. Compare the opportunities for debt financing a drug company vs. a public utility. Bondholders, in making their debt agreements, seek protection from ex post contractual exploitation.[17] The company has a much wider range of legitimate initial choices of research direction and choice than does the public utility. The drug company's activities are more difficult to monitor. This implies that it will be difficult for the debt holders to write a contract with the equity holders to keep the equity holders from exploiting the bondholders. The drug company

---

17. C. Smith and J. Warner, "On Financial Contracting: An Analysis of Bond Covenants," *Journal of Financial Economics* 1 (1979): 111–61.

will find debt expensive. But with the public utility, the assets are cheaper to monitor and assess, and consequently the public will find debt inexpensive.

We emphasize that it is not the riskiness of the assets that are debt financed that matters, but their plasticity—the degree to which the equity holders can exploit the bondholders ex post by altering the asset outcomes. We predict that firms with more plastic assets will have lower debt ratios than will firms with less plastic assets. Our earlier example, the oil well, serves well the point that the issue is not risk. The oil well is very implastic but very risky, but we predict that oil recovery will be a highly debt financed business because it is implastic and easy to monitor.

Another theory of debt is that it serves as a device to allay stockholder-manager conflicts—monitoring done by bondholders aids equity holders in evaluating the decisions of managers. This argument implies that firms with more plastic assets, i.e., those more difficult to monitor, will issue bonds in order to enlist the bondholders to help monitor management. The "enlist the bondholders" theory thus stands in direct contrast to the "plasticity" theory of firm indebtedness. Unless there is an important difference between assets that are vulnerable to shareholder-manager conflicts of interest vs. those vulnerable to shareholder-creditor conflicts of interest, and we are not convinced there is, we strongly doubt that the monitoring of managers provided by debt holders is a powerful force on the debt-equity ratio.

Yet another possibility is that debt serves as a device to constrain managers from doing anything with the firm's income but pay it to security holders.[18] For example, in a firm with exceptionally large cash flows of quasi-rents or profits, managers could invest the proceeds toward self-aggrandizing but not profitable investments. If instead the firm is committed to large interest and debt repayments, these cash flows would have to be channeled to outsiders and to the rest of the market.

The "commit the quasi-rent" view combines the issues of moral hazard and vulnerability to holdup. A firm with quasi-rents is vulnerable to holdup. We would imagine also that in industries with large sunk costs, and consequently quasi-rents, the assets are also often fairly implastic, as in heavy manufacturing. The "commit the quasi-rent" view argues that quasi-rents call for some kind of mechanism to commit the firm to disburse its rents, but does not spec-

18. M. Jensen, "The Takeover Controversy: Analysis and Evidence," working paper no. MERC 86-01, Managerial Economics Research Center, Graduate School of Management, University of Rochester, New York, 1986.

ify to whom. The plasticity view argues that implastic assets are cheap to finance with debt. Then the question becomes, who is the likely suspect for the holdup? Ippolito argues that the presence of unions in heavy manufacturing is explained by the quasi-rents that arise in any economic endeavor with significant sunk costs and that the unions are simply trying to expropriate the quasi-rent.[19] Firms retaliate not with just debt financing, but also by making the union the debt holder by underfunding pension plans.

But the union expropriating the quasi-rent and the managers expropriating the quasi-rent are very different matters. It is not because the assets are difficult to monitor that unions are able to raise wages. They are simply exercising market power through cartels. But when managers expropriate a quasi-rent by making self-aggrandizing investments, the implication is that the shareholders are unable to judge whether the investments made by the managers are ex ante profitable or not. So if the problem is that shareholders are unable to judge managers' productivity, why try to solve the problem by adding more security holders and their monitoring problems, rather than make the managers stockholders to induce them to act like stockholders? The presence of higher monitoring costs on which this argument seems to depend appears inconsistent with a debt-financing solution given the monitoring problems created by debt financing.

Plasticity of resources also influences whether assets used by the firm will be rented (or leased) vs. owned. Renting an asset and debt financing an asset have important similarities. The renter or borrower obtains an upside value residual, while the creditor bears the downside prospects. Exogenous risks not affected by the behavior of the rentor-debtor are compensable through the rent as they are through debt. But the difficulty of detecting wear and tear, and diversion of use, constrain the degree of both renting and debt financing. These are simply aspects of plasticity. Whenever resources tend to be plastic, and moral hazard is severe, users will tend to be owners, not renters, and tend to finance with equity, not debt.

We acknowledge that we have no good measure of plasticity. "Firm-specific risk" (the residual variance left after market and industry correlated variance is eliminated) has been used and shown to be related to debt financing and also to concentrated holdings of stock by managers. It may well be related to plasticity, but since we argue that risk itself is not the issue, we are sure it is not a perfect measure. Nonetheless, some indications emerge of which circum-

19. R. A. Ippolito, "The Economic Function of Underfunded Pension Plans," *Journal of Law and Economics* 28 (1985): 611–52.

stances will lead to high debt ratios and which to low. In a professional service firm, such as law, architecture, medicine, engineering, or economic consulting, members may be so specific to certain customers that if they left the firm, remaining members and shareholders would hold an empty shell. To finance professional firms by outside equity would make the equity holder dependent on the unique insider members. But financing might be secured by the wealth of the "unique" resources. For the same reason, members will be faced with the problem of preventing some unique members from leaving and starting new firms after acquiring customer contacts and reputation while working as members. One precautionary device is to defer compensation to members until substantially later, even until retirement. But professional firms remain "black boxes" in that their internal contractual and control systems are yet to be analyzed and understood.

4. Contractual Arrangements and Market Conventions

Preceding sections have emphasized internal arrangements germane to corporate charters. But the potential for holdup and morally hazardous exploitation also has resulted in the evolution of some contractual and conventional arrangements of a more general, informal scope. These arrangements facilitate the advantages of intra- and inter-firm specificity.

4.1 Explicitly Rigid and Posted Prices

Posted prices, announced publicly and maintained until publicly revised, are prices at which the posting party will transact any amount. All parties obtain the same price; the price to a particular party cannot be changed while all others are getting better prices. The posting and stability of the price indicate reliability as a non-opportunistic buyer (seller) to all dependent sellers (buyers). An implication is that posted prices that are stable should be more commonly present where there is "dependency," i.e., reliance investments.

An example is the oil-gathering pipelines in California, where the pipeline gathering system is unique to several oil-well owners relying on the pipeline to transport oil to the refiners. The pipelines could opportunistically drop price under the guise of a temporarily reduced market demand, except that assurance against such behavior is provided by the stable posted price to all oil producers. Posted prices are present also in tuna and salmon fishing, where the fishing boats are reliant on a unique buyer-processor. Similarly, they, or a fixed-price guarantee, occur in many agricultural products where farmers plant crops relying on a unique buyer-processor.

Note all these situations arise where the classical economies of scale in processing (and pipelines) are large and where the costs of alternative suppliers of the same services are also large. Competition "for the market" rather than "in the market" determines the level of price, and the device which assures the multiple customers that they are not being monopolistically exploited in the posted price. Evidently, they are better able to determine whether the posted price is competitive than they would be to determine the competitiveness of varying prices.

"Most favored nation" clauses differ from posted prices in that the terms include more than prices. They are commitments made by a unique party to dependent parties and should be observed where such dependence exists. Where the dependent parties' products are not homogeneous, price protection alone is not sufficient to protect from quality alterations. An "advance notice" clause notifies the buyer of future price changes. This, too, shields the buyer from opportunistic price changes. The buyer is given time to seek new sources requiring less costly adjustment.

"Take or pay" clauses commit a buyer to taking a specified amount in the future. This protects a seller from a unique buyer who might strategically reduce the amount taken, for which the seller has geared the facilities, in order to force a lower price to expropriate composite quasi-rents of the seller. This provision is found in gas and oil pipeline contracts as a commitment by the buyer to a seller-producer, who is dependent on a unique buyer's transport facilities.

4.2 Implicitly Rigid Prices

Opportunistic price changes (intended to effect a holdup) are not clearly or cheaply distinguishable from price changes to which the parties would have agreed had the demand and supply environment been mutually foreseen. Variations in amount demanded are sometimes temporary and sometimes permanent. Should price be revised instantly to make the amount demanded equal the monetary amount supplied, i.e., instantaneously and continuously clear the market? Variations in such prices would tend to be dampened if there were buyers and sellers who believed that some of the variations were transient values from a stable underlying distribution, and they had sufficiently low storage or waiting costs to exploit the variation and stabilize the price.

However, the notion of a quickly equilibrating market price is baffling save in a very few markets. Imagine an employer and employee. Will they renegotiate price every hour, or with every perceived change in circumstances? If the employee were a waiter in a restaurant, would the waiter's wage be renegotiated with every new customer? Would it be renegotiated to virtually zero when no customers were present, and then back to a high level that would extract the entire customer value when a queue appeared? Obviously, prices and wages do not vary at every moment at which there is a change in the monetary demand or supply, as with the unimaginable waiter. But what is the right interval for renegotiation or change of price? The usual answer, "as soon as demand or supply changes," is uninformative.

A reason for wage and price "inflexibility" is protection of the expropriable composite quasi-rent of dependent resources. As stated earlier, to induce the coalition-dependent investment in the first place, the investor demands protection against the unique resource's subsequent attempts to expropriate that dependent quasi-rent. However, the investor is prepared—indeed desires—to have future revisions that both parties would have agreed to before the investment could they have foreseen that future change, or to which they would have subsequently agreed if the true state of demand and supply were readily known. But it is very difficult to later agree about what really is the current situation, because at the later time a false allegation could be made by the unique party as a subterfuge to capture some expropriable composite quasi-rent.

One protective device is to hold price or terms of trade constant until both parties agree that the new price is one they would have agreed upon if they could have foreseen the new demand and supply conditions prior to their investments. This underlies what the law calls "unconscionable" or "unfair" prices. The parties forestall costly expropriative behavior. The waiter in the restaurant case is identical to laborers who could refuse to pick a tomato crop at the last minute unless the farmer paid them the entire value of the crop. (This is a reason why farmers resist labor unions and opt for "family" labor instead.) If people were to renegotiate continuously and revise prices at every moment, the holdup possibilities would be severe in many, but not all, situations. If there were many alternative suppliers or buyers instantly available without sacrifice of composite quasi-rents, then quick price changes would be likely, as in markets like the stock market. But between an employee and an employer, momentary or even daily or weekly renegotiation would be susceptible to the disease of "holdups," "expropriation of composite quasi-rents," "unconscionability," "opportunism," etc.

Typically, prices are not varied in real emergency situations to exploit victims for the same reason prices are not continuously renegotiated in routine employment and rental situations. It helps forestall expropriative action and avoids expensive precautionary actions. The principle has wide applicability.

For example, imagine a remote highway repair shop which might charge a stranded motorist full dependent value (or full consumer surplus) for repairs. If that dependent value were to be expropriated in the event of a breakdown, travellers would take precautionary action to reduce breakdown prospects. These precautionary actions can be expensive and might even forestall travel through that region. A sense of "moral outrage" at people who charge an extractive, "exorbitant" price serves the social and economic function of deterring such behavior and thereby reduces dependence on more expensive means of avoiding breakdowns or leads to choosing not to travel at all. The equilibrium is a delicate one, however, and once such social capital is destroyed by a series of cheats it is not easily replaced.[20] The degree to which "moral outrage" is an efficient device for controlling socially costly behavior merits study.

Similarly, when a disaster isolates a community, the local grocer may deplete remaining inventory at the usual "competitive" price, despite the sudden increased demand. And the customers will tend to share resources. This price stability and sharing avoids the precautionary (costly) holding of larger than optimal inventories (hoarding) solely to avoid such interpersonal wealth transfers. Assurance against dependent value extraction is desired; i.e., people want prevailing prices to be those that would have been negotiated in advance earlier had a binding contract been feasible.

4.3 Layoffs and Unemployment Spells

Holdup threats are not effective against an independent, non-reliant resource. So the offers and prices to general resources should respond more readily to momentary transient observed market demands. Homogeneous and independent resource services will have prices that change more quickly and in smaller amounts in response to observed fluctuations, because neither party faces potential expropriative holdups. However, the more firm-dependent resources are exposed to this threat. They seek assurance that the unique-resource owners will not alter their behavior under a guise of a falsely alleged decline in the equilibrium price. As a result, price will not respond to every perceived momentary change and, more importantly, will not respond even at the moment of a change in the underlying demand or supply conditions, because those changes are initially undetectable from the background noise. It takes more reliable information to persuade both parties to adjust.

The more firm-dependent resources will face more rigid prices and more

---

20. V. Goldberg, "Fishing and Selling," *Journal of Legal Studies* 15 (1986): 173–80.

spells of unemployment, where rigidity is used as a means of reducing holdups. The unemployment is a side effect of the purpose of price rigidity—the prevention of holdups hidden under the allegation of a change in equilibrium conditions—and is the price paid when mutually dependent resources protect themselves from exploitation. Long-term contracts or conventions, which restrain future behavior and terms of trade, are as essential and characteristic of the "firm" as is teamwork. The price rigidity does not imply market power on either side, as once both parties agree that market conditions have changed, price will change.

An explanation for "layoffs" has been that they are devices to allay the threat of holdups.[21] To convince employees that an employer's proposal to reduce the work force is a response to decreased demand, rather than being an attempt at a holdup, the employer suspends operations, which is more costly if demand has not fallen. If demand has really decreased, a shutdown is more economical than a wage cut, because the implied required wage to justify continued operations would be lower than options believed available to employees elsewhere. The temptation to suggest that unemployment cannot be understood until an adequate theory of the firm has been worked out is too powerful to resist. Without an explanation of why and how firms' constituents contract with one another, it seems unlikely that unemployment, layoffs, and wage and price behavior can be explained.

4.4 Labor Unions

Labor unions, whether company or industry, can, by collective action, protect employees' firm-dependent values. Employees who have made their own investments in firm-specific skills in response to employer promises, or who have earned rights to future insurance and retirement benefits, want to monitor the employer's performance and restrain the employer from expropriating those firm-specific rewards. This is a major defense of unions, and if this were their only function, firms would not object to them. After all, an employer who borrows from a bank does not oppose monitoring by the bank, as the monitoring makes the loan cheaper. Despite this beneficial effect of organized employees, firms fear the reverse risk of employees expropriating employers' quasi-rents.[22]

---

21. R. E. Hall and D. M. Lilien, "Efficient Wage Bargains Under Uncertain Demand and Supply," *American Economic Review* 69 (1979): 868–79.

22. Ippolito, "The Economic Function of Underfunded Pension Plans."

4.5 First Refusals

A right of first refusal prevents a threat to sell a unique, relied-upon resource to some other user, a threat made solely to extract some of the composite quasi-rent. If the optioned resource really had a new, higher value alternative, then it could move for reasons unrelated to any threat of expropriative behavior. But it might threaten to leave, without really having a higher-valued alternative. The right of refusal permits matching a bona fide offer, and therefore, a threat to sell or remove services unless paid more to match a false outside alternative would not be effective. First refusal does not prevent a unique resource from simply terminating services, even without selling to someone else. Therefore, the optioned item should be one from which the service flow to the current user is not easily controllable by its owner. Nor is the option a device to transfer the risk of market value changes. Instead, the possibility of expropriative action by the unique resource is suppressed by a first refusal option.

5. The Variety of the Firm

5.1 Franchises

Some products are retailed under a common trade name by franchises, each of which is owned by a different party. Franchises exploit the informational economies of scale from the use of a national brand name, but do not exploit the market economies of scale that could result from common ownership with publicly traded shares. McDonald's, for example, has equity traded on the New York Stock Exchange and presumably could finance all of its hamburger stands with capital raised there, giving financiers the benefits of liquidity and diversification. But it chooses instead to place the risk for each individual unit on the residual claimant/managers of each unit. Evidently the productive outcomes from this arrangement are sufficiently superior to overcome the benefits of more marketable claims.

The behavior of each franchisee determines the quality of its product and therefore affects not only its own revenue but also the revenue of the fellow franchisees because of the shared brand name. A retailer-franchisee could, by providing inferior service, reduce its costs for a short-lived gain but harm the reputation and reduce demand for the product sold under the common trade name. Because of the interdependence, common ownership of the franchisor and franchisee would help protect interdependent value.

But the employer-employee relationship does not always provide the most appropriate incentives, especially where operations are not well standardized and rely on discretion. We would expect, for example, that gourmet restaurants (slow food, in contrast to fast food) would not be organized as national chains, because the discretion necessary is not easily monitored and standardized into repetitive management activities. Franchised operations are intermediate between the individual gourmet restaurant and the national chain of restaurants jointly owned. Apparently the franchises are sufficiently monitorable for the parent company to be able to make decisions whether the franchise should continue or be terminated on an intermittent basis, but not sufficiently monitorable to hire a manager to operate the unit.

5.2 Resale Price Maintenance

Some manufacturers depend on a network of retailers to provide services to create and maintain the value of the manufacturer's product and shared reputation for reliability of a known quality. When the provision of these services is difficult to monitor, producers can elicit the provision of the services anyway by locking in a differential between wholesale and retail prices by setting the wholesale price and also "maintaining" (setting) the retail price. Retailers will compete away any rent in the differential by providing the services consumers and the producer desire. If retailers who cheat (sell at prices lower than the maintained resale price—a behavior easier to detect than service provision) are penalized by termination, cheating is deterred, services are provided, and the producer and consumers are better off than if resale prices were not maintained. Without resale price maintenance, retailers would cheat on service provision to the point where no services were provided, and lower prices to the point where no services were paid for, but both customers and the producer would be worse off.

5.3 Joint Ventures

Joint ventures are formed where two usually pre-existing "firms" share in investments on which both will be interreliant. The rationale for joint venture is the interreliance of a unique resource or end product. The resource or product is likely research, invention, information, or anything that has both (1) significant economies of scale (like research or a pipeline) and (2) services on which both parties will rely. A joint venture is an efficient organizational device because it avoids duplication of effort (same pipeline built twice or same research done twice) and avoids the opportunity for expropriation which would result if only one party owned the resource and sold its services to the other.

5.4 Mutually Owned Teams

A "mutual" organization is one in which the equity holders and the customers are the same individuals. Mutual organization is common in banks (some are organized with depositors as owners, and some with borrowers as owners), insurance companies, nursing homes, country clubs, and some other social clubs. Mutuality enables the members to (a) prevent outside equity holders from expropriating value by lowering the quality of service, and (b) preserve for incumbents any gains from admitting new members. Mutuals do not permit anonymous alienability of members' ownership interest. A "mutual" member can sell ownership only by ceasing to be a consumer of the group's services, and in some organizations, such as country clubs, can transfer rights to membership only with the permission of the other members.

As Adam Smith so persuasively argued, in most productive activity the profit motive successfully aligns the interests of producers and consumers. In what kinds of economic activity is the additional inducement for this alignment provided by making the consumers explicitly also owners called for? Calling upon our developing theme, it is called for in those cases where information is expensive, expropriation is possible, and long-term relations between producers and consumers prevail, in particular in those cases where the fellow consumers influence the quality of what is produced.

For banks and insurance companies, mutuality removes the incentives for equity holders to take risks which would impair without compensation the security of an insurance fund or deposit, and qualifications for membership influence the quality of the product purchased. For example, one of the earliest (1690s) mutual insurance companies sold life insurance only for wives of clergymen, assuring that all members of the pool would have similar lifestyles (although they surely did not use this term). Alternative mechanisms for solving this same problem are (a) reputation acquisition, and (b) regulation. The force opposing mutuality in banks and insurance companies is that mutuality constrains the opportunities for diversification of risk by requiring the customers to be equity holders. In organizations such as the US Farm Credit System, a mutual credit organization, it seems unlikely that in the absence of the government umbrella, farmers would want to bear the regional, and in principle diversifiable, components of agricultural lending risk.

For social organizations, such as nursing homes and country clubs, the forces for mutuality are even more powerful. The mutual members themselves are the interdependent resources who interact and create the mutual's service and value. Increasing the number of members can affect each incumbent's realized social satisfaction and the level of congestion. The difference here is that the members are inputs to, not just buyers of, a product. The membership acting in consortium will maximize the average net yield per member. New members will often be charged more than their pro rata share of the club's capital facilities, and thereby incumbents will capture the value of admitting new members, and incumbents will admit new members to the point where they benefit despite increased congestion.

Social clubs are owned by members because the "social value quasi-rent" would be vulnerable to expropriation if it were owned by outsiders. An independent owner could admit new members without compensating existing members for the reduction in average quality. Quality is not just a matter of congestion. If it were, competition among clubs would result in the optimal level of congestion. This would imply that members could switch clubs at no cost. But the members create and obtain interpersonal social services; they themselves produce what the club is providing. Replacement of one club member with another not known to the rest of the group will result in lower quality to the remaining members. The members have "specific capital" in one another, and that specific capital could be expropriated by an independent owner. Mutual ownership tends to preserve the interspecific value for members.

This view of country club ownership bears on the general question of social relations. If people could be costlessly interchanged in social relationships, no expropriable social value would exist, just as in firms where employees have perfect substitutes. But neither firms nor social groups are costlessly created and altered. Social associates, such as marriage partners, result in highly specific interpersonal dependence. Why people are more attentive to social associates than to those who simply eat in the same restaurants or worship in the same churches is not easy to explain. We leave unanswered the question of why friendships are more costly and long-lived than relations with mere fellow consumers and acolytes. What is there about "friendships" that requires interpersonal dependence and, hence, results in expropriable composite quasi-rents?

6. Conclusion

The variety of contracts used to organize cooperative activity involving dependency reveals that the standard conception of the firm is too narrow. Teamwork is widespread and spans more than ordinary production; it extends, for example, to marriage, engagements, "live-ins," social clubs, churches, athletic leagues, and associations. Questions like "Is the National Football League a firm or is it 24 separate firms?" and "Is McDonald's one large firm or hundreds of firms?" and "Is the National Collegiate Athletic Association a firm, a cartel, a collusion, a coalition, or a cabal?" are not useful questions. Instead, the useful questions are why the various types of contractual arrangements are made among coalitions of owners of resources, and what are the consequences.

Many economists, lawyers, and judges, despite the dictum that "substance, not form" counts, nevertheless answer a question regarding how an organization ought to be allowed to operate by deciding whether or not the organization "is" a "firm." In litigation involving the National Football League, a judge declared the league to be 24 different firms, and therefore they were colluding. If, however, the league were declared a joint venture, or a single firm with franchises, the applicable legal rules would have been very different. In that proceeding at no time was it ever made evident what was the criterion for identifying or defining "a firm," let alone on what criteria the arrangement, whatever it be called, should be treated this way or that way.

The criterion surely must recognize the nature of and reason for the restraints of long-term contract—the existence of investments by parties mutually dependent on one another's continued association. Because such dependency and contractual arrangements occur in a great variety of forms, it is of little value to try to define the firm as any particular one of them. More important is an examination of each form of group activity to understand the reasons for and consequences of organizational form, whether it be in social clubs, sporting groups, marriages, or the production of goods and services for sale.

ADDITIONAL REFERENCES

Alchian, A. A. "Uncertainty, Evolution and Economic Theory." *Journal of Political Economy* 58 (1950): 211–21.

Coase, R. H. "The Nature of the Firm." *Economica*, n.s., 4 (1937): 386–405.

CONCLUDING REMARKS

Dedicating to me the 4th Saarland University Seminar on the New Institutional Economics is an honor I am happy to receive, and I do so fully aware that I am only one of many other economists who have also been effective in advancing understanding of the institutions called "the Firm." I am particularly impressed and gratified by Karl Brunner's gracious statement, for I know he does not engage in insincerity. And I am grateful to the officers of Saarland University and in particular to Professor Richter and to Professor Furubotn for their successful effort in arranging for not only this seminar but also the productive and stimulating seminars of the past three years.

A firm can be defined as a set of resources and their owners bound by a contractual coalition for more effective production. Such a coalition for achievement of any other particular shared objective is often called something other than "firm," e.g., a club, a mutual, a cooperative, a family, an association, a league, a set of franchises. So far as I can ascertain, the firm is distinguished from the other coalitions by its particular objective, increased market value of the group's activities. A family or club also seeks a shared objective, but that objective is not a larger market value of wealth. Any form of coalition that has that objective is usually called some kind of "firm" whether it be an association or set of franchises.

Alfred Marshall seems to have been the first, in 1890, who identified what now appears to be a key feature of a firm, viz., inter-resource specificity, which he defined in terms of its result, "composite quasi-rent." Though he did not use the concept for further formal analysis of the "firm," he did explicitly note the key problem, avoidance of the expropriation of the dependent composite quasi-rent. Yet the context in which he used it should have led, but unfortunately did not, to explaining the reason for and nature of the firm. Instead a technological feature of teamwork subsequently dominated the underlying conception. Joint activity, or teamwork, could not be handled by inter-individual sale of individual specific items, because there were no separable individual

Reprinted, by permission of the author, from *Zeitschrift für die gesamte Staatswissenschaft* (Journal of Institutional and Theoretical Economics) 143 (March 1987), 232–34.

specific items to sell. Because of the jointness or absence of individually specific and separable outputs, with resultant inter-dependence of marginal productivities, monitoring inputs is used as a surrogate measure of marginal productivity. Absent perfect monitoring, shirking, or what can be called a form of free-riding on other members of the group, must be controlled—a form of moral hazard problem. Much can be explained on this basis, but not enough.

A common, but not universal, consequence of teamwork is resource dependence, an excess of value achievable by some resources used in the team above that achievable outside the team once the resource has joined the team. This transformation of the situation, from one in which the resource gets an amount inside that barely exceeds what it could earn outside to a situation in which its exterior net value falls significantly after the resource has entered the team, has been appropriately called, by O. Williamson, the Fundamental Transformation. (There is in my mind no doubt that appropriate or suggestive names serve to economize on communication as well as attract attention, e.g., shirking, teamwork, bounded rationality, opportunism, impacted information, expropriable quasi-rent, resource specificity, and dependency. But they become helpful only insofar as they designate useful analytical concepts, as appears to have been the case for these at least. Even better, it would be interesting if the name of the person who first popularized a concept were used as the name of the popularized concept, as is done in physics and medicine. We could call it not the Fundamental Transformation, but the Williamson transform, or instead of teamwork, the Alchian-Demsetz force, and the Marshall effect to denote the creation of an expropriable quasi-rent, perhaps measuring the amount of that rent in units of Marshalls.)

Abandoning fantasizing, I note that about a decade ago Marshall's composite quasi-rent was reinvented or, so far as I was involved, may have been subconsciously recalled (as explained in the footnote to the paper with Woodward). The desire to prevent that expropriation by opportunistic behavior (here called a "holdup" to distinguish it from moral hazard shirking) suggested the binding and, hence, long-term contracts between the owners of resources that had become dependent and those that were unique. Though long recognized in the law as reliance investments, importance of the holding remained insufficiently noted by economists until law and economics became popular, wherein economists learned much from the law. With this understanding it was an easy step to the enlargement of the range of contractual implications for the organization of the firm, in which the essential ingredient became inter-resource specificity and dependence protected by long-term constraining contracts, rather than a technical institution characterized by a long-lasting series of spot, unconstrained exchanges among cooperative inputs.

This dependence among resource owners has been the common element in the concepts called asymmetric information with opportunism, dynamic inefficiency, time irreversibility, holdups, agencies, all attacking the same fundamental problem from different points of view or with different analytic tools.

The current and future directions of study seem to be toward the so-called non-standard firm—i.e., mutuals, clubs, cooperatives, labor-managed firms (e.g., professional law and engineering firms), associations, franchises, and leagues—in which, again, the form of inter-resource or inter-person dependence looms large as a critical ingredient. The organization of so-called labor-managed firms in socialist countries may prove to be amenable to analysis because the same problems occur whenever dependence and uniqueness among separately owned resources occur. With socialist firms, the absence of private property rights renders the analysis less amenable to standard treatment, but perhaps progress will be made.

Another direction of research is suggested by the joint paper delivered here with S. Woodward. To what extent can the resource or investment characteristics imply the contractual structure among the resource owners, as for example in whether the resources or their funding will be "rented" from renters or from bondholders rather than owned by the users or operators of the coalitions' activities, often called the firm's owners? We have attempted to define a concept or characteristic of resources of investment, one we name "plasticity," which we conjecture will be useful. Whether or not it is remains to be seen. In any event it will be an element in our future research agenda.

Some implications and consequences of the evolving understanding of "the firm" are easy to discern. The word "firm" will be less used to characterize a well-defined group within which cooperation is acceptable but across which it is deemed "anti-competitive" or undesirable. There can be cause for decrying some forms of intra-firm behavior, and conversely, there can be cause to encourage inter-firm cooperation. The decision or judgment no longer can be that whatever is across firms is anti-competitive (i.e., undesirable). Instead, the question will more transparently be "What are the effects?" and whether the cooperation is within or among firms will be ignored, simply because the boundaries of the firm are not well defined for that purpose. As a very simple example, the extremely rapid evolution of the product-identifying bar codes used by virtually all manufacturers internationally was the result of "inter-firm" cooperation. Alternatively one could argue that development was "within a new special-purpose large firm." More precisely, we now are led to inquire into what contractual coalition is being formed with what purpose and what effect and to worry less about "What is the Firm?" For example, the family is a contractual coalition formed usually under the conventional marriage contract. Similarly cohabitation exists under less binding, shorter-term contractual arrangements. Now that Pandora's Box is open, the "Firm" is dead, long live the new firms.

The paper with Susan Woodward is an attempt to encourage investigation of what we believe may be a useful characterization of some attributes of types of resources or investments that are made in the coalition called a firm. We regard it as an element in a research agenda. Perhaps in following years we will have good reason to honor someone who really advances our understanding.

THE FIRM IS DEAD; LONG LIVE THE FIRM
A REVIEW OF OLIVER E. WILLIAMSON'S
*THE ECONOMIC INSTITUTIONS OF CAPITALISM**
ARMEN A. ALCHIAN AND SUSAN WOODWARD

Once upon a time, the organization of cooperative economic activity we call the firm was a black box. Into this box went labor and capital, and out came products. The mechanism was driven by wealth maximization and governed by the laws of returns. Some venturesome economists have wondered what the black box contained, seeing as how market prices could guide all gains from specialization. What more could a firm do?

No one has been more venturesome than Oliver Williamson in his eminently readable and imperially titled book, *The Economic Institutions of Capitalism*, essentially a compendium, elaboration, and revision of certain of his publications in this decade. It summarizes his many significant insights that gave substance to Coase's suggestion that firms reduce transactions costs and presages a research agenda for himself and others. For those seeking a more accessible presentation of the transactions approach, the new book is both a more general and at the same time more precise exposition of Williamson's contributions.

Because the book is a summary of Williamson's contributions to the analysis of the firm, this review will of necessity, and deservedly, become a sort of analytic review of both (a) the prevailing transaction cost interpretation of agreements among owners of cooperatively used resources and (b) some important implications that are being derived from that model.

The emphasis in Williamson's book is not on capitalism's "free markets" but on the constraints that are voluntarily arrived at when transactors are free to impose restrictions upon themselves. The restrictions that interest

Reprinted from *Journal of Economic Literature* 26 (March 1988): 65–79, by permission of the American Economic Association.

The authors thank unnamed referees for improvement in content and exposition. The usual caveats apply.

*Oliver E. Williamson, *The Economic Institutions of Capitalism: Firms, Markets, Relational Contracting* (New York: The Free Press; London: Collier Macmillan Publishers, 1985).

Williamson are not "anticompetitive" (though some used to be presumed so by some economists) but rather those crafted in competitive markets and that minimize transactions costs both across markets and within firms.

1. The Puzzle

The traditional price-theoretic paradigm in which gains from trade depend on a comparative advantage in production (i.e., by marginal cost equalization across producers) is distinguished by two features: First, no one relies on some-one else for directions about what to do; market prices alone direct production and exchange. Second, production results from cooperative teamwork or cooperative production, leaving no role for contracts or any other constraints (such as rigid prices) on the options of cooperating parties. Yet in a wide array of economic activities, people rely on and follow the administrative directions of other people, and both explicit and implicit agreements restrict options. In other words, "firms" or organized and managed "coalitions" exist. Why?

An answer—transactions costs—has been developed in two complementary, but different, directions. One emphasizes the administering, directing, negotiating, and monitoring of the joint productive teamwork in a firm. The other emphasizes assuring the quality or performance of contractual agreements. Both activities prevail across markets and within firms, but to different degrees and with different opportunities for containment. Where these costs are high, market transactions tend to be replaced with internal production and direction and common ownership of more of the jointly used resources so that quality is controlled (managed) and monitored through and during the production process.

A. *Bounded Rationality and Opportunism*

The first three chapters concern how Williamson views bounded rationality and opportunism as a source of many transactions costs, both across markets and within firms. By "bounded rationality" Williamson means that people have limited information and limited ability to process it. This implies incomplete information about market opportunities, limited ability to predict the future and derive implications from predictions, and limited ability to prespecify responses to future events. People don't know everything, and so they make mistakes; moreover each person may know different things.

Opportunism follows from bounded rationality plus self-interest. When a conflict arises between what people want and what they have agreed to do for others, they will act in their own interest insofar as it is costly for others to know their behavior (others face costly information). Opportunism, not merely self-interest, is the original and deadly sin recognized by Williamson.

Opportunism covers more than the propensity for mutually reliant parties to mislead, distort, disguise, obfuscate, or otherwise confuse (p. 47) in order to expropriate wealth from one another. It includes honest disagreements. Even when both parties recognize the genuine goodwill of the other, different but honest perceptions can lead to disputes that are costly to resolve. The point is important because many business arrangements interpreted as responses to potential "dishonest" opportunism are equally appropriate for avoiding costly disputes between honest, ethical people who disagree about what event transpired and what adjustment would have been agreed to initially had the event been anticipated.

B. *Transactions, Exchanges, and Contracts*

The notion of a "transaction" includes both exchanges and contracts. An exchange is a transfer of property rights to resources that involves no promises or latent future responsibility. In contrast, a contract promises future performance, typically because one party makes an investment, the profitability of which depends on the other party's future behavior. The transactions that are the focus of Williamson's approach are contractual, not just spot exchanges or even a long-lasting series of spot exchanges. In a contract a promise of future performance is exchanged, and investments are made, the value of which becomes dependent on the fulfillment of the other party's promises.

For Williamson, transactions costs are more than the cost of finding other people, inspecting goods, seeking agreeable terms, and writing exchange agreements; they include, almost to the extent of ignoring the former, the costs incurred in making contracts enforceable by law or by self-enforcement and extends to the precautions against potential expropriation of the value of investments relying on contractual performance as well as costs of informing and administering terms of contractual relations. These costs are associated with the containment of opportunism.

Williamson defines ex ante costs as the costs of actions and tasks involved in establishing a contract. Ex post costs are those incurred in subsequently administering, informing, monitoring, and enforcing the contractually promised performance—features that dominate the transactions cost approach. Williamson labels the transition from precontract to postcontract the Fundamental Transformation. Options available in the former stage are lost in the latter; as a result, the value of some resources becomes dependent on particular unique other parties because of loss of significant substitutability by equivalent resources. Other terms used for this dependence are *asset specificity, interspecificity, reliance*, and Williamson's previously used term *idiosyncratic*.

The contract terms that make possible the Fundamental Transformation include both promises of performance and agreements on price. If price (or a price formula) were to be changed or renegotiated whenever either party proposed, no effective commitment of performance would be present. Precommitments to a price by both parties constrain the options and restrict future renegotiability, which is precisely the point of a contract—to protect dependent, reliant resources from malperformance and to guarantee them a prespecified compensation.

Although this is called a "transaction cost" approach, it involves identifying factors that make spot market transactions less viable, and transactions governed by contracts more viable. It also involves identifying the factors that shape contractual restraints. But we know what the behavioral factors are— bounded rationality and opportunism. Evidently, these can occur in various ways and circumstances, which call for different institutions for their management. Indeed, we submit that by drawing some distinctions among kinds of opportunism Williamson's analysis can be made more powerful.

II. Moral Hazard and Holdup

Paradoxically Williamson's exposition and, in part, the analysis do not distinguish analytically between the two kinds of opportunism: moral hazard and holdup. Fortunately, it only rarely leads Williamson to errors. But the distinction will help the reader get to many of Williamson's conclusions. In this section we set out the distinction.

A. *Holdup and Specificity*

Uncertainty about price or compensation arises when the value of a collection of resources dependent on continued association for their maximum product exceeds their summed market values. Resources dependent upon one another in this way are referred to by Williamson as "specific" or "interspecific," and those making investments specific to other assets will seek protection against reneging or "holdup" by the other parties. This view gives us insight into contracts, pricing policies, and agreements that constrain markets, and also gives us a theory of the types of assets the firm will own.

Alfred Marshall, in his *Principles*, was the first to identify these elements in the context of what he called "composite quasi-rent."[1] A quasi-rent is the excess above the return necessary to maintain a resource's current service flow, which can be the means to recover sunk costs. Composite quasi-rent is that portion of the quasi-rent of resources that depends on continued association with some other specific currently associated resources. Thus, composite quasi-rent is the amount those other currently associated resources could attempt to expropriate by refusing to pay or serve, that is, by holdup.

Marshall offered the example of a steel mill that locates near a public utility and makes an investment, the profitability of which depends on being able to buy power at some given price. Once the steel mill incurs costs that become sunk, the power company could raise power prices. The steel mill would continue to operate so long as the new marginal cost did not exceed marginal revenue, even though the sunk costs are not being recovered. Marshall recognized the danger of parties with sunk costs relying on those in a position to expropriate composite quasi-rents. But he assumed the threat was resolved by "doing what is right" or by "haggling." So far as we can ascertain, Marshall did not develop the importance of quasi-rent for understanding the organization of the firm.

Composite quasi-rent has been recently rediscovered by others in discussion of "time-irreversibility," "asymmetric information with uncertainty," "bilateral monopoly," "opportunism," "self-enforcing contracts," and "principal-agent relationships" to name a few.

If a resource can leave a team without cost or loss of its value, Williamson would say it is independent or is not team-specific, or is "redeployable." But if the remaining resources would lose by its departure, they are dependent (reliant is the term in legal proceedings) on it, and to them, the departing resource is unique because they cannot replace it with no loss. Resources that are mutually dependent are also mutually unique, and vice versa.

A landowner renting land as a site for a skyscraper is an owner of a resource that is unique but impotent. The landowner cannot cheaply alter the services of the land as a means of extracting some of the quasi-rent of the building from the building owner. But the owner of the building could refuse to pay all of the promised rent, nevertheless secure in the knowledge that the landowner has no feasible alternative use of the land. The landowner's remedies by law limit the

1. Alfred Marshall, *Principles of Economics* (1890; 8th ed., London: Macmillan, 1936), 453–54, 626.

expropriation the building owner could extract, but the expense of the remedies limit the protection afforded the landowner through such remedies. An
owner of a unique resource will be more tempted to exploit the situation as the
composite quasi-rent grows large and as the unique resource's flow of services
become more controlled (for example, by failing to pay the rent or failing to
show up for work). The more likely and foreseeable is this temptation, the
greater is the likelihood that precautionary contractual terms will be sought.
Obviously, dependency motivates a desire for reliable services from the unique
resource that is relied upon. Services can be obtained by (1) buying the services
or (2a) owning or (2b) renting the unique resource for self-service. Buying *services* exposes the purchaser to a holdup threat. Hence, the unique resources are
more likely to be controlled by (2a) ownership or (2b) rental for self-use. The
choice will depend on the ability of the owner to detect abuse or effects on the
resource consequent to the way it is used by a renter. With cheap detection,
the unique resource is likely to be rented rather than owned by the dependent
party. The two features—(a) dependency and (b) monitorability of use—are
important in determining whether the relied-upon services will be obtained by
ownership or by rental, and hence the degree of integration of ownership of
resources in a firm.

B. *Moral Hazard and Plasticity*

Moral hazard, a form of opportunism, arises in agreements in which at least
one party relies on the behavior of another, and information about that behavior is costly. The owner of a firm hires a manager and wants the manager to
maximize profits. The manager hires employees and wants them to follow directions. An investor lends money to a firm and wants the firm to act in that
debt holder's interest. Because it is costly for the principal to know exactly what
the agent did or will do, the agent has an opportunity to bias his actions more
in his own interest, to some degree inconsistent with the interests of the
principal.

The term *moral hazard* has been unjustly maligned for its moralistic over-
tones. In the finance literature, especially, it is often called *postcontractual
opportunism*. We resist. First, as we argue here, the events that can give trouble
ex post of the contract are not just those associated with moral hazard but also
those of holdup, which we believe are neglected compared with moral hazard
in most of the principal-agent literature. Second, the term *moral hazard* correctly implies that if everyone would simply agree to undertake a given standard of effort and abide by the promise, a more efficient outcome would result.

The term suggests that people cannot be counted on to do what they say they are going to do, and that failure manifests itself in prices and in contractual arrangements. It also indicates correctly that among the devices used to control such behavior are moralistic aggression and contempt.

Though moral hazard is involved in many transactions, it does not follow that they are regretted. For example, both the insurance market and the labor market experience moral hazard, but all parties are better off having made the transactions than not. The insured pay the full expected losses plus administration to the insurer, so all costs are compensated. The laborers earn their expected marginal product. The moral hazard loss simply measures what could be gained if magically either the cost of monitoring behavior by the insurer-employer were zero, or if people could be counted on to do as they promise.

Though criticizing Williamson for not analytically distinguishing between two types of opportunism, we note that the literatures on holdup and moral hazard are almost entirely unintegrated.

The degree to which resources are vulnerable to morally hazardous exploitation depends on what can be called their "plasticity" and on monitoring costs. We call resources or investment "plastic" to indicate that there is a wide range of discretionary, legitimate decisions within which the user may choose. For example, compare a drug research laboratory with a steel manufacturer. There are fewer options for discretionary behavior in steel manufacturing. The technology is largely determined by the nature of the plant. Absentee owners and debt holders have little cause to worry about the managers' turning the resources of the plant into personal consumption or increasing the riskiness of prospective outcomes. In contrast, a drug research firm could be working on some mundane project with a modest but sure payoff, or on some long shot with a slight chance of a high payoff. Research and development firms are plastic.

We conjecture as further illustrations that enterprises with intellectual research and capital—for example, fashion designers, professional service firms such as engineering, law, architecture, and computer software creation—are especially plastic and susceptible to moral hazard. In contrast, industries with less plasticity are railroads, utility services, airlines, petroleum refining (but not exploration), and other activities involving much in the way of "hard" resources. Interestingly, physical resources requiring large sunk costs, and consequently that are vulnerable to holdup, can be implastic and immune to moral hazard.

Cash is among the most plastic of resources, because it can be hastily exchanged for nearly anything. But this example serves well the point that plasticity must be combined with high monitoring costs to result in opportunities for moral hazard. Cash is plastic but very easy to track as it is used (once the records establish that it is there). Thus, we expect managers handling large cash balances to be subject to considerable controls and review by principals, but we observe that there are many large financial institutions operated by nonowner managers.

By "plastic" we do not simply mean risky. Oil that has only to be pumped and sold is highly implastic. The optimal rate at which to pump the oil depends on the pattern of prices over time, and there is little in the way of possibilities for exploiting an oil well either by increasing the riskiness of its value or by changing its product into personal consumption. But an oil well is a risky asset if the price of oil fluctuates.

c. *Two Expeditions Reunited*

The early explorers of transactions costs set out on two very different expeditions. One party, guided by the notion of moral hazard and adverse selection, headed off in the direction of insurance and risk and ventured successfully into generalized principal-agent conflicts. The implications of informational asymmetries and impactedness for behavior and market viability explained various aspects of insurance markets, the assignment of liability, the use of the firm for teamwork, some firm financing decisions, and conflicts of interest between owners and managers, between inside owners and outside owners, and between debt holders and equity holders. In particular, monitoring costs associated with moral hazard became a basis for explaining two different aspects of firms. The first aspect is the role of "management." Some firm members are managers while others are managed, because the party with comparative advantage in deciding what a particular worker should do is not necessarily the worker himself. This relationship is subject to moral hazard, and the desire to control the costs associated with it explains some aspects of firm organization. Second, monitoring costs will also motivate ownership of assets by their user. If the user of an asset is also its owner, the full consequences of how the asset is used falls on the user. When the owner and user are separate parties, the owner bears the costs of the user's behavior, even if the user is careless. Costly detection of care, moral hazard, is thus a source of asset specificity and will drive ownership of an asset by the user. Once the asset is owned by the firm (used by the owner), informational asymmetries regarding that user's effect on the resource keep it in the firm, that is, make it firm-specific.

The other party studying the firm headed off from industrial organization to look for explanations as to why firms vertically integrate. Chapters 4–10 recount Williamson's earlier vehicle for exploring beyond that territory: holdup and its prevention. Holdup could explain not only common ownership of assets and aspects of contracts but also contractual constraints on markets such as posted or otherwise inflexible prices, pay or take, first negotiation, and rights of refusal.

From these two different explorations the question arose: Does the essence of the "firm" lie in teamwork or in the nexus of long-term contracts (i.e., agreements restraining the behavior of transactors)? Williamson writes as if he believes teamwork always involves such contracts. We agree, because we can think of neither significant nor interesting cases where teamwork does not create dependencies calling for contractual restraints. The durability of the team-specific investments, especially accumulated team-specific information involved in teamwork, connects teamwork to contracts.

We observe that in most cooperative production (teamwork), people show up for work at the same place every day. (As a matter of fact, people often show up for play in the same locations, too, though less reliably, but for many of the same reasons.) Team members are more productive working together than working separately, and this differential at least partly depends on knowledge of one another's personal talents. This specific knowledge has lasting value, and consequently departure of part of the team can threaten the team's value. This special lasting knowledge makes the members of the team mutually team-specific. They will want assurance of performance and compensation before they will be willing to make any self-financed investments in the team's efforts—hence, long-term contracts. Teamwork and long-term contracts seldom appear without the other.

III. The Firm

To help explain Williamson's conception of the firm, we offer a provisional characterization. The classic, paradigmatic private property firm is a coalition among owners of separately owned resources whose value as a team exceeds the sum of the market values each could get separately. Some of this value derives from the durable and costly specialized knowledge they possess about each other. That value depends on continued association; the departure of any of the mutually dependent resources would diminish the value of the team. The desire to protect this value and secure a share of it will motivate contracts among inputs for the continuing services of the resources of the team.

It follows that the team members who own resources (human as well) whose values depend most heavily on the performance of the team (i.e., are the most team-specific) will be willing to pay the most for the right to control the team. By definitional consequence of being owners of such resources, they own the residual value. They are the ones who are called the owners of the firm, though no one literally owns all the resources used in the firm. The owners, or equity holders, as a precaution against moral hazard and holdup, will be common to all contracts with input owners, will possess the right to sell their contractual status, and will bear the residual value of team-specific resources. The more general, less specific, more substitutable resources (some of which are called employees) will be rented, because their value and reward are independent of the fortunes and behavior of the team. They must be, and are, paid no more or less than their opportunity value.

The differences between the value of the team and the summed values all the resources could command outside the team is a return to the entrepreneur's investment in the search for a successful team. It is, as such, much like the *expectational* return to investments in search for oil. Absent any team-specific investment on their own part, the other members will earn just their value elsewhere, unless they are able to collude to extract a successful team-assembling entrepreneur's quasi-rent and profit.

A. *Ownership Integration*

One form of protection from opportunism is common ownership of the dependent resources as one bundle, that is, ownership integration, sometimes misleadingly called "vertical" or "horizontal" integration, although these adjectives are unnecessarily restrictive. This is obvious enough when all the firm-specific resources are owned by one person. Problems develop if either (a) those resources are owned in common by several people (as in corporations and partnerships), or (b) the firm-specific resources are not all owned in common (as in joint ventures or cooperatives).

B. *Joint and Several Ownership in Common*

Chapters 11 and 12 apply Williamson's schema to the corporation. In corporations, stockholders jointly own the firm-specific unique resources. While predetermined shares of ownership preclude disputes over the division of the resulting value (at least in the idealized corporation), the shareholders may have different beliefs about the best choice of action, when dividends ought to be taken, or how much risk to take on. One way to get around this difficulty is to make the shares transferable. Then changes in beliefs and personal consumption plans can be accommodated through buying and selling, without affecting the operation of the firm itself.

Williamson sees the anonymity of stockholders as something of a problem. He describes stockholders as having "investments that are not associated with particular assets" (p. 305) and as "the only voluntary constituency whose relation with the corporation does not come up for periodic renewal" (p. 304). He argues that the "diffuse character of their investments puts shareholders at an enormous disadvantage" with respect to protection from opportunistic exploitation. "The board of directors thus arises endogenously, as a means by which to safeguard the investments of those who face a diffuse but significant risk of expropriation because the assets in question are numerous and ill-defined and cannot be protected in a well-focused, transaction specific way" (p. 306).

Anonymity is derived from limited liability and lowers the transactions cost associated with transferable shares. If shareholders were liable for debts of the firm, both creditors and shareholders would find it in their interest to investigate the wealth of each shareholder. They would also find it in their interest to inhibit sales by rich shareholders to poor ones, for such transactions would leave the remaining shareholders with enlarged liability and creditors with less security. Limited liability insulates both shareholders and creditors from differences in wealth among shareholders. The shareholders become a true *société anonyme*. These considerations explain why virtually all corporations with publicly traded shares limit shareholders' liability, and why closely held, non-traded firms often extend the liability of one or more shareholders through personal loan guarantees.

The flexibility and liquidity that enable diffuse ownership and anonymity of shareholders are surely among the great virtues of the modern corporation. But these desirable qualities come at a cost, because when ownership is diffuse, the shareholders must delegate operation of the firm. Delegation requires monitoring. The problem is not an absence of firm-specific capital on the part of any stockholder but simply the fact that the stockholders are numerous. But the potential for "political market failure" due to numerous stockholders is substantially abated by the opportunity for some shareholders to control blocks of shares.

If shareholders opt for concentrated ownership another cost arises: Because shareholders have limited wealth, substantial ownership of wealth in one firm implies that the shareholder with a large block has a less well diversified portfolio with an inferior risk-return trade-off and in some way must be compensated for this by the "outside" shareholders. Other things being equal, people prefer to diversify. Compensation may be in the form of higher salaries for owner-managers, or profits from trading on insider information.[2] The monitoring costs of different activities should thus explain why some firms are organized with substantial owners being managers (aligning the incentives of management and owners) and others with none. Personal, firm-specific investments made by managers result in both the desire of managers to own stock to protect their firm-specific investments and for various other forms of protection, such as golden parachutes.

We wish Williamson had seized this opportunity explicitly (rather than implicitly) to refute the myth that firms are owned, controlled, and administered by "capital" rather than "labor." He could have cited labor-owned firms: law, architecture, accounting, engineering, economic consulting, advertising, restaurants, computer software creators—the list is long. These are firms in which the human resources are firm-specific, and "labor" is the owner. To believe that "capital" is in some sense the "boss" and hires "labor" is to fail to understand the most basic forces that shape the firm: First, the leader of a team (management) is the member with the comparative advantage in deciding what the team and its members should do, and this manager need not be an owner or even part owner in the firm; second, ownership of the team is the residual claimancy on the most team-specific resources, which may be labor or capital. To start an analysis of firms by assuming the presence of "capital" or that capital hires labor is to beg the question of the basis for the existence of a firm.

c. Financing

The partitioning of income to assets owned in common may also take the form of separate debt and equity claims. In a brief but provocative and important paragraph (p. 307), Williamson suggests that the manner in which resources are financed will depend on the attributes of the resources. In other words, debt and equity financing will vary directly with the degree of firm-specificity and redeployability, a view in sharp contrast to theorems of the irrelevance of capital structure. We argue and here attempt to elaborate on that important contention. But the *type* of firm-specificity is at least as important as the degree. In particular, the distinction between holdup and moral hazard il-

---

2. Harold Demsetz and Kenneth Lehn, "The Structure of Corporate Ownership: Causes and Consequences," *J. Polit. Econ.* 93, no. 6 (1985): 1155–77.

luminates the issue considerably. Assets that are firm-specific and vulnerable to holdup will affect firm financing very differently from those that are firm-specific and also vulnerable to moral hazard. Moreover, there will be different effects on the degree of inside ownership, the potential for being publicly traded, and the optimal incentives for managers.

If a firm's assets are plastic and costly to monitor, moral hazard costs arise with debt (which, incidentally, limits the degree to which the tax advantages of debt can be exploited). Once indebted, the equity holders do not bear the full downside losses on projects. Their incentive is to increase risk taking, because the bondholders will bear part of the risks of downside losses, but the equity holders get all of the gains. Bondholders, aware of this incentive, design contracts between themselves and equity holders to control it. Debt contracts usually aim at controlling two potential forms of moral hazard opportunism. First, they often constrain the size of dividends that equity holders can pay to themselves, limiting the ability of equity holders to carry away some of the assets (in the form of a dividend) that secure the debt. Second, debt contracts constrain the degree to which the riskiness of the assets can be increased. For example, they might restrict sales of some assets and purchases of others. But the contracts are not perfect. Bondholders charge equity holders for the expected uncontrollable losses imposed on them. In choosing debt financing, equity holders are trading off the moral hazard costs of debt against the attraction of creditors who are risk averse as well as the tax advantages.

The theory of debt financing rests on the degree of asset plasticity as an explanation of the debt-equity ratio. Compare the opportunities for debt financing for a drug company versus for a public utility. The drug company has a much wider range of legitimate choices than does the public utility. The drug company's activities are more difficult to monitor. This implies that it will be difficult for the debt holders to write a contract with the equity holders to keep from being exploited. The drug company will find debt expensive. But with the public utility, the assets are cheaper to monitor and assess (and the returns to equity are regulated), so the public utility will find that the moral hazard consequences of debt are low.

It is not the riskiness but the plasticity of the firm's assets that drives the cost of debt financing. What matters is the degree to which the equity holders can exploit the bondholders ex post by altering the returns to assets. We predict that firms with more plastic assets will have lower debt-equity ratios than firms with less plastic assets. Our earlier example, the oil well, serves well the point that the issue is not risk. The oil well is very implastic but very risky; we deduce that oil recovery will be a highly debt financed business but that drilling and exploration will not.

Another view is that debt is a device to prevent holdups and to restrain moral hazard. There are two versions of this story. First, Richard Ippolito suggests that committing income to debt holders keeps strong unions from expropriating it. Second, Michael Jensen argues that if income is committed to bondholders, the managers cannot spend it, because they have less discretion over interest payments than over dividends.[3] The important point in both views is that when a quasi-rent is present, because of large sunk costs or a windfall gain, the quasi-rent is vulnerable to expropriation. Managers of a firm with exceptionally large quasi-rents or profits could invest the proceeds toward self-aggrandizing but unprofitable investments. Or the union could strike for higher wages. If, instead, the firm had committed to large interest and debt repayments, these cash flows would have to be channeled to outsiders.

The debt-equity decision can also be seen as a "flow" response to fluctuating financing needs (rather than as an optimal "stock") which seeks to avoid the suspicion of opportunism. If a firm's managers sold equity every time it sought additional financing, and bought stock back when it had cash balances, stockholders would find it difficult to distinguish between a true financing strategy and "insider trading." How can stockholders be certain that managers are not simply selling stock when on the basis of inside information they think the price is too high, and buying when it is too low? Only transacting stockholders would be harmed by this, but knowing this, investors who valued liquidity would be reluctant to buy. Perhaps this is a clue as to why nearly all transient fluctuations in financing of public traded firms are in debt and retained earnings, and almost none with equity issues.

D. *Incomplete Integration of Ownership*

In Chapter 12 Williamson explores corporate governance, in particular where integration of ownership of firm-specific resources is incomplete. Resources cannot be classified as purely firm-specific and dependent or not, and an absolutely nonoverlapping distinction cannot be made among (a) stockholders, (b) creditors, and (c) employees. If some stockholders own firm-specific resources not shared in common by all other stockholders, or if some

3. Richard A. Ippolito, "The Labor Contract and True Economic Pension Liabilities," *Amer. Econ. Rev.* 75 (Dec. 1985): 1031–43; Michael C. Jensen, "Agency Costs of Free Cash Flow, Corporate Finance, and Takeovers," *Amer. Econ. Rev.* 76 (May 1986): 323–29.

nonstockholders have some firm-specific resources in which ownership is not shared with stockholders, conflicts of interest among the otherwise homogeneous interests will arise.

Employees can be both dependent and depended upon. They may have agreed to make self-financed investments with firm-specific value; to develop skills or knowledge with firm-specific value; to purchase homes whose values depend on the firm's success; to accumulate rights to subsequent benefits, like pensions; to receive payment later for earlier underpayment when the employee's actual productivity was difficult to predict. Or employees may have high transfer or mobility costs to the next best work. If so, they will demand some protection from employer opportunism. And they may seek representation on the board of directors, or at least some control with respect to certain decisions affecting the probability of fulfillment of their contracts, though this incomplete and disproportionate sharing in equity relative to fixed payments will create divisiveness on other issues. Williamson concludes that whether labor serves on the board of directors depends on whether employees have made firm-specific investments.

Dependence does not typically stop at the boundaries of groups of cooperating people in what is conventionally called a "firm." Not to be ignored are some customers of the firm's products. A consumer who buys a product, the future performance of which depends on the firm's continued activity, will have become an owner of a firm-specific resource—much like Marshall's steel mill, or like a buyer of computers or automobiles for which future spare parts are valuable. When customer dependence becomes dominant, the firm will tend to be organized as a mutual, and the customers will own the firm. A subcontractor whose resource values depend on the prime contractor is a dependent part of a coalition, possibly one involving strong mutual interdependence. Though the resources of a subcontractor and a prime contractor may be separately owned, mutual dependence creates a coalition with contractual relationships similar to those "within" a conventional "firm." Owners of such firm-specific but separately owned resources would want representation or influence on the board, even though, again, this will create divisiveness and conflicts of interest.

Although firm-specificity can extend beyond the traditional boundaries of the firm, this does not imply that it is efficient for all, even slightly, firm-specific parties to be represented on the board of directors. As more parties are added, the commonality of objectives diminishes, and the cost of making decisions goes up; the cost of negotiating decisions must be traded off against the costs of a decision unfavorable to some parties. From an ex ante perspective, negotiating for control and representation should protect all parties willing to pay for protection before becoming dependent. If parties with repeated transactions unexpectedly find themselves mutually dependent, they will be without a contract to contain opportunism. They will have no choice but to negotiate, and to appeal to social institutions larger than the firm (for example, the law) to determine appropriate protection. But the practice of putting ex ante disinterested parties on the board is insidious. Advocates of membership on the board of directors by ex post interested, or firm-independent resources owners, are, possibly unwittingly, undetermining the viability of the corporate form by making it easier for owners of non-firm-specific assets to expropriate quasi-rents from firm-specific assets, thereby reducing the willingness to invest in assets organized as a corporation.

IV. Credible Commitments

Absent integration of ownership of all the interdependent resources, investments can sometimes be protected from opportunism by credible commitments. Williamson emphasizes the important role of credible commitments, as distinct from credible threats, in the entire transaction cost analysis. Indeed it is the major implication and message of this book. These commitments can take several forms with varying degrees of credibility and effectiveness, several of which Williamson explores. At the simplest level, a unique (relied-upon) party can post a hostage or a bond forfeitable upon malperformance. Less commonly recognized forms of credible commitments are often misinterpreted as monopolizing, or competitor-obstructing, devices. Some of the following examples are illuminated in Williamson's two chapters on credible commitments: reciprocity, take-or-pay, duplicative suppliers, product exchanges, posted prices, inflexible prices, most-favored-customer clauses, block-booking, blind-selling, blind-buying, buy-sell agreements, stock options, patent pools, joint ventures, premium profit streams supported by exclusive territories and resale price maintenance, franchise-specific investments, exhibition clearances, athlete trades among teams, and reserve and waiver clauses. All these can serve as means of creating competitive, economical mutual reliance and self-enforcing contracts.

We digress a bit to elaborate on one. Price stability can restrain opportunistic behavior by a resource owner who otherwise could alter the price of its services to extract composite quasi-rent from a reliant party. The resource owner, say a buyer from a dependent supplier (e.g., the only oil field pipeline gather-

ing system buying from several oil well owners, or a tuna or salmon canner buying from fishermen who serve only that canner), would desire to assure those
dependent suppliers that the buyer would not engage in opportunistic alteration of prices to expropriate quasi-rents of canner- or pipeline-dependent
investments by suppliers for whom there were no other economically readily
available buyers.

By publicly posting a price and holding it constant, a buyer can assure suppliers of no last-minute price opportunism. Such posted prices tend to be unresponsive to transient changes in demand and supply and are changed only
when the underlying demand and supply conditions have remained changed
for some time. Otherwise adjustments of price to *alleged* momentary shifts in
demand or supply could mask extensive opportunistic expropriation of dependent suppliers' quasi-rents. This implies that posted or stable prices would prevail where suppliers are in a position of substantial dependence with respect to
a buyer. Casual observation seems to support that implication, for example, in
pipelines for gathering oil and gas, for fishing boats selling to a cannery, and in
restaurants. Even restaurants that print or post menus daily seldom change the
price of their offerings in the middle of the evening. Williamson correctly emphasized that a clearer perception and appreciation of the problems that arise
when two parties separately own interdependent resources would help redirect
the inhospitable gaze of economists and lawyers away from the restraints-of-
trade paradigm to one in which reliability of future performance is the focus.[4]

Williamson's Chapter 10, on the organization of work, contains a withering
examination and critique exposing the emptiness of the so-called radical economics interpretation of power and hierarchy in business firms. It is, however,
a very constructive chapter with focus on the organization of employees and on
the means whereby people who become reliant on other people, whether on
their personal services or capital equipment, protect their investments from
holdup. This allows a double purpose of employee unions: to cartelize employees to restrict competition, but also to protect employees' human firm-specific
investments. Tenure, seniority, company "unions," company towns, layoffs and
shutdowns, rigid wage rates, and golden parachutes are some examples of devices or contractual clauses to protect firm-dependent human capital.[5]

4. Armen A. Alchian and Susan Woodward, "Reflections on the Theory of the Firm,"
J. *Institutional Theoretical Econ.* (Z. *ges. Staatswiss.*) 143, no. 1 (1987): 110–37.
5. Ibid.

v. Hierarchical Governance Patterns

Administration, direction, or management involves a flow of information through a chain of decisions, suggestions, orders, and so on, which Williamson calls the *governance hierarchy*. It takes on many forms, for example, putting-out, inside and outside contracting, federated groups, peer groups, employer-employee authority, and the unitary, multidivisional, or holding-company forms of governance which he calls U, M, and H forms. His attempts (in Chapter 11) to bring the U (unitary), H (holding company), and M (multidivisional profit center) organizational forms into line with his main argument are, in our opinion, novel and plausible but as yet a less successful portion of his published work. He associates them with the extent of firm-specific, nonredeployable resources and the extent of other safeguards against opportunism.

The stereotype U form has a unitary chief over subordinate functional divisions (production, sales, finance, engineering, etc.), of a single product firm, so Williamson associates the U form (unitary control) with greater viability where there is no major complex integration.

Williamson suggests that safeguards against opportunism (reflecting degree of specificity of resources) across firms are provided by integrating and using the M form rather than the U form. The U form suffered from inability to collect and utilize all pertinent information at one central headquarters. The M form separated the firm into separate profit centers to reduce the need for information flows across divisions and to permit a more independent ability to use information where it existed (in the divisions). This restrains opportunism of information and physical services across the divisions. The distinctive elements are (a) feasibility of decentralizing the flow of information while providing incentives to use the information to make better decisions and (b) safeguards against opportunistic use or concealment of information. As enterprises increased in complexity and integrated complementary activities to avoid potential opportunistic behavior by outside suppliers, the more integrated firm (whether vertical or horizontal) became more complex and difficult to administer by a central office.

The incentive to use information more effectively is sharpened if responsibilities are separated into semiautonomous profit centers which, in turn, are overseen by managers who monitor and evaluate division performance (instead of managing and administering the divisions), reward or punish division managers, and allocate investable funds among them. Thus, the argument goes, the M form evolved precisely for the same reason the "firm" evolved: to restrain opportunism among controllers of interdependent resources.

The H form (holding company) also divides the group into profit centers, and limits control by the top officer primarily to the amount of reinvestment of each center's income. The manager of each subordinate division controls its own reinvestment selections. The top holding group primarily retains dividend-like returns. Williamson seems to suggest that an H form is more likely among firms that have less operational and informational interdependence among the several divisions; however, a clearer identification of the resource, product, or production conditions that make one form rather than another the more viable seems to be the next item on the research agenda.

vi. External Government Controls

Government regulatory agencies can help not only to avoid "monopolistic prices" but also to prevent opportunistic holdups of the type illustrated by Marshall. Chapter 13 contains Williamson's critical review of regulatory experiences in some TV cable franchise bidding for natural monopolies. Though pre-contract award bidding is competitive, the Fundamental Transformation occurs in passing to the postaward stage. Williamson argues convincingly, at least to us, that postaward regulatory authority to restrain opportunism is not effectively or totally displaceable by bidding for franchises with long-term contractual commitments.

Chapter 14 opens with this statement: "Antitrust enforcement has been massively reshaped in the past twenty years" (p. 365). That reshaping is concisely reviewed with respect to merger policy, nonstandard contracting, and strategic behavior, a reshaping in which Williamson's analysis has had a part, and which is very briefly evaluated in Chapter 14. That chapter is convincing evidence that media pundits and politicians who believe that the policies of the Antitrust Division of the Department of Justice and the Federal Trade Commission have been altered by the Reagan administration, and who long for a return to the old antitrust policies, are wrong and are bound to be disappointed. Not the current administration but, instead, the advancing understanding of transactions issues is responsible because it is now the intellectual apparatus of economists. Regardless of the administration, economists will use the best economic understanding available and that, rather than some administration's biases, will guide future antitrust actions. To believe otherwise is to insult economists in those agencies and, worse, to believe economic understanding has no effect on government.

VII. Definitions and Boundaries of "Firms"?

A. *Future Forays into Terra Incognita*

The view of organizations arising from the concept of resource interdependence or firm specificity makes the boundary of the firm fuzzy; a bright line distinguishing "inside" and "outside" is missing. The interpretation of the firm as a nexus of long-term contracts among interspecific resources weakens the "firm" as a useful basic unit of analysis. Though we have used the word *firm*, we believe a better and more useful concept is a coalition: a set of resource owners bound by contractual relations that depend on the degrees of dependence and uniqueness. But definitions are for the taking; none is standard.

The old notion led to an intrafirm versus an interfirm conception of agreements in which "interfirm" relations were viewed inhospitably and with suspicion. An egregious example of the pitfalls of this line of thinking was the procedures in a 1982 antitrust suit within the National Football League. The disputants forced the judge to "determine" whether the 24 teams in the league were "one firm" or separate firms, presuming a clear distinction could be made. As the foregoing emphasizes, this approach ignores the nature and degree of dependence among the involved resource owners and the reasons for contractual arrangements to control free-riding on investments and to restrain opportunistic expropriation of dependent quasi-rents. The court "found" the league to be 24 separate firms and inferred they were therefore subject to court review as to legality of joint action. Instead the court could have ruled they were one firm, with 24 subordinate divisions.

This does not mean that that economists could have provided an analysis for the NFL case or reliably ascertained the effects of different rulings. So far as we are aware, economists have not adequately analyzed many mysterious arrangements in interteam sports, for example, trades rather than sales, or players' employment contracts. Moreover, the mysteries are not limited to team sports: trades or exchanges of products among members of an industry (e.g., exchanges of petroleum and its products, electricity, aluminum, gypsum, corrugated cardboard, and new automobiles) are not rare. We suspect the explanation for these arrangements lies in avoiding potential expropriative behavior where spot supplies are small, but we are not sure.

The institutions of capitalism are more than just firms, markets, and relational contracting. Dependence occurs in complex ways and motivates a large variety of precautionary arrangements. Joint ventures, mutuals, social clubs, cooperatives, and families, to suggest a few "capitalist" institutions, are, as we understand them, basically similar contractual arrangements in which (a) the joint venturers will be interreliant, but the assets, especially human capital, will not be owned in common; (b) the joint venturers will be dependent on the services of the venture (e.g., research, sociability, pipeline transportation); and (c) alienability of a member's interest is restricted. Without a joint, restrictive arrangement, one venturer could otherwise hold up the other dependent nonowner user of the services.

The country club is a complex and rich example of a cooperative firm. The customers (members) of the country club own the firm—the club. They are also the producers of the firm's product—sociability. The most important assets of the firm are not the grounds and building but the members themselves, who are now "owned by the firm." The members are mutually reliant on one another to produce the sociability that makes membership in the club worthwhile. Sale of membership is restricted to prevent entry of "undesirables," those whose sociability is not regarded as sufficient to exchange for reciprocal sociability. Members can sell their membership only back to the club, and new memberships can be admitted only upon consent of the group. Outside ownership of such a firm is not viable. The outside owner could admit, for a high price, new members who would destroy the composite quasi-rent created by the members themselves, or could raise the price to existing members to extract the quasi-rent.

viii. Social Restraints

That contracts are not sufficiently well enforced by resort to the law is emphasized by Williamson. Unique parties who could expropriate dependent quasi-rents resist the temptation, in part, because "it isn't right." Social opprobrium and the feeling of guilt may operate. Actions regarded as "unconscionable" or "unfair" can result in social ostracism or moralistic aggression. We believe it is important to recognize the forces of ethics, etiquette, and "proper, correct, reasonable, moral, etc.," standards of conduct in controlling business relationships. We do not believe contracts are observed (e.g., self-enforcing) only so long as the personal economic costs of contract violation exceed expropriable rents obtainable by violations. People do not always violate contracts whenever their own costs are less than their own gains from violation. Temptations of free-riding or stealing are resisted even when the net gains of free-riding or stealing are great. We don't know enough about how such "moral" forces operate to say more than that they exist and should not be ignored in seeking an understanding of how the economic institutions of capitalism, or any other -ism, evolve and operate.

One can see how morally aggressive, pejorative terms like "gouging" with reference to prices make economic sense. A remote auto repair shop servicing an unlucky traveler whose car's fanbelt has unexpectedly failed might charge far more than the full costs of replacing the belt, in order to extract almost the total value of an emergency repair to the unfortunate driver—the value of the service to a customer in dire straits. Or imagine an ambulance operator or a doctor charging a price reflecting the value of emergency service to a critically injured person. Not without reason is such behavior condemned. It is wicked and reprobate, and it's inefficient.

If such opportunistic expropriation were expected by travelers, they would travel less, or take expensive safety precautions to avoid expropriation. The avoidance costs would exceed the true cost of providing the emergency service, so society would incur greater costs if people did not act "responsibly, fairly, conscientiously, and ethically." Whatever the emotive language, "decent" behavior saves resources and enables greater welfare. (It is another question how such "responsible, nonopportunistic" behavior is induced in society, or why people "waste" their own scarce resources berating gougers.) This is consistent with the usual explanation for why professions (i.e., sellers of services whose buyers are in a position of trust and substantial dependence) typically promote and enforce professional codes of ethics to protect the clients or principals from "expropriative" unethical tactics.

IX. Evaluation

It is hard to decide whether the title or the content of Williamson's book is the more general. Williamson describes explicitly only some of capitalism's institutions. But the forces Williamson describes surely operate in all systems. Regardless, the analysis in Williamson's book will enable a broader, more profound understanding of coalitions, institutions, and contract structure, including the allocations and partitioning of property rights as well as a variety of "institutions" that lack contracts but establish and maintain behavior of a contractual type. A central message of the book bears repeating in Williamson's words:

> Upon observing that humans have a propensity to behave opportunistically, Machiavelli advised his prince that "a prudent ruler ought not to keep faith when by so doing it would be against his interest, and when the reasons

which made him bind himself no longer exist . . . [L]egitimate grounds [have never] failed a prince who wished to show colourable excuse for the promise." But . . . preemptive opportunism is . . . a very primitive response. . . . The more important lesson, for the purposes of studying economic organizations, is this: Transactions that are subject to *ex post* opportunism will benefit if appropriate safeguards can be devised *ex ante*. Rather than reply to opportunism in kind the wise prince is one who seeks both to give and to receive "credible" commitments. (p. 48)

The message of Machiavelli is to be reversed: Instead of opportunism, offer and seek credible commitments. It is clear Williamson's view is that the main purpose served by economic organization is not monopoly, efficient risk bearing, power, or the like but is transaction cost economizing, in no small part by use of credible commitments.

Even economists who have read the original articles will find Williamson's *The Economic Institutions of Capitalism* provocative, informative, edifying, and very much worth reading.

REFERENCES

Because Williamson's book contains an extensive bibliography through 1984, we have merely added some other and more recent citations.

Allen, Franklin. "On the Fixed Nature of Sharecropping Contracts." *Econ. J.* 95, no. 337 (Mar. 1985): 30–48.

Barzel, Yoram. "Transaction Costs: Are They Just Costs?" *J. Institutional Theoretical Econ.* 141, no. 1 (Mar. 1985): 4–16.

Baysinger, Barry D., and Henry N. Butler. "The Role of Corporate Law in the Theory of the Firm." *J. Law Econ.* 28, no. 1 (Apr. 1985): 179–91.

Behrens, Peter. "The Firm as a Complex Institution." *J. Institutional Theoretical Econ.* 141, no. 1 (Mar. 1985): 62–75.

Bonus, Holger. "The Cooperative Association as a Business Enterprise: A Study in the Economics of Transactions." *J. Institutional Theoretical Econ.* 142, no. 2 (June 1986): 310–39.

Brickley, James, Sanjai Bhagat, and Ron Lease, "The Impact of Long-Range Managerial Compensation Plans on Shareholder Wealth." *J. Acc. Econ.* 7, nos. 1–3 (1985): 119–29.

Carlton, Dennis W. "The Rigidity of Prices." *Amer. Econ. Rev.* 76, no. 4 (Sept. 1986): 637–58.

Cecchetti, Stephen G. "Staggered Contracts and the Frequency of Price Adjustment." *Quart. J. Econ.* 100, no. 5, suppl. (1985): 935–59.

Crew, Michael A., and Keith J. Crocker. "Vertically Integrated Governance Structures and Optimal Institutional Arrangements for Co-generation." *J. Institutional Theoretical Econ.* 142, no. 2 (1986): 340–59.

Drèze, Jacques H. "(Uncertainty and) the Firm in General Equilibrium Theory." *J. Econ.* 95, suppl. (1985): 1–20.

Frech, H. E., III. "The Property Rights Theory of the Firm: Some Evidence from the U.S. Nursing Home Industry." *J. Institutional Theoretical Econ.* 141, no. 1 (Mar. 1985): 146–66.

Gilley, Otis W., Gordon Karels, and Randolph M. Lyon. "Joint Ventures and Offshore Oil Lease Sales." *Econ. Inquiry* 24, no. 2 (Apr. 1985): 321–40.

Holmstrom, Bengt, and Laurence Weiss. "Managerial Incentives, Investment and Aggregate Implications-Scale Effects." *Rev. Econ. Stud.* 52, no. 3 (July 1985): 403–25.

Jensen, Michael C. "Agency Costs of Free Cash Flow, Corporate Finance, and Takeovers." *Amer. Econ. Rev.* 76, no. 2 (May 1986): 323–29.

Kahneman, Daniel, Jack L. Knetsch, and Richard Thaler. "Fairness as a Constraint on Profit Seeking: Entitlements in the Market." *Amer. Econ. Rev.* 76, no. 4 (Sept. 1986): 728–41.

Levy, David. "The Transactions Cost Approach to Vertical Integration." *Rev. Econ. Statist.* 67, no. 3 (Aug. 1985): 438–45.

MacDonald, James M. "Market Exchange or Vertical Integration." *Rev. Econ. Statist.* 67, no. 2 (May 1985): 327–31.

Masten, Scott E., and Keith J. Crocker. "Efficient Adaptation in Long-Term Contracts." *Amer. Econ. Rev.* 75, no. 5 (Dec. 1985): 1083–93.

Mathewson, G. Frank, and Ralph A. Winter. "The Economics of Franchise Contracts." *J. Law Econ.* 28, no. 3 (Oct. 1985): 503–26.

Olmstead, Alan L., and Paul Rhode. "Rationing without Government: The West Coast Gas Famine of 1920." *Amer. Econ. Rev.* 75, no. 5 (Dec. 1985): 1044–55.

Poster, Philip K., Gerald W. Scully, and Daniel J. Slottje. "Industrial Policy and the Nature of the Firm." *J. Institutional Theoretical Econ.* 142, no. 1 (Mar. 1986): 79–100.

Rogerson, William. "The First-Order Approach to Principal-Agent Problems." *Econometrica* 53, no. 6 (Nov. 1985): 1357–68.

Rubin, Paul H. "The Theory of the Firm and the Structure of the Franchise Contract." *J. Law Econ.* 21, no. 1 (Apr. 1978): 223–34.

Schultze, Charles L. "Microeconomic Efficiency and Nominal Wage Stickiness." *Amer. Econ. Rev.* 75, no. 1 (Mar. 1985): 1–15.

Singh, Nirvikar. "Monitoring and Hierarchies: The Marginal Value of Information in the Principal-Agent Model." *J. Polit. Econ.* 93, no. 3 (June 1985): 599–609.

Telser, Lester G. "Cooperation, Competition, and Efficiency." *J. Law Econ.* 28, no. 2 (May 1985): 271–95.

Titman, Sheridan. "The Effect of Forward Markets on the Debt-Equity Mix of Investor Portfolios and the Optimal Capital Structure of Firms." *J. Financial Quant. Anal.* 20, no. 1 (Mar. 1985): 19–27.

Vickers, John. "Delegation and the Theory of the Firm." *Econ. J.* 95, suppl. (1985): 138–47.

Williamson, Oliver. "Reflection on the New Institutional Economics." *J. Institutional Theoretical Econ.* 141, no. 1 (Mar. 1985): 187–95.

Woodward, Susan. "The Economics of Limited Liability." *J. Econ. Theory and Inst.* 141, no. 3 (1985): 601–11.

DEVELOPMENT OF ECONOMIC THEORY
AND ANTITRUST
A VIEW FROM THE THEORY OF THE FIRM

A basic implicit theme seems to characterize many of the papers of this conference, and also underlies much of the recent advance and reinterpretation of the proposed role for antitrust or "competition" policy. It can, I believe, be characterized in the following way. According to all texts and earlier economic theory, the gains from cooperative production came from specialization in production with subsequent exchanges. The principle of those gains from trade, usually stated in terms of comparative advantage or of specialization, is really nothing more than the principle of marginal cost equalization. This principle stated more fully is that no producer should produce a rate of output at a marginal cost higher than for any other producer. More abstractly if X is the sum of two outputs from two separate processes, A and B, then the inputs, Z, used in producing A and B should be allocated so as to equate the marginal products of Z in each process A and B. The "processes" can be individuals, firms, or countries as producers.

The reason for terminology like "comparative advantage" was an earlier confusion between marginal cost of a product and total possible output of that product by a producer. The "specializer" was the lower marginal cost producer, not the producer with the largest production potential. Nothing was implied about how the producers produced what they did, beyond the conventional cost curves. Internally they were black boxes which magically yielded rates of output under various cost conditions. The only useful way in which these producers interacted was by purchasing and selling of finished or component products—all in accord again with the above-stated principle. Quite correctly that specialization, via equalization of marginal costs, is a source of gains from "cooperation," a cooperation restricted solely to the buying or selling goods or services.

Reprinted, by permission of the author, from *Zeitschrift für die gesamte Staatswissenschaft* (Journal of Institutional and Theoretical Economics) 147 (March 1991): 232–34.

Under that reason for trade in markets, business owners (indeed all people) had no purpose in talking or negotiating or contracting with "competitors" except to alter the terms of trade, i.e., monopolize; hence, any sharing of information or agreements among competitors on either the buying or selling side, no matter how, was implied as pointless except for affecting exchange rates, i.e., prices. It follows that an antitrust doctrine based on that principle of the source of the gains from cooperative actions (trade across markets) looked askance at inter-firm communication or cooperation—an activity that the rationale for trade could not explain except as a way to restrict trade or alter prices. Whatever the political reasons for the adoption of the Sherman Act in the U.S. as an expression of general governmental policy about inter-firm activity, I believe that until very recently the basic political-economic doctrine enshrined in the Sherman Act and its parallels in other countries—and partly in the common law—was this interpretation of the source of gains from trade—equalization of marginal costs among competing producers by heeding the common market price. It all flowed from the analyses of Smith, Ricardo, et al.

Recently with the awareness that (1) cooperative activity with a "firm" yields an output greater than could otherwise be achieved and that (2) the underlying factor in that source of gain in the firm is "teamwork" with almost always inevitable dependence among the resources, a revolution in antitrust law was started. This second source of gain from cooperation is a fundamentally different source, previously ignored. That added gain comes mysteriously from teamwork, a form of cooperative production in which no summable separable total of products are involved, and in which effectiveness of that cooperative productivity rests on reliable continuity of services from specific uniquely related, interdependent suppliers of productive services. Because the fundamental way in which that teamwork increases output is still mysterious (i.e., not yet implied by deeper axioms), its fundamental status and significant implications for policy remain hidden.

However, given the existence of the teamwork-specific reliance characteristic, one can immediately see that the cooperation is not merely that of a specialization with exchange of separably produced goods and services. Jointness of effort and activities in teamwork by definition and fact involves more cooperation among individuals than that of simple market exchange. It follows that people can communicate, interact, and correlate their actions outside of markets for reasons other than affecting only terms of exchange among independent parties. Interaction, communication, and agreements can have purposes other than affecting terms of trade, contrary to Adam Smith's and current antitrust's presumptions that "business people rarely meet except to set prices." They meet to negotiate binding agreements to facilitate increased reliable interreliant investments in teamwork. They meet not merely to change the division of the pie but to enlarge the pie they can consume.

Unfortunately antitrust law was written when this second source of gains from cooperation was not well perceived and appreciated. However, with the recent developing understanding of this second source, antitrust actions are being altered. For example, at the most primitive or obvious level, research activities across firms are being recognized as not necessarily "cartelizing." Coalitions are being distinguished from "collusions." The sheer force of obvious gains from joint research, a classic example of teamwork among researchers, is now being propounded as acceptable exceptions to the antitrust laws.

The analysis of the organizational relationships among resource owners, where the resource values will become specifically dependent on resources owned separately, implies a thorough revision of antitrust doctrine. That revision is now being thrust into the litigation of sports leagues and joint ventures. The revolutionary implications should be obvious to one familiar with the recent understanding of the gains from teamwork reliant on reliable services of all in the team. Prior to this analytic advance, the U.S. Congress exempted professional sports from antitrust legislation. The excuse was that sports provided a service rather than a good! Yet, before laughing, let's look at substance rather than form or words. The Congress exempted interdependent teamwork, among both players and teams.

They did a "right" thing by simple common sense—a degree of common sense that still hasn't invaded the economic literature, which rightly insists on consistent analysis.

But the U.S. courts are still confused. They tend to associate interdependence with vertical arrangements and not with what are called horizontal. Probably vertical refers to "non-competing" cooperators in a line of production, while "horizontal" is supposed to mean competitors of similar products. However, I believe the fundamental distinction should be that based on the presence or absence of specifically dependent resources investments. It is probably true that often sequential stages in production involve investments in sequential dependent resources, whereas specific dependence among producers of similar goods is rare, though not entirely absent (as, for example, in common sources of information collection among "independent" real estate agents or mortality data for insurance firms, or research efforts with pooled knowledge among otherwise separate chemical and drug firms, or standardization of computer systems among computer producers).

Nor have the courts been so successful in abandoning the confused and logically inseparable "distinction" between price and non-price competition.

THOUGHTS ON THE THEORY OF THE FIRM
A TRIBUTE TO EIRIK G. FURUBOTN*

It is splendidly appropriate that Eirik Furubotn's superb and valuable contribution to increased international communication of economic analysis can be
acknowledged and celebrated in this journal. His success in helping to resusci-
tate this journal into major status is the kind of contribution that, unfortunately, usually passes unnoticed. He has enabled much to be published about
the structure, allocation, and partitioning of private property rights in various
organizations called "firms." Corporations, mutuals, cooperatives, and a vast
variety of organizational forms—all differing in the particular combination
and permissible recombination or further partitioning of component elements
of private property rights—have been analyzed. In this brief token of tribute
to Eirik, I express a few thoughts and conjectures that may stimulate others to
work in a similar direction—much as he has done for me.

First, and at the most elementary and basic level, consider the ancient matter of the source of gains from *cooperation* in production. Beginning with Adam
Smith we have learned that cooperation through specialized production according to comparative advantage with cooperation in exchange of the independently produced goods yields a larger vector of output than if each person acted self-sufficiently. The gains from cooperation in production were
available because of comparative, not absolute, advantages among the producers. Also, the gains were asserted to be greater, the greater the extent of specialization into narrow, more specific detailed component activities—such as
Smith's example of pin-making with drawing of pins, putting on heads, sharp-
ening the points, etc. The greater the particularization in component tasks, the
greater the gains. Smith, as is well known, attributed the gains from cooperative production, which enabled specialization, to increased dexterity, time
saved in passing between tasks, and invention when minds are concentrated
on a single process. I venture to assert that all three of these are wrong. They

Reprinted, by permission of the author, from *Zeitschrift für die gesamte Staatswissenschaft*
(Journal of Institutional and Theoretical Economics) 149 (June 1993): 365–69.

*On the occasion of his 70th birthday.

apply equally to non-specialized production—even that of passing between tasks. But Smith's arguments, though logically flawed, were psychologically persuasive.

It is now recognized, though not as widely as deserved, that what is called the principle of comparative advantage is really the principle of maximizing the aggregate output from several sources by equating the marginal costs in each source. If one converts the measures of a producer's comparative advantages between two products into costs, it will be seen that the comparative advantage is a comparison of the marginal costs of the two compared producers. This means the conceptions of absolute advantage and comparative advantage are equivalent to the comparison of the total and the marginal yields of producers.

The general principle is that "if product X" can be produced by two or more processes each requiring inputs of Y, then the total X ($= X_a + X_b$) from processes a and b is maximized if Y is exhaustively allocated to process A and B (i.e., $Y = Y_a + Y_b$) such that the first derivatives of X with respect to Y in each process are equated. (This assumes, quite plausibly, that the second derivatives are negative, as usual.) That is the principle of comparative advantage expressed mathematically as a standard maximization problem. That setting of rates of production at which marginal costs are equated is the basis of the gains from trade by specialization. At unequal marginal costs, the difference is a gain that could be obtained by equating the marginal costs.

What is called the absolute advantage refers to the difference in X_a and X_b with equal amounts of Y applied to each.

The comparative advantage refers to the differences in their marginal products dX_a/dY_a and dX_b/dY_b (in processes A and B, respectively—when each use an equal amount of Y or at equal outputs of X). The principle of gains from production of X by A and by B when using input Y requires that the Y and X in each process be such that the dX/dY in each process are equated—not the averages, X_a/Y_a and X_b/Y_b.

For this mathematically true proposition, there is no need for any conceptions of learning by doing, or of saving time between, or of "concentrating thoughts on methods of improvement." It all comes from avoiding the waste of a disparity between marginal costs of the producers. In fact, if the source of the gain were improvements in ability by learning and practice and repetition, there would be generalized "jacks-of-all-trades," not concentration on specialized tasks. The reason is diminishing marginal returns, i.e., diminishing marginal improvements, implying that it did not pay to concentrate practice on one activity when the marginal yield fell below the marginal yield available in other activities. That kind of learning by doing would imply no specialization, and instead would imply generalization. Smith's gains from specialization are inapplicable.

But I used that introductory example of gains via cooperation in production as a lead-in to the question of why the production is done in firms by joint productive effort called "teamwork." I shall arbitrarily define a firm as a group of people in teamwork and not one-person enterprises. I do so because of interest in the way in which *cooperation* among people yields a larger output. My interest is not in how several persons each working alone can be made more productive. The kind of cooperation Smith explored was that of technologically isolated production, with cooperation occurring through exchange of the separately produced goods. Under that source of the gains from specialized production associated with cooperation in exchange of goods, there is no need for cooperation in production or of communication among producers of the same kind of product. No producer's activities affect technological abilities of others. Market values may be affected, but not physical productive abilities. There is no reason—related to increased gains from cooperative specialization—for competing suppliers to communicate. No one would want to tell others about improved techniques—the secrets of superior ability. Therefore, communication among competitors is viewed with suspicion, as an attempt to suppress market competition—a view Smith captured in his businessmen's dinner conversation. The cooperation in production is between suppliers of inputs, not among suppliers. The producers could be single-person enterprises.

That is the view that permeated economic theory until the mid twentieth century. It promises to persist, despite its flawed basis as the basis of governmental anti-trust and economic regulatory policy, into the twenty-first century. Why flawed? Because the bases of gains from cooperative production are not all captured by that long-dominating interpretation of specialization among technologically independent producers. The flaws are the inadequate recognition of teamwork and of the value of commitment to perform as promised. It is these two—already the subject of a very extensive literature—to which I turn now in an attempt to emphasize their general role in the economy, rather than to attempt to delve deeper into the details of each.

Earlier I defined a firm as productive enterprise of two or more persons. Why then do firms exist? If, as is contended, they involve teamwork, there is no exchange of separate products in the firm. I emphasize the premise that teamwork is involved—a production process involving more than one person's resources and in which the product is not an aggregate of components separately produced by identifiable producers. The only measure of output is a marginal measure—the increase in the total conglomerate product consequent to a unit more of one of the inputs. The firm is a set of separately owned resources working as a team. It certainly does not exist to reduce costs of transactions in the kind of cooperation via exchange explored by Smith.

Logically, having defined firms as we did, there is no alternative. The firms exist because they *are* teams. And hence, firms exist because teamwork is more productive. The question then is not, why do firms exist? but instead, what is the nature of contractual relations among the team members? This may all seem like a definitional exegesis of no empirical content. On the contrary, the definitions delineate the issues. Asking why "firms" exist without clearly denoting what is meant by a "firm" creates opportunities for dispute or non-refutable generalities.

The answers to the questions about types of contracts are being supplied by extensive research, both empirically about existing contracts within team members and "theoretically," from first principles about moral hazard—whether called "opportunism," asymmetric information, time inconsistency, principal-agent problem, composite quasi-rent expropriation, or whatever. What is common to all these is the dependency of some of the team members on other members. Indeed, it is almost, but not quite, possible to assert validly that every team involves some interdependency. The alternative and valid assertion is that if some dependency is involved then there is interest in the question of the contractual basis among the team members. In other words, given some dependence, there is interest by a reliant party in obtaining a commitment of promised performance from the relied-upon party. Indeed what distinguishes a "contract" from an "exchange" is that the former contains a commitment about future action—a restriction on at least one of the parties. Exchange contracts are records or specifications of exchanges of title with no future performance specified. Reducing the costs of "exchanges" may be of interest, but among members of a firm, the agreements about future performance are what the contracts contain. These firms do not exist to reduce transaction costs. They exist because they are organizations for teamwork. The contracts among the members are means of "reducing costs of ensuring performance." That may be called "reducing transaction costs," but the firms don't exist to reduce those costs. The contracts do that. Teamwork and dependency lead to a desire for commitment among the team members. The firms that we see surviving have discovered a set of contractual relations among the members enhancing fulfillment of promised performance about work and distribution of the resulting product value.

Not forgetting our earlier remark about anti-trust regulatory law, it appears that here too there is no need for communication among firms. Hence communication is viewed with suspicion. Unfortunately, the restraining committing contracts within firms have led to laws and regulations restraining the restraining clauses and contracts—often without recognition of the usefulness of the clauses in enabling the parties to obtain the gains from interdependent teamwork—by preventing subsequent opportunistic expropriation of dependency values. But beyond this, there are reasons for firms to communicate and to make contracts among separately owned teams. Though separately owned, they are not necessarily also independent in the sense of not being reliant on other teams. For example, a single supply source for inputs to a team makes the team dependent upon the supplier. As protection multiple suppliers may be obtained initially, but at higher cost than a contract that restrains the single supplier from not performing as promised. Examples are contractual hostages and legally enforceable penalties or restrictions on other parties the supplier might serve. Joint ventures may be undertaken between two firms that are reliant on each other—placing the mutually relied-upon elements in the joint venture. These actions would, under the Smithian non-teamwork source of gains from equalization of marginal costs, appear to be "monopolistic" or "anti-competitive."

The legacy of the Smithian gains from cooperation by exchange has dominated for too long. One source of change, aside from the research of economists, is the lower cost of transactional and geographical movements. That is probably far more effective in moving the beliefs and laws than academic research and writings. After all, who would attribute the demise of socialism to the scribblings of Nobel laureates rather than to the empirical competition of the systems themselves? Still, we must be content with the smaller effects of published research.

VERTICAL INTEGRATION AND REGULATION
IN THE TELEPHONE INDUSTRY

Technological changes in the local exchange and interexchange markets have made vertical integration significantly more important for efficient competition in the telephone industry today than it was when the Modification of Final Judgment (MFJ) took effect. It would therefore improve consumer welfare to lift the line-of-business restrictions.

Vertical integration refers to the extent to which resources in successive stages of the production and sale of a good are owned in common within a single firm. All firms are vertically integrated to some extent. What determines the efficient extent of integration? What resource must be integrated for efficient operations? If there were no problem of ensuring reliability of promised performance in transactions across markets, firms would be smaller and more specialized. Even the work performed in a small factory could be divided among many firms, each specializing in only a single operation. The gradually completed product or service could be sold and resold as it moved through successive stages of production. In practice, these transactions are themselves costly; to ensure reliability of performance to dependent downstream firms, related resources are owned in common—that is, they are integrated in ownership.

Vertical disintegration is efficient if the desired successive services can be easily specified, measured and enforced. For example, automobile makers may buy such things as finished seats from outside suppliers because their inspection is relatively easy. But automobile makers are hesitant to use outside sources to supply sheet metal parts, which ordinarily are discovered to be out of tolerance only when a car body does not fit together correctly. The limits of vertical disintegration delineate the resources that must be commonly owned within a firm for efficient performance from those resources that can be owned by different firms.

Regulation can lead to an inefficient degree of vertical integration. The social losses of such inefficient organization may not be apparent even to careful

Reprinted from *Managerial and Decision Economics* 16 (July–August 1995): 323–26. Copyright 1995 by John Wiley and Sons, Ltd. Reproduced with permission.

observers. Inefficiency may take the form of either excessive or insufficient vertical integration. The most common way these inefficiencies are discovered is through deregulation, whereupon various forms of the old and new organizations compete in the marketplace. Efficient organizational forms survive the transition from a regulated to an unregulated environment.

An example of regulation-induced inefficient vertical integration can be found in the trucking industry. Under the old regulation, common carriers had to travel fixed routes and adhere to filed tariffs. Private carriers were limited too, being allowed to carry only the goods of the truck's operator. Regulation resulted in many firms operating their own trucks, rather than submitting to the high tariffs and inflexibility of the common carriers. This was a regulation-induced vertical integration into trucking. Many of the firms involved were unable to utilize their trucks to full efficiency, having many partial loads and empty back hauls. Deregulation resulted in a change to a more natural degree of vertical integration, allowing specialized trucking firms to customize their services to the needs of their clients' firms. Trucking became more efficiently organized once the regulatory pressure towards integration was removed.

An example of inefficient vertical disintegration can be found in the same industry. Combination truck-rail transportation (where truck trailers are loaded at a customer's premises, travel by road to rail heads, are sent by rail to the receiving city and again are delivered by road to their ultimate destination) are efficient where cities are geographically spread out as in the West. However, regulation discouraged railroads from direct participation in trucking, reducing the prevalence of intermodal transportation. With deregulation, this efficient integrated form of shipment became more common.

The U.S. telephone industry provides a textbook example of all varieties of vertical integration, both efficient and inefficient. The various relationships between research design, manufacturing, system network management and toll and local services displayed by the old Bell system seemed to be perfect examples of the limits of both vertical integration and disintegration. We now know, however, that many of these vertical relationships may be better explained as regulatory artifacts.

Wiring cities for telephone service and then connecting cities across long distances with trunk lines created overwhelming technical-contractual incentives for the Bell System to integrate vertically. The extent to which it was profitable to wire a city depended on the ability to connect reliably to other cities as well as the extent of the telephone networks in those cities. Coincidentally, the value of the long lines depended upon the extent to which cities so joined were wired. These effects, known as network externalities, were nowhere greater than they were in the telephone industry at the turn of the century.

Bell also found it necessary to integrate into the manufacturing of telephones and other telecommunications equipment, first by buying a partial ownership stake in Western Electric in 1887. Long-term exclusive-dealing contracts reinforced that partial ownership, but eventually Bell and Western Electric found it necessary to merge completely in order to resolve technical-contractual difficulties.

Bell's integrated structure evolved with technology, providing the United States with telephone service unmatched in quality or ubiquity anywhere in the world. Regulation, however, also led to an inefficient form of vertical integration. Technological advances lowered the cost of interexchange service relative to intraexchange service, but regulatory demand for low residential rates led to continued high long-distance charges and profits necessary to provide revenues to the operating companies with which to subsidize intraexchange service.

Under the integrated Bell System before 1982 the subsidization of local rates with revenues from long-distance service was initially done by the imposition of station-to-station rather than board-to-board regulatory accounting. The difference between these alternatives is that in station-to-station accounting part of the fixed costs of local switching and transmission facilities are allocated to interexchange services, while with board-to-board accounting only the (smaller) marginal costs of those activities are allocated to interexchange services.

This subsidy for local services led to artificially high prices for interexchange services. That, in turn, made entry attractive to new competitors. The Bell System resisted that entry (which it considered to be a form of "cream skimming"), and that resistance led to the antitrust suit that broke up the Bell System.

The MFJ, by mandating equal access to the local exchange for all interexchange carriers, should have permitted market and technology to determine the proper level of vertical integration. But the MFJ went further and precluded vertical integration by the Bell companies except in a few instances (e.g., Yellow Pages) where it was thought that the vertical integration would serve to subsidize local telephone calls. Although this redistribution may be a valid public policy goal, it is not the only benefit to vertical integration in the telecommunications industry. Quality assurance is a significant benefit from vertical integration that has become increasingly important in the telecommunications industry since divestiture.

The human tendency to take private advantage of incompletely written or imperfectly monitored contracts gives rise to problems referred to variously as post-contractual opportunism, holdup, shirking or moral hazard. These terms denote the behavioral causes of difficulties in framing and enforcing agreements between firms whose self-interests naturally diverge. If this divergence of interests is too strong to be overcome contractually, the various functions may be taken internally within a single firm by vertical integration.

Contractual problems induce vertical integration largely because of difficulties in reliably specifying and measuring performance. For example, the separate functions of making dough and baking are usually performed by the same firm. The baker's trade is dependent on the quality of the bread. In order to ensure the quality of the finished product, the baker must verify that the dough is properly prepared. If it is costly to determine the quality of dough objectively, and if the quality of dough cannot be costlessly inferred from the quality of the finished bread, vertical integration between the baker and the supplier of dough can align their interests better, thus avoiding intermediate and costly inspection and ensuring a more reliable quality of bread. This benefit of vertical integration is both a single point of accountability and an enhanced alignment of interests.

The benefits of a single point of accountability and better alignment of interests arise almost everywhere. For instance, when customers receive an unexpectedly poor meal from a particular fast-food outlet like a McDonald's restaurant, they reduce the expectation of the franchisor's quality assurance program and therefore reduce the demand for its meals. An offended customer does not have to (and cannot) determine which of McDonald's many suppliers was responsible for the poor meal. By assuming the role of quality assurer, McDonald's enables consumers to economize on search and is rewarded with a correspondingly valuable brand name so long as McDonald's remains accountable and efficient.

The preceding examples illustrate that differing degrees of vertical integration solve the problem of assuring quality, depending upon how difficult it is to infer at what stage the poor quality originates. Similarly, vertical integration in the telephone industry benefits consumers by establishing a single point of accountability. Customers benefit from being able to call one firm's service department; they spend less time being told that it is some other firm's fault that their call from Washington to Chicago did not go through or was of unacceptable quality.

Developments in the interexchange market under equal access now reveal that a carrier's reputation for quality and reliability is critical to its success. Thus the most efficient competitors (actual and potential) in interexchange services are those with the least cost of building and sustaining such a reputation. These benefits from vertical integration appear to have grown even more important in this industry in the dozen years since divestiture. Nevertheless, the social costs that the line-of-business restrictions created (by precluding the efficiency gains from vertical integration) were deemed small relative to the benefits from deterring the Regional Bell Operating Companies (RBOCs) from using technical or regulatory advantages in a socially harmful manner.

Except for regulatory intervention, rapidly emerging technologies for the provision of both interexchange service and local exchange service now encourage efficient, large-scale "bypass" of traditional supplier networks and, more fundamentally, make moot the prevailing distinctions between interexchange and local exchange service. Narrowband copper cable and hierarchical switch architecture represented the only feasible design for a major telephone system until almost 1990. With fiber optics, two-way coaxial cables and fast microelectronics with digitalization and signal compression, an alternative horizontal network design is possible, with individual controllers at each *customer's* location directing calls on a common broadband buss linking customers across relatively large geographic areas. Each customer becomes the unique element. All other items serve any number of other customers, no matter where on the network.

In the absence of regulation, this kind of technological change would alter the degree of vertical integration in the industry. Without any clear long-distance "gateways"—central points equivalent class 3 switches—long-distance and local service facilities would become integrated throughout the system. With no "toll" lines and no "toll" switches, long-distance would become a service transported throughout the network, with every function potentially involved in every call. There would be nothing to be separately owned or controlled, no clear break point between interexchange and local exchange facilities and service. The point for logical vertical disintegration would disappear. Every line, switch and employee would be producing part of a seamless single "telephone" facility, and divided responsibility for separate functions would become contractually and technologically infeasible. But services could be distinguished and provided competitively, as with taxis, buses or trucks on the road network. A series of vertically integrated telecommunications firms would compete with one another.

In such a system local and long-distance communication would no longer require different equipment. Any switch could potentially be connected to any other regardless of its "level." These connections would simply reflect least-cost approximations of ideal interconnections given geography, population distribution, usage patterns and the relative cost of lines and switches. Calls might be completed through a variety of different physical links of lines and switches, billed centrally and perhaps never pass through any of the traditional long-distance "gateways." Indeed, the distinction between local and long-distance service would no longer need to be manifested in special facilities— the distinction would be more in the customers' minds than in the facilities they would be using.

Recently, MCI announced its intention to integrate vertically into local access, not only by building its own fiber rings in metropolitan markets with which to offer broadband switched service[1] but also by acquiring a substantial block of Nextel, a company that has exploited technology and the regulatory process to convert its special mobile radio frequencies into a virtual substitute for cellular telephone capacity.[2] These transactions, along with AT&T's proposed acquisition of McCaw Cellular,[3] are dramatic evidence that the old distinction between local and long-distance service no longer has the technological basis that it once had.

Telephone companies will vertically integrate if there are economies obtainable from allowing their customers to look to any supplier for all their telephone-supplied services. Vertical integration identifies for consumers a single point of accountability for service quality. AT&T and MCI plainly comprehend these benefits. Their recent steps towards greater vertical integration testify to the fact that vertical integration is more important now to the efficient production of telecommunications services than it was a dozen years ago. Correspondingly, the costs of precluding vertical integration by the RBOCs are greater than at the time of divestiture. Indeed, there is a realistic threat that the

1. J. J. Keller, "MCI Proposes a \$20 Billion Capital Project," Wall Street Journal, January 5, 1994, A3.

2. MCI Communications Inc., "MCI Will Invest \$1.3 Billion in Nextel to Offer Nationally Branded Wireless Services," press release, February 28, 1994.

3. McCaw Cellular Communications, Inc., 1992 Form 10-K, p. 3; see also M. L. Carnevale, "AT&T-McCaw Link Stuns Baby Bells," Wall Street Journal, November 6, 1992, B1; J. J. Keller, "Cellular Move Underscores AT&T's Transformation," Wall Street Journal, November 6, 1992, B1; J. J. Keller and R. Smith (1993), "AT&T Agrees to Buy McCaw Cellular in Stock Swap Valued at \$12.6 Billion," Wall Street Journal, August 17, 1993, A3.

continuation of the line-of-business restrictions will permanently leave the RBOCs' customers with an inferior information-communications system.

The line-of-business restrictions should accordingly be eliminated. Technological changes have displaced the old narrowband hierarchical switch system that prevailed at the time of divestiture. To retain the MFJ's restrictions on vertical integration would be to deny consumers the benefits of cheaper and more reliable communication services.

BALDARELLI VS. H&R BLOCK

Q. I'm going to ask you a question. It is the kind of a question lawyers call a hypothetical question, asked to an expert witness, and I'm going to read this question so that the hypotheses, the assumptions set forth, will be clear. The assumptions are these:

1. A corporation named Acme does a tax preparation business through offices located in certain geographically limited territories. By tax preparation business, I mean the preparation of Federal and State income tax returns primarily for individuals.

2. In certain other territories, Acme franchises individuals to engage in the tax preparation business under the Acme name. In each case, Acme agrees that it will not open offices in the franchisee's territory or territories, and that it will not franchise anyone else to open offices in that territory or those territories. Under the franchise agreement, the franchisee has only a limited territory or territories, and he cannot set up Acme tax preparation offices elsewhere.

3. In each of the territories occupied by Acme or any franchisee of Acme, there are numerous other persons engaged in the tax preparation business under other names; that is, there is interbrand competition.

4. The franchisees pay royalties to Acme generally at the rate of between five and fifteen percent of their gross revenues, although one franchisee pays a royalty of only two percent of his gross revenues.

5. Franchisees may subfranchise others to open up offices under the Acme name within their respective franchised territories.

6. *Whoever owns and operates the offices, whether he be Acme, a franchisee, or a subfranchisee, will have a substantial opportunity to affect the quality of the services rendered to the public through those offices, either positively or negatively.* For example, the owner and operator of an office or of offices can influence the promptness with which customers are received and processed either by staffing their offices adequately or understaffing them. They can influence the quality of the work done, by hiring capable people and

Undated, edited testimony.

training them well, or by hiring less capable people and training them less well. They can influence the accuracy of the work done by double-checking it or not double-checking it.

Follow-on services such as being available in case of a later audit are also important. Lower quality services cost the operator less to provide than higher quality services.

7. Some of the quality of what a customer receives can be ascertained by him shortly after he first enters the office. For example, he can determine whether customers are being processed promptly or only after a considerable delay. Other aspects of quality the customer cannot readily determine. For example, the customer generally does not know when he has it done whether his return has been correctly prepared. That becomes known to the customer only imperfectly and after a substantial period of years, during which he has his work done by the particular operator. He will perceive the quality or lack of quality depending upon whether he is assessed for deficiencies or gets refunds that were not claimed, or he hears about others having or not having such experiences.

8. Generally customers do not inquire as to the price which they will be charged for their tax preparation. They usually learn the charge only after the work has been done. It is often impracticable to make a precise estimate of the cost of the services until they have been performed. Therefore, the customer generally orders the services before he knows how much he will be charged.

9. The amount of advertising paid for by the operator in any individual territory is an important ingredient in his success or failure, high advertising expenditures being positively correlated with success.

10. Repeat business from year to year and the recommendations of customers to others are extremely important ingredients in the success of the operator of any territory.

Q. Now, based upon the assumptions which I have read, will the Acme name perform an important economic function for the public?

A. The name Acme performs a very important economic function. It is an assurance of a particular quality of service and price, and it is a low-cost identifier of the supplier of that particular quality and service.

Q. And what are the bases for your opinion?

A. Consider what a trade name, if I may use that expression for the Acme name, does. It differentiates one supplier from another. Not all suppliers are exactly alike in their product, the service, the way it is rendered and the price. And as we learn about each supplier's performance from either first-hand experience or from trusted sources, we sensibly attach to the trade name under which he operates a reputation for a particular quality and kind of service. Once established, reputation can be quite valuable. We rely on the trade name to economically indicate a supplier of that quality. And it will be especially valuable if three features are present. I shall indicate what those three things are and illustrate them with an example where they are present and with a case where they are not present.

One feature is that the availability of, or the quality and particular performance features of a product or service one is going to purchase are not known exactly and are not easily knowable, or are knowable only at quite expensive cost prior to decision to purchase.

A second feature is that the exact price one is going to pay for whatever he buys is also not known prior to commitment to purchase.

The third feature is that once one has purchased the service, the consequences, if the service is not up to expectations, can be extremely serious.

I give an example of where those three features are not significant. Take the purchase of a head of lettuce. You go in a store and you can see the head of lettuce there. You can tell by its looks and its color whether it is ripe; you can feel it and tell by its crispness and generally feel whether it's a good head of lettuce. That's the first feature. The price is usually indicated right away, so much per pound, so much per head, so before you purchase the lettuce you know quite cheaply and quite accurately what the price is and what the quality is going to be. That's the second feature. But once you purchase the head of lettuce and get home, you may find it's not up to snuff. It may be a bad head of lettuce, but the consequences are trivial. You may lose a fraction of the head, or you lost part of the salad, but I regard those as trivial effects. That's the third feature. So in the case of purchase of a head of lettuce, none of those three factors appears to be significant. And it is, I think, relevant evidence that you rarely find a head of lettuce with a trade name on it.

But take an income tax service, where I assume some of these factors, maybe all, are significant. Suppose I go to some income tax preparation office. I can tell by carpets and the furniture and the kind of people waiting on me whether it's likely to be a clean, quick service. But as the person starts to fill out my form, I can't tell just how good the service is going to be. I've probably already decided to accept their services, and now they are filling out the form, asking me questions about whether I've had expenses for children, or child support, or for alimony, or whether I've paid taxes in some other state, whether my pension is taxable. They ask a lot of questions, and at least I know I can't tell whether a person's doing a good job or not doing a good job. I'm acting on faith and other sources of information that they are doing a good job. I can't tell myself. If I could, I'd probably fill out my own form.

Secondly, I don't know (and even they may not yet know) what they're going to charge me. That depends upon complications of my case, and whether it's a long-drawn-out inquiry, and how difficult. In fact, if I ask them in advance what the price will be, they will tell me it depends upon the service. So I believe that in this income tax case, both the first two features are notable. I lack knowledge as to the exact quality of what I am going to get, prior to commitment to purchase, and the exact price is also not known prior to commitment to purchase.

And the third factor is significant here too. If the product is not up to snuff, and turns out not to be properly filled out, I may be in serious trouble. At least I may spend a day or so with the auditors, who may audit my return, and that's a day's wages lost, if that's the least that happens to me.

I may have fines or penalties to pay because of poor income tax preparation. On the other hand, I may have overpaid and never know that. So the consequences of a bad performance can be serious.

Where any of those three factors are significant, the established reputable trade name performs an important function. It gives that quality assurance, prior to purchase, and some assurance about the price. It is a direct substitute for personal first-hand knowledge about how to perform a service or how to detect good performance, without having to incur the cost of becoming an expert. This gives a cheap source of information about sources of reliable qualities of particular items.

In summary, where any of those three factors are present, the trade name should be especially valuable.

Q. Based upon the assumptions that have previously been stated, do exclusive geographically limited territories tend to have any effect upon the quality assurance information feature of the Acme name that gives it economic value from the point of view of the consumer?

A. Yes. Exclusive territory provides a strong economic motivation for the independent-operator-franchisee in that territory to produce and to continue to produce the good service that will give that trade name a good reputation and give it economic value in which he, as the franchisee-operator, can share.

Let me add one more feature, which I believe is in the questions you first formulated. In the present circumstance, the local independent operator, the franchisee in this territory to which he has an exclusive right, can materially and substantially affect the quality of the service provided. That is, both the franchisor, in this case Acme, and the particular franchisee in the local exclusive area, both of them can affect the quality of the product the customer gets. In particular, the local franchisee can affect it. That is extremely important, and I don't want to let it pass without emphasizing it, because what I'm going to say later will rest heavily upon that. This is absolutely crucial here. If that were not present, much of what I say would not follow.

The local franchisee plays an important part in affecting the quality of the service. He can make it or he can break it. When I say "he can make it," he can make a good service. And good service promotes repeat customers. In fact, the test of good service is that the customer would say, "That's the kind of service or product I would like to have again when the occasion arises." A test of good service is that the customer wants to have it again.

The prospect of that kind of good service and hence of repeat customer business induces giving good service. Providing and getting a reward for a good service is tied to the exclusive territory, because in that case, there will be no other independent franchise operators—under the same name and therefore indistinguishable from him in that same territory—who could come in and take away customers or leech off or share the rewards of his initial good services. Under the exclusive territory, the franchisee bears more fully the long-run rewards of his good services.

If he did not bear or reap those long-run effects, his current operation would be different, because there is another set of effects, what I will call the partial or the immediate, short-run effects, as distinct from this long-run repeat business.

In the short-run, immediate period, he could have provided less expensive service, which would make the service less good and lose the long-run business.

He could gouge the customer now by raising the price now and lose that long-run business. But both these two actions would give an immediate higher income, sort of a short-run, temporary, quick killing—and I use the word killing advisedly now—because he would be killing off that future business that would otherwise be obtained by good current services under his trade name. The long-run effects and the short-run effects both must be considered with the exclusive territory. He takes both into account. At least his self-interests make him take into account the long- and short-run effects.

So, under the exclusive territory, his self-interests are harnessed to the long-run interests of providing good service.

That good service he provides will strengthen the reputation of the trade name under which he operates and will raise the value of that trade name in which he will share. He helps create that value, and this is an important point which is often overlooked, not just by buying a building or some furniture but by his own time and effort. That kind of reputation is one you build by your own effort and ingenuity and hard work.

But that repute is a wealth, once it is created. It is the goodwill, so-called. You won't find it in the balance sheet, like a building. You may find goodwill—one dollar or trivial amounts—but for good reasons conventional accountants do not put that in his balance sheet as his wealth.

But it is true economic wealth. It is the present value of all cost savings he provides customers when they can rely on him for predictable quality and price. The future business he will generate by his good action comes because he provides that assurance more cheaply. That wealth in which he will share is the incentive which harnesses his interests to long-run service and which he is induced to provide by this exclusive territory.

So to conclude this long statement, the exclusive territory enables, in fact induces, the franchisee to provide a good service. The public benefits by getting this good service. The franchisee benefits by sharing the trade name, and the franchiser also benefits.

In that sense, an exclusive territory can be a socially beneficial device which motivates the franchisee to perform his good service.

Q. I would like to make one change in the assumptions previously related to you: suppose an Acme franchisee starts off believing that he has an exclusive territory, and after three or four years of building up the name in the way that you have described, he learns that other Acme franchisees are going to enter his territory. And he goes to the lawyer and shows him the franchise agreement, and this franchisee who started building the territory then learns that, in fact, he does not have exclusivity under his agreement.

Under those circumstances, what is your opinion as to what would happen with regard to that Acme name and the reputation associated with the Acme name in that particular territory?

A. The good reputation of that trade name would be severely eroded and its economic value ultimately destroyed.

Q. Why?

A. It is almost the reverse of what I already stated, and I will try to state it briefly: without the exclusive territory, this franchisee now will no longer bear the full long-run consequences of his actions, which were the beneficial long-run effects. Others can now come in, under the same trade name in that territory, and capture some of the customers who return to that particular trade name because of the initial good services associated with that trade name.

Since only a smaller fraction of the customers that he generated will return to him, he will not, therefore, bear the full weight of the beneficial effects of his current actions.

But the short-run effects, those which would induce him to try to make a quick killing, still persist and are less outweighed by the diminished long-run prospects. The longer-run effects are gone, but the short-run effects still persist. So he is now induced, whether he wants to or not, to now cut costs by hiring poorer labor, or by being open less often, or by cutting corners on the way he provides the service, or by charging a higher price more often, which will give him a higher current earnings. That will be the more likely behavior, because his rewards structure has been changed. He does not become more evil or less socially minded. It is just that the reward structure has changed, and the good circumstances are driven out by the poorer quality. The good does not flourish anymore under the trade name. The trade name loses its reputation. Under those circumstances, the local franchisee will no longer have that good trade name to share with the franchisor.

In summary, without the exclusive territory, the trade name of the franchisee and franchisor will suffer.

Q. Again using the original assumptions that I stated, except for one that I would like to change, I would like to ask you another question. The assumption that I will change is this: instead of the franchisor having new franchisees or exclusive geographic franchises, suppose he offers that franchisee a non-exclusive geographically unlimited franchise.

First of all, would qualified individuals be likely to be willing to become franchisees on that basis?

A. It is not at all likely. It is very unlikely. I can't imagine why anybody would do that. In fact, I would predict that he would probably demand to have an exclusive territory as a condition of performing the business.

Without it, for the reason I have given, he just wouldn't get off the ground.

Q. All right, now assume that you could find someone willing to be the first franchisee in a territory and that he would be willing, despite what you have said, to become a franchisee on a non-exclusive basis. And assume also that at the outset he is the only franchisee in a given territory.

Under those circumstances, do you have an opinion as to whether the new franchisee having a non-exclusive territory would be likely to develop it effectively?

A. Yes, he would not be likely or able to develop it effectively.

First, he would not be bearing those full long-run effects of his good services. In fact, he would be facing the imminent threat, indeed the virtual certainty, of others coming in under the same trade name in the same area and capturing or leeching off the good services which he has provided. When that happens, any initial reputation he may have built up by good service and the delusion that he will be able to retain that service will be destroyed.

Q. Under the assumption heretofore stated, would a franchisee be economically better off with a smaller geographically limited franchise than with non-exclusive geographically unlimited franchises?

A. Yes, he would be much better off with a geographically limited exclusive territory than he would with the open territory. Under the exclusive territory, he has an opportunity to help develop that trade name reputation, which will acquire a value which he will share. That represents his goodwill; he will be able to protect it from others who otherwise would have come in to share it and destroy the reputation of that name.

Without an exclusive territory against such entrants under the same name, he does not have an opportunity to develop that trade name and share in it, because the trade name won't survive. All he can do without exclusive territory is to earn the normal rate of return he would get on the ordinary labor or servicing as an employee, or on any investment he might make in the way of building, space or furniture. He could get the same return on investments and stocks, bonds or savings accounts.

So he lacks the opportunity to capitalize on his time and effort to build up a reliable, desirable service to consumers and identify by that trade name. Without such service and a valuable trade name to identify its supplier, a value in which he can share, he and society lose. That is what he has lost when he does not have exclusive territory under the conditions we specified here.

Q. One of the assumptions to this point was that the trade name would be eroded and ultimately lose its value to the franchisee if there were a non-exclusive, geographically unlimited territory.

Now, let's assume for the moment that despite that deterioration of the name on a non-exclusive basis, that name could somehow or someway continue to draw customers to tax preparers operating under the Acme name, even though many Acme franchisees with the same name might be operating alongside one another in the same territory.

Now, under those circumstances, which I know are not what you regard as likely, might a franchisee be worse off by having a geographically limited territory than if he were one of a large number of franchisees, all of whom could open offices under the same name, wherever he and they chose?

A. No, he would suffer no economic injury. In fact, he would be better off with the exclusive territory, even under that condition, which I can't imagine can be done. But if it is done in some magical way, he is better off with the exclusive territory, suffering no economic injury.

Q. Would you explain why?

A. As I understand the question, to make sure that we're not at cross-purposes, this franchisee can go into some other territory, others can come into his territory.

If he enters into the new territory, because in that new territory the trade name is already established and present, others can also enter that territory and go into it. They will continue to enter that territory, opening new stores and multiplying the number of stores so long as the number of customers they get from those new offices attracts enough business to cover the cost of the offices and the franchise fee the operator must pay. More will come in until those returns for the business just match the cost of opening an office and paying the franchise fee, leaving nothing but the normal rate return on their labor and investment of equipment.

So quickly, and I believe it's very quickly in this case, there would be such a large number of new offices in that territory, in which all can go, that there'd be no prospect of his having any share of value in the trade name thereafter. Franchisees might flood in excessive amounts, and they may even end up with losses by having gone into that area. But the expectation is that very quickly there will be enough offices opened up that the business will have been spread thin over all of them, so that the revenues just cover the cost of performing the service and the franchise fee being paid to the franchisor.

Now, I don't know how that trade name is going to be maintained, but if by magic somehow it's maintained, that's an important extra ingredient here; the trade name still has a value, still attracts customers, and they're still getting good service, because that's what we've assumed magically. The value of the trade name, which formerly the franchisees held in that territory, is now absorbed into the higher cost of all those franchisees doing business. They bring in an extra number of offices until those extra costs just absorb that—the value of that trade name. That's why none of them makes any profit in that new area. They'll continue to come in until the trade name value is now spread over all of them, but none of them is gaining anything, because each is incurring an extra cost to get it. So in that circumstance, the public is worse off, because resources are diverted from other, more useful things into too many outlets. Too many of these outlets are now being created just to absorb or get rights to the value of that trade name, and that's a loss to the public. Some of the customers may be better off because they have stores closer to them, but there's an excessive number of outlets, with too little of other more valuable goods.

Q. Are there any other economically desirable consequences that you know of from exclusive geographically limited franchises under the assumptions heretofore stated?

A. There are a few others. It will prevent the franchisee from biting off more than he can chew. He would be tempted to try to grab now a large territory for the sake of getting now a right to later development and capture the value of that later on. But the risk this runs is that he will grab off a larger territory for the sake of getting hold of it, to develop it later, and spread his efforts so thin to hold the rights that he won't develop the smaller area which he should develop at first. So trying to get rights now for later development, in order to get first claims on it, will mean that he will take too large a territory and simply be unable to digest it, because it takes his time and his effort to develop it. He's not just buying resources.

A second effect of the exclusive territory is that if it's a contiguous, relatively homogeneous or closed area, say a hundred offices in Northern California rather than two offices in each of fifty states, the cost of managing and monitoring and supervising these offices is cheaper. With a closer set of offices, transportation and communication costs are cheaper. He can monitor and supervise the offices more carefully. He can also transfer personnel or effort from office to office as peak demands or seasonal demands or daily demands should fluctuate.

Third, in advertising, which may be an important feature of the business. Promotional work in a geographically limited area is easier than it would be spread over many widely dispersed areas.

Fourth, if a franchisee in one area, discovers some new way to give better service or to create more business or better business, he will share it with franchisees in other territories. He knows they aren't going to use it against him, so he's willing to tell somebody in some other territory, "I've learned the following ideas of how to give a better business, or how to run a better business, and if you'll trade knowledge with me, I'll trade with you." So they both benefit and provide better service, and they will do so so long as they know they're not going to use the items against each other.

3

THE BEHAVIOR OF GOVERNMENT AND NONPROFIT ORGANIZATIONS

PRIVATE PROPERTY AND THE RELATIVE
COST OF TENURE

Private property and consumer sovereignty have effects that can be more vividly revealed by case studies than by a statement of principles. I should like, therefore, to examine a special labor market whose product is regarded as unique, so that special employment relations are necessary to preserve the quality of that product. I am speaking of the collegiate market for professors. The special employment relations in the professors' market is tenure, whereby the professor has job security except for immoral acts, loss of mental competence, or financial disability by the college. The professor is assured of his job security so long as his teaching reflects his search for the truth. I shall pass over the questions of how one determines dishonest expounding of the search for the truth and how incompetence and immorality are established. And I shall not dispute the meaning of financial inability. But assuming they are answerable questions, we can concentrate on the question of why tenure is desirable and viable.

Why is this kind of security deemed necessary for the professor? That is, for what is it necessary? Let me quote some of the arguments. I quote first from the Statement of Principles of the American Association of University Professors, a statement endorsed by many other academic professional associations.

> Institutions of higher education are conducted for the common good and not to further the interest of either the individual teacher or that institution as a whole. The common good depends upon the free search for truth and its free exposition. Academic freedom is essential to these purposes and applies to both teaching and research.
>
> Tenure is a means to certain ends; specifically: (1) freedom of teaching and research and of extramural activities, and (2) a sufficient degree of economic security to make the profession attractive to men and women of ability. Freedom and economic security, hence tenure, are indispensable to

Reprinted from Armen A. Alchian, *Economic Forces at Work* (Indianapolis: Liberty Fund, 1977), 177–202. This article was previously published in *The Public Stake in Union Power*, ed. P. D. Bradley (Charlottesville: University of Virginia Press, 1959): 350–71.

the success of an institution in fulfilling its obligations to its students and to society.[1]

I give another quotation.

The modern university . . . is a unique type of organization. For many reasons it must differ from a corporation created for the purpose of producing a salable article for profit. Its internal structure, procedures, and discipline are properly quite different from those of business organizations. It is not so closely integrated and there is no such hierarchy of authority as is appropriate to a business concern; the permanent members of a university are essentially equals. . . .

Free enterprise is as essential to intellectual as to economic progress. A university [my italics] must therefore be hospitable to an infinite variety of skills and viewpoints, relying upon open competition among them as the surest safeguard of truth. Its [my italics] whole spirit requires investigation, criticism, and presentation of ideas in an atmosphere of freedom and mutual confidence. This is the real meaning of "academic" freedom. It is essential to the achievement of its ends that the faculty be guaranteed this freedom by its governing board, and that the reasons for the guarantee be understood by the public.

When the [scholar's] opinions challenge existing orthodox points of view, his freedom may be more in need of defense than that of men in other professions. The guarantee of tenure for professors of mature and proven scholarship is one such defense. As in the case of judges, tenure protects the scholar against undue economic or political pressure and ensures the continuity of the scholarly process.[2]

What are the reasons for tenure? Apparently it is necessary to insure efficient searching for the truth because of the special nature of the product, truth, and because the university is different from ordinary business entities. However, my conclusion is that the reason for the general acceptance of tenure is not that the search for truth has some special characteristics which distinguish it from other products, but that, instead, its acceptance springs from the special own-

1. American Association of University Professors, "Academic Freedom and Tenure," *AAUP Bulletin* 42, no. 1 (Spring 1956): 42.

2. Association of American Universities, *The Right and Responsibilities of Universities and Their Faculties* (March 1953); reprinted in the *University Bulletin* of the University of California 1, no. 33 (April 20, 1953): 162–64.

ership arrangement and financial structures of our colleges. Economic analysis has driven me to this conclusion, that it arises from an absence of the ordinary kind of property rights that exist in profit-seeking businesses.

What is the economic analysis or what are the theorems that yield this conclusion? The simplest and most fundamental postulates and theorems of economics are sufficient. The first theorem says individuals act so as to further their own interest, even when acting as members of a group. The second fundamental theorem of economics says the lower the relative price of any good or source of satisfaction, the more will be purchased. These are called the first and second fundamental theorems of economics to suggest that their power is comparable to that of the first and second fundamental theorems of physics.

A person can further his interest—or as we say in the jargon of economics, he can increase his utility—in many different ways. He can increase his pecuniary wealth and personal consumption expenditures. He can further his interests or satisfaction by having more pleasant working conditions, a bigger and plusher office, a more beautiful and cooperative secretary, a jovial, friendly, and lenient employer, cleaner and more elaborate washrooms, more convenient and automatic equipment with which to work, music in the factory, or, if he is the employer, he might have more responsible employees with desirable personal and cultural characteristics. The lower the costs that must be paid for any of these, the more he will buy them, in exactly the same way that a person revises his purchases of types of food in response to their prices. A person will always spend some of his personal wealth on his job environment, but every dollar so spent means a dollar less for expenditure at home. If the costs of things bought for home consumption were to rise relative to costs of business-connected sources of personal satisfaction, he would buy more of the latter.[3]

What this all says is that a person has at least two ways to spend money. He can take it out of the business, if he owns it, and spend it at home and wherever he pleases. Or he can spend it in the business, not merely for the sake of increasing the net profits or income of the business but for the personal benefits he gets in the course of his income-earning activity. He can always take a smaller salary or profits in exchange for better working conditions or for greater job security. The less of any one of these things he must sacrifice to get the other, the more of the other he will take. The more personal take-home wealth he must sacrifice to get pleasanter working conditions, the poorer will

3. For an excellent illustration of this, see G. S. Becker, *The Economics of Discrimination* (Chicago, 1957).

be his working conditions. For example, if he sacrificed no profits or salary, he would indulge in job choices exclusively on the basis of security and working conditions.

People differ in their preferences for various ways to spend their personal wealth at home, and they differ in their business-connected expenditures. Some will be willing to buy more in the way of attractive working surroundings than will other people in the same wealth position. Some will want their business-connected sources of personal satisfaction more in the form of congenial employees, and others will place a greater emphasis on physical surroundings. It all depends upon their personal preference patterns. But if the cost of beautiful secretaries should rise, everyone will be induced to cut down somewhat on the amount of beautiful secretarial services, regardless of his relative preferences for beauty and efficient secretarial work. Of course it is possible that some employers may attach no significance to degree of beauty, but as long as some do, the effect will be noted. Only if employers attached no value whatsoever to beauty—perhaps such as might happen if the employer's wife were in some way to be in control of secretarial hiring—would it not follow that more would be bought at a lower price?

To be more explicit, suppose that a certain secretary was capable of producing $0.80 of pecuniary income per hour. At $1.00 an hour the employer would have to sacrifice $0.20 of personal profits which he could have used in any way he saw fit in or out of the business. Let us suppose that he decided the extra attractions of the secretary were not worth the $0.20 per hour sacrifice of profits that he could have taken home and devoted to, say, his wife's beauty. Now, modify the system so that he is not allowed to take home all the profits. As an extreme, suppose that he can take home only one fourth, $0.05 per hour. Now the attraction of the secretary, formerly not worth $0.20 per hour, need be compared only with $0.05 of sacrificed domestic expenditures. The cost to him of business-connected satisfaction has fallen from $0.20 per hour to $0.05 per hour. The employer will find his satisfaction enhanced if he spends more in the business, getting a larger portion of this personal satisfaction through business-connected expenditures or costs. Not only will he hire a prettier secretary but he will enlarge all business costs that in any way provide personal satisfaction.

A word of caution: it has not been said that he would have spent nothing for secretarial beauty before a tax or confiscation of profits. All that is implied is that he would have bought less of it before, not none of it. Everyone always is willing to buy some pleasantness of working environment depending upon the costs of domestic consumption. What is being said here is that more will be bought as the domestic-consumption sacrifice or price is made lower. And not only will secretarial beauty be more extensively purchased, but *every* source of personal satisfaction obtainable through business-connected costs will be increased. And the increase will be greater, the greater is the cost of taking profits home.

Significant also is that there is inefficiency when his profits are taxed. The business is using up $1.00 worth of resources to provide a benefit worth less than $1.00. The business owner is spending a dollar to get $0.80 worth of pecuniary service via typing and $0.05 worth of extra pleasure of beauty. Formerly he got $1.00 worth of typing services, whereas now he gets a total satisfaction worth only $0.85, a loss of $0.15. But that loss is not imposed on him. Instead it is borne by the whole of society as a consequence of not using resources in their most valuable ways as judged by consumers. It is possible to have provided just as much typing service and beauty and still have other things too. This, of course, is merely the well-known efficiency aspect of the competitive, free-price system under private property.

The task to which we turn now is to see what affects the relative prices of these various sources of satisfaction, some of which are domestic, business-free expenditures and others of which are business-connected cost-covered expenditures. In particular, we shall consider the effects of profit-seeking privately owned institutions as compared with nonprofit organizations on the cost ratios of various forms of business-connected sources of satisfaction, and the particular form of business-connected source of satisfaction to which we shall devote most of our attention is tenure.

An ordinary privately owned profit-seeking business, whether it sells shoes or news, whether it be a proprietorship or a corporation, is operated for the sake of increasing the wealth of the owners and not for the common good. That the business will survive only if it benefits other people as a consequence of its owner's search for personal profits does not deny this latter objective. In other words, the test of survival of such a business is not that it intends to serve the public interest or common good, but instead that it produces profits— which the owner can take out of the business if he wishes. To make profits the business must be taking resources from less useful alternative activities and putting them to work in more valuable channels. From this difference in usefulness, as judged by the consumers, arise the profits. If the owner fails to satisfy this condition, he will suffer a loss in his personal wealth, which will compensate other people for the reduction in the value of output which he has caused. Thus the owner is forced to bear through smaller profits or through losses the true economic costs of his actions. Loss of personal wealth is a powerful dissuader, while profits are a powerful persuader to pay heed to other people's preferences.

Any employer who may be induced by an employee to produce a service inefficiently will find that consumers punish him by making him bear the costs through losses. And this dissuades the employer from supporting inefficient behavior. But no one employer can prevent the employee from continuing his inefficient activities elsewhere if any other member of the community will agree to bear the costs out of his personal wealth. In summary, the profit-seeking owner who satisfies the consumer best makes profits, and he can use the profit in any way he likes, at home or in the business. His range of choice of places and ways in which he can spend the income of the business is not confined to business avenues or working conditions only.

This kind of private ownership or private property right, common as it is, is not universal. A non-profit-seeking business is the name usually given to an entity or institution administered by individuals acting in the capacity of trustees and who *cannot* appropriate the net wealth gains directly to themselves as profits nor completely as higher salaries. Nor can anyone else take the wealth out of the business as an owner could and spend it on as wide a range of alternatives as he could with his own personal wealth. The administrator is a trustee, and not for any particular person's private wealth. There is no owner in the conventional sense; there are merely managers, administrators and operators. This does *not* mean that no one can further his own interest through the ways the wealth of the organization is spent. But what it does mean is that since there is no residual owner who can spend the net profits more efficiently at home and in the business than in the narrower range of business-associated sources of personal benefits, the inducement to increase profits is reduced. In fact, it is turned into an inducement to reduce them to zero, but not into losses. Avoidance of losses is still a binding, effective constraint on the activities of a non-profit-seeking institution that relies upon sales to consumers for its income.

In a non-profit-seeking enterprise, the administrator must spend all the income in the business for salaries, materials, building, etc. Some of the expenditures will contribute to future income, and some will be spent in ways to enhance the working environment or to acquire personal satisfaction through business cost expenditures. This all is merely an application of the earlier stated principle about buying more of these things that are cheaper and less of those that become more expensive. It is more expensive in a nonprofit organization to take the profits home, and the ruse of raising the administrator's salary to equal the profits is not completely available. If it were, then the non-profit organization would be the same as a profit-seeking institution. But the fact which we have to accept is that the profits cannot all be taken out in this way as cheaply as in a privately owned profit-seeking organization. And so in conformity with the second fundamental theorem of economics, a greater portion of the business expenditures will be spent for business-connected sources of personal satisfaction than in a profit-making organization. Of course, the particular kinds of business-associated or business-cost activities that will in any case be most increased depend upon the particular tastes and preference patterns of the administrators. But whatever ones are increased most, all will be increased.

It is easy to cite many examples. Medical insurance in the business, especially if it is proportional to salaries or status, becomes more attractive since this substitutes for domestic, personally purchased medical aid. Life insurance for all the employees is now a cheaper way of getting it for the administrator—without sacrificing so much profits. And if the key officials like coffee, the coffee break is longer and more elaborate. If they like baseball, the company will have a box at the ballpark for its employees, with you-know-who going most often. Company cars will be newer. Athletic facilities in the plant will be more common because their cost via the business has fallen relative to take-home profits. The administrator can devote more of his time to community affairs and act more like a statesman and less like a grubbing profit seeker. Some, or even all, of these things will be found in a profit-seeking business, but since their cost is even less in a nonprofit organization relative to profits, these things will be more common and on a larger scale.

For example, an administrator of an automobile company, if non-profit-seeking, would find it more in his interest (than in a profit-seeking business) to lower prices and sacrifice some revenue and profits in order to create a backlog of orders, or, as they say, a waiting list. His production scheduling and inventory problems would be eased. Prestige and personal benefits could be gained by his being able to favor and obtain various acceptable favors from certain customers by special priorities. He would be willing also to increase costs and lower profits if in that way he could reduce internal management nuisances and employee-relations problems. Unproductive but congenial workers who would be fired in a profit-seeking business will be more readily kept. Firing a person is an unpleasant task, but in a profit-seeking business it is even more unpleasant not to fire them.

His employment policy will be *less* closely related to productivity in a pecuniary sense and more oriented toward satisfying his own welfare through non-
pecuniary forms, e.g., employees who agree with his point of view, or employee cultural characteristics, or special employment arrangements which are
conducive to administrative ease. But insofar as employment policies reflect
considerations other than productivity in the business, some employees without these side characteristics will feel unjustly discriminated against if they are
not promoted or are fired when doing what they think is consistent with the
avowed purposes of the enterprise. They will demand less "arbitrary" hiring,
firing and employment policies and will seek to protect themselves from the
inefficient practices of the employer. But the policies they seek will reduce
efficiency. Weakened as the consumer controls are on the employer because of
the elimination or reduction of the available profits, they are even weaker on
the employees. The less such policy costs the administrator-employer, the
more he will be induced to accept it. He will be more ready to accept employment policies that mean a quieter, more peaceful, even if less profitable, life.
And one of the forms of employment policy that will be pressed on him, and
more willingly brought now, is greater job security for the employees.

At any given wage rate, the greater the job security an employee can get, the
better for him and the worse for the employer. An employer who grants a long-
term contract must bear the consequences of changes in the employee's productivity. If the employee proves to be less productive than anticipated, the employer suffers and the employee is the gainer. If the employee proves to be
better than anticipated, the employee can quit his job and go elsewhere and get
a higher pay. The risks are not symmetrical. Hence at the same wage rate, an
employer prefers shorter-term to longer-term contracts. And since the employer cannot revise wages downward, else the whole objective of security
would be negated, he will offer a lower wage guarantee than he expects the
employee's productivity to be.

If we look at our private colleges and universities, we find that they are typically non-profit-seeking institutions. Whatever the attitude of the administrator of the college toward academic freedom and exposition of the truth, his
ability to impose his own standards of acceptable employee behavior is enhanced above his ability to do so in a profit-seeking enterprise. His actions do,
of course, affect the status of the college and the attraction it has for students
or for donors. Yet since he does not have a right to keep the profits for personal
expenditures, he is not so severely affected by the loss of profits caused by the
unpopularity of his decisions. Of all the forces that can be brought to bear on

him, one is now weakened, and this one is the personal wealth effect. Students and their parents are less able to punish him so severely for behavior not in conformity with their desires, since the profits incentive is attenuated, as it is not in a profit-seeking owned institution. As said earlier, it is in just such situations that the administrator will more frequently evidence arbitrariness in hiring and firing people. And similarly, in just such institutions would we expect employees to react most strongly and seek protection from this apparently capricious behavior by the college administrator who seems to be paying even less attention to the criterion of truthful teaching. It is perfectly true, however, that those administrators who already stand for the truth are even more willing to retain teachers of the truth who present the unpleasant truth. But what all this means is that those who would defend such teachers from discharge by keeping them despite their statements are more easily able—that is, at lower cost to themselves—to grant tenure. Those who do not want such teaching are more insulated from the pressure of their customers' withdrawal of purchases, since the losses of profits are not all imposed on him as his costs. But whatever his degree of opposition and whatever his attitude toward the truth, the cost imposed on him for granting tenure is lower in a nonprofit organization. Therefore, because the demand for it is larger and because the gains to the employer from opposing it get smaller, the probability of tenure is increased in nonprofit organizations.

It is not necessarily the college president or board of governors whose capricious behavior is made cheaper as a source of personal satisfaction. Many college staffs have attempted to protect themselves from this by having fellow faculty members decide on new appointments, retentions and promotions. This is called democracy, but it is not clear that this makes any difference. Who is to protect the individual faculty member from the equally-cheap-to-exercise personal preferences of his colleagues when they assume the administrative powers?

Everyone wants security, if the cost is zero. And the higher the cost, the less they will want. But there is a particular set of employees who will most desire tenure. These are older people whose productivity is nearing or past its peak. By securing tenure at existing current wages, they will be assured of continuing employment, despite declining productivity, at a high wage rate. At the same time, all current employees on short-term contracts will be happy to switch to a tenure contract if no cut in pay is involved, for then it would appear as though they had obtained job security without any cost to themselves with all the cost being dumped on the employer. An employer will, of course, resist this, but the extent will depend upon the cost, and in a nonprofit institution, the costs imposed on the administrator are lower than the same person would bear in the same kind of business if it were a profit-seeking enterprise. Hence the extent to which employers are induced to resist this demand is reduced, and tenure is more likely to exist, as are other forms of inefficiency.

But it should not be assumed that all the costs of tenure will be shifted by the employer to society at large. Actually they have also been shifted onto *some* of the employees. Nothing is guaranteed in a tenure contract as to the rate of advance of pay. The employer, once he has granted tenure, may subsequently resist pay increases until the margin between pay and productivity reflects the risk-bearing aspect mentioned earlier. As a partial defense the employees insist on provisions about the rate at which pay will advance. But the beginning rate under tenure will be lower than under nontenure as a result of the risks of long-term contracts. In such arrangements, who prove to be gainers and losers—since this is essentially a vast insurance-type gamble? Individuals who live longest and turn out to be below average in productivity growth gain at the expense of the short-lived in this profession and those whose productivity increases the most. Those who had short lives received less of their total productivity. The risk the employer bore was that they, later in life, would be less productive and at that time their wages would not be decreasing. Hence in the earlier part of his career the employee is underpaid in the gamble that later he will overcollect.

Another gamble also occurs. Those who proved to be most productive will have received less than they would have received without tenure, even though they earn more than the average worker. And those who turn out to be below average in productivity growth will earn more than they would have received without tenure, but still they earn less than the average of better workers.

Mobility is penalized because every new job means the task of resolving some doubt in the new employer's mind. This implies that older and less able people, who are now getting a reward more than they are worth, will find very few new job offers elsewhere at equivalent or better wages, since no new employer is likely to induce a person to leave a job at which he is currently being overpaid. On the other hand, the better men will be paid less than they are worth and so should be receiving offers from other employers who will propose to narrow the gap.

This does not mean that new employers want to hire only the best people; rather, it means that they will find the better people are more willing to move because of the discrepancy of their wages and productivity. Tenure benefits the older, less able people at the expense of the younger, more able and shorter-lived individuals.

If one goes one step farther and assumes that in such a nonprofit organization the older people are in authority, as seems likely by virtue of the weaker pecuniary productivity rewards because "profits" are less efficiently used, one would expect the interests of older people to be given greater consideration than those of younger people. This would be evident in the way facilities and privileges were rationed among the many employees.

The drive for tenure involves compelling most, but not all, employees to accept the tenure system. In many colleges all staff members must acquire tenure—as it is euphemistically stated—at the end of a fixed number of years outside the tenure system. Any member who wants to continue without tenure at a higher wage for a nontenure appointment is not allowed to do so. To permit this would undermine the position of those in the tenure situation exactly in the same way that a nonmember of a cartel is able to undermine the cartel.

Furthermore, if wages are tied to rank, and rank to tenure, it becomes impossible for the younger, more able men to bargain for higher pay without tenure. They are prevented from foregoing tenure in the interests of a higher current wage. In this way, tenure is harder to break. If this is so, why should anyone be allowed to teach without tenure? For two reasons: in the first place, a trial period gives the administrator and his colleagues a better idea of what a person's productivity will be—or was. Also, they can get a better idea of whether he will be a compatible, docile, agreeable colleague or will be obstreperous and overly competitive in what he seeks to do. And if one's colleagues are involved in determining appointment and promotion, these issues become even more pertinent. This system has been called democratic. Indeed it is democratic, along the same lines of democracy that would prevail if auto manufacturers were to be the democratic deciders as to who could make cars, or as in fact the medical profession does in deciding who can be a doctor. The question of democracy is a red herring. The correct question is whose tastes and preferences are to be satisfied and who is to bear the gains and the costs, the consumer or one's fellow employees? The second reason for not insisting on tenure for every member is that a nonprofit institution may become a "loss" institution and will then have to curtail expenditures. This will mean cutting the staff. But who is to go if all have tenure? To protect those who do have tenure, a buffer, the nonpermanent group, is created to absorb the possible shock.

There is one more institutional factor that also enhances tenure's viability.

In addition to student fees, colleges get income from current gifts and from current income from past gifts—the endowment. Consider the extreme of endowed income, where the income is dependent upon how well the endowment is invested and not upon current activities of teaching and research, which do affect student fees and current gifts. Colleges with endowments can and do sell their services at prices less than the cost of the education received by the student. No longer is the old constraint of no losses binding on the administrator. It will be recalled that under a profit-seeking owned institution, increments in profits are sought, but under a nonprofit institution costs are magnified until they equal income. In each of those cases the extent to which profit or income was sought depended upon their costs relative to other sources of satisfaction that could be obtained with the money available to the institution. Now as we introduce another feature, a source of income independent of how well one uses the money to enhance current income; it will be even more in the administrator's interest to devote some more of the income of the institution to sources of satisfaction that do not bring the pecuniary income. In addition, he can more cheaply devote more of his own time to nonpecuniary income-obtaining activities and more to leisure or statesmanship. He can be consciously or unconsciously less efficient in the way he spends the organization's money. Of course, he is still efficiently pursuing his own interests at the new relative costs of various activities. He can use more assistants; he can delegate to assistants tasks that he would have performed himself; he can also delegate to less able persons and committees. The faculty can be brought more and more into administrative work if they complain about the way he is doing things. He can let them do it, and even if it is more inefficient in the usual sense, it will give him a quieter, more placid life among more friendly fellows. And tenure will again be still less costly, and the demand for it will be still greater, exactly as outlined earlier. Activities which would not be tolerated by consumers are now more viable, hence more common.

How can the validity of the preceding analysis be established? That it follows directly from the simplest and most powerful economic theorems is subject to a logical test. But more pertinent, for present purposes, is the question, Is it empirically valid? What empirically observable results, if observed, would refute the analysis, and what would be consistent with it? First, non-profit-seeking schools will be observed to have a higher incidence of tenure than will private profit-seeking schools. And there are both types, so this can be checked. There are hundreds, if not thousands, of privately owned profit-seeking schools. Some survive entirely from student fees. Some of our best accounting and engineering schools are profit-seeking, financed entirely from student fees, as are some girls' colleges. Schools of advertising, art, music, theater, television, design, secretarial work, foreign languages, law, nursing, beauty-shop work and barbering are straight profit-seeking institutions. Here student consumer sovereignty exists jointly with the explicitly imposed costs of inefficient behavior. If tenure is not more frequent in nonprofit educational institutions the analysis is refuted.

Second, the preceding analysis implies that the incidence of tenure is corre-lated with the ratio of total income that is covered by endowed income. If such a test were made and the evidence refuted this empirical proposition, the im-mediately preceding analysis would be conceded to be wrong. However, noth-ing is implied to the effect that teaching or research will be better or worse as a larger fraction of the income is endowed nor is anything said about the quality of teaching between private profit-seeking and nonprofit organizations. The relationship in that respect may be positive, negative or zero and still be con-sistent with the preceding analysis, even if there were agreement on a measure of good teaching and good research.

It is implied also that tenure should be observed more frequently where rank and pay are tied to tenure than where rank and pay are not tied to tenure. I have not gathered these observable pieces of evidence, but I can illustrate the idea by noting that the extension service at my university teaches much the same courses as the regular university, and in it we had full-cost pricing for the stu-dent and no tenure nor is pay related to age. The summer session, which oper-ates on the same basis, also operates with no tenure. Furthermore, it does not invite full professors to teach, because they don't earn their way compared with the younger, lower-salaried men. The truth is sometimes concealed by assert-ing that the young men "need" the jobs.

Purposely excluded from this discussion have been the state-owned schools, not because I teach at one and presented this analysis at another one. Rather, I can't decide whether the taxpayers should be regarded as customers or as en-dowers. I *conjecture* that they are close to endowers and so would predict that tenure would be more common than at profit-seeking private and in nonprofit private schools that are wholly supported by tuition fees, and I would expect tenure to be less frequent than in the most heavily endowed private schools.

Another, and possibly humorous, implication is that the eagerness with which the administrators devote themselves to seeking new sources of reve-nue, as distinct from gifts, should be inversely related to the fraction of the total income that is endowed. Although with less eagerness, because less rewarding than in a private profit-seeking institution, it will still pay the non-profit-seeking institution to spend some of its money so as to enhance its total revenue. Recall that this was not denied earlier; instead it was merely stated that the rewards obtained from revenue sources were less captureable, hence less valuable, than in a private profit-seeking institution. Now, if I may indulge in a bit of byplay, I would predict that football would be more avidly used as a source of income, the smaller the fraction of income covered by endowment. But I shall not pursue that further here.

Other lines of reasoning have been advanced for tenure. It is not entirely clear whether these other reasons attempt to explain why tenure ought to exist, or why it does exist. The analysis presented so far sought to explain why it developed and why it continues to persist. It did not seek to justify tenure. Essentially the analysis said that it developed because it was one way to further the interests of people working for nonprofit institutions. However, some proponents of tenure argue that it ensures a higher probability of the truth being taught, or that it gets more of it taught. And some argue that it is necessary if the truth is to be sought and taught. With respect to the first argument, more truth may in fact be taught, but the reason is that if tenure is granted, more resources are devoted to teachers than would otherwise be diverted to them. But by what criterion is this judged desirable—except that of inducing a greater demand for one's services?

Or maybe the argument is that greater job security enhances the teaching of the truth. It certainly does, but it also induces one to take his job less carefully and to devote more time to one's politics or social ambitions. The net effect is by no means necessarily, nor even more probably, favorable to greater truth. Neither theoretical analysis nor empirical evidence suggests that result nor is there anything in economics to imply that compulsory lifetime contracts are more efficient than shorter-term voluntary contracts. In truth quite the contrary is implied.

Could it not be argued alternatively that it is indeed fortunate that colleges are not privately owned profit-seeking enterprises, for then tenure would not have survived, and without it the search for the truth would have been dissuaded? Therefore these arrangements have grown up in order that the inefficiencies of tenure can be borne in order to preserve the exposition of truth. This would make a virtue of a necessity, if tenure were necessary. To argue that it is, is to ignore the relevance and effect of competition. If there were but one employer of teachers from whose decision there could be no escape, then suppression of the truth would be cheap. With alternative available employers, suppression by one would not prevent other employers from hiring the intimidated individual and paying him to speak his piece. It would pay another employer to hire him if what he had to say were wanted by other people. A new employer may pay less than the former employer. However much this may be distressing to the employee, there is no cause for anyone else to be concerned. No one has any right to compel another person to support him in the style he would like to have, merely because he is, or believes he is, seeking the truth. And yet that is exactly the position taken when one argues that no person ought to be discharged for teaching the truth.

The news industry is an excellent example of the effect of competition. Any newspaper or radio station owner who prints or broadcasts false news will be hurt by other competitors who reveal the truth—not just the polite superficial truth, but all the truth in its most lurid details. While the *New York Times* may be justly proud of its wide coverage, it is debatable as to whether it prints as much truth in depth as some of the more sensational papers, which are sensational primarily because they print more of the facts of some events. Competition among newspapers for profits by catering to the customers' pocketbooks brings out the truth. A news agency could suppress honesty and truth only if it were a protected monopoly, but it would not succeed in the face of competitors who would seek profits by appealing to the consumer's desire for the truth. The truth in news reporting is not the result of tenure for reporters or editors, nor of a code of ethics, and by no stretch of my imagination can I understand why reporters are not just as much in search of the truth as are teachers.

Competition does exist among our schools. Schools that do not satisfy students' desires will lose their students; the repute of the school will decline among those people who want honesty in teaching. People who do have different ideas about the truth or who care more for indoctrination in some other ideal will support schools that satisfy their demands, as they are entitled to do. We must acknowledge that such schools have a valid place in our society unless we were to seek to impose our tastes on everyone—a position somewhat incompatible with voluntaristic, individualistic principles.

A criticism of this substitution of competition for tenure is that students and parents can't tell good teaching from bad teaching. I do believe they have ways of discerning good from bad; they can also tell the difference between hard and easy, interesting and dull. And they reveal their choices unmercifully, but in accord with the rules of success that are imposed on them by the colleges that ask of them only grade points unweighted by difficulty or severity or importance of material. As long as we weigh grades only by hours of class work, we should hesitate to say that students cannot discern good from bad or truth from falsity. Furthermore, to the extent that students pay less in fees or tuition than the course is worth, to that extent will they sensibly tolerate inefficiency and bad teaching. Would one say that students who go to the Massachusetts Institute of Technology or the California Institute of Technology do so without knowledge of the best engineering schools? If the students can't tell good from bad teaching, one has to wonder how they manage to choose among colleges?

It may be true that some students can't tell a true theorem from a false one. But so long as some students can detect the difference, they will challenge the teacher. And, furthermore, a teacher will challenge a colleague's teaching when he thinks he detects error in it. The ethic of not criticizing one's colleagues, or competitors, in the fashion of the medical profession, is a very dangerous one to the discernment of the truth. Of course, some of the ideas taught are incapable of being proven true or false. They are recital of doctrines and preferences, and economists certainly are not free of this fault. We shouldn't be alarmed if we then find students unable to detect truth from falsity; there may be none to detect. There may be just accuracy of note taking.

What if consumers do not want the truth and instead want romance and illusion? The theater and the movies are much more efficient at that than the teachers are. Fiction writers may have outclassed teachers for many centuries. And in any event, so much the worse for tenure, for then those who want tenure to foster the truth, if such it did, would be trying to impose their preference on other people. To assert that some college officials do not always want the truth and that some alumni or outsiders criticize the teacher and seek to get him fired is certainly true—and commendable. If the truth harms or offends some people, in a free society why should they not have the right to use their resources to combat it? Others may desire the truth even more, and be willing to pay for it. When I buy a house, the fact that I outbid the other bidders means that someone else did not get what he otherwise would have got. And so it is with the bidding for the truth. If someone prefers to buy up the time of teachers to induce them not to speak the truth, he is entitled to do so. And if he tries to buy up a college president in order to persuade him not to continue to hire a certain teacher, he is entitled to do so. Teachers have no claim on the resources of society or of any person. The crucible of the truth is open competition among ideas, although ideas are costly.

A question still hangs over my head. Why do non-profit-seeking subsidized schools exist if they are less efficient, as revealed by the willingness to make inefficient labor contracts. The answer, I think, lies in two places. One is our

state school system, in which the state, through its taxing power, not only subsidizes education but also administers the state schools on a non-full-cost-
tuition basis. Even the most efficient private profit-seeking business would
have a difficult time surviving, if survival is possible, in any endeavor where the
taxing power is used to support a competitor. The nonstate, nonowned private
schools can survive only if they too are given subsidies. If the tax-supported
education were instead given to students as tuition grants in the fashion of the
GI educational benefits, there would be a chance for the private profit-seeking
school to provide us with a test of efficient education and truth seeking.[4] But
barring that change in our educational structure there seems little hope for
avoiding the inefficiencies of the non-profit-seeking nonowned educational
system. The efforts of many people to help education will take the form of
grants to institutions if they are nonprofit, whereas such grants would not
occur if they were profit-making. If they were profit-seeking, the grant would
merely go into the owners' pockets. Under a private profit-seeking school
arrangement, givers would be induced to give to students or to set up charities
for students rather than for schools, much on the lines of the Guggenheim and
Carnegie grants. But if nonprofit institutions exist, it will be possible to aid
education via grants to schools, although such grants will be less efficient than
direct grants to students.

The answer lies, second, in that special and legal advantages given to a non-
profit institution have enabled it to grow and survive, and with it the particular
feature developed in this analysis. The persistence of the nonprofit college
arises, not from its ability to support tenure and the search for the truth, but,
rather, from legal and tax advantages given it, and the granting of gifts to the
college rather than to students. And even with these aids it is highly doubtful
that it will be able to survive against the tax-subsidized support of the state
schools. Admittedly, these last remarks about the reasons for the existence of
nonprofit schools are based on personal conjecture.

In sum, the conclusion suggested is that tenure is neither necessary nor
efficient. Its survival depends upon the absence of private ownership and also
is encouraged by subsidization of education by noncustomer income sources.
Without a private profit-seeking system and without full-cost tuition, the demand for tenure increases, and the cost of granting it appears to be cheaper because the full costs are not imposed on those granting it. Competition among

4. M. Friedman, "The Role of Government in Education," in R. Solo, ed., *Economics and
the Public Interest* (New Brunswick, N.J., 1955).

schools, teachers and students provides protection to the search for the truth without tenure. Just as in the dissemination of news, the exposition of the search for the truth is tested in the open market for ideas and empirical verification. Truth is not something given the stamp of authority or validity by appointed persons. Authority cannot establish what people will believe is the truth. The individual must do that. Truth then is no higher an objective than voluntary individualism. The two are not incompatible. Indeed, what does one mean in the absence of the other?

As a test of whether or not my exposition has been even moderately successful, let me quote a passage from a far better than average defense of tenure. If the passage now appears humorous or transparent I will have passed the test.

> The demand we of the academic world make for academic freedom is not made primarily for our own benefit. We enjoy the exercise of freedom; but the purposes of liberty lie, in a democracy, in the common welfare. It has recently been said, "With regard to some occupations, it is eminently in the interest of society that the men concerned speak their minds without fear of retribution. . . . The occupational work of the vast majority of people is largely independent of their thought and speech. The professor's work consists of his thought and speech. If he loses his position for what he writes or says, he will, as a rule, have to leave his profession, and may no longer be able effectively to question and challenge accepted doctrines or effectively to defend challenged doctrines. And if *some* professors lose their positions for what they write or say, the effect on many other professors will be such that their usefulness to their students and to society will be gravely reduced."
>
> We ask then for the maintenance of academic freedom and of the civil liberties of scholars, not as a special right, but as a means whereby we may make our appointed contributions to the life of the commonwealth and share equitably, but not more than equitably, in the American heritage.[5]

5. American Association of University Professors, "Academic Freedom and Tenure in the Quest for National Security, Report of a Special Committee," *AAUP Bulletin* 42, no. 1 (Spring 1956): 54–55.

ECONOMICS OF TENURE

The collegiate market for professors is a special labor market whose product is regarded as unique, so that special employment relations are necessary to preserve the quality of that product. The special employment relations in the professors' market is tenure, whereby the professor has job security except for immoral acts, loss of mental competence, or financial disability by the college. The professor is assured of his job security so long as his teaching reflects his search for truth.

Why is this kind of security deemed necessary for the professor? That is, for what is it necessary?

"Free enterprise," states the American Association of University Professors in their Statement of Principles, "is as essential to intellectual as to economic progress. A university must therefore be hospitable to an infinite variety of skills and viewpoints, relying upon open competition among them as the surest safeguard of truth. When the [scholar's] opinions challenge existing orthodox points of view, his freedom may be more in need of defense than that of men in other professions. The guarantee of tenure for professors of mature and proven scholarship is one such defense. As in the case of judges, tenure protects the scholar against undue economic or political pressure and ensures the continuity of the scholarly process."

Private Business—Profits

Apparently, then, tenure is necessary to insure efficient searching for the truth because of the special nature of the product, truth, and because the university is different from ordinary business entities. However, this paper will attempt to show that the reason for general acceptance of tenure is not that the search for truth has some special characteristics which distinguish it from other products, but that instead its acceptance springs from the special ownership arrangement and financial structure of our colleges.

The simplest and most fundamental postulates of economics yield this conclusion. The first postulate says individuals act so as to further their own inter-

Reprinted from UCLA *Daily Bruin*, April 4, 1963, 5–8.

ests, even when acting as members of a group. The second states the lower the relative price of any good or source of satisfaction, the more will be purchased.

An ordinary privately owned profit-seeking business, whether it sells shoes or news, whether it be proprietorship or corporation, is operated for the sake of increasing the wealth of the owners and not for the common good. That the business will survive only if it benefits other people as a consequence of its owner's search for personal profits does not deny this latter objective. In other words, the test of survival of such a business is not that it intends to serve the public interest or common good, but instead that it produces profits—which the owner can take out of the business if he wishes.

Administrators—Elaborate Coffee Breaks

This kind of private ownership or private property right, common as it is, is not universal. A non-profit-seeking business is the name usually given to an entity or institution administered by individuals acting in the capacity of trustees and who cannot appropriate the net wealth gains directly to themselves as profits nor completely as higher salaries. The administrator is a trustee not for any particular person's private wealth. There is no owner in the conventional sense; there are merely managers, administrators and operators. This does not mean that no one can further his owner interest through the ways the wealth of the organization is spent.

It is easy to cite many examples. Life insurance for all the employees is now a cheaper way of getting it for the administrator—without sacrificing so much profits. And if the key officials like coffee, the coffee break is longer and more elaborate. If they like baseball, the company will have a box at the ball park for its employees, with you-know-who going most often. The administrator can devote more of his time to community affairs and act more like a statesman and less like a grubbing profit seeker. Some, or even all, of these things will be found in a profit-seeking business, but since their cost is even less in a non-profit organization relative to profits, these things will be more common and on a larger scale.

Cost and Tenure

If we look at our private colleges and universities, we find that they are typically non-profit-seeking institutions. Whatever the attitude of the administrator of the college toward academic freedom and exposition of the truth, his ability to impose his own standards of acceptable employee behavior is enhanced above his ability to do so in a profit-seeking enterprise. His actions do, of course, affect the status of the college and the attraction it has for students or for donors. Yet since he does not have a right to keep the profits for personal expenditures, he is not so severely affected by the loss of profits caused by the unpopularity of his decisions. Of all the forces that can be brought to bear on him, one is now weakened, and this one is the personal wealth effect. Students and their parents are less able to punish him so severely for behavior not in conformity with their desires, since the profits incentive is attenuated, and it is not in a profit-seeking owned institution.

As said earlier, it is in just such situations that administrators will more frequently evidence arbitrariness in hiring and firing people. And similarly, in just such institutions would we expect employees to react most strongly and seek protection from this apparently capricious behavior by the college administrator who seems to be paying even less attention to the criterion of truthful teaching. It is perfectly true, however, that those administrators who already stand for the truth are even more willing to retain teachers of the truth who present the unpleasant truth. But what all this means is that those who would defend such teachers from discharge by keeping them despite their statements are more easily able—that is, at lower cost to themselves—to grant tenure. Those who do not want such teaching are more insulated from the pressure of their customers' withdrawal of purchases since the losses of profits are not all imposed on him as his cost. But whatever his degree of opposition and whatever his attitude toward truth, the cost imposed on him for granting tenure is lower in a non-profit organization.

Therefore, because the demand for it is larger and because the gains to the employer from opposing it get smaller, the probability of tenure is increased in non-profit organizations.

Security at Zero-Cost

It is not necessarily the college president or board of governors whose capricious behavior is made cheaper as a source of personal satisfaction. Many college staffs have attempted to protect themselves from this by having fellow faculty members decide on new appointments, retentions and promotions. This is called democracy, but it is not clear that this makes any difference. Who is to protect the individual faculty member from the equally-cheap-to-exercise personal preferences of his colleague when they assume the administrative powers?

Everyone wants security, if the cost is zero. And the higher the cost, the less they will want. But there is a particular set of employees who will most desire tenure. These are older people whose productivity is nearing or past its peak. By securing tenure at existing current wages, they will be assured of continuing employment, despite declining productivity, at a high wage rate. At the same time, all current employees on short-term contracts will be happy to switch to a tenure contract if no cut in pay is involved, for then it would appear as though they had obtained job security without any cost to themselves with all the cost being dumped on the employer. An employer will, of course, resist this, but the extent will depend upon the cost, and in a non-profit institution, the costs imposed on the administrator are lower than the same person would bear in the same kind of business if it were a profit-seeking enterprise. Hence the extent to which employers are induced to resist this demand is reduced, and tenure is more likely to exist, as are other forms of inefficiency.

But it should not be assumed that all the costs of tenure will be shifted by the employer to society at large. Actually they have also been shifted onto some of the employees. Nothing is guaranteed in a tenure contract as to the rate of advance of pay. The employer, once he has granted tenure, may subsequently resist pay increases until the margin between pay and productivity reflects the risk-bearing aspect mentioned earlier. As a partial defense the employees insist on provisions about the rate at which pay will advance. But the beginning rate under tenure will be lower than under non-tenure as a result of the risks of long-term contracts. In such arrangements, who prove to be gainers and losers—since this is essentially a vast insurance-type gamble? Individuals who live longest and turn out to be below average in productivity growth gain at the expense of the short-lived in this profession and those whose productivity increases the most. Those who had short lives received less of their total productivity. The risk the employer bore was that they, later in life, would be less productive and at that time their wages would not be decreasing. Hence in the earlier part of his career the employee is underpaid in the gamble that later he will over-collect.

Tenure Benefits the Old

Another gamble also occurs. Those who prove to be most productive will have received less than they would have received without tenure, even though they earn more than the average worker. And those who turn out to be below average in productivity growth will earn more than they would have received without tenure, but still they earn less than the average of better workers.

Mobility is penalized because every new job means the task of resolving some doubt in the new employer's mind. This implies that older and less able people, who are now getting a reward more than they are worth, will find very few new job offers elsewhere at equivalent or better wages, since no new employer is likely to induce a person to leave a job at which he is currently being overpaid. On the other hand, the better men will be paid less than they are worth and so should be receiving offers from other employers who will propose to narrow the gap.

This does not mean that new employers will want to hire only the best people; rather, it means that better people are more willing to move because of the discrepancy of their wages and productivity. Tenure benefits the older, less able people at the expense of the younger, more able and shorter-lived individuals.

If one goes one step further and assumes that in such a non-profit organization the older people are in authority, as seems likely by virtue of the weaker pecuniary productivity rewards because "profits" are less efficiently used, one would expect the interests of older people to be given greater consideration than that of younger people. This would be evident in the way facilities and privileges were rationed among the many employees.

The drive for tenure involves compelling most, but not all, employees to accept the tenure system. In many colleges, all staff members must acquire tenure—as it is euphemistically stated—at the end of a fixed number of years outside the tenure system. Any member who wants to continue without tenure at a higher wage for a non-tenure appointment is not allowed to do so. To permit this would undermine the position of those in the tenure situation exactly in the same way that a non-member of a cartel is able to undermine the cartel.

Furthermore, if wages are tied to rank, and rank to tenure, it becomes impossible for the younger, more able men to bargain for higher pay without tenure. They are prevented from foregoing tenure in the interests of a higher current wage. In this way, tenure is harder to break. If this is so, why should anyone be allowed to teach without tenure? For two reasons: In the first place, a trial period gives the administrator and his colleagues a better idea of what a person's productivity will be—or was. Also, they can get a better idea of whether he will be a compatible, docile, agreeable colleague or will be obstreperous and overly competitive in what he seeks to do. And if one's colleagues are involved in determining appointment and promotion, those issues become even more pertinent.

This system has been called democratic. Indeed it is democratic, along the same lines of democracy that would prevail if auto manufacturers were to be the democratic deciders as to who could make cars, or as in fact the medical profession does in deciding who can be a doctor. The question of democracy is a red herring. The correct question is whose tastes and preferences are to be satisfied and who is to bear the gains and the costs, the consumer or one's fellow employees? The second reason for not insisting on tenure for every member is that a non-profit institution may become a "loss" institution and will then have to curtail expenditures. This will mean cutting the staff. But who is to go if all have tenure? To protect those who have tenure, a buffer, the non-permanent group, is created to absorb the possible shock.

Empirical Observations

The validity of the preceding analysis is empirically verified. First, non-profit-seeking schools will be observed to have a higher incidence of tenure than will private profit-seeking schools. And there are both types, so this can be checked. There are hundreds, if not thousands, of privately owned profit-seeking schools. Some survive entirely from student fees. Some of our best accounting and engineering schools are profit-seeking, financed entirely from student fees, as are some girls' colleges.

Schools of advertising, art, music, theatre, television, design, secretarial work, foreign languages, law, nursing, beauty shop work and barbering are straight profit-seeking institutions. Here student consumer sovereignty exists jointly with the explicitly imposed costs of inefficient behavior. If tenure is not more frequent in non-profit education institutions the analysis is refuted.

The analysis further implies that tenure would be observed more frequently where rank and pay are tied to tenure than where rank and pay are not tied to tenure. This can be illustrated by noting that the extension division at the University teaches much the same courses as the regular university, and in it we find full-cost pricing for the student and no tenure nor is pay related to age. The summer session, which operates on the same basis, also operates with no tenure. Furthermore, it does not invite full professors to teach, because they don't earn their way compared with the younger, lower-salaried men. That fact is sometimes concealed by asserting that the young men "need" the jobs.

Tenure Protects Truth

The analysis presented so far sought to explain why it developed and why it continues to persist. It did not seek to justify tenure. Essentially the analysis said that it developed because it was one way to further the interests of people working for non-profit institutions. However, some proponents of tenure argue that it insures a higher reliability of the truth being taught, or that it gets more of it taught. And some argue that it is necessary if the truth is to be sought and taught. With respect to the first argument, more truth may in fact be taught, but the reason is that if tenure is granted, more resources are devoted to teachers than would otherwise be diverted to them. But by what criterion is this judged desirable—except that of inducing a greater demand for one's services?

Or maybe the argument is that greater job security enhances the teaching of the truth. It certainly does, but it also induces one to take his job less carefully and to devote more time to his politics or social ambitions. The net effect is by no means necessarily or even probably favorable to greater truth. Neither theoretical analysis nor empirical evidence suggests that result nor is there anything in economics to imply that compulsory lifetime contracts do so. In truth quite the contrary is implied.

Truth Through Competition

Could it not be argued alternatively that it is indeed fortunate that colleges are not privately owned profit-seeking enterprises, for then tenure would not have survived, and without it the search for the truth would have been dissuaded? Therefore these arrangements have grown up in order that the inefficiencies of tenure can be borne in order to preserve the exposition of truth. This would make a virtue of a necessity, if tenure were necessary. To argue that it is, is to ignore the relevance and the effect of competition. If there were but one employer of teachers from whose decision there could be no escape, then suppression of the truth would be cheap. With alternative available employers, suppression by one would not prevent other employers from hiring the intimidated individual and paying him to speak his piece. It would pay another employer to hire him if what he had to say were wanted by other people. A new employer may pay less than the former employer. However much this may be distressing to the employee, there is no cause for anyone to be concerned. No one has any right to compel another person to support him in the style he would like to have, merely because he is, or believes he is, seeking the truth. And yet that is exactly the position taken when one argues that no person ought to be discharged for teaching the truth.

The news industry is an excellent example of competition. Any newspaper or radio station owner who prints or broadcasts false news will be hurt by other competitors who reveal the truth—not just the polite superficial truth, but all the truth in its most lurid details. Competition among newspapers for profits by catering to the customers' pocketbooks brings out the truth.

A news agency could suppress honesty and truth only if it were a protected monopoly, but it would not succeed in the face of competitors who would seek profits by appealing to the consumer's desire for the truth. The truth in news reporting is not the result of tenure for the reporters or editors, nor of a code of ethics, and by no stretch of one's imagination could you understand why reporters are not just as much in search of the truth as are teachers.

Truth or Romance?

Competition does exist among schools. Schools that do not satisfy students' desires will lose their students; the repute of the school will decline among those people who want honesty in teaching. People who do have different ideas about the truth or who care more for indoctrination in some other ideal will support schools that satisfy their demands, as they are entitled to do. We must acknowledge that such schools have a valid place in our society unless we were to seek to impose our tastes on everyone—a position somewhat incompatible with voluntaristic, individualistic principles.

A criticism of this substitution of competition for tenure is that students and parents can't tell good teaching from bad teaching. There are ways of discerning good from bad; they can also tell the difference between hard and easy, interesting and dull. Would one say that students who go to the Massachusetts Institute of Technology or the California Institute of Technology do so without knowledge of the best engineering schools? If the students can't tell good from bad teaching, one has to wonder how they manage to choose among colleges?

What if consumers do not want the truth and instead want romance and illusion? The theatre and the movies are much more efficient at that than the teachers are. And in any event, so much the worse for tenure, for then those who want tenure to foster the truth, if it did, would be trying to impose their preference on other people. To assert that some college officials do not always want the truth and that some alumni or outsiders criticize the teacher and seek to get him fired is certainly true—and commendable. If the truth harms or offends some people, in a free society why should they not have the right to use their resources to combat it? Others may desire the truth even more, and be willing to pay for it.

Ideas Are Costly

If someone prefers to buy up the time of teachers to induce them not to speak the truth, he is entitled to do so. And if he tries to buy up a college president in order to persuade him not to continue to hire a certain teacher, he is entitled to do so. Teachers have no claim on the resources of society or of any person. The crucible of the truth is open competition among ideas, although ideas are costly.

In sum, the conclusion suggested is that tenure is neither necessary nor efficient. Its survival depends upon the absence of private ownership and also is encouraged by subsidization of education by non-customer income sources. Without a private profit-seeking system and without full-cost tuition, the demand for tenure increases, and the cost of granting it appears to be cheaper because the full costs are not imposed on those granting it. Competition among schools, teachers and students provides protection to the search for the truth without tenure.

Just as in the dissemination of news, the exposition of the search for the truth is tested in the open market for ideas and empirical verification. Truth is not something given the stamp of authority or validity by appointed persons. Authority cannot establish what people will believe is the truth. The individual must do that. Truth then is no higher an objective than voluntary individualism. The two are not incompatible. Indeed, what does one mean in the absence of the other?

COMPETITION, MONOPOLY, AND THE PURSUIT OF MONEY

ARMEN A. ALCHIAN AND REUBEN A. KESSEL

The Problem

Generally speaking, the observations of economists on the subject of monopoly fall into two classes. One set of observations, which flows directly from monopoly theory, is that resources in the competitive sector of the economy would be underutilized if used by monopolists. The other, which does not arise as an implication of either monopoly or competitive theory, consists of a series of observations of empirical phenomena: that monopolistic enterprises, by comparison with competitive enterprises, are characterized by rigid prices, stodgy managements, and relaxed, easygoing working conditions. Alternatively, it is alleged that employees of competitive enterprises work harder, managements are more aggressive and flexible, and pricing is more responsive to profit opportunities.[1]

Reprinted from Armen A. Alchian, *Economic Forces at Work* (Indianapolis: Liberty Fund, 1977), 151–76. This article was previously published in Universities-National Bureau Committee for Economic Research, *Aspects of Labor Economics* (Princeton: Princeton University Press, 1962), 157–83. Copyright 1962 by the National Bureau of Economic Research.

1. Hicks concludes: "The best of all monopoly profits is a quiet life." This conclusion appears in a theoretical paper on monopoly; yet it does not flow from the theory presented.

Preceding the foregoing quotation is: "Now, as Professor Bowley and others have pointed out, the variation in monopoly profit for some way on either side of the highest profit output may often be small (in the general case it will depend on the difference between the slopes of the marginal revenue and marginal cost curves); and if this is so, the subjective costs involved in securing a close adaption to the most profitable output may well outweigh the meager gains offered. It seems not at all unlikely that people in monopolistic positions will often be people with sharply rising subjective costs; if this is so, they are likely to exploit their advantage much more by not bothering to get very near the position of maximum profit, than by straining themselves to get very close to it. The best of all monopoly profits is a quiet life." John R. Hicks, "Annual Survey of Economic Theory: The Theory of Monopoly," *Econometrica*, January 1935, p. 8.

To regard this second class of observations as not an implication of either monopoly or competitive theory is only partly correct. More correctly, these observations are inconsistent with the implications of the standard profit or wealth-maximization postulate. For analyzing the behavior described by Hicks, the pecuniary wealth-maximization postulate is clearly inappropriate and should be replaced by a utility-maximization postulate.

Utility Maximization, Not Wealth Maximization

That a person seeks to maximize his utility says little more than that he makes consistent choices. In order to employ this postulate as an engine of analysis, one must also specify what things are regarded as desirable. This is the class that includes all those things of which a person prefers more rather than less: money, wealth, love, esteem, friends, ease, health, beauty, meat, gasoline, etc.[2] Then, assuming that a person is willing to substitute among these variables—that is, he will give up wealth in return for more peace and quiet, or better-looking secretaries, or more-cordial employees, or better weather—the behavior described by Hicks can be analyzed.

Economics cannot stipulate the exchange value that these things have for any particular person, but it can and does say that whatever his preference patterns may be, the less he must pay for an increase in one of them, the more it will be utilized. This principle, of course, is merely the fundamental demand theorem of economics—that the demand for any good is a negative function of its price. And price here means not only the pecuniary price but the cost of whatever has to be sacrificed.

For predicting the choice of productive inputs by business firms, where only the pecuniary aspects of the factors are of concern, the narrower special-case postulate of pecuniary wealth is usually satisfactory. But this special-case postulate fails when a wider class of business activities is examined. Therefore we

2. The following impression is not uncommon. "To say that the individual maximizes his satisfaction is a perfectly general statement. It says nothing about the individual's psychology of behavior, [and] is, therefore, devoid of empirical content." T. Scitovsky, "A Note on Profit Maximization and Its Implications," *Review of Economic Studies*, 1943, pp. 57–60. But this is also true of profit or wealth maximization—unless one says what variables affect profit or wealth and in what way. And so in utility maximization, one must similarly add a postulate stating what variables affect satisfaction or utility. This leads to meaningful implications refutable, in principle, by observable events. For example, an individual will increase his use of those variables that become cheaper. Utility maximization, like wealth maximization, is not a mere sterile truism.

propose to use the general case consistently, even though in some special cases simpler hypotheses, contained within this more general hypothesis, would be satisfactory.[3]

An example of the power of the generalized utility-maximizing postulate is provided by Becker.[4] He shows that under the more general postulate a person, deliberately and even in full knowledge of the consequences for business profits or personal pecuniary wealth, will choose to accept a lower salary or

---

3. Failure to give adequate heed to the special-case properties of wealth maximization may have been responsible for some complaints about the inadequacy of economic theory and may even have led to the curious belief that people themselves change according to which postulate is used. For example, Scitovsky says:

"The puritan psychology of valuing money for its own sake, and not for the enjoyments and comforts it might yield, is that of the ideal entrepreneur as he was conceived in the early days of capitalism. The combination of frugality and industry, the entrepreneurial virtues, is calculated to insure the independence of the entrepreneur's willingness to work from the level of his income. The classical economists, therefore, were justified in assuming that the entrepreneur aims at maximizing his profits. They were concerned with a type of businessman whose psychology happened to be such that for him maximizing profits was identical with maximizing satisfaction.

"The entrepreneur today may have lost some of the frugality and industry of his forefathers; nevertheless, the assumption that he aims at maximizing his profits is still quite likely to apply to him—at least as a first approximation. For this assumption is patently untrue only about people who regard work as plain drudgery; a necessary evil, with which they have to put up in order to earn their living and the comforts of life. The person who derives satisfaction from his work—other than that yielded by the income he receives for it—will to a large extent be governed by ambition, spirit of emulation and rivalry, pride in his work, and similar considerations, when he plans the activity. We believe that the entrepreneur usually belongs in this last category" (ibid.).

Aside from the dubious validity of (1) alleged differences between the entrepreneurs of the "early days" of capitalism and those of today, and (2) the allegation that the early entrepreneur was one whose utility function had only a single variable—wealth—in it, the more general analysis obviates the urge to set up two different and inconsistent behavior postulates, as if people were schizophrenic types—utility maximizers when consumers and wealth maximizers when businessmen.

The special-case property of the wealth-maximizing postulate has been noted by M. W. Reder ("A Reconsideration of the Marginal Productivity Theory," *Journal of Political Economy* [October 1947]: 450–58). But in suggesting alternatives he did not postulate the more general one, which includes the valid applications of the special-case postulate as well as many more, without leading to the invalid implications of the special-case postulate.

4. Gary S. Becker, *The Economics of Discrimination* (University of Chicago Press, 1957).

smaller rate of return on invested capital in exchange for nonpecuniary income in the form of, say, working with pretty secretaries, nonforeigners, or whites. The difference in money return between what an entrepreneur could earn and what he does earn when he chooses to discriminate is an equalizing difference that will not be eliminated by market pressures. If these persisting, equalizing differences exist, their size, and consequently the extent of discrimination, will differ when institutional arrangements lead to differences in the relative costs of income in pecuniary form relative to income in nonpecuniary form. Thus, if one can determine the direction in which relative costs are affected by activities or variables that enhance a person's utility, then it should be possible to observe corresponding differences in behavior.

Monopolistic versus Competitive Behavior

The wealth-maximizing postulate seems to imply that both competitive and monopolistic enterprises pursue profits with equal vigor and effectiveness, that their managements are equally alert and aggressive, and that prices are just as flexible in competitive as in monopolized markets. Both the competitive and monopoly model imply that the assets of an enterprise, be it a monopolist or competitive firm, will be utilized by those for whom these assets have the greatest economic value. One might object to this implication of similarity between competition and monopoly by arguing that when a monopolistic enterprise is not making the most of its pecuniary economic opportunities it runs less risk of being driven out of business than a similarly mismanaged competitive enterprise. The answer to this is that despite the absence of competition in product markets, those who can most profitably utilize monopoly powers will acquire control over them: competition in the capital markets will allocate monopoly rights to those who can use them most profitably. Therefore, so long as free capital markets are available, the absence of competition in product markets does not imply a different quality of management in monopolistic as compared with competitive enterprises. Only in the case of nontransferable assets (human monopoly rights and powers like those commanded by Bing Crosby) does classical theory, given free capital market arrangements, admit a difference between competition and monopoly with respect to the effectiveness with which these enterprises pursue profits.[5]

5. For a statement of this position, see Becker, *The Economics of Discrimination*, p. 38. Becker argues that, insofar as monopoly rights are randomly distributed and cannot be transferred, there are no forces operating to distribute these resources to those for whom

The preceding argument implies that there is no difference in the proportion of inefficiently operated firms among monopolistic as compared with competitive enterprises. (Inefficiency here means that a situation is capable of being changed so that a firm could earn more pecuniary income with no loss in nonpecuniary income or else can obtain more nonpecuniary income with no loss in pecuniary income.) As Becker has shown, discrimination against Negroes in employment is not necessarily a matter of business inefficiency. It can be viewed as an expression of a taste, and one's a priori expectation is that discrimination is characterized by a negatively sloped demand curve. From this viewpoint, discrimination against Negroes by business enterprises, whether competitors or monopolists, would not lessen even if managements were convinced that discrimination reduced their pecuniary income. Presumably, the known sacrifice of pecuniary income is more than compensated for by the gain in nonpecuniary income. But if discrimination does not constitute business inefficiency, then the frequency of discrimination against Negroes ought to be just as great in competitive as in monopolistic enterprises, since both are presumed to be equally efficient. This implication is apparently inconsistent with existing evidence. Becker's data indicate that Negroes are discriminated against more frequently by monopolistic enterprises.[6] But why do monopolistic enterprises discriminate against Negroes more than do competitive enterprises? One would expect that those who have a taste for discrimination against Negroes would naturally gravitate to those economic activities that, for purely pecuniary reasons, do not employ Negroes. Free choice of economic activities implies a distribution of resources that would minimize the costs of satisfying tastes for discrimination. Consequently the managements of competitive enterprises ought to discriminate against Negroes neither more nor less than those of monopolistic enterprises.

If there is greater discrimination by monopolists than by competitive enterprises, and if it cannot be explained by arguing either that people with tastes for discrimination also have special talents related to monopolistic enterprises or that monopolists are in some sense less efficient businessmen, what, then, explains Becker's data and similar observations? More generally, what is the explanation for the contentions that monopolists pursue pecuniary wealth less

---

they are most valuable. Consequently monopolists, when rights are nontransferable, would be less efficient, on the average, than competitive firms.

6. Ibid., p. 40, Table 2.

vigorously, do not work as hard, have more lavish business establishments, etc.? It is to this problem that this paper is addressed.

Monopoly and Profit Control

Stigler and others have pointed out that monopolies, both labor and product, are creatures of the state in a sense which is not true of competitive enterprises.[7] Monopolies typically are protected against the hazards of competition, not simply by their ability to compete but by the state's policy of not permitting competitors to enter monopolized markets. Laws are enacted that encourage and lead to the creation of monopolies in particular markets. Monopolies so created are beholden to the state for their existence—the state giveth, the state taketh away. Accordingly, they constrain their business policies by satisfying the requirements that they shall do what is necessary to maintain their monopoly status.

Public utilities are an example. Under this head one should include not only gas, electric, and water companies but all franchised and licensed industries. Railroads, busses, airlines, and taxis fall in this category of business for which permission of a public authority is required, and for which rate and profit regulation exists. For many other businesses, entry regulation exists: commercial and savings banks, savings and loan associations, insurance companies, and the medical profession. All these are formally regulated monopolies, since they are licensed and operated with the approval of the state. Their cardinal sin is to be too profitable.[8] This constraint upon monopolists does not exist for firms operating in competitive markets. This difference in constraints implies differences between the business policies of competitive firms and those of monopolies. The remainder of this paper is devoted to indicating specifically the character of the constraints that are postulated and exploring the observable implications of this postulate.

Even a firm that has successfully withstood the test of open competition

7. George J. Stigler, "The Extent and Bases of Monopoly," *American Economic Review* (June 1942), Supplement Part 2, p. 1; H. Gregg Lewis, "The Labor Monopoly Problem: A Positive Program," *Journal of Political Economy* (August 1951): 277; C. E. Lindblom, *Unions and Capitalism* (Yale University Press, 1949), p. 214; and Milton Friedman, "Some Comments on the Significance of Labor Unions for Economic Policy," in *The Impact of the Union*, ed. David M. Wright (Harcourt Brace, 1951), p. 214.

8. The notorious suggestion of the medical profession that doctors not drive around town in expensive Cadillacs when visiting patients is an example of the point being made.

without government protection may manifest the behavior of a protected monopoly. Thus a firm like General Motors may become very large and outstanding and acquire a large share of a market just as a protected monopoly does. If, in addition, its profits are large, it will fear that public policy or state action may be directed against it, just as against a state-created monopoly. Such a firm constrains its behavior much in the style of a monopoly whose profit position is protected but also watched by the state. This suggests that the distinction between publicly regulated monopolies and nonregulated monopolies is a false distinction for this problem. As the possibility of state action increases, a firm will adapt its behavior to that which the state deems appropriate. In effect, state regulation is implicitly present.

The cardinal sin of a monopolist, to repeat, is to be too profitable. Public regulation of monopolies is oriented about fixing final prices in order to enable monopolists to earn something like the going rate of return enjoyed by competitive firms. If monopolists are too profitable, pressures are exerted to reduce profits through lowering prices. Only if monopolists can demonstrate to regulatory authorities that they are not profitable enough are they permitted to raise prices.

Implications

If regulated monopolists are able to earn more than the permissible pecuniary rate of return, then "inefficiency" is a free good, because the alternative to inefficiency is the same pecuniary income and no "inefficiency." Therefore this profit constraint leads to a divergence between private and economic costs. However, it is easy to be naive about this inefficiency. More properly, it is not inefficiency at all but efficient utility maximizing through nonpecuniary gains. Clearly one class of nonpecuniary income is the indulgence of one's tastes in the kind of people with whom one prefers to associate. Specifically, this may take the form of pretty secretaries, of pleasant, well-dressed, congenial people who never say anything annoying, of lavish offices, of large expense accounts, of shorter working hours, of costly administrative procedures that reduce the wear and tear on executives rather than increasing the pecuniary wealth of the enterprise, of having secretaries available on a moment's notice by having them sitting around not doing anything, and of many others. It is important to recognize that to take income in nonpecuniary form is consistent with maximizing utility. What is important is not a matter of differences in tastes between monopolists and competitive firms, but differences in the terms of trade of pecuniary for nonpecuniary income. And given this difference in the relevant price or exchange ratios, the difference in the mix purchased should not be surprising.[9]

If wealth cannot be taken out of an organization in salaries or in other forms of personal pecuniary property, the terms of trade between pecuniary wealth and nonpecuniary business-associated forms of satisfaction turn against the former. More of the organization's funds will now be reinvested (which need not result in increased wealth) in ways that enhance the manager's prestige or status in the community. Or more money can be spent for goods and services that enhance the manager's and employees' utility. There can be more luxurious offices, more special services, and so forth, than would ordinarily result if their costs were coming out of personal wealth.

For the total amount of resources used, these constrained expenditure patterns necessarily yield less utility than the unconstrained. The man who spends a dollar with restrictions will need less than a dollar to get an equivalent satisfaction if he can spend it without the restriction. This constrained optimum provides the answer to the question, If a person does spend the wealth of a business as business-connected expenditures for thick rugs and beautiful secretaries, can they not be treated simply as a substitute for household consumption, since he can be regarded as voluntarily choosing to spend his wealth in the business rather than in the home? The answer is that business spending is a more constrained, even if voluntary, choice. This whole analysis is merely an illustration of the effects of restricting the operation of the law of comparative advantage by reducing the size of the market (or range of alternatives).

Employment policies will also reflect the maximization of utility. Assume that an employer prefers clean-cut, friendly, sociable employees. If two available employees are equally productive, but only one is white, native born, Chris-

9. Usually in economics, consumers are presumed to maximize utility subject to fixed income or wealth. What is the wealth or income constraint here? In one sense it is not merely wealth or income that is the pertinent limitation. Many people have access to the use and allocation of resources even though they don't own them. An administrator can assign offices and jobs; he can affect the way company or business resources are used. In all of these decisions, he will be influenced by the effects on his own situation. Therefore to gauge his behavior by the usual wealth or income limitation is to eliminate from consideration a wider range of activities that do not fall within the usual "wealth" or ownership limitation. By straining it is possible to incorporate even this kind of activity with the wealth constraint but we find it more convenient for exposition not to do so. In this paper, in a sense, we are discussing the institutional arrangements which determine to what extent constraints are of one type rather than another.

tian, and attractive, the other will not get the job. And if the other employee's wages are reduced to offset this, it will take a greater cut or equilibrating difference to offset this in a monopoly. Why? Because the increase in take-home profits provided by the cost reduction is smaller (if it is increased at all) in the monopoly or state-sheltered firm. Thus one would expect to find a lower fraction of "other" employees in "monopolies" and other areas of sheltered competition.

What this means is that the wages paid must be high enough to attract the "right" kind of employees. At these wages the supply of the "other" kind will be plentiful. A rationing problem exists, so that the buyer, when he offers a higher price than would clear the market with respect to pecuniary productive aspects, clears the market by imposing other tests, like congeniality, looks, and so on. For the right kind of employee the price is not above the market-clearing price. In a competitive situation this price differential would not persist because its elimination would all redound to the benefit of the owners, whereas in monopoly it will persist because the reduction in costs cannot be transformed into equally large take-home pecuniary wealth for the owners.

The question may be raised, Even if all this is true of a regulated monopoly like a public utility, what about unregulated, competitively superior monopolies? Why should they act this way? The answer is, as pointed out earlier, that the distinction between regulated and unregulated monopolies is a false one. All monopolies are subject to regulation or the threat of destruction through antitrust action. And one of the criteria that the courts seem to consider in evaluating whether or not a firm is a "good" monopoly is its profitability.[10] It behooves an unregulated monopoly, if it wants to remain one, not to appear to be too profitable.

The owners of a monopoly, regulated or "not," therefore have their property rights attenuated because they do not have unrestricted access to or personal use of their company's wealth. This suggests that the whole analysis can be formulated, not in terms of monopoly and competition, as we have chosen to for present purposes, but in terms of private property rights. There is basically no analytic difference between the two, since an analysis made in terms of monopoly and competition identifies and emphasizes circumstances that affect property rights. The same analysis can be applied to nonprofit organizations, governments, unions, and state-owned and other "nonowned" institutions, with almost identical results.

10. See Aaron Director and Edward H. Levi, "Trade Regulation," *Northwestern Law Review* (1956): 286 ff.

One word of clarification—the contrast here is between monopoly and competition, not between corporate and noncorporate firms. We are analyzing differences in implications for behavior that arise from factors other than the corporate structure of the firm. Although there may be differences between corporate, diffused ownership firms and single proprietorships that may affect the many kinds of behavior discussed in this paper, we have been unable to derive them from the corporate aspect. Nor are those features derived from considerations of size per se—however much this may affect behavior.[11]

The preceding propositions stated that more of some form of behavior would be observed among monopolies. But more than what and of what? More than would be observed in competitive industries. It is not asserted that every monopolist will prefer more than every competitor; instead, it is said that whatever the relative tastes of various individuals all those in a monopolistic situation pay less for their actions than they would in a competitive contest. And the way to test this is not to cite a favorable comparison based on one monopolist and one competitor. Rather the variations in individual preferences must be allowed to average out by random sampling from each class.

Tests of the Analysis

What observable populations can be compared in testing these implications? One pair of populations are the public utilities and private competitive corporations. Public utilities are monopolies, in that entry by competitors is prohibited. Yet, as indicated earlier, the utility is not allowed to exercise its full monopoly powers either in acquiring or in distributing pecuniary wealth as dividends to its owners. The owners therefore have relatively weak incentives to try to increase their profits through more-efficient management or operation beyond (usually) 6 percent. But they do have relatively strong incentives to use the resources of the public utility for their own personal interests, but in ways that will count as company costs. Nor does the public utility regulatory body readily detect such activities, because its incentives to do so are even weaker than those of the stockholders. The regulatory body's survival function is the

---

11. We were originally tempted to believe that the same theory being applied here could be applied to corporate versus noncorporate institutions, where the corporate form happens to involve many owners. Similarly the size factor could also be analyzed via the effects on the costs and rewards of various choice opportunities. Subsequent analysis suggests that many of the appealing differences between corporate, dispersed ownership and individual proprietorship proved to be superficial.

elimination of publicly detectable inefficiencies. Furthermore, the utility regulatory board has a poor criterion of efficiency because it lacks competitive standards.

Public utility managements, whether or not they are also stockholders, will engage in activities that raise costs even if they eat up profits. Management will be rational (i.e., utility maximizing and efficient) if it uses company funds to hire pleasant and congenial employees and to buy its supplies from salesmen who have these same virtues. They cost more, of course, but how does the regulatory commission decide that these are unjustifiable expenditures—even though stockholders would prefer larger profits (which they aren't allowed to have) and customers would prefer lower product prices? Office furniture and equipment will be of higher quality than otherwise. Fringe benefits will be greater and working conditions more pleasant. The managers will be able to devote a greater part of their business time to community and civic programs. They will reap the prestige rewards given to the "statesman-businessman" class of employers. Vacations will be longer and more expensive. Time off for sick leave and for civic duties will be greater. Buildings and equipment will be more beautiful. Public utility advertising will be found more often in magazines and papers appealing to the intellectual or the culturally elite, because this is a low-"cost" way of enhancing the social status of the managers and owners. Larger contributions out of company resources to education, science, and charity will be forthcoming—not because private competitors are less appreciative of these things, but because they cost monopolists less.[12]

12. We could compare a random sample of secretaries working for public utilities with a random sample of secretaries working for competitive businesses. The former will be prettier—no matter whom we select as our judges (who must not know what hypothesis we are testing when they render their decision). The test, however, really should be made by sampling among the secretaries who are working for equal-salaried executives in an attempt to eliminate the income effect on demand. Another implication is that the ratio of a secretary's salary to her supervisor's salary will be higher for a public utility—on the grounds that beauty commands a price. Other nonpecuniary desirable attributes of secretaries also will be found to a greater extent in public utilities (as well as in nonprofit enterprises) than in private competitive firms. In a similar way, all of the preceding suggested implications about race, religion, and sex could be tested.

Another comparison can be made. Consider the sets of events in the business and in the home of the public utility employee or owner having a given salary or wealth. The ratio of the thickness of the rug in the office to that of the rug at home will be greater for the public utility than for the private competitive firm employee or owner. The ratio of the value of the available company car to the family car's value will be higher for the public

Job security, whether in the form of seniority or tenure, is a form of increased wealth for employees. Since it makes for more pleasant employer-employee relations, it is a source of utility for employers. The incentive or willingness of owners to grant this type of wealth to employees and thereby increase their own utility is relatively strong because profits are not the opportunity costs of this choice. The owners of a competitive firm, on the other hand, would have to pay the full price either in profits or in competitive disadvantage. Therefore the viability of such activities is lower in that type of firm. The relative frequency or extent of job security should be higher in monopolies and employee turnover rates lower. Also, the incidence of tenure in private educational institutions will be less than in nonprofit or state-operated educational institutions—if the foregoing analysis is correct.[13]

The relative incidence of employee cooperatives will also provide a test. Some employee cooperatives are subsidized by employers. This subsidy often takes the form of free use of company facilities and of employees for operating the cooperative. For any given set of attitudes of employers towards employee cooperatives, costs are lower for monopolists with "excess" profits. Consequently their frequency will be greater among these enterprises.

Inability to keep excess profits in pecuniary form implies that monopolists are more willing than competitive enterprises to forgo them in exchange for other forms of utility-enhancing activities within the firm. Fringe benefits, cooperatives, and special privileges for certain employees will be more common. Employees whose consumption preferences do not induce them to use the cooperatives or fringe benefits are not necessarily stupid if they complain of this diversion of resources. But their complaints do reflect their differences in tastes and their ignorance of the incentives and reward patterns that impinge upon owners and administrators. Instead of complaining, they might better seek benefits of special interest to themselves. But since this involves a power play within the firm, the senior people are likely to be the ones who win most often. Hence one would expect to find such benefits more closely tailored to the preferences of the higher administrative officials than would be observed in a competitive business.

Wage policies will also differ in monopoly and nonmonopoly enterprises. If

---

utility than for the private competitive firm. And similarly for the ratios of secretary's beauty to wife's beauty, decorations in the office, travel expenses, etc.

13. See Armen A. Alchian, "Private Property and the Relative Cost of Tenure," *The Public Stake in Union Power*, ed. P. Bradley (University of Virginia Press, 1958), pp. 350–71.

business should fall off, the incentive to resort to fringe or wage reductions (unpleasant under any circumstances) will be weaker for a public utility because the potential savings in profits, if profits are not below the maximum permissible level, cannot be as readily captured by the management or stockholders. One would expect to find wages falling less in hard times, and one would also expect a smaller turnover and unemployment of personnel. The fact that these same implications might be derived from the nature of the demand for the utility's product does not in itself upset the validity of these propositions. But it does make the empirical test more difficult.

Seniority, tenure, employee cooperatives, and many other fringe benefits—instead of increased money salaries or payments—can be composed of mixtures of pecuniary and nonpecuniary benefits, though the inducement to adopt them despite their inefficiency is enhanced by the relatively smaller sacrifice imposed on the owners of organizations in monopolistic situations, as defined here. The relative cost of take-home wealth for the owners is higher; hence they are more willing to utilize other consumption channels.[14]

Constraints on the opportunity to keep profits that are above the allowable limit reduce the incentive to spend money for profitable expansion of services. An upper limit on profits, with strong protection from competition but no assurance of protection from losses of overexpansion, will bias the possible rewards downward in comparison with those of competitive business. An implication of this is "shortages" of public utility services. Despite the fact that prices are above the cost of providing some services, the latter will not necessarily be available. It is better to wait until the demand is already existent and expansion is demanded by the authorities. The possible extra profits are an attenuated inducement.

But these implications hold only if the public utility is earning its allowable limit of profits on investment. If it is losing money—and there is no guarantee against it—stockholders' take-home pay will be curtailed by inefficiency. Until profits reach the take-home limit, profitable and efficient operations will be desirable. If the state regulatory commission is slow to grant price increases in re-

---

14. The other commonly advanced reasons for such benefits or "inefficiencies" are the income tax on pecuniary wealth and the influence of unions. The former force is obvious; the latter is the effect of desires by union officials to strengthen their position by emphasizing the employee members' benefits to the union administration, as is done in many fringe benefits. But whether or not these latter factors are present, the one advanced here is an independent factor implying differences between monopoly and competition.

sponse to cost increases, the utilities should find their profits reduced below the allowable limit during a period of inflation. As a result there should be a tightening up or elimination, or both, of some of the effects predicted in the preceding discussion.[15] One would expect the opposite to occur during periods of deflation.

The present analysis also suggests that there may be an economic rationale for the "shock theory" of wage adjustments. This theory asserts that the profit-reducing wage increases imposed by labor will shock management into greater efficiencies. Suppose that monopolies are induced to trade pecuniary wealth (because they are not allowed to keep it) for nonpecuniary forms of income financed out of business expenditures. This means that under the impact of higher wage costs and lower profits the monopolies can now proceed to restore profit rates. Since some of their profit possibilities have been diverted into so-called nonpecuniary forms of income, higher labor costs will make realized profits, broadly interpreted, at least a little smaller. In part, at least, the increased pecuniary wages will come at the expense of nonpecuniary benefits, which will be reduced in order to restore profit levels. Actually, the shock effect does not produce increases in efficiency. Instead, it revises the pattern of distribution of benefits. Left unchanged is the rate of pecuniary profits—if these were formerly at their allowable, but not economic, limit.

Evidence relevant for testing the hypothesis presented here has been produced by the American Jewish Congress, which surveyed the occupations of Jewish and non-Jewish Harvard Business School graduates. The data consist of a random sample of 224 non-Jewish and a sample of 128 Jewish MBAs.[16] The 352 Harvard graduates were classified by ten industry categories: (1) agriculture, forestry, and fisheries, (2) mining, (3) construction, (4) transporta-

---

15. This analysis suggests that, with the decline in profitability of railroads, the principle of seniority advancement in railroad management has become relatively less viable. Similar arguments are applicable for other fringe benefits. With respect to negotiation with unions, it implies that railroad managements will more vigorously resist giving the unions extravagantly large concessions because these costs are being borne by owners.

The analysis also implies that unions do better in dealing with monopolistic as contrasted with competitive industries.

16. The existence of these data became known to the authors as a result of an article that appeared in the *New York Times* on the first day of the conference at which this paper was presented. Subsequently the American Jewish Congress released a paper, "Analysis of Jobs Held by Jewish and by Non-Jewish Graduates of the Harvard Graduate School of Business Administration," which contains the data reported here.

tion, communication, and other public utilities, (5) manufacturing, (6) whole-sale and retail trade, (7) finance, insurance, and real estate, (8) business services, (9) amusement, recreation, and related services, and (10) professional and related services.

Categories (4) and (7) must be regarded as relatively monopolized. Therefore, if the hypothesis presented here is correct, the relative frequency of Jews in these two fields is lower than it is for all fields combined.[17] The relative frequency of Jews in all fields taken together, in the entire sample, is 36 percent. These data show that the frequency of Jews—74 MBAs—in the two monopolized fields is less than 18 percent. If a sample of 352, of whom 36 percent are Jews, is assigned so that 74 are in monopolized and 278 in nonmonopolized fields, the probability that an assignment random with respect to religion will result in as few as 18 percent Jews in monopolized fields (and over 41 percent in nonmonopolized fields) is less than 0.0005. This evidence, therefore, is consistent with the hypothesis presented.

One might object to classifying all finance, insurance, and real estate as monopolized fields. This classification includes the subcategories of banking, credit agencies, investment companies, security and commodity brokers, dealers and exchanges, other finance services, insurance, and real estate. Of these, only insurance and banking are regulated monopolies. If only these two subcategories are used, then there are 6 Jews among a group of 39, or a frequency of less than 15 percent. If a sample of 352, of whom 36 percent are Jews, is assigned so that 39 are in monopolized and 313 in nonmonopolized fields, the probability that an assignment that is random with respect to religion will result in as few as 15 percent Jews in the monopolized fields (and over 39 percent in the nonmonopolized fields) is less than 0.005. This evidence is also consistent with the hypothesis presented.

Applications to Labor Unions

This application of monopoly analysis need not be restricted to public utilities. Any regulated activity or one that regulates entry into work should show the same characteristics. Labor unions, because of their control over entry or because of exclusive union representation in bargaining, have monopoly potential. Insofar as a union is able to use that potential to raise wages above the

---

17. Similarly, one would expect Jews and Negroes to be underrepresented among enterprises supplying goods and services to monopolists for the same reason that they are underrepresented as employees.

competitive level, unless the jobs are auctioned off, the rationing problem is a nonprice one. A "thoroughly unscrupulous" agent could, in principle, pocket the difference between the payment by the employer and the receipts to the employee, where this difference reflects the difference between the monopolistic and the competitive wage. The moral pressures and the state regulation of union monopoly operate against the existence of thoroughly unscrupulous union officers. But so long as the fruits of such monopoly are handed on to the employed members of the union, the state seems tolerant of monopoly unions. Because of the absence of free entry into the "union agent business," competitive bidding by prospective union agents will not pass on the potential monopoly gains fully to the laborers who do get the jobs.

The necessity of rationing jobs arises because the union agents or managers do not keep for themselves the entire difference between the monopoly wage and the lower competitive wage that would provide just the number of workers wanted. If they did keep it, there would be equilibrium without nonprice rationing. If any part of that difference is captured by the laborers, the quantity available will be excessive relative to the quantity demanded at the monopolized wage rate. The unwillingness of society to tolerate capture of all that difference by the union agents means that either it must be passed on to the workers, thus creating a rationing problem, or it must be indirectly captured by the union agents—not as pecuniary take-home pay, but indirectly as a utility derived from the expenditure of that difference in connection with union business.

To the extent that the monopoly gains are passed on, the preceding rationing problem and its implications exist. But to the extent that they are not, the union agents or persons in control of the monopoly organization will divert the monopoly gains to their own benefit, not through outright sale of the jobs to the highest bidder, but through such indirect devices as high initiation fees and membership dues. This ties the monopoly sale price to the conventional dues arrangement. Creation of large pension funds and special service benefits controlled by the unions redounds to the benefit of the union agents and officers in ways that are too well publicized as a result of recent hearings on union activities to need mention here.[18]

18. Relevant for the analysis of monopoly power is the character of the protection afforded by the state. For utilities, the state actively and directly uses its police powers to eliminate competition. For other monopolies—and this is especially relevant for union monopoly—the state permits the use of private police power to eliminate competition. The powers of the state passively and indirectly support these monopolies by refusing to

The membership of monopoly unions will tolerate such abuses to the point where the abuses offset the value of monopoly gains accruing to the employed members. We emphasize that these effects are induced by *both* the monopoly rationing problem and by the desire to convert the monopoly gains into non-pecuniary take-home pay for the union officers or dominant group. We conjecture that both elements are present; part of the monopoly gain is passed on to the workers, and part is captured as a nonpecuniary source of utility. When the former occurs, the rationing problem exists, and the agents or those in the union will exclude the less desirable type of job applicants—less desirable not in pecuniary productivity to the employer but as fellow employees and fellow members of the union. Admission will be easier for people whose cultural and personal characteristics conform to the interests of the existing members.[19] And admission will be especially difficult for those regarded as potential price-cutters in hard times or not to be counted on as faithful members with a strong sense of loyalty to the union. Minority groups and those who find they must accept lower wages because of some personal or cultural attribute, even though they are just as productive in a pecuniary sense to the employer, will be more willing to accept lower wages if threatened with the loss of their jobs. But these are the very types who will weaken the union's monopoly power. All of this suggests that young people, Negroes, Jews, and other minority or unorthodox groups will be underrepresented in monopolistic unions.[20]

There exists a symmetry in effects between nonprice rationing of admission to monopolistic trade unions and the allocation of rights to operate TV chan-

---

act against the exercise of private police power. This suggests that there ought to exist a link between those who have a comparative advantage in the exercise of private police powers (gangsters) and monopolies that eliminate competition through "strong-arm" techniques.

19. If the employer is the nonprice rationer—i.e., if the employer does the hiring and not the union, as is true for airplane pilots—he too will display a greater amount of discrimination in nonpecuniary attributes than with a competitive wage rate. If the wage rate has been raised so that he has to retain a smaller number of employees, he will retain those with the greater nonpecuniary productivity. If the wage rate would have fallen in response to increased supplies of labor but instead is kept up by wage controls, then the supply from which he could choose is larger, and again he will select those with the greater nonpecuniary attributes—assuming we are dealing with units of labor or equal pecuniary productivity.

20. See Reuben A. Kessel, "Price Discrimination in Medicine," *Journal of Law and Economics* (1958): 46 ff.

nels, airlines, radio stations, banks, savings and loan associations, public utilities, and the like. In the absence of the sale of these rights by the commission
or government agency charged with their allocation, nonprice rationing comes
into play. This implies that Negroes, Jews, and disliked minority groups of all
kinds will be underrepresented among the recipients of these rights. The symmetry between admission to monopolistic trade unions and the allocation of
monopoly rights over the sale of some good or service by a government agency
is not complete. The rights allocated by the government, but not by trade
unions, often become private property and can be resold. Therefore this analysis implies that entrance into these economic activities is more frequently
achieved by minority groups, as compared with the population as a whole,
through the purchase of outstanding rights.

The chief problem in verifying these implications is that of identifying relative degrees of monopoly power. If the classification is correct, there is a possibility of testing the analysis. A comparison of the logic of craft unions with
industrywide unions suggests that the former have greater monopoly powers.
Therefore if this classification is valid, the preceding analysis would be validated if the predicted results were observed.

For classic economic reasons, we conjecture that the craft unions are more
likely to have monopolistic powers than industrywide unions. Therefore we
would expect to observe more such discrimination in the first type of union
than in the second. And included in the category of craft unions are such organizations as the American Medical Association and any profession in which
admission involves the approval of a governing board.[21]

Conclusions and Conjectures

This analysis suggests that strong nonrestrained profit incentives serve the
interests of the relatively unpopular, unorthodox, and individualistic members
of society, who have relatively more to gain from the absence of restrictions.
Communists are perhaps the strongest case in point. They are strongly disliked
in our society and, as a matter of ideology, believe that profit incentives and private property are undesirable. Yet if this analysis is correct, one should find
communists overrepresented in highly competitive enterprises. Similar conclusions hold for ex-convicts, disbarred lawyers, defrocked priests, doctors
who have lost their licenses to practice medicine, and so forth.

21. For evidence of the existence of discrimination, see H. R. Northrup, *Organized
Labor and the Negro* (New York: Harper, 1944), chap. 1; and Kessel, op. cit., pp. 47 ff.

The analysis also suggests an inconsistency in the views of those who argue that profit incentives bring out the worst in people and at the same time believe that discrimination in terms of race, creed, or color is socially undesirable. Similarly, those concerned about the pressures towards conformity in our society, i.e., fears for a society composed of organization men, ought to have some interest in the competitiveness of our markets. It is fairly obvious that the pressures to conform are weaker for a speculator on a grain or stock exchange than they are for a junior executive of AT&T or a university professor with or without tenure.

REVIEW OF
THE ECONOMICS OF DISCRIMINATION

To say that this is the best book on the manifestations of discrimination would be no great compliment, since so little has been done elsewhere. But praise is due Becker for having written so superb an analysis in a relatively unexplored but important field. The reader will gain a richer understanding of discrimination. Furthermore many preconceptions and errors will be removed—to judge by this reviewer's experience. The theoretical analysis is beautifully, if concisely, presented, and many of the empirical implications are tested and measured. In other instances, illustrations are given of how to test the implications with observable quantitative data.

Were this review being written for a professional economics journal much would be said about its theoretical model. Emphasis would be placed on the fact that Becker has used the classical economic postulate that people try to maximize their utility—and not their wealth. Thus he treats wealth as one component or variable in a person's decision or utility function. Other components are of a non-pecuniary nature, such as the working environment and the kinds of people with whom a person associates in earning his wealth. This last attribute—the personal features of one's employees or employers—is such that some individuals are willing to pay something in the form of a reduced income to be associated with some people instead of with others. When discrimination occurs, the discriminator must in fact either pay or forfeit income. This simple, but powerful, way of looking at the matter gets at the essence of prejudice and discrimination. Thus an employer who prefers to have blonde employees rather than equally productive brunettes will act as if employing a brunette costs him more than blondes. Only at lower wages for brunettes than for blondes would he hire brunettes. This price difference becomes a basis for measuring discrimination.

Becker compares this approach with others commonly used and shows

Review of G. Becker, *The Economics of Discrimination* (Chicago: University of Chicago Press, 1957), reprinted from *Journal of the American Statistical Association* 53 (December 1958): 1047–48.

wherein the others are inconsistent or inadequate. He then shows that this application of basic economic ideas is fruitful. He shows that tastes for discrimination are an important part of the theory explaining actual discrimination, but the analysis is not simple. Tastes for discrimination can result in market price discrimination as well as in market segregation, two frequently confused concepts. Becker is careful to keep segregation distinct from discrimination phenomena, even though both are implied by a taste for discrimination. For example, groupings of Negroes and whites constitute segregation, but that does not mean that the rents for similar housing must be different. The latter implies discrimination, whereas the former does not. Becker is careful to note that no emphasis should be placed on the distinction between discrimination in "favor of" as distinct from that "against." In other words a theory based on "hatred" of one group is not easily distinguished empirically from one based on love of the other group. But at the same time, conclusions about normative issues may depend on whether hatred or love is assumed to motivate decisions.

But this review is written primarily for statisticians. What is there in Becker's book that would interest them? Aside from the book's general excellence as an analysis of "discrimination," its interest to statisticians as professionals is as an example of the application of available observable quantitative data to what are frequently regarded as non-quantitative subjective phenomena. The book serves as an example of the fact that statistical analysis can be applied to measuring sociological phenomena, in a sense more profound than merely counting how many people do or do not say they have certain tastes or preferences. A measure of the effects of these tastes can be made, as Becker shows.

For example, the effects on the income to labor and capital consequent to discrimination among Negroes and whites is revealed. He shows that under conditions that appear to be satisfied, white capitalists suffer from discrimination against Negroes while white laborers gain. He obtains different implications about the effects on incomes of two minority groups, Indians and Negroes, consequent to differences in the degree of segregation. The wide range of phenomena covered can be suggested by listing some of those explicitly discussed by Becker: discrimination by minorities, discrimination by single employers and by the group of employers, differences in discrimination between competitive and monopolistic employers, discrimination by employees and by unions, discrimination by consumers and by government. The effects of these tastes for discrimination are tested with market phenomena comparing North and South, different industries, retailing versus manufacturing, different professions, and farming versus urban occupations. In each case measurements are made and hypotheses tested.

If Becker had had an eye on royalties, more elaboration of obvious intermediate steps would have produced easier reader acceptance. Nevertheless this book is a major contribution to our understanding of discrimination and to its measurement.

THE MEANING OF COLLUSION

1. What Is Collusion?

Not every joint action, explicit or tacit, is collusion. A partnership is not collusion. Yet some mergers are regarded as collusive behavior. What effects are deemed undesirable and serve to separate permissible "cooperation" from impermissible "collusion"?

The standard test of economic theory is social efficiency—the extent to which output is that at which marginal costs reach price rather than only marginal revenue. Marginal revenue is less (though often trivially less) than price at any output. The profit-maximizing output that equates marginal cost with marginal revenue tends to restrict output *inefficiently*. That is, some of a good X is not produced even though the marginal cost (value of forsaken alternative output) is less than the value (as indicated by price) of more X.

Sellers in an industry, each of whom sees a marginal revenue higher than the marginal revenue for the *group as a whole*, will produce closer to that socially efficient output than if they paid heed to group marginal revenue. But if they heeded the group marginal revenue, the net income of the *group* would be greater. Since that group marginal revenue is farther below price than the individual seller's marginal revenue, attention to the group marginal revenue would lead to smaller output and hence greater divergence from the socially optimal output rate of the group.

Any group pricing action designed solely to heed the group's marginal revenue involves some costs, yields no social benefit and only transfers income to that group. Hence social policy will treat such collusion as undesirable. That is why (horizontal) collusion for price-fixing is held illegal, whereas horizontal mergers for achieving lower costs are held desirable and are not called "collusion."[1]

This previously unpublished May 1976 article appears here by permission of the author.

1. Query: How should policy treat a merger that reduces costs because of better joint management (as in legal partnerships, for example) but that at the same time leads to greater divergence from "marginal-cost-equal-to-price" output? Social gains of lower

THE MEANING OF COLLUSION   425

II. Sources of Potential Revenue Increases by Collusion

The revenue gains from an effective collusion to influence price (costs of achieving a collusion ignored) are larger, the greater the difference between each seller's marginal revenue and the marginal revenue to a group whose revenue he affects by his output and pricing. By acting more in accord with the *group* marginal revenue and somehow sharing in the group revenue, the individuals will enhance their wealth. A collusion for monopsony (buyers) interchanges marginal revenue and marginal cost, etc.

Factors affecting the (relative) size of gross potential revenue gain are:

1. Elasticity of group demand (or supply to group, if buyers). I conjecture the less the elasticity of group demand, the greater is the difference between group and individual marginal revenues. However, the validity of this conjecture must be empirically determined.

2. The homogeneity of the product among sellers. Homogeneity implies greater price cross-elasticities among the sellers and greater elasticities relative to the group (i.e., the higher their individual marginal revenues are above the group marginal revenue). Hence the larger is the potential gain from a collusion.

3. The greater the number of sellers, the greater the elasticity of each, and the greater the potential gains from collusion.

4. Entry costs. Greater economic costs of entry of new firms or new resources by existing firms is presumed to permit a longer-lasting revenue gain. The lower the costs of acquiring political power to control entry, the greater the potential revenue increases.

5. Low costs of discovering prices and alternative offers and bids via greater publicity of prices in other exchanges helps both buyers and sellers by reducing price search costs of both parties, thus reducing time and resources in finding best bids or offers. Low costs of price discovery also reduce durability of effective collusion by making individual sellers' demands more elastic with respect to competitors' prices—or suppliers more elastic even if buyers are trying to collude. Greater publicity is an information device—as a real estate agent serves as a means of informing both buyers and sellers of real estate about opportunities (at lower cost to both parties).

-----

production costs are possibly dissipated through greater misallocation of resources from this output to other less valuable output. This is the difficult empirical question that calls for what is typically called "merger policy," but this is not an issue here.

III. Factors Affecting Ability to Agree on Optimal Price and Product Mix

Whatever the potential gains from an effective collusion, the ability to agree on a uniform optimal price will depend on:

1. Homogeneity of product. The more homogeneous the product and the smaller the range of products or services in the mix, the more likely the colluders can agree on an optimal price and product mix. The more diverse their revenue or cost conditions, the less likely is one uniform price or product mix to be agreeable. Of course, if total revenues (or purchases) were pooled and managed through one pooling agency, some of this disagreement would be avoided, though there would then exist the problem of deciding who gets what fraction of the pooled proceeds.

2. The number of colluders. The more colluders, the less likely is a uniform price-product mix to be optimal. This is similar to the preceding point, where increased numbers are another source of greater diversity among participants.

3. The size and frequency of purchases (sales). The smaller the individual purchases and the greater their frequency, the more decisions must be made, and the relative gains on each are smaller. With a few big sales, the optimal price to each can be more acutely adjusted.

IV. Enforcement Costs

Whatever the potential gains and agreeability, the costs of enforcement will hamper effectiveness of a collusion. The higher those costs, the less likely the collusion can be effective, or even reached. The costs are affected by several factors.

1. The less the cost of altering the product mix of any one selling outlet, the greater the ability to cut price by an effective improvement in quality of product because the costs to detect such violations are greater.

2. The more difficult it is for a party outside the particular transaction to detect the quality or price cut, the greater the gains from violating the collusion and the greater therefore must the costs of enforceability the colluders expect to incur.

3. The greater the costs of effectively specifying the product mix in the detail necessary to identify product or price alteration, the less effective is any agreement on price or quality, since within those ambiguous bounds of price

or quality, competition can continue. The greater that ambiguity, the less effective is agreement.

4. Greater losses that can be imposed on violators for any level of costs to non-violators make the enforcement more effective. For example, if an association exists, membership in which is of high value, threat of expulsion will be a loss threat without requiring side payments, fines or fees.

5. The lower the costs of measuring shares of sales of each member, the more effective the detection of violations. Sudden shifts in shares during alleged collusion are indicative of secret violations, with large increases indicating violations by the gainer of shares.

6. The greater the "customer loyalty," i.e., the greater the propensity of a customer to return to a seller in the absence of price changes, the less the gain from violations. Hence enforcement costs are lower.

7. The lower the costs of effectively assigning customers and suppliers to each other by geography or by pooling of sales, the more effective the enforcement.

8. Legality of prices. If prices are set and must be observed legally, then public notice of prices serves to alert customers to any illegally high or low price. "Illegal" action is subject to legal fines on violators.

v. Empirical Tests Indicating Presence or Absence of Effective Collusions—And Empirical Tests of No Discriminatory Power.

A. *Test Indicating Absence of Effective Collusion*

1. If alleged colluders experience profits increase and shares of sales decrease and others in the industry outside of the collusion do not, collusion was weak. Outsiders should gain more profits and shares in accord with collusion effectiveness in raising prices. They don't have to curtail output.

2. Relative prices among colluders change as much during collusion as before or after. Collusion wants to avoid constant costly renegotiation. A control group is needed to perform this test.

3. Advertising prices, *where prices vary and differ* among sellers is evidence of *no* collusion. If all colluders charged the same price, they would advertise the *same* price. But a collusion would not have advertising of the same goods at prices that differ from day to day among colluders. That would be inconsistent with the control of price. Pricing differences might occur—but not be publicly advertised. If varying prices that are advertised are to be consistent with a collusion, one would have to have some pricing *formula* on how to alter the prices

to obscure the pretension of a collusion. On the buying side, colluding buyers would not advertise their varying offer prices to suppliers.

4. Relative price of a good (relative to close substitutes) should change during collusion period.

B. *Tests Indicating an Effective Collusion*

1. Detection of a policing device used with penalizing effect on violators.

2. Detection of an effective means for determining price and output, e.g., pooling, allocations, some rule for price setting.

3. Relative shares and profits of colluders should be more stable during collusion (omitting initial period when efficient reallocations of output may occur) than before or after, *and* relative shares and profits of colluders should be more stable and uniform than relative shares of non-colluding firms.

4. Collusion shields members (and non-members) from random vagaries of market. If collusion lasts long enough, investors will note decreased variance in returns, and market prices of stocks will adjust so that risk premium is reduced relative to risk premium of market as a whole and to non-colluders.

5. A once-and-for-all upward adjustment in market value of firms in industry vis-à-vis stock market. As a whole the upward adjustment would be strongest for non-colluders.

6. Increased service and associated benefits to buyers suggest attempts of individuals to compete more in non-price features. This should disappear after collusion. Such extra forms of competition should indicate weakness or evasion of collusion while indicating presence of attempt to effectively collude.

ELECTRICAL EQUIPMENT COLLUSION
WHY AND HOW

Man sensibly tries to collude with other people to avoid mutually costly competition. At the same time he tells himself that he should rise above the collusive habit and shun it. For example, the recently revealed collusion among sellers of heavy electrical equipment to the government has evoked sermonizing condemnations of business transgression. But, perhaps fortunately, collusion is as immune to preaching as is sex.[1]

At the birth of economics as a formal science, Adam Smith explicitly recognized the incentive to collude. But Smith went on to indicate some places wherein the economic system makes collusion difficult and wherein it makes it easy—aside from laws and doctrines of immorality. Smith showed how some forms of property rights or institutions make collusion less viable or profitable. Is there a similar explanation that will suggest why the "electrical equipment" collusion was tempting? Is there some reason why the instinct to collusion was provided with an especially favorable environment? Or was it that the particular sellers involved were simply less "moral" or more predisposed toward lawbreaking than the mass of the rest of us?

The purpose of this note is to see how economic theory implies that the viability of collusion is stronger among sellers who are selling to an institution not characterized by private property and in particular one that is characterized by public ownership. In the present instance, the buyers against whom the collusion was *successful* were almost always governments, government agen-

Reprinted, by permission of the author, from Armen A. Alchian, *Economic Forces at Work* (Indianapolis: Liberty Fund, 1977), 259–69.

This paper is the result of some luncheon discussions among W. Meckling, N. Breckner, G. Becker, and A. Alchian and represents another stride forward in the effort to blame "government" for all evils of the world as an antidote to the strawmen who praise it for all virtue. Alchian is the reporter because the rest were employees of only one public agency, but he accepts no liability or responsibility for any misstatements of fact or logic.

1. "The catastrophe resulting from the destruction of the instinct to collude would be second only to that resulting from the elimination of the sexual urge" (Y. Hamparsoom, *The Origins of Near-Eastern Philosophy* [Erevan, 1886], p. 137).

cies, or governmentally owned public utilities. What is interesting is that economic theory implies that one should expect a greater chance of effective collusion precisely in these cases.

By an involved line of analysis it can be shown that gains and the viability of collusion are greater for sellers to governments than among buyers selling to private businesses. The reasoning is not based on any antagonism toward the government by the sellers. Instead it reflects the fact that the rewards and costs of public administrators of public property are less correlated with their cost-cutting, dollar-saving, careful-buying activities than are those of counterpart administrators or owners of privately owned businesses. Quickly, we insist that this does not mean that owners and administrators of private property are more intelligent, more alert, or more honorable than public administrators. No difference is assumed in these respects. We shall skip over the chain of logic that shows how all this can be derived from the fundamental law of economics—"the lower the cost of any source of personal gain, the more will that source be utilized" (or its converse, "the higher the cost of some source of personal utility the less will that source be utilized").

What is embarrassing about all this to an economist is that although this general understanding permeates economics, its import seems not to be widely enough appreciated. Perhaps I am wrong in saying it has not gained wide acceptance. But I certainly confess to a lack of evidence of such a state.

Perhaps the easiest way to put meat on the bare bones of the analysis is to ask why governments typically use the sealed-bid system of buying and no private firms use it. One would think that if the sealed-bid system were so good, the private firms would use it, too. Or that if it really weren't good the government would abandon it and imitate the private firms.[2]

In the absence of a sealed-bid system, a public administrator could easily tell a "friendly" seller what were the best bids so far received and then give the sale to the friend at one dollar less. The advantage of being the last bidder—*and of knowing what the other bidders have offered*—is obvious. Each competitor would like to be last, and he would like to make sure that no concealed bidders were around to take advantage of a friendly administrator who thereby could gain in nondirect, and possibly nonpecuniary, ways. Remember, we do not postulate that public administrators are "bad guys" or "good guys." Instead they are like me . . . and you. Both taxpayers and competing sellers have incentives to in-

---

2. We say no private firms use it—which means obviously that we know of no cases where they do.

sist that the bidding be open, that each bidder have equal opportunity to make his best offer, and that the public administrator buyer take the lowest offer.

It would appear that the sealed bid is a wonderful device. For example, each competing seller would state the minimum price he would take. If he didn't, he might lose the contract. Thus it would seem that this system is very effective in squeezing the competing sellers. However, there are two flaws with that line of reasoning. In the first place, a private buyer without sealed bids can get equally effective "squeezes" simply by asking the potential seller to name a price, and then all the buyer has to do is (1) make it clear that he is a serious buyer—i.e., he is not just trying to decide whether or not to buy at all—and (2) tell each competing seller that he does not intend to return to report his best price from among the various sellers. At least he is under no compulsion to do so. As the buyer walks out the door, the seller knows he must make his best bid. This "seller" may try to play it coy in the belief that the buyer will not get better offers elsewhere. Notice, however, that exactly the same kind of "game" can be played with the sealed bid. And this is the second flaw in the preceding argument. There is no reason to presume that the sealed-bid prices are really the minimum selling prices of each seller. Each competing seller can use some strategy and try to beat out merely the conjectured next best price. In sum, it is no trick at all for a private buyer to duplicate all the merits of the sealed bid— and then some. He can resort to even further attempted squeezes of the lowest bidder, who may not know he is already lowest.

The sealed bid, then, is a device to compensate for a well-recognized problem in government arising from public ownership—that of making the administrator act as aggressively and effectively in watching costs and performance as a private owner or even the administrator or manager of a privately owned business. Private property owners (and the capital markets enable private property owners more effectively to) induce their agents to act in ways consonant with the interest of the owners. We say *more* effectively (not with perfect or complete effectiveness) than for public property owners.[3]

3. We skip over the derivation of the implication that we are using as a premise here, namely that private property ownership implies more effective inducements and incentives than does public ownership to watch for the interests of the "owners." Some may take this on faith, and others by logical implication. We care not which at the present moment. And we simply ask the reader to accept it for purposes of the present exposition. If it be wrong, in fact, then our entire analysis collapses. And of course what we are leading up to is the fact that this premise implies such collusion as was observed will occur more frequently in sales to the government.

The sealed bid is, unfortunately, only a crutch. Even with it, the public property owners—the governments—can't run as fast as private owners. Given the desire to collude, collusion is more viable against the government than against privately owned firms, even with the sealed bid. The reason is not hard to see. Although the sealed bid makes conniving by the public property administrators with the seller more difficult, it does not change the basic structure of the incentive system in public ownership and governments as compared with private ownership. Illegal activity by public administrators in conniving with competing sellers is thwarted by the sealed-bid system, but it does not offset the weaker incentives and lesser rewards for aggressive, price-conscious, dollar-saving activity. For example, the authors act quite differently in their capacities as public employees and as private individuals. When buying typewriters for themselves they shop more extensively and exert more effort to obtain the best price—in order to keep the savings for alternative personal uses.[4]

How much of the saving will accrue to the public employee or to his supervisor or even to his "boss" if he, by extra effort, manages to save extra dollars? They revert to the general fund, not to him. Where they do revert to his own budget, he will act more carefully. But the reduced incentive is clear-cut. And furthermore, with the sealed-bid system it is improper for the buyer to continue negotiations and efforts to find still lower prices—even if he were to have as much incentive to do so. What the sealed-bid system and public ownership accomplishes is the *avoidance* of that kind of activity as well as of conniving. It puts purchasing on a plateau of uninspired routine mediocrity. The councilman, the politician, or the bureaucrat in responding to prices suggested for paving a road or building a sewer, a school building, or an electric circuit does not respond to the prospects of "savings" by extra unpleasant laborious activity, not to the extent he would if it were his own road, sewer, building, or electric circuit.

The sellers are not fools. They know that the initiative, care, perspicuity, and incentive of public agents are quite different from those of private purchasers. Care in being ethical, conformity with the rules, not bargaining hard (to avoid the appearance of trying to connive as well as because of reduced incentive) are manifest symptoms of public agencies. Any experienced salesman of computing machines, automobiles, furniture, or paper knows how the public agency buyers differ from the private buyers.

But at this point the thoughtful reader will be impatient to interject that even

4. Veterans of the military will remember well the sudden transformation that followed the expression, "You're on your own time."

though the buyers may be different, we have overlooked the fundamental nature of competition. Competition does *not* pit buyer against seller (whether it be electrical equipment, paper, or labor). Instead, it is the competition *among the sellers themselves* in trying to get business away from each other that aids the buyer. It is not the buyer who somehow by some mystical "bargaining" power makes a seller cut prices. Instead, it is the other sellers who make better offers that the buyer reflects back to still other sellers and that make the latter sellers compete. It simply is not seller against buyer. It is seller against seller. It is not the nasty, aggressive, loud, "pushy," threatening buyer who gets prices down. It is competition among sellers. A person who wants to buy a car need not go into a showroom and start trying to be a hard, tough bargainer. He need merely let it be known he intends to buy and is willing to listen to all offers and will then take the one that is best for him.[5] The sellers can think up more devices or special devices to attract his business than the buyer could ever think up.

But if this is true, have we not destroyed our earlier argument? Will not sellers compete among themselves and destroy the collusive agreement if the attitude of the buyer is irrelevant? We did not say the buyer's attitude was irrelevant. In fact, it is responsible for whatever effectiveness there may have been. What is being said is that the competition among sellers is intensive *to the extent that it will pay* each seller to be competitive. And this reflects the incentive and *ability* of the buyer to accept special competitive offers from sellers. To see why, ask the question, What will enable a collusive agreement to be effective? Or to put it conversely, What prevents collusive agreements from being viable?

A collusive agreement to restrict competition means that the members believe they can divide up this larger income so that each gets more than he would in the absence of the agreement. Some people believe that our laws against collusion prevent such collusions. Perhaps they do, just as they prevent gambling. But there is another, more powerful force that destroys collusive agreements even in the absence of laws. First, there is an incentive for each and every member, secretly and individually, to violate the agreement. We need not belabor this point except to state that the policing of agreements is extremely difficult and expensive—sometimes so expensive as to consume all the potential gains of the collusion.[6]

5. Allen F. Jung, "Price Variations Among Automobile Dealers in Metropolitan Chicago," *Journal of Business* 33, no. 1 (January 1960): 31–42.

6. A classic, though not widely understood, example of collusion beset with secret violations is the collusive agreement among colleges not to pay the free-market price for

Secret rebates, extra service, and better quality are illegal if offered to the public agency administrators (let alone the problem of keeping them secret). Judgments of quality and service are easy for a private buyer to make and defend as compared with the defense which a public buyer must put up for buying from one seller rather than another at the same or higher price. As we indicated earlier, sellers will, when they know that buyers are more likely to be responsive to special or secret inducements, be very adept at devising methods for secretly offering better terms to the buyers. In public buying, such secrecy is illegal and unethical, as well as difficult to keep secret, whereas it is legal, ethical, and easier to keep secret (from other sellers) in private buying. This means that in bidding for public contracts the incentives to collusive agreements— which are always present—are less likely to be thwarted by secret terms between buyers and sellers.

But there is another potent force against viability of collusive agreements. Outsiders who are capable of producing the items being sold collusively will be attracted by the lure of profits. To admit them into the collusion would mean sharing the profits with so many newcomers that the gains would be (quickly?) dissipated. If admission is denied, they can undersell the conspirators and take away their sales directly. Since this *can* happen when the collusion is against a government, why is it assumed not to be present, or weaker as a force, in the case of collusion against the government than against private buyers? Here is where the buyer's incentives and attitudes are critical. A private buyer will have more incentive to detect collusion, and he will have more to gain by encouraging *new* producers. Even if he is not aware of the collusion, the incentives on the private buyer to seek out and stimulate new sources of supply are greater than for the public buyer. The private property buyer has more to gain by exerting effort and ingenuity in attracting *new* competitors than does a public property agent. In fact, a public property agent runs the risk of criticism in seeking out new firms to produce something for fear that such favoritism can be interpreted as conniving. And basically his rewards are less for such actions. In purest formal terms, the spread of information about the collusion is more rapid under private property than under public property. And information is

_____

talented athletes. This collusive agreement is the foundation of the National Collegiate Athletic Association. The violations of the agreement form the main items on the agenda of all of its meetings. We leave the question open as to how this collusive agreement manages to survive—although we think we know the answer. In many other areas collusion is *aided* by laws. Guess where!

not a free good; it costs something to disseminate it or to obtain it. Commitments can be made by private buyers to new potential suppliers, whereas a public agency would be readily accused of seeking special favors from special firms. Any politician or government employer or administrator will provide illustrative stories.

To put the issue bluntly. If the buying agent of a private firm failed to thwart a collusion, he would not survive as long as would a buyer in a government agency faced with the collusion. Can you see how behavior in the two cases would be different? Can you see why a buyer would be fired in the first case? And let alone in the second? This implies that if one examines the record in the electrical-equipment case, he will find that the public buyers who were paying the "cartel" prices were regarded as completely blameless, innocent parties, or even praised if they brought the collusion to the attention of the Federal Anti-Trust Division. But the buyer for a private firm would be criticized and demoted if he failed to quickly detect *and* circumvent the collusion.

We summarize. Collusion against the government is more viable because two things are reduced: (1) the possibility of secret violations and (2) the extent to which information about the collusion will be disseminated and used as an inducement to outsiders to enter into competition and thwart the collusion. The attenuation of these forces reflects the existence of public ownership and is inevitably present.

None of this says that public ownership should be abandoned on this count alone, any more than marriage should be abandoned because of some of its inherent disadvantages relative to bachelorhood. But at least the faults or weaknesses should be discerned if understanding of the real world is desired.

How would one verify these implications of economic theory? In the first place, the fact of sealed bids serves as verifying implication—if they are present in public property agencies more than in private buying. In the strongest form, we would assert they are to be observed *only* in public property agencies (or, for reasons basically similar, also in nonprofit firms and profit-regulated government firms—e.g., public utilities). But we prefer to leave out this embellishment.

Second, it should be observed that of all the collusions that have been recorded, more of them are directed against government than against private property firms—after allowing for the relative proportion of government and private buying activity. However, there might seem to be one biasing factor in this particular piece of evidence, namely, that a collusion will be destroyed without legal action by private firms. But this is, of course, exactly what the preceding analysis implies. There is, however, a complicating factor that does have a biasing weight: legal suits involve costs—in the one case borne by the private firm, whereas in the government case it is borne by the public at large. However, this biasing effect can be overcome by the third testable implication. And this is that the life length of such collusions, as are verified to have existed, should be greater for those directed against the government than against private firms. This life-length test may appear to be biased against the preceding analysis by the fact that the public bears the legal prosecution costs in the public agency case.

Government agencies would resort to legal suit more readily, since they don't have to bear the economic costs. Hence, the life of such collusions should be shorter, because legal suits are more likely to be used to destroy them—if one believes that private firms have to resort to a suit to break collusion. But the preceding analysis denies this. Suits are clumsy, expensive, and less effective for private firms as devices to break collusion than are direct market operations or secret "deals."

We do not deny the birth of collusive agreements in the private sphere, nor do we assert that they last forever or for a long time in the public sphere. Just how long is long? We can't answer that question, but we note only that there is no necessity of proving immortality of certain forms of life to show why those forms will prosper in one area relative to another area. It suffices to show that collusion is more viable among sellers to governments than to private property institutions. Even then, whether collusion will survive very long or be profitable will depend upon economic costs for outsiders to enter the business— barring legal obstacles such as government licensing or union restrictions.

DOLLARS OR SCHOLARS

THE ECONOMICS OF COLLEGE FOOTBALL

ARMEN ALCHIAN AND WILLIAM MECKLING

Louisiana State University recently applied to Phi Beta Kappa for recognition as a university qualified for a PBK chapter. Recognition was refused. Not because its library was inadequate, nor its staff incompetent, nor its students below standard, nor its administration hostile to the search for truth. No, and not because its racial policies were abhorrent. The reason was much more important. Louisiana State had given disproportionately greater financial aid through scholarships to athletes than to non-athletes. Scholars must admit that such devotion to principle by PBK is exceptional. Why is it exceptional? Surely consistent intolerance of discriminatory treatment would indicate that PBK should withhold chapters from colleges giving disproportionate aid to Catholics, Jews, or women, as many schools do. Indeed, Harvard gives preferential treatment to students whose fathers were newsboys, Stanford gives preferential treatment to residents of Utah, and UCLA gives preferential treatment to veterans. Clearly the principle of objecting to preferential treatment of certain groups has *not* been applied consistently to colleges which give preferential treatment. Why? Some of the answers attempt to give the impression that the situation is complex. When one wishes to conceal a simple point, one should direct attention to all the other facts of the world, their complexities and complications. The world is not simple; hence, obviously it follows that simple explanations are not acceptable. I expect the reader to see through that fallacy. In fact, a major purpose of education is to learn to distinguish between simplicity of explanation and complexity of events.

Wherein does preferential treatment of athletes differ in principle from that of Catholics, Jews, women, or veterans? Simply in this—athletes have a tremendous financial value to the college. Football and basketball players come to college, the public pays to see them perform, the profits fill the college treasury, and these funds are used to benefit the *entire* college. New gymnasia, dor-

Reprinted from *Claremont College Quarterly* (Winter 1960): 37–41.

mitories, social centers, buildings, and faculty can be obtained. The net profits run into the hundreds of thousands of dollars for the larger colleges. Do not be misled by statements that the profits are earmarked for athletic purposes. This merely channels that amount of money into athletics, thereby releasing funds from the general college budget that would otherwise have been spent on athletics. These released funds can then be spent on buildings and faculty salaries. The conclusion is inescapable: the profits whether or not earmarked for athletics redound to the benefit of everyone associated with the college at the expense of the individual football players.

In the high tide of its fortunes, the Pacific Coast Conference (PCC) colleges and other conferences in the National College Athletic Association (the NCAA) entered into a collusive, monopolistic pact agreeing to restrict how much they paid athletes to play football for them. As everyone knows, cartelized, collusive agreements are illegal. But the colleges, under the fiction that college football players are not professionals and are not employees of the university, have remained legally immune from prosecution for monopoly. Football players are not called professionals, because the colleges have agreed among themselves not to call a student a professional so long as he doesn't earn more than they will allow him to earn. The word "scholarship" is substituted for wages. A strange definition of professionalism. It used to mean pay for play. And on that basis, college athletics is unquestionably professional. Professionalism has entered because football is an extremely profitable activity for the universities. But, if professionalism were recognized openly instead of concealed, and if there were no collusive agreements among colleges limiting how much they will pay, these very productive athletes would be able to demand and get pay that matches the value of their services—just as a welder or engineer can get higher wages from employers if the employers do not gang up and agree not to pay competitive wages. Free, open competition would drive up athletes' pay to the value of their services, thus enabling them to obtain pay commensurate with the value of their contribution. But if this occurred, the colleges would lose a very large chunk of their net receipts, because their exploitive power over the players would be gone. Like any other business, they would then be paying honest competitive wages and keeping smaller profits. Suppose every employer of a welder entered into a pact, agreeing to limit the pay of welders. This is exactly what the colleges have done—every college now in the National Collegiate Athletic Association—the basic core of the collusive, monopolistic combine.

But again the NCAA and the Pacific Coast Conference are (or were) organizations, and each member of that collusive group would find it even more profitable to secretly exceed the agreed-upon restrictive pay limits. So long as only a few schools succeed in breaking the pay limits, they will benefit not only at the expense of the athletes but also at the expense of the schools that do not break the pact. The temptation to break the code is strong, and since mutual destruction is the effect if all members break it, strict enforcement of the pact on pay limitations is absolutely essential. Small wonder, then, that a school caught breaking the pay limit of the code is severely punished.

Even though every member of the conference would gain from secret evasion, some stand to gain more than others. And this explains why the Conference had so much trouble agreeing upon a new restrictive limit after the recent so-called scandals. A level of pay that is high enough for one college to attract what it deems an adequate number of good athletes may not be high enough for other colleges with less attractive locations or lower social, academic, or athletic repute. The newer college is at a disadvantage compared with the older colleges. And colleges in metropolitan areas with enormous potential gate receipts will be able to offer higher pay and still make profits, as compared with schools in less populated areas. From these differences arise the complicated conflicts of interest about the acceptable pay limit. Although only a compromise is possible, that is better for the colleges than no restrictive agreement at all.

Once a compromise limitation is agreed upon, the incentives to violate it secretly are so great that every avenue of enforcement will be needed. Phi Beta Kappa, by withholding or, even better, by withdrawing recognition from the evasive colleges, apparently believes it should and can restrain them. Is a college willing to go without PBK for the sake of *extra* profits obtained by breaking the restrictive code? PBK, or some people in it, seems to believe this is a proper way to use its prestige and power. Note that PBK does not propose to punish schools that exploit one class of students—the athletes. Instead it stands ready to help the colleges continue their restrictive collusive exploitation of football-playing students. And for whose benefit? For the benefit of the faculty.

Are the faculties who benefit from these restrictive agreements perhaps unwittingly trying to conceal the truth by diversionary tactics? Is that why they say that only outright full pay would be professionalism? Is that why a president of one of the PCC universities argued that morality is involved? He said, "We place high value in our society in having a man's word as good as his bond. If an institution of higher learning will not work to honor a compact freely agreed to, then it has debased itself and its purpose." One can't help wondering whether such compacts which violate the fundamental tenets of a society of free people deserve to be honored. Since when did honor among monopolistic conspirators justify monopolistic exploitation?

One of the university presidents also said that "a university is measured most exactly by its educational standards and performance, by the training which it affords to young men and women who seek to improve their minds by acquiring knowledge and wisdom, and by the examples it sets for them in matters of character and content. In the whole educational enterprise which is measured by these standards there is an important place for intercollegiate athletics. But its place cannot be justified if such importance is attached to victory on the athletic field as to produce practices which lead to cheating." Who, for the sake of victory and profits, is cheating against free, open competition—a fundamental basis of our free society?

Another group says that if the football players were paid what they were worth, their sense of value would be destroyed with such high incomes. Do these advocates really propose to justify stealing by saying they can use the money better than the present owners? And I must confess that such opinions are advanced by some respected colleagues—on another campus.

Another group thinks playing football is different from other things because the players are students. But students are working as waiters and clerks and research assistants in university cafeterias, bookstores, and laboratories. Why are students paid full competitive wages for services rendered by the university in all other lines of profit-making endeavor, but not in football? The answer is simple. Collusive pacts in the other services would have to include every business firm in our economy—a clear impossibility. But in the exclusively collegiate lines of activity, such as college football, the colleges have been able to stand together under the auspices of the National Collegiate Athletic Association—the ultimate protective association.

Still another extremist group, the Ivy League, is attempting to confuse the issue by advocating that the Pacific Coast colleges avoid professionalism by revising their schedules to play colleges like Cal Tech, Johns Hopkins, and Reed. But none of them wants that. All of them *want* to go on exploiting the athlete. It's in their interests to do so. They gain from it.

Now I have reached the end of my story. The moral I would leave is not "Intelligence is more honorable than honesty." Nor "Thou shalt not steal." Instead the moral I would suggest is "Trust other people to put their interest first."

THE BASIS OF SOME RECENT ADVANCES IN THE
THEORY OF MANAGEMENT OF THE FIRM

Attacks on the theory of the firm—or more accurately on the theory of behavior of individuals in the firm—have called attention to logical inconsistencies in the profit-maximizing criterion and to empirical evidence refuting its implications in a wide class of firms. The empirical evidence seemed overwhelming that individuals working within a firm as managers or employees (and even as employers) pursued policies directed at, for example, increasing sales, gross assets, employees and expenditures for various equipment and facilities beyond those that yield a profit maximum.

Attempts to defend the profit-maximizing theory by rigorously treating profits as capital value increments, rather than as current transitory rates of net earnings—so as to avoid the short- and long-run pitfall—removed some conflicting evidence. Similarly a defense asserting that the aberrations are temporary deviations in a search process does eliminate some more of the embarrassing evidence. However, the defense is not adequate; a vast class of behavior conflicting with wealth maximizing remains to be explained.

The observations of behavior that refute the profit- or wealth-maximizing theory are the "facts" that some managers incur expenditures apparently in excess of those that would maximize wealth or profits of the owners of the firm. Managers of corporations are observed to emphasize growth of total assets of the firm and of its sales as objectives of managerial actions. Also managers of firms undertake cost-reducing, efficiency-increasing campaigns when demand falls; under wealth maximization they would already have been doing this. Managerial actions not conducive to the greatest wealth to the stockholders are taken to be well-established facts—and with which there appears to be no quarrel. Baumol emphasizes the managerial objective of sales increases, even to the extent of postulating that sales maximization is an objective. Penrose emphasizes the growth of the asset size of the firms. None of these can be made consistent with stockholder wealth maximization. If one postulates

Reprinted from *Journal of Industrial Economics* 14 (November 1965): 30–41, by permission of the publisher, Blackwell Publishing Ltd.

asset growth or sales maximization he will explain some cases but reject a lot of others in which that simply does not hold. Similarly, attempts to posit asset or sales maximization subject to a minimum wealth or profit constraint also runs into the objection that it implies the firm will not make *any* sacrifice in sales no matter how large an increment in wealth would thereby be achievable. Observed behavior simply does not support that attempted revision of the theory. Thus the Baumol type of attempt to modify the theory flounders—which in no way diminishes the importance of the insistence on recognizing inadequacies in the then existing state of theory.[1]

Attacking any theory is easy enough, since none is perfect. But the wide class of empirical observation that is explained by economic theory should caution one against sweeping that theory aside and setting up new *ad hoc* theories to explain *only* or *primarily* those events the standard theory will not explain. What is wanted is a generalization of economic theory to obtain an expanded scope of validity without eliminating any (or "too much") of the class of events for which it already is valid. Too many new theories happen to be *ad hoc* theories, valid only for a smaller class of cases. And among recent attempts to increase the power of the theory of the firm one can find some sparkling examples. Though there is no point in our giving attention to those failures, credit is due them as reminders of the areas in which economic theory awaits valid generalization.

Deserving our attention here are those in which scientific progress toward a more generalized and valid theory is realized. Two recent works serve as good examples. Especially distinguished is the contribution in Oliver E. Williamson's *The Economics of Discretionary Behavior: Managerial Objective in a Theory of the Firm*, a doctoral thesis (which won a Ford Foundation award). The other is Robin Marris, *The Economic Theory of Managerial Capitalism*. Now that we have some advances we can look back and determine what prior works served as foundations for the advance. Especially noticeable as pathbreaker was Gary Becker's *Economics of Discrimination*, also a doctoral dissertation completed almost ten years ago. From Becker to Marris and Williamson there are worth noting here the works of Downie, Baumol, Penrose, March and Simon, Averch and Johnson, Cyert and March.[2]

---

1. William J. Baumol, *Business Behavior, Value and Growth* (New York: Macmillan, 1959); Edith T. Penrose, *The Theory of the Growth of the Firm* (New York: John Wiley, 1959).

2. Oliver E. Williamson, *The Economics of Discretionary Behavior: Managerial Objectives in a Theory of the Firm* (Englewood Cliffs, N.J.: Prentice-Hall, 1964); Robin Marris, *The Economic*

Perhaps the nature of the advance can be characterized by asserting that the old schizophrenia between consumption and production behavior has been replaced by a consistent, more powerful criterion of utility maximizing. In a sense the utility theory underlying individual behavior in the consumption sphere has swallowed up producer or management theory—with, if we judge the recent literature aright, significant improvements in economic theory. Rather than concentrate on a detailed statement of who said what (and why he should or should not have said it), this paper is an attempt to indicate the nature of that advance—as a sort of survey review of the recent literature.

A means of advance was made explicit by Becker, who insisted that non-pecuniary sources of utility be included in the utility function of an income earner. An owner, manager or employee is prepared to sacrifice some pecuniary income as a source of utility if he is offered enough non-pecuniary goods, which also contribute to utility. Becker concentrated on race, religion and congeniality of colleagues or employees as a source of non-pecuniary utility. He emphasized the production trade-offs or transformation rates between money income and working conditions (including color of colleagues and other non-pecuniary goods), and he pointed out that changes in the trade-off rates would affect the extent to which a person chose non-pecuniary sources (goods) of utility relative to pecuniary income.

There is, of course, nothing novel in this proposition. One can find it in Adam Smith. But with the growth of formalism and rigor of mathematical modes of analysis, it seems to have dropped out of the theory. Becker's dissertation stimulated applications of the principle to see if different kinds of institutions implied different trade-off rates between pecuniary and non-pecuniary incomes to managers and employees. Thus, a paper by the present author and R. Kessel applied the analysis to profit-limited and -regulated businesses—public utilities, for example—and derived the implication that discrimination against racial and religious groups is greater in profit-controlled firms. Any

Theory of Managerial Capitalism (New York: Free Press of Glencoe, 1964); Gary Becker, The Economics of Discrimination (Chicago: University of Chicago Press, 1957); Jack Downie, The Competitive Process (London: Gerald Duckworth, 1958); Baumol, Business Behavior, Value and Growth; Penrose, The Theory of the Growth of the Firm; J. G. March and H. A. Simon, Organizations (New York: John Wiley, 1958); H. Averch and L. L. Johnson, "Behavior of the Firm Under Regulatory Constraint," American Economic Review 52 (December 1962): 1052–69; Richard M. Cyert and James G. March, eds., A Behavioral Theory of the Firm (Englewood Cliffs, N.J.: Prentice-Hall, 1963).

firm already earning the maximum *allowable* profit found it almost costless (of profits) to "buy" that kind of discrimination. Evidence was also presented to corroborate the analysis. Averch and Johnson applied the principle to investment activities of owners of public utilities and derived an implication about the extent to which investment in cost *increasing* activities would be induced.[3]

Marris says the managers will be induced to sacrifice some increment of owner's profits for the sake of the increment of size of firm (and consequent increment of managerial salary). Managers' salaries are larger in larger firms. Therefore they will have an incentive to enlarge the firm beyond the owner's wealth-, or profit-, maximizing size. Marris makes explicit that stockholders are not blind to this; the costs of their detecting this effect and exerting controls are large enough to make it more economical for stockholders to tolerate the reduced wealth than to incur the costs required to keep the managers more strictly in line with the stockholder's wealth-maximizing criterion.

Unfortunately Marris's analysis appears to be slightly marred by a logical confusion between rates of profit *per unit of investment* and absolute growth of wealth (profit)—in view of the fact that the investment is a discretionary *variable*.[4] If I am correct in my understanding, the implication derived by Marris, wherein the manager will seek a growth rate of assets beyond that which maximizes the above-mentioned ratio, is completely consistent with simple wealth maximization *to the owners*. Diminishing marginal rate of return on *additional* investment calls for setting that marginal rate of return equal to the rate of interest—maximizing neither the marginal nor the average rate of return per dollar of (variable) investment. However, it would be a simple task to set the analysis aright by formalizing into the manager's opportunity set of choices among wealth to stockholders versus wealth to managers the costs to stockholders of enforcing a stockholder's wealth-maximizing criterion on the managers.

Marris says he uses a utility-maximizing approach wherein the person has his utility increased not only by higher salaries but also by greater security in his continued incumbency. In a strict sense, this is a wealth-maximizing, rather than a utility-maximizing, approach for the manager. It is that because a

---

3. Adam Smith, *Wealth of Nations*, book 5, chapter 1, articles 2 and 3; Armen A. Alchian and Reuben A. Kessel, "Competition, Monopoly, and the Pursuit of Pecuniary Gain," in *Aspects of Labor Economics*, Universities-National Bureau Committee for Economic Research (Princeton: Princeton University Press, 1962).

4. Marris, *Economic Theory*, 254–60.

greater security is an increase in wealth. If risk of loss of future receipts is re-duced, the present value is increased. Hence Marris uses a wealth function in which two components of greater wealth are made explicit—the projected future receipts and the probability of their being realized.

Competing with the utility-maximizing approach is a wealth- or growth-of-wealth–maximizing criterion. Marris devotes most of his book to an exposi-tion of a model in which the growth of the firm is constrained by internal sav-ing out of its business-generated income. As it turns out, a wealth growth–maximizing criterion is a wealth-maximizing criterion. Although Marris offers interesting observations it is his utility-maximizing proposition that makes his approach most fruitful—in this reviewer's judgment.

As of the present moment, the best formulation of a theory that seems to be both more general and more valid than the wealth-maximizing theory is the utility-maximizing approach more fully presented by Williamson. He postu-lates that the manager can direct the firm's resources to increase his own utility in at least three ways. First, he can get a higher salary by obtaining greater prof-its for the owners, as in the older profit-maximizing model. Second, he can direct the firm's resources so as to increase his salary at the expense of a de-crease in profits. In particular, if the manager believes that a large firm is cor-related with higher salaries (holding profits constant as a *ceteris paribus* condi-tion), he will strive more to enlarge the gross asset size of the firm.

Third, the manager can sacrifice some increments to stockholder profits in order to increase expenditures for his own non-pecuniary emoluments within the firm. The extent to which these three avenues are used depends on the costs to the stockholders of detecting and policing the manager's behavior and effec-tiveness, i.e., on the costs, of enforcing contracts. In the modern large corpo-ration these costs are higher than in the single-owner enterprise (and are ab-sent in the owner-operated enterprise).

The third of the avenues listed above is formally admissable if one uses a utility-maximizing theory rather than a pecuniary wealth-maximizing postu-late. By doing so, the manager's behaviour is interpreted as choosing among opportunities to obtain increments of non-pecuniary goods in his utility func-tion (e.g., pretty secretaries, thick rugs, friendly colleagues, leisurely work load, executive washrooms, larger work staff, relaxed personnel policies in-volving job security, time off for statesmanlike community activities, gifts of company funds to colleges, out-of-town hotel suites, racial and religious dis-crimination in personnel policy, etc.). The utility-maximizing theory is appli-cable and useful if, and only if, (1) we can identify some of its components (besides direct pecuniary wealth) *and* if (2) we can identify circumstances that involve differences in the costs of each of the various types of managerial non-pecuniary "goods." By satisfying these two conditions, we can deduce the relative extent of such activities in each of those circumstances.

One circumstance is the type of ownership of the firm, e.g., corporate ownership, non-profit firm, public utility (with a restricted profit rate) and governmentally owned organizations. In this context, the contributions of the recent literature lie in the clues about the differences in relative costs among various types of organizations.

In conformity with the familiar fundamental theorem of demand, the lower the cost of a good or activity (whether it be a traditional type of economic good or one of a more general class of goods, like pleasant surroundings and those mentioned above), the more it will be demanded. This is all merely standard economic theory applied in a broader nexus of utility affecting components and is in no way an abandonment of the traditional basic theorems.

Williamson and Marris provide advances along the second and third avenues, indicate how to test the theory and provide examples of tests. Williamson considers emoluments and staff preference as two ways of spending beyond the profit-maximizing rate. The preference for larger staffs exists because salaries to a manager are correlated with a larger staff under a manager— a phenomenon best explained, to my knowledge, by Mayer.[5]

The approach used by Williamson is expressible as a maximization of the manager's utility, which is a function of several specified variables (e.g., size of staff and profits of the firm). The utility is subject to constraints on the choices he can make about staff and profit. Williamson postulates that profits are affected by the size of the staff (at first profits and staff size are positively related for increasing staff up to level and thereafter negatively related for larger staffs—given the demand environment of the firm). The owners of the firm, by detecting and policing their employees' actions, seek to induce them to select the maximum profit combination, which maximizes owners' utility. Unfortunately for the owners, there are costs of detecting and policing his actions so as to make sure he does select that point. Once these costs are recognized, it

---

5. Thomas Mayer, "The Distribution of Ability and Earnings," *Review of Economics and Statistics*, May 1960, 189–95. Mayer's explanation, in terms of the dependence of marginal product of managers upon the size of assets affected by the managers' decisions, avoids many of the superficial, misleading or downright erroneous explanations relying on convention, prestige, privilege of rank, etc.

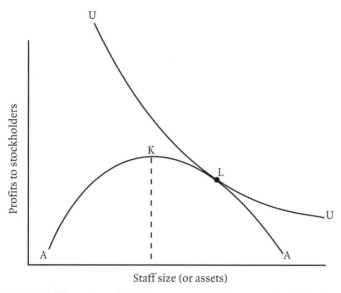

FIGURE 1. *Stockholder profits and staff size as sources of utility or pecuniary income to manager shift equilibrium beyond maximum profit size.*

is obviously better to avoid some of these costs if the profits saved are less than the costs. Cash registers, sales books and accounting systems are in part devices to enable more efficient detecting and policing of employees' deviations from profit maximization. The greater the costs of this detection and policing, the greater the profits managers will sacrifice for the sake of staff size and other means of increasing management utility.

Perhaps Williamson's analysis can be most easily illustrated, without doing it too much violence, by his graphic technique. In Figure 1, the vertical axis measures profit to the owner-stockholders. The horizontal axis measures staff (or emoluments) to the manager. Curve AA is the feasibility curve portraying the opportunity set of combinations of profits and "staff" open to the manager. The initial positively sloped portion indicates joint increases in staff and profits; the negative portion indicates staff can be larger than the profit-maximizing level indicated at the point K. One typically shaped utility curve is drawn UU. Profits to stockholders enter the manager's utility function insofar as larger profits imply larger salaries to the manager. Similarly, staff enters as an argument in the manager's utility or wealth function in that this too is correlated with salary as well as with emoluments. The familiar conflict of interest between stockholders and manager or between owner and employee or between taxpayer and government employee is portrayed by the utility curves of the employee-manager's utility function, which contains the firm's staff or emolument component, whereas only the profit or net value of the firm enters the stockholder's utility function. Point L is chosen by the manager. That point K is not chosen reflects the costs that must be borne by stockholders if the manager tried to detect and prevent all deviations from point K. The opportunity set bounded by AA would be vertically bounded on the right by the dotted line straight down from K if, and only if, detection of profit-maximizing actions and the policing were costless.

Any events, circumstances or factors that affect the feasibility curve (taxes, changes in business conditions) can shift the optimum tangency point. (Similarly, anything that shifts the shapes of the utility map will shift the equilibrium position.) Williamson derives the implied effects of corporate tax changes on the position and shape of the opportunity set bounded by AA. He also analyses the effects of a decline in business conditions on the curve AA. Williamson shows that the decrease in demand (and profitability) implies an increased effort to achieve greater *efficiency* in staff size—such as presumably would already have been achieved if the managers were maximizing profits of the stockholder owners. Thus the results differ from those of profit maximization, and they are more like those that seem to be observed in reality.

The significant point is that the equilibrium or solution values involve staff size, corporate expenditures and emoluments beyond the maximum profit combination of profits and staff or emoluments. Thus the owner's profit-maximizing hypothesis is apparently replaced with a more general utility-maximizing postulate for the manager with the indicated resultant implications. A fixed total tax shifts the AA downward vertically; this leads to a solution with smaller gross size of firm, emoluments and staff. Williamson points out that a firm with several subdivisions could in effect impose a fixed tax on each subdivision—calling it an overhead cost—thereby inducing the subdivision managers to shift their actions more toward profits and less toward staff and gross asset size. The lower the profit to the subdivision, the greater the marginal rate of substitution in consumption for managers between profit and other "goods." The tax does not change the feasible or opportunity rate of substitution between salary from larger profits and gains from the size and staff, because the slope of the AA curve is unchanged as it is shifted vertically downward. This leads to the leftward revision of the tangency point between the curve AA and the utility line. Marris, as we said, came close to the same result;

in fact his book presents a diagram much like Williamson's, but the axes are different, and no utility-maximizing approach is involved.

The significance of the utility-maximizing approach for the sales maximization approach is rather interesting. Sales maximization, advanced conjecturally by Baumol, is constrained by a "minimum-requisite" profit. Unfortunately, this minimum-requisite profit squares neither with the rest of economic theory nor with the facts of life. Managers do not maximize sales regardless of how much they could increase profits if they sacrificed some increment of sales. While sales maximization subject to the postulated constraint gives *some* implications that agree with observed events, it also implies many other things that are refuted by all available evidence. The hypothesis cannot be held out as a serious proposition. Instead, Williamson's model seems to explain the facts that Baumol was seeing and emphasizing. He saw some firm's managers with their eyes on sales—even to the point of increasing sales beyond what everyone would have agreed was the profit-maximizing level. Williamson makes this sensible, in that the incentive to increase sales is not treated as a single criterion for maximization, but rather as *a* means of the manager increasing his salary—in much the same fashion as a larger staff under the manager has the same effect. Substitution between these various components (salaries correlated with firm's profits, sales, assets, employees, etc.) affecting the manager's income or utility is the crucial factor, and Williamson emphasizes the factors making the substitution rate non-zero.

Without tarnishing the brilliance of Williamson's work, we can point out a bit of ambiguity. The derivation or basis of his profit-staff feasibility curve AA is not clear. In particular, he does not indicate exactly what is being held constant as a constraint defining the opportunity set. Furthermore, pecuniary and non-pecuniary benefits are mixed together on his emolument and staff division, thus making the utility isoquant an ambiguous concept. However, this can be easily corrected, formally, by adding a new dimension by which he can separate the pecuniary from the non-pecuniary goods to the manager. This would require at least a three-dimensional graph and a more detailed mathematical formulation.

One could then include business expenditures designed to increase, not the manager's pecuniary salary, but rather the *non-pecuniary* benefits available within the firm, like those mentioned above in the "third avenue." If quantities of these non-pecuniary benefits were explicitly included in the utility function and also indicated along one of the axes of the graph, we could draw iso-utility curves, showing combinations of pecuniary and non-pecuniary goods that yield a constant utility to the manager. Then the tangencies of the utility function with the feasibility function (production function of wealth and non-pecuniary benefits) would yield the solution values of profits and types of non-pecuniary managerial benefits for the managers.

If one formulates his analyses in this way, the changes in taxes and especially of changes in ownership structures (which affect the costs for owners to detect and punish non-profit-maximizing behavior by their employees) will be reflected in the feasibility set or production function on which the managers can operate. For example, the incentive to achieve maximum feasible profits for any given level of emoluments depends upon the costs of the owners' detecting that full realizability and appropriately rewarding or punishing the manager. If a large corporation with many stockholders involves higher detection and policing costs, the inducement for managers to depart from the objective of their employers is increased. In effect the profit-emolument curve is lowered and made flatter, pushing the manager toward greater emolument and less profit to stockholders.

This model can, and has been, applied to profit-limited public utilities and to non-profit corporations. A lesson to be drawn from these applications is that we can readily improve our analysis of managerial behavior if we first categorize firms according to whether the firm is a public utility (with constraints on the retainable profits) or a non-profit organization (rather than according to size or simply to corporate versus non-corporate firms). Much loose talk and erroneous blanket generalizations about managerial behavior would be avoided if the differences between *types* of corporate ownership were recognized. Drawing inferences from the behavior of managers of *large* (public utility firms) and applying those inferences to managers of non–public utility firms is not generally justified. What is more viable in one firm is not so viable in another. A further temptation to compare the small manager's behavior with that of a large non-profit or public utility is to confound size with different forms of ownership. Improvements in this direction await merely the application of some routine intellectual toil.

This model certainly can be applied to government ownership, where it may serve to shock some people who think that more government ownership or regulation will solve the problem of making managers conform more to the criteria they are "told" to seek.

The approach in the literature reviewed here is in stark contrast to that which attempts to use new types of utility functions, such as lexicographic or

discrete utility functions. Lexicographic functions rank goods by some criterion and assert that those of a lower rank provide no utility until those of a
higher rank achieve some critical amount. For example, there may be no utility
of non-pecuniary goods (via prestige, leisure, emoluments, pretty secretaries,
etc.) until profits or income achieve some minimum level. Furthermore, increments of the higher-ranking goods beyond the critical level have zero utility, so
that, in effect, substitution among goods is denied. The analyses covered in this
review retain the classic utility function but revise the types of constraints on
the opportunity set of choices open to the utility maximizer (instead of revising the utility function). It is difficult for this reviewer to place much hope in
this lexicographic type of utility function—in view of the clear-cut refutation
of its implications. The refutation of some of the implications derived with the
classic utility functions seems (now that one examines these new analyses) to
be the result of the postulated constraint system. By revising the constraints,
rather than the utility function, new implications are being derived. Instead of
postulating classic constraints of private property with zero costs of detecting
and policing employee behavior, a more general theory can be derived from
more general or varied types of property constraints. Perhaps unwittingly the
literature of managerial behavior is enlarging the realm of formal economic
theory to be applicable to more than conventional, individual private property
systems.

Another apparent "casualty" of the utility-maximizing approach under the
revised constraints is the "satisficing" or "aspiration" approach. The discussion by Marris is especially effective in bankrupting "satisficing," perhaps even
more than Marris intended. As he points out, in one sense it amounts to a statement of a constraint rather than an objective. That is, certain conditions must
be satisfied (i.e., losses not incurred). In another sense it indicates a "maximum"—given the costs of getting more information about the possibility and
location of still superior positions. As Marris suggests, the subject faced with a
problem involving effort in finding the solution sets up a tentative solution or
target as an aspiration or satisficing level. If he happily succeeds in exceeding
that level, he raises his "aspiration," target or "satisficing" level. And conversely. In this sense the word is simply a name of the search process for maximizing some criterion—not a replacement or substitute.[6]

There is no sense in trying to summarize a review. Instead a couple of personal impressions are offered. First, and least important, it is embarrassing

6. Marris, *Economic Theory*, 266–77.

that some economists feel compelled to preface or defend their work by an attack on the irrelevancy of existing economic theory. Even more embarrassing is their subsequent erroneous use of that theory.

Second, it is a genuine puzzle to me why economics has no "field" or section (analogous to the "fields" of money and banking, international trade, public finance, labor, etc.) devoted to "property rights." The closest thing to it is the field known as comparative economic systems; yet even there the fundamental role of the particular set of property right, as a specification of the opportunity set of choices about uses of resources, seems inadequately recognized. Especially puzzling is this in view of the fact that Adam Smith's *Wealth of Nations* is heavily concerned with exactly such questions. Perhaps the answer is that the whole of economics is the analysis of property rights in non-free goods. But if that is so, it is puzzling why it has taken so long to bring rigourous analytical techniques to bear on the implications about behaviour under different forms of property rights. In any event, a substantial start has now been made—even if it has not been explicitly recognized. Hence one of the major points of this paper has been to try to make explicit and emphasize this basis which, I think, underlies the advances of analyses here reviewed.

INCENTIVES IN THE UNITED STATES

WILLIAM H. MECKLING AND ARMEN A. ALCHIAN

Incentives are the prizes in the game of life—the goals individuals seek—the carrots. Through the ages of Tutankhamen, Alexander, Caesar, Louis XIV, and the Atom, they have remained the same. Men want, and have always wanted, exorbitant wealth, tyrannical power, idolatrous prestige, lavish consumption, and undisciplined leisure. And the men of Kharkov and Karachi are not different from the men of Kalamazoo. The specific objects of wealth or power may differ between Kalamazoo and Kharkov. But if Kalamazoo teems with thieves and brigands while Karachi is serenely industrious, the explanation lies not in differences in goals. Differences in goals will not explain differences in the way individuals pursue their goals.

What does explain the disparities? Differences in the relations between costs and goals. It is trite, but nonetheless important, that there is not enough wealth, power, prestige, etc., to go around. As all economists are aware, this scarcity becomes evident as costs. In seeking prizes, individuals must make sacrifices; for example, they must forego leisure or forego consumption. The existence of costs is universal—once again whether it be Kharkov, Karachi, or Kalamazoo. But the specific relations between costs and goals differ from place to place and from era to era. An hour of foregone leisure will not yield the same reward in Karachi as in Kharkov or Kalamazoo. There are two reasons for this. First, the technological circumstances—the resources and knowledge—are different. Second, the rules of the game—the mores and laws—that condition the hunt are different. The observed relation between cost and rewards—the relation that the contestants see—is a product of these two sets of factors. The technological circumstances imply a basic relation which in turn is conditioned by the rules of the game.

Observed cost-reward relationships are important because they govern individual behavior. Contestants perceive the schedules of prizes and costs and adapt accordingly. If the road to riches is dishonesty and deception, dishonesty and deception will flourish. If the state levies taxes on incomes, people will

Reprinted from *American Economic Review* 50 (May 1960): 55–61.

take more leisure. If the tax is limited to money incomes, the do-it-yourself club will flourish. If the tax exempts income from owner-occupied housing, the ranks of proud homeowners will swell. If corporate risk sharing is more efficient, the corporate organization will flourish.

But in trying to improve their lot individuals do more than merely adapt to given cost-reward relationships. They try to alter the schedule of prizes and costs to their own advantage. How? By changing the rules, especially through government. By pressing for advantageous legislative, administrative, or judicial action, individuals can and do use the power of government for personal gain. Thus economists describe the effects of reduced demand for an industry's product in terms of a new equilibrium with lower prices and lower output. But in a society where government can be summoned to the aid of distressed suppliers, that description is incomplete. For the industry may induce government to artificially maintain demand or subsidize losses.

Constitutional government is an attempt to limit this prerogative; but constitutional limitations are not and cannot be immutable. Even if legislative amendments were prohibited, experience suggests that *de facto* limitations are at the mercy of the courts which themselves adapt to social pressures. Of course, to get favorable changes in rules, individuals must incur costs. And the extent to which people attempt to change rules depends on the relation between the costs of changing rules and the potential rewards.

During the twentieth century a number of developments in the United States, such as the growth of corporations, technical progress, and urbanization, have had important effects on cost-rewards relationships, including the costs of changing the rules. But to us the one that overshadows all others in significance is the growth of government activity.

During the past sixty years, a dramatic metamorphosis has taken place in the role of government in the United States. By any standard, there has been an astonishing expansion, not only of the federal government, but of all governments during the twentieth century. To quote Solomon Fabricant:

> In 1900 one out of 24 workers was on a government payroll, in 1920 one out of 15, and in 1940 one out of 11. The current ratio . . . is one out of 8. The trend is sharp and clear. (p. 14)

> Today government holds 20 per cent of the nation's capital assets (exclusive of roads and streets and most military and naval equipment) not 7 per cent as in 1900. (p. 9)

The sixfold rise in government employment between 1900 and 1949, and the similar increase in capital assets, great as they are, understate the rise in total volume of resources used in producing government services. . . . The physical volume of goods and services purchased by government from private industry went up more than a thousand per cent between 1903 and 1949. (pp. 24–25)[1]

The facts disclosed by Fabricant, striking as they are, tell only part of the whole story. Transfer payments are not included. These were about 12 billion dollars in 1949, or 6 per cent of individual income compared with less than 1 per cent in 1900. (Ibid., p. 9) Furthermore, Fabricant's data do not reflect the growth in government during the last ten years. Expenditures of government have doubled since 1949, the year on which his statements were based. Today they are about 30 per cent of gross national product.

National defense accounts for a significant part, but by no means all, of this increase. In 1903 defense expenditures were 10 per cent of total government expenditures. Today they are on the order of 35 per cent.[2] In 1900 there was no Old-Age and Survivors Insurance, no Old Age Assistance program, no unemployment compensation, no Commodity Credit Corporation, no Federal Housing Administration, no urban renewal program, and no Reclamation Bureau.

Growth in expenditures is only one facet of the expansion of government. Important transformations have also occurred in regulation and control. The twentieth century has witnessed the birth and growth of the Securities and Exchange Commission, the Federal Communications Commission, the Federal Aviation Agency, the Federal Reserve Board, the Federal Deposit Insurance Corporation, the National Labor Relations Board, and minimum wage and hour laws. At state and local levels, planning and zoning commissions, building codes, public health regulations, and licensing have proliferated.

The fact of large government growth or change itself does not justify our concentration on this change. If the increased importance of the corporate structure or of urbanization or of complexity of modern technology were even

---

1. Solomon Fabricant, *The Trend of Government Activity in the United States Since 1900* (New York: National Bureau of Economic Research, 1952).

2. Including military assistance, stockpiling, NASA, and the lion's share of AEC expenditures. See Otto Eckstein, *Trends in Public Expenditures in the Next Decade*, CED Supplementary Paper, April, 1959.

more spectacular, we would still emphasize government activity. Increased corporate activity, greater urbanization, and increased complexity do not reduce the role of the marketplace or private property as institutions through which individual wealth, prestige, consumption, or leisure is determined. But the growth in government that has taken place does have that effect. Government as a taxer, a spender, an employer, and a regulator supplants the marketplace and private property, thereby changing patterns of individual behavior. Standards of behavior required in the marketplace lose viability with the expanded role of government.

Public Finance and Incentives

The wherewithal to support governments in the United States comes mostly from taxes on individual income, corporate income, sales, and property, and from miscellaneous excise taxes. All of these have important effects on cost-reward relationships. Even if tax laws were in a sense ideal, taxes would alter basic cost-reward relationships. Individual income taxes inevitably alter the rewards for foregone leisure. Corporate income taxes increase the cost of doing business as a corporation vis-à-vis alternative organizational forms. Sales taxes increase consumption costs relative to holding wealth. And so on!

But in practice the laws are not ideal. As we have noted, most home-produced income, to the delight of farmers, is not taxed as individual income. Income from owner-occupied dwellings is largely exempted. Income spent on interest, charity, medical services, and employment fringe benefits is largely exempt. Co-operatives and so-called nonprofit corporations are exempted from corporate income taxes. Depletion provisions make the rate on extractive industries less than on other industries. Income taken in the course of conducting business—private airplanes, private cars, pretty secretaries, and thick rugs—is exempt from individual and corporate taxes. Certain forms of consumption, e.g., eating at home, are often exempt from sales taxes. The property tax turns out to be largely a tax on land and buildings.

In 1900, when government was small, such tax provisions would have been of little consequence. Government being what it is today, however, the effects are by no means trivial. Cost-reward relationships are effectively rewritten, and the contestants must revamp their style of play accordingly.

Government expenditures also affect basic cost-reward relationships. Farm price supports, various "low-cost" lending schemes, water, power, and reclamation projects, and postal subsidies to publishers and advertisers are some obvious examples. Unemployment insurance alters the rewards in seasonal industries. Old-Age and Survivors Insurance penalizes employment after age sixty-five.

To economists these kinds of individual adaptation to taxes and expenditures are a familiar subject, and we need not dwell on them further.

Incentives Within Government

When government employs a significant fraction of the wealth and of the labor force and buys an even greater share of the output, cost-reward relationships within government deserve attention. The prizes for various forms of behavior in government are markedly different from those in private markets. Private firms buy inputs and sell outputs, and the test of survival is the relation between the value of the two. Government buys inputs, but the inputs are paid for by levying taxes, while output is given away. The problem is identical with the familiar problem of divergence between private and social costs. Once tax receipts reach the Treasury, they are owned by no one. To the individuals entrusted with their expenditure, the costs of using these funds is not equal to their value. They are not required as a condition of survival to see that value of output exceeds the value of inputs.

Specific cost-reward relationships in government employment reflect these circumstances. The bulk of government employees fall into three categories: employees under civil service or merit systems, teachers, and military personnel. In all of these cases, seniority is the key to success, and a premium is placed on job security. These systems owe their origin and survival to the fact that private and social costs diverge in government. Civil service and merit systems originated as answers to the spoils system. Why should government be marked with the spoils system? Why should politicians hire and promote unqualified people? Because the cost to them of doing so is not equal to the social cost (which, incidentally, is not to say that civil service is any improvement). Elaborate procedures to ensure competitive bidding are another device conceived as an answer to the same problem.

Incentives and Government Regulation

Regulation is still another government activity affecting rewards and associated costs. The spectrum of government regulation runs from national minimum wage and hour laws to licensing itinerant fruit dealers. Frequently regulation confers valuable privileges on selected groups of individuals. Licensing of banks, insurance companies, security dealers, radio and television stations, airlines, taxicabs, and doctors are examples. Sometimes the valuable privilege consists of nothing more than the right to operate a monopoly, as in the case of medicine and taxicabs. Other times a scarce resource is given away, as in the case of radio, television, and airlines. Frequently, a government agency is interposed between the consumer and the producer with the power to decide which producers are acceptable. An applicant producer not only must show that customers demand the service he proposes to offer but must also satisfy whatever other criteria the regulatory agency adopts, e.g., that he is of good character. In technical terms, the money price of licenses is raised to infinity by legal prohibition of purchase; consequently, other kinds of activity that lead to obtaining a license become more rewarding. The reward for favorable personal impressions on the regulatory agency has increased. Statesmanship, conformity, sociability, prestige, political influence, civic-mindedness, and the like replace money as means to rewards. Where a monopoly is granted, as in medicine, constant vigilance is required against interlopers. Both the public and the politicians must be convinced in perpetuity that the monopoly is in their interest. Again statesmanship, conformity, sociability, prestige, political influence, etc., take on added importance.

Where valuable privileges are conferred, profit regulations are often imposed. Public utilities and nonprofit corporations are privately owned but profit restricted. Since the restriction takes the form of some percentage of investment (zero in the case of nonprofit firms), the firms actually operate on a cost-plus basis. What is restricted is only the money profits that can be taken out of the business. Potential profits can be turned to personal gain, however, by disguising them as costs. The cost of rewards taken in the form of business-connected purchases has gone down. Thick rugs, pleasant offices and colleagues, and even such seemingly mysterious activities as community affairs participation by officials, support of charity, and extensive fringe benefits become sensible.

Incentives to Political Action

A striking change in public attitudes toward the role of government has attended government expansion in the twentieth century, as Solomon Fabricant notes:

President Cleveland had vetoed an appropriation of $25,000 to buy seed corn for Texas farmers ruined by a drought. Even a democratic President, vetoing the appropriation . . . could state "I can find no warrant for such an appropriation in the Constitution, and I do not believe that the power and duty of the general government ought to be extended to the relief of individual suffering which is in no manner related to the public service or benefit. A prevalent tendency to disregard the limited mission of this power and duty should, I think, be steadfastly resisted, to the end that the lesson should be constantly enforced that, though the people support the government, the government should not support the people."[3]

That the above statement, which was made in his first term, was not "political suicide" is about as eloquent a testimonial to the change in attitude as one could find. The change is not a change in the ends for which men strive; i.e., wealth, power, and prestige. It is a change in the relation between costs and rewards for political action. Nineteenth-century attitudes severely proscribed the use of the state as a means to individual ends. The twentieth century has seen this proscription eroded away. Behavior which society formerly held to be unacceptable has become standard practice.

The change in attitude toward the role of government has increased rewards for exerting organized political pressure—not only to recognized types of union and industry groups but to doctors, teachers, fishermen, golfers, senior citizens, parents, et al. The services of professional lobbyists, public relations experts, and lawyers are more rewarding. Mass communication media—radio, television, newspapers, and magazines—are more earnestly courted because of their influence and power. Contributions of time and money to political campaigns have larger pay-offs. These are kinds of behavior that are efficient in bringing about changes in the rules of the game.

If it appears that we are pointing a fickle finger at government, the impression is correct. If it appears that this is also a condemnation, that impression, too, is correct. But the condemnation does not derive from the economic analysis. For the analysis merely identifies the changes in cost-reward relationships over the last half-century and develops the implications for individual behavior. It is an ethical judgment that leads us to condemn the kinds of behavior that this has induced. And it is on the basis of an empirical judgment that we assert that cost-reward relationships have changed, not goals or incentives.

3. Cleveland's statement is from "Veto of the Texas Seed Bill, Feb. 16, 1887," in *The Writings and Speeches of Grover Cleveland*, ed. George F. Parker (New York: Cassel Publishing, 1892).

MARKET PRICES, PROPERTY AND BEHAVIOR

I. Analysis and Advocacy

Scientific economics has developed along different lines in various countries and at different times—primarily because of some breakthrough in analytic method or advocacy of some new policy. For example, the portion of economics concerned with the theory of demand was advanced when the Austrians (as we call them) formulated the utility or choice theoretic foundations of demand and value theory. Recently, reduced costs of computational services and algebraic analysis have enabled reformulation of production theory in terms of matrix theory and of input-output matrices. This has encouraged beliefs about the possibilities of broader as well as more detailed optimization of output.

Much economic theory was developed in the course of attempts to advocate some policy; however, the logical and empirical validity of the theory could be established, not by reference to good or humanitarian intentions, but only by empirical verification against the facts of the world. For example, the writings and theory of Adam Smith, Karl Marx and John Keynes were directed to advocacy of a policy or socio-economic system. These writers were not exclusively analytical; they did not restrict themselves to non-normative scientific propositions. But that has not prevented their theories from being tested in the crucible of empirical, factual scientific validity. To the extent their contributions were scientifically and objectively supported, they have contributed to the advance of economic analysis.

And in the course of time we have all learned more valid economic theory. Economists are in the same situation as physicists, chemists and biologists; the conjectured theories or interpretations must stand the *test of empirical validity*. Laws of chemistry and physics respect no particular socio-economic system. They are universal. And the same is true for economics.

The scientific, empirical objectivity and generality inherent in economic analysis make it applicable to *all* societies and enable economists to act as sci-

This previously unpublished paper was presented at Conference of Soviet and Western Economists, Repalto, Italy, September 1967, and appears here by permission of the author.

entists in pursuit of demonstrable theorems. And that, I believe, is the axiomatic premise of a meeting such as this. If there is no such premise that is valid, then I would advise us to adjourn and to relax on the beaches of Rapallo admiring the pretty girls . . . on which I am sure we can all agree.

Recently, the effectiveness of prices in guiding behavior has attracted attention. In particular the possibility of making prices a more effective incentive and guide to production decisions has been evident in the socialist states. Also, in capitalist states interest in prices and exchange as guides and incentives to production and employment has been revived now that the so-called Keynesian models, which ignored prices, have been modified. The role of prices in determining employment, output and the use of resources has been analyzed more carefully from new points of view. I shall, as a means of eliciting from the socialist economy economists their discerned, tested theorems and analysis, give a brief exposition of some kinds of analysis pursued by capitalist economists— in the hope that an exchange of such expositions will, as with physicists and chemists, enable us to formulate a more powerful and valid economic theory.

II. Guides to Productive Activities

In many areas of economics we have common interests, and we could explore known or conjectural theorems. For example, the Russians, as an outgrowth of their political and cultural objectives in a centrally planned and directed economy (here was *their* motivation!), have discerned theorems in production and allocation theory. Their linear programming and input-output analyses have paralleled or preceded similar studies in capitalist countries induced by the use of centralized economic controls during our common efforts of World War II. The results of this work have been mutually discussed, especially at development conferences in which attempts are made to see if increased centralized planning and coordination of activity are means of achieving economic growth. As we already know, many conferences and studies implicitly assumed that necessary data were readily available, that the demands of consumers and of various means of production were well known and that the individual would sacrifice all concern for his own interests in stating and fulfilling official plans.

But Soviet economists and leaders, such as Lenin, recognized that solid bridges to socialism are built not merely on enthusiasms directly but, with the aid of enthusiasm, on personal incentives *effectively guided* by or related to *appropriate* values of output. For example, Soviet economists have detected several alternatively formulated cost accounting or valuation systems for guiding "output" and for rewarding personal activity and efficiency. One system of cost accounting and rewards encourages technological stagnation; another encourages understatement of plans. Improvements are sought so as to channel behavior more to conform to the selected criterion of increased profitability. Unless given appropriate criteria to follow or achieve, one would neither contribute nor gain as much as he could. With incorrect criteria he may be induced to actions that increase his welfare by reducing that of others rather than by jointly increasing mutual benefits.

We read of Soviet discussions of decentralized implementation of a planned economy, of greater control by the consumer, of greater control by the plant managers, of improved coordination of plans and prices, and of prices that are more decentralized and compatible with plans. I point this out because exactly this same problem occurs in so-called capitalist countries. It may seem strange to Soviet economists that capitalist economists would also study means of establishing prices that are more responsive to local conditions in order to make "profitability" a more effective index and guide to activity.

But if you Soviet economists claim any distinction or novelty in discerning these difficulties, let me challenge your dubious uniqueness. We in the capitalist world also see similar problems. Unemployment occurs, not because some devil produces it but because we individually follow inappropriate economic signals, prices and indicators. So, like the Soviets, we capitalist economists also worry about prices as production and employment guides and about how to make them perform "better."

In the mathematical analysis of economics, economists (both capitalist and socialist!) have assumed a special constraint in the derivation of demand functions—that of private property constraint. It was Slutsky who developed this demand theory in its most notable form. And Konus rescued cost-of-living indices from the morass of the theory of averages. What did Slutsky postulate as the constraint on the individual utility maximizer? He postulated a market exchange economy with the individual spending his own wealth at market prices. This gives a private property theory of demand, a capitalist application and a socialist one, since in both economies the consumer allocates his income among marketable options of consumption at his volition.

This theorem of demand has become known as the negative demand function. The lower the cost to a person of engaging in any desirable activity (desirable to him), the more will he do so. In special contexts, this can be interpreted to say that the lower the price at which a good is available, the greater will be the amount demanded by consumers. Putting it in opposite terms, we can say that for any rate of consumption or activity by any person, there is some increase in price, or cost to him, of that consumption or activity that will induce him to engage in less. And in this formulation we are not referring to costs as merely the market money price and the activity as merely the purchase of consumer goods. The theorem refers to every desired activity—resting, playing or bullying people. The greater the sacrifice imposed on one who engages in some activity, the less he will engage in that activity. This law—the law of demand—holds in all societies and is a beautifully verified law of economics.

Though the consumer choice in response to market prices is identical in both socialist and capitalist economies, differences arise in the realm of *production management*. In a socialist economy producers obtain raw materials and labor services but are not subject to "private property" constraints, as are consumers of final products or producers in a capitalist society—at least for those who happen to be operating privately owned firms.

Perhaps I should hasten to add that we so-called capitalist economists really are not mere capitalist economists. Much, though probably not the majority, of our production is conducted and organized via institutions other than that of the private property capitalism. For example, almost all of our formal academic education is provided by organizations that are not privately owned or operated for private profit. In some instances, that education is provided via not-for-profit organizations; these may appear to be private property organizations, but they, in fact, do not possess all the essential characteristics of private property, as I shall try to explain later. Nearly one-fourth of our gross national product is organized via socialist enterprises, i.e., the government. And much of our economic theory is directed to the analysis of those portions of our economy. And almost all of us here work for publicly owned or not-for-profit institutions. It should not be surprising that our attempts to advance and generalize economic theory are directed toward including socialist organizations.

But that is the fact. In the United States we talk about wasteful use of water, of air and water pollution as the Russians do, for example, about potential pollution of Lake Baikal. We talk a lot about inefficient education, congested roads, dirty public parks, rude bureaucrats, inefficient postal service and racial discrimination, to name a few examples. All of these are cases in which producers or plant managers are believed to be doing an "inefficient" or unsatisfactory job. Such a complaint could be merely the dissatisfaction with a world in which other people don't devote their entire energies to *our* personal benefit. On the other hand, it may reflect a belief that people are behaving in ways that they would not if the total social value (and costs) of their actions were more fully impressed upon them as costs of benefits to which they would respond. When the costs are imposed on people *other* than the responsible person, the responsible party will use resources for one purpose even though they could obviously have been used elsewhere or in some other way with a greater value. He may be acting in *ignorance* of that higher-valued alternative use or he may act *despite* knowledge of it, since others bear the costs. He ignores, though he is not ignorant of, those forsaken values or costs imposed on other people. But if the damaged parties could pay him to perform that preferred alternative service, he would do so, to his own benefit also. Or if he had been damaging them by his actions, and if they could make him aware of those costs by having to bear them, he would heed those potential costs and revise his behavior.

Now I assume it is a fact that we see this kind of individually "irresponsible" behavior—in the sense of not being responsive to the costs imposed on others or of the benefits sacrificed—and that we regard it as behavior of the type that we seek to avoid in an economic and social system. As economists, we know that if the prices of various goods more closely reflect the value of the benefits that would accrue to other people, then the costs a manager must pay to get resources, or to get people to work, more closely reflect the damages done to them or the value of opportunities forsaken by those productive workers and goods in performing this work. And the manager, out of the greater value of the product, will be able to pay for the cost of that service—called reward or wages for their work. Thus the value of the gross social product is pushed closer to the maximum profitability by inducing activity to be directed more toward its higher-valued uses (net of the costs of such activity). And all this is true regardless of whether the norms, or prices, are determined by individual market negotiations or by a central planning agency responsible for assigning the norms. Yet in either case there are ethical and practical difficulties. If values are set by a central planning or evaluation agency, some people will object that the conception of the appropriate values differs from that of other individuals in the community and that the central agency is not fully informed in any event. If values are set by the market, some may contend that the best prices are not costless to find, because of the cost of communication among *all* people; the negotiated and effective prices are not immediately and fully reflective of highest-valued uses; there *are* costs of communicating and negotiating with every conceivable potential demander or buyer of some goods; and these may in some cases be so high that market prices fail to reflect potential values.

III. Property Rights and Market-Revealed Values

Efficient production (i.e., maximizing the value of output as judged by appropriate norms of value) involves solving several general problems: (1) discovering the appropriate norm of value, (2) discovering the appropriate costs to be used in production decisions and (3) inducing managers and people to respond appropriately to those norms of value and costs.

A little thought will show that the second problem is simply the first one restated. In any situation of scarcity—i.e., one in which there are more uses for goods than can be simultaneously satisfied—any allocation of the available goods will *imply* a set of *costs*. For each resource in any one use, the highest-valued of all its alternative uses is the implied measure of cost. When some good is used in one particular way, cost is, by definition, the highest value forsaken. This proves that the first and the second questions are merely different formulations of the same question. But the one question that both formulations express still remains. What is the *appropriate* measure or criterion of value? Is it a value expressed in a price set by a central agency or one revealed by open market forces with negotiation among potential buyers and sellers? I do not want here to discuss these two alternatives and their implications. Instead I wish to go on to the third question: Whatever may be deemed the appropriate value, what affects the extent to which managers of resources heed it as a guide to allocative decisions? Under what conditions will they have more incentive to maximize that value and under which will they have less reason to do so?

In more general terms, "Under what conditions will managers respond more to the net value (net of costs) of output and try to maximize that value?" In a capitalist economy this question can be posed as follows: "What conditions enable market prices of a good to reflect most accurately the highest social values of that good?" This question involves (1) the incentive of potential, alternative users to reveal the values they place on various uses of the good—and this reflects the security of the benefits or rights the buyer would obtain, (2) the visibility or availability of the price as the norm of value—and this reflects the costs of getting all potential demanders to reveal their use values of whatever might be produced and (3) the willingness or incentive of the "seller" to heed or respond to discerned prices as the reward for a particular assignment of goods.

I discuss each in turn. (1) If an umbrella, for example, were offered for sale, no buyer would offer as much as he otherwise would if he thought it would, with very high probability, be stolen within a few days. No one would offer as much for the umbrella if he were unable to retain possession or control over the subsequent use of the umbrella. Only if all the potential subsequent beneficiaries of that umbrella had to reveal their valuation and contributed toward its purchase or toward the benefit to the producer would the true total value of the umbrella be effective in its production and allocation.

(2) Even with secure rights to the purchased item, if some potential users or demanders were unable to communicate with potential producers—possibly because the demanders were prohibited from making market purchases or had to incur prohibitive costs in communicating or negotiating an exchange—the value that would be revealed to the potential producer would not reflect the total value. If markets were prohibited or if the hours at which exchanges could be consummated were limited, some people would find it more expensive to express their bids. Closing the "market" to some potential users restricts the ability of price to reflect more fully the total use value. I hasten to admit that there is no reason for saying that it is "good" to permit highest-use values to be revealed to potential producers; it may be that the good is deemed by some religious or state or paternalist authority to be an improper good (e.g., alcoholic liquors in the United States from 1919 to 1933, gambling services, production and sale of marijuana). In many instances, some products are prohibited from being produced for sale to consumers because some "higher" authority deems such goods "improper."

The difficulty of revealing all demands can be thought of in two terms—the difficulty of revealing (a) values of uses and (b) costs that are imposed on other people. If you pollute the water or air I use, and if I demand more clean water and air, I will want to impress on you the value of the cleaner air and water that you are destroying. If I am unable to identify every source of pollution of water and air, or if it is too expensive to discover and negotiate with every source, then I may simply accept the pollution in order to avoid the still higher costs of identifying and negotiating with and policing every contract with every source of pollution. Furthermore, there may be 1,000 beneficiaries of clean water, but if only a few take action, the extent to which they will incur expenses to avoid excessive water pollution will be restricted. The costs of getting everyone together may exceed the value of having cleaner water. Transactions and negotiation costs (excluding the market price to be paid, once the negotiation about price is completed) may be too great relative to the value of the service about which negotiations may be conducted. High transactions costs thus will attenuate the extent to which market prices are effective or reflective of total social values of goods and services.

(3) The availability to the seller-producer of the market price proceeds is nearly the obverse of the availability of the good to the demander-purchaser. If an agent responsible for the allocation or disposition of some good can not be rewarded commensurately with increased net values and proceeds, or if there is no person for whom he is acting who can claim that net sales proceed for himself, then the price will be less influential in directing his allocation or disposition of the goods at his disposal. He will be less willing to seek out every possible opportunity for a better or higher market price or use-value to the potential demanders; after all, what the demander would give up as inducement would not so fully go to the allocating agent. Or more precisely, the less the market price is correlated with the profitability to the allocator for some sale or allocation of resources at his disposal, the less will he be responsive to the market price potential.

From these considerations, it follows that the degree of reliance that may be placed on markets and market prices, or indeed even on prices set by some authority, depends on the nature of the authority over the income obtained by some managerial agent consequent to any allocation of resources. Even more, the willingness and efficacy with which the allocative agent will seek the highest available prices for the uses to which he can allocate goods depend upon the extent to which the price will determine the rewards he can obtain. In technical terms, property rights play a significant role in the extent to which prices will reflect highest values of uses and the extent to which allocative authorities will respond to those prices.

In most countries, consumer valuation of goods reflects a valuation based on private property in the bid for goods. And in most countries, market prices are used as a rationing device and as a guide to managers in deciding how much to produce. However, productive goods are less likely to be allocated and used according to market-revealed values, where centralized controls or prices are set by central agencies, because in those cases we note that there is less likely to be private property in the goods subjected to those prices. More likely, socialized industries or mutually owned or not-for-profit enterprises will be operative. And of course this makes good sense. There is less likelihood that resources can be controlled via direct controls or via prices set by some central agency if those resources are privately owned. The incentive would be stronger for an owner to seek out other higher-valued uses or exchanges. To reduce that incentive, either his rights of private property are eliminated or the new privately owned goods will more likely be those for which such controls are absent, leaving this portion of the economy to be dominated by non-private property.

Let me protect myself by noting that nothing said so far implies that a correlation between effectiveness of market prices and private property is good or bad. That correlation is purely a scientific, empirical fact of life. If it is regarded as bad, then either market prices or private property rights will be suppressed or made illegal. One may argue, as many do in socialist and capitalist states, that market prices should not be allowed to influence, let alone dominate, the allocation of resources in certain kinds of uses. For example, often it is asserted that in education, research and defense, the market price or exchange-revealed values should not be allowed to control production and allocation of goods. One reason is the contention that the amount of goods and their values in various uses should not depend so much upon the distribution of marketable wealth. Another contention, and one alluded to earlier, is that some activities should not be allowed even though some individuals, in their narrow interest, would want them. Prostitution, some forms of gambling, alcoholic liquor, uses of drugs, types of religion, salacious pictures and antisocial and "treasonable" literature are a few examples of prohibited activities. Private property would enable people to circumvent or modify those prohibitions. Another contention, already mentioned, is that even if private property effects were desired, in some cases the costs of using the market to reveal individual demands and to enforce contracts would be prohibitive relative to the value of the goods so allocated. Traffic problems on roads are an example. Hence a standard centralized, politically imposed solution may be more economic.

I shall consider it agreed that the foregoing and ensuing discussions in no way pertain to the desirability of various forms of property rights. Instead they pertain to the scientific implications of the presence or absence of various forms of property rights—much as chemists can analyze the effects of various chemicals. In the ensuing discussion I shall investigate some forms of property rights to show the differences in responsiveness to market prices and the incentive to seek out highest market prices.

IV. Exchangeability, Discrimination Among Risks and Values of Rights

By authority or rights I mean the expectations a person can have that the decisions he makes will determine what is done with those resources over which he has that authority. I call this authority a property right—a legal right or socially enforced expectation that decisions about specified goods over which a person has such rights will in fact be honored. And it could be a state or private property right. I might have called it a personal right or a personal accountability, in the sense that all potential users of that good are accountable to the person in charge who has the authority or right to make decisions about what will be done to that good. If he can also *exchange* rights over some good for rights to some other goods on mutually acceptable terms with some other property holder then we call that right a private property right. Even if the exchangeable right is held jointly and exercised as a joint decision (as in a partnership or corporation or mutual cooperative), the right is still a private property right. The joint owners can exchange rights to various goods with other people—limited only by their ability to find some other party willing to make the exchange. Quiet thought will suggest that this is not the case for state or communal property.

Risk Bearing

If we examine more closely what the rights of "public" or government ownership are, we shall find a significant difference, even if there are some similarities. In publicly owned enterprises, as in a jointly owned private enterprise (corporation), not every rights holder has a right to manage nor even to walk in and take away some fractional share of the assets on the grounds that he is one of the owners. Each "owner" in a public or government enterprise has a right to share in the decisions that will be made—usually by the selection of politicians to select people to manage the enterprises. Also he has a right to a pro rata share in the net profitability or losses of the enterprise. How and to what extent does he participate in that sharing? If the *publicly owned*, socialist enterprise is profitable, the excess of social product over costs means that the state expenditure budget for this product can be lower. Less state revenue need be spent on that factory. Everyone's taxes can be smaller than if the enterprise were less successful. Or the net profits can be used to finance other activities for the benefit of everyone else in the community who is, of course, a pro rata rights holder in this enterprise. The gains to any person of the profits of the enterprise that are used to reduce taxes or produce other goods will depend upon the extent to which his taxes are reduced below what they would have been and the extent to which he benefits from the use made of the surplus or profits in producing other goods. The net distribution of those profits depends upon the tax structure and on the way those profits are used for other purposes. Some people may be especially benefitted by a particular tax revision and some by the particular use of the funds. That is determined by the political process.

Exchangeability and Discrimination Among Rights

For state-owned enterprises, no single members or subsets of the public can trade among themselves any subsets of the jointly held rights. I cannot exchange my rights to the income or control over a state-owned auditorium for your share of rights in a state-owned athletic field. Nor can I trade my portion of state-owned rights for some of your private property rights to consumption goods (which *are* individually exchangeable for other rights to privately owned consumption goods).

If I could trade my rights in one state enterprise for your rights in another, what would we be exchanging? To be meaningful, we would have to exchange prespecified classes of authority or consequences. Such an exchange would specify that in transferring my rights of a share of public ownership of the auditorium to you in exchange for your rights to a furniture factory (for example) I would acquire the potential benefits or costs or consequences that would have accrued to you from the activities of the furniture factory, while you get all the public ownership consequences to me of the activities of the auditorium.

What are these consequences? If the enterprise earns a profit, the gains can be used for the state budget expenditures, thereby expanding state services or reducing taxes, or they can be used to produce other goods or to raise wages of the enterprise employees. In any case my rights to a pro rata share of the tax reduction, consequent to the use of the auditorium, would be transferred to you. Your tax and income for consumption would be more dependent or concentrated on the enterprises in which you now have a double ownership share and less dependent on the enterprise in which you transferred your public ownership rights to me. It is the rights to a share in the decision authority and to the benefits produced by the profits of one enterprise that you would be exchanging for rights to similar effects that would accrue from the operation of some other enterprise. The influence you could exert in the enterprise in which you have acquired a second share is increased, and it is reduced in the enterprise in which your former share of public ownership has been transferred to me. Both of us have concentrated our rights on a smaller subset of economic activities. To permit such exchangeability and concentration there must be explicit specification of the rights accruing to each member of the public so that transfers would have some meaning. I shall assume that the meaning of an exchange is that which I have just discussed: (a) specification of the rights to the selection of the manager, (b) benefits of the disposition of the surplus or burdens of making good any losses and (c) the transferability of these specific identified component rights.

The proposition can now be derived that differences in managerial behavior between publicly and privately owned enterprises are affected by the ability of people to sell or exchange shares of property rights in various enterprises or resources and to *concentrate* differentially such rights to consequences of operations of various enterprises on subgroups of the public. Let me be clear about this. It is not that there are no other differences nor that this difference I single out has not been noticed before. Instead I am merely emphasizing its unique importance.

If such rights are exchangeable, it follows that unit pro rata shares of rights of public ownership to each enterprise will not necessarily exchange on a *one-for-one* basis. Some enterprises are larger. Further pro rata shares in enterprises that are, or are expected to be, more profitable will be exchanged for more than one pro rata share in a less profitable or less efficient enterprise. After all, a share in the rights to a more profitable or efficient enterprise will give more benefits to the share owner than will the less efficiently operated firm. A share in a publicly owned dam may be exchangeable only for six shares in a publicly owned golf course. The ratios of exchange are the market prices of the shares. Furthermore, these exchange rates among shares will not only reflect the *present* profitability of each enterprise but will reflect *expected* profitability *in all the future years.* Thus not only will current profitability be compared among enterprises, but the future profitability expected consequent to present actions (such as investments revision of fixed assets, long-term planning) will be compared. Furthermore, these capitalized exchange rates (market prices) will change over time as future prospects change. This is known as the present value effect of future anticipated effects, sometimes called "capitalization" of resource values—a phenomenon from which capitalism may have obtained its name. I am not arguing that this is good or bad, or that the market price of shares will necessarily reflect absolutely accurate foresight. In fact they will not. But whether the accuracy of foresight is reflected in the *changes* in relative exchange rates of various enterprises, these prices reflect the fact that some people will choose to *concentrate* their holdings in fewer enterprises than in uniform pro rata shares in all enterprises of the economy. The people will discriminate among enterprises.

Specialization in Control and Risks via Exchangeable Property Rights
Concentration of one's rights holdings in a few enterprises will result in variations in the values of his rights *relative* to the mass of the public as a whole. This is what happens in the capitalist system. These exchanges are what the "stock markets," to mention only one market, facilitate.

Without in any way establishing the superiority or inferiority of transferrability and capitalization, let us examine two implications of that transferrability and capitalization: (1) concentration of effects are more directly on persons responsible for them and (2) "comparative advantage" effects of specialized applications of (a) knowledge and of (b) risk bearing are enabled.

The concentration of consequences of personal activity is easy to illustrate. Suppose there are 100 people in a community, with 10 separate enterprises. Suppose that each person, by devoting 1/10 of his time to some one enterprise could produce a saving or gain of $1,000. Since the individual is a 1/100 part-owner he will acquire $10. Suppose, further, that he does this for each of the 10 different enterprises, in each of which he has 1/100 part. His total wealth gain will be $100, with the rest of the product, $9,900, going to the other 99 people.

However, suppose everyone owns 1/10 of *one* enterprise only (this means that ownership has been reshuffled from pro rata equal shares in all 10 enterprises to a concentration in one enterprise by each person); a person will now devote his whole time to the one enterprise, where he again produces $10,000. (We assume that his productivity is proportional to the number of hours of work and is the same in all lines of work. Other assumptions relying on advantages of specialization will change the arithmetic and would strengthen the main principle being elaborated.) Of this he gets $1,000. The remainder, $9,000, goes to the owners of the other 9/10 share. Now $1,000 of his wealth is dependent upon his own activities whereas formerly only $100 was. If we go to the extreme where the 10 enterprises are subdivided into 100, with each person a sole owner of one enterprise, then his wealth increase will depend even more upon his own activities.

If public ownership rights were separable and exchangeable, they would soon be "privatized" by a movement toward specialization of ownership of the type in the second example. Why? First, the wealth a person can get would be more dependent upon his own activities. However, it is possible that many people may prefer to collect a major portion of their wealth gain from other people's activities. If this were the case, the total wealth gain would decrease since everyone would have less incentive to work. But it suffices that there be at least one person who prefers to make himself less dependent upon other people's activities. He will then be prepared to buy up some ownership rights and pay a higher price for them than they are worth to some other people. That he values them more highly is precisely another way of saying that he values self-dependence more than they do or that he prefers more wealth to less wealth—even if it requires some work by him.

Comparative Advantage in Rights Specialization

The second reason for specialization of property rights is the specialization of control and productivity. The preceding example did not utilize interpersonal differences of abilities, knowledge or attitude toward risk. But people do differ in these respects. It can be shown with the famous, long-standing logical theorem of gains from specialization and comparative advantage that specialization in various tasks—including that of managing *and* bearing risks—will increase wealth.

Usually the illustrations of comparative advantage are based on "labor" productivities with no references to risk bearing or to managerial productivities. But people differ in their "talents as property right holders." What are the functions of "rights holders," regardless of whether they are "public" or "private"? They bear the risks and consequences of value changes, make the decisions of how much to invest, how to produce and who shall be employed in what tasks as laborers and managers. The ability to do these things is affected by attitude toward risk bearing, ability to detect different people's differential productive abilities, foresight and responsiveness to changing values of output. The talents to do these are sensitive to the particular industry, type of product or productive resource and vary among people. The differences in skills of people as property rights holders make pertinent the principle of comparative advantage through specialization in property right or managerial functions.

If property rights are transferable, then specialization of property rights will occur. People will concentrate their selected rights in those areas in which they believe they have a comparative advantage. Just as specialization in typing, music or various types of labor is more productive, so is specialization in ownership. Some people specialize in electronics industry knowledge, some in airlines, some in dairies, some in retailing, etc. Under exchangeable property rights, people more effectively utilize specialized knowledge about electronics, devote more of their effort and study to detecting which electronic devices show promise, which are now most efficient in various uses, which should be produced in larger numbers, where investment in electronics should take place, what kinds of research and development to finance, etc. Non-exchangeable property rights attenuate such specialization—though not among employees in the publicly owned venture.

v. Property and Responsiveness to Market Values

The separability of property rights and the ability to redistribute them via exchange implies that their market exchange values will reflect the differential productivity of such resources. For example, a mine in the extractive industry with a high quality of ore could show greater profits than a less richly endowed mine even if the manager were less efficient. To correct for the effects of natural and geographic endowments in favored mines relative to the less favored mines, it is necessary to provide some means for estimating the size of the effects of that natural superiority.

I shall outline one method for accomplishing this objective. Suppose property rights to the mine can be exchanged. The higher exchange value of rights to the superior mine over the value of rights to the inferior mine is an estimate of the larger profitability due to the superiority of the ore or other natural features. If anyone thought the higher value of such rights failed to reflect fully the natural superiority and advantages, he would purchase those rights and capture that higher value in the form of a greater flow of net receipts. If the incumbent manager failed to operate the mine sufficiently efficiently to yield the profits estimated by the value of the property right to be available from that mine, the rights holders would replace him with a manager who would. And that new manager would be paid more only if he could operate the mine more efficiently. In other words he would be paid out of the enhanced profits—if those profits were concentrated to the rights owners. And then no manager could let the natural advantage of the mine compensate for his own inefficiencies or wasteful actions. If there were no known managers who could operate the mine more efficiently, the exchange value would fall to correct its earlier overestimate of the natural advantages.

This is, of course, the method of providing incentives and rewards to managers and resource allocators to respond to market prices in a capitalistic system. My purpose in reciting it here is not to recommend it, but rather to emphasize that it depends upon prices set in an open market in which people can buy and sell (i.e., exchange) separable property rights. In the absence of that structure of *exchangeable* property rights there would be no market prices to reflect the highest profitability value of resource use, and there would be less incentive for managers to respond to market prices. Further, if incumbent managers could escape the control of market prices, they could more readily respond to personally advantageous criteria—which are less sensitive to valuations placed on the goods by the rest of society. (Incidentally, it would, of course, be inefficient to give higher prices or extra income to the inferior mine in order to enable it to operate, since that would divert resources to mines where productivity is lower. Instead the superior mine should be worked harder, and the inferior mine should be operated only if the product is so highly valued as to cover the higher costs of the inferior mine.)

Illustrations are plentiful. In the United States we have public utilities. These are often privately owned, but the rate of profit available to the owners is legally limited to 6 percent on the invested capital. In such a public utility suppose the manager's secretary retires. He realizes that if he has a choice between two equally capable (insofar as performing business-type secretarial services is concerned) women who apply for the job, he would gain more personal satisfaction by hiring the more attractive woman even if she were more expensive. If he had hired the less attractive woman at a lower wage, the reduced costs and larger profits would not have increased the profits available to the owners, for they are limited to 6 percent. In the profit-limited public utility the enhanced profit if realized would be taken away either by forcing him to lower prices or by taxing his extra profit. So he will choose the more expensive secretary for his *profit-limited* firm, and the less expensive, but equally productive (of business services) secretary for the unlimited-profit business. Clearly the profit-limited firm will be staffed more with prettier, more expensive women, while the for-unlimited-profit firm will have homelier ones.

This is all implied in the simple theory of demand so clearly laid out by Slutsky: The lower the cost of a good, the more of it will be purchased. In our present applications of the cost, forsaken profit to the employer in the unlimited-profit business is higher than in the profit-limited firm. So a manager buys more beauty in his employees where that is cheaper (in terms of the costs he bears—not in terms of the total true real costs, part of which are borne by the consumers in the form of higher prices for the services of the limited-profit business). This is merely an extension of Slutsky's formulation. He utilized a private property constraint in which the price paid was all borne by the purchaser. In the present example, the price to the employer (purchaser) is not all borne by the purchaser. Part of that cost is transferred by the profit limit to consumers of the service.

There are other differences in behavior implied for this limited-profit (limited property right) enterprise. Inefficient, lazy employees will cost him less—since there is less incentive to avoid reduced profitability. If he replaced the inefficient workers with better ones, the increase in profitability would merely be taxed away. As a result, limited-profit firms have smaller labor turnover, less firing, more job security and more nepotism. Furthermore, the managers can devote more time to non-business activities. They can be more active in community, political and cultural affairs, since the sacrificed profitability is not borne by them as heavily as if the enterprise were operated without legally limited profits.

We also have not-for-profit and publicly owned enterprises. The following proposition is derivable: The incentive to respond to market price and to seek out and satisfy the most profitable production is stronger in the private for-profit enterprise than in the profit-limited, not-for-profit or publicly owned enterprises, where managers will tend to use prices that are *lower* than the true worth of the services provided. Why? The loss of maximized value of service is not borne by the manager or owner as fully as if the enterprise profits were specialized on a subgroup of the population. But why should not the price possibly be too *high*, rather than too low, as the proposition asserts. Because by *under-pricing*, the manager will have an *excess* demand to ration, and he can then utilize rationing principles (other than a higher market price) that do redound more fully to his personal benefit—as the competing customers offer to pay non-money supplements or rewards to the manager to enhance their probability of getting some of the available goods. Some customers may "offer," for example, to "pay" more to the seller in the form of a greater tolerance with slow-moving, surly salesmen, greater submissiveness, willingness to stand in line while the sellers relax and an acceptance of inferior products and poorer service. The customer will offer to behave more in ways that please the manager. The manager would be more willing to sacrifice many of these non-money blandishments and put his services to the higher-price uses if the increased profitability could have more effectively increased his own wealth.

I should like to elaborate on one such case in greater detail for your possible interest and amusement—the universities. In the United States, universities are typically not-for-profit organizations, or they are state-owned enterprises. The university insists on low tuition, i.e., a price for its services far below the value to those who are provided the education. Every so often some naive person proposes that a university charge a higher tuition fee to provide more income to the university. Invariably the faculty and the university administrators oppose this almost as a matter of life or death. Why? The standard reply is the allegation that poor students would be unable to obtain an education. Now this is of course patently false, as can be seen when it is noted that the universities also strongly oppose a proposal to grant scholarships to students to cover tuition

MARKET PRICES, PROPERTY AND BEHAVIOR   477

costs and then let the students pay the market price for their tuition. What is the alternative reason for wanting to have too low a price?

Costs of education can be covered in several ways: by (1) providing large endowments or by (2) having funds paid directly to universities out of the state budget, but they can also be covered by (3) granting scholarships or tuition payments to students and then permitting the students to pay the funds to the university chosen by the student. This would compel the university managers (faculty and administration) to respond more to the students' demands and judgments of services—as proposed by Soviet economists who seek to have managers made more responsive to consumer demands. Our famous Ford Foundation, however, has preferred to make large grants directly to the endowment of colleges thereby permitting the colleges to continue a low-tuition system. The Ford Foundation might instead have established many large scholarship grants from which students could pay the costs of their selected colleges. But I suspect, because the Ford Foundation is heavily dominated by faculty people from universities, scholarship endowment grants have not been utilized; instead, as I said, grants were made directly to the colleges. What are some of the consequences? The answer can, I think, best be discerned using our earlier principles derived from our analysis of what enables a decentralized market system to operate more effectively.

Universities are, as we said, marked by zero or low tuition fees. (I shall be extreme and put things in "black and white," but you can interpret it in less extreme terms.) The faculty imposes course grades as criteria of entry and of permission to remain in school. We, of the faculty, impose required courses with examinations. Students are severely restricted in their ability to transfer from course to course, to drop courses in mid-term and to repeat courses until they obtain passing grades. They must behave in specified ways, or they will not be allowed to have university services. A student must stand in line for hours to register and pay his bills (can you imagine a department store making you stand in line to buy and to pay your bills!), he must continue to behave in an exemplary manner and he must not belong to fraternities that discriminate against certain races. Can you imagine a private for-profit store engaging in such customer exclusionary tactics and suffering the loss of monetary wealth? Of course, if a student offered to pay $100 for the privilege of staying in my class a second time after failing it, I would accept, except for my contract with the university which, for not mysterious reasons, prohibits such behavior. Yet my golf teacher, my teachers of music, typing, shorthand, driving, dancing and electronic computer programming are all delighted to continue teaching me so long as I pay the market price. They do heed and respond to market values and prices. They do not seem to care if I take only part-time schooling or get drunk periodically. But we teachers at zero-tuition, not-for-profit schools are less tolerant. Tolerance would be wasteful—to us. We mistreat students with greater success, the lower the tuition is. The cost of our doing so is lower, the lower the tuition is relative to costs of education or the value of it to the student.

The land and facilities of the university are internally assigned on a non-price basis. Faculty offices, parking lots and use of classrooms are distributed so that those in charge of the allocation get better facilities than if the highest-valued market prices were collected and turned over to the university administration or added to the state or university budget. The enhanced profits would give less benefit to any administrator than if he were a manager for a privately owned enterprise. Hence parking spaces are more frequently allocated not by pricing but by hierarchical status.

Compare all this with the operation of a department store; the employees or managers do not control or select customers in that way. And the fact that education is a different kind of service is not the reason. The property rights arrangement is the explanatory difference.

I (a member of the faculty) could survive with a market-clearing price for tuition and admission to the university. But students would insist on better treatment, else they will transfer their custom to a competitor, and competitors will exist at market-clearing prices. Therefore, intentionally or not, with foresight or not, we faculty *say* we keep the tuition fees low to accommodate less wealthy, more needy but deserving students. Yet low fees enable us (faculty) to select students according to non-money criteria. My utility is enhanced as I select the better learners and smarter people who obviously "deserve" a higher education.

The same general principles of analysis could be applied elsewhere. My imagination easily conjures the following fantasy. If food were rationed at zero price, chefs and dieticians who prepare and serve the food could see that only the most deserving got the best food, while those who were less appreciative would get standard food without luxurious and expensive desserts. Or if we were couturiers and dressmakers, we would let only the most beautiful women have the best clothes. The average woman can wear a shapeless, less expensive dress. Why waste hundreds of dollars on a woman of hopeless figure, while there are women who, if beautifully dressed, would provide external benefits to the rest of society. Clearly, on the external-benefit count alone, clothing should be distributed as is education. That the beautiful and the shapeless alike should both have to pay would never cross our minds. After all how could a *poor* beautiful woman pay? Certainly she could not borrow and pay out of later proceeds, for how could she earn more? Education, of course, could readily be financed by borrowing; after all, education is productive of income—but beauty, no. We must therefore provide zero-priced beautiful clothes to the prettiest women, while education can be sold at market-clearing price, with repayments out of later enhanced income. Couturiers have long advocated that the state finance dressmaking with zero prices for clothing so that they too can select their clients with the gracious social beneficial care that we educators employ. But not until the designers get tax or endowment support for non-profit dress design and manufacturing plants will they be able to ignore market prices and values as cleverly as do educators.

Enough of these parables! Their purposes were many: (1) to demonstrate that the problem of inducing managerial behavior that is more responsive to market prices is not one confined to any one country nor one particular industry; (2) to illustrate the way in which the kinds of property rights in the institution affect the responsiveness of managers to marketable prices; (3) to illustrate how in such circumstances the managers can create a facade of excuses for justifying their inefficient behavior.

But one purpose was *not* that of showing that a private property system which induces the closest responsiveness to market prices is the best system. I could not honestly do so, because my own behavior would belie it. I work for a socialist institution—the University of California. I could have been an economist for a private for-profit business firm and subjected myself to all the incentives and controls toward different types of behavior than I now experience. But I did not. Could it be that I prefer the socialist environment despite the so-called inefficiencies in responding to the consumers' interests? I do as a producer, but as a consumer I prefer to buy from private property firms because they are more responsive to my demands and less responsive to my personal characteristics and behavior habits. They are much more tolerant of what I propose to do with the purchased goods. They are more willing to work out special arrangements to satisfy my personal interests, far more than is the socialist post office, socialist golf course or socialist bus system. Clearly as a producer I have chosen the socialist environment, but as a consumer I prefer the capitalist. But of course the particular choice I have made is not one that is open to society at large. The two are inconsistent for the group as a whole.

VI. Conclusion

In this paper I have tried to present some ideas and tentative propositions pertaining to the issue of how to make prices more effective in directing people in the way productive resources are used. I suggested a correlation between the kinds of property rights to goods and the way their managers allocate and use the goods. I believe it is not possible to know what interpretation or meaning to give to market prices without specifying the prevailing set of property rights in those goods. Once the kinds of property rights are identified, it is then possible to make some statements about their meaning *and* their potential effectiveness as guides to resource users. To try to analyze the role of market prices and how to make them more effective indices and incentives to efficient or profitable activity—without specifically considering the kinds of property rights—is to overlook a basic factor affecting behavior. None of this implies that one form or another of property rights is the proper or superior kind. But it does imply that the kinds of rights have a significant differential effect on the extent to which prices and values will be revealed and made effective in controlling behavior of people with respect to economic goods and even with respect to social and cultural behavior.

We Western economists, and I suspect the Soviet economists also, are only just beginning to recognize this and are only just beginning to develop the theory and understanding of the effects of various kinds of property rights on the role of market prices and human behavior. What that study will eventually teach us and where it will take us is still to be discovered. I hope our discussions will give us all some clues, suggestions and conjectures about valid theorems and means of testing them.

CUSTOMS, BEHAVIOR, AND PROPERTY RIGHTS

On doing business with Americans you would probably get better advice by asking or copying the Chinese who are already doing business with us, those living in Singapore, Hong Kong, Seoul, Taipei, and those in the United States.

But I may be helpful if I tell you about some U.S. customs and behavior different from the behavior that is common here in China, not because of differences in desires or ambitions, but because Americans live in a private property system (or what in the United States is called a capitalistic system), whereas you live in a public, or government-owned, system of economic firms (which in the United States is called a socialist system).

The competition and behavior that are allowed and which get one further ahead differ in those two systems. The systems of rewards and penalties differ. These differences exist even though we have some public institutions, and you have some private institutions. For example, our democratic government is a public institution. Much of our educational system is public. We have state universities and state schools, though we also have many private schools and universities. Our postal system is public and so are the roads, airports, water, power, and fire protection systems. But nevertheless, about 80 percent of our national product is created and exchanged through a private property system, without central control and planning.

And you have some private property systems. Here in China you have some private rights to livestock and to fruits and vegetables grown in "private, self-reserved plots." You can sell those products to whomever you wish in the farmers' free markets for whatever price consumers and your competing sellers make possible. In the United States that kind of right is held over almost all economic resources—land, houses, machinery, automobiles, businesses, and so forth.

What I mean by a private, or market, economic system is one in which all

This previously unpublished paper was presented at Peking Institute of Foreign Trade, 1982, and appears here by permission of the author.

rights to select uses of all economic goods and human services are assigned to individuals as private property. That means each person must choose, and each must accept, the consequences of how his goods are used. The same is true in selecting what work he will do. He must estimate which of all the possible uses are most valuable, whether for his use or for that of someone else who offers to pay more for its use. When he buys he must offer something he owns, not someone else's property or something that no one owns. People compete by offering their wealth, which they earned by being productive for other people, who in turn . . . and so on and so on. In the United States we call that "putting one's money where his mouth is."

The university where I work—the University of California—is a public, or government, institution. There I compete for equipment by arguing and over-stating its value to me. I am not allowed to offer some of my own wealth to buy. The administrator, or controller, of the resources used in the university must decide on some other basis. The ways I compete to affect his decisions are different than if I could offer him some of my private property, and the way he makes decisions is different than if the resources were his. You can see that one way I learn about how socialism works is by studying my university, UCLA. In the same way, I believe you can learn how business is done in the United States by carefully studying what happens in your private institutions, your private plots, and farmers' free markets. You can see that persons desiring to get some of those vegetables or livestock must compete by offering something of value to the seller as evidence of its worth and as an incentive to the seller to respond. However, your private plots are not quite as private as they are in the United States, because we can sell the land by private agreement. But still it is a way to start to learn about the U.S. system.

Let me tell you a true story. The Russians who visited the United States to study our economy repeatedly asked, "Who directs the farmers to produce how much of this or that?" They seemed unable to understand the meaning of our answer: "No one and everyone." This meant no *one central* authority gave direc-tions. Instead, everyone had an influence by the offers they made in the market. Another thing the Russians didn't realize was that market prices are set by free competition, not by political authorities. Prices are competed to a level that eliminates both shortages and surpluses, so we have no lines, no shortages, no ration coupons from factory managers or state officials. The reason we don't is not that we are richer. It is that prices are allowed to be competed up to that level which restrains the amount demanded to equal the amount that can be produced at that price. And that price is equal to the costs of the amount supplied. The result is the same as yours here in China for vegetables and livestock from your private plots and farmers' free markets.

I am just identifying, not defending, differences. Now what are some lessons we can deduce from those behavioral differences?

First, to know what is most profitable (which in the United States is the same thing as saying what is most valuable), you must not look for those things for which there are shortages, with people lined up on waiting lists or using ration coupons. That doesn't happen, because we don't have shortages, which as you know are caused by price controls, not by being poor. Shortages, as you know, are not the same things as scarcity. Our prices are set by open competition, just as in your farmers' markets.

Prices are competed to that level at which people want to buy exactly the amount which it pays to produce at those prices—not more, not less. Prices that are controlled by politicians are typically set so low that people demand more than can be produced for those prices. That, not poverty, is what creates shortages. That calls for rationing, which is controlled by and gives power to the politicians. That's the way it is in the United States when politicians take control.

Second, success in doing business in the United States will depend on how you deal with *private* customers, not just with government officials. You must persuade private customers to buy your products or services with their own money. If they prefer blue to black bicycles, you had better paint them blue. If they prefer pink or green to white soap, offer it to them, or someone else will. It is not just what you can produce, but the form, color, design, variety, manner of service, location, delivery, and promptness. You must act like private producers, not government employees, or you won't attract customers in the United States.

You must cater to your customers' whims. You must price so as to avoid shortages, which means that you must not set prices so low that there will be shortages and queues. If you do, frustrated customers will be unhappy, while those who do get the goods will resell them at a higher price, keeping the difference for themselves. Other sellers will be charging prices that avoid shortages and just barely covering their costs because of competition from still other suppliers. You must price the same way private firms do in the competitive market.

If you set prices the way public firms usually do, you will not succeed. My observations in the United States suggest that public institutions and managers tend to underprice their output because that makes it appear that their goods are highly desired, when in fact if they were priced at their costs, they would not survive. That is certainly true of all the public institutions in the United States, universities, the post office, transportation systems, and power and water systems. They survive because the government supports them with tax-collected money.

Third, I don't know any way to get that private-firm pricing behavior by exhortation, cajoling, or political pressure. The incentives of even the highest political authorities in the United States—and I would suspect in any government—are not directed at wealth or profit maximizing for the enterprise they operate, but, like anyone else, at their own personal benefits which are achieved by forsaking the stated objectives of the enterprise they are managing. No owners exist to oversee and control those managers. Perhaps you will find a way. But with your permission and forbearance at my rudeness, I doubt that you will. Unless you create a private firm, with managers who are responsible to people who own rights to the value of the enterprise, you will not successfully compete in the United States. I wish it were otherwise, but honesty requires I not tell you something I believe to be false.

You may have to give your factory managers ownership rights in the special resources used in those factories, with rights to accumulate their own wealth from a successful business. I digress to remind you that it was precisely that development in Czechoslovakia which threatened the Russian political regime and made the Russian army enter to stop the economic reform. They were more interested in political control than in economic production. I do not know enough to conjecture about Chinese political interests to make any forecasts, but I will predict that unless those who are placed in the position of doing business with consumers in the United States have some rights in their ventures similar to those of their private competitors, they will not succeed against that competition. For example, I can think of not one product made in a public firm and sold to American consumers through a public firm that has survived in the United States on any significant scale.

Fourth, as Chinese trade expands with the United States, American politicians will complain that you are selling us more than we are buying from you. You should ignore our American politicians, who don't know that international trade involves many countries. No one buys from another exactly the same amount sold. Instead three- or four- or five-way trade—called multilateral trade—

occurs, and one country's imbalance with another country is matched by its opposite balance with still another. But some politicians who understand that fact are really representing some American producers who are being displaced by the foreign imports. We American consumers welcome those imports. So if American politicians complain about your success, you know how to answer them.

Fifth, I predict it will be profitable to sell your "scenery" and "memories of China" to American tourists, as you have already started to do. Merely for looking at your country, Americans will pay billions of dollars. China has much to teach us. That is one reason I am here. Millions of Americans will offer you billions of American dollars for a visit here. You won't have to export anything. Just build hotels with that excellent service and cuisine for which you are famed. Switzerland is an example. They collect millions from tourists who wander around the country looking at it. We do that to the Japanese who visit the United States taking pictures, playing golf, and taking home almost nothing else. That is an inexhaustible resource to be exploited.

Another way to export those same services is to encourage the making of motion pictures by American film producers and actors. Labor costs are relatively high for making motion pictures in the United States because the labor unions are exceptionally strong in that industry. Therefore motion picture production sites are a potentially profitable form of export. Even better, the pictures will be made by Americans who will come here, much like tourists. You will obtain income both for those who work in making the pictures and for providing the Americans with accommodations while they are in China.

Another reason for predicting that tourism and motion picture sites will be a profitable activity is that it is almost inconceivable that quotas and tariffs would be imposed on those exports to the United States. The U.S. government would have to restrict travel to China.

This suggests one way to avoid tariffs and quotas on your *other* exports to the United States—cloth, for example—is first to establish a strong tourist business, attracting many Americans. After that is established and investments are made by Americans in hotels in China, you can threaten to restrict travel to China unless the quotas on other Chinese exports are reduced or removed. That will put one American special-interest group, the American tourist group, against another American special-interest group, the producers of cloth in the United States. Those two pressure groups will fight each other and reduce the probability of quotas on other imports from China. That's how to play politics in the United States, probably played the same way everywhere.

I am beginning to tell you how to act politically in order to do business in the United States. However, I shall stop, because I am not an expert on that subject. And furthermore, that might suggest that in order to succeed in doing business in the United States you must become deeply involved in political contacts and activity. I believe that is not true. But in any event, I am not an expert on that subject.

Let me finish by saying that I hope someday some of you will come to the United States and tell us how to give academic talks in China.

AN ECONOMIST LOOKS AT
SECONDARY EDUCATION IN CALIFORNIA

"Shortages of educational facilities" are the first thing an economist sees when looking at secondary education in California. He sees this first because his training has habituated him to inquiring about the allocation of economic resources to the various desires of consumers, and about the process effecting that allocation. His attention is easily attracted by the complaints about teacher shortages and building needs: "the need far outstrips the supply." Yet the economist is also aware that all "needs" are relative things. My wife's need for a new car increases as her needs for housing and clothes and food are more fully satisfied. But her need for a new car is decreased if she is unable adequately to satisfy her desires for food, clothing, and housing. Now this is an annoying way of saying that our "needs" can be increased and decreased simply by varying the price we must pay to satisfy them. The higher the price of a service or commodity, the less we "need" it; the lower the price, the more we "need" it. Absolutely no individual commodity whatsoever is exempt from this law. It follows that the simplest way to create a shortage is to charge too low a price for the desired service. And the simplest way to remove a shortage is to raise its price. The clear lesson is that the price of teachers—that which is short in supply—is too low. At the price the school system sets on the teachers' pay, it finds that it wants to hire many more teachers than are available. Simply by raising the pay scale, the various boards of education would reduce their "needs," and the shortage would disappear overnight.

I am fully aware that I must be taxing the patience of the tolerant reader who has read this far without losing his temper. "Surely," the reader must be saying, "the writer is living in an ivory tower. Doesn't he know that raising pay is out of the question? Let him listen to the boards of education. And what does he mean by saying that the needs for teachers would be reduced by raising their pay? What does he expect the students to do, disappear? They have to be taught. Everyone recognizes that as a need. No amount of economic double-talk will

Reprinted from *California Journal of Secondary Education* 29 (January 1954): 35–38.

conceal that fact." Well, the facts are that the economist is aware of all this, and yet the assertions in the first paragraph are still correct. Let's see why.

Admittedly boards of education are lagging in their pay raises. That is exactly why there is a teacher shortage. There is no solution to the problem, short of higher pay and more money spent for facilities. It is economic nonsense to think that some other solution exists. And if it is a fact of life that boards will not increase pay, then the shortage will remain, and there is no sense in beating our brains out trying to eliminate it by other methods. Let the parents stew, and let the children not be given the more expensive education that their parents would like them to have at costs lower than those at which it can be made available. Propaganda and public appeals to college students to enter the teaching profession (despite higher pay elsewhere) will never solve the problem; they may even make it worse by advertising that teaching is an underpaid profession, relative to other opportunities. The wisest thing California does toward getting more teachers is advertising its pay scale in those other states where salary rates are lower. While this aggravates their problem, it helps to increase the supply in California. As other states find their problem of supply becoming more acute, they may raise their pay scales, thus putting even greater pressure on our own boards to meet competitive rates. In summary, only by higher pay (except for normal interstate migration) will the teacher shortage be reduced.

Turn now to the assertion made at the beginning, that the needs will be affected by the higher pay. Just as the higher pay will increase the supply of teachers, so will it reduce the needs. Higher costs of education will induce an allocation of facilities and personnel into more important tasks and out of less important ones. For example, kindergarten might be contracted and resources diverted into elementary and secondary teaching. This does not require that kindergarten teachers become secondary teachers—a chain of substitutions will accomplish this end. The variety of offerings in the schools would have to be curtailed as costs rise. For example, it could be suggested that driver training, physical education, art, music, etc., might be curtailed in order to shift those funds and facilities into "reading, writing, and arithmetic." Secondary education for adults, vocational education, or night schools could be put on a paying basis. Fees for the courses could be raised to cover the costs so that no funds would be diverted from the satisfaction of more urgently desired offerings at the lower levels. Any adult offerings that do not pay their way could be dropped, thereby saving the money for the more urgently desired courses in elementary and secondary schools. This would mean that children would not be deprived of education in order that adults might get night classes to satisfy hobbies or improve their vocational opportunities. Let the reader be warned that the above list of substitutions is merely illustrative of the process by which "needs" will be redefined.

As it is now, the modification of course offerings in view of revised "needs" (considering costs) is seriously hampered in two respects. First, pressure to re-evaluate the wisdom of current offerings is reduced. Second, the capability of revision is reduced. The pressure for course revision is increased if one is forced to realize that *courses not offered are the costs of those offered*; and if substitution of one course for another is not readily possible because of unavailability of teachers, the incentive to re-evaluate course offerings in terms of the forsaken courses is weakened. Only if one sees that by abandoning a certain course he can be sure of offering a different one will he be compelled to calculate the course "needs" (in view of costs).

When, as now, prices offered for teacher services (or buildings) are too low to satisfy all the "needs" for education, what will determine which of the "needs" or desires are to be left unsatisfied and which to be fulfilled by a revision of offerings? It will depend heavily upon the personal choices of the new supply of teachers and those recruited temporarily. They will be able to pick and choose what they would like to teach—by picking the job which offers them what they want. School administrators, because of inadequate pay scales for teachers, will be unable to counter this effect, and so our new supply of teachers will unwittingly determine what course revisions we shall have. And it is therefore not surprising that the tendency is to offer more and more courses that are pleasant to teach but less essential. (Older, more permanent teachers will not have this freedom.) Of course, there are exceptions, but they *are* exceptions. The general validity of the preceding argument is attested to by every commodity in the economic system. Let price be set too low, and the commodity will disappear from the market place; instead, resources will go to uses that are pleasant, though not so desirable. For example, with price control during the war, utility-type clothing and low-cost items disappeared and luxury types flourished. We now have the same phenomenon in a new field.

All this says that with prices too low, an evaluation of relative needs is hampered, and the ability of the board of education to control the curriculum despite (new) teacher preferences is attenuated. (If this were an objective unanimously and highly desired, it might be best not to expose this analysis.)

Where does this discussion bring us? We now see that as prices or costs are raised, needs—really desires—are revised and reduced to the more "fundamental" wants. I am not arguing that it is good to be poor; I am merely saying that given the funds available, higher revealed costs and prices will force us *and* *enable* us to re-evaluate and satisfy our desires more efficiently and sensibly. This can be done only by eliminating the less desired courses in order to see that children get the more desired courses. The alternative is to give all the children a curriculum that, considering the time available for teaching, is less satisfactory.

But all this, while helpful, is not enough for the parent who wants his children to get better education than could be provided even if the pay scale were raised and the current teaching curriculum revised. How can a parent get more money (economic resources) diverted into education? Unless the state or county or city assesses extra taxes, these desires will go unfilled. The individual parent is hamstrung. There is no way he can offer to pay more money to the school system and have it used for educating his own child. Nor could a group of parents in a given school area band together and offer more in order to get a new building or more or better teachers. And exactly because of this, no parent can control the amount or quality of education, short of sending his child to a private school. But if he adopts this recourse, he is penalized because he must still pay taxes as if he were sending his children to public schools. Even though he fulfills his responsibility to his children and to society by paying for their education, he must still contribute to the state. (This is why private schools at the elementary and secondary levels are so rare, as contrasted with colleges.)[1]

The current dilemma of public education—the shortage of teachers and facilities—is a built-in feature of all organizations which sell their services at too low a price and offer to pay too little for the requisite facilities. And as if we wanted to really ensure that there be no escape from this bind, the individual members of the community are restrained from getting more of the service, if they want it, by virtue of a penalizing tax system. The irony of the situation seems to have escaped the attention of society: this vast socialist industry (and this is what public education is) is directed by elected boards who, while emotionally and vocally professing to be staunch opponents of socialism and defenders of individualism, adopt policies which can be rationalized only on the

---

1. A tax remission scheme equivalent to contributions to private schools would enable willing individuals to obtain more educational facilities if they "needed" them. In essence, until some non-penalizing method is found to enable individuals to contribute more to schools in order to get more education, the political facts of life will always restrain consumer sovereignty in this regard.

basis of furthering socialist objectives. And this is done not of necessity, but because of a lack of careful analysis of the economics of public education. Public education is an established part of our life; the present discussion is not an attack on this institution. It is an attempt to reveal how an ignorance of fundamental economic principles is seriously reducing its effectiveness and efficiency.

COST EFFECTIVENESS OF COST EFFECTIVENESS

Why has a cost-effectiveness system only recently been applied to defense and government actions? Why had cost-effectiveness evaluation systems not previously been in use, as has long been the case in the private business sector? The answer is not that politicians and military people are slower, less discerning, and less rational—rather that the rewards and punishments imposed on businessmen who ignore this particular kind of cost-effectiveness calculus are more severe. As a matter of fact, cost-effectiveness analyses of one type or another have always been used in government and defense activities. But since the resulting decisions seemed to reflect too little concern for some factors and too much for others, "inappropriate" (that is, different) weights were given to the various components of costs and benefits. The pertinent question, then, is what were the presumably correctible weights of the old system that the new was supposed to have corrected? And does the new system have new dangers or defects of its own that, hopefully, are less grievous than its added benefits?

1. Cost-Effectiveness Concept

There should first be agreement on what is meant by the new cost-effectiveness principles. Cost-effectiveness studies, as they are now commonly called in government, refer to a means of comparison, choice, and implementation of decisions among available, considered options with the assumption that the appropriate criteria are being used. An "assumption that the appropriate criteria are being used" is crucial; for without it, the description would be practically empty, because all selections of actions are based on something, ranging from a random choice generator or one's personal whims to a dictum from higher authority. A crucial feature of cost-effectiveness studies as currently recommended is that the appropriate criteria of cost and of effectiveness be used and that *all* costs and predictable effects of the *relevant decision* be given their appropriate weight in the choice.

Reprinted from *Defense Management*, ed. Stephen Enke (Englewood Cliffs, N.J.: Prentice-Hall, 1967), 74–86.

That the emphasis upon explicit or appropriate cost-effectiveness studies comes from economics does not mean that only narrow material effects, distinguished from some allegedly noneconomic effects, are the appropriate criteria. Beauty, truth, dignity, religious and personal freedoms, security of life, democratic processes, tolerance for disparate views, and so forth, are sometimes thought to be noneconomic factors or objectives that must be given separate weight. Thus sometimes it is contended that considering only economic values without remembering social, cultural, political values confines the decision maker to an incomplete, and probably biased, cost-effectiveness criterion. However, there is no exclusivity or conflict among economic values, political values, social and cultural values. Economic (that is, trade-off) values merely reflect and measure the trade-offs between the other values and goals. Any good capable of providing more desired political, social, cultural, esthetic, religious, nutritional objectives has economic value. Every good that helps achieve any goal is an economic good with (economic) value, for *the rate at which some amount of good can be substituted or traded for some of another good in achieving those various goals is precisely what is meant by its (economic) value or price.* To repeat, economic value is simply a measure of trade-offs or rates of substitutability between means (goods or resources) for achieving these various goals.

But a mythical difference between economic and other values must not be allowed to obscure a significant distinction between (a) effects for which it is possible to measure trade-off rates or values directly *via* market prices (market exchange rates via production or sale), (b) effects that can be quantified in some physical sense but cannot be valued in any generally accepted or valid way (as when the effect is not purchasable in the market), and (c) effects that cannot even be quantified in a way that would be valid for everyone (the impact on the probability of war, on morale, on morality, and so on).

Although already explained by Charles J. Hitch and Roland N. McKean,[1] this interaction of effects is worth repetition and emphasis, because there are still allegations that cost-effectiveness principles reduce everything to the dollar sign and ignore technological and social values. Vivid examples of the misunderstanding of the functions and implications of cost effectiveness are the charges that if we had used cost effectiveness in the nineteenth century we would still be using sailing ships, or that cost effectiveness will mean losing the war without going bankrupt.

---

1. Charles J. Hitch and Roland N. McKean, *The Economics of Defense in the Nuclear Age* (New York: Atheneum Publishers, 1965).

II. Defects of Old System

What were believed to be some of the correctible faults of the prior system?

1. *Span of Costs.* The wrong span of costs of a weapon system was used. The full cost of a system considered for procurement was not viewed as comprising the stream of payments now and in the future; usually only the present expenditures were given serious weight. This way of thinking resembles buying a car as if the initial down payment were the cost. Piecemeal expenditures were treated as total costs. Often, as a result, future expenditures were obligated and in time often become excessively large. A better allowance for the subsequent expenditures would have encouraged different and more efficient procurement decisions. To reduce this error, recent cost-effectiveness systems have promulgated a forecast spanning several years, with all expenditures in that interval counted in costs.

2. *Component Costs.* The old system was even worse than buying a new car by contemplating only the initial down payment. It made decisions independently about interdependent or component parts of a system—as if a family car were to be bought by four different members of the family, each being responsible for buying a different part of the car. Each would consider the cost to be only the payment on their particular part. In defense programming, decisions about bombers were made by one command, about fighter defense escorts of the bombers by another, about personnel by still another, and about air bases by another. Defense performance tasks were not costed as a task. Only the components were costed as end-items. Moreover, the Air Force, the Army, and the Navy sometimes acted as though the others did not exist. This is not to say that the agencies did not discuss, dispute, and argue with one another and in Congress for the right to be responsible for certain tasks. It says instead that the defense of the continental United States or the strategic striking power was not costed or evaluated by combining all strike forces into one performance or program package. Therefore, the costs of these general functions were not costed in ways that enabled a rational calculation of the approximate worths of such performance capability. And thus the next inadequacy is suggested.

3. *Disregard of Incremental Gains and Costs.* The size of any program or even of a purchase (for example, a new bomber type) was not systematically treated as a variable. "Requirements" and "priorities" were bandied about as though they had to be met regardless of the costs (that is, sacrifices of other "requirements and needs"). As a result, the gain in one avenue of defense expenditure obtainable by spending less in some other avenue was not systematically considered.

Because budgets and plans were specified in terms of inflexible requirements and needs, evaluations of trade-offs or of substitution between amounts of weapons and levels of goals were not elicited. The opposite error to thinking in terms of "requirements" and "priorities" was the specification of a total "essential" budget that presumably met our "needs"—with the implication that one dollar more would not contribute to greater defense, and that one dollar less would mean loss of all defense capability. The "requirements" or "priorities" extreme is tantamount to a "damn the cost" extreme, whereas the budget limit implies "damn the effectiveness." This approach was not at all conducive to systematic exploration and evaluation of the cost effectiveness of various programs.

4. *Incentive Systems.* Even if the above faults are recognized, there remain difficulties arising from the *context* in which cost-effectiveness studies are used. For many institutions, a change of context often changes or frustrates effectiveness. In the present instance, the absence of (1) a market and of (2) private-property rights in the resources being allocated means that the effectiveness of a cost-effectiveness analysis in a private-property system cannot totally be transferred to government or socialist systems. The extent to which various costs and effects are discerned, measured, and *heeded* depends on the institutional system of incentive-punishment for the deciders. One system of rewards-punishment may increase the extent to which some objectives are heeded, whereas another may make other goals more influential. Thus *procedures* for making or controlling decisions in one rewards-incentive system are not necessarily the "best" for some other system. In other words, the application of cost-effectiveness studies and principles (as used in a private-property, competitive-market context) to socialistic or governmental arenas involves some serious, undesirable side effects.

Of course the danger of serious, undesirable side effects does not mean that the achieved and desired effects may not be worth the costs; it should also be remembered that ancillary steps can reduce the undesirable side effects. In fact, this paper is intended to direct attention to such ancillary precautions—not to undermine cost effectiveness. Gratuitous meaning should not be read into these remarks. It is not here being contended that government or socialistic action is less desirable than a private-property, capitalistic context. The proposition is that various criteria differ in effectiveness.

In the competitive, private, open-market economy, the wealth-survival prospects are not as strong for firms (or their employees) who do not heed the market's test of cost effectiveness as for those firms who do. In the private, market-oriented sector of our economy, such behavior would mean a loss of wealth to other business firms. As a result, the market's criterion is more likely to be heeded and anticipated by business people. They have personal wealth incentives to make more thorough cost-effectiveness calculations about the products they could produce and offer for sale. In the government sector, two things are less effective. (1) The full cost and value consequences of decisions do not have as direct and severe a feedback impact on government employees as on people in the private sector. The costs of actions under their consideration are incomplete simply because the consequences of ignoring parts of the full span of costs are less likely to be imposed on them. Their decisions are conditioned by a different span of the resulting costs. The costs they bear more fully are the costs to which they give greater (though not necessarily, of course, exclusive) weight. (2) The effectiveness, in the sense of benefits, of their decisions has a different reward-incentive or feedback system: for example, a general who could save the economy one billion dollars, with unreduced defense capability over a ten-year span, has less incentive than in a market economy to heed that savings, particularly if it will impose a severe cost on him. Whatever his motivations and understanding of the "national interest," it is fallacious to assume that government officials are superhumans, who act solely with national interest in mind and are never influenced by the consequences to their own personal position.

Even if everyone could be imbued with a selfless spirit and attitude, what criterion or test of their wisdom, superiority, or efficiency would be ultimately decisive? Small-scale tests of wars or deterrence as a means of testing efficiency of decisions are not readily available. In the private civilian sector, open-market competition among competing buyers and sellers provides a continuing, effective test and a criterion of production and allocation decisions. None is so readily available for the military nor for a very wide class of government action. Again, a precautionary disclaimer. This is neither criticism of government nor praise for the private-sector decisions; it is not an innuendo that government should do less. The fact is that some tasks are delegated to governments or nonmarket group action because of a dissatisfaction with the appropriateness of the private-property market process for allocating some resources.

In sum, the old system of decisions characterized by (a) incomplete, biased concepts of cost, (b) failure to properly categorize the item, service, or program to be costed, and (c) failure to consider trade-offs among programs, their components, and the goals being sought led to what was believed to be inefficient military-defense programming and procurement. But the reward-punishment incentive system characterizing government activities must not be forgotten. It is worth examining just how the new cost-effectiveness system proposes to avoid or modify disabling characteristics.

III. Obstacles to Effectiveness of Cost Effectiveness

It is clear now in which ways the new cost-effectiveness system calculus and its implementation are intended to be improvements. (1) The new system analyzes the costs of a whole program or function—not merely components or parts of a program. For example, the strategic strike force, the continental defense, the supply or logistics mission may be a basis for assemblage and comparisons of costs. This concept of costs has been characterized as program packaging. (2) Most programs are costed for at least five years into the future in order to give greater assurance that the full time-span of costs will be reflected in the present estimates of total costs. Initial outlays can no longer be officially interpreted as the relevant costs. Inherent in a combination of these two changes is the greater ease of comparing trade-offs among programs. (3) Program changes, which inevitably will occur as the future unfolds and greater information is discerned about capabilities and events, are to be implemented by "program-change proposals." Any proposal to change (substantially) a program can be initiated by any agency but must be approved by higher authority, usually the Office of the Secretary of Defense. This provision for program-change proposals is designed to ensure that costing continues to be done on a program basis and that coherence among components of a program is maintained.

In effect, the Defense Department now operates (on paper, at least) along the command and decision lines of a business firm. New products or production programs must be costed on an end-product (not simply on an input) basis. Competition among various possible products that a firm could produce is resolved by top management in the light of estimated realizable marketability and product costs. And so decision and control over procurement for various types of functions for arming the military is resolved at the high level of the Office of the Secretary of Defense. Operating details, as in a business, are delegated to lower-level management. The parallel is excellent—up to a point. Unfortunately, some ingredients in the business firm's environment are missing in government. Two of these merit some examination and notice.

1. *Program Definition.* The program being costed is not one that can be readily identified as the pertinent, complete package. Is the appropriate program

defined as that of Defense, or the Air Force, or Air Defense, or Strategic Offense, or Minutemen system, or a single launch complex, or a single missile? The more narrowly it is construed, the more will there be interdependencies with other associated complementary programs that are likely to be ignored. Simply to consider a larger or more broadly defined program than before does not in itself ensure a more appropriate basis for costing and decisions. The larger the scope of the program, the greater will be the span of trade-offs and adjustments that are presumed to have been considered within the analysis. But the larger the scope, the larger is the uncertainty about the costs. At the extreme, one could call the whole government a program, and we would end up with something like the federal budget proposal. A smaller program enables more explicit comparisons of alternative programs. But then the smaller the program, the less are the interdependencies explicitly and analytically taken into account. These considerations are not criticisms of a cost-effectiveness calculus; instead they are warnings against the belief that cost-effectiveness calculations for some program automatically lend that particular program the aura of the "appropriate" size program for decision making. However sophisticated may be our cost-effectiveness analyses of particular program packages, we still must recognize the unresolved problem of the appropriate scope of the defined program.

2. *Reward-Incentive System and Centralization of Control.* The government decision context lacks competitive markets and private-property rights as incentive and control mechanisms for the decision makers. That these are missing is, of course, news neither to the Defense Department planners nor to those who are expanding the role of the new cost-effectiveness systems with centralized control. But the question still stands about the extent to which the new system can effectively overcome the absence of these two features and yield a better system.

Unfortunately, centralization of decisions in a single office over the three military sectors is not analogous to the centralization of business decisions in the head of the firm. In the private economy, other competing firms can duplicate or take different points of view about the nature of desirable products. But there are not two departments of defense to provide the competitive survival and selection of preferred products. The existence of a market in which the results of competing independent producers or decision makers can be exposed to evaluation is crucial to business efficiency. Without competitors a monopoly situation develops, and centralization within a monopoly does not ensure that alternatives will be tested and explored with the efficiency of competing firms. In a government agency, the incentives of the managers to maximize the capitalized wealth of the agency are weaker than if there were identifiable owners of the agency who could reap the capital gains. Their incentive to maximize the wealth or economic efficiency of their decisions is reduced, since their own wealth and welfare are less tied to the resulting effects. This is, of course, precisely why the five-year programs are being advocated over a one-year program plan. But the incentive for decision is still not the same.

A quiet, uncomplicated life without so much bickering and fighting about wealth values of alternative products is more viable. Centralization under government contexts implies less exposure and testing of differences of opinion, easier suppression of alternatives, less effective response to costs, and less flexible adjustments of programs despite more exhortations to the contrary.

The new cost-effectiveness system offers no discernible protection against the tendency it has to facilitate or encourage greater centralization of the decision processes. The risks inherent in centralized control are well known: belief by the superior in his own superior judgment (otherwise, why would he be there?), reduced incentive to consider alternatives, less motivation for subordinates to risk testing alternatives not acceptable to the superior. In sum, centralization of decision making—a valid achievement within a privately owned business firm competing with others in an open market—has its dangers in government. A danger of centralization of government authority in conjunction with cost-effectiveness studies is the belief that properly formulated studies of cost effectiveness will provide a proper test that can dispense with the checks and balances of the decentralized political process. But, as has been stressed, government cost-effectiveness studies are not policed and tested in the political sector with the same enforcement system that pervades the private sector's market-exposure tests. There is a vast difference between properly formulated studies and realized results that correspond (a) to actions inherent in behavior responsive to those studies and (b) to the incentives and punishments policed by an open-market, private-property competition. Men can be less expected to heed a broad cost-effectiveness concept if punishment for failure to do so is weaker. To provide this "heed," a centralized system of estimation and conceptualization of costs and effects is used to police and select among alternatives, but the former system of effective political checks and balances is thereby weakened.

3. *Costs of Current Decisions vs. Costs of Programs.* Program packaging for estimation of costs of procurement, production, and operation necessarily involves long time spans of estimates. The five-year or eight-year span of projection is popular and certainly better than the one-year, expenditure-cost

identification. Yet beware. The danger here is the belief that if a decision is taken now, it will necessarily incur the costs forecasted. Attention is drawn not simply to errors of estimate, but instead to the fact that the cost estimated is the pertinent cost *if and only if* the program is carried out in its entirety over the projected future. A program that is expensive over five years may involve only a small cost if initiated *and then terminated* at the end of one year. The well-known mistake of paying regard to sunk or past costs (which the cost-effectiveness system is intended to avoid) may be matched by the opposite error of regarding full-time costs as the *incurred* and inescapable costs of a present decision to procure equipment. What the full-time cost estimate tells us is the costs that will be incurred if and only if the program is carried out. Neither that cost nor the past expended costs are valid for present decisions; present decisions are not *now binding* upon the completion of the entire projected program. The costs incurred in the *selection* of some plan are not the costs incurred if that plan is carried through to fruition.

Of course, cost estimates of contemplated full programs are not irrelevant. They are useful for a comparison of the costs that will be expended for the selected plan if it is ultimately implemented over the projected interval. After a *plan* has been selected on the basis of that full time-span cost estimate, there is a temptation to stay with the plan thereafter; for after all, was it not the best one? Yes, but only if there is no uncertainty about the future. Where there is uncertainty, it may be wiser (more economical) to adopt a more expensive (full-time costs basis) action with a sufficiently lower *first-year* incurred cost than a less expensive one (full time-span costs) with a higher first-year incurred cost. For example, it may be better to lease for the first year and then buy in the next year if the postponement means a sufficiently good chance for a better procurement decision. Decisions are not made once and for all. With new developments and possibilities springing up each year, attention should be given to the costs of providing for revisions of plans. In other words, the five-year plan period with costs for the full period is a *forecast period*, not a commitment or budget-decision period. Therefore, in addition to full program costs, one should also compute and heed the costs that will be *incurred* by the current decision.

As an experienced colleague, Roland McKean, points out, the costs incurred by the act of marrying Miss A or Miss B (who has an exquisite taste for luxury) are relevant (even) to one's present choices about which girl to date. But it would be absurd to fall into the trap of regarding the full cost of marriage as being incurred by one date. As in research and development, it is possible and desirable to date several girls to acquire more information about each before making a permanent procurement.

4. *Research and Development vs. Procurement.* The distinctions developed in the preceding paragraphs become especially important if, as is suspected to be the case, the five-year cost-forecast interval tends to become a *decision interval.* If the five-year foresight becomes a five-year commitment, as if one were committed to that plan, flexibility and adaptability are unnecessarily restricted. Especially important are the dangers arising from inclusion of research and development activity in a procurement program. There has long existed in the military an unfortunate confounding of research and development decisions with the procurement or production decision. Research and development activity decisions are typically geared to some "optimally" designed end-item that is supposed to result from the planned research and development. Furthermore, that contemplated end-item is treated as a requirement or need. If there were not foreseeable need for that projected end-item, the research and development activity would not be supported. A justification of this basis for decisions about research and development makes the untenable assumption that the results of research and development are foreseeable with sufficient accuracy to determine the nature and function of the end-item. It is difficult to imagine a more plausible, yet fallacious, assumption.

It is one thing to know desirable directions of changes in performance capabilities; it is quite another to know in which ways that greater capability can be performed—let alone discovered. To desire faster planes is sensible. To ask for research to obtain faster planes is sensible. But to specify the kind of plane and the other joint attributes that it should yield is simply muddleheaded. To do so presumes knowledge about how and *when* the greater speed will be achieved, and about what trade-off between speed and other characteristics will be worthwhile. Such information is simply not available. Yet the research and development activity decision is tied to the criterion of full time-span costs for an item yet to be produced, a procured and operated end-item—as if all the costs were irrevocably incurred at the initial research and development stage. This kind of tie is not always desirable. Any decision system should avoid an implicit tie.

The official dogma of the Department of Defense is that research and development is *not* included in decisions about operational mission programs, at least until the project has passed the program definition stage and until the weapon system to be procured has reached a highly developed stage of engineering. But the history of the TFX decisions is sufficient, without going back to our rocket development program, to foster doubts about the meaningfulness of such doctrines of proscriptive behavior intended to separate decisions about production of operational end-items from research and development decisions.

Program packaging in terms of missions of military tasks is sensible, but the acquisition of knowledge, if always included in a mission or program package, amounts to a defective program definition. Acquisition of knowledge is itself a function or mission, and there is no obvious reason for distributing its cost among all the missions or programs, like some kind of overhead cost. To divide it and immerse its costs and activities in other program packages is exactly what the general principle of cost effectiveness of coherent, alternative programs is intended to avoid.

5. *What Type of Effectiveness?* Cost-effectiveness analysis found its hardest going in obtaining acceptance of the cost concept as a valid criterion. Less difficult was acceptance of the effectiveness criterion. More recently, however, the objective or criterion of effectiveness has been more and more difficult to identify. Number of targets destroyed and probability of being able to launch a counter strike given that the opponent has launched the initial attack are examples of two relatively simple criteria. But these are no longer, if they ever were, the only pertinent criteria. They are, instead, component variables of the utility or criterion vector. Unfortunately, the difficulty, or impossibility, of discovering or formulating an acceptable effectiveness criterion has led many observers to use an "approximate" criterion so that an explicit answer could be obtained. In other words, the criterion has been formulated so as to facilitate the analytic method. And, of course, that is precisely why the "big" issues seem always to be settled without formal cost-effectiveness analyses; there simply does not exist a formalized cost-effectiveness analysis capable of giving answers to those problems. It has not been possible to formulate the criteria in explicit, generally acceptable terms. The criterion vector itself is still open to debate. There is a tendency to be impatient with decisions not based on a formal analysis of an explicitly characterized problem because of the belief that such analysis is better than an informal, nonstructured "judgment" about the relevant problem. Uncertainty about objectives, let alone the means of best achieving them, attenuates (though it does *not* eliminate) the relevance of cost-effectiveness studies without objectively measurable objectives.

National military strategies are still open. Is our military capability to be a method of preserving a set of friendly governments, or one of "containing" communism on the assumption that communist countries can be friendly and compatible with continuing coexistence? And so, the discussion could lead on and on into a host of unresolved issues, which certainly should be part of a full cost-effectiveness study.

6. *Nondefense Activities.* An increasing portion of nondefense government activities will surely be submitted to cost-effectiveness evaluations by higher authorities in the government. The people in the Bureau of the Budget are insisting on more thorough analyses of programs by departments prior to inclusion in the budget request to Congress. Centralization via presidential authority has always existed. What will be the effect of this enlarged scope of formal cost-effectiveness application? Most of the features mentioned earlier and regarded as potential dangers seem to apply here, even though a major advantage of this cost-effectiveness emphasis is that it will expose proposed activities to cost-effectiveness concepts broader than those viewed by the proposing agency. The interest of each director of an agency is to enlarge his realm of activity. The natural bias toward overestimating benefits and underestimating costs is not easy to avoid. A more clear-cut exposition of the cost-effectiveness or benefit study conducted by the lower-level agency will enable the higher authority to compare various proposals with less parochial interest in the competing proposals. Therefore, it is possible to conjecture that the cost-effectiveness estimates should be less biased toward the interests of the operating agency.

But there is the *danger* that duplication of services by various agencies will be avoided. We have in mind the duplication among regulatory agencies. Currently, many regulatory agencies control our banks. In each state a state agency and national agencies exist. Banks can be authorized by either. This competition among the regulators provides a protection from unacceptably capricious regulatory actions. Take another example; presently one regulatory agency regulates surface transportation and another regulates air transport. Had all been subjected to control by the same regulatory agency, it is safe to conjecture that the airlines would have been less free in attracting traffic away from rail and bus. The cartelizing propensity of regulatory agencies with respect to the industry being controlled (that is, protected from competition) is too well known to warrant being neglected. Clearly, the advantage of cost-effectiveness studies being cleared and policed by higher authorities is not without its dangers.

Now we clearly do not know how much centralization of review of cost-effectiveness studies will lead to these faults. Although experience and adequate measure of the effect is lacking, the danger is in no way eliminated, nor is the net advantage of cost-effectiveness studies at high levels of centralized authority automatically denied. Even driving a car has its dangers—but actions have been taken to reduce such dangers, at the expense of the other desired performance qualities. And it would seem similarly appropriate to devote some effort to reducing the prospects of those disadvantages in cost-effectiveness applications.

If all our foreign-aid or all our agricultural-aid programs, to name but two, are evaluated in terms of cost-effectiveness analysis at a higher level, the analysis of these programs as a package or as an integrated whole pushes toward centralization of decision about such activity in one agency—a not unmixed blessing. Exposure to alternatives actually undertaken enables better choices. Mere recognition of this danger is not sufficient. Some institutional system to protect competitive choices and behavior, in order to induce exposure of alternatives to some kind of realistic, public testing and evaluation, is desirable. Unfortunately desirability does not mean feasibility, and it is not clear how such a context might be provided. Like much else in this essay of evaluation, it is easier to detect dangers and undesirable forces than it is to suggest ways of eliminating or attenuating them. It can only be hoped that some awareness of these dangers will stimulate some caution or action intended to reduce those disadvantages.

IV. Effectiveness of Cost Effectiveness

Yet no one doubts that the new system has, in fact, achieved greater responsiveness to cost. What is the explanation?

The conjecture is offered that the proponents of the new cost-effectiveness analyses have a zeal for what we would all regard as desirable or good cost-effectiveness studies. The current proponents and executors understand the relevant concepts of costs and the obstacles to better decisions about programs and procurement decisions. And they have succeeded in achieving a level of authority from which to apply their desirable criteria.

But what will happen when new people inherit this new centralized cost-effectiveness machinery along with its system of control? Is there anything that suggests that it will be inherited by men equally able to enhance a career by using these more economically general cost-effectiveness studies? And even for the present incumbents, is there anything to assure that those now in command will be prepared seriously to modify approved plans if their prior plans look "bad"? Will not they, too, begin to observe the general laws that characterize viable political behavior?

RELATED READINGS

Dulles, Eleanor L., and Robert D. Crane, eds. *Detente: Cold War Strategies in Transition.* New York: Frederick A. Praeger, Inc., 1965.

Herzog, Arthur. *The War-Peace Establishment.* New York: Harper & Row, Publishers, 1965.

Hitch, Charles J., and Roland N. McKean. *The Economics of Defense in the Nuclear Age.* Cambridge: Harvard University Press, 1960.

Kahn, Herman. *Thinking About the Unthinkable.* New York: Avon Books, 1962.

Levine, Robert A. *The Arms Debate.* Cambridge: Harvard University Press, 1963.

Martin, Thomas L., Jr., and Donald C. Latham. *Strategy for Survival.* Tucson: University of Arizona Press, 1963.

Peck, Merton J., and Frederic M. Scherer. *The Weapons Acquisition Process: An Economic Analysis.* Boston: Harvard University Graduate School of Business Administration, 1962.

AN ECONOMIC ANALYSIS OF THE MARKET
FOR SCIENTISTS AND ENGINEERS

A. A. ALCHIAN, K. J. ARROW, AND W. M. CAPRON

Introduction

In the years since 1950, at least until very recently, there has been widespread discussion of a "shortage" of scientists and engineers in the United States. Industrial leaders, public officials, educators, and scientists and engineers themselves have all voiced concern, and in some cases advocated various policies, both public and private, designed to alleviate the problem.

In order to bring out more clearly the issues involved, we have sought to explain some of the accepted principles of economic theory that are relevant to the problem. More specifically, this paper has several purposes. First, our review of a large number of the public statements about the "shortage" has convinced us that a useful purpose will be served if we can clarify the several senses in which the term "shortage" has been used. Rarely in the course of the public discussion has the term been clearly defined.

Second, we attempt to explain how one could determine the extent to which there has in fact been a shortage in any of the senses of that term which are susceptible of objective application. This assessment is based only on a rough reading of the readily available data and is therefore of necessity qualified. A third and more significant purpose of our work is a series of suggestions for further research on the supply and demand of scientific and engineering manpower and on the markets in which their services are bought and sold.

For these purposes it is necessary to analyze the mechanism of the market, and we begin with a brief re-capitulation of the standard analysis. An understanding of the market mechanism provides insight not only into the meaning of a "shortage" but also into the social issues of what the market for scientists and engineers "ought" to be. Our fourth purpose is to clarify these social issues and make some conjectures and policy suggestions about them.

"An Economic Analysis of the Market for Scientists and Engineers," RM-2190-RC, RAND Corporation, June 6, 1958.

CHAPTER I
THE CONCEPT OF A SHORTAGE

There are several different situations, all of which have, at some time or another, been called a "shortage." (1) Many people say there is a "shortage" if firms want to but cannot hire more engineer-scientists of a given quality at the same salaries they are currently paying; that is, there are unfilled vacancies in the usual usage of that term. Such a shortage will result from wage control or other restrictions that prevent prices from rising; it may also result from sluggishness in market adjustments when there are rapidly rising demands, as we shall suggest in Section 4 below. (2) But some people assert that a shortage exists when they mean simply that engineer-scientists are more expensive than they used to be, absolutely or at least relatively to other salaries or other costs. (3) Still others use the term "shortage" to mean that there are fewer engineer-scientists than there "ought" to be, according to some criterion. We will elaborate these meanings in the following sections, for their policy implications are very different. By way of a necessary preamble, we will sketch quickly the determination of salary levels in the market.

1. Supply and Demand in the Determination of Prices

For simplicity of exposition, we will suppose for the moment that there is only one type and one quality of engineer-scientist. For any given firm (or the government or any other hiring agency), we will define *demand at a given salary* as the number of engineer-scientists it would choose to hire if it were permitted to hire as many as it wished at that salary. We assume that the choice by the firm is a considered, rational one. That is, at any given instant of time, the firm may have more or fewer engineer-scientists than is profitable but will revise its market demand accordingly.

The number of engineer-scientists that it would be rational for the firm to choose is determined by the relation between the value of an additional engineer-scientist in increasing the revenue of the firm and the salary level. So long as the revenue that can be obtained from the services of an additional engineer-scientist (net of the additional expenses directly attributable to his work, such as office space and equipment) is greater than the given salary, it will pay the firm to increase its employment. As more engineer-scientists are hired, the uses that the firm will find for them will be of less and less value, since it will, of course, put them first to the more valuable uses. The point will

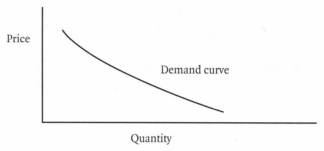

Price

Demand curve

Quantity

FIGURE 1.

eventually be reached when the value to the firm of an additional engineer-scientist will not exceed his salary. The number of engineer-scientists hired at this point is the demand of the firm at a given salary.

For each given salary level, there will be a corresponding amount demanded by the firm. The higher the salary level, the less will be the demand. We can graph all these demands by putting price (salary) on one axis (the vertical axis has become conventional) and number demanded (quantity) on the other, as in Figure 1. The relation between price and quantity demanded is known as the *demand curve* or *demand function* or demand schedule of the firm.

The *market demand at a given salary* (referred to simply as the demand when the meaning is clear) is the total of the quantity demanded by all the firms in the market. Such a market demand can be found for each given salary; it will decrease as the salary increases. The relation between market demand and salary can be graphed the same way as that between the demand by the firm and salary; this relation is referred to as the (market) demand curve or function and can also be illustrated by Figure 1.

The *supply at a given salary* would correspondingly be the number of individuals who are willing to take positions as engineer-scientists at that salary: usually the higher the salary, the greater the supply. Since for each salary there is a corresponding supply, the relation between salary and supply, the *supply curve or supply function*, can be represented graphically as in Figure 2.

In many discussions of the engineer-scientist "shortage," the very concept of a supply curve (relation between supply and price) seems to be denied. It is often alleged that because the individual scientist or engineer, practicing or potential, is motivated more or less strongly by non-economic forces (e.g., fascination of the job, desire to make exciting new discoveries, interest in knowing more for its own sake, desire to be free of routine) changes in salaries cannot

Price

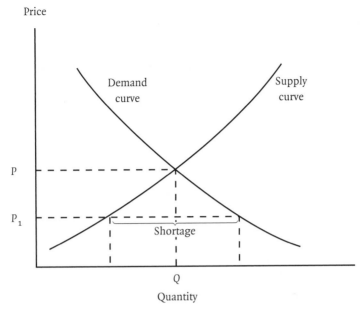

FIGURE 2.

be expected to produce changes in supply. It is said, for example, that many sci-entists will not leave an interesting job for a less-interesting, better-paying po-sition; that many university scientists refuse to forsake the campus for the in-dustrial laboratory even for substantially greater pay. These points are intended as a refutation of the relevancy of the application of the usual types of eco-nomic analysis to this market. This view rests on a misunderstanding. All of the above factors will be reflected in the position and shape of the supply func-tion, but they do not indicate that the function does not exist or cannot be de-fined. For example, the argument about university scientists, if valid, implies that the supply of university professor-scientists available to industry is very unresponsive to price changes. But it is not true that there is *no* level of indus-trial salaries, no matter how high, for scientists that could attract more profes-sors from the campus. All that is necessary for the market mechanism to work in such cases is for changes in the differentials in salaries to cause some shift of scientists and engineers to jobs that now pay more. In addition, while as we shall see the market mechanism "works" even if the total currently existing number of people of a specific skill is completely fixed (unaffected by price changes), an increase in salaries will call forth some increase in supply whenever an increase in supply is possible. None of this means that minute changes in salaries cause a vast reshuffling in jobs, that every engineer is always ready to move regardless of all other personal and professional conditions, etc. All that is asserted is that there are always individuals who are "on the margin" and for this reason will find the scales tipped by economic considerations; in short, individuals are enticed by sufficiently large differentials. Whether or not these individuals are worth so much in the new job as to justify such a differential is left to the judgment of the employer, whose job it is precisely to make these decisions. (Policy issues affecting supply are considered more fully in Chapter IV.)

Because each level of skill has an associated training period, the effect of a change in salary on numbers of engineer-scientists will not be felt immediately. For simplicity of exposition, we shall ignore the delay in response for the time being but will reconsider it later.

Consider now the price level designated by P in Figure 2. *At this price*, the market demand is satisfied by and equal to the supply offered. If all firms hire as many engineer-scientists at this price as they wish, they will in total hire the number Q. But there will be precisely Q individuals who wish to work as engineer-scientists. Hence the situation will be in balance, and we will refer to P and Q as the *equilibrium price* and the *equilibrium quantity* demanded and supplied, respectively. If the price P in fact prevails and each firm and individual acts as it wishes, there will be no reason for the situation to change in the absence of outside forces affecting either the value of an engineer-scientist's contribution to the revenue of a firm or the willingness of individuals to become engineer-scientists at any given salary level. On the other hand, at any price other than the equilibrium price, there will be tensions somewhere in the market system. Some firm or some individual potential engineer-scientist (possibly both) will find that his desires at the given price are not in fact satisfied.

It is to be expected then that, under ordinary circumstances, the price prevailing in the market will not stay put at any price other than the equilibrium price because of competition among engineer-scientists and among firms. If there is no interference with the operations of the market and its participants, there is a tendency for the actual price at which transactions take place—the salary at which engineer-scientists are in fact hired—to approximate the equilibrium price at which the supply offered equals the amount demanded.

We have so far considered the special case where there is only one type of engineer-scientist. In the real world, of course, there are many. Even within any one type, first-rate scientists are not the equivalent of those of lesser ability and, strictly speaking, should be classified as a different commodity. Though the essential principles of the preceding analysis are not changed, they have a more complicated expression, and the advantages of graphical presentation are lost.

To illustrate the complications, suppose that we classify chemical engineers into two grades of ability. Then the demand by a firm for first-rate chemical engineers at any given salary will not be a single number but will depend upon the salary to be paid to second-rate chemical engineers. To see this, consider any position for which the firm has decided to hire a second-rate engineer. A first-rate engineer in this position would create a greater return for the firm, but the difference in returns is not as great as the difference in salaries. Now suppose that the salary of second-rate chemical engineers rises while that of first-rate chemical engineers remains constant. The difference in salaries then decreases, and there will usually be some positions for which the salary difference becomes smaller than the difference in returns, which remains constant. In these positions, the firm will now wish to hire first-rate engineers where it formerly hired second-rate ones. Thus the demand for first-rate chemical engineers at a given salary will increase as the salary of the second-rate chemical engineers increases.

This means that the demand for first-rate engineers is a *function* of the salaries of both first- and second-rate engineers. Of course, the same is true of the demand for second-rate engineers. The supplies of the two are likely also to depend upon both prices. If a second-class chemical engineer can make himself into a first-class one by further training, then he will have an incentive to take the trouble and bear the costs if the salary difference is sufficiently great but not otherwise. Thus a rise in the salary of second-class chemical engineers while the salary of first-class engineers remains constant will decrease the supply of first-class engineers and increase that of second-class engineers.

Equilibrium now requires both that the supply of first-rate chemical engineers equal the demand for them and that the supply of second-rate chemical engineers equal their demand. These two conditions must be satisfied by the two salaries to constitute an equilibrium set of prices.

Similarly, we may discuss the determination of equilibrium for any number of related types of engineer-scientists. The general principles are the same as for a single type. For expository reasons, we will confine most of our discussion to the latter case, but it is, of course, understood that in many empirical studies the interrelation of the demands and supplies for different categories will have to be considered.[1]

2. The Economists' Use of the Term "Shortage"

If an economist is told that a particular commodity is "short," he expects to find, when he looks at the market, that buyers wish to buy more of the commodity *at the going market price* than is being supplied at that price. In other words, the price is such that the demand is greater than the supply. This situation can persist only if there is some obstacle preventing the market price from rising to the equilibrium price where demand equals supply. A shortage is represented in Figure 2. If for any reason the price stays at some point such as P_1, instead of rising to P, supply will be less than demand. One can say that supply is short of demand—that there is a "shortage." Or one can say that demand is in excess of supply—that there is "excess demand." The two expressions denote exactly the same thing.

What could prevent the price from being bid up to where the amount the buyers would want to buy is just equal to the amount offered? An obvious case occurs when a government imposes a price ceiling. As was seen during World War II, if such ceilings are to be successfully maintained it is usually necessary to accompany them by a rationing system so that the supply, inadequate to satisfy the demand *at the price fixed*, can be allocated. Prices and income no longer are allowed to do the rationing.

In addition to legalized price control, various private actions may keep prices artificially low. Possible impediments restricting prices may appear on either the demand or supply side of a market. One form of such action is illustrated by the emergence of the "gray market" for steel after World War II, even after price controls had been removed. The gray market was of course a manifestation of a "shortage" situation. Buyers wanted *at quoted prices* more steel than was available; hence they were willing to pay for steel more than the market prices asked by the major steel producers. For reasons not presently germane, the management of the major steel companies chose not to accept prices which would have cleared the market. Had they done so, the "excess demand" or, in other words, the "shortage" would have been eliminated.

---

1. See Appendix 1 to this chapter for an elaboration.

3. A Special Issue: Government Control Over Research and Development Salaries

The suggestion has been made that the government, particularly the Department of Defense, has created a shortage of the kind just described through its regulations of salaries paid by contractors.[2] There are two types of control that restrict the freedom of contractors with regard to salaries paid and could conceivably set an upper bound on salaries below the equilibrium price. In the first place, in all government contracts there is some measure of control over the costs incurred for particular purposes; on cost-plus-fixed-fee contracts, which are characteristically used for research and development work, the government is required to review and approve all cost elements, including wage and salary schedules. In the second place, the Air Force, at least, has special regulations that require explicit approval of any salary in excess of $25,000 and review of all salaries above $15,000 on an individual basis.[3]

The mere existence of such regulations does not prove that the government is creating a "price control shortage" but does show that it has some price control type of power over salaries paid by contractors. The critical question is whether or not the salaries offered by employer-contractors to scientists and engineers have been influenced to a significant degree by the existence or administration of these regulations.

To our knowledge, there is insufficient evidence to answer this question. That the Department of Defense has never actually turned down proposed salaries as being too high is not conclusive evidence that the regulations have had no effect in artificially keeping salaries down and thereby creating a shortage; the absence of such cases might mean only that employers have correctly anticipated the limits to which contracting officers are willing to let salaries rise. There have been publicly expressed complaints on the part of industry regarding these regulations, but, as far as we are aware, they have been directed to a fear that the government is attempting to usurp management's prerogatives and have not specifically suggested that the regulations as administered have in fact depressed salary levels. In response to these criticisms, Department of Defense officials have vigorously denied any intention to interfere with contractors' internal management decisions. They have repeatedly asserted that the only purpose of the regulations is to insure that public funds are not

---

2. James C. DeHaven, "The Nationalization of Research and Development in the United States," The RAND Corporation, P-853, April 30, 1956, Santa Monica, California.

3. As of this writing, June 6, 1958.

used to pay artificially inflated salaries—in their terms, to insure that salaries are not "out of line." We have not discovered any precise definition of this phrase, but presumably the contracting officer is expected to see that the salary paid to any given engineer or scientist on a government contract is the same as the salary he would command if he were employed on other work.

Despite the absence of sufficient information to draw firm conclusions, we suggest that no matter how the government chooses to use its salary-control powers it cannot create in the whole market a true "price control shortage." The government, directly and indirectly (through its contractors), hires only a fraction of the total number of engineers and scientists employed, though the fraction rises to about half in research and development. If the government were at all rigid in maintaining price controls on its contractors, it would find itself losing engineer-scientists to privately financed research and development activity. For example, if the government should decide not to permit salaries to be paid today above the levels prevailing in, say, 1950, its contractors would very quickly find that they were unable to obtain personnel. Since there is no evidence that this has happened, apparently the government has not pursued the policy, irrational from its point of view,[4] of preventing salary rises. We would tentatively suggest from this indirect evidence that at most the administration of these regulations has prevented salaries paid by government contractors from rising more rapidly than salaries paid for work in the private sector. At worst, then, the government may have caused some lag in the adjustment of salaries to levels appropriate to the situation of increasing demand.

It would be desirable to have more evidence bearing on this question. Among other things that should be undertaken is a program of interviews with government contractors in an effort to find out what, if any, impact these regulations have actually had on their wage and salary policies. To get significant answers, these interviews would have to be very skillfully conducted because contractors may not themselves be conscious of the effect of these regulations and their administration. Another kind of relevant information would be a comparison of the rate, magnitude, and timing of salary increases in the public and private sectors, respectively. Such information should be examined in conjunction with information regarding changes in demand in the two sectors.

---

4. However, apart from the "shortage" issue, it is rational from one point of view for the government to exploit its mass buying power to hold down salary levels somewhat. See Chapter III, Sect. 2.4.

4. Dynamic Shortages

Suppose that the price of a commodity that uses engineers in its production has increased. This means that the contribution to value of output made by engineers is now higher than formerly. Assume further that each firm producing this commodity was in equilibrium before the increase in the commodity price, that is, that it had as many engineers as it wished to hire at a given salary level. This means that before the price rise each firm chose not to hire another engineer, because the net returns attributable to hiring him were not equal to his salary. Under the new conditions, however, the number of engineers that it would pay the firm to hire at the previous salary has gone up. In the terminology introduced in section 2, the demand by each firm at any given salary has risen, and therefore the market demand has risen. The change from the old situation to the new is illustrated in Figure 3.

Hence D_1 represents the original demand curve for engineers. Curve D_2 represents the new demand arising from some change in external conditions, in this instance, the rise in the price of the commodity in whose production the engineers are engaged. To avoid misunderstanding, let us recall that for present purposes we are defining demand as the amount which the firm would choose to buy after careful calculation. At any given moment of time, the firm may not be fully aware of what its demand (in our sense) is and seek to hire

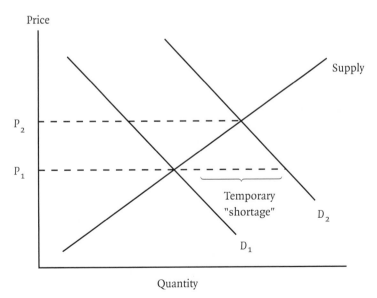

FIGURE 3.

more or fewer engineers. But we do assume that the firm will gradually become aware of any such errors and correct them.

In Figure 3, P_1 represents the equilibrium price when the demand curve is D_1. Let us assume that in fact P_1 was the price prevailing just before the shift in the demand curve. After the demand curve has shifted to D_2, the price that would bring supply and demand into equilibrium is P_2. It is indeed reasonable to suppose that the price or salary level prevailing on the market will eventually become P_2. But this process typically will take time. In this section, we wish to examine what happens during the interval.

Consider the situation of a firm just after the shift of the demand curve to D_2. A comparison of Figures 2 and 3 shows a strong analogy, not to say identity. At the moment of the shift, the market is experiencing a shortage, which is in many respects comparable to what it would face under price control. Each firm seeks to hire additional engineers at the price it currently pays, but there are no more engineers available at this price. We do not assume that each firm recognizes fully its demand, that is, how many engineers it would be best to have under the new conditions. All that is required is that each firm realize it wants more engineers than it now has. Then there will be unfilled vacancies so long as the firms do not raise salaries above what they are currently paying.

We have sketched the first response of the market to a shift in demand, which is a perception by the firm of unfilled vacancies. Before going on with the subsequent steps in the process by which the salary eventually rises to its equilibrium level, let us ask if there is any evidence of a shortage in the sense just described. In view of all the discussion of the "shortage" problem, it is remarkable how little direct evidence is available. The National Science Foundation in 1953 asked officials in large companies whether or not they were experiencing a shortage of engineers and scientists for research and development purposes.[5] As far as the reports go, no clear definition of the term "shortage" was supplied to these officials. It is plausible to suppose that a respondent to the survey would interpret the term to mean the existence of unfilled vacancies with salaries equal to those of engineers and scientists now employed by the firm and performing equivalent services. But the survey would have been more useful if the term had been given a careful operational definition in the questionnaire. At least half of the firms reported that they were unable to hire enough research scientists and engineers to meet their needs, although, except for the aircraft industry, there was no industry in which all firms reported such a shortage.

5. See National Science Foundation, *Scientific Manpower Bulletin No. 6*, August 1, 1955.

The picture given by the National Science Foundation study is similar to that given by Dr. G. W. Beste in a study of the chemical industry.[6] Referring to the Ethyl Corporation, Dr. Beste states, "We employ 370 chemical engineers today but need an additional 39. This 39 represent the accumulated deficiency of the last five years."[7] The meaning of the term "deficiency" is not explained, but it is perhaps fair to assume that it means the inability to fill vacancies at salaries then being paid to employees.

Fragmentary evidence suggests to Dr. Beste and to the respondents to the National Science Foundation's survey that there is a shortage as manifested by unfilled vacancies but that this shortage is not large. Such a situation is to be expected when the demand curve has shifted and the price does not immediately rise to the level that would equate supply and demand.

We will trace briefly the sequence of events that will be observed in the market as a result of the shift in the demand curve from D_1 to D_2. At the moment, any individual firm may not have fully calculated how many more engineers it could profitably hire, but we may suppose that it will be aware of wanting more engineers than it now employs. It will begin by seeking to hire more engineers at the going salary but will find that there are none to be had. Its advertised vacancies find no takers; its offers are refused. In any event, the firm becomes aware that in order to hire additional engineers it must pay higher salaries. The original decision to hire more personnel must be reconsidered in the light of new information about the necessary salaries. The firm will have to calculate whether or not the additional product derivable from additional engineers will be sufficient to cover the higher level of salaries. In the situation envisaged, the firm will indeed eventually decide to hire some additional engineers at a higher salary, but the decision will take time. First, there must be recognition of the need for higher salaries, then approval must be obtained from various echelons of management, and finally orders must be issued to hire.

Thus the time lag in the firm's reaction is spent partly in learning about the supply conditions in the market and partly in determining the profitability of additional hiring under the new supply conditions. This, however, is only one

6. G. W. Beste, "A Case Study of the Shortage of Scientists and Engineers in the Chemical Industry," presented at the second meeting of the National Committee for the Development of Scientists and Engineers, June 21, 1956.

7. Actually, this deficiency turns out to be largely the product of two years, 1955 and 1956. It is typical of the lack of historical perspective in the engineer-scientist shortage discussion that such short-run phenomena are made the basis for discussion of long-run policies.

step in the process of adjustment. First of all, the firm may not yet have fully adjusted to the new demand curve; it has hired some more engineers than before but possibly not as many as would achieve maximum profitability. But second, even if the firm had hired as many as would be profitable at the new salary level, the market as a whole would still not be in equilibrium, because the firm is now paying a lower salary to its old employees than to the new ones, and there is really more than one price being paid for the identical services rendered by different individuals. The multiplicity of prices is characteristic of disequilibrium situations, but in any well-developed market it cannot persist indefinitely. What happens is that other firms, also experiencing shortages, bid for the services of the engineers belonging to the firm we have been considering. While old employees will probably have some reluctance to move, this reluctance is certainly not absolute but can be overcome by a sufficiently high salary offer. That engineers do change jobs in sufficient numbers to suggest a responsiveness to market forces has been shown by Blank and Stigler.[8] However, we would again expect a lag in information. An employed engineer may not be in touch with current salary offers, and it may take some time before he is aware that the salary he is receiving is below what he might receive elsewhere. We would, however, certainly expect that he will become informed eventually and that the discrepancy between his actual and his possible salary will tend to be reduced over time. While some individuals will not be tempted to move even in the presence of considerable possible salary increases, many would be willing to do so; either they will in fact move or the hiring firm, to keep them, will raise their salaries to the competitive level. Thus the initial tendency within the firm for new employees to enjoy higher salaries than old ones will gradually be overcome as the salaries of the latter are raised in response to competition.

Thus, we see that it takes time, on both the demand and supply sides of the market, to adjust to the new situation created (in our example) by an increase in demand for the final product whose production requires, among other things, the services of scientist-engineers. The total time it takes demand and supply to adjust to the new situation is dependent on how costly it is for firms to decide exactly how many more employees they want at various higher salaries, and how costly it is for the employees to become aware of higher salary alternatives elsewhere.[9]

8. David M. Blank and George J. Stigler, *The Demand and Supply of Scientific Personnel*, New York, National Bureau of Economic Research, 1957, pp. 29–30.
9. We might note that in some markets, such as the organized exchanges for securities or commodities, information is available very quickly, indeed almost instantaneously,

There is another mechanism which will work to eliminate salary differences within a firm but at the expense of slowing down the firm's willingness to raise salary offers for new personnel. Salary differences within the firm are certain to be a source of morale problems to the extent that they are known, and clearly complete secrecy is out of the question. There will be pressure on the firm to increase the salaries of all its employees (in the same category) to the new higher levels. The lag in adjustment of the salaries of already-employed engineer-scientists is thereby reduced, but on the other hand the firm is made more reluctant to increase its salary offers to new employees because it realizes it must incur the increased cost not only for the new employees but also for the old ones. In effect the additional cost caused by the salary rise is recognized by the firm to be much greater if it has to extend the increase to all employees.

The total lag in the response of salaries to a shortage (in the sense of an excess of demand over supply) is then compounded first by the time it takes the firm to recognize the existence of a shortage at the salary level being paid, second, by the time it takes to decide upon the need for higher salaries and the number of vacancies at such salaries, and finally either by the time it takes employees to recognize the salary alternatives available and to act upon this information or by the time it takes the firm to equalize without outside offers. The details of this adjustment process have not been well studied, and they would form a useful field for research. For many purposes, however, a simple model suffices to bring out the most important implications of the above picture for economic analysis and policy.[10]

We have thus far been sketching a way of looking at the response of the market to a single shift of the demand curve. We have suggested that the price will tend to move to the new equilibrium price but with a lag. This analysis has been preliminary to our main purpose, which is to consider a situation of continuing change in demand (or supply). We suggest that this has been the case for engineer-scientists in the period beginning about 1950. For example, if the demand curve is rising steadily, then as the market price approaches the equilibrium price, the latter steadily moves away from it. There will be a chronic

---

but this is clearly accomplished only because it has been found worthwhile for those who buy and sell on these markets to pay the costs of the operation of such exchanges. No such exchange exists for scientists and engineers, and one can understand why: the product is not homogeneous, and each unit of supply is controlled by a different owner (i.e., the individual scientist or engineer himself).

10. See Appendix 2 to this chapter, Part I.

shortage in the sense that as long as the rise in demand occurs, buyers at any given moment will desire more of the commodity at the average price being paid than is being offered, and the amount of the shortage will not approach zero. The price will increase steadily and indefinitely but always remain below the price that would clear the market. This condition will continue as long as demand is increasing.[11]

To sum up, in the market for engineer-scientists or for any other commodity we expect that a steady upward shift in the demand curve over a period of time will produce a shortage, that is, a situation in which there are unfilled vacancies in positions whose salaries are the same as those being currently paid to others of the same type and quality. Such a shortage we will term a *dynamic shortage*. The magnitude of the dynamic shortage depends upon the rate of increase in demand, the reaction speed in the market, and the responsiveness of supply and demand to price changes. From the earlier discussion, the reaction speed may be expected to vary from market to market. It depends partly on institutional arrangements, such as those that determine how often prices are changed, that is, the prevalence of long-term contracts, and partly on the degree to which information about salaries, vacancies, and availability of personnel becomes generally available throughout the market. In the case of an organized exchange, such as those for securities or certain agricultural products, we would expect the information to be passed on so rapidly that the reaction speed is virtually infinite and dynamic shortages virtually nonexistent. In the following section we will advance evidence for the hypothesis that the engineer-scientist market for the last seven or eight years has shown a dynamic shortage in the sense just defined.[12]

5. Dynamic Shortage in the Engineer-Scientist Market

The preceding analysis has been very abstract. Though we have referred to the market for engineer-scientists for the sake of concreteness, actually everything said would be equally applicable to any other market. We want to argue here

---

11. See Appendix 2 to this chapter, Part II.

12. A. Alchian dissents in questioning the desirability of using the "dynamic shortage" approach of Sections 4 to 6 because the phenomena can be alternatively explained by the usual analysis, wherein price always equates effective demand and supply. In the usual analysis the path of price and quantity adjustments is explained by market period, short-run and long-run demand, and supply shifts; and not by a lagged response to a hypothetical demand and supply that would exist if foresight were perfect, knowledge free, and costs independent of how quickly one wants to do something.

that because of the special character of the engineer-scientist market and the demands made on it over the last few years, the magnitude of the dynamic shortage may well have been sufficient to account for a great proportion of the complaints. It should be made clear that we are not arguing that the market is subject to unusual imperfections. Rather the very way in which the market performs its functions leads to the shortage in this particular period.

A dynamic shortage is a possible explanation of the observed tensions in the engineer-scientist market because (1) there has been a rapid and steady rise in demand, (2) the responsiveness of supply to price is low, especially for short periods, and (3) the reaction speed on the engineer-scientist market may, for several reasons, be expected to be slow. The hypothesis stated in the previous section would imply that under such conditions a dynamic shortage could be expected. And we believe that such a shortage would largely explain such reactions as intensified recruiting and attempts at long-range policy changes observable in the industries affected.

(1) The market on which the tensions seem to be focused is not the engineer-scientist market in general but the market for engineers and scientists for research and development purposes. It is a matter of common knowledge that there has been a very rapid increase in demand in this market. During the year 1951 the number of research engineers and scientists in industry rose from 74,028 to 91,585, an increase of 17,557 or 23.7 per cent.[13] Such an increase is clearly capable of putting a strain on the smooth functioning of almost any market.

The increase in demand is, in turn, to be explained chiefly by the action of the government in contracting for research and development work by private industry. The increase in the number of research engineers and scientists employed on government contracts during the year 1951 was 15,547, so that virtually the whole increase in employment of research engineers and scientists was due to government demand.[14] The importance of the increase in government demand as the chief explanation of shortages has also been stressed by some observers, such as Dr. C. B. Jolliffe, of the Radio Corporation of Amer-

13. See United States Department of Labor, Bureau of Labor Statistics, *Scientific Research and Development in American Industry: A Study of Manpower and Costs*, Bulletin No. 1148, 1953, Tables C-5 (p. 62) and C-11 (p. 68). This source gives the January 1952 employment and the percentage increase; the other figures were calculated from these two.

14. *Ibid.*, Table C-13 (p. 70), shows that the number employed on government contracts in January 1952 was 45,425 and that this figure was an increase of 52 per cent over that of January 1951. The figure in the text is calculated from these two.

ica.[15] Dr. Jolliffe also states that the type of research and development done on military contract is more complicated than the usual industrial work. This would imply that there is some differentiation between the markets for engineer-scientists in military and in other research and development, so that the full force of the increased demand would fall on the former.

(2) While the increase in demand is an essential condition for a dynamic shortage, its magnitude is also regulated by the responsiveness of supply to price and by the reaction speed. We discuss supply problems at some length in Chapter IV. To summarize the conclusions relevant here, we may say that the responsiveness of the supply of engineer-scientists to price changes may be expected to be small but not zero over short periods of time, owing to the length of time it takes to train new personnel. Over longer periods, higher salaries will certainly elicit a greater supply, though again because of the importance of non-economic factors in choosing a career and because of the uncertainty of rewards in the distant future, the responsiveness of supply will be less than for commodities such as manufactured goods. Hence while it would be totally incorrect to deny the influence of price on supply, the responsiveness is sufficiently low to add to the possibility of a dynamic shortage.

(3) There are three reasons why it might be expected that the speed of reaction in the engineer-scientist market would be slower than that in the markets for other commodities, such as manufactured goods, or even than in other labor markets. They are the prevalence of long-term contracts, the influence of the heterogeneity of the market in slowing the diffusion of information, and the dominance of a relatively small number of firms in research and development.

While there exists a wide range of prices for the services of engineers and scientists, typically the price is a salary paid for the services of an engineer or scientist over some specified or indefinite period of time. Thus, for the engineer-scientist already employed by the government, a university, or a private industrial firm, there will be no instantaneous adjustment in the price he receives even in the face of demand changes, since contracts are not sub-

15. C. B. Jolliffe, "Electronics: A Case Study of the Shortage of Scientists and Engineers," delivered to the President's Committee for the Development of Scientists and Engineers, June 21, 1956. In discussing his own company, Dr. Jolliffe says, "We could use one thousand more right now without any question. Where could we use them? Mainly on military contracts because it is here—rather than in consumer and industrial electronics—that the pinch is tightest" (p. 6).

ject to daily renegotiation. Even in the absence of specific contractual elements of this sort, reaction is slowed down because of the greater job security which comes with long service with a particular employer. Professorial tenure is an extreme and institutionalized form of this phenomenon.

We have had several occasions to note that the market for engineer-scientists is not a single one. The heterogeneity of the market may interfere with the diffusion of information because an individual engineer-scientist may not know which market he belongs to. He may be aware that an associate is getting a higher salary, which may suggest that he ought to look around for another position. But he may very well wonder whether the associate's higher salary is perhaps due to superior ability or to the fact that somewhat different skills are being rewarded more highly at the moment. Because of his doubts he will be delayed in ascertaining his alternative opportunities. Thus the length of time before he actually does achieve a higher salary, either from another firm or from his own, will be longer, and the reaction speed will be correspondingly less.

Finally, one special characteristic of the market for engineers and scientists in research and development is that the typical buyer is large; in one instance a single buyer, the government, directly and indirectly accounts for about half of total demand.[16] Since the engineer or scientist bargains as an individual, there is room for the large buyer to delay salary rises. A large firm with large competitors has an incentive to keep salaries down rather than bid engineer-scientists away from competitors up to a certain point. Any one firm in an industry dominated by a few large ones will fear that increasing salaries in order to attract more engineers and scientists may set off competitive bidding that will end up with no substantial change in the distribution of engineers and scientists among firms but a considerably higher salary bill. This is especially likely to be the attitude of firms if the total supply of the engineer-scientists for which they are competing is not likely to change much in response to higher prices.

The desire to avoid competitive bidding sometimes takes the form of "no-raiding" agreements drawn up among otherwise competing firms in the same

16. Bureau of Labor Statistics, Bulletin No. 1148, presents some relevant figures for 1951. In that year, seven companies spent 26 per cent of the total expenditures on research and development in industry (p. 21), and the government financed 46.8 per cent of all such expenditures (Table 4) in addition to research performed directly by the government.

industry. Such a situation exists to some extent in the electrical equipment and electronics industries, dominated by General Electric, Westinghouse, and the Radio Corporation of America, and in aircraft, where a handful of firms account for the bulk of the research and development and of output.

But in no case do the large firms dominate the research and development market to such an extent that "no-raiding" agreements or other devices to limit competition in hiring can be effective indefinitely. If nothing else happens, the competition of smaller firms forces the large firms to match their offers. There is no evidence that attempts by the large firms to avoid competitive bidding can in the long run prevent the market price from reaching its equilibrium level. But they certainly can slow down the speed with which prices will rise in response to an excess of demand over supply and so, in accordance with the analysis of the preceding section, increase and prolong the dynamic shortage.

In short, the very rapid increase in demand for the services of scientists and engineers that this country has experienced ever since World War II and particularly in the past seven years has led to "shortage" conditions resulting basically from a failure of the price of such services to adjust upward as rapidly and by as large an amount as warranted by the increasing demand, given the supply schedule of such services. This lag in adjustment, so far as we can see, can be attributed to a significant extent, not to any successful overt attempt to control prices artificially, but to certain inherent characteristics of supply and demand conditions and of the operation of the market. While the relative rigidity of supply in the short run is unpleasant (from the buyers' standpoint), and the price rise required to restore the market to equilibrium may seem to be very great, it is only by permitting the market to react to the rising demand that, in our view, we can have any hope of calling forth the desired increase in supply in the longer run.

It must be recognized that the theory of a dynamic shortage rests upon much weaker empirical foundations than other aspects of economic analysis. The notion of prices adjusting to an excess demand is at best an approximation to reality. Observations that might provide direct evidence for the meaning and magnitude of a reaction speed are at best casual. It would be very useful to study the engineer-scientist market to test the hypothesis of a dynamic shortage. The following might be studied: (1) the existence of shortages for individual firms, in the sense that they are ready to hire but cannot find additional personnel at the same rates they now pay for comparable work, while they are not at the moment ready to pay higher salaries; (2) the existence of different salary levels for the same work both within the firm and among different firms; (3) the degree to which individuals are aware of alternative job opportunities with higher salaries and the extent to which firms are aware of the salaries necessary to attract additional personnel; and (4) the details of the process by which firms actually decide to increase salaries and to hire additional engineer-scientists.

6. Policy Implications of a Dynamic Shortage

The policy implications of a dynamic shortage are very different from those of a shortage due to price control. If we decide that in some important market artificially imposed restrictions either on the demand or on the supply side are resulting in price rigidity such that in the face of increased demand, price is prevented from rising sufficiently to restore the market to a balanced situation, then serious consideration should be given to removing such artificial restrictions. On the other hand, if we have a case of "dynamic shortage," we may ordinarily decide that all that is involved is a lag in adjusting to new circumstances that are inherent in the character of the market and the commodity. Only in cases where lags result in prolonged and serious departure from equilibrium and, at the same time, where there are workable policy measures to reduce these lags, should we propose intervention.

If we decide in a given case that we face a "dynamic shortage," what if anything should we do from a policy standpoint? First, should we take any action, assuming for the moment that there are measures we can take which will alleviate the situation? As long as the shortage is merely a symptom of a lag in adjustment and unless the lag results in a persistent maladjustment over long periods, there does not seem to be a particular reason for concern. As long as the movement of price in response to changes in demand is in the right direction, then presumably if demand does not continue to change rapidly, price will eventually adjust to the new situation. If however, we discovered that price adjustments were so sluggish that there continued to be an imbalance between supply and demand, then we would have reason for taking action. This then raises the second issue: if action is desirable, are there any policy measures available that will improve the adjustment process in the market without introducing undesirable interferences and imperfections in the market mechanism?

The fact is that none of the policy measures that have been advanced really bears on the movements of salaries in the market. Our analysis has shown that the elimination of the dynamic shortage can be achieved only by a rapid rise in salaries. The significant fact about the recent behavior in the market for scientists and engineers is that, despite the resistance to salary raises, they have been rising. If this process continues, and if demand does not continue to rise more rapidly than salaries, the dynamic shortage can certainly be eliminated.

Policy proposals, especially those emanating from employer organizations, are likely to minimize the role of price increases. Any attempt, private or public, to resist the called-for salary increases will only serve to perpetuate and even intensify the shortage. In fact such action might turn the dynamic shortage into one of the price-control variety. This is not to say, as we indicate below, that we may not wish to supplement the effect of relatively high salaries in leading to an increase in the supply of scientists and engineers in the long run, by various measures designed to improve the flow of information as to the probability that the demand will continue to be high, or by actions designed, for example, to increase the *potential* supply by improving our public schools.

Why, it may be asked, if short-run supply is relatively unaffected by prices, should we permit salaries of scientists and engineers to rise? All this does, it may be argued, is to increase the incomes of a special class in our society and results in boosting our national bill for research and development. There are two reasons why the "excess demand" should be eliminated by the necessary rise in salaries. One we have already indicated: today's salary increases serve as the "signals" which call forth the increase in supply in the long run. If the signals are prevented from appearing or are obscured by artificial controls, then the shortage may persist indefinitely. The second is that those using the services of scientists and engineers should be faced with the "true" price of these services if they are to use them economically. We discuss this problem at length in the following chapter under the heading "misallocation."

7. The Blank-Stigler Definition of a Shortage

In their recent important study of the engineer-scientist market Blank and Stigler address the issue raised in this paper:[17] has there been a shortage of engineers and scientists? Considering several definitions of the term "shortage," the authors settle on the following: "A shortage exists when the number of workers available (the supply) increases less rapidly than the number demanded *at the salaries paid in the recent past*. Then salaries will rise, and activities which were once performed by (say) engineers must now be performed by a class of workers less well trained and less expensive."[18] Blank and Stigler rely primarily on a comparison of the earnings of engineers with the earnings of

17. Blank and Stigler, *Demand and Supply of Scientific Personnel*, Chapter II, p. 2.
18. Ibid., p. 24. Italics by Blank and Stigler.

other professional groups and wage earners in order to test the hypothesis of a shortage of engineers. By definition a shortage exists if the relative earnings of engineers have risen.

The authors look at such data as are available going back to 1929, in more detail at the period since 1939, and in still greater detail at the post–World War II period. They say:

> We may summarize these pieces of information on engineering earnings as follows. Since 1929, engineering salaries have declined substantially relative to earnings of all wage earners and relative to incomes of independent professional practitioners. Especially since 1939 engineering salaries have declined relative to the wage or salary income of the entire group of professional, technical and kindred workers, as well as to the working population as a whole. After the outbreak of the Korean War there was a minor increase in the relative salaries of engineers (and of other college trained workers), but this was hardly more than a minor cross-current in a tide. Relative to both the working population as a whole and the professions as a separate class, then, the record of earnings would suggest that up to at least 1955 there had been no shortage—in fact an increasingly ample supply—of engineers.[19]

The Blank-Stigler conclusion that there has been no significant shortage must be viewed not only in the light of their definition but also in the context of their major concern with long-run trends, not short-run phenomena. It might be pointed out, however, that it is only in the post–Korean War era that there have been any complaints of shortages in this market. Therefore even if one is primarily concerned with the broad sweep of events, it seems proper to suggest that the period of real interest as far as possible shortage goes is that of the last few years, and with this interest in mind one may legitimately view "the minor cross-current" as being significant. The reason that Blank and Stigler adduce for dismissing the evidence of a shortage (by their own definition as tested by their own data) in the years since 1950 is that the relative change in salaries of engineers has been so slight that the shortage could not have been serious. But concluding that the market is a free, competitively working market, they do not consider the suggestion put forward here, namely, that even though there may be no obvious imperfections in the market, there may be a considerable lag in the adjustment of salaries in response to changes in demand.

19. Ibid., pp. 28–29.

It is worth noting just what the Blank-Stigler data do show. By their definition a shortage exists whenever the price of a given commodity rises. From 1950 to 1956 they show a rise in average starting salaries for college graduates with an engineering degree of 51.5 per cent (Table 14, p. 28). Since increases in starting salaries for college graduates in other fields have been roughly comparable (though none are quite so high for this same period), this merely indicates, by their definition, that there has been a shortage of college graduates in general, that is, a rise in their relative wages. (The same table shows that, for the period 1950–1955, starting engineers' salaries increased by 38.0 per cent compared with an increase for manufacturing wage earnings of 31.8 per cent.)

Blank and Stigler acknowledge that there has been considerable talk about a shortage of engineers and scientists, but having concluded that there has not in fact been a "shortage" of the price-rise type of any significance, they make no attempt to explain all the talk except to point to the use of the word "shortage" as embodying some social criterion. It may be their hypothesis that the recent complaints of "shortage" have been based solely on this use of the term.

8. Other Uses of the Term "Shortage"

Even the casual observer is aware that the term "shortage" has been used in many ways markedly different from the economist's. Perhaps the most common way in which "shortage" is used in everyday parlance is to describe those situations where a significant increase in demand and/or decrease in supply has resulted in a major price rise. Then, even if there is no shortage in the economist's sense (i.e., even if the price rises as much as required to clear the market under the new supply-demand conditions), many people who formerly consumed some of the commodity or service in question and now find the price so high they no longer want as much (or any) will describe the situation as one of "shortage." Actually, this is merely one way of saying that they can't get the given commodity at its old price. We can think of many examples of this use of the word "shortage." For example, the "servant shortage" during World War II was a case in point. Those for whom the increase in household servants' wages was more than they could afford to pay apparently found it more convenient to describe their change in circumstances as a result of a "shortage" than to admit baldly that they just couldn't afford to keep servants. As we have seen in previous sections of this chapter, the economist would not describe this change in the servant market as a shortage, since there is no evidence that prices did not rise sufficiently to eliminate excess demand.

It seems reasonable to explain a good deal of the current complaint about a shortage of scientists and engineers as a variant of the "servant shortage" phenomenon. Employers who find themselves losing engineers to other firms and at the same time find it uneconomic to try to keep these employees by offering them substantial salary increases may see the situation as a "shortage" rather than recognize that other firms can put these skills to more valuable uses.[20]

Many of the public statements by leading scientists, engineers, and businessmen directed to the "shortage" question seem to have implicit in them yet another definition of shortage. As we have seen, the economist defines shortage in relation to the equilibrium of a market; that is, he assumes the demand and supply functions as "givens" determined by the underlying supply of resources, the production possibilities, and consumer wants. Many of those who have expressed concern that our supply of scientists and engineers is insufficient seem really to be saying that the demand (and therefore the supply) *should* in their judgment be higher than it is. They appear to argue that, in their judgment, we *need* more people of this training in order to undertake various activities at the *proper* level. In other words, they are speaking in the same way as one who points to a dietary deficiency and says we *need* such and such an increase in calories per person in order to have "proper" standards of health. This is the statement of a physiological "demand," not an economic demand. Such statements are of course perfectly respectable. There can be no objection to an authority speaking of a "shortage" of proper food nor of his arguing that there is a "shortage" of scientists and that something ought to be done about it.

The only point we wish to make here is that it is not proper to interpret such statements as if the word "shortage" had any direct relation to a market shortage in the economist's sense of that term. This can be important, because the economist's prescriptions for removing a shortage, such as removing the imperfections preventing price from adjusting to its equilibrium level, will do nothing to meet the pleas of those using shortage in this other sense. For what they are saying is that, in their view, society should be willing to pay more for the services of scientists and engineers or, what amounts to the same thing, that the *demand* (in the economic sense) should be greater than it is. They may be arguing (quite correctly as we will indicate in Chapter III) that a private enterprise market economy tends to underestimate the value to the community of the activities of scientists and engineers and that the government should at-

20. While we lack specific evidence, we have the impression that the firms who have complained most insistently about a "shortage" have been those whose demand has not increased or at least has not increased as rapidly as that of other firms in their industry.

tempt to correct this undervaluation by extending its support of research. Or they may be arguing that more young people with the necessary ability and qualifications should pursue scientific careers for idealistic, non-economic motives. Finally, they may hold another position, which we will examine, namely that we *need* more scientists and engineers in order to hold our position *vis-à-vis* the rest of the world and particularly the Soviet Union in the battle for technological superiority.

While anyone may agree or disagree with any of these positions—for example, the view that consumer tastes *should* be such that there will be a large enough demand (in the economist's sense) to call forth, say, twice as many scientists—such a position is basically unassailable since it rests on a personal value judgment. And such statements may be successful in changing public attitudes sufficiently so that market demand is increased for the services of scientists and engineers, for example, by public approval of greater governmentally supported research and development activity.

Since these value judgments are not as a rule to be carried out at the expense of the one making the judgment, it is perhaps not surprising that some are extravagant by any sensible standards. Thus the International Business Machines Corporation is alleged to have estimated in 1956 that manning the computers then on order would "require" 7,500 mathematicians of whom 1,500 "should" be Ph.D.s.[21] At that time, the number of Ph.D.s in mathematics produced annually was approximately 250, of whom the great majority were not interested in computing. If these requirements are to be taken seriously, they would indicate a preposterous lack of foresight on the part of either the International Business Machines Corporation or its customers, roughly the equivalent of placing a city in the midst of the Sahara Desert and then complaining of a water shortage. The truth of the matter, of course, is that the computers are and will continue to be manned by people with lower educational qualifications.

The economist can contribute to the value discussion in two ways beyond his contribution as a citizen. First, he can remind us that ordinarily we can only get more of one thing by sacrificing something else. We can't increase the supply of scientists without having fewer people with other types of specialized training. Second, he can point out the significance of a freely operating competitive market as a standard for insuring that resources are used in the most efficient way. This particular contribution is so important that the next

21. See "Remarks of Dr. Alan T. Waterman at the Annual Air Power Symposium of the Air Force Association," press release of the National Science Foundation, August 3, 1956.

chapter is devoted to it. The market should operate so that no shortage in the sense described in Section 1 develops. But to the extent that institutional obstacles prevent the ideal competitive market in all its aspects from operating, the economist may find that the actual supply and demand conditions result, for example, in fewer scientists and engineers than the competitive ideal would supply. One might speak of this situation as a "shortage," although this is not the usual language of economics. For example, suppose that entry into the profession were limited by some type of licensing scheme. In the strict analytic sense, there would be no shortage, since the supply is constituted by those actually licensed. But the supply is monopolistically restricted and smaller than it would be if entry were free. The economist might then affirm that such restrictions should be removed or reduced in order to improve resource use; or, if the restrictions or other imperfections of the market cannot be removed, he might recommend government intervention or other measures to make the situation closer to what it would have been under perfect competition. Thus the economist can bring an argument of efficiency to support a looser argument of fairness. This position is close to the usage of the word "shortage" in the sense of demand and supply falling short of a standard set by value judgments, as just described.

We can summarize this section as follows:

(1) Many of those who have complained of a "shortage" of engineer-scientists are really complaining that they can no longer afford to hire as many as they used to, or as many as they would like to at the old salary levels. By the same token, those of us who drive Fords and Chevrolets may deplore the "shortage" of Jaguars and Cadillacs.

(2) Many of those who have expressed concern over the existence of a "shortage" seem in fact to be saying that the aggregate national demand for the services of scientists and engineers is less than it *ought* to be. In the language of the economist, they are *not* saying that the supply is too small, given the existing market demand; they are not asserting that the market mechanism is failing to work properly so as to "clear" the market. Instead they are reproving society for having "too low" a demand. Their view of what *ought* to be is based on their personal judgments, which may be influenced by a variety of factors such as our "technological race" with the Soviet Union, their view as to the tremendous advances which might be made if more scientists and engineers were put to work on various challenging and important problems in fields ranging from human disease to space travel.

(3) With one exception, the economist has no special competence in dis-

cussing these value judgments, let alone adjudicating among them. His role is to remind the community that more scientists and engineers cost something in the sense that other activities must be reduced if we are to have more scientists and engineers. The exception, which we deal with below, is his competence in demonstrating that a private market economy may at times operate so that the demand for scientists and engineers does not fully reflect their value to the community. In this sense he too may deplore a "shortage."

9. "Surpluses"

It is worth noting that people who talk about "shortages" are usually the same people who use the word "surplus" to describe the situation where demand has fallen (or supply increased). The term "surplus" (of supply) to refer to this situation, though commonly used, is extremely misleading. Just as people who use the term "shortage" are actually suggesting that supply ought to be increased (rather than price being allowed to rise to adjust demand to supply), those who complain of "surpluses" are really suggesting that supply ought to be reduced in order to keep prices up, rather than letting prices fall so as to increase the amount of the commodity demanded to the point where it matches the supply at the lower price. Whatever may motivate the choice of words, the terms "shortage" and "surplus" are extremely misleading in that they suggest policy measures that may not be justified by the true situation.

For example, there would be much talk about "surpluses" if the supply of servants should increase as a result of a fall in demand for their labor in other occupations. Household maids and chauffeurs would complain bitterly. But again the question must be asked, "a surplus at what price?" If at the old price, then this would mean only that people are complaining that the demand for their services in other occupations is not as great as it used to be. Rather than admit to the necessity of taking wages that reflect their lowered service value, they prefer to complain of a "surplus," implying that something is wrong with supply. Again, if demand did not fall but supply increased, the complaints of "surplus" would mean only that at the old higher price, demand was not great enough to employ the larger supply. At lower prices the amount demanded would be increased until the number available at a sufficiently low price was fully employed. This kind of complaint about "shortages" and "surpluses" can be heard about all kinds of things: wheat, butter, milk, servants, engineers, salesmen, paper, and so forth. Talk about "shortages" means that some people, buyers, for example, are distressed that others are now successful in draining away resources by offering more for them. Complaints about "surpluses," in turn, mean that sellers are distressed because new suppliers have so increased supplies as to enable buyers to get more at lower prices. Unfortunately the policy action that such complainants *seem* to demand is that other people be restrained from bidding away the resources that used to be had at lower prices or, in the case of surpluses, that competing sellers be prohibited from entering the market and providing more supply at lower prices to buyers. Actually no policy changes or action is necessarily called for at all. Price adjustments in response to demand and supply changes are the normal working process of a free price, private property system.

Appendix 1 to Chapter I

1. Supply and Demand with Interrelated Markets

In this appendix we will consider the supply and demand for a commodity on a number of interrelated markets. Suppose there are n services or other commodities which can be supplied from the same or related sources, for example, engineers of given training who can be used in different industries, or, in the long run, engineering students who can specialize in different ways. Let p_i ($i = 1, \ldots, n$) be the price of the service or commodity on the ith market, and let S_i be the supply forthcoming at any moment of time. The supply of any one commodity will depend not only on its price but also on the prices of all other commodities, since higher prices on other markets will draw supplies away from the given market. We can thus write,

(1) $S_i = S_i(p_1, \ldots, p_n)$, with $\partial S_i/\partial p_i > 0$, $\partial S_i/\partial p_j < 0$ for $i \neq j$.

In a linear approximation,

(2) $$S_i = \sum_{j=1}^{n} a_{ij} p_j + c_i \ (i = 1, \ldots, n),$$

with

(3) $a_{ii} > 0$, $a_{ij} < 0$ for $i \neq j$.

We will assume, for simplicity, that the demands for the commodities are independent, so that, for example, the demand for engineers by the petroleum industry will depend only on the salary for engineers in that industry and not on the salaries in other industries.

(4) $$D_i = D_i(p_i), \text{ with } \partial D_i / \partial p_i < 0,$$

or to a linear approximation, we have a demand equation for each industry.

(5) $$D_i = -b_i p_i + d_i, b_i > 0 \, (i = 1, \ldots, n).$$

On each market, there will be usually a "shortage," that is, the difference between demand and supply, which we will denote by X_i.

(6) $$X_i = D_i - S_i.$$

(Of course, X_i might be negative, in which case there is a "surplus.") As described in the text, we assume that on each market, the price moves as directed by the shortage X_i, rising if the shortage X_i is positive, decreasing if negative, and remaining stationary if zero. To a linear approximation,

(7) $$dp_i / dt = k_i X_i, k_i > 0 \, (i = 1, \ldots, n).$$

Substitute from (2) and (5) into (6).

(8) $$X_i = -(b_i + a_{ii}) p_i - \sum_{j \neq i} a_{ij} p_j + (d_i - c_i) \, (i = 1, \ldots, n).$$

For convenience, let,

(9) $$m_{ii} = -(b_i + a_{ii}), m_{ij} = -a_{ij} \, (i \neq j), n_i = d_i - c_i.$$

Then (8) can be written,

(10) $$X_i = \sum_{j=1}^{n} m_{ij} p_j + n_i \, (i = 1, \ldots, n).$$

From (9), (3), and (5), we see that,

(11) $$m_{ii} < 0, m_{ij} > 0 \text{ for } i \neq j.$$

The equilibrium situation is one of equality of supply and demand on all markets, that is, $X_i = 0$ for all i. Then (10) yields a system of linear equations which can be solved for the equilibrium price. The approach to equilibrium is described by equations (7) and (10). These combine to yield,

$$(12) \quad dp_{ii}/dt = k_i \sum_{j=1}^{n} m_{ij} p_j + k_i n_i \ (i = 1, \ldots, n).$$

(12) constitutes a system of simultaneous differential equations whose solution yields the time paths for each price. We will assume that the system is *stable*, that is, that each price approaches its equilibrium value.

Let us rewrite the above in vector notation. Let X be the vector with components X_i, p the vector with components p_i, K the matrix with diagonal elements k_i and off-diagonal elements 0, M the matrix with elements m_{ij} and n the vector with components n_i. Then (7), (10), and (12) can be written

$$(13) \quad dp/dt = Kx,$$

$$(14) \quad X = Mp + n,$$

$$(15) \quad dp/dt = KMp + Kn.$$

We have assumed that the system (15) is stable. The stability depends only on the matrix of coefficients of p, so that we will also say that KM is a *stable matrix*, which we will define as the matrix of a stable system of differential equations (with constant coefficients). Equivalently a stable matrix is one whose characteristic roots all have negative real parts. Also a matrix with the properties (11), that is, negative diagonal and non-negative off-diagonal elements, will be termed a *Metzler* matrix. Since the elements of KM are $k_i m_{ij}$, it follows from (7) and (11) that KM is also a Metzler matrix.

$$(16) \quad KM \text{ is a stable Metzler matrix.}$$

2. *Some Mathematical Properties of Stable Metzler Matrices*

As a preliminary to the subsequent analysis, we will need some mathematical properties of stable Metzler matrices. Note that for any matrix A we can choose a constant s so that $s + a_{ii} > 0$ for all i; then if A is a Metzler matrix, $sI + A$ has only non-negative elements, where I is the unit matrix. Such non-negative matrices have a number of convenient properties which will be used.[1]

LEMMA 1. A principal minor of a stable Metzler matrix is a stable Metzler matrix.

1. These properties are collected conveniently in Gerard Debreu and I. N. Herstein, "Nonnegative Square Matrices," *Econometrica* 21, no. 4 (Oct. 1953): 597–607.

PROOF: Let A be a principal minor of the stable Metzler matrix B; obviously A is a Metzler matrix. Choose s so that $sI + B$ is non-negative. The characteristic roots of $sI + B$ are s larger than those of B; since, by hypothesis, the real part of any characteristic root of B is negative, it follows that the real part of any characteristic root of $sI + B$ must be less than s. For any non-negative matrix, there is a real characteristic root λ_0 such that $|\lambda| \leq \lambda_0$ for all characteristic roots λ. Let λ_0 be this root for the non-negative matrix $sI + B$ and λ_1 the root for the non-negative matrix $sI + A$, which is a principal minor of $sI + B$. Then,

$$(17) \qquad \lambda_1 \leqq \lambda_0 < s.$$

If λ is any characteristic root of $sI + A$, then $|\lambda| \leq \lambda_1$; since the real part of λ is necessarily not greater than $|\lambda|$, it follows from (17) that the real part of λ is less than s. Since the characteristic roots of A are s smaller than those of $sI + A$, their real parts are all negative, so that A is stable.

LEMMA 2. If A is a stable Metzler matrix, then $Ax < 0$ implies $x > 0$ and $Ax \leqq 0$ implies $x \geqq 0$.

PROOF: Choose s as before so that $sI + A$ is non-negative; let $B = sI + A$. Let $y = -Ax > 0$. The characteristic roots of B are less than s in absolute value by the same argument as in the proof of Lemma 1. Then,

$$(sI - B)^{-1} y > 0.^{2}$$

If we substitute for B and y, we find that $x > 0$. The second part of the lemma follows by continuity.

LEMMA 3. If A is a stable Metzler matrix, then $-A^{-1}$ is non-negative.

PROOF: Let x be the ith column of $-A^{-1}$; then the vector Ax has -1 in the ith place and 0 elsewhere, by definition of an inverse. Hence $Ax \leqq 0$, so that $x \geqq 0$ by Lemma 2. Since x is any column, the lemma holds.

THEOREM. If A is a stable Metzler matrix, $b \geqq 0$, $y(0) \geqq 0$, and $dy/dt = Ay + b$, then $y(t) \geqq 0$ for all $t \geqq 0$.

PROOF: Suppose the set of times t such that $t \geqq 0$, $y_j(t) < 0$ for some j is non-null. Let t_0 be the greatest lower bound of such t-values. If $t_0 > 0$, then by definition $y(t) \geqq 0$ for $t < t_0$, so that, by continuity,

$$(18) \qquad y(t_0) \geqq 0.$$

2. Ibid.

If $t_0 = 0$, then (18) holds by hypothesis.

The functions $y_j(t)$, $\dot{y}_j(t)$ $(= dy_j/dt)$ are analytic. For each there is some open interval beginning with t_0 in which they have constant sign. By choosing $t_1 > t_0$ but sufficiently close,

$$(19) \qquad y_j(t),\ \dot{y}_j(t) \text{ have constant sign over the open interval } (t_0, t_1).$$

Let S be the set of indices j such that $y_j(t) < 0$ in (t_0, t_1); by definition of t_0, S must be non-null. If $\dot{y}_j(t) \geq 0$ over (t_0, t_1), then $y_j(t) \geq 0$ over the same interval by (18). From the definition of S,

$$(20) \qquad \dot{y}_S(t) < 0 \text{ in } (t_0, t_1),$$

where the subscript S means the subvector composed of components of S. Let B be the principal minor of A with rows and columns in S, C the minor of A with rows in S and columns not in S.

From the hypothesis as to the differential equation satisfied by $y(t)$ and (20), we conclude that

$$(21) \qquad 0 > \dot{y}_S \equiv By_S + Cy_{\bar{S}} + b_S \text{ for } t \text{ in } (t_0, t_1),$$

where $y_{\bar{S}}$ contains all components of y not in S. Since A is a Metzler matrix, C contains only non-negative components. By definition of S, $y_{\bar{S}} \geq 0$; hence $Cy_{\bar{S}} \geq 0$. By hypothesis, $b_S \geq 0$. Therefore, from (21),

$$(22) \qquad By_S < 0.$$

From Lemma 1, B is a stable Metzler matrix; by Lemma 2, then, $y_S > 0$ for t in (t_0, t_1). But this contradicts the definition of S. Hence, the supposition that the set of non-negative t-values for which $y_j(t) < 0$ for some j is non-null has led to a contradiction, and the theorem is proved.

3. The Adjustment Process with Steadily Increasing Demands

We shall now examine the process of adjustment described in Section 1 of the appendix when the demand is shifting steadily upward in time on some or all of the interrelated markets. For simplicity, we assume that the supply curve is not changing; however, the following analysis would remain valid if the supply were also shifting upward in time but not more rapidly than the demand. We will also assume that, to begin with, supply and demand are equal.

We shall then continue to assume that (2) holds, but (5) becomes

(23) $$D_i = -b_i p_i + d_i + e_i t, \, b_i > 0, \, e_i \geqq 0.$$

The definition of the shortage X_i remains as before, and the adjustment of prices continues to be described by (7). Then the following discussion remains valid with slight modification. A term $e_i t$ is added on the right side of (8) and, equivalently, of (10). Let e be the vector whose components are e_i. Then, in vector notation, (13) remains valid, while (14) becomes

(24) $$x = Mp + n + et.$$

M still satisfies (11). Further, we will assume that the system defined by (13) and (24) would be stable in the absence of trends, that is, if $e = 0$, so that (16) remains valid. The characteristic roots of KM are the same as those of $K^{-1}(KM) K = MK$, so that the latter is also stable; it is clearly a Metzler matrix, since it is derived from M by multiplying each column by a positive constant.

(25)   MK is a stable Metzler matrix.

Differentiate (24) with respect to time.

(26) $$\dot{x} = M\dot{p} + e,$$

where, it will be recalled, dots denote differentiation with respect to time. Substitute for $\dot{p}$ from (13) into (26);

(27) $$\dot{x} = MKx + e.$$

From (25), we see that the solution $x(t)$ of the differential equation (27) converges to a limit, which must be such that $\dot{x} = 0$.

(28) $$\lim_{t \to \infty} x(t) = -K^{-1}M^{-1}e.$$

The assumption that supply and demand are equal at the beginning can be expressed by saying that

(29) $$x(0) = 0,$$

where $t = 0$ is taken as the beginning of the process. Let $t = 0$ in (27); from (29) and (23),

(30) $$\dot{x}(0) = e \geqq 0.$$

Differentiate (27) with respect to time.

(31) $$d\dot{x}/dt = MK\dot{x}.$$

We can apply the theorem with y replaced by $\dot{x}$, b by 0, and A by MK; the hypotheses are satisfied, according to (25), (30), and (31), so that

(32) $$\dot{x}(t) \geqq 0 \text{ for } t \geqq 0.$$

Thus *the shortage on each market increases from the initial value of 0 toward the asymptotic limit given by (28)*. In particular,

(33) $$x(t) \geqq 0 \text{ for } t \geqq 0.$$

From (13) and (33),

(34) $$\dot{p}(t) \geqq 0 \text{ for } t \geqq 0,$$

so that the price on each market is increasing over time. Differentiate (13) with respect to time.

(35) $$d\dot{p}/dt = K\dot{x}.$$

Substitute for $\dot{x}$ from (26).

(36) $$d\dot{p}/dt = KM\dot{p} + Ke.$$

From (16) and (36), it follows that $\dot{p}$ converges to a limit as t approaches infinity.

(37) $$\lim_{t \to \infty} \dot{p}(t) = -(KM)^{-1}Ke = -M^{-1}e.$$

From (34) and (37), we conclude that *prices rise on all markets and the increase approaches a constant rate which will usually be positive on all markets, even those which do not themselves have an upward shift in demand; the limiting rate of price increase depends only on supply and demand conditions and is independent of the speeds of adjustment.*

At any time t, let $p^\star$ be the vector of prices which would clear the market, that is, make the shortage zero. From (24),

$$(38) \qquad\qquad 0 = Mp^\star + cn + et.$$

Multiply through in (38) by K.

$$(39) \qquad\qquad 0 = KMp^\star + Kn + Ket.$$

Substitute from (24) into (13).

$$(40) \qquad\qquad \dot{p} = KMp + Kn + Ket.$$

Finally, let q be the difference between the market-clearing price $p^\star$ and the actual price p, that is, $p^\star - p$. Subtract (40) from (39),

$$(41) \qquad\qquad -\dot{p} = KMq,$$

or,

$$(42) \qquad\qquad q = -(KM)^{-1}\dot{p}.$$

From (16) and Lemma 3, $-(KM)^{-1}$ is a non-negative matrix. Then from (34),

$$(43) \qquad\qquad q(t) \geqq 0 \text{ for all } t \geqq 0,$$

while from (42) and (37),

$$(44) \qquad\qquad \lim_{t\to\infty} q(t) = (KM)^{-1}M^{-1}e = M^{-1}K^{-1}M^{-1}e.$$

Thus *the actual price is always below the price which would clear the market, the difference approaching a limit which is less, the faster the speed of reaction on the different markets.* It can also be shown that the difference between the actual and the market-clearing prices widens as time goes on.

Appendix 2 to Chapter I—Part I

While there is, strictly speaking, no one market price during the process of adjusting supply to increased demand, a multiplicity of prices being characteristic, one could focus attention on the average price being paid for engineering services. The text discussion makes clear that the average price will tend to rise so long as there is an excess of demand over supply, but it will not rise instantaneously to the level that will bring supply and demand into equality (P_2 in Figure 3). Further, the forces that induce price rises will clearly operate more strongly, the greater the excess of demand over supply. Hence we find it reasonable to assume that *the rate of increase of price per unit time is greater, the greater the excess of demand over supply.* As a corollary, it will cease rising when the price is such that demand equals supply, which is our previous definition of equilibrium. Recall that demand and supply at any given price are defined as the quantities demanded and supplied after complete rational calculation.

Call the ratio of the rate of price rise to the excess of demand over supply the *reaction speed.* Then the amount of shortage will tend to disappear faster, the greater the reaction speed and also the greater the responsiveness of supply (or demand) to price.

Let p be the (average) price, k the reaction speed, D be demand, S be supply, and t be time. The movement of the market over time is determined, in the above model, by the following relations (using linear approximations for the demand and supply functions).

(1)
$$dp/dt = k(D - S),$$

(2)
$$D = -ap + c,$$

(3)
$$S = bp + d.$$

Equation (1) expresses the assumption in the text about the relation between price rises and the difference between supply and demand; equations (2) and (3) are simple assumptions about the nature of the demand and supply functions, as represented graphically in Figures 1–3.

Let X represent the shortage, that is, $X = D - S$. From (2) and (3),

(4)
$$X = -(a + b)\, p + (c - d).$$

Differentiate (4) with respect to time; then $dX/dt = -(a + b)(dp/dt)$. If we then substitute from (1) and replace $D - S$ by X, we have

$$(5) \qquad\qquad dX/dt = -k(a + b)X.$$

Thus, for any given shortage X, the speed of convergence is greater the greater $k(a + b)$. In particular, other things being equal, the smaller the value of b (which measures the responsiveness of supply to price), the slower will be the convergence of the shortage X to zero.

Appendix 2 to Chapter I—Part II

The steady upward shift may be represented by adding a trend term to the demand as given by (2) in Part I of this appendix.

$$(6) \qquad\qquad D = -ap + c + et,$$

where t represents time and e the rate of increase of demand with time for any given price. Let X be the amount of shortage, that is, $D - S$. From (3) and (6),

$$(7) \qquad\qquad X = -(a + b)p + (c - d) + et.$$

Differentiate all the terms of (7) with respect to time.

$$(8) \qquad\qquad dX/dt = -(a + b)(dp/dt) + e.$$

In view of the definition of X, (1) can be written

$$(9) \qquad\qquad dp/dt = kX.$$

Substitute from (9) for dp/dt into (8).

$$(10) \qquad\qquad dX/dt = -(a + b)kX + e.$$

Assume that at the beginning, there is no shortage, so that $S = D$, or $X = 0$. Then from (10) we see that $dX/dt > 0$, so that the shortage X starts increasing and must continue to increase (since if dX/dt ever reached zero, it would remain at zero thereafter). It is also easy to see that

(11)
$$\lim_{t \to \infty} X(t) = e/(a + b)k,$$

so that the shortages tend to a limit which is greater, the greater the rate of increase of demand, and the slower the speed of adjustment would have been with an unshifting demand schedule.

Let p' be the rate of increase of prices, that is, dp/dt. Differentiate (9) with respect to time and then substitute from (8).

(12)
$$dp'/dt = k\, dX/dt = -k(a + b)\, p' + ke.$$

By the same reasoning as with (10), p' must be increasing over time and approaching a limit. Since it is zero to begin with, it follows that p' must be positive for all t, so that, by the definition of p', the price p must be increasing steadily.

Let $p^\star$ be the price at any time which would clear the market, that is, which would make $X = 0$. In view of (7), $p^\star$ satisfies the equation

(13)
$$0 = -(a + b)\, p^\star + (c - d) + et.$$

Multiply through in (13) by k.

(14)
$$0 = -k(a + b)\, p^\star + k(c - d) + ket.$$

Let q be the excess of the market-clearing price over the actual price, that is, $q = p^\star - p$. Substitute from (7) into (9).

(15)
$$p' = -k(a + b)\, p + k(c - d) + ket.$$

Subtract (14) from (15) and use the definition of q.

(16)
$$p' = k(a + b)q.$$

Since p' is positive and increases from zero to a limit, the same must be true of q. Thus the actual price will always remain below the market-clearing price, and indeed the gap will actually widen with time, but the two time paths will approach parallelism.

The discussion to this point has dealt with a single market. In the real world there are a number of related markets. Firms in different industries or in different localities may in any given case compete for the services of engineer-scientists of certain specified skills. Therefore the firms in any one industry will find that the supply available to them depends not only on their own salary offers but on the salary levels in all industries buying similar skills. In short, the demand for engineer-scientists comes from a whole series of interrelated markets. This situation cannot be represented graphically, but the general conclusions just drawn remain valid. See Appendix 1.

CHAPTER II
THE ECONOMIST'S CONCEPT OF MISALLOCATION

Everything is limited; the fact that at every moment the total stock of trained engineers and scientists of various qualities is given raises two inescapable problems. First, what allocation among various tasks is a good allocation of these engineers and scientists? Second, how shall this allocation be brought about?

1. The Optimal Allocation

The first question can be made precise only if a "good" allocation can be defined. By "good" the economist means the greatest possible value of output that can be obtained, taking into account the willingness to work. The output of engineer-scientists is not a single thing but many: chemicals, airplanes, new ideas, and so on. The values of these different outputs reflect the desires of consumers, including the government, a collective consumer. Consumers' desires are revealed by their readiness to give up one thing for the sake of getting something else. This sacrifice of goods for the services of engineers is the exchange ratio that the market expresses as prices and wages.

Given the momentary tastes and preferences—no matter how these are determined or effected—an optimal allocation of engineer-scientists or of any productive resource is the one that will yield the highest level of satisfaction to the members of the community. By highest level of satisfaction is meant simply that it is impossible with any other allocation to produce a greater level of satisfaction for any member of society unless one hurts someone else in order to do it. Poor or inefficient allocation is one in which it is possible to revise allocations further such that some people are made still better off without anyone else being hurt. Clearly, if it is possible to improve things in this sense, then the existing allocation should be changed, and for this reason the existing arrangement is called "bad" or "inefficient." Economics uses the term "efficient" to denote this kind of goodness, and "inefficient" to denote its absence.[1]

1. We speak of the satisfaction of the community's desires without going into the distribution of those satisfactions among individuals. In evaluating a proposal for social policy, one might object to one which increases the average level of satisfaction but which affects some adversely while raising the level of others more than correspondingly. In considering the engineer-scientist market, however, we are considering such a small part of the economy that no policy changes discussed are apt to have a significant effect on total income distribution. We will therefore ignore distributional effects in subsequent discussion.

In time the stock of engineer-scientists can be made bigger or smaller. But if it is bigger, it is at the expense of fewer people trained in other skills, for example, doctors, lawyers, musicians, and carpenters. The fact that more engineers and scientists will result in a greater output of their kind of services is not sufficient to justify an increase in the stock of engineer-scientists. It must be greater than the sacrificed potential output these men would have yielded had they entered other occupations. Only then can we conclude that more engineer-scientists should be trained. Further, training new engineer-scientists is itself costly. It uses up resources that could be used for other purposes. These educational facilities, for example, could be used to train more psychologists, business managers, teachers, or skilled production workers, and these are but a few examples of the alternatives to increasing the supply of engineer-scientists. An efficiently operating economic system in signaling that more engineer-scientists are desired would simultaneously be making this comparison of relative alternative worths.

2. Optimal Methods of Allocation

Nothing in the preceding discussion suggests *how* an efficient allocation of existing engineer-scientists can be brought about. Nor does it suggest *how* the future supply can be modified in the appropriate directions. What is necessary is a mechanism that will enable our desires for the services of engineer-scientists and, indeed, for all other goods in the economic system to be realized and to function as controls over the training and kinds of work that people undertake. That such a mechanism exists in the operation of a free economy seems to have escaped the awareness of many people who are complaining about an engineer shortage. For example, a high-ranking general testified before a Congressional committee that in the race for the development and production of scientific weapons the Russian form of society has "a great advantage in that they can tell their youth what they are going to do, whether to go into scientific training, or whether to go into the army or the air force, and they can with their system make their services so attractive that men want to be part of them."[2] And from another high-ranking general, we have the following testimony offered to Congress: a Russian advantage is that "they can disregard public opinion, and that they have the power to induce a young man who may have

2. "Study of Airpower" Hearings before the Subcommittee on Armed Forces, United States Senate, Eighty-fourth Congress, Second Session, April 16, 20, 1956, Part 1 (GPO, 1956), p. 59.

engineering talent or scientific skill, to pursue any line of effort that they want."[3]

These are but samples of the common belief that the Soviet system has a more effective *and* efficient control mechanism than ours. Is it true that a free economy is weaker in its control technique or that it is less able, whatever the level of effectiveness of its control techniques, to achieve efficiency?[4] In fact, subject to several qualifications that we deal with later, an efficient allocation of resources can be obtained by an economy of competitively determined prices. But this fact seems to be widely ignored for several reasons. The system was not invented by anyone. It works independent of any common understanding that it has the property of efficiency and independent of any central, directive authority. For these reasons a person can easily fall into the trap of concluding that it lacks effective and efficient control.

In a competitive system, each individual is at liberty (a) to choose whatever kinds of training and jobs he wishes, given the market costs and incentives of getting that training and of working in those jobs; (b) to produce whatever goods and services he chooses; and (c) to consume or exchange them for whatever other goods he wishes at mutually agreed exchange rates with other people. Only by offering incentives in the form of freely acceptable or rejectable payments as rewards for services are individuals induced into certain skills. This mechanism for letting the tastes of the members of the community shape the allocation and supply of resources is termed the *free price, private property* system, or "capitalism" for short.

Trite as the foregoing may seem, it is important. Can a person or a society logically say that it wants or needs more scientists and engineers than it is willing to pay for? If one says he needs or wants more scientists than he can get at the amounts he is currently willing to offer, he is saying, in effect, that as much as he wants or needs such skills, he neither wants nor needs them as much as other things which he would have to give up. It is inconsistent to say that one needs or wants more of something than he now has at the price he must pay for

3. Ibid., p. 9.

4. We do not discuss a third criterion—that of the cultural and social milieu within which interpersonal problems are resolved—because acceptance of the principle of individual and personal freedoms and rights is so widespread as not to require elaboration. An understanding that a free private property individual-choice system is also a very efficient allocator of productive resources is what seems to be lacking; hence this is the feature emphasized in the present discussion.

it, if he prefers instead to have other things. What his statement really means is that he wishes he were richer so that he could have more of everything.

To be sure, the ability of the price system to insure that resources are as well directed as possible to the satisfaction of people's tastes depends on the presence of certain conditions. (1) The prices must be such as to make the amount supplied and the amount demanded of any good or service equal. In the engineer-scientist market, the salaries must be such that there are neither firms willing to hire more engineer-scientists at the wages asked by engineer-scientists than are available nor more engineer-scientists willing to work than are able to find jobs. (2) The rewards and costs of any productive activity, including training, must be reflected in the prices and incomes received and paid by economic agents responsible for that activity. (3) No market price should be controlled by a single agent acting either as a seller (monopoly) or as a buyer (monopsony).[5]

If any one of these conditions is not satisfied, there is presumptive evidence that the price system is leading to an inefficient allocation of resources. Our subsequent analysis in this chapter will therefore for the most part investigate the possibility that one or more of these three conditions is violated.[6]

3. Misallocations and Shortages

As we pointed out in Chapter I, an inequality between supply and demand at a quoted price in the engineer-scientist market takes the form of a shortage or, equivalently, of an excess of demand over supply. We will trace out in some detail how this kind of shortage of engineer-scientists is presumptive evidence of a misallocation of resources.

First consider the case where firm A has all the engineer-scientists it wishes at the current salaries while firm B would like to hire at least one more engineer-scientist. We assume that the market value of the outputs of the two firms reflects social value. (See Section 4.) This means that for firm A the net increase in value of the firm's output resulting from employment of another engineer-scientist would not exceed his salary. On the other hand, firm B would have an increase in output greater than the salary of a new engineer-

---

5. A fourth condition which plays a role in some contexts, though not especially here, is that there not be important economies of scale in production.

6. For a more detailed elaboration of the efficiency properties of a competitive system see, for example, J. E. Meade and C. J. Hitch, *Economic Analysis and Policy*, Oxford University Press, New York, 1938, or T. Scitovsky, *Welfare and Competition*, Irwin, Chicago, 1951.

scientist if it employed another one. It follows that the total value of the output of the two firms would be increased if an engineer-scientist were transferred from firm A to firm B, for the loss in output to firm A would be about equal to the going salary rate while the increase in output to firm B would be greater than that rate. Thus if some firms want to employ more engineers at wages high enough to attract them but are for some reason unable to do so, and if some other firms are not experiencing such a shortage, we have clear evidence that the total output could be increased by a reallocation of the existing supply of engineer-scientists.

When all firms are experiencing shortages, the argument is a little more complicated. In the preceding paragraph the essential point was that if two firms could get different values of outputs out of an engineer-scientist, total output would be increased if personnel were transferred from the low-output firm to the high-output firm; the "shortage" or lack of "shortage" at a given salary was a way of demonstrating the inequality in the productivities of the engineer-scientist in the two firms. If all firms are experiencing shortages, then all we can directly infer is that for each firm the output derivable from an additional engineer-scientist is greater than this salary. But we would expect that only by sheer accident would firms not differ in the productivity of an additional engineer-scientist, and hence even in this generalized situation there would be misallocation.

Only if salaries rise until there is no "shortage" of this type will this source of misallocation be eliminated. Less efficient firms, unable to match higher salary offers, will be forced to give up engineer-scientists to more efficient ones. The less efficient firms like to resist this force by calling it "pirating," for only in the absence of such "pirating" can they continue using engineer-scientists in relatively unproductive ways.

It should be observed that the preceding argument that shortages of this type are wiped out by competitive salaries does not depend upon the assumption that the total supply of engineer-scientists will be increased by a salary rise. The argument has rested solely on using a given number of engineer-scientists as efficiently as possible. But as we pointed out in the preceding chapter, salary increases (relative to other salaries) will increase the number of engineer-scientists, and this effect therefore provides an additional justification for letting supply and demand govern salaries. This supply argument is similar to the preceding efficiency analysis except that it rests on competition among different occupations for the limited supply of potential entrants rather than among firms for the supply of already trained personnel.

If there are complaints of a shortage in occupation A (say engineer-scientists) but no complaints of shortage in occupation B, then exactly the same argument holds, namely, that total national output will be increased if there occurs a shifting of actual or potential members of occupation B into occupation A. This shifting will be greater as time passes because, for one thing, the effects on students ready to undertake training can be considerable. The possibilities of such shifting are discussed in greater detail in Chapter IV.[7]

4. Divergence Between Social and Private Rewards and Costs

In a free economy it is prices that convey information about the desires of the people for different products and the alternative uses of resources. Normally if a man creates a product or renders a service, the laws of property permit him to charge a price (i.e., exchange products) so that his productive efforts will be motivated to supply those goods or services that have the greatest value measured by the price others are willing to pay. Similarly if a productive effort requires a commodity or a service to be supplied by someone else, a price has to be paid, and the producer will have an incentive to economize on the use of goods or services that have important alternative uses or that involve considerable dissatisfaction to the seller.

There are circumstances, however, in which individually desirable behavior is at variance with this principle. A classic case is that of smoke produced by an industry. An industrial process often involves the creation of a by-product that is of considerable disutility to other people and for which our legal structure does not require compensation. As far as the net creation of satisfactions to society as a whole is concerned, the dissatisfaction caused by the smoke should properly be offset as a cost of the output of the productive enterprise. But the individual producer does not take the effects of the creation of smoke into account, since he is not required to pay other people for their loss of clean air. Hence the industrial activity that produces smoke will be undertaken on a larger scale than is socially optimal, or, what amounts to the same thing, the

---

7. When comparing different occupations or firms, it is really not necessary that they have the same salary level, since occupations or firms may be more or less attractive irrespective of salary. The criterion for optimal allocation between occupations or firms is that the net gains, counting both income and the satisfaction of the individual in his job, be the same in both. In a free market, the salary differences automatically adjust in the direction of offsetting the differences in job satisfactions, so that it remains true that a "shortage" in one occupation but not in another is a signal of misallocation.

enterprise responsible for this activity cannot be expected voluntarily to add to its costs by using smoke abatement or elimination techniques. Not all the physical property damages that other people are forced to incur are charged to the individual who causes the damage.

The reason for this undesirable behavior is not some inherent defect in the pricing system nor is it that free markets and private property distort motives. The source of the difficulty is that private property rights are not widespread enough—in particular, property rights in smoke and fresh air have not been established because of the prohibitively high cost of doing so. If such rights were feasible and could be cheaply enforced, we could then prevent creators of smoke from dumping their smoke on our property or from taking away our fresh air in exchange for bad. Where property rights cannot or have not been established we cannot expect the voluntary exchange price system to operate—it simply doesn't exist. In this situation a substitute means of control is used, for example, special laws prohibiting certain kinds of action or taxes imposed on such action. Usually these special laws attempt to prescribe behavior of a type that simulates the behavior that would be observed if property rights were present.

Similar considerations may apply if a productive enterprise produces benefits for which it is not compensated. We shall argue below that this is true of research and development work (see Chapter IV, Section 1). In that case, the amount of productive activity will be smaller than if the value of services could be realized by the producer.

The divergence between social and private rewards and benefits is a cause of misallocation quite independent of the "shortages" we have been discussing. Indeed these two factors, the "shortages" and the failure of the property system to include all conceivable property rights, might work in opposite directions, at least for a while. Thus one possible explanation of the engineer-scientist market over the past decade is the following: the government became aware that the amount of research and development was too small because of the failure of the benefits of research and development to be adequately included in the private-property price system. In an effort to remedy this situation, it increased research and development expenditures rapidly and thus created increased demand and "shortages" (see Chapter I). Thus the effort to eliminate misallocations from one cause might have given rise to "shortages," which imply other misallocations. If so, it may be that the gains from increasing research and development expenditures outweigh the losses due to "shortages," which in any case can be expected to be temporary.

5. Monopoly and Monopsony Inefficiencies

As the rate of output of any product increases, the price at which it can be sold ordinarily decreases, other things remaining equal. If there is a seller of the commodity who is sufficiently large to affect price in this way, he will take account of this fact in setting his rate of output. He will be aware that an increase of, say, one unit in the rate of output will increase his total receipts by less than the selling price of that one unit because the price at which the entire rate of output is sold is now lower. This reduction must be subtracted from the selling price of the new unit of output. This means that the "effective" price received by the seller for increasing his rate of output by one unit is less than the actual selling price. In such a situation there will be a misallocation of resources because consumers are willing to pay for an additional unit of output more than the increase in receipts realized by the seller (who is taking into account the effect of the reduced price on his total receipts). The producer will spend more money to produce at a higher rate only up to the point at which extra receipts cover the extra costs. At this point, where extra receipts just equal extra costs, we will find that his selling price is higher than the extra receipts for the reason just given. If price is greater than the extra costs of increasing output, output should be increased, since the selling price measures the consumer's value of the increased output. But this seller is looking at his increase in receipts, not at price; hence he is not induced to produce at as large a rate as consumer desire. This means that resources that should be used to produce more of the commodity under consideration are in fact allowed to be used for production of other less desired goods. Any seller whose output affects selling price in this way is called a monopolist.

The same considerations apply to a buyer. If a buyer is sufficiently large in the market, an increase in his demand for what he is buying causes the purchase price to rise. The effective increase in total cost of his purchases will be higher than the price of the extra unit bought. He will curtail his demand below the social optimum. Buyers who behave in this way are called monopsonists.[8]

6. Effects of Uncertainty on the Optimal Allocation of Resources

It has been assumed up to now that all economic agents can predict the outcomes of their decisions to produce, enter training, take particular jobs, or consume. In two aspects of the engineer-scientist market the assumption of

8. See Chapter III, Sect. 2.4 for a discussion of the government as a monopsonist in the market for engineer-scientists.

certainty conspicuously fails to hold. By its very nature, the outcome of a research and development study, especially the research phase, must be uncertain; if the answers were known, there would be no need for the research. Further, the individual who decides to become an engineer-scientist cannot know with certainty what the salary level will be either at the time he finishes training or thereafter. However, how uncertainty distorts the workings of the market in general is a complicated and by no means thoroughly understood topic that is peripheral to our main theme.[9] Some specific implications for the engineer-scientist market are discussed later.

7. International and Intertemporal Comparisons of Efficiency of Resource Allocations

As we have seen, the theoretical efficiency of the price system is subject to some qualifications. It would therefore be very useful to supplement theoretical arguments with empirical observations. Direct measures of misallocations are extremely difficult,[10] but comparison of resource allocations and outputs in different nations or in the same country at different periods of time might serve the purpose. Some such feeling as this lies behind some of the comparisons between the United States and the Soviet Union as to the rate of training of engineer-scientists and also behind some of the demand projections based on past experience.

It may indeed be possible to show by observation that one allocation of resources will lead to a higher level of satisfaction in the community than another. However, such comparisons must be made with extreme care, since the allocation problems to be solved by two countries or the same country at different periods of time will usually be different. An economic system starts with given basic resources—land, labor supply, facilities for imparting skills, and capital equipment—and allocates them so as to satisfy the tastes of the community. Two situations (two nations or two time periods) may involve two different allocation problems because either the basic resources are different or the tastes to be satisfied are different. The mere fact that resource allocations—

9. See, for example, Armen A. Alchian, "Uncertainty, Evolution and Economic Behavior," *Journal of Political Economy* 58 (June 1950): 211–21.

10. Mention should be made of an ingenious attempt by Arnold C. Harberger, "Monopoly and Resource Allocation," *American Economic Review*, Papers and Proceedings, 44 (May 1954): 77–87. This is principally devoted to the effects of monopoly and does not bear on the divergence between social and private rewards and costs which is of more interest in the engineer-scientist problem.

for example, the proportions of engineer-scientists in the labor force—differ in two situations does not prove that either allocation falls short of optimality with respect to its availability of resources or its tastes. If one society is shorter of educational facilities than another, we would not be surprised if it had fewer engineer-scientists relative to manual labor, and we would not call it inefficient. Similarly, if one society valued handicrafts more highly relative to manufactured goods than another, it would be appropriate for the former to have a smaller proportion of engineer-scientists and other aids to manufacturing.

This argument does not mean that intertemporal and international comparisons are useless, but it does mean that judgments about efficiency of allocation have to be made in the light of possible resource and taste differences.

At the beginning of Chapter I we identified three meanings of "shortage." Two of these—unfilled vacancies and the "servant shortage," where people are merely complaining about the rise in the price of particular services—were discussed in that chapter. We now return to the more important third meaning in the light of the discussion in Section 4 of the preceding chapter.

Some people think society is not getting as much science and engineering service as it ought to have. It may be that the complainants think that other people are ignorant and should want or demand more than they do, perhaps through government service. Another opinion is that there are certain defects in the way in which the existing desire for research and development is transmitted to the marketplace via the private property system. Some defect prevents a full realization in the marketplace of the public's true demand for research and development. The same individual may hold both these opinions. But the two opinions are quite different in their value judgments and in their implications for policy.

1. Differences of Opinion

Differences of opinion can arise because of differences in knowledge about the existing situation or because, with equal knowledge, objectives and goals differ. Is there any basis for believing that the degree of information or awareness of the public of the usefulness of research and development or of engineer-scientists is incomplete or based on inadequate appreciation of the value of such services?

1.1 Comparison with the Soviet Union

One line of argument asserts that the Russians are producing more scientists and engineers than we, not only in absolute numbers and quality but also relative to their total labor potential. If they can produce at so high a ratio, then we must be inefficient if we are not also producing an equally large ratio of scientists and engineers.

The number of living graduates in science and engineering in the Soviet Union is about 70 per cent of that in the United States, but the number of new graduates in 1955 was more than twice as great. The difference in resources devoted currently to the production of scientists is especially striking in view of the difference in national income levels. This comparison has suggested to many that we are seriously underestimating our needs or, in more meaningful

TABLE 1. *Graduate scientists and engineers in 1954*

Country	Pure Science		Applied Science	
	Total number	Number per million of population	Total number	Number per million of population
United States	23,500	144	22,500	137
U.S.S.R.	12,000	56	60,000	280
Great Britain	5,200	105	2,800	57

Source: "New Minds for the New World," *New Statesman and Nation*, September 8, 1956, p. 279.

terms, that our allocation of resources in this area is currently below the optimal level. The logic of this international comparison must now be examined in light of our general discussion of such comparisons in Chapter II.

First we present a few figures. To give more perspective, we add some figures for the United Kingdom, where the resource allocation to the production of engineer-scientists is again very different, being much lower than in either of the other two countries. See Tables 1 and 2.

The figures, in combination with the observation that the rate of growth of national income has been higher in the Soviet Union than in the United States and higher in the United States than in the United Kingdom, might suggest that there would be a net economic gain by increasing the production of engineer-scientists at the expense of other occupations. However, there are several alternative interpretations of the facts. (1) The greater rate of production in the Soviet Union relative to their labor potential can be interpreted as a catching up from an initially suboptimal ratio. Of course once the educational institutions needed for this rapid rate of training have been created, one might expect them to continue to be used. But after some time, one could expect the discrepancy to disappear, apart from continuing differences in consumers' desires for engineering and science services and apart from differences in natural resource endowments. (2) One country may have a lower rate of production of engineer-scientists relative to its labor supply because its evaluation of different kinds of services may differ. That such a difference in social evaluation can lead to a difference in the number of engineer-scientists may be seen by a comparison with British experience. The relatively smaller number of engineer-scientists may reflect an inadequate appreciation by British employers of their market value, or it can be a rational adaptation to a different set of values and public

TABLE 2. *Soviet-American comparisons of scientific personnel*

	United States	U.S.S.R.
1. Living graduates in science—1955	1,536,000	1,158,000
2. Living engineers—1955	575,000	555,000
3. Science graduates—1955	59,000	126,000
a. Pure science	29,000	22,000
b. Engineering	23,000	59,000
c. Agriculture	7,000	20,000
d. Science teacher	★	25,000

Source: National Science Foundation press release, "Comparative Figures on U.S., U.S.S.R. Scientific Personnel," August 3, 1956.

★Not separated from other categories in United States figures.

preferences. It can be seen from Table 1 that in Great Britain, in particular, engineering is considerably less prized than pure science by those qualified for it, and this attitude may be consistent with other aspects of the culture of British university graduates. Similarly the Soviet Union clearly puts a greater value on economic growth as contrasted with current consumption than either we or the British do.[1] Such a different evaluation should rationally be accompanied by a greater stress on heavy industry and consequently on engineers and scientists.

(3) It may be that the country with the larger relative rate of production is overproducing in the sense that the alternative services that these trainees could have provided would be more socially valuable according to its (possibly suppressed) preferences. In sum, there may be a possibility of using international comparisons to make a judgment as to the possible undervaluation of engineer-scientist services in a free economy, but there are too many imponderables to make these comparisons currently reliable enough to serve as a basis for policy.

1.2 *Military Rivalry*

Another line of argument offered in support of the position that the American public *ought* to want services from engineers and scientists rests on the Soviet military threat. It has been said that only through advances in our technol-

1. Of course the social value structure in the Soviet Union is that set by the ruling group, not by the consumers as a whole as in the United States. The ends of the society are thus not only different but differently derived.

ogy can we continue to pay the price of preserving our national integrity and international security, that we can afford to see the Communists' population increase relatively to ours so long as we can maintain military superiority via more efficient technology. Hence we should place a tremendous value on scientific advance and on the technical knowledge of our population. The more rapidly Communists progress scientifically, the more rapid must be our own progress to maintain economic military superiority. Otherwise the costs of military superiority may exceed our willingness to pay, and we may thereby lose the "war."

This argument is certainly not without validity, but the policy implications have to be considered carefully. Let us spell out the steps of the argument in a little more detail. (1) The value to us of any increase in our military power increases if Soviet and Chinese military power increases. (2) An increase in the number of Soviet engineer-scientists is an increase in their military power. (3) One way for us to achieve an increase in our military power is to have more engineer-scientists. It would then follow that a sensible reaction to a Soviet increase in the number of engineer-scientists would be an increase in the number of ours.

Step 1 is undeniable; steps 2 and, especially, 3, however, have to be made more precise. As far as step 2 is concerned, an increase in the number of Soviet engineer-scientists implies some presumption of an increase in the quality of Soviet military technology. But an increase in the number of Soviet engineer-scientists might not increase their military power. Improved military technology is only one possible use for Soviet engineer-scientists, while they may increase their military power in ways little related to technical superiority, for example, numerical increase in the armed forces, or because they may increase the number of engineer-scientists in military research without increasing the total.

But let us suppose that there is an increase in Soviet military power because of increased efforts to improve military technology or any other reason. It could still be argued, from steps 1 and 3, that we should increase our supply of engineer-scientists. However the obvious point must be made, in connection with 3, just as it was in connection with 2, that it is not the total supply of engineer-scientists but the number used in military research and development that is relevant. That is, if it is felt for any reason that research and development for eventual military uses is becoming more valuable, this should be expressed in terms of an increase in the military demand for engineer-scientists. The government should increase its military research and development budget, and primarily let the market take care both of the long-run implications for the supply of engineer-scientists and of the current job allocation of the existing personnel. To take steps to increase the supply of engineer-scientists without an increased demand in the military research and development budget is not a rational response if the Russian danger is evaluated so highly. And, incidentally, to do this *alone* will be to generate an increase in supply that will depress earnings in this field, a prospect that promoters of more engineer-scientists should recognize.

In any case the United States' decision with regard to the amount of resources that should be allocated to military research and development or to military purposes in general will certainly be influenced by estimates of changes in Soviet military power, but there is no obvious and direct connection between this decision and the *manner* in which the Soviet Union achieves increases in her relative strength. In short, there is only a tenuous and indirect sort of inference possible for United States policy to be derived from Soviet policy with regard to the production of engineer-scientists.

It will be objected that in the short run, at least, the policy sketched above will involve drawing engineer-scientists from other uses to military ones, and that a better policy is to increase the total supply first so no one will suffer. But increasing the total supply also means drawing individuals from other occupations where they are also valuable. If the military danger is greater, then *all* other uses of trained personnel in and out of the engineer-scientist profession must be rated relatively lower. Not only should potential lawyers and doctors be diverted to the engineer-scientist profession but also engineer-scientists should be diverted from consumer goods to military work. Indeed, if time is important, it is the present uses of engineer-scientists that will have to bear the immediate impact, since turning others into engineers and scientists involves considerable delay.

We conclude that the national evaluation of military research and development should be expressed by an increase of expenditures for that purpose in the military budget at the expense of other, presumably less efficient, ways of achieving national security. The government should not hesitate to bid high for research personnel and to trust the workings of the free market system to distribute the impact among competitive uses and, in the long run, draw others into this work.

1.3 *Demand Projections*

A third line of argument that the American economy is in danger of not getting as many scientists as it ought to want rests on projections of past observed relationships between the number of scientists and other economic variables, such as gross national output. These almost all show that demand will exceed supply by a greater amount as time goes on. The argument then suggests that something drastic or special must be done to increase the supply and avoid the gap.

A sensible demand projection must really be intended as a prediction of the number of engineer-scientists that would yield a good allocation of our resources in view of their alternative use values. The projected inequality between demand and supply can be interpreted sensibly only as an estimate of the extent to which the economy will, if policy measures are not undertaken, suffer from a non-optimal number of engineer-scientists. There will not be observed any gap or unfilled vacancies, simply because the prices and wages will have risen enough to induce employers not to want to employ any more engineer-scientists than in fact do exist—even if the number that does exist is in some sense smaller than optimal.

The flaw in these systems of projections is twofold. First, they assume that the market price system contains some defect—which it may have but which these authors do not reveal. Second, the method of projection is presumed to be a valid indicator of the optimal number of engineer-scientists. Those who construct such projections attempt to determine the optimal number of engineer-scientists in the future by a comparison with the allocation in the present and near past. They seem to start by assuming that the present (or at least the recent past) situation is optimal or, at any rate, satisfactory. They do not conclude from this, of course, that merely continuing the present number of engineer-scientists will maintain an optimal position. Indeed, they argue that the resources of the economy, labor supply, and capital are growing and that the optimal allocation in the future will therefore require an increasing number of engineer-scientists.

In effect their procedure is to select some relation between the number of engineer-scientists and some other variable in the economy observed over the recent past and then to assume that this relation must hold in the future if continued optimality is to be maintained. For example, it might be suggested that the present ratio of engineer-scientists to the labor force be held constant for the future. Alternatively, and with equal plausibility, it might be the ratio of engineer-scientists to national income that is to be held constant. Neither of these is in fact assumed by those making the projections, and neither would lead to a conclusion that an imbalance will develop between supply and demand, though the assumptions are as plausible as those actually used.

To take an example, the projection made by the Manufacturing Chemists'

Association is based on the observation that over the past ten years, national income has been growing at an average rate of 4 per cent per annum while the number of engineer-scientists has been growing at an average rate of 6 per cent per annum. Hence, it is argued, to maintain the present rate of growth of national income it is necessary to maintain the 6 per cent rate of growth of engineer-scientists. This rate is then used to project the "needed" number of engineer-scientists over future years. The authors of this projection assert that anything less than this number of scientists will diminish the growth rate of national income.

Obviously there are a great many alternative assumptions upon which to base such projections, and they lead to widely different conclusions. The amount of information about the economy that can be summarized in the handful of figures used for the projections is a very small fraction of the total amount dispersed throughout the individual firms in the economy and brought together by means of the price system. Even though the latter does not indeed guarantee optimality, the data and individual decisions to which it responds are so vast that one must indeed be hesitant to criticize the resulting allocation on the very narrow basis employed in the usual demand projection.

The unreliability of demand projections may be suggested by the fact that as recently as 1948 the Bureau of Labor Statistics was forecasting a glut in the engineer-scientist market. That such forecasts are not yet reliable enough to serve as a serious basis for policy becomes apparent when one considers the general unreliability of economic forecasts even for a single year, not to mention the startling failure of the United States population forecasts.[2]

We do not argue that carefully made projections of demand may not be of some use. Because of the long training period for engineer-scientists, a forecast of the optimum number of engineer-scientists and the resulting wages would help in inducing the appropriate number of entrants into engineering

2. J. S. Davis, "Our Amazing Population Upsurge," *Journal of the American Statistical Association*; L. R. Klein, "A Post-Mortem on Transition Predictions of National Product," *Journal of Political Economy*, Vol. 54 (1946), pp. 289–308; M. Sapir, "Review of Economic Forecasts for the Transition Period," *Studies in Income and Wealth*, Vol. 11, National Bureau of Economic Research, 1949, pp. 275–351. The post-war forecasts made in the post-war period and used as a basis for economic policy by the United Kingdom have been equally useless; see E. Devons, "Planning by Economic Survey," *Economic Journal*, September 1952. Norwegian and Dutch experience seems to have been better; see H. Theil, "A Statistical Appraisal of Postwar Macroeconomic Forecasts in the Netherlands and Scandinavia," *Proceedings of the International Statistical Institute*, Summer 1955, pp. 1–16.

and scientific education. Much more effort should be made to exploit the allocative information that is already available in the economy. But we should be a lot surer than we are today that forecasts have a reasonable degree of accuracy before any serious policy decision is based on them. And the forecasts must be tested against the past and for a period in the future before they can be taken seriously.

It is easy to forecast better than, say, the average college entrant, but it is not nearly good enough to excel this low standard. Personal forecasts of college entrants can be expected to conflict a good deal, with extreme forecasts cancelling each other as far as they induce movement toward particular occupations. But if there were an official or quasi-official forecast, most students might be influenced to move toward particular occupations. In these circumstances we would be running a much greater risk of extreme movements, of "putting all our eggs in one basket," and hence the standard that an official forecast should meet must be for higher than simply improving upon the average individual forecast.

2. Possible Defects in Economic System

In addition to the preceding complaints about shortages of scientists and engineers is still another that rests on the belief that there are defects in our economic system that prevent the true demands of the public for scientists from being accurately transmitted to the marketplace so as to affect market demand and supply. Four such defects in the current property system have been alleged at different times to apply to the engineer-scientist market. Two defects are presumed to lead to an understatement of the true demand in the marketplace and at least one to an exaggeration of demand.

2.1 *Weakness of Private Incentives for Research and Development*

A distinguishing characteristic of research and development is that it ends up primarily with new knowledge as its product. Knowledge, in turn, is a commodity that cannot be owned except in a very imperfect way. Once it is revealed, knowledge ceases to be private property. The man who buys it knows that he runs the risk of having his property expropriated and is reluctant to pay its full value. This effect makes itself felt all the way back to the inventor or the researcher whose incentive to uncover new ideas does not fully reflect their potential value simply because ideas do not fall in the class of private property. This problem is an example of the divergence between private and social rewards, along the line described in Chapter II, Section 4.

Desirable as it might be to have such value capturable by the inventor in order to encourage future invention, it would mean necessarily that the use of new ideas would be restricted. Unlike other commodities, coal or labor for example, there is no need to forsake any of the valuable uses of a new idea, because its use in one place does not preclude its use in another. This means that nothing is sacrificed currently when new knowledge is used. Of course the *discovery* of knowledge is not costless. Discovery involves the use of resources that could be used for other purposes—that is to say, the sacrifice of the forsaken output is the real cost of the discovery. Hence, in order to get new knowledge these costs must be met, and they are met in the hope that the use of the discovered knowledge will enable one to recover the costs. Unfortunately the use value of the discovered knowledge is difficult to capture, and if we disregard the incentives for future invention, it is undesirable to restrict its use in order to be able to charge for its use, simply because its use costs society nothing. This dilemma, which does not exist for other commodities, has been in part resolved by the granting of limited-life patents, which are intended to induce discovery and some dissemination of new useful knowledge. The disadvantage, of course, is that a patent restricts the use of newly discovered ideas. Thus the grant of limited-life patents is a compromise between the conflicting goals of fullest incentive to discover and fullest use of discovery.

The difficulty of turning knowledge into private property is one of the important economic characteristics of research and development. A second characteristic is the high degree of uncertainty about what knowledge will result. There is alleged to be so much uncertainty *vis-à-vis* other forms of investment, that private firms value research and development less than its true worth to society as a whole, and this even when the knowledge discovered can be retained and used by the inventor as his exclusive property. From the point of view of society as a whole, the many losses or failures can be canceled out against the successes, but an individual cannot engage in enough of these independent ventures to secure this averaging effect. Therefore in view of these imperfections—indeterminate proprietary status of knowledge and the uncertainty of success—it has been argued that special consideration should be given to research and development. Indeed in certain fields (e.g., medicine, agriculture, aeronautics, and military research), these considerations have already been strong enough to lead to government support. In addition to outright grants for research is the offering of prizes for the discovery of new knowledge or techniques. For example, prizes have already been awarded for the invention of the chronometer, the technique for extraction of sugar from beets, and for canning food.

Because of the incompleteness with which risks can be shifted, it is likely that there will be some discrimination against more risky activities, among them research and development. As shown earlier, the non-appropriable nature of the product constitutes another and probably even more important cause for undervaluing research and development. Of course, it must be recognized that neither uncertainty nor non-appropriability is peculiar to research and development, and the degree to which the latter is inhibited depends in part on the degree to which alternative uses of resources share in these properties. Most forms of business investment involve some risk. To the extent that they embody new ideas, new products or services, there is an element of non-appropriability. Success inevitably breeds competitors who copy these ideas and so eat away the profits. If all other uses of resources were as risky as research and development and if the difficulties of appropriating the product were as great, there would be no discrimination. However, on the average, research and development activities belong to the more risky class of investment activities, and the difficulties of "ownership" operate more sharply than in at least some other forms of investment. The degree of the undervaluation of research and development is clearly very hard to establish, and it would be difficult to assemble relevant empirical evidence.

2.2 Government Contracting Practices

A second source of demand falsification is alleged to exist in the government's contracting policies for research and development. For obvious reasons the government has increased markedly its emphasis on research and development of improved weapons during the past few years. This increased demand for military research and development is expressed through its contracting procedures with private contractors who carry out the research and development. The contractual arrangement can in principle take three forms.

A cost-plus-fixed-fee contract requires that the contractor engage in research and development work in a given area for a given period of time, in return for which the government agrees to pay all costs up to a tentative maximum, depending upon subsequent developments, and a fixed fee. In a fixed-payment-for-fixed-results contract, the government announces a fixed payment price, independent of what the contractor's costs happen to be, and the payment is made if and only if certain definite results are achieved.[3] A third form

---

3. This contract is hypothetical as far as military research and development work is concerned, but it is, of course, the normal form of commercial contract and is used by the

of contract is the fixed-price-for-fixed-time contract; here the contractor agrees to perform research and development in a given area for a given period of time and receives a fee specified in advance. The contractor keeps all that he does not spend in performing the research. However, if there is recontracting on the basis of the actual costs, as is in fact the case, the fixed-price-for-fixed-time contract really becomes identical with the cost-plus-fixed-fee contract. Hence our three forms of contractual arrangement reduce in current practice to two.

The fixed-payment-for-fixed-results contract gives the contractor every incentive for efficiency. The cheaper he gets the desired result, the more he makes; the quicker he gets it, the more he enhances his chance of getting future contracts. But, of course, the widespread application of this contractual form in research and development (R & D) is impeded by the exploratory nature of R & D as distinct from the later phases of development and production. The desired result can be specified, if at all, only by constraining the contractor from striving for novel results. Surely this is the last thing to do when what we want from exploratory R & D are truly new and promising ideas and equipments. This form of contract cannot be drawn when the fixed result cannot be specified. Moreover, even if the desired result were couched in very general terms, acknowledging the inability to specify, the underlying uncertainty about whether, when, and at what cost the result would be possible would impose great risks upon the contractor. For these reasons the fixed-payment-for-fixed-results contract is usually inapplicable to R & D and defective where applicable, explaining the widespread use of the cost-plus-fixed-fee contract.

If we consider only the contract itself, the incentive effects of the cost-plus-fixed-fee contract are troublesome. The immediate reward does not vary with the accomplishment, reducing the incentive to do the work well. However, there are two principal factors beyond the terms or forms of the contract itself which influence favorably the performance by the contractor. One is the possibility of future contracts with the government, and the other is the effect of research under government contract on other areas of the firm's work. (1) The government rationally allocates its contracts to those whom it expects to do best, and its expectations of future performance are certainly affected in good measure by past performance. Hence even under a cost-plus contract there is a positive incentive to maximize the probability of success with given resources.

------

military in the purchase of ordinary commodities. A fixed price is stated to be paid for an article only if it meets the specifications laid down in the contract.

In addition there is the possibility of research and development contracts leading to future *production* contracts on items successfully developed. This *expectation incentive* to *efficient* effort, however, is diminished by the uncertainty of this reward. First, success as such is much easier for the government to judge than the efficiency with which the success is achieved. Second, the government's contract allocation depends on many other factors in addition to past performance, and the fields in which the government demands research and development may change. (2) Research work in any part of a firm will increase the stock of knowledge of the firm, more, usually, than is actually embodied in the distributed reports. This is true, in particular, of government-financed research. Hence the firm's reward from a government contract will in fact exceed the government's payment, since there will be a net *spillover* effect of the research on other parts of the firm's activities.

The less a contractor is interested in future government contracts, of course, the greater is his incentive to direct the expenses reimbursable under his government contract toward the services that promise to have the greatest "spillover" effects upon his non-government work. There then can be some distortion of his demands for this and other reasons. Because the prospect of future contracts is uncertain, there will be a bias toward forms of expenditure that do not involve long-term commitments. For example, more consultants may be used relative to regular employees because their services can be terminated more quickly and easily. Or, a factor directly related to the "shortage" of engineer-scientists, advertising may be used as a partial substitute for higher salaries in attracting personnel. Either form of expense is currently reimbursable. But the advertising can be stopped at any time with little embarrassment, in contrast to the painful process of reducing salaries and staff once they have been swollen. The spectacular growth of advertising for engineer-scientists in recent years is directly related, we conjecture, to the "dynamic shortage" phenomenon discussed in Chapter I.[4]

4. A study of help-wanted advertisements in the *New York Times* for the years 1940, 1946, 1950, 1956 showed (1) a great increase in the space devoted to advertisements for scientists and engineers; (2) an increase in ads for scientists and engineers relative to other types of labor; (3) the increase occurred in the form of display (institutional) advertising; (4) no significant increase in the proportion of the conventional style of classified help-wanted advertisements for scientists and engineers occurred after 1946; (5) about 90 per cent of all display advertising had been purchased by government-financed research and development contractors (typically on cost-plus-fixed-fee contracts). C. A. Mahon and Associates, *Development Report: The "Shortage" of Scientific and Engineer Manpower in the*

It must not, of course, be concluded that we should replace cost-plus contracts, for they serve to lessen the burden to the contractor of the uncontrollable risks of research and development, that is, those risks which would exist even if the contractor were as efficient as possible. This is not the place to expand policy proposals, but the above analysis suggests that it is worthwhile to explore the possibilities of contractual forms that might reconcile better the rival claims of improved risk-bearing and improved efficiency. One can imagine a contract that provides for a fixed fee in any case, plus some percentage of the costs, plus additional compensation depending on the degree of success in the research work. Such a feature, known as "coinsurance," is employed in similar circumstances, such as insurance against medical costs, where it is desired to increase the incentive of the individual to economize. This principle is frequently applied to production contracts, where it is much easier to implement than in research and development, and it may be possible to broaden its applicability. But where "success" is so difficult to appraise objectively, the payment of additional compensation by the government will always be scrutinized suspiciously lest it reflect any bribery of government contracting officers. Our traditional zeal to prevent corruption hence poses a formidable obstacle to reforms that will allow contracting officers greater flexibility in giving differential rewards.

2.3 Possible Wasteful Utilization of Engineer-Scientists

A third form of demand falsification which has been very widely alleged in the discussion on shortages is the use of engineer-scientists in jobs below their full capacity. For example, it is alleged that many engineers are doing work that is essentially draftsmen's work. Such wasteful use of trained personnel is held to contribute to the observed shortage.

To the extent that the complaint is valid, it might well be explained as part of the misallocation due to shortages of the sort discussed in Chapter I. In a shortage situation the current market price does not reflect the value of an engineer-scientist in alternative uses. Hence a firm may calculate that an engineer-scientist is being used in an activity where the output attributable to him is at least as great as the salary being paid to him, and yet from a social point of view he could be used more profitably elsewhere.[5]

United States, 1957, ASTIA Document No. 098930, Development Report AFPTRC-TN-57-25, Air Force Personnel and Training Research Center, Lackland Air Force Base, Texas.

5. In this discussion we are ignoring a special dynamic problem alleged to exist, namely the hoarding of engineer-scientists by some firms, based on expectation of future

This behavior is rational for a firm that does not face a shortage. Hence, if some firms face shortages and others do not, we would expect the firms that do not face shortages to use their engineer-scientists in a manner that would appear wasteful to the other firms. However, it would not be rational for a firm facing a shortage to use engineer-scientists in relatively unskilled uses. For such a firm, the supply of engineer-scientists available to it is temporarily fixed. Hence the salary the firm is paying should be irrelevant to it in deciding where to use engineer-scientists, since they can all be used in activities that have net outputs attributable to engineer-scientists above the actual salary level (otherwise they would not be said to have a shortage). A firm faced with a shortage therefore has a powerful incentive to economize, more so than even the price mechanism would provide. It is possible however that such firms may act irrationally, since their cost accounting methods use the market salaries and do not consider the scarcity of engineer-scientists to the individual firm.

It may well be that the so-called wasteful utilization of engineer-scientists is like a lot of other cases where the engineer sees waste and the economist does not. There must be some reason why firms use engineers when they could use draftsmen or other lower-paid employees; the practices complained of seem to antedate the current shortage. After all, there are great differences in ability among engineers, and it is certainly possible that those used for inferior purposes are in fact well placed according to their capacities.

2.4 The Government as Monopsonist

As we have seen in Chapter II, Section 5, the price system can lead to a distorted use of our resources if the buyer or seller affects prices by his rate of purchase or sale. It is certainly true that the government is the source of over half the expenditures on research and development. Presumably its demand for inputs is large enough to affect the prices paid for scientists and engineers. If so, then as we have shown in Chapter II, Section 5, there will be an incentive

contracts. In a tight market for manpower, it is not surprising that some firms should behave this way, particularly if they must demonstrate the capacity to perform additional work before they can successfully bid on a contract. In this situation it would be improper to describe as irrational a firm that used highly trained personnel temporarily on tasks requiring much less training or even leaving them idle. While this practice may not be irrational from the viewpoint of the individual firm, it can contribute to the appearance of a shortage which may not "really" exist from society's point of view.

for the monopsonist to restrain purchases below the most desirable level. As we pointed out above, the government, even if it has the market power of a monopsonist, need not behave as one. It is not a profit-making organization and hence is not under the same impulse as a private monopsonist to increase its profits. However, it is under political pressure to reduce its spending, which does give it one incentive to exercise its monopsony powers. But the government's criterion should be the welfare of all individuals rather than the desire simply to hold down its budget by such demand restriction. These two objectives will diverge when the government uses its powers to restrict wages.

It may be asked how it is possible for the government to act like a competitor. One alternative, desirable from many points of view, is to have many decision-making units in the government, where choices can be made as to the desirability of individual research or development projects. The individual units will then act like competitors, since no one of them can exert discernible influence over the engineer-scientist market. They will compare the benefits derived from each proposed project with the costs calculated at the current salary levels and disregard the impact on the salary levels paid by either the government in general or private industry. Indeed, in practice the situation is not too far removed from the above; there is independent behavior among the services and among smaller units within them, particularly for research.

Of course, in the government there will ultimately have to be a centralized budgetary review. But putting the emphasis initially on the desirability of individual projects rather than on a total research and development budget will make it easier for the Bureau of the Budget to disregard monopsonistic considerations in its final budgetary allocations.[6] Hence, it should in principle (with exceptions to be noted below) disregard the power the government has over the market for research and development services and let government units respond solely to current prices, as if each were a small firm. That is, each unit should let a research and development contract if, at current salaries, the expected cost of the contract does not exceed the expected benefits; it should not take into its calculations the possible impact of this contract on the salary level of all engineer-scientists.

It is not easy to determine whether or not the government's demand for research and development has in fact been restricted by these monopsonistic

---

6. We are not suggesting that the Bureau of the Budget review the merits of each project.

restrictions. Nevertheless, we will advance the following hypotheses: (1) the government is to some extent following a monopsonistic policy of restricting demand below the level suggested by cost-benefit comparisons at current prices; (2) under conditions of demand exaggerated for other reasons there may be some justification for such a policy as a very rough corrective, though great care must be taken lest the form such a policy takes make matters worse; (3) in any case, the transition to a more nearly optimal policy should be sought, and a revision of the government's budgetary methods in determining the volume of research and development can help to this end.

(1) It is natural to assume that the defense agencies, operating as they do under budgetary restraints, will take account of the higher costs they would face if they expanded their scale of operations. There is also a second and perhaps even stronger motive, the fear of raising engineer-scientist salaries in private industry. There are clear indications that the government has a tendency to restrain its own contract work and its salary bids in order to avoid disrupting private industry. The second motive, even though not strictly speaking monopsonistic in intent, has the same effect in restraining the government's demand for research and development.

(2) Any measure that restricts a demand exaggerated for other reasons will then move the actually realized amount of research and development closer to the intended amounts. The weakness of this corrective device is that the criterion for deciding which part of the demand to restrict is not fully reflective of social worths as revealed by market prices. Which effect will predominate is not, of course, something that can be settled here.

However, care must be taken that the technique used to hold down government demand does not intensify the misallocation unduly. If the government paid competitive salaries at all times but restricted somewhat its total expenditures, the effects would be those sketched in the preceding paragraph; the magnitude of any otherwise "excessive" demand and consequent inefficient resource use would be reduced. But suppose instead the government freezes the salaries it will pay in civil service or authorize to be paid on government research and development contracts. Then the government will indeed not compete so effectively in the market with private firms, but if its own desires are expanding, it will find that there will be a "shortage" for itself and its contractors. Under a salary freeze the corrective forces of the market would be restrained, and the "shortage" with its accompanying misallocation could be permanent.

The last situation occurs in fact only to the extent that civil service salaries are sluggish in responding, and there are regulations with regard to contracting that can be interpreted as attempts to fix salaries. The effects are rather a slowing down of the response of prices than a complete freeze and have been discussed in Chapter I.

(3) In any case, whatever actions may be partially justified because of exaggerated demand, optimal allocation requires that these departures cease as prices respond so as to bring supply and demand into equilibrium.

CHAPTER IV
SUPPLY PROBLEMS

1. The Short Run

Because the training period for engineer-scientists is long, a change in salary levels can have no immediate effect on the number of qualified individuals with suitable training. It would be going too far to assert that the total supply is completely uninfluenced by price, since individuals with such training may be drawn from other occupations back into the field. But in general the total supply is not very expansible in the short run. But changed demand will after a period of time elicit a greater response in supply. Thus over the past few years the supply may well have been below some kind of long-run normal because of past variations in price and other variables before the Korean War that now affect the current supply of engineers. The rise in population and the change in long-run expectations are factors that have been operating for some time and now may be expected to produce increases in the number of engineer-scientist graduates. To the extent that the short-run supply curve is thus shifting upward, the strain on the market mechanism to eliminate "the shortage" (see Chapter I) is thereby reduced. But these factors operate slowly.

Moreover, we must also consider that the market is not a single whole. Even within a single specialty, the willingness of scientific and engineering personnel to move from one firm to another, especially when geographical changes are involved, is limited. In the short run, then, the supply curve relevant to a firm or a locality may be very steep; that is, the supply is unresponsive to price changes. The adjustment process will then be slowed down. This effect operates much more strongly for older and more settled employees than it does for new entrants. The immobility of employed personnel arises from family connections and other social relations, moving costs, attachment to a particular job, geographical preferences, and from pension plans and similar incentives. The last set of causes might be the objects of policy-making. Indeed, it may be well to call attention to the social advantages of raising salaries as against bestowing fringe benefits that encourage immobility. But the other causes of immobility should, in a non-totalitarian society, be regarded as data, at least in the short run. In the absence of direction of labor, the motives for immobility can be overcome only by salary incentives or by some other forms of persuasion aimed at overcoming the distaste for change.

Of course, there is nothing peculiar to the engineer-scientist market as far as the immobility of experienced personnel goes; the situation is the same in any labor market. If, however, the demand for a particular type of labor is stationary or shifting slowly, all necessary adjustments can take place in the market for new entrants. In the case of rapidly growing demand, however, the hypotheses of Chapter I imply that the immobility of experienced personnel becomes more serious in slowing down the response process. In principle, if the future areas of expansion of demand are known, there will be a net gain to the economy in providing such information to guide job choices. However, the chances that such forecasting will be sufficiently accurate are very small.[1]

It is in this context that we must examine the great proliferation of advertising to attract engineer-scientists. Advertising shifts the supply curves to the right for particular firms; that is, it increases the number of engineer-scientists available to the advertiser at any given salary level. It is thus an alternative to raising salaries as a means of attracting personnel. It is primarily useful for drawing already employed personnel, particularly by overcoming the dislike for change noted above. It is therefore not surprising that there has been a very rapid rise in such advertising in view of the importance of moving experienced personnel about the country to meet the rapid increase in demand. It has been suggested that the government through its regulations imposes restrictions on the salaries paid by its contractors (see Chapter II, Sect. 3, above). If this is true and if advertising expenditures are not restricted, the contractor will have obvious incentives to increase the latter to compensate for the salary restrictions. Whether or not the government's regulations really restrict salary increases is debatable, but clearly there is some inhibiting effect on the spreading of information about salaries as a technique for drawing personnel. Advertising the non-economic advantages of employment to a certain extent compensates for the lack of explicit salary information.

2. Effect of Salaries on the Long-Run Supply

As we have seen above, in the case of engineer-scientists the response of supply to prices must be lagged because of the very considerable period of training. At the very least, the period is four years for an engineer and several more for a scientist with the Ph.D. degree. In one sense, the period may be considerably longer, since an engineer-scientist will normally have to have a strong training in mathematics and science in high school, and his decision to undertake such training must be at least partially made some years before his entrance to college. The student deciding whether or not to enter an engineer or

1. See Chapter III, Sect. 1.3.

scientist career takes into account, along with other variables, the salary he expects to receive. Indeed, what is relevant is the salary he expects to earn over his lifetime. The supply, then, will be a function of *anticipated lifetime earnings.*

(1) There is little reason to doubt that anticipated lifetime earnings is a significant determinant of the student supply.[2] Undoubtedly a considerable proportion of those going to college are motivated in their choice of careers by the higher level of earnings thereby opened to them, including among others those of engineer-scientists. We may thus assume that the student supply of engineer-scientists will change markedly if their anticipated lifetime earnings change relative to those anticipated in other occupations. It would, of course, be desirable to check this assumption more directly. For example, it should be possible to find out directly by questioning those going into each vocation as to the income they anticipate as well as the income they might expect to receive if they were to choose some alternative career.

(2) The relation between expected lifetime earnings and current salaries is not too well known. The simplest hypothesis is that the entering student assumes that (or at least acts as if) current salaries will continue to prevail throughout his productive lifetime. Under these conditions the supply available tomorrow is responsive to changes in today's salaries so that the response of supply to changes in current salaries will be conditioned by the length of the training period. But actually this assumption of *static expectations* probably overstates the influence of current salary levels on future supply. We may expect that a rise in current salaries will not have the same impact on anticipated earnings and therefore on supply when it first occurs as after it has remained in effect for a number of years. There are two reasons for this sluggishness in response. In the first place, it is rational for the entering student, in the presence of uncertainty, not to take the salary levels of any one year as a thoroughly reliable guide to the future. Instead, it is reasonable to use some sort of weighted average—current salaries, of course, being given the most weight—as representing the most up-to-date information, but with the past also taken into consideration to hedge against the possibility that the current salaries may represent a random aberration.

A second reason for a lagged response of anticipated earnings to current

2. It is convenient to talk as if the student has a consciously formed anticipation of future salaries, but of course the argument does not really rest on this assumption. Impressions of the relative incomes of different occupations may be formed, possibly not even consciously, in many ways.

salaries is the manner in which such information reaches the student who is choosing his career. While he may have some up-to-date knowledge as to starting salaries (even this is doubtful), his knowledge of salaries at more advanced levels (which of course also enter into expected lifetime earnings) must necessarily be imprecise. Indeed, it is by no means easy to acquire such information even by research. His information must necessarily be derived from general impressions that will usually be based ultimately on salary levels averaged over some previous few years.

For these reasons, a student's anticipation of lifetime earnings will tend to be somewhat insensitive to changes in salaries in any one year and responsive only to salaries that have shown some staying power. The effect can be roughly described as that of a lag between changes in current salary levels and changes in anticipated lifetime earnings, and hence in student supply. Thus the response of trained supply to changes in current salaries will, in effect, be lagged by a period which is longer than the training period, the extra lag being due to an understandable slowness of response of expectations to current salaries.

To sum up, the trained supply of engineer-scientists will respond to changes in current salaries only with a considerable lag. Even then the response will be blunted, partly by non-economic factors in occupational choice and partly by the informational lags between changes in current salaries and changes in expectations. From a policy point of view, there is of course a strong case for making information on salaries of all occupations available to students confronted with occupational choice. Such information will improve both the allocation of resources, by enabling students to make better predictions of the prices that measure the social usefulness of an engineer-scientist, and the speed of response, by reducing the cost of information. And as we have seen, if it were possible to predict future earnings with a reasonably high degree of accuracy, such information would be even more useful than that on current salaries.[3]

3. The Measurement of Anticipated Lifetime Earnings

The student making a choice of careers may think that his income any given number of years hence will be the same as the average income of those who have been currently engaged in that career for an equal number of years. He will thus suppose that his income five years after entering the profession will equal the average current salary of those who entered five years earlier, and similarly for all other years.

3. See Chapter III, Sect. 1.3.

Let us illustrate by considering a student who has just received a B.A. in chemistry or chemical engineering and is considering whether to take a job immediately or to go on for a Ph.D. The American Chemical Society has compiled the median base monthly salaries of male chemists and chemical engineers for 1955 by length of experience and by level of formal academic training.[4] We will assume that a Bachelor enters the profession at age 22, a Ph.D. at 25. Thus the American Chemical Society's median salary for a B.A. in his first year is assumed to be expected by the graduate at age 22, that received by a B.A. in his fifth year is expected at age 26, and so forth. On the other hand, the salary expected by the student at age 25, if he goes on for his Ph.D., is that received by Ph.D.'s with one year experience, while the salary expected at age 29 under the same conditions is that currently received by Ph.D.'s with five years' experience. Between ages 22 to 24, the student, if he goes on for his Ph.D., expects to receive nothing.[5] (See Table 1.)

Thus an individual who has just received his B.A. and is deciding whether or not to continue for the Ph.D. is choosing between the two income streams presented in Table 1. Economic theory suggests that the individual should compare the present values of the two income streams, the future income being discounted at a suitable rate of interest. If the rate of interest used is 5 per cent, the present value of the differences is $11,000, so on purely economic monetary or pecuniary grounds, there would be an advantage in continuing for the Ph.D. if it requires no more than three years. (See Table 2.)

Before discussing the implications of computations of this type, two cautions should be noted. (1) The present values are fairly sensitive to the specific assumptions. For example, suppose that it takes four years instead of three to complete the Ph.D., then the present value of the anticipated difference be-

---

4. A. Fraser, "The 1955 Professional and Economic Survey of the Membership of the American Chemical Society," *Chemical and Engineering News*, Vol. 34, No. 15, April 9, 1956, pp. 1731–81.

5. This is not quite accurate. On the one hand, the Ph.D. student must in many cases pay tuition and other educational costs, so his anticipated income would be negative; on the other hand, most students have some income, either in the form of scholarships and other aid or in the form of part-time employment. The anticipated income of zero assumed here may then be tolerably accurate, but it should be possible to secure more definite information by sample surveys. Data of this type have been collected for medical education; see S. Counts and J. M. Stalnaker, "The Cost of Attending Medical School," *Journal of Medical Education*, Vol. 29, February 1954.

TABLE 1. *Expected annual earnings of male chemists and chemical engineers by level of training and age (in dollars)*

Age	B.A. at 22	Ph.D. at 25	Net Income of Ph.D. above B.A.
22	4300	0	−4300
23	4460	0	−4460
24	4800	0	−4800
25	5100	6500	1400
26	5240	6700	1560
27	5520	7090	1570
30	6300	7800	1500
35	7320	8880	1560
40	8100	10100	2000
45	8940	10900	1960
50	9120	11400	2280
55	9700	10900	1200
60	10000	10300	300
65	8520	9600	1080
over 65	7800	9000	1200

Source: A. Fraser, *The 1955 Professional and Economic Survey of the Membership of the American Chemical Society*, American Chemical Society, 1956. Figures presented are based on linear interpolation of data in Table 22C, p. 46.

TABLE 2. *Present value of income (in thousands of dollars)*

Degree	5%	6%	7%	8%
B.A. at age 22	127	107	93	80
Ph.D. at age 25	138	115	97	83
Ph.D. at age 26	130	108	91	77

tween Ph.D. and B.A. incomes would fall to $3,000. Present values are also very sensitive to the interest rate chosen; the present value of the salary difference if the Ph.D. requires three years with an interest rate of 7 per cent would be $8,000. (2) The correct choice of interest rates is usually not easy to determine. If a person can lend and borrow at the same rate, then that is the appropriate rate, but for most people the rate at which they can lend (e.g., the rate on savings deposits or government bonds) is considerably lower than that at which they can borrow. This difference represents primarily the uncertainty of the lender as to the borrower's ability to repay; it is the premium paid by the borrower on insurance against his defaulting. For a student who can finance his education (and his living costs during the period of education) without borrowing at all, it is only the lending rate that is relevant. But one who has to borrow money for his additional training should calculate his anticipated lifetime earnings with the borrowing rate of interest. This rate may be very high; indeed, for some people credit to finance education may be unobtainable, so the effective interest rate is infinite. Since additional education means postponement of income, and since a rise in interest rates will affect the present value of earnings in the distant future more than those in the present, a higher interest rate will reduce the economic advantage of higher education. We will return to the question of the appropriate rate of interest shortly.

Suppose that the computation of anticipated lifetime earnings has met the above objections, with the rate of interest taken to be the general rate of return on new investment in the economic system. What inference can be drawn from the results? A simple hypothesis about the relation of supply to anticipated lifetime earnings is that a person will choose from among alternative occupations that which yields the highest anticipated lifetime earnings. Under this *purely pecuniary economic* hypothesis, students with the requisite ability will choose the Ph.D. if it leads to higher lifetime earnings, and the B.A. in the contrary case. In such a case the anticipated lifetime earnings for the two would have to become equal eventually. For in the first case, the supply of B.A.'s would, after a few years, decline, compared with that of Ph.D.'s, and hence the normal workings of the market mechanism would increase the salaries of the former compared with the latter. This process would continue until the anticipated lifetime earnings in the two categories were equal. The adjustment takes time because of the lag caused by the period of training, but certainly a difference in anticipated lifetime earnings could not persist over long periods under the purely economic hypothesis of supply.

In fact, the previous computations show that the anticipated lifetime earnings for Ph.D.'s and B.A.'s are not greatly different, especially if the appropriate interest rate is 7 or 8 per cent. These results tend to confirm both the purely economic hypothesis and the assumption that the interest rate appropriate to individual choices is the same as that on investments in general. Some additional evidence is provided by a recent article, which compares the earnings of chemical engineers (B.A.) with those of building construction workers.[6] Among other results, the author finds that the cumulated earnings of chemical engineers who graduated in 1929 or 1934 reached 100 per cent of those of building construction workers in seven years, while it is estimated, by extrapolation, that chemical engineers graduating in 1951 will require at least thirty years before their cumulated earnings equal those of building construction workers. Cumulated earnings are the same as the present value of future income discounted at a zero rate of interest; the calculation for 1951 would suggest that if a reasonable discount rate were used, the anticipated lifetime earnings of chemical engineers would now be below those of building construction workers. (It should be immediately remarked that a much more careful study would have to be made before these figures could be considered more than indicative; there are many correction factors to be applied to raw wages data, e.g., for irregularity of employment.)

The finding that anticipated lifetime earnings increase only slightly or not at all with additional post-graduate education has here been exemplified in only two cases, and much additional research of the same type will be necessary to establish its general validity. Similar studies have usually shown, on the contrary, that additional education does lead to higher anticipated lifetime earnings, as in Stewart's comparisons for 1929 and 1934 just cited. Such a result must have one of two possible explanations: either, as suggested above, the use of the market rate of return on investment in finding the present value of anticipated lifetime earnings is not correct or factors other than anticipated lifetime earnings affect occupational choices. Undoubtedly, both considerations are relevant. Let us take the latter first. It is commonly noted that an individual may prefer one position to another because of differences in job satisfaction. In the present case, however, it would ordinarily be presumed that the positions open to a Ph.D. would have more satisfaction attached to them than those open to a B.A. Presumably the educational process itself is a source of some satisfaction. Thus, as far as differences in satisfaction go, the anticipated lifetime earnings would have to be *higher* for B.A.'s to prevent them from going on to the Ph.D. Since there are no overt restrictions that prevent working toward the Ph.D., there must be some factors which differentiate those who do go on from those who don't. The most obvious and important one is ability. It is

6. P. B. Stewart, "Does Chemical Engineering Pay?" *Chemical Engineering*, September 1956, p. 192.

surely true that there is a difference of ability on the average (though certainly not uniformly distributed): the difference between the expected lifetime earnings in the two cases is probably a payment to scarce skills, an ordinary phenomenon of the price system analogous to the higher value of unusually productive farm land. The problem of differences of ability, of course, applies to all similar comparisons, such as those frequently made between high school and college graduates.[7]

Let us return to the question of the rate of interest. The chief problem, as indicated earlier, is that individuals may be effectively barred from undertaking additional education because of pressing cash needs and an effective rate of interest on borrowing which is higher than the prevailing returns on comparably risky investments. In effect, decisions in different but comparable parts of the economy are then made on the basis of different rates of interest, and the effect is the same as if they were made on the basis of different prices for the same commodity. (Indeed, the rate of interest is simply a particular price, that paid for deferring payments.) As explained in Chapter II, particularly Section 2, lack of uniformity of prices leads to a misallocation of resources. In the present case, society would be underinvesting in the production of certain skills whose productivity is higher than the general run of investments. Society would thus benefit by drawing resources from elsewhere to increase the number of more highly trained people. This conclusion is strengthened, the more it is held that society will benefit in general from a better educated citizenry in ways that will not be reflected in private earnings.

To sum up, there are two possible (not mutually exclusive) explanations for

---

7. From the point of view of the individual making an occupational choice, differences of ability imply that comparisons of anticipated lifetime earnings computed on the basis of *average* earnings are not relevant. Thus an individual who has average ability for a Ph.D. surely has considerably more than the average ability of B.A.'s. Hence he should assume in computing his anticipated lifetime earnings for a B.A. that the salaries he receives will be higher than the average now being received. Thus it may be that the purely economic hypothesis is valid for each individual when the formation of anticipations takes account of differences of ability as well as average earnings. It may be more to the point to compare the average discounted earnings for Ph.D.'s with the upper quartile of discounted earnings for B.A.'s.

For an instructive comparison of earnings of individuals of comparable ability but different levels of training, see Dael Wolfe and Joseph G. Smith, "The Occupational Value of Education for Superior High-School Graduates," *Journal of Higher Education* (April 1956), pp. 201–13.

a higher anticipated lifetime earning in professions requiring more extended training: the scarcity of the necessary ability and special financial limitations. The first is inevitable in a free price system and necessary to insure the proper utilization of resources;[8] the second, on the contrary, implies social inefficiency. The ideal way to remove the financial obstacles would be to grant loans for education whose interest rate really discriminated according to the risk of the individual case, that is, more or less according to ability. It would be a worthwhile research study to find out why such a market has not in fact arisen, whether or not one could be made practical, and what role, if any, fellowships would play in connection with it.

The apparent downward trend in differences in anticipated lifetime earnings that are attributable to education may be explained by the rise in income levels, which reduces the financial limitations on entry into training for the professions. However, it would add greatly to our understanding of the workings of the engineer-scientist and other professional markets if the details of the trend could be studied more carefully. In particular, it would be very interesting to know to what extent, and at what points in the process of training, additional training actually gives rise to an increase in expected lifetime earnings. Once this is known, we may be able to analyze the relative importance of ability and financial limitations to higher training in explaining these earning differences.

4. Salary Structure

In computing expected lifetime earnings, one must take account of the normal rise in salary with experience. As one would expect, we also find that for those with any given number of years' experience there is a range of salaries, presumably reflecting the range of talent and ability represented by those with the same number of years of experience. One special issue has been raised about the salary structure in research and development. It has been suggested that at upper levels of talent and experience the salary range which actually obtains for non-administrators is distorted, and that their salaries tend on the average to be below the value of their marginal productivity to their employers. Those who

8. As we have indicated earlier, we are not concerned here with income inequalities but solely with inefficiencies. However, it may be remarked that an egalitarian concern with income inequalities associated with scarce skills should be met with some general measure, such as the income tax, rather than any deliberate effort to hold down a particular class of above-normal incomes.

hold that such may be the case suggest that in our society and probably in most cultures there is a tradition that the order-giver should have a higher salary than the one to whom the orders are given. In other words the salary structure matches the organizational hierarchy, the highest salaries being paid to executives. However, there is good reason to believe that for most activities the traditional relation between position and salary reflects relative productivity because of the important, indeed crucial, role played by the decision-maker and order-giver. However, large-scale industrial research and development is a relatively new activity and one which is very different from other types of business activity. Those holding that the salary structure may be distorted somewhat at its upper end are suggesting that there is a "cultural lag" here; that it is taking time for us to recognize that in the case of scientists and engineers with extraordinary talent, the traditional hierarchical relationship between position and salary may be inappropriate. It is further suggested that given the difficulty of measuring the marginal productivity of those engaged in research and development, such a "cultural lag" can persist for a long period, and the value of the researcher with superior talent may not be fully appreciated and reflected in relative salaries.

This view is countered with the assertion that competitive forces are such that no such distortion in relative salaries (as between first-rate scientists and administrators) as suggested can persist for any significant length of time in our society. If the director of a laboratory always gets more than any of the scientists working for him, this is because his contribution to the organization is greater than that of the scientists or engineers.

Unfortunately there is no conclusive evidence on the basis of which we can settle this question. Those holding the view that the ordinary salary structure does not reflect relative marginal value productivity to the firm point to the recent recognition by a very few industrial firms that a few of their most talented scientists who do not hold any administrative positions should receive compensation equal to or greater than that given the top administrators in the research program. Those holding the contrary position say that there is no reason to think that there has been any particular delay but instead that the relative value of the contribution made by the scientists *vis-à-vis* the administrator has recently increased, calling for the changed relationship of salaries.

5. Non-economic Factors in Occupational Choice

In many discussions of occupational choice, and in particular in suggested policies for the engineer-scientist "shortage," there has been embedded a hypothesis that the determinants of entry into the profession are so exclusively non-economic that salary levels are essentially irrelevant. On the other hand, economists, in analyzing this and other similar markets, have usually tended to emphasize, as we have, the role of salary movements in changing the supply of engineer-scientists.

The question of the relative importance of economic and non-economic factors in the supply of engineer-scientists and other professionals can be asked in several different contexts, and only confusion results in not keeping them clearly separated. We may be interested from the viewpoint of *explanation* or from that of *policy* determination. Under the heading of explanation, we may seek to explain occupational choice by the individual or merely the total number choosing to enter the profession. Under the heading of policy, we may be concerned with the feasibility of alternative policies or with their ethical implications. Our remarks will be illustrated by some reference to two recent studies, by Eli Ginzberg and others and by Morris Rosenberg.[9]

It clearly emerges from these studies that an individual's choice among occupations depends upon many factors of environment and personality of which anticipated lifetime earnings is only one. In Ginzberg's formulation, the occupational choice of an individual is the result of a series of decisions that result in gradual elimination of alternatives, the decisions being made at different stages of maturity and under different emotional and environmental pressures. Only in the final stages is there evidence that the student is significantly aware of the income alternatives. Rosenberg's analysis is particularly concerned with the relation between choices of occupations and the values held by individuals. Thus, engineering students tend to be about average with respect to the importance of self-expression and of extrinsic rewards but very low with regard to the importance of other people. Cross-section studies of this kind do not cast much light directly on the influence of earnings expectations, since the earnings in different occupations do not vary within the period of observations. Nevertheless, the answers to the questions asked suggest that if we explain a given individual's choice as a function of his personality traits and other non-economic influences and of anticipated earnings, the former variables in

---

9. E. Ginzberg, S. W. Ginsburg, S. Axelrad, and J. L. Herma, *Occupational Choice,* New York: Columbia University Press, 1951; M. Rosenberg, with E. A. Suchman and R. K. Goldsen, *Occupations and Values,* Ithaca, New York: Cornell University Press (in press). In both studies, the basic data are answers to questionnaires by students; the first study begins with eleven-year-olds and continues through graduate school, the second treats only college students.

the aggregate will contribute more to the explanation than the latter for fluctuations in relative earnings such as are experienced in not more than a decade or so.

The economist stresses the role of earnings in occupational choice, not because he denies the influence of non-economic factors but because of a different range of interests and consequently a different set of relevant variables. (1) He is not usually interested in the explanation of individual choices, nor is the present concern over the engineer-scientist supply concerned with such explanation directly. What is of concern is the set of variables that controls the total supply, although, of course, the total supply is simply the aggregate of individual choices. (2) But not all of these factors may be variables in the aggregate. Suppose, for example, that intelligence is one of the factors that determine individual occupational choice. Intelligence is a variable from the individual viewpoint, since it is not the same for all. But if the distribution of intelligence in the population is constant over time, then intelligence is not a relevant variable for explaining variations in the total supply over time.

It follows from (1) above that the variables (2) that are not variables in the aggregate are of no interest to the economist. Thus, in general, if the personality and the non-economic variables that are so important in determining individual occupational choice have distributions over the population that are constant in time, the fluctuations in total supply are to be explained purely by variations in relative earnings of different occupations.

Does this mean, for the present purposes, that the literature on the non-economic determinants of occupational choice is irrelevant? Not quite. For one thing, the importance of non-economic factors in individual choice implies that the responsiveness to price changes may be fairly low. The logic of this remark, pursued further, may suggest methods for using the questionnaire responses on occupational choice to help make inferences as to the price-responsiveness of supply (of course, in conjecture with time series data). For another, it is not necessarily true that the distribution of non-economic attributes over the population is constant in time. It is widely argued by sociologists that cultural attitudes do alter over time. The attractiveness of different occupations is clearly not independent of these attitudes. As predilections for creativity become more common we may, for example, have a shift from business to science. The content of the educational process impinges upon the successive stages of occupational choice by emphasizing the more or less attractive aspects of professional work and by providing (or not providing) the knowledge by which the student can appreciate the relation between his talents and those useful in different occupations. Surely the quality and nature of education must be taken as variables. Thus a historical explanation of variation in the supply of engineer-scientists should take into account social variables as well as prices, though doubtless over sufficiently short periods the former change too slowly to be significant.

When we turn to policy, the first observation is, of course, that any historical explanation is automatically useful in policy formation. Suppose, for example, we are contemplating a policy that will shift the demand curve, an expansion of government aid to research and development. In order to predict the effects of such a policy, it is important to know the supply curve as extrapolated from past history. But there is also the possibility of policies designed to alter supply conditions. The class of variables that are relevant here need not be identical with those relevant to historical explanation. Some of the latter variables may represent forces that are not under the control of policy in any known way. Slow changes in the nature of basic culture patterns, for example, are probably not easily influenced, at least in our present state of knowledge. It is for this reason that the economist is likely to stress the importance of salaries, which can be influenced by government and other policy, either directly or through variation of demand conditions.

Nevertheless, some of the suggestions for dealing with the engineer-scientist problem have been based on the assumption that some of the non-economic variables can be controlled. In particular, education has come in for a good deal of scrutiny. It is held that the quality of secondary education in science and mathematics can greatly influence future choices of career. There is strong evidence that a person's assessment of his own abilities and his image of the skills needed in his chosen profession are related. Students sometimes modify the image of the occupation to fit their capabilities. This means that some occupational choices are made on distorted information, and where the distortion is not entirely subjective or idiosyncratic a better flow of information could possibly improve the direction of occupational choice.

It has been proposed that deliberate attempts be made to stress the "good" aspects of engineering and science in secondary and even primary schools and so change the preference patterns of students. Such propaganda is an example of a policy of whose efficacy we have little evidence. It is doubtful that much should be invested in these procedures before their effectiveness is tested. Such policies also raise an ethical question which goes beyond the scope of the present discussion. Is the use of propaganda to influence the willingness of students to enter particular professions a deprivation of freedom of choice?

Can we draw any conclusions from this discussion? As far as policy is concerned, apart from formal education, we know little of how effectively non-economic variables could be manipulated for the purpose of influencing supply, even if such manipulations were deemed consistent with democratic principles. On the research side, the complicated interrelations among the social and psychological variables that enter into occupational choice are prime subjects of study both for their own interest and for the better prediction of total supply. Further means may ultimately be suggested for having occupational choices made under more rational conditions, that is, with a better understanding of the implications. Of course, such information should not stress any one profession but give equal weight to all.

6. Education

The role of education in the supply of engineer-scientists has appeared to many commentators as peculiarly important among the non-economic variables. As we have suggested above, education is clearly important in the determination of the choices that successively narrow down the alternative occupational possibilities of an individual, and at the same time, the nature and quality of education seem to be appropriate policy variables since the government has considerable control over them.

Both the aims of the educational system and the efficiency with which they are carried out will affect the career choices of students. Comparison with the Soviet and British educational systems shows the importance of the curriculum in this regard. In Soviet secondary education (ages 14–17), physics, chemistry, and mathematics are compulsory for all and take up 40 per cent of the curriculum. It has also been observed that the number of science teachers in the Soviet Union is over 250,000 as opposed to 150,000 in the United States and 20,000 in Great Britain.[10] This stress on science in the educational system of the Soviet Union is undoubtedly a major factor in their relatively rapid growth in the engineer-scientist area.

These facts do not imply that the United States should change the curriculum of its educational program. That is a matter of social policy about the kind of citizenry that is desirable that far transcends such simple comparisons.

As for the efficiency with which our educational system attains its ends, there have been two kinds of complaints. A general one is that low standards

10. Figures are drawn from "New Minds for the New World," *New Statesman and Nation,* September 8, 1956, pp. 279–82.

in schools impair the potential supply for all occupations that demand a more rigorous training. The other more specific complaint is that mathematics and science training in high schools is so deficient that students who might otherwise become engineer-scientists are effectively debarred from doing so for lack of training in mathematics. These two arguments of course merge into one another: inadequate training implies low standards.[11]

The first complaint is frequently tied in with the argument that the American concept of universal and near-uniform high school education is responsible for deterioration of standards. It should, however, be observed in this regard that the supply of engineer-scientists in Great Britain is much smaller proportionately than in the United States, despite the very great differences in educational opportunities resulting from an examination at an early age that sharply segregates students according to ability. Despite all the public discussion of changing educational standards, we have little real evidence about historical trends. International comparisons may be of some help. The European system, which apparently has high standards for a minority, eliminates at an early age the majority from the potential supply of engineers, scientists, and other skilled professions. The American system, which has lower standards, retains a much larger proportion of the student population in the potential professional supply to the college age. It is not obvious *a priori* which system is more conducive to an increased supply of engineer-scientists or, what is not necessarily the same thing, to an improved allocation of manpower among occupations.

We are on safer ground when talking about deficiencies in mathematics and science instruction in high schools. Obviously an improvement here would benefit both the quality and the quantity of engineer-scientists, and perhaps in a way that could hardly be objected to, that is, as an increase in knowledge which can be achieved without impairing other areas of knowledge and without incurring higher costs. We argue that the allocation problem in this area can to a large extent be remedied by a proper application of the price system.

One prominent complaint about the quality of mathematics and science instruction seems to be the inadequate supply of highly qualified teachers. While there are complaints about the supply of teachers in general, the consensus seems to be that the problem is especially acute in mathematics and science be-

---

11. For a sparkling analysis of the fallacious arguments frequently advanced in support of the belief in deterioration of educational standards, see H. C. Hand, "Black Horses Eat More Than White Horses," *AAUP Bulletin* 43, June 1957, pp. 266–79.

cause of the competition of industry for individuals with these skills. As we have seen repeatedly, scarcities in particular areas have to be met by corresponding price rises. But this is not permitted to happen in elementary and high schools. In many communities, the salary schedule for teachers has become uniform, with the number of years of service and of formal academic training providing the only basis for pay differentiation. The pay is independent of the subject taught, or, for that matter, level of teaching skill or competence in subject matter. This situation is indeed unique; it would be hard to point to any other occupation in which distinct specialties and skills are not rewarded by different salaries.

The efficiency of the price and wage system in guiding, allocating, and controlling the supply and use of teachers is greatly weakened. If more teachers are wanted in a particular skill, the wages of all teachers must be raised to attract the specially desired ones. But if this is done, the salaries of many teachers are increased above the level required to attract them in the desired numbers, and money is wasted in unnecessarily raising the salaries of many skills. Shortages in particular skills are eliminated by creating surpluses elsewhere. Or if salaries are not raised to a level sufficient to wipe out the shortages in special areas, science classes will have to be eliminated, or inadequately trained teachers will have to be employed.

A policy of pay differentiation by specialty may be criticized as being unfair, but such criticism is not defensible. To say that there is a scarcity of mathematics and science teachers means that society values their services more highly than their present pay in education, and we have seen the importance of paying according to value. The problem is no different from that of any other pay differentiation by occupation, as between, for example, janitors and teachers, or teachers and principals.

4

LAW AND ECONOMICS

ON PRIVATE PROPERTY AND FREEDOM

A non-trivial source of the recent student-administrative malaise at the Berkeley campus of the University of California is an intellectual confusion between free speech and free resources. And it is ironical that a university with a powerful faculty should suffer from intellectual confusion. The difference between free speech and free resources has long been recognized in economics, political science and law. Freedom of speech is the right to use one's resources to communicate whatever he wishes with whoever is willing to hear him. It does not include a right to appropriate the use of other people's property to communicate with them. Nor does it include a right to communicate or express ideas to people against their desires. Thus, free speech does not permit a guest in my house to remain and talk regardless of my preferences. It does not permit an employee to talk to other people on the employer's premises if the employer does not so desire. It does not entitle a customer in a store to talk as he wishes without consent of the owner. Nor does it authorize a teacher to talk in class regardless of the desires of his employer. Permission to do so is usually given, but it is not a part of the right of free speech. No restriction against individuals using resources *other than their own* for the purpose of communication is a denial of free speech. Yet at the present time some students, faculty, administrators, legislators and publicists do not understand this simple, but basic, principle.

What has happened on the Berkeley campus of the University of California (but not on the other eight) is that some students and faculty have sought (1) to acquire the right to use the resources or property of other people (2) in order to express ideas publicly, that is, to communicate with other people without receiving prior approval by the intended listeners. This group wants to acquire rights to university resources for public communication of its ideas. Now, one easily can sympathize with a desire to communicate and especially with the urge to control more resources. But to claim that the right of free speech warrants a right to those resources is to argue that resources can be taken by anyone who wants to use them for communication. In sum, those who seek access

Reprinted, by permission of the author, from *Farmand* (March 1966).

to university resources for expression of ideas want to express their ideas for free (in the *economic* sense); they want *other* people to provide the wherewithall and the resources (such as paper, ink, space or facilities) with which to express ideas and communicate as if resources were free.

University property is not a free resource. It is an economic resource to be used at the direction and control of the Regents and those to whom they may delegate authority. In simplest terms, the advocates of the so-called free speech movement want someone else to provide both facilities (resources) and captive listeners by having the main avenues of campus thoroughfare designated as areas of such communication. That they could instead express themselves by hiring a hall is ignored.

And on this point, many of the students, faculty and administration, at the highest level, and even jurists remain confused. As evidence of this fundamental confusion, one can cite the so-called foul speech movement wherein some people carried placards upon which passersby could not help but see obscene words. The basic difficulty was not the *use* of obscene language but the public use of obscene language on placards that people could not avoid seeing. No matter what the placards may have said, they were directed to people who were not necessarily desirous nor willing to be exposed to that communication. Had the foul speech been conducted in private among only those desirous of engaging in such discussion, with no others involved even as inadvertent listeners, there would not have been any violation of free speech. Unpleasant, immoral or improper words are irrelevant to the concept of free speech. Filthy speech in private voluntary communication is not a travesty of free speech. The travesty is for the university administrators to think free speech is restricted to decent speech *and* that it includes the right to public discussion or communication with captive or unwilling participants. It is a travesty to think students are given "free speech" by the administrators' benevolent paternalism in permitting student or faculty to publicly use university resources to express ideas consonant with public decency—and for two reasons. First, public decency is not germane to free speech; it is relevant only for a voluntary audience which was led to believe it would hear only a certain class of communication or ideas and therefore had agreed to participate. No one who breaks that agreement by communications not consonant with the agreement can validly claim that his rights of free speech were being suppressed.

Second, it is a mistake to think that university administrators have anything to do with the right of free speech. Such a thought confounds the rights of free speech with a benevolent paternalism that tolerates acceptable uses of its resources. To ask the administrators to ignore the use to which university property is put is to ask the administration to surrender control of the resources assigned to them by legislative authority. To surrender that control to someone else is to grant that other person authority over the use of the resources—that is, to grant them certain property rights. Under the guise of seeking free speech rights, the students and those who aided them (in this particular cause) were in fact seeking to acquire property rights to university resources.

Incidentally, the university administration has recently granted students and faculty permission to use university facilities for political campaigning. But use of university facilities for commercial purposes by students or faculty is still prohibited. Why? What is it that merits use of university facilities for the benefit of politicians and those seeking government jobs and funds but which denies such merit in use of those facilities for union activity or commercial activity? All contribute to social benefit; all are motivated by private gain; all are equally honest. Could it be that political control of university facilities reflects a self-righteous belief of politicians that they, and no others, deserve to be allowed the use of university facilities? We leave the answer to this digressive, cynical question to others and return to our main theme.

The issue is fundamentally one of the control of university property, not of free speech. The students and faculty already have free speech rights—regardless of what they can do with university property. The free speech right is afforded by the rights to use the university's private property.

Before concluding, I should emphasize that nothing in this note implies that the administrators of the University of California acted wisely several years ago in refusing, or only reluctantly permitting, outside speakers on so-called controversial subjects. Fortunately, in very recent years substantial improvement has been accomplished in permitting greater tolerance for the airing of such points of view by students and outside speakers. While most of us feel that the university is a place where discussion of controversial ideas should be encouraged and tolerated, we should realize that the issue of free speech is not involved. The right of free speech does not rely on employers or governments tolerating or permitting employees' or citizens' use of the institution's property for communication. To think it does is to believe paternalist control is the basis of a free society.

The "free" speech advocates seem to be learning that the use of public property for "free" speech is not a grant of "free speech," because public authority can always declare some particular speech to be an inappropriate use of its property. The advocates might also be on the verge of concluding that private property rights protect and enable free speech by reducing the possibility of authoritarian censorship, compared with public property in which benevolent paternalism of the authorities is easier to invoke. In any event, one conclusion is clear: the more quickly the university community distinguishes among the concepts of free speech, free resources, property rights and benevolent paternalism in the use of property, the quicker will it restore within the university those institutions that characterize the ideals of our civilization.

ECONOMIC LAWS AND POLITICAL LEGISLATION

What is the fundamental premise of economic theory that I believe is informative? It is a conception of the animal called man. Law, political science, sociology, and psychology are social sciences. You would expect them to have the same conception, but they do not.

Many sociologists vision man as a pawn of convention and custom. He is what custom and society make him. And society and custom are left unexplained. Psychologists flirt with a man who has a hierarchy of goals or drives. He satisfies one before embarking on another. That conception provokes such an empty question as which drive or goal is more important. Political science and politicians espouse a man who is other-person oriented, who strives and sacrifices for the benefit of other people—to eloquently serve the public. All those conceptions are fatally defective. They are refuted by facts or are empty. Is the economists' man any more valid? The evidence says yes, in the extensive range of events now being made explainable—a range that began to be explored in the past few decades. Success has led to its adoption by lawyers and legal scholars with remarkable advances.

Briefly, the conceptions on which economic theory rests are: (1) Man seeks a multitude of goods and goals, not just one. He seeks bread, clothing, play, music, honesty, popularity, health, reputation, status, friends, athletic ability, knowledge, contentment, beauty, etc., etc. Obvious enough! (2) He strives for more than he has of these—a situation the economist calls scarcity. Also obvious. (3) He balances, substitutes, trades off, degrees of attainment of each relative to others, depending on feasible tradeoffs. In other words, he substitutes among the quantities of each according to the opportunities available—not satiating himself in one before striving for any of the next. Not so obvious to many so-called social analysts.

Indeed it is often denied. But it is true that he chooses a little *less* of this goal or good if he can have enough *more* of some other. He is not an all-or-nothing seeker. There is no minimum about of any good that is an absolute necessity.

Reprinted, by permission of the author, from *The Interaction of Economics and the Law*, ed. Bernard H. Siegan (Lexington, Mass.: Lexington Books, 1977), 139–48.

He does not have a hierarchy of amounts of goals or goods. All are attained to some degree; he compromises, depending on (a) his tastes for more of this relative to more of that and on (b) the feasible tradeoffs. We forsake some personal integrity if we get more of other things, like good looks, athletic strength, high grades, or good recommendations. It is the principled person, the one track, one goal seeker—no matter how much of other goods are sacrificed or forsaken—who drives us to despair.

The total amount we can claim from other people or produce ourselves is defined by our "wealth." In some societies that "wealth" is primarily in the form of exchangeable private property authority to goods and to services. But it also includes persuasive personalities, persuasive forensic oratorical powers, persuasive power in whatever form it may be; good looks, physical strength or skill in applying physical force on other people, political talents, that is, ability to acquire access to governmental coercive power to control people and acquire resources.

I remind you that in no place did I mention that man was concerned only with his own situation or that he was a pleasure seeker. In his possessive interest, we assumed he has some personal self-interest, not only that. Sometimes for some simple problems, we can usefully assume he is totally interested in his wealth only, with no concern at all for others, but that is not the conception of man that underlies economic analysis.

Private property (production and use) was the constraint on one's attained degrees of goals and goods. By private property authority, entitlements, or rights of person A to a good X, I mean: (1) Person A has reliable private authority as against other persons to select uses of the good X. (2) He may exchange that authority with some other person for authority over some other good at mutually agreeable terms of trade.

I use the word "authority," not "power," to suggest a socially recognized or sanctioned control status, not one exercised by sheer force nor a natural inviolate right. Other people may alter the authority. But until they do, person A can do what he wants with his property, and that includes trading it for some ownership in other goods at mutually acceptable terms. Don't worry about my not including any clause such as "subject to not injure any other person or his property." In the first place, he has no authority to affect some other person's property, or its use, by the use of his own goods. In the second place, his use of his private property does not mean that other people are left uninjured or no worse off. If he produces a better lecture and outcompetes me, I therefore have a lower income. He is injuring the exchangeable value of my services by altering other people's demand for my services. That is permissible under the private property authority. Under private property entitlements one has no authority over what others must continue to offer in exchange for goods or services. No one "owns" rights to other people's offers nor their custom. We each bear the uncertainty of the exchange, market value of goods and services that are "ours"—that we choose to own.

Any perceivable present or future changes in valuations by other people for my goods are capitalized into the present price. Let a manager in a firm be foolish; let him be smart—whatever he does will have future consequences, and if foreseeable, the consequences will be imposed on him now. The exchange value of the goods will be quickly altered to reflect anticipated future consequences. The owner suffers the loss now. If he is an employee, the employer suffers the loss now and is motivated to take corrective monitoring action over the responsible agent.

Capitalization of all foreseen future consequences into the present market price for some good, with the change in present value being borne by that private property owner, is an essence of capitalism. Capitalization into the present price is the crux of the connotation of the word "capitalist" in the term "capitalist system." It is not some presence of capital goods or equipment. It is not that capitalists (who are simply people who have private property entitlements) control the economic system. They (we) do, of course, by making bids and offers in the market. Since we all are capitalists (at least we own our own labor), we all affect the economic system and its outcome.

But capitalization of the foreseeable future consequences of one's present acts is not what happens—certainly not in the same degree and quickness—to resources that are not marketable or not held as private property. Let a New York City (or Socialist) mayor tolerate a couple of years of deficits. What wealth does he or someone else own whose capitalized value of the anticipated benefits and costs are so *fully* borne? The present capitalized value of future taxes or future implied consequences are not so clearly capitalized into the present price of some private entitlements. If the City of New York were a private stock corporation with common shares, the common share prices would drop immediately upon irresponsible financial activities. The behavior of Lindsay, Beam, and other mayors is not explicable by their personalities or odd tastes for irresponsibility, but rather by their constraints and rewards. The mayor of Los Angeles pleads for federal aid to New York. Does the mayor of Los Angeles see that trouble for New York enhances Los Angeles as a living area? Does he see rising stock prices of Los Angeles Incorporated? No, but local landowners do. Would stockholders of General Motors worry about the value of their common shares if their president pleaded for aid for American Motors on the foolish grounds that if American Motors fails, General Motors would fail?

I am not saying no cities are private. Most cities *are* private. What do I mean by private cities? I mean places where people sleep, eat, work, and recreate. If you live in an apartment, you are living in a private city. Its streets (hallways, elevators) are policed by the owner. Its residents are monitored and admitted or evicted by an owner. I am not being silly nor unrealistic. You work in factories or stores with other people. So you occupy two cities, one for sleep and one for work. And you may even recreate in a third private city where streets and living quarters are privately owned and policed with power of expulsion. For example, apartments, trailer courts, hotels, shopping centers are cities—private cities.

If a private city is successful as a working productive place of factories, the Socialist city—being a government—will tax the private city, but it will not return its share of sales taxes to the private city for operation of its streets and policing. Irvine found out. Rancho Santa Fe learned that too. The extending of political controls over private apartments in the form of rent controls, tenant unions, and tenant favors can be interpreted as constraints imposed—or found helpful—by politicians desirous of reducing private competition to Socialist cities operated by politically adept people. The consequent use of publicly owned, politically administered housing is not surprising. If the private city gets too big and threatens to become a place where people sleep, eat, and do everything in one private city, the Socialist city will eliminate it by force—before individual preferences and open competition eliminate the Socialist city, much as the Socialist postal system will not, indeed cannot, survive with private competition. Why? Because, for one reason, capitalization of effects of better or worse use of resources now and in the foreseen future are more quickly, fully, and perceptively thrust on responsible agents.

I digress momentarily because I am displaying my prejudice against political power—not politicians—but political power. Yet, we cannot survive without political power and controls, or so I believe. And even if we could, we would not want to.

Frequently, my friends complain about the movement toward more socialism. Are Socialists more effective in persuading the public about socialism versus capitalism? If more people understood capitalism, would the move toward socialism be slowed or reversed?

I do not know. But my belief is that the move toward socialism and a wide span of government power is not the result of a rising ideology that socialism or government political power is better than capitalism. Rather, it is the result of competition by people adept in political competition. Those adept at the political processes advocate, for self-serving reasons, more government control or expropriation of or brokerage power over private wealth. Those adept at economic market activity advocate more use of the capitalist system, again for self-serving reasons.

The Tartars did not plunder because they believed plunder was a better system. Instead, they were better at it. People excelling in one form of behavior will, of course, extoll it and denigrate other forms. To excel is to extoll. I am good at golf and terrible at bowling. So golf is a good game; bowling is a poor sport. Those who are better at being productive and in outcompeting others in offers of exchange will denigrate the politically or militarily adept. Those who are superior at military or physical coercion (or intellectual pursuits) will use it more and extoll it and condemn producers. Neither necessarily understands what the other does. Indeed we have no theory of Socialist or government behavior. Our theory and analysis and understanding of capitalism is so far advanced over that of socialism that if that were what counted, socialism would be long forgotten.

Some ideologists contend expanding political power is a result of increasing economic complexity and interdependence. I believe that is naive. Primitive, noncomplex, independent societies are militarized and run by government: Socialist states. No inherent sweep of increasing political power over society occurs in history. It has been strong from time immemorial—but fluctuating like a drunk meandering in a wide corridor. We should expect a society initiated as ours was, at the extreme of little political power (little by any historical standards), to regress toward greater political activity simply because people adept at that form of activity find a wide territory ready for exploitation.

Do not misunderstand. I am not saying that is bad. I, too, would delight in having political power. It just happens that I have not been successful. The best I can do is ride the politician's coattails on the state payroll as a highly paid professor—not unlike the high Mayan priests.

History reveals a contest among people of differing relative talents and modes of competition. The politically adept, who may say they prefer capitalism and indeed do, will nevertheless seek greater government authority. Some businessmen who believe in socialism nevertheless work effectively in the capitalist sphere. Need I name some very successful businessmen who espouse socialism? Businessmen who think they would be good politicians advocate greater political authority—out of self-serving interest rather than ideology. We who are good at political power acquisition will exploit and extoll it without necessarily being for socialism *per se* nor advocating political power because we happen to believe political power is a better way to order society. Instead, it permits us to better achieve enhanced status.

Education about socialism or capitalism will not, so far as I can see, change the future much. To change the move toward socialism, we must change the ability of various forms of competition to be successful. I know of no way to reduce the prospective enhancement from greater political power-seeking, but I do know of ways to reduce the rewards to market-oriented capitalist competition. Political power is dominant in being able to set the rules of the game to reduce the rewards to capitalist-type successful competitors. It is rule maker, umpire, and player: by taxes, regulations, controls, national planning and directives, lawsuits, etc. But I have been unable to discern equivalently powerful ways for economic power to reduce the rewards to competitors for political power! Each capitalist may buy off a politician, but that only enhances the rewards to political power.

As I read history the influence of political power is typically greater than that which characterized early U.S. history. We may be simply regressing toward the mean of civilizations, and that is not a prospect I enjoy. To look to the presumed good old days of our past century or two, when people were far apart and we were less interdependent, is to forget the power of Elizabeths, Williams, Henry, Charles, Ivan, Murad, Lo, and countless smaller heroes.

Some, but not necessarily most, of my colleagues in academia are searching for ways to reduce political power of those who succeed in acquiring it or to make it less rewarding. I have no principles to bring to bear. Nor have I found anyone who does.

But what I do have is economic theory and economic analysis, permitting some implications about the effects of legislation in a capitalist society. What the effects are in a socialist economy is less sure, because economic theory is best developed in understanding feasible responses and adjustments in a capitalist system as people adapt or adjust to legislation.

Economics views the law as a price list or menu. That is why economic theory will not let me say punishment is not a deterrent even if not a totally prohibitive deterrent. The price of a Rolls Royce is a deterrent, if not a complete deterrent. Some people pay the price. Economics does not say any activities are bad and hence ought to be stopped. It says if you want to restrain them, you can raise the price—the cost of doing that action. Still, behavior in a capitalistic system is, by definition, more difficult to control by political authority because private property gives us more extensive authority over our lifestyles. That is why, whatever the legislated law, it does not follow that its intent will be achieved. Legislated law is overpowered by economic laws of capitalism, which often nullify or pervert intended effects. So political forces are more and more designed to reduce the scope of private property rights, a bleak future. To see to what extent legislated law can be thwarted by economic law requires some notion of the intent of the legislation or order. Some legislation enhances property entitlements and their exchange ability in the market. Here intent and results may go hand in hand. Sometimes the legislated law reflects an attempt by the politically adept and powerful to achieve more wealth and power. I will take cases of each.

Laws against theft are obvious attempts to enhance private property authority and the operation of the economic laws of behavior under a capitalist system. Laws providing for adequate payment for eminent domain appropriation are other examples. So are laws unitizing oil fields to enhance private property rights over the underground pools. Extending national boundaries to 200 miles is another.

Establishing property authority to some resources may be too expensive, as it is alleged to be for some wild animals, running water, air, and electromagnetic radiation. This argument gives politicians enhanced power and authority on sound economic grounds—or does for some cases. But is it valid for all water, all space, all radiation? Radio and TV spectra could economically be controlled by private property rights to broadcast bands over designated areas. But in the 1920s, Hoover, the advocate of private property, declared them government property—when he was a politician. Our subsequent, disquieting history of commercial radio and TV has been a result of that analytical error, and what I think was undesirable policy. The consequent use of radio and TV for political purposes here and abroad is well known.

Surely control of our air quality is necessary. No ways yet exist to subject it to adequately defined and simulated private property authority. But are the effects of legislation and administrative edicts requiring cleaner air understood? The legislation and edicts are designed to improve the quality of life. But whose life? And at what cost? Let me give you a sample of some analysis of this particular issue. It shakes up my well-meaning friends who futilely implore me to donate to cleaner air efforts, to reduce disease and make the atmosphere more pleasant.

If the air in the polluted portions of the Los Angeles Basin were somehow magically and costlessly removed, who would benefit? The landowners. The increased value of living with cleaner air will be evidenced by larger immigration and bidding up of land prices, possibly until the advantages of the better air are all bid in the offerings for the land. Landowners benefit in being richer. Occupants paying higher rent get cleaner, healthier air but by paying higher rents have less to spend on food, clothing, and other goodies. The net effect may be to make nonlandowning residents no better off or possibly worse off, because for the better air they must pay more and sacrifice other goodies. Would you be willing to pay to have the smog reduced? How much for each incremental reduction? Would you be willing to pay to change your lifestyle without improving your overall situation? There is more. Indeed, some of us landowners in the less smoggy area will lose wealth as our land values decline as people move back into the smog-free areas.

Still, there is a positive benefit if the smog could be removed or reduced costlessly. The benefit is not necessarily to the residents in the area now freed of smog, but more to those who live elsewhere or who subsequently move to the Los Angeles area. They are the ones who will benefit—and along with the landowners may get all the benefit—while the tenant residents are literally made worse off. Whether you should regard this as a perverse effect or an intended effect, I leave to you.

The answer is not to abandon the effort to heed costs and values of environmental use. The moral is to more clearly perceive and understand effects of alternative methods before deciding what to do. Indeed, in some instances more pollution of the air and water will get more than it loses.

A second class of legislative laws change our lifestyles away from those permitted by a capitalistic system. These also enhance the politicians' welfare by increasing demand for their services, assigning more power to them, and increasing their wealth. Safety requirements on cars, drug sale admissibility under the pure food and drug laws, blue-sky laws, energy-use edicts, security sale regulations, warranty and guaranty obligations, occupational safety and hazard laws, minimum wage laws, and compulsory social security are examples. I believe the consequences of these laws are not comprehended by the public, which is not to say that their effects were not foreseen and desired by some people.

Consider safety requirements on cars. Sam Peltzman, in an extensive study, concluded that the result has been no reduction in number of deaths but more property damages. Seat belts, collapsible steering columns, dual braking systems, resistant windshields, and improved bumper requirements have induced us to drive faster and less carefully with more pedestrian deaths and property damage. These results are neither surprising nor undesirable. If safety is increased per mile driven, people will sensibly drive more miles. They will trade off some of the greater safety for less attentive, easier, more extensive driving. Since we cannot control all goals and objectives attained by a person, if we impose more of one on them (safety), they will trade *some* of it away for *more* of other good things (travel) to restore a balance of values—which they can do by adjusting their manner and extent of driving. An increase in the number of people killed and amount of damage done does not mean the law has been ineffective or undesirable. On the contrary, it has been extremely effective in unintended and possibly desirable ways.

Safer airplanes in the past half-century have induced more people to fly more; as a result we have more deaths from air travel than if flying were less safe. The greater number of deaths was worth the extra miles of travel and time released for other activities. In less offensive words, greater extent of travel and of time for other uses was substituted for some of the greater safety per mile of travel. Man compromises, as I said earlier. Give him a lot more of this, and he will trade off *some* marginal amount now worth less to him than some extra of other things whose amounts had not increased. Restraining him from doing so requires totalitarian control of lifestyles.

Take strict liability laws, wherein a manufacturer must bear the losses or gains of uncertain performance. If risk bearing is undesirable, manufacturers will have to be recompensed to carry that risk. Without those laws, consumers could, if they wish, buy at a lower monetary price and bear some of that risk themselves, or pay more (have less of other goods) for higher quality goods. Under *strict* liability laws that option is closed off; all consumers pay more for less risk. So how do they respond? By being less careful with the product once purchased, thereby raising costs of "required" standards. People who are more careful or less risk-averse will suffer. As an exercise, try to predict effects of a *compulsory uniform* insurance system for breakdowns of automobiles. What would that do to the purchase price of a car?

Occupational-safety and hazardous-occupation regulations make jobs safer—and more expensive. Employees get safer jobs and lower money salaries. Consumers will not pay more for a product produced under safer conditions. Employees *are* more willing to work in the safer jobs, so the wage will become lower in those jobs. If you think riskier jobs do not command higher wages than less risky jobs, try hiring some people for some job and then make the job more hazardous; watch their response. Occupational-safety laws reduce money income to those in the jobs made safer and raise them in jobs that were formerly the safer jobs. People forced to have so much safety are willing to forsake some money income or other rewards in the competition for that safer job. Also other working conditions will deteriorate if too much of one form of payment—greater safety—is provided, as people substitute by tradeoffs, as we stated earlier. This is one reason low-pay jobs have poor working conditions as well. That is *preferred* by workers. Those of us on low income have less of and poorer quality *everything*, not just some things. We *prefer* that balanced package.

Political legislation prevents banks from paying high competitive explicit interest on deposits, because, presumably, they would compete excessively and offer too much interest, increasing the risk of bankruptcy. The error in this is that they compete in other ways to enhance income, letting the combined risks reach the same level as formerly. The possibilities are plentiful. People substitute unless their entire lifestyles are controlled. Forcibly increasing one facet of their lifestyle or one good in their entire basket of goods does not prevent their compensating for that in the other goods, if they can buy and sell other goods.

Subsidies of education to students permit parents to divert funds from their children's education to other activities. Thus the low tuition subsidy at the University of California is in large part a gift to parents paid for by the general taxpayers—undoubtedly the intent of low tuition.

Minimum wage laws ostensibly devised to raise wages of the lowest wage earners do not. The number of employees an employer can profitably hire is reduced. Some lose jobs and must work at lower paying jobs exempt from the law, or if none is exempt, work as self-employed, for which there is no minimum wage law, or simply leave the workforce, or substitute poorer working conditions for the higher wages. Even those who retain jobs are not better off in the long run. Some who would be displaced will offer to work (at the higher wages) with less nonmonetary pay—stricter discipline on the job, poorer circumstances such as less time off, fewer coffee breaks, vacations, or fringe benefits. Employees will offer to forsake some of those things for the higher required wage rate to retain existing jobs, rather than take the inferior alternative of working in jobs not covered by the law, or becoming self-unemployed or departing from the labor force into "leisure." Economic law is not suppressed by legislated law.

Another class of political activity which directly enhances welfare of the adept political competitors is inflation. It is a tax without legislation. Expenditures are financed by explicit taxes and by printing new money—usually by first selling newly printed bonds indirectly to the Federal Reserve in exchange for newly printed money. That, *and that alone*, is the source of persisting inflation, the politician's best friend. After printing more money to pay for promised benefits to their constituency—and thus maintain their hold on office—they then legislate vain attempts to restrain the consequent inflation by imposing wage and price controls or an incomes policy—the same thing under a different name. But again economic law is not suppressed by legislated law. Inflation is not, and simply cannot be, restrained by wage and price controls. Inflation reduces the purchasing power of money. Price controls reduce purchasing power of money by creating shortages and forcing greater resort to nonmoney, nonmarket means of competing for goods and resources. Money loses some of its value when money will not buy the amount you want to buy at those prices. So you resort to other means of competition to establish claims to goods and services—like standing in line, supporting political candidates, spending time in protests and political action, and side favors of a variety too great to list, and of course, of reduced quality of goods and services—until the quality is reduced to just what the limited money price is worth to the producer. Is that what the legislation intended, and what economic law brought about?

Then, to benefit themselves, politicians gleefully insist they must do something about the shortage—as if it had not been caused by the price controls and the initial inflation in the first place—as we should all have learned (but did not) during the gasoline and oil fiasco in 1974 and from the current natural gas shortages caused by price controls. But instead politicians and the politically adept have sought self-serving advantage in the situation created by their legislation. So they decreed we could not use power for outdoor lighting. They knew better than any of us that my value of *some* outdoor light exceeded the value to me of *some* more indoor light. They knew. They did not like my preferences. So, to make up for the loss of an outdoor light, I lighted *two* on the inside to be as well off. In doing so, I did not think I was being antisocial. Had I not used the power, what basis is there for believing it would have been used elsewhere to greater value? None. Indeed, there is *assurance* it would have been used elsewhere with less value—where the user had to pay only the low legal price that understates its true use value.

More recently the same "only the kings shall wear purple and silk stockings" political authority appears in the California public utility commission's directive that outdoor swimming pools shall not be heated with natural gas because they are luxuries. The gas will instead be diverted to industry, making, I presume, *more* beer and aluminum cans rather than for *some* arthritic swimmers. My contrast of beer with arthritic swimmers is of course unfair. I have no basis to conclude that some *more* beer is in any sense less desirable than some *extra* swimming by arthritic people. But your friendly politician will pretend, indeed assert, he can, if he is carefully tuned to vote-getting or political staying-power of gas-use allocations.

The Federal Energy Agency's mandates for smaller cars with more miles per gallon will result in less comfortable, less durable, less resalable cars, but then they know what we prefer. What sparked that drive for mandated kinds of cars? The initial inflation with price controls jointly with environmental legislation. But economic law took over and the present results are evident. Did you realize that you, who must drive more-expensive-to-operate cars in California in order to reduce pollution, are doing so for the benefit of special landowners and people who now live in areas not plagued with smog? Know it or not, it is true. Do you know that using less gasoline for cars permits more petroleum for plastics, perfumes, and heating of vacant rooms? Getting back those rights from politicians will be done only by paying the politicians to return the rights. That is how political activists confiscate wealth.

REVIEW OF

PUBLIC LAW PERSPECTIVES ON A PRIVATE LAW PROBLEM: AUTO COMPENSATION PLANS

I deliberately wreck your car. Fortunately for both of us, I had earlier contracted with you to pay you in advance an amount sufficient to induce you willingly to accept the damage. I bore the cost. But suppose I had not made a contract in advance. Should I pay you afterwards? If so how much? Or should society at large pay you for the damage? These are the questions which Blum and Kalven discuss in their fine lectures given at the Yale Law School in 1964, as the Shulman Lectures, and now published in book form.

The problem posed by Blum and Kalven is how to compensate for automobile damages. Shall first fault and then damages be established, with payment from the faulty party to the injured? Or shall the injured be awarded a payment from society at large, on the ground that fault cannot or is too difficult to be established? Blum and Kalven skillfully force attention to the issues of whether or not the fault system is so hopelessly out of sorts with the modern world as to be futile, and whether our common law system is rapidly moving us to a compensation (instead of fault) system.

According to Blum and Kalven, many discussions of compensation schemes simply beg these questions, and instead concentrate on the kind of general compensation system to use. But Blum and Kalven effectively spike that easy superficiality and salvage the basic issue. They establish a strong case that the fault system is not archaic nor out of place and further that the drift of common law and insurance schemes will not get us to a general compensation system.

They discuss some implications of a general compensation plan, under various payment schemes: increased scope of coverage but smaller payments to severely damaged parties; a schedule of awards by classes of damages; a so-

Review of Walter J. Blum and Harry Kalven, *Public Law Perspectives on a Private Law Problem: Auto Compensation Plans* (Boston: Little, Brown, 1965), reprinted, by permission of the author, from *George Washington Law Review* 34 (1966): 820–23.

cial security, minimum guaranteed, satisfactory subsistence level so that damages are compensated only enough to bring the injured party back to some minimum satisfactory level; exclusion of a basic minimum amount of damage from compensation.

Blum and Kalven investigate the rationale for a switch from fault liability damages to accident insurance, wherein no fault criterion is used preparatory to payment of damages. They convincingly show that this system would be tantamount to a social insurance alternative; and in this discussion of the social insurance method, Blum and Kalven are at their destructive best: destructive because first they expose the fallacies of thinking that the defects of a fault system of torts and damages will be cured by switching to a general social security system; second, if moving toward a social security system is the purpose, as some say, it is difficult to understand why auto accident victims should be singled out for special treatment; third, such a switch would do much to destroy the incentive effects of damage assessments; and fourth, it would increase fraudulent claims.

Since this reviewer is an economist, he must direct himself to the economics of the lectures. Economics is the study of resolution of conflicts of interest in the face of scarcity, not the resolution of conflicts arising from "violation" of the law. It is a study of means of acting jointly in the face of people's conflicts of interests, usually in mutually agreeable ways. But if the laws or property rights, defining the spectrum of goods and actions related thereto, are not clearly delineated, conflict of interest will be accompanied by conflict over who shall have the as yet unspecified rights and how he shall retain them. This question should be separated from the question of what should be done if clearly demarcated rights are violated by others. In sum, the specification of property rights as rights of people who decide about the uses made of goods and the enforcement of those rights against violators are two separate issues. In trying to resolve the latter we sometimes are led to "weaken" the former. This is precisely the issue in Blum and Kalven's lectures.

Damage trials and legal actions are tantamount to ex post facto contracting. They are means of simulating action in the interest of property rights. Because of difficulties, proposals are made to switch to social security—to socialize the risks and damages; i.e., if private property rights cannot always be enforced, we should socialize them.

What is interesting to this reviewer is how this line of reasoning crops up in so many places, often without adequate consideration of an alternative route—that of strengthening the property rights. The gradually increasing economic value of water, of the radio spectrum, of airspace for airplanes all tend toward socialized control and general public ownership (analogous to a general auto damage compensation system), not because of any inherent reasons for doing so, but because legislation has prevented the common law evolution of enforceable private property rights to water, radio spectrum uses, and airspace. But economic methods do exist for creating and enforcing such property rights. Because of legislative failure to use such devices, the switch to general ownership (compensation) is suggested as inevitable and proper. Yet, if more analyses were made of these cases of control of water and radio-TV along the lines made by Blum and Kalven of auto accident insurance and damages, we would probably long ago have moved more toward a less socialized system control of water and radio-TV.

A particularly impressive feature of the Blum-Kalven lectures is the unusual display of awareness of economic analysis. Whether known to the legal profession or not, it happens that economists find the law journals an especially fruitful area for teaching graduate students. We turn them loose on the law journals to detect basic errors in economic analysis. To mention but a few: legislation and decisions on fair trade practices, tie-in sales, discriminatory pricing, and monopolistic practices are rife with elementary errors of economic analysis—but probably not more than in political science or in other disciplines (not to mention the business literature). Yet if we allow a reviewer the privilege (some would say duty) of carping here and there, we would make the following few remarks.

Blum and Kalven, in dealing with narrower economic problems, surprised this reviewer in calling forth the deep-pocket principle. That seems to be a political principle rather than an economic one. The concept of the superior risk bearer as the person on whom to place risk seems a caricature of the principle that, with free contractual exchange of various types of risks, risk bearing will be allocated among the members of the community on a voluntary basis: presumably, a greater amount will be borne by those with less dislike for risk. But nothing more than this can be said.

One possible source of serious misinterpretation may be worth pointing out. This pertains to the "allocation of costs." It is possible to allocate costs in the sense that the action giving rise to some costs can be measured or identified. But to allocate the costs in the sense of imposing that loss of value on a particular person is quite a different matter. The economist, in allocating cost, is trying to allocate costs in both senses. Presumably, the person responsible for the decision to take an action should bear the costs. But that depends on one's social philosophy. And any interpersonal assignment of costs is affected by the system of property rights, their transferability, and the ease of enforcement of people's rights to use property. (You will notice we avoid the erroneous, but common, impression that there is a difference between property rights and human rights. There is not. Property rights are simply the rights of people to use property. Occasionally, even distinguished legal philosophers fall into this confusion when speaking as advocates for legislation.) Once property rights are made explicit, rigorous, and easily transferable, then the assignment of costs to people is a result of voluntary arrangements among the individuals—independent of who has what rights. With explicit transferable property rights, the law has nothing more to do with who shall bear the costs. That depends upon the individual's own preferences. Usually, it turns out that we choose to have the cost borne by the person responsible for the action. And this is the invariable result with private property rights—except where charity is involved. If I own some land, you can dump garbage on my land if you pay me for the "damage" done to my land. You bear the cost even though I own the land. In fact, because I, or some other identifiable person owns that land, you will bear that cost—just as surely as if you owned the land itself. It makes no difference who owns the land—just so long as someone does. If, however, the land is not owned by me or anyone else but only occupied by me, and you dump garbage, I may bear the cost if I cannot make you compensate me for the damages. I may complain about being forced to bear some costs of "your" action against my will. The law is then asked to decide who shall bear the cost. The law asks the economist, who can say only, "It beats me." All we know is that, under different systems of property rights, costs of actions will be borne by different people. Whether we choose a private property system because we like the way the costs (not rights) are assigned or despite the way they are assigned is a moot question, at least so far as I have been able to ascertain. To ask an economist how costs should be borne is to ask him what kind of property and social system we ought to have. Give us another 3,000 centuries.

CORPORATE MANAGEMENT
AND PROPERTY RIGHTS

Though we know securities regulation is what securities regulators do, we may not know the "why." Why should exchange of corporate property rights be permitted only under restricted conditions, whereas exchanges of noncorporate rights—such as rights to nonprofit corporations or to proprietorships in houses and lands—are not equally regulated? What is there about corporate rights that calls for distinctive treatment?

Varied answers can be offered by economists. Securities in a corporation are homogeneous and purchased by many people; each potential stockholder in a corporation would bear a cost of independently discovering essentially the same information about the firm—a cost repeated for each potential buyer in some degree. If this information is required from each firm and made public, information search costs are reduced. For houses, or privately owned noncorporate enterprises, the turnover of identical rights is sufficiently small that potential costs savings are insufficient to justify the costs of compulsory revelation of "all" material and relevant data.

One may wonder why we insist that all public, corporate firms reveal information. Why not let those that choose to do so file "full-disclosure" reports; potential buyers could then ignore those which do not. Stockholders could then decide whether the change in stock values consequent to reduced information costs about the corporation is worth the cost of general disclosure. This would permit buyers to act on less information if they wish. It is hard to see how one can argue against such optional behavior unless he takes a paternalistic attitude—a position not without its advocates.

Another argument for compulsory disclosure is the reduction in fluctuation in security prices (as distinct from later or earlier fluctuation), but strong theory or evidence to support that proposition—or indeed even to deny it—is lacking.

From Armen A. Alchian, *Economic Forces at Work* (Indianapolis: Liberty Fund, 1977), 227–57. This article was previously published in *Economic Policy and the Regulation of Corporate Securities*, ed. Henry Manne (Washington: American Enterprise Institute, 1969), 337–60, and is reprinted by permission of The American Enterprise Institute for Public Policy Research, Washington, D.C.

Another basis for regulation of conditions under which corporate securities may be sold rests on the ingenious phrase "separation of ownership and control," which allegedly implies something about behavior in the corporate world. Writers who have tried to put content in that phrase have elaborated by saying "no group of stockholders would be able under ordinary circumstances to muster enough votes to challenge the rule of management."[1] Or "barring blatant incompetence, management can count on remaining in office. . . . [S]o long as management possesses the confidence of the board (of directors), that body will usually not actively intervene to dictate specific policies."[2] "Control lies in the individual or group who have the actual power to select the board of directors," and these presumably are some group other than the stockholders.[3]

Competition is said to be so restricted by the market power of large corporations as to change the role of competition; behavior by managers and employers is so insulated from the wealth-increasing interests of the owners that the conventional view of managers operating to increase owners' wealth is no longer germane.[4]

Though these pronouncements lack empirically refutable content, their emotional impact rivals that of a national anthem.

The empirical evidence for the "separation" theme, if we judge by the data brought to bear, is the dispersion of stockholdings in our largest corporations, combined with management advantages in a proxy fight. Recent data suggest the dispersion of stockholdings over holders with small proportional amounts has increased.[5] Yet surely the music about separation of ownership and control requires more lyrics than that stockholding is dispersed among many stockholders with no holders having, say, ten or more percent of the holdings. If that were all there were to the theme, it would mean merely that the expression "separation of ownership from control" had replaced the expression "dispersion of stockholdings." I would have thought that anyone propounding or testing a phenomenon to be called the separation of ownership from control would identify it with more than a measure of degree of stock ownership dispersion.

1. R. J. Larner, "The 200 Largest Nonfinancial Corporations," *American Economic Review* (September 1966): 779.

2. P. A. Samuelson, *Economics*, 7th ed. (New York: McGraw-Hill, 1966), pp. 89–90.

3. A. Berle and G. Means, *The Modern Corporation and Private Property* (New York: Macmillan, 1933), p. 69.

4. C. Kaysen, "Another View of Corporate Capitalism," *Quarterly Journal of Economics* (1965): 43.

5. Larner, op. cit.

The expression probably was meant to convey behavioral implications. What are they? Is it that more dispersed holdings give less certainty to any one holder that his preferred use of the corporate resources will be the actual one? Or that the agent he prefers as the manager is not the one who is? Or that the probability that a *private* proprietor of $10,000 of goods can determine the use of those resources is higher than the probability that the preferred decision of an individual with a $10,000 interest in a million-dollar enterprise will be the one executed. But note that though his power of decision making on $10,000 is reduced, it is increased over the remaining $990,000. Any of these might denote the behavioral phenomenon implicit in the expression "separation of ownership from control." But I suspect that is not what is meant.

For clues to the meaning, we can note that a necessary attribute of ownership is the bearing of the value consequences of resources. We can interpret control to mean the authority to control decisions that will affect the value of resources. What must be meant by those who speak of separation of control from ownership is a reduced ability to the owners to revoke and reassign delegations of decision-making authority that will affect value.

In other words, it is assumed that the probability that any majority can be formed *to reassign* authority is lower the greater the dispersion of stock ownership. This may rest on two factors: (1) Knowledge of negligence or inefficiency by an agent will be more expensive to disperse over a majority. (2) The knowledge of harmful managerial decisions will be less influential on each stockholder, as the proportionate interest of the largest stockholders is smaller and the number of stockholders is greater. In this sense, a manager's deviations from stockholders' interests are less likely to be "policed." This is one empirically meaningful interpretation of the expression "greater separation of control from ownership."[6]

But some features of group ownership cut against this argument. A greater number of owners implies a greater variety of owners, some with more knowledge of the particular business. We cannot assume legitimately that when there is one stockholder, he is the person most able to detect deviant behavior. Specialization of knowledge is not to be ignored; the corporate form enables a greater utilization of specialization of expert business knowledge. Despite the

---

6. Notice that one of the premises underlying this was *not* that in a group decision process one subgroup can exploit another, such as occurs in political voting for, say, a tariff or licensing restriction on entry into a profession.

difficulty in reconciling several points of view, the variety of talents, and special knowledge, may more than compensate. Committees are not entirely vehicles for blocking action.

Corporate voting mechanisms are frequently alluded to both as a principal cause and as "evidence" of a separation of stockholders from "control," as the management with its accessibility to proxy rights at corporate expense is alleged to dominate the voting.[7] No minority group can be formed to fight the management. The picture is completed with an etching of a monolithic management group with common interests, no interpersonal conflicts of interest, and capable of perpetuating itself in office. (One is reminded of the naive cartel theory in which a group of erstwhile competitors agree to share a market, apparently with no conflicts of interest to be resolved and suppressed.)

But in fact, if a management group is exploiting stockholders by operating an enterprise in a diversionary manner, within the group opportunities will arise for some to gain personally by eliminating that "inefficient" behavior. Management cannot be adequately analyzed if it is regarded as a single person; there is competition within the management; managers can move to new jobs; and they compete for jobs by superior performance on present jobs. For example, few of us at the University of California strive to produce superior products in research and teaching because the taxpayers of California are uppermost in our interests. It is the appeal we offer to other potential employers that induces us to act as if we were trying to satisfy our present employer's interests. Only if my future were irrevocably tied, like that of a slave, to my present employer would my behavior match that of the folklore indolent manager.

While we can leap from a monolithic view of management to the idea of effective separation of management from stockholder interest and control, we cannot do so if we recognize other significant management constraints. If that leap were valid, then I conjecture the tenure of office of management in "management-controlled" corporations, as they are called, should be greater than in other corporations. Is the management more able to stay in office at unaffected salaries? Are stockholder profits in such corporations smaller? Is management compensation greater? Is the transition probabiiity matrix of larger dispersed corporations different from others? I know of no empirical tests of these possible implications. Yet they are, I suspect, testable. And testing is precisely what should be done. Is what I have called the superficial analysis of the "separation" thesis incorrect, or is the alternative which does not

---

7. Berle and Means, op. cit., p. 139.

dismiss so readily the competitive forces valid? Absent any empirical evidence in favor of the former, I shall, perhaps mistakenly, not reject the latter.

In sum, demonstration of greater dispersion of stockholdings, along with our proxy system, does not establish that bearing-of-value consequences have been separated from the effective control of the decision maker, nor that the wealth of the stockholder is less well guarded.

There seems to have been an embarrassing delay or unwillingness to formulate the thesis in such a way as to make it refutable or testable. One would have expected the advocates to have presented evidence. But in thirty years, we remain with almost no empirical evidence. So, presumed implications still remain to be validated by empirical study, and I know of only one—the survival test, which is given almost no attention.

Since we observe an increased dispersion in corporate ownership, we should wonder why stockholders whose interests are less heeded by the top management would purchase stock in such corporations. Perhaps other advantages of the corporate form more than offset losses to stockholders imposed by the increased divergence of managers from stockholders' interests. This could be correct, but the fact that the dispersed ownership has increased certainly does not lend support to the implications of the general thesis that managerial activity in these situations will be less consistent with the shareholders' interests. However, although absence of a theory does not prove the phenomena are absent, the concomitance of unspecified implications, little evidence, and inadequate logic is certainly not conducive to confidence.

Weaknesses in Theory of New Corporate Economy

Some analytical and conceptual mistakes have been committed in attempts to deduce a "distortion" in managerial behavior. It has been said that profits accrue to those who bear risks and make innovative decisions. Indeed, you can find economists who have referred to profits as rewards or penalties for innovative activity, with the value effects serving to induce such innovation (or eliminate it) by rewarding the risk takers. But it is something else to say that managers who select the innovative uses are those who bear or should bear consequent value effects. Whether or not they do depends upon prearranged contractual relationships with respect to property rights.

The economic concept of "profits" refers to a particular value phenomenon—unpredicted value changes. Whoever has the title to goods is the person who bears the profits and losses. "The owner" is the name given to that person, and he is bearer of the profits or losses. It does not advance rigorous analysis to talk about profits as the "reward" both to the owners *and* to managers who exercise delegated decision authority in determining uses of resources. This careless conjunction, common in the lay literature, leads to sentences like ". . . if the courts, following the traditional logic of property, seek to insure that all profits reach or be held for the security owners, they prevent profits from reaching the very group of men (managers) whose action is most important to the efficient conduct of enterprise. Only as profits are diverted into the pockets of control do they, in a measure, perform their second function" (i.e., inducing innovation).[8]

To believe that employed managers, with delegated authority to determine uses of someone else's resources, are the bearers of resultant profit or loss is to lose sight of the essential attributes of the ownership-agency relation. Managers do *not* bear those realized profit gains or losses. Owners do. The manager does not acquire those realized profits any more than does the designer or builder of a profitable apartment house acquire or share in the realized profits—all of which go to the apartment owner. Profits (or losses) from the construction of an apartment house are borne by the owner, not the architect or builder. The profits they initiated are not theirs and are not distributed to them unless they initially had a contract to share in them—i.e., unless they initially had become co-owners in the assets. Yet, although that is true, it does not follow that the wealth or income of the architect or builder is unaffected or that he is left unrewarded. A profitable apartment brings more demand for its architect or builder. This increased demand leads to higher incomes for the architects and builders or managers.

It is one thing for agents with delegated authority to be rewarded for creating profits for owners; it is a far different thing for delegated agents to share in *those* profits. Profit receivers do not give up any of their accrued profits when their agents are subsequently paid higher incomes for future services. The *past, realized* profits are not redirected or redivided to the managers in the form of new subsequent contractual terms. Rather, the initial realized profits of the resource owners were smaller because people anticipate that the wages of the superior manager will be bid up in efforts to obtain his services. No *prior* contractual provision explicitly arranged between the parties is necessary for the superior manager to realize a gain for superior services. His revealed superiority is reflected in his higher market value.

I conjecture that confusion has arisen from the impression that a person gets what he produces—a manifestly false, if not empty, proposition. Instead

---

8. Ibid., p. 350.

he may get, via a contract, in the context of competition for his services, an amount commensurate with the most optimistic employer's belief of what he is *expected* to produce. If he prefers a different kind of contractual reward, viz., one in which his reward is contingent upon realized results, then he can become a co-owner of the resources whose values are to be affected and part of which value is to be his.

In sum, the fact that delegated agents are paid to produce value changes in goods by the way they use them, does not in any sense imply that the agents deserve or will obtain part of *that* value change. This stands even though their subsequent contracts reflect their earlier performance in successfully producing past profits.

Belief that earlier realized profits must be shared among the owners and the so-called responsible superior managers or innovators results from a failure to recognize anticipatory capitalization in the market's valuation of resources. If the manager had to be rewarded by a payment out of the initial profits realized by the initial employer, then those who worry about separation of ownership and management functions would indeed have pointed out a problem.[9] But that is not the way a market values resources.

Neither is that the logic of economic theory or the logic of conventional profit theory, despite some assertions to the contrary.[10] The conventional and still valid wisdom presumes competitive market capitalization of foreseeable future events and assumes that once a manager displays evidence of a superior activity, the market (i.e., other people) will not ignore the implications about the future demand and costs for his services. Ignoring or denying the forces of open competitive market capitalization is, in my opinion, a fundamental error in the writing about ownership and control and about the modern corporate economy. Neither the role of competition in the markets for capital goods and services nor its logic is upset by the presence of large corporations with dispersed ownership.

Not only is market valuation ignored in the misinterpretation of the role of profits, but it is ignored also in the contention that the modern stockholder's wealth is less well protected in the dispersed ownership corporation than in the concentrated ownership corporation. We have only to ask if anyone would pay as much for a share of stock in a corporation with dispersed ownership if he knew his wealth would be given less diligent interest by corporate managers.

---

9. Note that I refer to a separation of *functions*, not a separation of interests or a loss of control.

10. Berle and Means, op. cit., pp. 341–51.

He would pay less in the knowledge he was to get less. The lower bid prices for stock would protect investor-owners from the foreseeable losses anticipated from less diligent concern for the wealth. Yet corporations have thrived, and they would not have if the dispersed ownership corporation suffered from this value discounting.

Resolution of these two conflicting interpretations lies in the possibility that either (1) the alleged greater diversionary activity is a myth or (2) the dispersed large corporation is so advantageous in other respects that the diversionary tactics of the managers are financed out of those advantages while the stockholders get as much as they would in less dispersed corporations. If the former were true, the whole issue would collapse. If the latter were true, it would imply only that the *forms* (but not value) of managerial behavior and of rewards in the dispersed ownership corporation are different and more costly (inefficient), but the managers would reap no extra gain. The consumer of products of those corporations would be paying a higher price than he otherwise would (but still, a price lower than if there were *no* dispersed ownership corporations). But could it not still be argued that the stockholders could have received a larger return? It would seem not, for if they could have, the number of dispersed corporations would have increased, thus lowering returns to the equivalent of what is being obtained in less dispersed ownership corporations. Let me elaborate on these points.

Managers do not reap some special or additional gain or economic rent from their ability to engage in diversionary tactics. Awareness of greater diversionary capability by managers or employees results in lower pecuniary salaries as managers and employees compete for the jobs permitting diversionary tactics.[11] Competition among managers and employers in seeking attractive, easy, or secure jobs implies a lower pecuniary reward in those jobs. A job with more leisure yields a lower wage; one with greater security yields a lower wage; one with more leisure and a given wage will have its security competed down. Substitution among the various facets of jobs occurs so that, on *net* of all considerations, the advantage of one job over another is competed away. All the various facets constitute "forms" of payment to the employee, whether the facets be leisure, wages, types of colleagues, working hours, vacation provisions, extent

11. Unless you believe, with Kaysen (op. cit.), that executive compensation is not within control of the stockholders. If I knew what that really meant, I might test it. If it means what I suspect it was intended to mean, I think it is wrong. But then, ask yourself, Does an owner "have control" of the wages he pays—in any kind of firm?

of surveillance by the employer, etc. Pecuniary salary will be lower for the same reasons that salaries of people working in factories or shops in more pleasant surroundings will be lower than they would have been with less attractive working conditions. Stockholders need not be activists in bringing this about.

This argues that the dispersed ownership corporation implies a difference in the vector or form of payments to managers and employees. But not all forms of "compensation" to employees are equally costly. The form of compensation in a dispersed corporation may indeed represent a higher cost vector to the corporation, but if the corporation can earn enough because of its advantages, it can in equilibrium bear this higher cost vector of a managerial "salary." This does not mean the employees or managers are getting a more valuable or preferable return than in less dispersed corporations. Instead they are being paid with a different, higher cost (i.e., less efficient), vector of rewards—one that costs more to provide but is no more preferable on net than in other corporations or businesses. It is different simply because the cost of controlling the various facets of the vector and changing it to a different one (say one with higher wages and less leisure) is greater than the saving. The higher costs of such vectors (of given attractiveness to employees) can be financed out of the advantages of this type of corporation. If the costs of these forms of rewards to managers had not been higher, one might think there would have been larger earnings for the owners. But this would not be an entirely correct conclusion, for the number and scope of such corporations would have been greater, with consequent lower prices to consumers. The higher cost salary vectors, if indeed they are more costly, simply mean a sacrificed output potential for consumers—evidenced by higher prices than would have been paid for the larger output if the dispersed ownership corporation could police and control its managers' and employees' behavior as efficiently as is alleged for a smaller, less dispersed corporation.

To repeat, all this argues that the dispersed corporation changes the *forms* (and efficiency) of payment to employees and managers. It does *not* imply lower wealth for the stockholders nor higher earnings for employees and managers than in less dispersed corporations. If employees tend to be thieves, and if employers or employees are aware of this tendency, contractual money salaries will be adjusted so that part of the total salary is taken as legitimized "theft." The employers do not necessarily lose. The higher policing costs are borne by (i.e., discounted to lower wage offers to) the employees whose past conduct determines their present reputation and beliefs about future behavior. Similarly, if dispersed corporate ownership permits managers greater scope for anti-stockholder activity and if the stockholders or the employees are aware of this tendency, the terms of employment compensation will be adjusted.

The resultant implication is that in large, dispersed-ownership, for-profit corporations, we should expect different types of managerial and employee behavior and rewards than in small and closely held corporations. The large corporate pattern should reflect the greater costs of policing and revising delegated authority, but *without* necessarily resulting in lower wealth for the stockholder than in less dispersed corporations. These effects, insofar as they are foreseen or predictable, on the average will be reflected in anticipatory behavior and therefore in the valuation of initial capital investments or in stock prices on subsequent stock transfers. The stockholders are not any the poorer or their wealth less well secured.

How valid is this competitive market equalization process in reality? We do not know. But that does not mean that we can gratuitously assume it is absent or weak, as does most of the writing on the "ownership and control separation" theme. Nor can we cavalierly assume the opposite.

Do dispersed ownership firms have historically lower rates of growth of stockholders' wealth (allowing for dividends and capital value growth) than less dispersed ownership firms? I have yet to see a test of this, though it appears this should be a feasible evaluation. With attention to the "regression phenomenon" and with controls for types of industry, this should make a fine project for several doctoral dissertations—several, because of the value of replication and competitive testing of results.

Let us consider the presumed monolithic structure of management in the business firm. In reality, the firm is a surrogate of the marketplace, but differs in that longer-term general service contracts exist without continuous renegotiations at every change of type of service. To analyze the firm as a single-operator institution within which it is assumed there is not the competition that exists in markets is to miss a significant portion of the competitive processes. Though a firm may continue with unchanged name, and possibly even the same stockholders, the internal shifting of personnel within, as well as among, firms is market competition. The many people within a firm competing with each other and with people in other firms should suggest that the unit of analysis for competitive activity is the individual rather than an institution, which serves as an internalized market. Top management of a firm engages in screening employees, techniques, and proposals for new products which, if performed externally by separate firms, would be clearly evident as market functions. But when these functions are performed within the firm, the competitive market forces are hidden from obvious view and mistakenly ignored by careless analysts.

More significant than the rise and fall of firms, for purposes of behavioral analysis, is the rise and fall of individuals within firms. For many purposes (though not all) we can think of a firm (call it General Electric) as a market-place, as if it were a city within which individuals engage in atomistic competition. Competition among cities takes the form of individuals moving among cities and exporting ideas that have passed the test of profitability. While it is not correct to carry this analogy too far—and just how far "too far" is, I don't yet know—the analogy is very good in some respects. The long survival of some firm or of a few firms cannot be interpreted as evidence of a lack of market competition either within or between firms.

If it be argued that corporations with dispersed ownership or with so-called management control have separated the interests of stockholders from those of managers, we should expect differences in the rates of transition of individual employees within and between firms. We should perhaps expect a lower turnover of management in the dispersed corporation. Do we have any evidence of it? I am embarrassed to admit I have been unable to find that evidence. However, I shall cite some evidence later for implying different types of behavior. For example—to continue to speak of a mythical firm called General Electric—the directors and president are quick to fire or demote a division chief whose profit record shows inferiority to some other potential division head. Replacement of an inefficient division head may be quicker within General Electric than if the division manager owned the division. The internal capital and personnel market may be, nay is, more efficient than the external open market. That assertion I make in complete confidence as a challenge to anyone who with equal aplomb asserts the contrary. I could go on and assert that there is greater mobility of managers and technical personnel within General Electric than among firms in an atomistic market economy, that new ideas are internally evaluated more quickly, cheaply, accurately, and on a broader scale than in a society made up of several firms aggregating the same size. I could assert that the labor market within General Electric is superior to the atomistic, so-called pure competitive market and is superior because there are specialists within General Electric who are rewarded more fully for collecting and evaluating information about people. Thus the usual outside employment agencies that specialize in providing personnel information would be less efficient than the personnel employment agencies operating within General Electric. But what the truth is, I do not know.

Further, the investment funds (capital) market *within* General Electric is fiercely competitive and operates with greater speed to clear the market and to make information more available to both lenders and borrowers than in the external "normal" markets. In fact I conjecture that the wealth growth of General Electric derives precisely from the superiority of its internal markets for exchange and reallocation of resources—a superiority arising from the greater (cheaper) information about people and proposals. Many "knowledge effects" that would be externalistic in an ordinary market are converted into beneficial internalities within the firm as incentives and rewards to those producing them.

The foregoing is intended to suggest that the traditional theory of profits, of private property, markets, and competition is not obsolete, and also that the "separation of ownership from control" theme still lacks validly deduced and established implications about exploitation of stockowners' wealth. Long before the wide dispersal of stockholdings in a corporation, potential conflicts of interest among stockholders were recognized. Political theory if not legal history tells us much about the probability of subgroups exploiting the remainder by the group decision process. Furthermore, the conflict of interest between principals and their agents has long been recognized, though I presume, quite safely, that it is not that idea which the "separation of ownership and control" is supposed to designate.

If I appear to be defending the old theory as adequate, let me beg off. Inadequacies in the old theory exist, but they derive from its use of a wealth-maximizing instead of a utility-maximizing postulate. The wealth-maximizing postulate is usually appropriate (or less inappropriate) when applied to the "firm" as a unit of analysis. But in seeking to explain individual behavior within the firm, utility-maximizing criteria are more general and powerful than wealth-maximizing criteria. But this, I believe, would be equally true for the old-fashioned small firm.

Instead of a change in the modern society, it is the change in the objectives of economic theory that points up inadequacies in the old theory. We want now to interpret individual behavior, not merely firm survival as an entity. Although I say this is a change in objectives, I should be the first to assert that good old Adam Smith did exactly that in his *Wealth of Nations*. The adherents of the theme of a new modern corporate economy are saying what Smith said about corporations. Yet they are denying that the old competition theory is applicable. A somewhat strange twist, indeed.

There have been changes in our economy. But I do not believe that the idea of a replacement of a competitive era by an era of "market-power" large firms will enrich our theory or understanding of behavior.

My impression is that moves toward an economy with less open-market competition reflect a diversion of competition to the political processes, as resort is made to greater governmental control over economic access to markets and terms of exchange. Much of what passes for the new corporate economy should more accurately be called the new mercantilist, or the new "political" or politically regulated, economy, since it involves more political competition and the greater use of political rewards and penalties. And this move to political influence has occurred in both small and large firm industries. The "solution" (if such a "political" economy is a problem) usually is more political controls and political competition. This is beneficial to those most adept at political competition, for they would benefit from increased demand for their services as political competition displaces market competition in controlling economic activity. All this is, of course, what the "obsolete" economic theory implies.

Suggested and Tested Bases for Analysis: Hierarchical Control and Types of Property Rights

Advances in economic theory could be obtained by more explicit recognition of the political rewards-penalties structure in our economy. Advance could also be made with recognition and analysis of two other features—the hierarchical control task within a firm and the types of property rights prevailing in the firm. The hierarchical control structure has been analyzed in the context of a utility-maximizing criterion by O. Williamson.[12] For fear of flattering him justifiably, though unnecessarily, I shall merely note that the problem of inducing workers at the various hierarchical levels to gear their work to a specified common goal, as against individual interests, becomes more severe as the number of hierarchical layers or number of co-workers increases. The problem of surveillance, information handling, and filtering is a difficult one even when there is perfect consonance of goals among the workers. Since large enterprises are usually of a corporate form with more dispersed ownership, it is easy to confound the effects of dispersed ownership with the problem of hierarchical control, and I conjecture this has been done.

12. O. Williamson, "Managerial Discretion and Business Behavior," *American Economic Review* (December 1963): 1032–57.

Property Rights

But even if the confusion between stockholder dispersion and hierarchical controls is avoided, hierarchical control objectives are different in nonprofit or publicly owned enterprises (e.g., government agencies) from those in privately owned corporations. One objective—profitability—or effects on wealth of the owners will be given less weight in the former group. Profitability, combined with rights to profits, provides a clearer and stronger criterion for behavior of subordinates in for-profit corporations than in government agencies or not-for-profit enterprises. Absent that criterion and absent the "property" right to capture profits, resort is made to more detailed operating procedures and internal regulations.

The theme of separation of ownership and control in large dispersed corporations has been illustrated with public utilities and transportation companies as well as with unregulated firms. The corporate managers' behavior has been characterized as resembling that of administrators of universities, philanthropic foundations, nonprofit corporations, unions, and government agencies. This suggests, and economic theory does indeed imply, that in corporations which are *not* profit-seeking or are *not* privately owned (at least in the sense of having salable, marketable shares of ownership) behavior will deviate from that in a profit-seeking corporation. It deviates because "stockholders" in nonprofit or public utility corporations have less incentive (costs of doing so aside) for responding to market, competitive pressures for "efficient" or profit-making types of behavior. I shall try to elucidate this relatively neglected *basis for analysis of the kinds* of property rights and their relationship to economic and cultural behavior, because I believe something can be deduced and verified about the relationship between behavior and the types of property rights.

Crudely and broadly, let me identify one attribute of property rights in goods as being the probability of the effectiveness of my decisions about the use of those goods. That is, the greater the uses for a given good *and* the greater the probability that my decision about uses will be effective, the greater are my property rights in that good. Rights will be weaker if they have not been specified or explicitly recognized or if they have a small probability of being enforced by society.

Specification and identification of rights are not costless. For example, water is a good to which property rights are loosely specified, in part because of the high costs of doing so. But costs are high or low only *relative* to the value of the rights which could be specified. If the value of some right to a good rises, as that of rights to fresher water has during recent decades, the costs of specification, identification, and assignment of rights become more worth incurring. In general, the higher the value of potential rights to a good relative to costs of specifying those property rights, the greater will be the clarity of specification, identification, and assignment of rights in that good.

This proposition that the increase in value of potential rights to goods leads to a stronger specification of rights does not indicate what form the specification and identification will take, or to whom the rights will be assigned initially, or whether they will be transferable. It does not say whether title will be taken by the state or will be assigned to individuals as private property; it does not say whether the rights will be transferable among people or whether the goods are transferable among alternative uses.

You will rightly regard the proposition as obvious insofar as it is precise enough to have meaning. Anyone knows it doesn't pay to keep track of worthless things, while for more-valuable goods greater safeguarding costs are more worth incurring. But the influence of this proposition on our legal evaluation or development of property rights structures is by no means obvious and direct. The development of water law in the several states well illustrates the tortuous and hesitant progress toward more explicit specification and clear assignments of rights over water. The hold of precedent is rightly strong; adaptation to the changed values of rights and changed costs of specification is often inordinately delayed—or so it would seem from an examination of individual cases. Let me cite an example. In California, billions of dollars of wealth are being wasted simply because of the slowness in the adaptation of water law to changes in values of potential rights over water. A multibillion-dollar aqueduct, from Northern to Southern California, is being built now, ostensibly to bring water to Southern California. But, in fact, the aqueduct is being built now not to bring more water to Southern California but to establish or identify now who is to have rights over Northern California water in the distant future. Building the aqueduct now to capture the present flow of water is justifiable only as a means of presently establishing one's right to the future flow of water. All that cost could be deferred if rights to water use were legally established and made transferable by paper records rather than by concrete and steel devices.

With but slight imagination, we can perceive what would have happened had rights to future lumber, oil, gas, iron ore, and coal been assigned and controlled in that way. No imagination is required for what has happened to our radio-frequency spectrum, where a government board controls the use; private rights which had begun to arise in common law and which evoked judicial protection for exclusive use and exchange were thwarted by government agents who denied this policing activity and the legality of exchangeability. Small wonder that the resultant mess occurred. Federal allocative authority over assignment and use was established instead of property rights enforcement via market competition. The alternative of exclusive, exchangeable private rights, facilitated by state enforcement, to portions of that scarce valuable property—radio-frequency spectrum—was not allowed to be established.

As you may know, lumber rights once were acquired not by title to standing trees, but by cutting the trees into lumber. If trees were not cut, the landowner could not count on clear title to the lumber. In some agricultural areas, land title could be established only after the claimant had stripped the trees from the land, in order to manifest its use for agricultural purposes, as a legal precondition to title acquisition. Small wonder we stripped some of our Midwestern forest lands.

Yet these results have been interpreted by famous historians as failures in the private property, capitalistic competitive system. In fact, these results occurred where we did not have private property, capitalist market, competitive controls over those resources. The law did not permit the title acquisition and exchange rights that would enable economic competition to induce economic use of resources. As I view that history, the symptoms were not those of a private property, capitalist, competitive system, but of a different legal system of distributing and identifying rights which granted rights that induced "undesirable" behavior. Use values (of water or lumber) for future times or for different people and in different ways simply could not be realized; current possessors or competitors seeking rights in the resources were told they could not retain or capture rights to those future higher-valued uses.

This suggests that while we endeavor to regulate people's activities by imposing more regulation, with consequent enhancement of the role of political competition, it would be wise to examine the behavioral effects of the legal system of establishing, identifying, and transferring various types of property rights. For example, in a "not-for-profit" organization, the so-called owners or trustees do not have the right to decide to use or divide the wealth of the organization for their personal use—a right which is held by stockholders of a for-profit private property corporation. And in mutuals or cooperatives, while the "members" can vote to dissolve the enterprise and divide the proceeds among the members, they often cannot sell their rights. They can only abandon their interests in return for the initial investment, in contrast with private, for-profit corporate stockholders who can sell rights at open-market prices.

Whereas the present capital value—or wealth effect—is thrust on a stockholder as the value of his salable stock changes, in a "nonprofit" or "mutual" or "cooperative" enterprise, a member without transferable capital value rights bears the future consequences of current decisions only if he remains a member until the time of the future consequence.

In a for-profit private property corporation, current stockholders gain or lose wealth when the future consequence is anticipated and reflected in stock values. If members consume capital or are less diligent in preserving the future earning power, they bear more of the cost immediately. These problems are present also in mutual associations and nonprofit organizations, since their managers do not have to answer to anyone whose capitalizable wealth is at stake. Absent property rights that permit capitalization of future events into present market values, stockholders have less incentive to be concerned with potential capital value effects, and so the manager is less responsive to implicit capital value effects.

To avoid misunderstanding, let me emphasize that the proposition is that the capitalization of future effects into present values, combined with the ability to *capture* that market wealth by selling to a second party, provides an effective stimulus to the control of actions that affect present capital values.

There is a difference in incentive effects between a capitalizable, salable wealth right and a right to a stream of future receipts which will be obtainable only if one retains the claim into the future. For example, a mutual shareholder in a savings and loan association, or an "owning" managing-director of a nonprofit institution, can legally reap the future rewards for present action only by remaining with the enterprise, whereas a stockholder could immediately capitalize and reap the gain by selling his interests. Market capitalization and sale provide a different reward or punishment for present actions than is the case in the absence of capitalization possibilities. In sum, the wealth effects are more immediate to the stockholder than to the mutual shareholder or owner of an enterprise without capitalizable, salable property rights.

Before discussing noncapitalizable rights, let us consider a situation in which stockholders' rights to capture profits are restricted. The profits of a public utility are usually controlled by the state and limited to some maximum set by a regulatory agency. The *managers* will have incentives to strive for profits above the legal limit if the managers can conceal them from the regulators and capture them. And they can, to some extent. Higher earnings might be absorbed into cost-enhancing activities easing the life of the managers. Better offices, more congenial colleagues, and a more relaxed business operation with shorter hours are means of "converting" potential profits into "higher cost" activities. Or, also, the managers can engage in discriminatory hiring practices, by heeding more the race, creed, and color of potential colleagues.[13]

This higher-cost activity in a public utility is a form of profit conversion and is a form of activity which would reduce survival prospects for firms with less restricted property rights. We should expect to see greater clusterings of employees according to race, creed, and religion, for example, in not-for-profit enterprises than in for-profit private enterprises. Empirical studies provide corroborative evidence. In sum, legal limitations on profits or on access to markets harm the interests of the relatively unpopular, unorthodox, or individualistic members of society. Given this fact, there is an inconsistency in the view of those who argue that market competition brings out the worst in people, if they also believe that discrimination in terms of race, creed, and color is undesirable.

The reason is simple. Any open-market competitors who were to discriminate in this high-cost way would be outcompeted by others who did not engage in such discrimination. But if the explicit net earnings are already at the upper legal limit in a public utility, there is less to gain by avoiding discrimination in favor of less productive, but more popular, colleagues. Remove the prospect for stockholders capturing *greater* capitalizable profit, and the incentive to use lower cost, less discriminatory production techniques is reduced. No escape from this same *implication* is obtained by reliance on a regulatory body, for its members also lack the possibility of capturing capitalized wealth increments.

All this, though obvious, bears exposition because some of the "separation of ownership from control" discussion seems to be drawn from observations on behavior in public utilities. Here it is not the "widely dispersed ownership" but a legally imposed profit restriction which induces stockholders to permit more management behavior deviating from the wealth interests of the stockholder.

If, with restrictions on capturable profits, we combine restricted or licensed *entry* into the market, as is typically the case for public utilities, then monopoly rent appears as a supplement to competitive economic profits. Monopoly rent, which regulatory folklore says belongs to the consumer, will be captured in the form of taxes or as an easier, more convenient, and better life for employees, managers, and regulators, or even possibly with higher than competitive wages. Unions, for example, find these public utilities relatively easy pickings

13. A. Alchian and R. A. Kessel, "Competition, Monopoly and the Pursuit of Money," *Aspects of Labor Economics* (Princeton, 1962), pp. 157–83.

insofar as the union can share in the monopoly rent. It follows also that public utilities will display more discrimination by race, creed, color, and age; they will display greater tenure of job, fewer firings, and other attributes at the cost of the consumers who could otherwise have had lower prices. And for this there is empirical corroborative evidence.

In addition to profit-limited firms, with or without market-entry restrictions, there is another class of property arrangements that manifest similar behavior. These are the nonowned firms without stockholders, known as nonprofit institutions, mutual associations, cooperatives, union-type associations, governmental enterprises. All lack private ownership rights in the enterprise; there are no capitalizable, alienable shares or rights. There are people who make decisions as to how certain resources shall be used in the enterprise and within the scope of activities of the enterprise, but no one nor any group has the right to divert the wealth of the organization to their personal benefit by taking it out of the enterprise. And furthermore, although rights to manage that enterprise can be bestowed on other parties, they are not salable. The implications are profound.

A nonprofit (i.e., not-for-profit) enterprise may be successfully originated by some organizer-managing director. But increases in his wealth cannot be extracted from the enterprise for use outside the enterprise, nor can he sell his management rights. His only way to convert profits to his personal benefit is appropriately to use the enhanced wealth in the enterprise. Again, fancier offices, better-looking secretaries, more on-the-job fringe benefits, very liberal expense-account policies, and higher salaries all have served as conversion tactics. If he were the owner, he would have capitalized that net-earnings stream into a presently capturable wealth. Since he cannot, he dissipates the potential profitability via business-connected expenditure to obtain more nonpecuniary, non-take-home sources of utility. He substitutes on-the-job advantages for personal, at-home consumption.

Nonprofit, or not-for-profit, enterprises differ from profit-restricted enterprises in two respects. First, in the former, profits are not legally restricted; these enterprises just "happen" to make profits, according to the legal fiction of the situation. Second, there is no restriction on entry. The nonprofit enterprise is entitled to retain any available economic profits in the face of open-market competition. But neither the organizer nor anyone else can capitalize the profits into personal take-home wealth. However, the self-perpetuative, organizing-director, trustees, or board of directors can take higher salaries or put profits into an endowment if profits accrue more rapidly than the director-manager can ethically divert them to personal benefit. Had it been a for-profit enterprise, with salable stock, the present *and future anticipated* earnings could have been distributed or, if retained, captured by the initial stockholders via the higher market value of salable stock. We would expect nonprofit enterprises, insofar as they are profitable, to manifest and distribute their net earnings via business-connected costs. Their "costs" may appear to be higher, but in fact those "costs" may be distributions of profits; the higher "costs" are not necessarily signs of inefficiency or higher real costs.

Mutual associations of the sort that exist in the savings and loan business and in insurance provide evidence of the effects of an absence of private property rights. The legal fiction is that depositors or insurees are mutual "owners." The mutual shareholders acquire shares that often cannot be liquidated by redemption, and there is no possibility of marketing them at a value reflecting the profitability of the mutual organization. Mutual shareholders are limited in their voting power to a maximum number of votes, usually a very small percentage of all votes. Proxies can be solicited, but no one can start with a large or significant base of his own votes. There is less gain in raiding a mutual association or waging a proxy battle to put in new management as a means of improving profitability, because if such an attempt were successful, the potential gains would not be reflected in capitalized market values of salable shares. The winner of a proxy battle would have to take on some managerial position and reward himself by a salary collected during his tenure of office. Not only is his salary subjected to a higher tax rate, but, more fundamentally, a series of future net earnings is a less powerful incentive than the choice between that course and capturing the currently capitalized present value.

However, the organizing manager-directors of mutual associations do have some means, even if roundabout, by which some of the profits can be capitalized. One way is for the operator-organizer to own private, for-profit accessory companies selling insurance and other complementary services to the mutual. The mutual's purchases of such services can be made from these side companies which charge higher-than-competitive rates, thereby siphoning off the net earnings and enabling their conversion into capitalizable stock values of the service companies.

Market competition by other potential managers for the mutual manager's job will be ignored because the director, to whom an appeal must be made, is the manager himself. And any potential savings from the more efficient potential manager would be given little weight, since the present director cannot capitalize the value of the potential savings. I am not asserting that mutual shareholders are incapable of controlling the managers, just that their costs of doing so are greater and the gains are smaller than for privately owned corporate institutions.

Evidence for these "higher cost" or "aberrant" activities of mutuals (not necessarily indicative of less able, efficient, or alert management) has been obtained by A. Nicols in a study of mutual and private-stock savings and loan associations.[14] Reported costs per dollar of new loans, turnover of management, nepotism, and responsiveness of interest rates to changed market conditions show that the mutuals had higher costs, higher nepotism, smaller management turnover, and slower response via interest rate changes.

This does not mean that the managers are less alert or less informed of the possibilities. They exploit those possibilities in ways that yield benefits they can capture; the wealth potential is being exploited in ways other than take-home, capitalizable wealth for nonexistent stockholders.[15]

14. A. Nicols, "Stock versus Mutual Savings and Loan Associations: Some Evidence of Differences in Behavior," *American Economic Review* (May 1967): 337–46.

15. A study of this is provided by B. Weisbrod in his investigation of nonprofit hospitals. He identifies what he regards as nonprofit maximizing behavior, and the analysis is rather suggestive. A stronger test could be provided if one were to make a similar study of proprietary hospitals. B. Weisbrod, "Some Problems of Pricing and Resource Association in a Nonprofit Industry—Hospitals," *Journal of Business* 38 (January 1965): 18–28.

PRIVATE RIGHTS TO PROPERTY

THE BASIS OF CORPORATE GOVERNANCE

AND HUMAN RIGHTS

I.

My friends believe I make outrageous statements as if I really meant to. I do. Which may be why I was invited to make some more tonight. And I shall. Or perhaps you couldn't afford a professional comedian, say Don Rickles, so you thought you'd settle for an amateur. And you have.

I haven't the joke-telling talents of the late Senator Dirksen, whose jokes awakened his after-dinner audience. And his punch line summarized the point of his talk. But I have no prepared jokes—or none with a point—perhaps because I have no memorable theme, which is what you should expect of a talk in Washington, D.C.

So tonight I will annoy you with my annoyance at the widespread failure to appreciate how private property rights operate in our society—in controlling our economic product, our social behavior and our culture.

II.

My annoyance is that the present political attack against our private rights to property is affecting our behavior and standards of propriety in directions I dislike. That's a triple-threat proposition. First, private rights to property are being suppressed and replaced by political forces; second, the scope and degree of property rights affect our cultural mores and behavior differently than do political forces; third, I don't like any of that. I once foolishly thought all that was so obvious as to require no exposition, let alone emphasis. But I was wrong.

Controlling uses of economic goods (and other people are economic goods also) is what property rights (whether private or political) are all about. Control means that one's decisions dominate those of any other person's.

Let me elaborate some aspects of private rights of property—or what are

This previously unpublished lecture was presented at the Southern Economic Association Convention, November 9, 1978, and appears here by permission of the author.

called private property rights. If rights include (1) the right to decide among an unrestricted domain of uses, (2) the right to delegate or sell rights to any other person and (3) the right to obtain salable rights in exchange, then we have, I submit, a regime of private property rights.

Private property is often assumed to require that all these rights to a good be held by one person. However, it is the access to and the exercise of each of the component rights which, if they exist someplace for some people, even if partitioned among several people, or if held as a set in common by a group of people, constitute a private property control system. Not required is that the entire set of rights over a good be held by *one* person. And the components may each be held by different people. So long as the component rights over a good are held by some persons and are salable, the set is "private" property. Of course, the rights should be secure and cheaply transferable.

III.

A feature deserving emphasis is salability of rights. Then each person can decide in which rights, to which goods, to specialize his wealth. If he finds some other party valuing some rights higher than he does, salability permits concentration of rights to people who value them most highly. And this concentrates control over selected resources on those who believe and *bet* they are able to forecast more accurately the values of future uses. But neither (1) forecasting who has superior use selection talent nor (2) having a greater risk bearing willingness requires (3) superior talent in selecting more valuable uses.

People differ in their talents to perform these tasks. This implies potential gains by exploitation of comparative advantages in exercise of these rights. With *transferable* property rights, we can more fully specialize our holding of those particular *components* in which we believe we have a comparative advantage. It is the specialization in particular components of rights that, I believe, warrants emphasizing.

Specialization includes deciding on uses, monitoring effectiveness of uses, risk bearing and forecasting values. Since different resources and uses represent different prospective probability distributions of outcomes and since the outcomes of uses of some goods are more sensitive to monitoring, salable separation of the component rights permits specialization. For example, I believe (bet) that someone else can and will make better decisions about how to use some of my resources. He may have better information, analytical power and energy or even desire to work on that task. He may (indeed, will) divert some of the results of the use of the resources to himself rather than fully to me. Yet the value to me can exceed what I could have achieved had I decided on the uses. Therefore, I invest in assets operated by someone else because of my greater willingness to gamble, or because of differences in beliefs or in costs of borrowing, or in confidence in selecting uses. He is to make the decisions about how the company is operated—how the assembly of inputs is to be used and revised. This requires, as does all specialization, sufficiently effective monitoring to ensure that the agency relation between us is performed as anticipated. And, of course, competition by potential new specialists may provide adequate monitoring.

Yet we are often told that separating use decisions from risk bearing is an undesirable *separation* of "control" from "ownership." An ancient argument for private property is that those who decide on uses should and do bear the market value consequences of their decisions. Else their incentives to make responsible decisions will be weakened. If their decisions and results are not tied together, the rationale for permitting people to control the use of resources by private property rights is lost.

But if the nexus between risk bearing (often called "ownership") and use decision is removed, the presumptive effectiveness and acceptability of private property as a socially useful system of control are reduced. Hence it is argued— and still is by some commissioners of the SEC—that the modern large corporation tends to separate ownership from control and cannot be functioning with proper attention to the feasible market values of the corporation. This assumes the managers' incentives have insufficient dependence on the interests of consumers and stockholders.

Their premise is that managers are less responsive to the interest of consumers and owners than under the classical system of owner-manager–operated firms. The argument is that the insiders' control of the voting rights reduces stockholders to bystanders whose wealth is managed by the insiders. The dispersed voting process renders them as helpless as citizens in controlling politicians—or such at least is the case for all except a few holders of a substantial portion of the corporate stock.

The director-managers use the corporate resources just as government employees can use government resources—except that the explicit code of ethics applicable to government employees has not yet been applied to the corporate managers. That separation of ownership from control destroys the legitimacy of corporate *private* property rights and of the modern corporation as an acceptable means of social control. To restore that lost legitimacy, some substitute principle is required. A sense of social responsibility and high social ethical inculcation must guide the corporate managers who have escaped the yoke of private property rights of corporate owners. This is the modern doctrine of corporate *social* responsibility and governance.

This interpretation was elucidated elegantly and influentially by Adolf Berle in 1933 in *The Modern Corporation and Private Property*. It was the textbook in the first upper division course I took in Economics in 1934. I was much impressed by it. I believed it. I taught it for a long time. I now believe it completely wrong because of at least five fatal flaws: (1) a failure to recognize specialization in performance of private property rights, (2) the failure to recognize the effect of monitoring by covenants and (3) by competition among managers, (4) the widely shared erroneous belief that salable private property stockholder rights in the large corporation are essentially no different than political voting rights and (5) a failure to recognize that a corporation firm is a set of contracts, a contractual coalition of resources each owned by different people—with no owner of the corporation.

IV.

A. *Specialization in Rights*

The confusion about the separation of "control" (use decisions) and "ownership" (bearing risk of market value) probably reflects a failure to understand an elementary principle of social activity—gains of specialization—a principle known to all economists, knowledge of which is almost sufficient to define an economist. That confusion is like the belief that middlemen increase costs to consumers by separating consumers from producers, when in fact the middlemen, by specializing in the communication task, more effectively (at lower cost) correlate the interests and actions of consumers and production. For example, consider the separation of the consumption from the production of bread. A consumer who grew his own wheat, ground it into flour and baked his bread could make bread in whatever form with whatever special features he was able to make. When he permits commercial specialists to intervene and perform these separate tasks in producing bread, does he lose control? Consumption *is* separated from production. But the available variety of bread exceeds his own and comes at lower cost. Separating—specializing in consumption and production—benefits consumers. Consumers still influence production. Though some people believe that producers decide what bread consumers eat, they should ask what determines which bread the baker can profitably continue to produce. With specialization the consumers can "not" bake their cake and yet eat it too.

This separation, more correctly, specialization, in the elements of the rubric of rights called private property does not destroy or weaken the effectiveness of private property. These rights can be held separately by different people more effectively than if they were all held by one person who had all the specialized knowledge and talents of the several people who, under the modern situation, hold and exercise these component rights "separately"—but not independently!

How does the modern corporation establish *interdependence* among interests of the different holders of the separated components of private property so that separation enables *specialization* in property rights with a gain to all parties?

B. *Contractual Covenants*

Ancillary contractual provisions or covenants provide monitoring and interdependence in this agency relationship. Potentially divergent-interest actions are restrained. And insofar as they are not prevented but are foreseeable, the losses are imposed on the party who makes decisions that are less in accord with what the other party would have made had the other party the ability or talent to perceive and execute those more valuable decisions. As more fully articulated by M. Jensen and W. Meckling (*Journal of Financial Economics*, 1976), this is especially pertinent when an outside investor purchases some of the common stock while the inside operator retains the remaining shares.

A "manager-investor-owner" who performs all the functions himself forsakes the potential advantages of specialization. If an employee-manager, despite the best monitoring controls of the stockholder, is expected to divert corporate value to himself, the stockholder will take that into account by a lower wage paid to the employee. The stockholder will not suffer a loss. But insofar as the employee-manager is expected to engage in that diversionary activity, the employer will monitor his actions or performance. To offset that agency monitoring cost, there must be more than compensating advantage in having a separate manager and stockholders. If, for example, the manager can operate the enterprise better than the investor, then the gains from that specialization can more than offset the monitoring costs. In this case the investor and the manager both gain from specialization despite the costs of monitoring potential diversionary tactics of the separate manager. The monitoring costs are real costs, while the diversionary effects are transfers of wealth from the investor to the manager, which transfer is offset by the lower payment accorded the manager initially or afterwards.

Both parties achieve improved positions compared with not being able to separate and specialize in the bearing of residual value and in choosing of uses of enterprise resources. For an introduction to the history of the remarkable development of accounting to police the agency relationship between stockholders and operator-managers, I recommend Ross Watts, "Corporate Financial Statements, A Product of the Market and Political Processes" (*Australian Journal of Management*, 1977). I also recommend a recent and highly amusing and instructive analysis of forces affecting the role of accounting theory and practice by Ross Watts and Gerald Zimmerman, "The Demand and Supply of Accounting Theories: The Market for Excuses" (*Accounting Review*, 1979).

c. *Managerial Monitoring by Competition*

Competition among managers exposes an unanticipated degree of diversions and restrains such diversions and imposes the costs on the perpetrators. I do not here have time to detail the process whereby this intermanagerial competition monitors diversionary activities that work against equity holders. You need only think about competition among economists within and between universities. In the managerial world of the business corporation, the competition, I believe, makes ours pale by comparison.

Not only will this competition tend to control the wages and salaries paid to under- or overperforming managers and detect the better ones, but their results will also be reflected in the capital markets in the values of stock in the companies which they manage. This will reveal to stockholders excessive diversions and induce replacement by conscious direction by stockholders or by intermanager competition within or across firms or by both. I strongly recommend the very perceptive soon-to-be-published analysis of this by E. Fama, "Agency Problems and the Theory of the Firm."

d. *Voting Rights*

It is erroneous to view stockholders as similar to voters in a government. Their rights are significantly different. I have searched the legal literature in vain for a *useful* analysis of the relevant differences between governmental and private property rights. The difference, if any, is typically taken to be something that everyone knows and doesn't require elaboration. That may be true. But it would be helpful if one could formulate an analysis.

Sometimes the distinction is suggested as being in the individuality, i.e., the extent to which *one* individual holds the rights to all possible uses of a good. Then, if the rights are shared with other people, it appears difficult to distinguish between the case of thousands of stockholders of a large corporation and the thousands of citizens of a city government. The process of controlling the use of the resources—through voting to select an agent—is similar in the corporation and in the city. People vote some manager or mayor and supervisors into office. The control appears the same when one looks only at the *act* of voting or the delegation of the use decision. Indeed, fallacious statements to the effect that in a democracy people own the government's resources just as stockholders do in a corporation are induced by that appearance.

However, there is a difference. I cannot sell my share of rights to the Tennessee Valley Authority, the Federal Reserve System, the Post Office or city golf course. If they were privately owned, each of us could decide whether or not to hold rights to them. You might object that a stockholder of General Motors can not sell his interest in only the Cadillac Division; he holds rights in the whole corporation. And the same is true of government property. In a city I cannot divest myself of ownership rights to the city golf course, just as I cannot divest myself as a General Motors stockholder from the Cadillac Division. But the point is that you can't sell even all or any of your interest in a city. I agree that would be possible in a world of many small, independent governments; *if* landowning were a necessary condition for membership in any city, *and if* all consequences of the use of government property were fully thrust on the exchangeable value of the land, *and if* land were salable as private property, *and if* all the land in a given city were homogeneous or easily categorized into classes of land, parallel to types of corporate securities, then holding land would be equivalent to holding corporate stock rights. But I know of no such world, with the possible exception of a community called Buenaventura in California, whose city manager, upon analyzing the role of city government, concluded its role was to do whatever increased the value of the land—a not unreasonable conclusion, for an "open, small city," and possibly even for a large city like New York, which seems bent on the opposite goal.

In any event, that close an approximation to salable rights in government property is hardly to be expected in any real government, even though politicians profess that government resources are owned by the people. But as I still say, I'll sell my rights to Yosemite National Park or Washington, D.C., for a nickel. That absence of salability is the difference, and it is present for rights to corporate wealth.

It is that difference and not a difference in numbers of sharing holders of rights to some resource that makes private property rights different in their effect from government property rights. What difference does salability make? The variable capitalized exchange value depending on one's actions makes an exchangeable right of use influential on how the resources are used.

E. *Specialized Assets of Contract and Stock Holding*

Many of the misconceptions about separation of ownership and control of the corporate firm rest, in part, on a misconception of the firm. A firm is not an alternative to the market, as is commonly asserted. Rather it is a result of contractual activity in the market. It is a set of contracts between several parties about certain of their goods. The activities of the firm are the contractually authorized activities of the parties in the contractual coalition. Obviously no one owns a set of contracts. Instead there are owners of the various assets involved in the contracts. Someone may have a more central role in all the contracts, a common party to all the contracts with rights to a residual value of the organization's value net of other member claims. Then that common party is usually called the "owner of the firm" or "the employer" or the "capitalist." But he doesn't own all the assets used in the coalition. He owns only certain types of the assets used in the contractual organization. If all this seems odd, consider that there are no owners of New York City. There are only owners of the different jointly used resources.

Who, according to the contracts, is assigned the responsibility for selection of uses of the resources jointly used in the firm? Is he also the monitor of behavior, i.e., the judge of whether the services provided by each party are worth continuance of the contract with that party? Yes. By the term "owner," I submit we usually mean the central agent who is common to the contracts with all the cooperating input owners, who is the use director and the monitor, and who also bears the residual value rights. But this sense of "owner" should be carefully noted.

Once upon a time I believed that the residual value claimant was the one who put up sufficient collateral in the form of resources in the firm to cover prospective losses, thereby assuring the other contracting parties of fulfillment of their expectations. More recently, under instruction from colleagues Ben Klein and Earl Thompson, I learned that guarantees of promised prospects could be in the form of any kind of collateral. However, in fact, a special kind of asset in the firm is typically owned by the stockholders of the firm. To see what kind, consider the fact that the promised or anticipated income of each cooperating input may not be realized for one reason or another. Bad luck in the joint output, poor planning or even cheating on the contractual terms by some members imposes losses on others. For some input owners, the alternative income in other still-available activities is virtually the same as initially anticipated in this firm. They cannot be cheated nor suffer substantial capital value loss. However, inputs whose alternative incomes are substantially less than their anticipated earnings here—or of their costs of having been made available to this firm—are sunk by high initial installation costs, which the owner can only *hope* will be recovered by future income in his firm.

In other words, any inputs *specific to this contractual organization* are susceptible, by definition, to large losses in the event of bad luck or dishonest contract behavior by the other parties. It is these inputs for which the owners also will be those whom I have called the owners of the firm. These are the more specific inputs, with a high appropriable quasi rent after they have been made available to the firm. Those asset values are the most affected by the actions of the joint group. Their owners will therefore demand greater control or direction over the group's actions. They will be, or will appoint, the directors and managers. Other input owners whose value would not (or only trivially) be reduced below prior or alternative rewards—since they can cheaply switch someplace else at the same income—do not care as much what the firm does. They exert their control by walking away at little or no loss to themselves. But the specific resource owners are unable to avoid loss by withdrawing their resources. Hence they will, *prior to joining the firm*, contract for power to decide what is done with the resources in this organization.

Under the corporate form of the firm, they are called the stockholders. They own the *specific* resources *and* the resulting variable residual value, *and* they have the right to vote—i.e., to control the use of the specific resources. That voting power does not give them power to control the use of the generalized resources, since the owners of generalized resources can move them to similar valued uses elsewhere. Voting rights in selecting managers and directors are valued by owners of the more specific resources who are, by definition, the stockholders—with none held by the owners of the general resources used in the firm, i.e., labor, power, insurance, land.

Bondholders whose claims are highly specific to the firm will also demand voting rights when their claims are threatened by inadequate assets. The implications of this for industrial democracy—meaning the transfer of voting rights (i.e., property rights) from those owning resources specific to the firm to those who own *generalized* inputs—should not be missed. The proposal for industrial democracy is simply a proposal to transfer wealth of stockholders to employees, or, more accurately, to transfer a share of the stockholders' specific asset wealth to the providers of generalized, nonspecific resources—the employees. And it has no other viable economic function. That is why it does not appear voluntarily. One caution: In calling the employees generalized, I do not mean that some human services may not be specific to the firm. This is what an insider manager may be. Or some employees may have become so specific to the firm by having incurred costs of acquiring information of value only in this firm. They also claim a share of the ownership of the firm, expressed as being entitled to some shares of the common stock or of options or of tenure.

V.

While the preceding analysis is disconcerting news to the Securities and Exchange Commission, especially to its chairman, Harold Williams, if one judges by the thrust of SEC restrictions placed on the marketability of shares and SEC espousals about social responsibility, the analysis nevertheless rests on a solid analytic foundation and is empirically supported. Articles by Henry Manne, to whom much of the prior analysis is due and who is known as the wolf at the house of the three pigs known as S. E. and C., contain more details, and the work like that started by Eugene Fama and his students has brought more thorough understanding of the significance of salability of rights in the capital markets.

So, I revert to the main theme: Under private property rights of people to goods and resources, the anticipated future effects of one's current actions are capitalized *now* in to his wealth and hence his current and future exchange opportunities. Precisely for that reason do I like the name "capitalism" to denote a private property rights regime. It suggests the capitalization into present market-values of foreseeable events of current actions, which induces the private property rights owner to be responsive to the foreseeable distant effects and even the unforeseen effects.

I wish I had invented the name capitalism. It is felicitous and appropriate, certainly more than the term "free enterprise," for even when political restrictions are imposed on some users, there can be free enterprise in political competition. The capitalization effect is a pervasive, powerful characteristic of a private property system, i.e., a capitalist system. When private property rights are weakened, political agents who determine uses of goods are not so keenly subjected to the capitalized value effects of their current decisions. Not only do they affect opportunities of other people, they bear less of the consequences of their decisions about those uses.

I digress momentarily to recognize that the reason we academics analyze a capitalist market system in our classes is that we have a valid theory of many, though certainly not all, of its features. We have no equally strong theory of the operation of the socialist sector. None of that is a justification of capitalist systems. It is a happenstance that the opportunity set, or budget constraint, under private property can be expressed algebraically by a linear function of quantities and prices. That so-called budget constraint is of course a private property constraint. I call it not Walras' Law but Moses' Law—Thou shall not steal. And that analytical formulation plus aid from people like Slutsky, Fisher, Hayek, Samuelson, Friedman, Arrow, Coase and Tobin has taken us a long way. But we have found no comparable constraint for socialism. No Anthony Downs, Bill Niskanen, Buchanan or even Tullock has found a comparable formulation for the socialist or political constraint—nor has one come from among political scientists. That's too bad. If we had been able to formulate the constraints of socialism, rather than of capitalism, we would be teaching the socialist system and probably calling it optimal.

That situation is galling to my few economist acquaintances beyond the Iron Curtain who must persist in seeking a theory of socialist economics. With envy they see how a market system works. They try to figure out how they can make a market system operate behind the Iron Curtain. But when they realize, as they do, that it requires private property rights, they throw up their hands and say, just as we do, that's "*politically* impossible."

VI.

The empirical evidence for behavioral and cultural effects of types of property rights has been slowly, but impressively, accumulating during the past two decades to persuade those who already didn't believe it from casual evidence or who weren't persuaded by Adam Smith's famous chapter on university teachers in non-proprietary institutions. For banks, hospitals, airlines, oyster farms, insurance companies, managers, public utilities, unions and air force bases, systematic empirical evidence is becoming overwhelming. Implied differences occur, and no amount of pleading, rules, directions and instructions completely simulate the incentive response to *salable* capitalization.

VII.

Surprisingly, perhaps, I have so far made few normative statements about property rights. But I will now annoy you with some normative statements—or opinions—or jokes—about the failure to value our private property rights as a necessary condition for the exercise of human rights and, indeed, of freedom.

I am prepared and will go so far as to define the freedom of people in a society by the extent to which they may exercise private property rights over the resources in the community. The greater the set of resources controlled by such rights and the greater the proportion of the community entitled to hold such rights, the greater the freedom (however poor or rich each person may be determines their wealth, not their freedom). Under this definition freedom is but one element in the vector of the good life. We trade *some* of this freedom away for more of other desirable things, just as we do for any other good.

Our political leaders, current and past, sanctimoniously revile foreign politicians for suppressing human rights. Russia, South Africa, Chile, Poland, you name them. And rightly so. But our politicians make a joke of their own actions. At the same time they are criticizing other countries, they are imposing more restraints on our human rights by reducing private property rights, which I regard as fundamental to the exercise of human rights, civil liberties and the dignity of man.

The Russians restrict the ways in which people can use goods, such as by not permitting people to own photocopiers or CB radio or TV resources to communicate with others except by government approval. That is done by prohibiting people from having private property rights to the resources that would enable them to act as they prefer. Yet our politicians are advocating and achieving policies and legislation that are restrictive of our human rights by denying us the exercise or availability of private property rights over some economic resources.

Let us try to laugh at a few of the jokes being played on us. You all know the minimum wage law restricts many teenagers in choosing preferred occupations. The politicians may say minimum wage rates are for the overriding social good. But that, of course, is precisely what Kosygin, Idi Amin and Fernando Marcos say about their proposals. As President Marcos of the Philippines put it last September: "Who is to tell us what our public and social interest is? Not the Americans. The American government restrains its citizens' right to private property over some goods because of some 'social' good. But what the social good is for the Philippines is not an American's conception of the public or social interest. We try to do what is best for our society, expecting a judgment someday from God, not from the Americans." And of course, he is exactly right in what he says, because he could have added, You Americans restrict your cars to 55 MPH; we don't. No other country has such slow speed limits to save gasoline. We Filipinos could condemn your 55 MPH speed limit because while travelling, it forces you to drive an extra hour to save less than $2 an hour and to violate your minimum wage laws. If someone wants to use gasoline that he paid for in order to have faster travel, why not? He's compensated the rest of society for the value of the gasoline consumed.

He could have added, You prohibit manufacture and sale of automobiles that average less than, say, 20 miles per gallon. You are restricting the rights of people to use resources to lead the life-style they wish and can afford—to express their human rights. Why is it not a human right to ride in luxury in a big, powerful car with a quiet motor if the rider prefers that to the other things he could have with the same costliness of resources? Why do you American politicians force Americans to ride in small, uncomfortable and less safe cars that use less gasoline and thereby, with the income saved, induce Americans to eat more food and visit more theaters? That violates their human rights. If people had private property rights to buy and sell resources and decide on their uses, those human rights—their freedom—would not be reduced.

Of course, he would have been right. Our automobile regulations are especially nasty jokes. The automobile is like the horse of olden days, the provider of individual freedom and mobility and protection from politicians. That's why horse thieves were hung. Mobility—to move to another jurisdiction, to live in one and work in another, to escape taxes, to escape forced bussing or to escape controls—is aided by the privately owned automobile. But the auto is the politicians' enemy. Politicians prefer government-operated rapid rail transit—it's fixed in place. How much harder for the public to escape to new jurisdictions! Politicians want heavy taxes on gasoline not only because the demand is inelastic, which makes a gasoline tax a fine substitute for the old salt tax, but a tax also restricts the use of automobiles. What a joke—on us.

We prohibit the selling of labor services to a steel mill that is riskier and noisier than some government employees say it should be. But if workers prefer to work in a noisier mill for higher wages to have bigger cars, more clothes and better education, rather than to work in a quieter place and have fewer clothes and less education, why can't they? Their human rights are denied by the repression of their economic property rights. Others may say that the workers' tastes are wrong, that they should not be so stupid or uninformed to take such a tradeoff or that it should not be available. Many politicians claim that the individual chooser is stupid, ignorant or has no choice and that he has to be protected from his own follies or those of the bad employers—as the Russian workers must be protected from the revolutionary doctrines trying to sprout in Russia. It all depends upon what you pour into the bottle of "social or public interest."

I conclude with Carter's latest cruel joke—his "voluntary" price controls, which are as voluntary as death. They are restrictions on our human rights, our rights to use and exchange resources with others as we see fit. Of course he contends the social interest is overriding and there is no excuse for getting a higher exchange value than he believes appropriate. He thinks—no, be-lieves—inflation is caused by asking higher prices for what we sell. (You might wonder why people will buy at those higher asked prices.) If the "social inter-est" verbiage is persuasive enough to be influential in the price control advo-cacy, it is strong enough to be used in any restraint, even the wearing of blue jeans or Adam Smith neckties.

In sum, the biggest joke I can tell you is the one being played in the United States—on the public—by politicians proclaiming a concern for the human rights of foreigners while deliberately reducing them at home through a politi-cal erosion of private property rights in order to increase the political power of the politically powerful. Now, if that joke can't provoke more laughter than that, I had better stop.

If you wanted to hear funny jokes you should have met in Las Vegas, where the Western Economic Association meets. But if you wanted to hear some good economic analysis you should have known better than to expect it here in Washington, D.C.

ON CORPORATIONS

A VISIT WITH SMITH

Slowly opening the door I peered into Adam Smith's study, preserved as in his time, even to one shocking feature. At the desk was Smith himself, turning pages of his *Inquiry*. Looking up, he said, "Come in. Don't be startled. I am resurrected. Today, 200 years after this publication, I was granted a, shall I say, one-day sabbatical leave. Don't disbelieve me, else I disappear. Be seated. Who are you and from where?"

Recovering my wits, I told him.

He asked, "Where is Los Angeles? In Spain or one of its colonies?"

"No sir, though it once was. It's a large city on the Pacific shores of the United States of America, some 4,000 miles away."

"Ah, yes, the United States, grown that much. I thought it would. You say you arrived yesterday. Surely you must be exhausted. When did you start?"

"Yesterday."

"No. I meant, not from London, but Los Angeles. The ocean voyage must be an ordeal of months."

"Yesterday, sir; I flew from Los Angeles."

"Come now. I am the Angel, not you."

For the next few hours my powers of explanation were taxed to the limit. But he soon grasped—and seemed to believe—electricity, petroleum, aluminum, plastics, radio, television, anesthesia, and what, even to me, was an astonishing history of technological developments. But the electric lights, installed in his study for pilgrims like me, made him believe.

"Tell me about Los Angeles. How large is it?"

"Seven million."

"No, no. I meant not the United States—the City of Los Angeles."

I repeated, "Seven million."

"Seven million! Impossible! The streets, full of garbage, sewage, manure! The air laden with smoke and soot! Seven million people in a city, intolerable

This previously unpublished speech was given at the Mont Pelerin Society meeting, St. Andrews, Scotland, August 1976, and appears here by permission of the author.

noise, and excessive fire danger. I remember what was happening to London and Glasgow."

It was a struggle, but I think I convinced him that cities are now much cleaner, healthier, quieter, safer, and with a better environment than those he had known.

"You say you came alone from London? How did you avoid bandits, high-waymen, and kidnappers? Travel on the ground is dangerous, though flying might be safe from bandits and kidnappers."

My task got harder, but when I described highjackings of airplanes, he was reassured. Society was still believable.

He soon (how could I hide it?) learned I was an economist. The chase was on. He quizzed me on the state of economics and concluded that we had hardly moved beyond his *Inquiry*. (He kept calling it the *Inquiry*.) My counter that theory today is more rigorous, compact, and elegant than in his time evoked, "Elegance is for tailors. How useful is elegant economics?"

I changed the subject. He was astounded that economists were, in 1976, honoring the 200th anniversary of his *Inquiry* by a pilgrimage of economists to St. Andrews. (I did admit that golf had something to do with it.)

He conjectured such honoring might mean that the book's lessons had been learned and applied: "I presume people have learned to avoid tariffs, state-created monopolies, political restrictions on trade, cross-subsidies, low tuition for education, hidden taxes, government growth, inflation, and joint-stock companies. That would make the *Inquiry* worth honoring."

"Well, uh, you see, well, sir, not quite. Like religious pilgrims we are memo-rializing the virtues of an unattainable ideal—a hope. Regrettably all those sins, like the works of the Devil, are still with us in more clever guise."

"Ah, yes, of course, they would persist. Man is still human. Political power is still used. That insidious and crafty animal, vulgarly called a statesman or politician, applies police power to achieve his ends. And why not? All men strive and in different ways. Some are superior in production and exchange, some in intellect, some in military coercion, some in personality and rhetoric. The militarist extolls the military, the politician extolls government and social-ism, the artist extolls art, and the intellectual extolls intellect. Each exploits his own talents as he may."

And he continued, "These skills provide rewards—some by increased pro-duction, and some by exploiting or appropriating wealth. I advocated greater scope for competition in productivity, more in accordance with freer individual choice and exchange and less for compulsion through political forces. But I recognized both exist. I did not expect government—which means the people who are superior at achieving and wielding military or physical force—to sacrifice its power to people superior in productive ability. On the contrary, I expected government to use that power for its own benefit and for those who helped it—the army or the electorate. After all, there is no natural law that denies political power a natural or honored role in competition."

Smith continued: "You say 50 states are joined as the United States. Mobility from state to state should make it difficult for the politically powerful people in any state to tax heavily or control strongly, because the people taxed can easily move to a nearby state; of course, immobile resources like land and buildings could not escape such taxation. But surely, the state politicians would in 200 years have learned to collude and prevent escape by mobility."

"Right. We call it revenue sharing."

"And cartels or government monopoly must surely still exist in many industries: transport, news, and the post office, again because of convenience for the politically powerful."

"Professor Smith, your perception is undiminished. Are you sure you have not been resurrected several times before?"

"No, this is the first. Let me make some more conjectures. You still have zero tuition? The faculty still cleverly argues that it is for the students' benefit?"

"Yes, but I have my students read your timeless exposé in your *Inquiry.*"

"Thank you. That was fun, and it annoyed my colleagues. You said you have refrigeration to preserve foods. I predict, therefore, that the salt tax has disappeared. You say that electrical energy and petroleum are prime sources of energy. I conjecture you now have heavy taxes on electricity and on petroleum. The tax on petrol for your automobile must be a replacement of the old hated salt tax."

"Quite right. Of course, the politicians allege the tax is necessary to save energy."

"Yes, just like in the 18th century. The salt tax conserved salt—they said."

"And," Smith continued, "joint-stock corporations. I wrote that they were typically monopoly privileges and could not otherwise survive except in businesses of routine, requiring large investments. So if they have survived, these must be the ones with monopoly rights. You know, in my time, an *incorporated* joint-stock company was one recognized by the Crown and thereby granted access to the Crown's and Parliament's law and courts for suits. A joint-stock company could be unincorporated, but only because the law of equity outcompeted the common law and accommodated unincorporated companies in their legal problems. Companies were associations, and therefore there was the danger they might suddenly be interpreted as conspiracies by the Crown, which suspected any association as a potential plot or conspiracy against the Crown. Therefore, an association would seek approval by the Crown for exemption from its suspicion."

"Your prediction was not correct, Professor Smith."

"The joint-stock company has become common?"

"Not only common, but by far the major contractual form of association. The private partnership, or copartnery, as you put it, is minor. The advantages of continuity of existence, limited liability with flexible financing and assemblage of funds, have been overwhelming, far exceeding the costs of, as you put it, 'negligence and profusion . . . in the management of the affairs of such a company.'"

"So you say they have very often (rather than seldom, as I wrote) succeeded without exclusive privilege. Why was I wrong? Could it be that the joint-stock company I was analyzing is not the modern 20th-century type of corporation, but the 18th-century corporation? Some in my time were regulated, some were designed for such public services as charity, education, religion, some for improvement of the Airedale species, for ruling golfers by the Ancient and Honorable Golfers of St. Andrews, and for the general purpose of public benefits, as the Crown so cleverly put it."

He continued, "I emphasized that early corporations were monopolistic, politically protected guilds of craftsmen or dwellers of a city whereby the corporate body could make laws—called bylaws—which all in the area must observe. Thus the corporation of glovers, hatters, or coopers controlled all who might exercise their skills—the terms of trade, the quality of product, and the sources of supply—alike with merchants in the burg. Political or governmental power of these corporations was extensive. Corporations were identified with restriction and monopoly tied to the local political power. Yet in my *Inquiry* I did not confuse the joint-stock company with these regulated or government corporations when I suggested the joint-stock company has very limited value and could not survive against the private firm or private copartnery—with unlimited liability and smallness of membership. I wrote, 'that a joint stock company should be able to carry on successfully any branch of foreign trade, when private adventurers can come into any sort of open and fair competition with them, seems contrary to all experience.'

"But," Smith continued, "I did say there was a place for the joint-stock company. If the business is routine and can be reduced to rules, if the endeavor is

654 LAW AND ECONOMICS

for more general utility than the greater part of common trades, and if the amount of capital exceeds that which can easily be collected into a private co-partnery, the joint-stock company has a useful role. I exampled that with banking, turnpikes, canals, and insurance. And I knew of no others, not even refining of copper, lead, glass grinding, linen making, or manufactures."

"Yes, sir," I interjected, "I have studied your great book carefully. But I believe your examples are inappropriate. Banking and insurance are not reducible to simple routine and details. Selecting loans is a delicate, uncertain activity. Insurance is not routine either. Your writings would then appear to say that joint-stock companies would not survive even in those areas with a monopoly privilege."

"Aye."

"But, sir, the other two reasons are really beside the point. What is of 'greater utility' than a common trade? And 'easy' availability of funds empties the analysis. For it says the joint-stock company will be perfectly reasonable where absence of easy collectibility of funds does not permit a private copartnery. Collecting one pound for a venture that looks profitless is hard; collecting a million for one that looks profitable is easy. Did you, sir, with all due respect, mean that only for small ventures is the private copartnery feasible?"

He was silent. I continued: "What might have misled you when you wrote, '. . . the greater part of these proprietors seldom pretend to understand any thing of the business of the company; and when the spirit of faction happens not to prevail among them, give themselves no trouble about it, but receive contentedly such half yearly or yearly dividends as the directors think proper to make them. This total exemption from trouble and from risk, beyond a limited sum, encourages many people to become adventurers in joint stock companies, who would, upon no account, hazard their fortunes in any private copartnery' [p. 699]. I will say, Sir, that several modern-day economists who profess to the opinion your work is obsolete use exactly that same argument as an alleged weakness of the modern corporation."

Smith ignored that last bit of byplay. He responded, sticking to the subject: "Upon reconsideration, I see I should never have written that. How empty. What does it mean to 'receive contentedly,' and what does it mean for directors to pay what they 'think proper'? No, there is nothing there of content. Nothing to deduce negligence and profusion. Instead, there is the contrary. I should have realized that stockholder-investors will invest only as much as will give them at least a prospective competitive return. Foreseeable negligence, profusion, carelessness, or diversion of funds will lower what investors are willing to pay for a share and will impose the cost of managers' negligence on the initial promoter. He, in turn, will pay less to managers who compete for access to offices of 'negligence and profusion.' The question then is whether the advantages of the joint-stock company are sufficiently great to offset that negligence and whether the investor-stockholders have sufficiently effective means to detect and restrain negligence to warrantable proportions. If so, the joint-stock company may flourish. If not, it would not. And it has."

Smith continued, "I should have recognized that even in the 18th century the unincorporated joint-stock company continued to grow despite the restriction on incorporated joint-stock companies in the Bubble Act of 1720. The advantages of limited liability, continuity, and access to courts were achieved by privately executed deeds of settlement among stockholders and notice to the company's creditors of this limited liability. The Courts of Equity, rising above the rigidity of the common law, recognized these deeds, expanded the law of agency, and permitted the unincorporated joint-stock companies to have access to courts for suits and settlements. Despite the Bubble Act, which restricted incorporations of new joint-stock companies with limited liability, unincorporated joint-stock companies continued to grow and flourish."

I interrupted him. "Sir, you will be gratified to learn the Bubble Act was repealed in 1820, despite the century-long interim of pontifications by politicians alleging imagined faults and dangers of joint-stock companies. The current modern-day assault on the multinational corporation and the vertically integrated or so-called concentrated industry is no more sophisticated or accurate than those earlier attacks on the joint-stock company. Not until 1862 was the joint-stock company—as a company of venturers sharing jointly held rights to the value of a common stock, or pool, of resources—recognized formally as a right rather than as a privilege granted by the government. That Parliamentary Act of 1862 culminated a series of acts to repeal the old Bubble Act of 1720 and to permit incorporation of joint-stock companies with limited liability under the law."

I hurried on, seeking some graceful explanation of Smith's falsified forecast. "The 18th-century joint-stock company differed from the modern one in the votes held by stockholders. From one vote per person, it moved to one per unit share of the equitable interest in the corporation wealth."

Smith responded, "The one-vote, one-person rule was a feature of the regulated corporations—guilds and burgs—for establishing rules under which members as well as nonmembers could or could not conduct trade on their own account. These were governmental bodies, dispensations and privileges granted by the Crown to further foreign policy, foreign trade, or domestic order. Many chartered or regulated corporations were composed of merchants and craftsmen, who were given these governmental privileges in return for aid to the Crown, either directly or indirectly, as sources of support alternative to the landed gentry and nobility on whom the Crown could not rely. The one-vote-per-person rule in the regulated corporations was initially carried over to the joint-stock companies, which at first were a series of single ventures of ships but later were a continuing stock of wealth. As the joint-stock of wealth developed, with disproportionate shares by stockholders, the one-vote-per-man system moved toward one-vote, one-share. Indeed, the one-vote, one-person rule was widely shed by the time of the *Inquiry* . . . though not fully."

I interjected, "Sir, the one-vote, one-man system might have been injurious to the joint-stock company, but the matter calls for care. The modern joint-stock company has a variety of investors, not all with voting rights. Not all common stock has voting rights, though sharing in every other respect the identical rights. Some investors hold voteless warrants, as rights to subscribe to common stock. Some with preferred stock have interests exceedingly akin to common stockholders, or they may be essentially bondholders. In either case these are without voting rights. Yet all share in the fortunes of the company. Though all can be damaged by unforeseen negligence and diversion, so long as some people have voting rights whose interests are parallel to those without voting rights, incentives exist to monitor and restrain the manager.

"The one-vote, one-share principle is not the only way interests of investors are protected. In the modern joint-stock company, matters are even more complicated. Votes can be separated from the common stock—by proxy—ostensibly without sale or without consideration. Though outright sale of voting rights is illegal, transfers via proxy rights, without explicit consideration, are legal. Also, creation of shares of equitable interest without votes—in effect, sale of votes to other shareholders—is legal. As usual our politicians, administrators, and courts do not always understand what is happening and resist developments until they become so common under some other guise that they are finally sanctioned, as was done for the joint-stock, limited liability company. And then the sanction or recognition is incorrectly proclaimed—in a self-serving intent—to be a political privilege, as if political power creates that contractual institution."

I continued to monopolize the discussion. "Sir, as you said, politicians exercise power to obtain wealth by exploiting the joint-stock corporation. They do so by arguing that the corporation is a creature of the state, requiring some service from the state without which it could not exist. But why one should have a contractual right only if authorized by the state is hard for me to understand. Except, of course, that requiring the government's charter of incorporation is simply a method of exercising political power over economic wealth and individual liberty."

Smith smiled and said, "It's the old variety of forms of competition for wealth, so you should not be surprised that some people compete in ways which Nature permits, much as I might dislike those ways. Clearly, my prognosis of the joint-stock company was wrong. I accurately identified abuses and features of the regulated and chartered corporations, which were essentially monopolistic governmental bodies. However, I underestimated the flexibility of the joint-stock company as a means of obtaining funds, and its advantages of limited liability, of continuity, and of providing a variety of types of investment interests. And especially did I not foresee its ability to anticipate and control negligence and profusion. Perhaps if I had foreseen the extent to which a market for saleable shares of stock in various companies at publicly known prices—the formal stock market—would be developed, and the extent to which control would be closely related to equitable interests, and the extent to which the costs of foreseeable negligence and profusion would be borne by the parties themselves, and the extent to which the institutions of agency would be developed, I would have been optimistic about the joint-stock company."

"Ah, but Professor Smith, I do believe your pessimistic view of the joint-stock company is correct, but for a different, more general reason. My pessimism arises from the ability of the politically powerful to extract private wealth. Joint-stock corporations are taxed by lawsuits, regulations, and restrictions on their permissible activity. National incorporations, instead of state incorporations, are proposed to whose benefit you can imagine. Political power directs the wealth of joint-stock companies to uses congenial to the politically powerful. It engages in regulation of products, of contracts assigning liabilities or risks, of wages and prices, of occupational safety and hazards. It places restrictions on the saleability of shares of stocks, on rights to acquire stock in other companies, on employee selection, retention, and termination, on pension funding. It specifies detailed data reporting, industrial democracy, and labor codetermination laws and makes national planning proposals presaging even greater mercantilist controls. These all are revocations and reductions of private contractual agreements which make the future of the private property market system, and hence of the joint-stock company, not one about which to be optimistic."

I continued, "People are less certain as to what contractual terms the courts and legislature will tolerate. The value of corporation stock—indeed, of all contractual responsibilities and agreements—is being eroded. The politically motivated legislation in Europe for corporate codetermination is not simply to transfer wealth of stockholders to employees. The rights assigned to employees will not be saleable. Capital valuation and transferability of wealth will be destroyed; foreseeable future events will less fully be capitalized and impressed on present actors. The result will enhance the politically powerful and reduce the role of individual private preferences. The attack is on the institution of private property and on the right to make private contractual agreements, not on the facades, such as the large corporation or concentrations of wealth. Not just an appropriation of current wealth, but reduction of the scope of private property, private contract, and the market price as a social, economic control is the effect. In contrast to some government actors who simply appropriate private wealth, the modern attack is on the private property system itself. The control of wealth and behavior of people by voluntary contractual exchange values of alienable property in the market is being replaced by political force. Capitalism is being weakened.

"Professor Smith, you were right in your pessimistic prognosis for the joint-stock company. But right, not for the reasons you state, but for a reason that is transparent throughout your whole book—the conflict and competition from the politically powerful, who are not only rule enforcers but rule makers whose tolerance for established private property is low. More than the corporation, the more basic institutions—private property and contractual agreements—are being weakened. Capitalism is being destroyed. The situation has been excellently stated by two perceptive economists:

> Bureaucrats and politicians can and do use their positions in government to bestow benefits on others, but they do so in exchange for votes, for campaign funds, for favors, for job offers, etc., all of which yield benefits indirectly.
>
> Individuals who have rights benefit from stability in those rights. The more confident owners are that they will be able to retain rights, the more valuable those rights will be. . . . Stability in private rights is by its very nature a constraint on what government (i.e., bureaucrats and politicians) can do! The more difficult it is to enact laws, issue administrative rules and regulations, or make court decisions which revoke or abrogate individual rights, the more restricted is the domain of the bureaucrat and politician. To

the extent that government's power to revoke or abrogate rights is limited, the market for the services of individuals in government is limited.

Revocation and abrogation of rights is the currency in which politicians and bureaucrats deal. Like all of us, they are constantly searching for ways to expand the market for their services. To do so, they must effectively break down the system of private rights because it limits their market. Our individual interest in having rights which are immutable, is in direct conflict with the interest of bureaucrats and politicians who want to be able to alter rights at will."[1]

Smith smiled tolerantly and remarked, "Very well put. But you used a term 'capitalism.' What an ingenious expression. Congratulations. It emphasizes that under a private property system any change in the *capital* value of any resource, human or nonhuman—the present market valuation of the foreseen future consequences of an act—will be impressed on the owner. Immediate market *capitalization* of future consequences into the present price makes the owner more heedful of what to do with his resource. Responsibility is sharpened as uses of a resource are made more fully responsive to the value of foreseeable future consequences of any action. Not only the future consequences but the consequences for anyone in the public who might have a use for that resource are impressed on the owner through the effects on the marketable capital value of that resource. I wish I had thought of that expression—'capitalism.' What a beautifully expressive name. Who devised it?"

I could not bring myself to disillusion him. Instead I said, "It's my time for golf at the Old Course. You will join me? Good. You can test some modern clubs and balls. Let's go."

BIBLIOGRAPHY

The foregoing account of a visit to Adam Smith's study is based on records in the following:

Blackstone, William. *Commentaries on the Laws of England*. Vol. 8. London, 1800.
Cooke, C. A. Corporation, Trust and Company. Cambridge: Harvard University Press, 1951.
Dienstag, Mark A. "Adam Smith and the Eighteenth Century Company." Manuscript. University of Miami School of Law, 1976.

1. Michael Jensen and William Meckling, "Can the Corporation Survive?" University of Rochester Public Policy Working Paper Series #76-4, May 1976.

Holdsworth, W. S. *A History of English Law.* Vol. 8. New York: Little, Brown and Co., 1926.

Hunt, Bishop C. *The Development of the Business Corporation in England, 1800–1867.* Cambridge: Harvard University Press, 1936.

Jensen, Michael, and William Meckling. "Theory of the Firm: Managerial Behavior, Agency Costs and Ownership Structure." *Journal of Financial Economics* (1976): 305–60.

———. "Can the Corporation Survive?" University of Rochester Public Policy Working Paper Series #76-4, May 1976.

Levi, Leone. *The History of British Commerce and the Economic Progress of the British Nation, 1763–1878.* 2nd ed. J. Murray, 1880.

Manne, Henry. "Some Theoretical Aspects of Share Voting." *Columbia Law Review* 64 (1964): 1427.

———. "Mergers and the Market for Corporate Control." *Journal of Political Economy* 73 (1965): 110.

———. *Insider Trading and the Stock Market.* New York: Free Press, 1966.

———. "Our Two Corporation Systems: Law and Economics." *Virginia Law Review* 53 (March 1967): 199–223.

Pollock, Frederick, and Frederick Maitland. *The History of English Law before the Time of Edward I.* 2nd ed. Cambridge: Cambridge University Press, 1898.

Scott, William R. *The Constitution and Finance of English, Scottish and Irish Joint-Stock Companies to 1720.* Vols. 2 and 3. Cambridge: Cambridge University Press, 1910.

Smith, Adam. *An Inquiry into the Nature and Causes of the Wealth of Nations.* New York: Modern Library, 1937.

Williston, Samuel. "History of the Law of Business Corporations before 1800." *Harvard Law Review* 2 (1888): 105–24, 149–66.

CONSTITUTIONAL BASELINES BY VIRTUAL CONTRACT

A GENERAL THEORY AND ITS APPLICATION TO REGULATORY TAKINGS

WESLEY J. LIEBELER AND ARMEN ALCHIAN

Cooperation [a legal rule], if it is to be defensible, must be reconstructible as the outcome of a rational choice by the parties whose behavior and well-being is to be affected by it.[1]

I. Introduction

Time and time again the Supreme Court has been asked to decide when state regulation runs afoul of the Takings Clause, which bans taking private property for public use without just compensation.[2] Despite many opportunities, the Court has failed to articulate a coherent concept of the Takings Clause.[3] The main reason for this lack of coherence is the Court's failure to define the terms of the Clause itself, or even to recognize the need to establish the *constitutional* meaning of those terms, which would provide a baseline standard against which the Court could decide whether a particular state regulation constituted a taking or not.

The principal terms at issue here, undefined by the Constitution itself, are

Reprinted from *Supreme Court Economic Review* 3 (1993): 153–88; originally published by George Mason University Press. Copyright 1993 by the University of Chicago Press.

Professor Liebeler thanks his classes in Law and Economics and in Constitutional Political Economy for the last two years. They suffered, but contributed much to the analysis reflected in this article. He also thanks an anonymous referee for helpful comments, and acknowledges his intellectual debt to David Gauthier.

1. Jules L. Coleman, *Afterword: The Rational Choice Approach to Legal Rules*, 65 Chi Kent L Rev 177, 182 (1989) ("Coleman, *Afterword*").

2. US Const, Amend V.

3. The Court has often admitted it has not been able to develop any "set formula" for determining when "justice and fairness" require that economic injury caused by public action be compensated. See *Penn Central Transportation Co. v City of New York*, 438 US 104, 124 (1978); *Kaiser Aetna v United States*, 444 US 164, 175 (1979); *Hodel v Virginia Surface Min. and Reclamation Assn., Inc.*, 452 US 264, 295 (1981); *Keystone Bituminous Coal Ass'n v DeBenedictis*, 480 US 470, 495 (1987).

"private property," "taking," and "just compensation." The Court instinctively turns to state law for definitions,[4] but the constitutional meaning of those terms cannot be left to state law without emasculating the Takings Clause. If a state can change the meaning of these terms as it sees fit, the Clause places no limits on state power. There must be a constitutional baseline definition of private property and a definition of taking that specifies how and how much a state can change the definition of property without being required to pay.

The most obvious basis on which to define the terms of the Takings Clause is the common law at the time it was adopted, since the common law provided the principal legal context for the Constitution. But it is widely claimed that defining private property in its Blackstonian sense would freeze the common law and "allow no room for change in response to changes in circumstances."[5] Many proponents of a "changing" or "living" Constitution argue against any disciplined definition of constitutional terms on similar grounds.[6] For two reasons, this problem is greatly exaggerated in takings cases. First, the Court does not focus precisely enough on the role the state seeks to perform through the regulation at issue. Second, there has been a general failure to appreciate the relevance of recent advances in applying the economic theory of contracting to land-use conflict, which, like many contracting problems, results from the specialization of particular assets to each other. These points strongly undercut the argument that reliance on the common law to define constitutional baselines allows no room for change in response to changing circumstances. We discuss each point in more detail before proceeding with our discussion of the Supreme Court's recent decision in the *Lucas* case.[7]

A. *The Roles of the State in Regulating Property*

1. The state has been deeply involved in defining the existing structure of private property rights. This was done and continues to be done largely under the processes of the common law, subject to constitutional constraints. We put the process of adjusting land-use conflicts through nuisance law in this category. We consider the nature of this process more fully in Part V.

---

4. See, for example, *Lucas v South Carolina Coastal Council*, 112 S Ct 2886, 2900–01 (1992).

5. Id at 2921 (Stevens dissenting) (quoting Justice Marshall's concurring opinion in *PruneYard Shopping Center v Robins*, 447 US 74, 93 [1980]).

6. See 112 S Ct at 2921–22 (Stevens dissenting); *Miller v Schoene*, 276 US 272 (1928), discussed below in text following note 56 and in text following notes 100–101.

7. *Lucas v South Carolina Coastal Council*, 112 S Ct 2886 (1992).

2. Some regulation simply enforces existing private property rights more effectively. Common law nuisance doctrine prevented people from using their land in ways that unreasonably interfered with their neighbors, for example, by emitting unreasonable amounts of noise, smoke, dust, etc.[8] Much of today's environmental regulation provides more effective ways of doing this under circumstances in which the "neighbor" may be miles away and what constitutes an "unreasonable" emission might be less than it once was because of the interrelated acts of other persons.[9] Such enforcement of existing property rights is the ultimate expression of the police power. Since it does not involve a taking, compensation is not required.

3. Regulation may create new private property rights where none existed before. Examples include private property rights in the electromagnetic spectrum, patents, copyrights, making "free" roads into "pay" roads, and the creation of private property rights in land to protect beavers from overkilling.[10] Compensation is not required in such contexts because private property was not taken; the Takings Clause does not prohibit the "taking" of communal or state property. As with environmental regulation, the state has great leeway for adaptation without running afoul of the Takings Clause.

4. The state may use regulation in its role as an agent to make deals that could not be made privately because of high transaction costs. Examples would include the use of eminent domain for highway construction, zoning and similar land-use regulations, the transfer of two parcels of land from David Lucas to the State of South Carolina for beach protection purposes, or a statute providing for the destruction of infected cedar trees to protect apple orchards.[11] It is in such contexts that the Takings Clause is most important.

Each transfer or reassignment of rights in this last category will constitute a taking, many of which will require explicit compensation. In some cases, however, implicit in-kind compensation will render explicit compensation unnecessary.[12] In other cases, the value of the amount taken will be so small that the

---

8. See, for example, *Sturges v Bridgman*, 11 Ch D 852 (1879), discussed in Ronald Coase, *The Problem of Social Cost*, 3 J L & Econ 1, 8–10 (1960) ("Coase, *The Problem of Social Cost*").

9. See Tom Horton, *Chesapeake Bay—Hanging in the Balance*, National Geographic 2–35 (June 1993).

10. See Harold Demsetz, *Toward a Theory of Property Rights*, 57 Am Econ Rev 347 (1967) ("Demsetz, *Property Rights*").

11. For the last example, see *Miller v Schoene*, 276 US 272 (1928).

12. See Richard A. Epstein, *Takings: Private Property and the Power of Eminent Domain* 195–215 (Harvard, 1985) ("Epstein, *Takings*").

transaction costs of effecting compensation would exceed the social benefits of making it. Both these exceptions to the requirement of explicit compensation provide considerable room for government to respond to changing circumstances while remaining within the bounds of the traditional common law definition of private property.

B. Specialized Assets and Opportunistic Behavior

Recent developments in the economic theory of contracting also help us understand why defining private property in terms of the historic common law will not prevent the law from changing in response to changing circumstances. Assets are specialized if their value is interdependent—if the value of each depends on what is done by or with the other—and there are significant transaction costs involved in making them independent, i.e., in moving one set of assets to another otherwise less preferred location. Consider the relationship between a cement plant owned by one party and land owned by others on which the plant necessarily deposits noise and dirt if it operates.[13] Other examples would include cedar trees located close to apple orchards while harboring a disease fatal to apple trees,[14] Catholics and non-Catholics in a jurisdiction that bans contraceptives[15] or in one that requires children between the years of eight and sixteen to attend public schools,[16] or an unborn child and its putative mother.[17]

Such specialization creates possibilities for opportunistic behavior in which one party to the relationship attempts to extract wealth from the other that could not have been extracted absent the interdependence. For opportunistic behavior to occur a person must have committed specialized wealth to another party in such a way that the other party's behavior can affect the first person's subsequent wealth.[18] The specializer cannot then walk away from the relationship and be just as well off somewhere else. "An economist would say that the first party's wealth is not entirely 'salvageable' elsewhere; it will be lower if the second party doesn't behave as expected."[19] When assets are specialized in this way, one or both parties can extract wealth from the other until the party from

13. See *Boomer v Atlantic Cement Co.*, 26 NY2d 219, 257 NE2d 870 (1970).

14. See *Miller v Schoene*, 276 US 272 (1928).

15. See *Griswold v Connecticut*, 381 US 479 (1965).

16. See *Pierce v Society of Sisters*, 268 US 510 (1925).

17. See *Roe v Wade*, 410 US 113 (1973).

18. See Armen A. Alchian and William R. Allen, *Exchange & Production: Competition, Coordination, & Control* 170 (Wadsworth, 3rd ed, 1983).

19. Id.

whom wealth is being extracted finds it advantageous to move his assets else-where. Economists call that amount a quasi rent—the return to an asset in ex-cess of that required to keep it in its current use. Thus, opportunistic behavior might be called "quasi-rent seeking."

Assets can be specialized by contract,[20] by location (as in land-use conflicts), or in other ways, as the above examples suggest. In each case, however, the spe-cialization is a function of the high costs of making the value of the assets independent of each other.

Rational people will not specialize assets to each other by contract without taking precautions against future opportunistic behavior. They have three basic options: (1) contract terms guarding against opportunism, (2) ownership verti-cal integration, or (3) not making the contract. The first two measures are ex ante (before-hand) precautions taken to reduce the possibility of future wealth loss.[21] In land-use conflicts, assets are specialized by location, which creates precisely the same problem—opportunistic attempts to appropriate wealth—that is asso-ciated with specialized (reliance) assets in contract situations. Opportunistic be-havior is a more serious problem in land-use conflicts than in contract cases, however, in part because land's relative immobility exacerbates the problem of specialization and in part because locational specialization, unlike contract spe-cialization, does not require the advance consent of affected parties. We can buy a parcel of land next to you without your consent, but we cannot make a noncon-sensual contract with you. Moreover, ex ante precautions available in the com-petitive contracting process are typically less available in land-use conflicts. Ex ante ownership integration might be available in some land-use cases if spe-cialized parcels could be purchased before their owners become aware of the specialization problem. But absent earlier ownership integration (coupled with subdivision, for example), ex ante contract solutions to land-use conflicts are much more difficult to effect than they would be in the typical contract case.[22]

20. See Benjamin Klein, Robert G. Crawford, and Armen A. Alchian, *Vertical Integra-tion, Appropriable Rents, and the Competitive Contracting Process*, 21 J L & Econ 297 (1978) ("Klein, Crawford and Alchian").

21. An example of ex ante precautions are the orders Odysseus gave to have himself tied to the mast—not to be released even on his own orders—and wax placed in the ears of his men as they passed the island on which lived the Sirens, the "enchanters of all man-kind." See Homer, *The Odyssey*, Book XII.

22. For an example of problems caused by specialization and attempted opportunis-tic behavior, see Wesley J. Liebeler, *What Are the Alternatives to Chicago?* 1987 Duke L J 879, 880–88 (discussing *Aspen Skiing Co. v Aspen Highlands Skiing Corp.*, 472 US 585 [1985]).

The difficulties in arranging private ex ante solutions to land-use conflicts lead us to conclude that nuisance law should be viewed as a substitute for the ex ante contractual precautions the personae in the competitive contracting process would take before entering contracts involving specialized (reliance) assets. Nuisance law can be seen as a set of virtual contract provisions that existing owners of land involved in conflicting uses would have made had they been able to contract for them ex ante, i.e., before they found themselves in the specialized relationship that underlies all land-use conflicts.

To be an effective substitute for these ex ante contracts, nuisance law must be structured from the point of view of the owners of the land involved in conflicting uses *before they know they are owners of particular pieces of land*. While we metaphorically speak of such a position as a state of nature, we are simply proposing an exercise of the mind (involving role reversal) to discern what contracts rational persons would probably have made to deal with ex post problems created by specialization, if they could have made such contracts before they actually became involved in those situations. Coherent answers to these questions—which strikingly track the common law—will help us understand why the historic common law provides appropriate constitutional baselines for conflicting resource uses. While we cast our discussion in terms of land-use conflict, the underlying ex ante analysis applies to a wide range of constitutional issues, the scope of which is only suggested in the examples of specialized relationships discussed above.[23]

In Part IV we sketch the parameters of a property rights system that would emerge from ex ante contracts made by rational persons exercising equal liberty under zero transaction costs, knowing they would face generalized ex post specialization caused by high transaction costs. The ex ante or idealized result of these contracts would be a perfectly competitive equilibrium under which the value of interaction was maximized to each person, subject to equal rights in others. This equilibrium would be the result of contracts by each person to forgo actions for which the marginal social cost exceeds marginal social benefit and to permit to others actions for which the marginal social benefit

23. See text accompanying notes 9–13 above. For additional issues to which the ex ante analysis can be applied, see Cass R. Sunstein, *Lochner's Legacy*, 87 Col L Rev 873 (1987), which discusses the baseline problem in the context of economic regulation, campaign financing, statutory "entitlement" benefits, state action, judicial review of agency inaction, standing, race and gender discrimination, and the nature of individual preference.

exceeds marginal social cost. Such contracts, however, place each person in a prisoner's dilemma—it is in everyone's individual self-interest to break these contracts *no matter what anyone else does.*

This would be a matter of little consequence if ex post transaction costs were negligible. But they are not. In the ex ante contracting position, people know they will face generalized ex post specialization caused by high transaction costs and that each person will have a strong incentive to break the ex ante contracts designed to solve the opportunism problems created by ex post specialization. To solve these problems they would contract ex ante for ex post property rights designed to bring the results of ex post interaction as close to the ex ante perfectly competitive equilibrium as is cost effectively possible. This can best be done by a property rights system that concentrates the costs and benefits of human actions on those who take the actions, i.e., by efficiently internalizing externalities.[24] A commitment to such concentration of costs and benefits would also discourage rent seeking—attempts to structure involuntary transactions to make some people richer by making others poorer—the very nature of which is to deconcentrate costs and benefits by allocating benefits to some people and their costs to others.[25]

They would also adopt ex ante precautions against ex post opportunism. The most effective precaution would prohibit involuntary ex post interaction—typically caused by legal rules or externalities from the voluntary acts of others—that could not be reconstructed as a voluntary contract, perhaps ex ante, between those who would be affected by such interaction.[26] Since rational people would not interact unless they believed it would make them better off, we would not expect them to contract ex ante to accept ex post interaction that would make them poorer than they would have been in its absence, once again possibly viewed ex ante.

We claim the terms of the virtual ex ante contracts described above would track the common law quite closely;[27] they also illuminate the underlying principles of that body of law. To the extent this ex ante analysis is consistent with

---

24. See Demsetz, *Property Rights* at 348 (cited in note 10).

25. See James M. Buchanan, Gordon Tullock, and Robert D. Tollison, eds., *Toward a Theory of the Rent Seeking Society* (Texas A&M, 1980).

26. See Coleman, *Afterword* at 182 (cited in note 1).

27. See Epstein, *Takings* at 22–24 (cited in note 12); *Bryant v Lefever*, 4 CPD 172, 175–76 (1879).

those principles, it may inform the articulation of constitutional baselines to evaluate the actions of courts and legislatures alike. If those agencies stay within the terms of those principles, they can alter private property relationships without effecting takings. If they move beyond them compensation will be required.

In Parts II and III we develop the facts and opinions in *Lucas v South Carolina Coastal Council*,[28] a recent regulatory takings case that we use as a context for our discussion. We develop the core of our ex ante analysis in Part IV, using as context the facts in *Boomer v Atlantic Cement Co.*,[29] and expand it in Part V by applying it to *Lucas* and to *Miller v Schoene*,[30] which is well known for its strikingly expansive concept of the police power.

II. The Facts and Lower Court Opinions in *Lucas*

In December of 1986 David H. Lucas paid $975,000 for two residential lots on the Isle of Palms near Charleston, South Carolina. Lucas was a contractor and manager and part owner of a residential development on the island. The lots, on which Lucas intended to build single-family houses, were two of the last four vacant lots in the development.

South Carolina first began to regulate coastal development in 1977. The Coastal Zone Management Act, which was first enacted that year, required owners of coastal zone land that qualified as a "critical area" (beaches and immediately adjacent sand dunes) to obtain permits for new uses from the newly created South Carolina Coastal Council. The lots Lucas bought, however, were not in the critical area defined by the 1977 statute. He was free to build single-family housing on the lots when he bought them in 1986. Since they were part of a development that was coming to an end, such housing had already been built on most of the lots in the area.

In 1988 the state adopted the Beachfront Management Act (BMA), which absolutely forbade the construction of permanent habitable structures in a zone that included Lucas's lots. Lucas promptly sued in state court, claiming the BMA took his property without just compensation. He did not challenge the BMA's validity "as a lawful exercise of South Carolina's police power, but contended that the Act's complete extinguishment of his property's value entitled

28. 112 S Ct 2886 (1992).
29. 26 NY2d 219, 257 NE2d 870 (1970).
30. 276 US 272 (1928).

him to compensation regardless of whether the legislature had acted in furtherance of legitimate police power objectives."[31] The trial court found there were no restrictions to prevent building single-family houses on the lots when Lucas bought them. In its view, by permanently prohibiting such use, the BMA "deprive[d] Lucas of any reasonable economic use of the lots, . . . eliminated the unrestricted right of use, and render[ed] them valueless."[32] It found Lucas's lots had been taken, and ordered the Coastal Council to pay just compensation of $1,232,387.50.

The South Carolina Supreme Court reversed, based on Lucas's concession that the BMA was "properly and validly designed to preserve . . . South Carolina's beaches."[33] It believed a regulation designed to prevent a serious public harm did not require compensation regardless of its effect on the property's value.[34] Two dissenters believed the state could prohibit noxious uses, like nuisances, without compensation, but found that the BMA was not primarily designed to prevent such activity. Thus, they believed "compensation will be necessary when the act deprives an owner of economically viable use of his land."[35]

Recalling the categories set forth in Part I.A above, we can facilitate the analysis of *Lucas* by asking whether the BMA was (1) addressed to a legitimate nuisance problem, (2) designed to enforce existing property rights more effectively, (3) aimed at creating new private property rights where none existed before, or (4) an example of the state's "brokerage" function—the transfer of existing rights that could not be made privately because of high transaction

---

31. Id at 2890. We quote the Court's description of the Lucas claim in full to show how the position Lucas took in the state court, albeit based on *Agins v Tiburon*, 447 US 255 (1980), may have hindered correct analysis, because compensation is typically not required if the state acts within the scope of its police power. The police power is sometimes confused with the public use requirement. "Meeting the public use limitation does not allow the state to take private property without just compensation. Satisfying the police power limitation, in contrast, does allow it to take without compensation." Epstein, *Takings* at 109 (cited in note 12). To be more precise, we might say that satisfying the police power permits the state to *act*, rather than *take*, without compensation. Technically there is no taking if the state stays within its police power.

32. 112 S Ct at 2890.

33. Id; *Lucas v South Carolina Coastal Council*, 404 SE2d 895, 896 (SC 1991).

34. 112 S Ct at 2890.

35. 404 SE2d at 906.

costs. Clearly the BMA was not addressed to item (2) or (3). Nor, as Justice Scalia suggested[36] and as the South Carolina Supreme Court found on remand,[37] was there a legitimate nuisance issue involved. This leaves the conclusion that the BMA was an example of the state's brokerage function. The state wished to acquire land from Lucas and others to improve the quality of its beaches. Since Lucas's loss was not so small that the costs of effecting compensation would exceed its social benefits, and since Lucas was hardly compensated in kind, compensation should have been paid according to our analysis.

III. *Lucas* in the Supreme Court

The United States Supreme Court reversed in an opinion by Justice Scalia, which was joined by the Chief Justice and Justices White, O'Connor, and Thomas. Justice Kennedy concurred. Justices Blackmun and Stevens each wrote dissenting opinions. Justice Souter would have dismissed the grant of certiorari for reasons not relevant here.[38]

A. *The Opinion for the Court*

Justice Scalia noted first that prior to Justice Holmes's opinion in *Pennsylvania Coal Co. v Mahon*,[39] the Takings Clause was thought to reach only a "direct appropriation" of property or "the functional equivalent of a 'practical ouster of [the owner's] possession.'"[40] In *Mahon*, however, the Court saw the Clause would be meaningless if government could redefine property through repeated, uncompensated qualifications. Holmes believed "the natural tendency

---

36. 112 S Ct at 2901: "It seems unlikely that common-law principles would have prevented the erection of any habitable or productive improvements on [Lucas's] land; they rarely support prohibition of the 'essential use' of land."

37. *Lucas v South Carolina Coastal Council*, 424 SE2d 484 (SC 1992) ("Coastal Council has not persuaded us that any common law basis exists by which it could restrain Lucas's desired use of his land; nor has our research uncovered any such common law principle.").

38. Because of uncertainty whether Lucas had been deprived of his entire economic interest in the property, Justice Souter did not believe this was a good case in which to decide what constitutes total deprivation and the relationship between total deprivation and nuisance abatement. 112 S Ct at 2926. There was also considerable exchange on the question of whether Lucas had exhausted his administrative remedies. We do not discuss this question since it is not relevant to the substance of the takings claim addressed by the Court.

39. 260 US 393 (1922).

40. 112 S Ct at 2892.

of human nature [would be] to extend the qualification more and more until at last private property disappear[ed]."[41] He concluded that "while property may be regulated to a certain extent," regulation would be a taking if it "goes too far."[42] Unfortunately the Court has never identified the boundaries of this limitation.

Justice Scalia noted two areas, however, where the Court had found regulatory action to be compensable "without case-specific inquiry into the public interest advanced in support of the restraint."[43] One is regulation that prompts a physical "invasion" of property.[44] The other is regulation that, supposedly as in *Lucas*, "denies all economically beneficial or productive use of land."[45] As coherent baselines protecting private property from the dangers of the gradually encroaching regulation Holmes so presciently described in *Mahon*, these aren't much. They let government do whatever it wants as long as it doesn't physically eject us, or extract that last minuscule right of use which if left might avoid denying us "all economically beneficial or productive use."[46]

It is particularly jarring that one of the two circumstances that triggers the

41. Id at 2893.

42. Id.

43. Id.

44. The case usually cited for this conclusion is *Loretto v Teleprompter Manhattan CATV Corp.*, 458 US 419 (1982), holding that a New York law requiring landlords to permit cable companies to place cable facilities in their apartment buildings amounted to a taking. This law may have been designed to prevent landlords from skirting rent control by installing their own TV systems and charging above-market prices for TV services. This would be a way indirectly to increase controlled rents toward market levels. See William A. Fischel, *Exploring the Kozinski Paradox: Why Is More Efficient Regulation a Taking of Property?* 67 Chi Kent L Rev 865, 901 (1991).

45. 112 S Ct at 2893. *Agins v Tiburon*, 447 US 255 (1980), is usually cited to support this conclusion. It said:

> The application of a general zoning law to particular property effects a taking if the ordinance does not substantially advance legitimate state interests or denies an owner economically viable use of his land.

Id at 260 (citations omitted).

46. Predictably, given the precedents, one Justice (Blackmun) opined that Lucas had no complaint, for the state had left him with the right to pitch a tent on lots for which he had, quite reasonably at the time, paid almost a million dollars. See 112 S Ct at 2908. To presage our ex ante analysis below, which asks parties to reverse their positions in cases like this, consider what the Justice's view might be had he received attention from the state like that accorded Mr. Lucas.

Court's categorical requirement of compensation equates loss of all economic value with physical invasion that might cause only the most trivial economic loss. One possible way to bring these two rules together might be found in Holmes's language about regulation that "goes too far." Holmes may have meant that regulation goes "too far" when it takes more value from particular individuals than should be permitted in a society guided by rationality. This is suggested by his phrase "the petty larceny of the police power," which he wanted to use in another takings case[47] but which he was dissuaded from using by his colleagues.[48] The idea is that the police power can be stretched beyond its scope as determined by principle without triggering compensation, as long as the value of that which is taken is so small as to constitute only petty larceny by the state. There really is a taking, in other words, because the state has acted beyond the scope of its police power, but because the value of that which is taken is so small (de minimis, perhaps) it is not cost effective to compensate.

This makes economic and legal sense in that rational parties would not insist ex ante on compensation if the transaction costs of effecting it exceeded its social benefits, at least if the state's petty larceny were random and widespread. When a regulation commits larceny greater than petty—i.e., when it becomes cost effective to compensate—it goes "too far" and compensation is required. This provides a coherent way out of the peculiar result of equating confiscation with trivial physical invasion. Physical invasion would not be compensated unless the economic loss reached some threshold level at which we could reasonably conclude the transaction costs of effecting compensation would about equal its social benefits. Economic loss from regulation (without physical invasion) would be compensated at the same level. This would achieve parity between physical and regulatory takings and provide a coherent standard for setting the point at which compensation would be required in each case. As we shall see, this is precisely the result suggested by our analysis below.[49]

If Justice Scalia believed a taking resulted whenever regulation denies all economically beneficial use of land he could have ended his opinion much ear-

47. *Jackman v Rosenbaum Co.*, 260 US 22 (1922).

48. See Mark DeWolfe Howe, ed, *Holmes-Laski Letters* 457 (Harvard, 1953).

49. See the discussions in text following note 88 and in the paragraph following note 98 below.

lier than he did.[50] He want on, however, to deal with the problems created by Lucas's failure to claim that the BMA was beyond the state's police power, commonly thought to be a condition of compensation. While there was confusion as to the exact meaning of "police power," it is clear that the Coastal Council did not wish to pay Mr. Lucas for his lots.[51] The state's supreme court agreed, concluding that the act was within the state's police powers "to mitigate the harm to the public interest" from Lucas's building houses on his lots.[52] It based this conclusion on a series of Supreme Court cases decided between 1897 and 1962 (the *Mugler* line)[53] upholding a wide range of state regulations that diminished the value of particular properties without providing compensation.[54]

Justice Scalia conceded that many of the Court's earlier cases had said government could abate "harmful or noxious uses" of property without compensation. But he did not believe those cases justified the state court's conclusion that the BMA was within the police power simply because the legislature claimed the law was aimed at preventing harm to the state's beaches. Preventing harm to beaches was not equivalent to abating a harmful or noxious use simply because the legislature said it was.[55]

The Court faced a real problem at this point, for the *Mugler* line of cases clearly supported the South Carolina Supreme Court's conclusion. In *Miller v Schoene*,[56] for example, the Supreme Court upheld a Virginia law requiring destruction of cedar trees to prevent the spread of disease to apple trees owned

---

50. The conclusion that a taking occurs when an owner has suffered total loss of value comes at the bottom of 112 S Ct at 2895, seven pages into the opinion. The opinion proceeds for six more pages after that.

51. 112 S Ct at 2896–97.

52. Id at 2896.

53. The first case in this line was *Mugler v Kansas*, 123 US 623 (1887), which upheld a Kansas prohibition law even though it lessened the value of Mugler's brewery.

54. Other cases in the *Mugler* line include *Hadacheck v Sebastian*, 239 US 394 (1915) (upholding Los Angeles ordinance banning operation of brickyard after houses had been built around it even though it lessened value of brickyard); *Miller v Schoene*, 276 US 272 (1928) (upholding Virginia law requiring destruction of cedar trees that harbored a disease fatal to apple trees); and *Goldblatt v Town of Hemstead*, 369 US 590 (1962) (upholding town ordinance preventing operation of quarry below water level).

55. 112 S Ct at 2897.

56. 276 US 272 (1928).

by others. The Court approved the legislature's decision that the apple trees were more valuable and saving them was in the public interest. It said:

> And where the public interest is involved preferment of that interest over the property interest of the individual, *to the extent even of its destruction*, is one of the distinguishing characteristics of every exercise of the police power which affects property.[57]

The *Lucas* Court was willing neither to follow the approach of *Miller v Schoene* nor to overrule the *Mugler* line. The resulting attempt to make us believe *Miller* could possibly be consistent with the Holmes opinion in *Mahon* made it more difficult for the Court, enmeshed in questions of harm, benefit, property law, and nuisance, to articulate a standard to distinguish state regulation within the police power from that which effects a taking. This is the somewhat convoluted core of the Court's opinion, which requires a more detailed examination.

Justice Scalia began by attacking the noxious use doctrine the state supreme court had used to uphold the BMA. He thought the *Mugler* line of cases, holding that harmful uses could be abated without compensation, was simply using the noxious/harmful-use formulation to describe the scope of the state's police power. He saw no difference from the Court's "more contemporary statements that 'land use regulation does not effect a taking if it "substantially advance[s] legitimate state interests.""[58] He thought:

> The transition from our early focus on control of 'noxious' uses to our contemporary understanding of the broad realm within which government may regulate without compensation was an easy one, since the distinction between 'harm-preventing' and 'benefit-conferring' regulation is often in the eye of the beholder. It is quite possible, for example, to describe in *either* fashion the ecological, economic, and aesthetic concerns that inspired the South Carolina legislature in the present case. One could say that imposing a servitude on Lucas's land is necessary in order to prevent his use of it from

57. Id at 297–80 (emphasis added). While the Virginia law had declared the cedar trees to be a public nuisance, the Court thought it "need not weigh with nicety" whether they were a nuisance under common law or "whether they may be so declared by statute." Id at 280. The Court said the legislature could proceed as long as it was "controlled by considerations of social policy which are not unreasonable." Id.

58. 112 S Ct at 2897.

'harming' South Carolina's ecological resources; or, instead, in order to achieve the 'benefits' of an ecological preserve. . . . [59]

The Court thus concluded that identifying noxious or harmful use required a subjective valuation of competing land uses. This made it impossible to identify harm, and thereby harm-preventing regulation, "on an objective, value-free basis."[60] Since noxiousness/harm is in the eyes of beholders, the Court concluded that the noxious use doctrine was too subjective to identify legitimately the type of regulation for which compensation would be required.

It followed:

> A *fortiori* the legislature's recitation of a noxious-use justification cannot be the basis for departing from our categorical rule that total regulatory takings must be compensated. If it were, departure would virtually always be allowed. The South Carolina Supreme Court's approach would essentially nullify *Mahon's* affirmation of limits to the noncompensable exercise of the police power.[61]

To be sure, a legislature's declaration against harm[62] should not except it from the Court's categorical rule requiring pay for total takings. But a contrary rule would little affect *Mahon*; its main nullifier is not in South Carolina. That honor goes to the Court in Washington for limiting serious review of regulation to that which confiscates. Coupling that rule with *Mahon* says regulation goes too far only when there is nowhere farther for it to go.

The Court's conclusion that the distinction between harm and benefit was too subjective legitimately to identify regulatory takings required it to find another way to do that job. It concluded that a confiscatory limitation could not be newly legislated without compensation. Rather:

> [It] must inhere in the title itself, in the restrictions that background principles of the State's law of property and nuisance already place upon land ownership. A [confiscatory] law or decree . . . must, in other words do no

---

59. Id at 2897–98 (emphasis in original).

60. Id at 2899.

61. Id.

62. Or, as in *Miller v Schoene*, 276 US 272 (1928), a declaration preferring property that the legislature says is worth more than other property it requires to be destroyed in the name of the public interest.

more than duplicate the result that could have been achieved in the courts—
by adjacent landowners (or other uniquely affected persons) under the
State's law of private nuisance, or by the State under its complementary
power to abate nuisance that affect the public generally, or otherwise.[63]

Relying on the Restatement (Second) of Torts,[64] the Court then noted that the inquiry required by this formulation necessitated analysis of the degree of harm
Lucas's houses might cause, the social value of the houses, their suitability to
the neighborhood, and who could most cheaply avoid the costs of conflicting
interaction.[65] Thus the Court came full circle. It first refused to identify regulatory takings as those which conferred benefit because the distinction between
benefit and harm was too subjective. It sought an "objective, value-free basis"[66]
on which to identify takings in the state law of property and nuisance. It then
interpreted that law as relying heavily on subjective estimates of the value of
competing land uses. It returned to the eye of the beholder.

The Court is right to be reluctant to define, assign, or transfer private property rights on the basis of an "evaluation of the worth of competing uses of real
estate"[67] or on the degree of harm they might cause. A harmful or noxious use
is present in virtually every social activity. The occupancy of a rented house is a
nuisance and harmful to the owner who is thereby denied the occupancy of the
house. But rent payments offset that harm and suddenly transform a "harmful"
use into part of a desirable, beneficial package. The owner of the house loses
something but gets something worth more in return; the harm is more than
compensated by a benefit. Our doctors consider our visits a nuisance, but we
pay enough to induce them to bear this harm. No doubt Lucas's decision to
build houses harmed those who value beaches highly; his decision not to build
would harm those who would eventually buy them. To build or not to build de-

---

63. 112 S Ct at 2900. The principal "otherwise" was litigation holding parties not
liable in cases of actual necessity, as in preventing the spread of fire. Id at n 16.

64. Section 826 of the Restatement of Torts (ALI, 1939) adopted the so-called "balance
of utilities" test, which in defining nuisance said: "An intentional invasion of another's
interest in the use and enjoyment of land is unreasonable . . . unless the utility of the actor's conduct outweighs the gravity of the harm." See Jeff L. Lewin, Boomer and the American Law of Nuisance, Past, Present, and Future, 54 Albany L Rev 189, 210–12 (1990) ("Lewin,
Boomer").

65. 112 S Ct at 2901.

66. Id at 2899.

67. Id at 2898.

pends on the action of those who wish to affect the result; those harmed the most would pay the most to produce the result they prefer.

We are, of course, describing market processes, within which the holders of private property rights contract to allocate harms and benefits in ways that move resources to their most highly valued uses. The legal function most basic to this process is to define and enforce private property rights. Once that is done the appropriate uses of particular resources will be decided by voluntary exchanges among the holders of those rights. Government has little role as long as such exchanges are not foreclosed by high transactions costs. If those costs are high, government can act as the agent between Lucas and those who wish to pay, through higher taxes or fees, to move his lots to beach-front use.

When government acts in that role, there is no need for a court to consider which use of property is the most highly valued. That can and should be done by structuring a surrogate market transaction to provide us the best information as to whether or not the state's action could be reconstructed as a voluntary contract between rational persons affected by that action. There was no claim that Lucas was compensated in kind. Under our interpretation of the Holmes "too far" test, payment should be made whenever its social benefits exceed the transaction costs of making it. Those transaction costs were so low in the *Lucas* case that this condition seems clearly to have been met. Under these circumstances Lucas should have been compensated and that right should not have depended on his loss being total.

B. *Justice Kennedy's Concurrence*

Justice Kennedy believed the Takings Clause protected "reasonable, investment-backed expectations," but admitted there was "an inherent tendency towards circularity in this synthesis, . . . for if the owner's reasonable expectations are shaped by what courts allow as a proper exercise of governmental authority, property tends to become what courts say it is." He thought the common law of nuisance "too narrow a confine for the exercise of regulatory power in a complex and interdependent society"; it could not "be the sole source of state authority to impose severe restrictions" on land use. In his view, "reasonable expectations must be understood in light of the whole of our legal tradition."[68]

Justice Kennedy made the need for principled baselines clearer than any of the other opinions in this case. The only way to avoid circularity is to base con-

---

68. Id at 2903.

stitutional definitions on principles outside the Court's own ipse dixit. The principles of the common law—which we claim are captured by our analysis of ex ante contracting developed in Part IV below—provide this basis.

c. The Dissents

Justices Blackmun and Stevens both believed the Court's common law nuisance standard had unwisely frozen the common law by outlawing legislatures from defining new types of harm. Justice Blackmun said:

> In determining what is a nuisance at common law, state courts make exactly the decision that the Court finds so troubling when made by the South Carolina General Assembly today: they determine whether the use is harmful. Common-law public and private nuisance law is simply a determination of whether a particular use causes harm. . . . There is nothing magical in the reasoning of judges long dead. They determined a harm in the same way as state judges and legislatures do today. If judges in the 18th and 19th centuries can distinguish a harm from a benefit, why not judges in the 20th century, and if judges can, why not legislators?"[69]

This question deserves a better answer than Justice Scalia's response that courts have less leeway than legislatures in determining state law.[70] True, but why is less leeway better than more? After all "the great office of statutes is to remedy defects in the common law as they are developed, and to adapt it to the changes of time and circumstance."[71] The real question is whether changes of time and circumstance require the Court to be more suspicious of certain kinds of legislation, or state court decisions for that matter, than it was at various times in the past. We think so.

The rise in interest-group politics and the vast expansion of government and governmental regulation over the last fifty years greatly increases the opportunity for people to manipulate the state to increase their own wealth at the expense of others, to engage in rent seeking.[72] The Court's refusal meaning-

69. Id at 2914 (citation omitted).

70. Scalia wrote: "There is no doubt some leeway in a court's interpretation of what existing state law permits—but not remotely as much, we think, as in a legislative crafting of the reasons for the confiscatory regulation." Id at 2902 n 18.

71. Id at 2921 (Stevens dissenting) (quoting *Munn v Illinois*, 94 US 113, 134 [1876]).

72. See Harold Demsetz, *The Growth of Government*, in *Economic, Legal, and Political Dimensions of Competition* 99 (Elsevier Science, 1982); Richard A. Posner, *Taxation by Regulation*, 2 Bell J Econ & Mgt Sci 22 (1971).

fully to review economic regulation since its abdication of that responsibility in the 1930's,[73] and the corresponding erosion of limitations on the police power, have removed practically all judicial limitation on such rent seeking. That Justice Stevens believed the Lucas majority was seeking to interfere with such rent seeking is suggested by his charge that the Court's decision would "represent a return to [Lochner] . . . when common-law rights were also found immune from revision by State or Federal Government."[74] He thought this would freeze the common law in its 19th-century form, which would prevent changes in response to changing circumstances.[75]

The Lucas baseline is hardly so rigid as to require adherence to early common law; indeed, its baseline of current state law is remarkably limp. Moreover, that baseline has two additional defects. First, it provides no guidance by which to judge the performance of courts; they have changed the common law in ways that could easily be viewed as takings.[76] Second, as charged by the dissenters, it truncates the role of legislatures in revising the common law in ways that may be socially desirable.

We need constitutional baselines to assess the work of both courts and legislatures. Those baselines must capture the essence of the institutions—primarily the common law—that provided the context in which the Constitution was created. These baselines must be able to identify and permit principled adaptation to changing circumstances, and to distinguish it from rent seeking—the unprincipled manipulation of government to enrich some at the expense of others—which should be banned.

In the rest of this article we seek to describe and derive such a set of baseline standards that reflect the essential core of the common law process. While

73. See Bernard Siegan, Economic Liberties and the Constitution (U Chicago, 1980); David Bernstein, The Supreme Court and "Civil Rights," 1886–1908, 100 Yale L J 725 (1990); Note, Resurrecting Economic Rights: The Doctrine of Economic Due Process Reconsidered, 103 Harv L Rev 1363 (1990).

74. See 112 S Ct at 2921 (Stevens dissenting) (quoting Justice Marshall's concurring opinion in PruneYard Shopping Center v Robins, 447 US 74, 93 [1980]).

75. 112 S Ct at 2921.

76. See Barton Thompson, Judicial Takings, 76 Va L Rev 1449 (1990). An example of a probable judicial taking is Prah v Maretti, 108 Wis 2d 223, 321 NW2d 182 (1982), holding that plaintiff stated a common law claim by alleging that building a house on adjacent land would interfere with the flow of sunlight to his solar collectors. The court said the previous contrary rule "reflect[ed] factual circumstances and social priorities that are now obsolete." Id at 189.

these baselines will be useful in many areas of constitutional law, we focus primarily on the problem of regulatory takings, the problem involved in *Lucas* itself.

IV. A Contract Theory of the Common Law

We attempt now to explicate a contract theory of the common law. We believe the essential core of common law processes can be discerned by asking what kind of property rights system would emerge from ex ante contracts made by rational persons exercising equal liberty under zero transaction costs, knowing they would face generalized ex post specialization caused by high transaction costs. Think of the ex ante position as a Hobbesian state of nature from which we desire to move to a state of civil society.[77] In the state of nature (ex ante) each person has complete freedom, with no obligations or duties to others. Since there is no cooperation each person's efforts to advance his own interest imposes costs on others with whom he interacts that exceed any benefits they might obtain from such interaction. To increase the chances that the ex ante contracts will survive ex post, ex ante contractors will agree to enter the contracting process on the basis of equal liberty. "A cooperative venture for mutual advantage"[78] based on the concept of equal liberty would have greater survival prospects than one formed on any other basis.[79]

77. Our argument follows David Gauthier, *Moral Dealing* 130–37 (Cornell, 1990) ("Gauthier, *Moral Dealing*").

78. See John Rawls, *A Theory of Justice* 4 (Belknap, 1971).

79. This condition that the contracting proceed on the basis of equal liberty for all parties is an important part of the ex ante model. This is not an implausible claim that all parties have equal strength in a state of nature. Equal liberty is rather a condition, agreement to which greatly increases the chances that the ex ante agreement will survive ex post. Unequal liberty implies coercion of some persons by others. A social contract based on coercion will not be neutral and will have less chance of commanding adherence ex post than one based on equal liberty in the ex ante contracting process. Because ex ante contractors desire their contracts to endure ex post, they would agree to conduct their contracting under conditions of equal liberty. See David Gauthier, *Morals by Agreement* 190–232 (Oxford, 1986) ("Gauthier, *Morals by Agreement*").

A related problem is the nature of our ex ante agreement on the extent to which we could avail ourselves ex post of wealth obtained ex ante in ways that imposed inefficient externalities on others. The imposition of such externalities is equivalent to the exercise of coercion. For reasons similar to those sketched in the preceding paragraph, we would probably agree ex ante to prohibit bringing wealth to ex post interaction unless it had been obtained without taking advantage of others. Since our ex post institutions will be de-

Conditions in the state of nature are the ultimate expression of the problem of externalities, which it is the principal purpose of an effective property rights system to internalize.[80] Hobbes offered three rules by which rational parties might contract their way out of this unhappy condition.

1. Each person should endeavor peace.
2. Each person must be willing when others are too to lay down their right to all things [liberty] and be contented with so much liberty against others as he would allow others against himself.
3. Each person must keep his covenants.[81]

Since ex ante transaction costs are zero, exchanges in the hypothetical state of nature will capture all possible gains from trade. There will be no externalities. No exchange will be made unless it makes all affected parties better off, i.e., unless social benefits exceed social costs.

These conditions will not exist ex post; there transaction costs mean interaction will affect parties in three possible ways. First, ex post interaction could produce gains for all affected parties; this would be Pareto optimal and Pareto superior, both collectively and individually rational.[82] Second, it could help some but hurt others, with the winners gaining more than the losers lose. This would be Pareto optimal but not Pareto superior, collectively but not individually rational. Third, such interaction could help some and hurt others, with the losers losing more than the winners gain. This would be neither Pareto optimal nor Pareto superior (Pareto pessimal?);[83] it would be neither collectively nor individually rational.

Rational actors would seek ex ante to establish property rights that cost-effectively identified which of these three categories characterized particular ex post interactions. They would favor interactions in the first category, consisting of voluntary exchanges with a low level of externalities. Since there would be

---

signed to minimize taking advantage of others (imposing external costs on them), we are really saying wealth acquired ex ante could be brought to ex post interaction if it were obtained in ways permitted by our ex post institutions. This raises large and interesting questions, which thankfully are beyond the scope of this paper. See id.

80. See Demsetz, *Property Rights* at 348 (cited in note 10).

81. See Gauthier, *Moral Dealing* at 133–35 (cited in note 77).

82. See Coleman, *Afterword* at 181 (cited in note 1).

83. See Richard A. Epstein, *Forbidden Grounds: The Case Against Employment Discrimination Laws* 326 (Harvard, 1992).

few if any benefits from regulating such arrangements ex post, such regulation would be banned by ex ante contract.[84]

Our second and third categories of interaction are partly involuntary since they both involve losers, a result to which rational people would not agree voluntarily. Losers are created by negative external effects either from the voluntary acts of others or from state action. We would outlaw interaction in the third category, since it reduces social wealth, but permit interaction of the second type because of its positive wealth effects.

But there are two problems. First, how do we distinguish these two types of interaction, which differ only in that one ups social wealth while the other cuts it? This is the problem of valuing competing uses, the way the *Restatement* would identify nuisance,[85] which plagued Justice Scalia in his *Lucas* majority opinion. Second, assuming we correctly place an interaction in the second category, what do we do about the losers? Typical efficiency analysis would leave them as it found them; after all, the transaction as a whole increased social wealth. Thus, if the land on which Lucas wanted to build is worth a bit more as a beach than a housing site, the state could allocate the land to beach use without compensation.

We analyze these questions using a model developed by David Gauthier to explicate Hobbes's second law of nature.[86]

We use Figure 1 to examine the arrangements that might be made by a group of persons in a state of nature to improve their circumstances with respect to certain land they have at their joint disposal. C_1 represents the benefits any one of them (P_1) could obtain from using all or part of the land as long as the others did not interfere. C_2 represents the costs to the others of P_1's use of the land.

P_1 receives large benefits as long as the others accept the costs of his actions; thus he will tend to take more actions, moving to the right on OX to increase his benefits (C_1), but also increasing costs to the others (C_2). But the others will not passively accept these costs. Everyone will try to benefit from using the land and in so doing they will generate costs for others. Absent cooperation, each person's attempt independently to maximize his returns produces more costs than benefits.

---

84. This forces the conclusion that the vilified case of *Lochner v New York*, 198 US 45 (1905), was correctly decided. The legions who disagree have the burden of explaining the benefits of collective interference with voluntary transactions where transactions costs are low or zero, as they typically are in relations between employers and employees.

85. See note 64 above.

86. See Gauthier, *Moral Dealing* at 134 (cited in note 77).

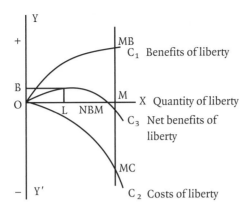

FIGURE 1.
Source: David Gauthier, *Moral Dealing* at 134.

Suppose each person is exercising a quantity of liberty—engaging in acts regarding the land—equal to OM. Since these acts are imposing costs on everyone, no one will be receiving benefits measured by C_1. Net benefits can be determined accurately only by offsetting costs; those net benefits are shown by C_3. If everyone is engaging in quantity of acts OM, net benefits (NBM) will be negative.

An example of acts producing these results might be taking corn or livestock others have raised. Everyone doing this uses his own resources unproductively and prompts others to defend themselves, also wasteful if cheaper ways to stop the taking can be found. Rational persons could quickly improve things by contracting reciprocally to reduce their claims to liberty. Each would agree, for example, to stop taking sheep raised by his neighbor in return for his neighbors' agreements to stop taking sheep raised by him. Such contracts would move the group jointly to the left on line OX to point L, where the joint value of their interaction is maximized.

This network of contracts by which each member of the group "agrees to renounce certain of his rights, to stand out of the way of others, in return for their reciprocal renunciations"[87] is our property rights system. In our hypothetical zero-transaction-cost ex ante contracting process, we would contract for ex post property rights that would bring and keep us as close to point L (which, as determined ex ante, is a perfectly competitive equilibrium without externalities) as would be cost effectively possible. The cost-effectiveness constraint means we would rationally accept ex post deviations from point L; we

87. Id.

would attempt to move toward it only as long as marginal benefits exceed marginal costs. It is not, in other words, rational to try to eliminate *all* ex post externalities, which was Coase's point in discussing the trains.[88]

We suggested this willingness to forgo internalization unless it is cost effective is the underlying meaning of the *Mahon* "too far" test: regulation goes "too far" and compensation is required when the marginal transaction cost of making compensation falls below its marginal social benefit. We return to this point below.

v. The Model Developed: *Boomer v Atlantic Cement Co.*

To show the continuity of private and public law, we develop the property rights generated by our network of ex ante contracts using the facts of a torts case, *Boomer v Atlantic Cement Co.*[89] We apply this analysis to *Lucas*, a public law case, in Part VI.

Atlantic built and operated a cement plant in the Hudson valley that deposited large amounts of dust on nearby land owned by Boomer and others. The plant cost \$45 million to build; it was equipped with the most advanced pollution control equipment available. Plaintiffs sought an injunction against its operation, claiming that the discharges were a nuisance. The court set their damages at a little more than \$710,000. While the historic remedy in a New York case like this would have been an unconditional injunction, the court ordered an injunction to be entered only if Atlantic failed to pay plaintiffs the \$710,000 by a certain date. Atlantic paid and continued to run its plant. We believe this result is consistent with the property rights that would be adopted by (virtual) ex ante contracts between the *Boomer* plaintiffs and Atlantic—the group that together would eventually own the cement plant and all the surrounding land adversely affected by its operation.

We consider this group ex ante, in such a way that they are removed from the interests associated with the particular land parcels they eventually own; we do this to unspecialize them, as it were.[90] This would put them in the same posi-

---

88. See Coase, *The Problem of Social Cost* at 29–34 (cited in note 8).

89. 26 NY2d 219, 257 NE2d 870 (1970).

90. We seek to establish an Archimedean point for judging the relations between Atlantic and the *Boomer* plaintiffs. An Archimedean point is represented by:

... a rational actor freed, not from individuality but from the content of any particular individuality, an actor aware that she is an individual with capacities and prefer-

tion as parties considering specializing their assets by contract. The question to be addressed is what precautions would those parties take before entering such contracts.[91]

We can move to this initial position by asking what contract they would make with one another if they did not know which particular parcels they would later own. Or we could ask what costs each owner would agree to accept from other nearby owners knowing ownership relations might be reversed. These devices will be familiar to parents who have divided goodies among their children by requiring the one who divides them to let the others choose first. They are designed to remove the problems created by the way in which these particular parcels of land become specialized to each other ex post, which led Atlantic to argue it should be permitted to discharge dust without payment, and the neighbors to argue the plant should be closed, even though neither result appeared to be in the parties' joint interest.

To concentrate the benefits and costs of each other's acts, and create incentives to use the land more efficiently, members of our hypothetical group would contract initially (ex ante) for each party to have wide-ranging rights to exclude others. None of them would wish to have to obtain permission from others to use the land assigned to them in ways that did not have significant effects on their neighbors—as would be required in communal ownership, for example. The high costs and low benefits of such a system, resulting in part from strategic behavior problems, would prevent its adoption by ex ante contract.

They would not, however, contract for complete, fixed or unchangeable exclusion. Exercising equal liberty in the contracting process, and assuming each person's land use generates roughly equal externalities, each person would contract to accept costs arising from others' use of their land until the marginal cost to him of such use equalled the marginal benefit to him of the others' contracts to accept equal costs from him. All members of the group would make

---

ences both particular in themselves and distinctive in relation to those of her fellows, but unaware of which capacities, which preferences. Such a person must exhibit concern about her interactions with others, and this concern leads her to a choice among possible social structures. But her concern is necessarily impartial, because it is based on the formal features of individual rational agency without the biasing content of a particular and determinant set of individual characteristics.
Gauthier, *Morals by Agreement* at 233 (cited in note 79).

91. See Klein, Crawford, and Alchian (cited in note 20).

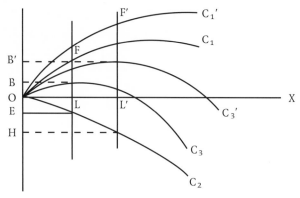

FIGURE 2.

similar reciprocal contracts, producing a result that conforms closely to the common law's live and let live rule.[92] This would leave each member at point L in Figure 2; joint benefits would be maximized and costs of OE would be distributed equally.

How would the group contract ex ante to deal with the possibility that one parcel might become particularly valuable in a use—like cement production—that generates significantly greater external effects than do the uses of the other parcels? With externalities no longer even close to equal, it becomes impossible to make ex ante reciprocal (in-kind) contracts to equalize even roughly the ex post costs and benefits of obligations to receive and rights to emit externalities across all parcels. The ex ante contract will have to provide either that those who end up with ordinary parcels will have to accept external costs from the high externality generator that exceed any reciprocal benefits received from that party or that such party will have to compensate them at least enough to equalize their costs and benefits. Since we have supposed these contractors are rational persons who by definition act to maximize the expected value of their

92. See Epstein, *Takings* at 231–32 (cited in note 12). The closeness of the fit between the results of these ex ante contracts and the common law's live and let live rule is shown in the following statement of Lord Justice Bramwell:

> But these natural rights [to use one's land] are subject to the rights of adjoining owners, who, *for the benefit of the community,* have and must have rights in relation to the use and enjoyment of their property that qualify and interfere with those of their neighbours, rights to use their property in the various ways in which property is commonly and lawfully used.

Bryant v Lefever, 4 CPD 172, 176 (1879) (emphasis added).

preferences, they would surely insist on being paid to accept these extraordinary costs. Perhaps they would contract for a little extra to salve the wounds of the (ex post) involuntary nature of the exchange. The court did this in *Boomer;* plaintiffs' recovery was nearly four times greater than the trial court's initial determination of permanent damages.[93]

Similarly, the New Hampshire Mill Act required payment of 150% of market value for upstream land involuntarily flooded when a dam was built to create a mill pond.[94]

It is also possible they might contract that no extraordinary costs (those in excess of OE in Figure 2) could be externalized by anyone without the consent of all those on whom they might fall. This was the effect of the position taken by the *Boomer* plaintiffs when they asked for an unconditional injunction against Atlantic's operation. Had they obtained it, one suspects they would have sold Atlantic their rights under it at a price considerably in excess of the monetary damages the court awarded, although it is conceivable that the surplus they were receiving from the particular plots they owned was so large they would not have sold at any price Atlantic was willing to pay.[95] But it cannot be denied that an unconditional injunction would enable them to behave opportunistically to extract quasi rents from Atlantic, which could have been a rather large amount since the plant had just been built for some $45 million and had little value for any use but producing cement.

Creating a huge gap between Atlantic's costs and benefits is hardly an effective way to internalize externalities and could be counted on to reduce future productive investment. The question is whether rational actors would so contract ex ante. We doubt it. It seems most probable that the actual result in *Boomer* avoided wholesale rent seeking by the plaintiffs by (generously) fixing their damages and permitting Atlantic to continue operations upon their payment. Requiring Atlantic to compensate for the mitigated damages caused by its ex-

---

93. See Lewin, *Boomer* at 218 (cited in note 64).

94. See Epstein, *Takings* at 174 (cited in note 12).

95. See *Estancias Dallas Corp. v Schultz,* 500 SW2d 217 (Tex Civ App 1973). An elderly couple living next to property in Houston on which a large apartment complex was built got an injunction against continued operation of the complex's air conditioner which had been located near their house. It was enforced even though the cost of moving the air conditioner exceeded the decline in the market value of plaintiff's property by a factor of up to sixteen. See Jesse Dukeminier and James Krier, *Property* 964–68 (Little, Brown, 3d ed, 1993). We thank our colleague Jesse Dukeminier for calling this case to our attention.

ternalities also provides an incentive for it to take cost effective measures to reduce those external costs. This would be important for efficient resource allocation wherever transactions costs were high.

An initial agreement to require someone like Atlantic to compensate its neighbors for the external costs it generates in excess of OE on Figure 2 will also produce information as to whether its activities increase total wealth or not. The fact that Atlantic paid the damages and kept running the plant strongly suggests that the plant's social benefits exceeded its social costs. The activity that increased external costs from OE to OH also increased benefits. This is shown on Figure 2 by benefit curve C_1', which in turn creates the new net benefit curve C_3'. While the external costs associated with the level of activity L' have risen from OE to OH, benefits to the actor generating that increase in costs have risen from F to F'. As a result net benefits increase from B to B'.

This appears to have been the result in *Boomer*. That conclusion would be conclusive if plaintiffs represented the recipients of all the plant's significant externalities and if their damages were covered by the amount the court awarded. The *Boomer* court in effect created a surrogate market that effectively produced information about the relative costs and benefits of the competing land uses involved. This information showed that continued operation of the plant fell within our second category of ex post interactions rather than the third. The winners gained more than the losers lost; social wealth would be increased by running the plant and there would not be any individual losers.

But requiring compensation for the losers did more than that. If the damages really covered plaintiffs' losses from the externalities, it moved this interaction into our first category of interaction. If running the plant made Atlantic richer (by creating the new benefits curve C_1') and legally hurt no one (because they were compensated), the plant's operation is both Pareto optimal and Pareto superior, both collectively and individually rational.

These points can be seen in Figure 2. Assume we start with everyone at point L, where the joint value of all interaction is maximized. We then observe someone, A_1, exercising greater amounts of liberty (doing things proscribed by ex ante contract) to move from point L to point L'. Such acts increase the costs of those affected by his action from OE to OH. If A_1 is still operating along an individual benefit of liberty curve equal to C_1, the net benefits to A_1 and those affected by his acts will decline along C_3, decreasing social wealth.

This scenario is highly probable, for each of us is in a prisoner's dilemma at point L. Even though we contract ex ante not to exercise liberty to the right of point L (joint marginal cost exceeds joint marginal benefit beyond that point),

CONSTITUTIONAL BASELINES BY VIRTUAL CONTRACT   689

it will be in the strict self-interest of each to violate that agreement and seek a greater and unequal liberty for himself.[96] Starting at point L, you would be richer if you cheated and no one else did. But that would be true even if everyone else cheated too. We each have a strong incentive to cheat no matter what anyone else does. Unless we can prevent this nonproductive pursuit of individual self-interest, "Covenants are in vain, and but Empty words; and the Right of all men to all things remaining, we are still in the condition of Warre."[97] This sorry scene is familiar as the rent-seeking characteristic of factions and interest-group politics.[98] Internalizing externalities by requiring compensation to losers from involuntary interaction, at least where such compensation is cost effective, would reduce the incidence of rent seeking (or taking advantage) and help maintain the integrity of the social contract.

One final note before applying this analysis to Lucas and some of the cases in the Mugler line. We have already noted that it would not be cost effective to compensate everyone who loses in an involuntary interaction, and we related that evident proposition to Justice Holmes's formulation that a regulation that goes "too far" requires compensation. That idea might be better expressed by saying that an externality that becomes too great requires compensation. Sometimes the transaction costs of determining the loss and making compensation would exceed the social benefit of doing so; sometimes they would even exceed the compensation itself. It is no more rational to require compensation in those cases than it would be to try to wipe out all private theft. No sensible person would contract ex ante to do either. The fact that there is an optimal amount of everything presumably justifies the petty larceny of the police power. The problem is keeping it petty.

vi. Further Applications

We briefly apply our contract theory of the common law, and through it of constitutional baselines in takings cases, first to Lucas and then to Miller v Schoene,[99] a prominent case from the Mugler line.[100]

The ex ante contract theory of the common law makes short shrift of cases

96. See Gauthier, Morals by Agreement at 79–82, 157–89 (cited in note 79).

97. See Gauthier, Moral Dealing at 135 (cited in note 77) (quoting Hobbes).

98. See Federalist 10 (Madison) in Clinton Rossiter, ed, The Federalist Papers 77 (Mentor, 1961).

99. 276 US 272 (1928).

100. See notes 53–54 above.

like *Lucas*. As in *Boomer*, the ex ante group would contract for wide-ranging rights to exclude others from the property they turned out to own, rights for its use without interference from others unless that use generated extraordinary external costs, and for rights to transfer such property to others.

While this ex ante contract defines the structure of ex post property rights, it does not determine the use to which particular pieces of property are to be put, nor does it in any sense prevent individual owners from using their property in ways that "harm" others. It only proscribes "harm" generated by extraordinary external costs, which we defined above in our discussion of *Boomer*.

Suppose the beach-front lots owned by Lucas are flanked on either side by similar lots owned by Smith, Ricardo, Marshall, and Stigler. Those four decide they want to use their lots as undeveloped beach front, perhaps charging admission to permit others to rent their beach for short periods of time. But Lucas wants to build houses on his lots which would "harm" his neighbors by interfering with the uninterrupted sweep of pristine beach, the availability of which would enable his worthy neighbors to charge higher admission prices. While the neighbors are harmed, and while they have every right to offer to buy the Lucas lots, under our ex ante contracts and under the common law they would have no legal recourse against Lucas's building his houses. Nor would Lucas have any such resource against them even though the use to which they put their property may have harmed him by denying him ready access to nearby fellow homeowners.

Unless we adopt some theory of the state nowhere to be found in our Constitution, its police power with respect to the use of the Lucas lots in the circumstances here described is no greater than that held by Smith, Ricardo, Marshall, and Stigler as individuals, save for the power of eminent domain. The state can force Lucas to sell if it wishes to put his property to a public use and if it pays him just compensation. The fact that its functionaries prefer empty beaches to beach-front housing is no more relevant from a constitutional standpoint than are the preferences of the dismal four.

This is basically what Justice Scalia suggested in *Lucas*, although the Court could not be convinced to put aside the unfortunate nonsense that limits an otherwise sensible rule to cases in which the larceny of the police power has become total. Would anyone argue that Smith, Ricardo, et al., would be free of liability if they got together and destroyed 99% of Lucas's houses, or perhaps destroyed them totally but graciously did not object to his pitching a tent on his land? If not, then why is the state?

Miller v Schoene involved a conflicting use between apple and red cedar trees;

rust spread from cedar trees and killed trees in apple orchards that were important sources of wealth in Virginia. The legislature found the apple trees more valuable than the cedar trees and provided for destruction of the latter whenever found to threaten apple trees, but the state provided no compensation for the cedar trees. Rational persons would no doubt contract ex ante to allow ex post preservation of the more valuable resource, but they would want convincing evidence as to which resource was more valuable and would want to internalize the cost of such preservation by making sure it was visited on those who benefitted from it. We suspect they would be particularly concerned about these issues if they knew the legislature was to be influenced heavily by owners of apple orchards, as it was in Virginia for years. But they would also be concerned about rent seeking by owners of cedar trees who in a straightforward market transaction would be able to extract large quasi rents from owners of apple orchards.[101]

Generous compensation for real loss in value to be paid by the apple orchard owners—not by the Commonwealth of Virginia—to those whose cedar trees were destroyed to protect apple trees would solve this problem nicely. It would avoid rent seeking on both sides, determine whether the apple trees were in fact more valuable than cedar trees in each particular case, and, when they were, protect the more valuable resource. Since the number of parties on each side of these localized conflicts[102] were few and the cost of determining the value lost by destroying the cedars apparently low, there is no reason to suppose the transaction costs of effecting compensation would exceed its social value. Our model suggests the Virginia statute should have been struck down for failure to provide for compensation. Such compensation would effectively identify the most valuable resource. It would also focus costs and benefits, particularly if it were required to be paid by the benefitted parties. This would conform well with the set of property rights for which we would expect rational persons to contract ex ante and with the result we would have expected in *Miller v Schoene* if the Court had given due regard to the common law.

---

101. See Warren Samuels, *Interrelations Between Legal and Economic Processes*, 14 J L & Econ 435 (1971); James Buchanan, *Politics, Property, and the Law: An Alternative Interpretation of Miller et al. v. Schoene*, 15 J L & Econ 439 (1972); Warren Samuels, *In Defense of a Positive Approach to Government as an Economic Variable*, 15 J L & Econ 453 (1972).

102. Apparently the rust could move from cedar trees to apple trees only if the latter were two miles or less distant from the cedars; at least the statute applied only to cedars within that distance from apple trees. See 276 US at 278.

VII. Conclusion

The need to define the terms of the Constitution by reference to materials outside the document itself has long been clear; the quarrel is over which materials are relevant. The context in which the Constitution was written and adopted—principally the common law of that time—is the most obvious source of definitional material. As we saw in *Lucas*, however, there is an objection that reliance on Blackstonian common law freezes at a particular point in earlier times the very process by which the common law itself was developed and thus prevents the growth of that law to meet changing circumstances. The Court's opinion in *Lucas* relied primarily in defining its constitutional baseline of decision on the law of South Carolina as it had been structured by its courts and legislature until just before it adopted the Beachfront Management Act, and on the *Restatement (Second) of Torts*. The legitimacy of those materials as sources to define the terms of the Constitution of the United States is not apparent.

We claim the ex ante contracting process described in this article is a model that can be used to structure neutral baseline definitions that will be true to the context that produced our Constitution and at the same time permit the common law to develop in accordance with the principles of its original creation. This is not a claim that the common law was created by a process in any way resembling the ex ante contracting process. It is a claim that such a rational contracting process, which aims at maximizing the value of the preferences of each person involved in it, could be expected to produce a result quite similar to one that had developed over time and survived in an environment of relative freedom, which we take to be a description of the common law.

The ex ante model coupled with the theory of specialized assets produces surprisingly useful results. We do not claim perfection. But if our competition is the *Restatement (Second) of Torts* and the law of South Carolina on the day before the Beachfront Management Act was adopted, our analysis might survive.

5

THE ECONOMICS OF GIFTS

THE ECONOMICS OF RATIONAL ASSISTANCE

ARMEN A. ALCHIAN AND WILLIAM R. ALLEN

Economics sometimes has been described (and condemned) as the study of selfish behavior. The conception of the "economic man" has been ridiculed as a bloodless abstraction which constitutes a calumny on real people who are warm in spirit and generous in heart. For (most) real people are not wholly self-centered creatures, coldly calculating only how best to aid themselves even at the cost of injuring others, if need be.

This is but a parody of the "economic man" notion specifically and of the concern of economic study generally. Economics, accurately conceived, is directed to the analysis not of *selfish* behavior as such, but of *efficient* behavior. The basic question asked by the economist is not, "In light of the egocentric avariciousness of people, how can one best skin one's neighbor?" Rather, he asks, "In light of the scarcity of resources, how can one squeeze the greatest return—which can take myriad forms, e.g., goods, power, utility, inner glow of contentment—from given productive services, talents, and environment? Or, alternatively, how can one achieve his desired goals with the minimum cost?" His goals can involve not only his own immediate welfare, but also that of other people.

Giving with Efficiency

We can usefully illustrate the matter by considering the granting of a subsidy or gift. The *motivation* of the giver may be as humanitarian and philanthropically pure as can be, but what of the *efficiency* with which the aid is given?

Suppose that a university—call it U.C.L.A.—wishes, for reasons good or bad which we shall not consider here, to subsidize the veterans in the student body by providing campus housing. U.C.L.A., it can be imagined, possesses a substantial amount of land on which are placed a number of war-surplus barracks. The barracks are renovated into a total of 1,000 apartments. The rent is set at $30 per month, which exactly clears the veterans' market; i.e., at $30, the veterans, of whom there are more than 1,000, wish to take 1,000 apartments.

Reprinted from *The Freeman* (November 1960): 20–24.

(If the price is set at less than $30, there is at the outset a messy problem of administrative rationing, for at such a low price, more than 1,000 veterans will demand apartments.) The U.C.L.A. administrators decree that no non-veterans are allowed to occupy apartments, so non-veterans do not apply.

The land being devoted to veterans' housing has some alternative valuable uses, e.g., as parking space, playing fields, or simply scenic lawn; so there is a *cost* involved in the housing program. The major question is now in order: for the given cost borne by U.C.L.A., are maximum benefits being bestowed, or, stated differently, could benefits equivalent to those actually bestowed be attained at smaller cost to U.C.L.A.?

Maximizing the Benefits

For the moment, concentrate on maximizing benefits. Are the beneficiaries of the subsidy as well off as possible with the resources being made available to them?

As things stand, the veterans must take their assistance in a specified form, i.e., a barracks apartment, or not receive aid at all. And with more veterans than apartments, some veterans receive nothing. Now, if the apartments were to be opened to the whole student body, the market-clearing rent presumably would be higher than $30; suppose it to be $40. Some veteran might feel that, instead of living in the barracks at $30, it would be preferable to sublease his barracks apartment for $40 and apply the excess proceeds to the renting of a more desirable apartment in town at, say, $60. In this fashion, the veteran would in effect obtain a gift in the form of money ($10) which he then expends as he pleases.

Who gains and who loses by this subleasing procedure?

Before subleasing was allowed, the veteran had the alternatives of (a) a barracks apartment at $30 or (b) a town apartment at $60. But now the veteran is presented with an *additional* alternative, viz., (c) rent and sublease a barracks apartment, gaining a $10 profit, and live in a town apartment. Although the town apartment may be more conducive than a barracks apartment to gracious living, the veteran might prefer alternative (a) over (b); i.e., he might prefer the inferior apartment plus an extra $30 to spend on other things over the more expensive apartment. But in comparing alternative (a) with (c), staying in the barracks apartment would provide only an extra $20 for other things, and this extra $20 might or might not be sufficient to compensate for the poorer apartment. Finally, we certainly can say that if he prefers alternative (b) over (a), he will prefer (c) over (a), for a town apartment plus an extra $10 (i.e., alternative c) is preferable to a town apartment without an extra $10 (i.e., alternative b). In any event, the subleasing alternative cannot hurt the veteran, and it may help him.

Non-Veterans Also Gain

Has the non-veteran student who is subleasing from the veteran at $40 been helped or hurt? He may feel envious that he is not a member of the privileged group eligible for the barracks at $30, but this is true whether or not subleasing is permitted. Prior to subleasing, his only alternative was a town apartment at $60, but with subleasing he can now rent a barracks apartment at $40. He may prefer the latter. The subleasing offer has given him, too, an additional alternative, and his accepting the new alternative is evidence that he is better off by moving into the barracks.

U.C.L.A. also is involved. The university is financially indifferent, for it receives $30 per apartment whether or not the apartment is subleased.

It appears that no one is hurt by the subleasing practice, and the veteran and the other student are both better off. Why, then, are administrators generally loath thus to widen the alternatives of those they are intending to aid? If the university wants to put valuable resources at the disposal of veterans, why does it prevent the full potential benefits being realized by restricting the use to which the veterans can put the subsidy? Perhaps administrators would consider it "untidy" and "inappropriate" to provide veterans' housing which is occupied by non-veterans. Or perhaps the administrators feel that they know what is best for the veterans, and barracks-living at $30 is deemed by them to be preferable for veterans to town-living at $60 and a $10 profit.

The moral is plain. A free price system enables men to use their resources in the ways they consider best. If it is felt that welfare is enhanced by broadening the alternatives available, a free price system enlarges welfare.

Alternative Land Use

Consider another possibility, which presents some additional complications. Suppose that the land now occupied by the barracks could be rented by U.C.L.A. at a rate equivalent to $50 per month for each apartment—or the land could be sold and the proceeds invested in acceptable fashion at a rate of interest equivalent to $50. With 1,000 apartments, this alternative income, as rent or interest, is $50,000 per month, compared with $30,000 when the land is used as barracks apartments for veterans.

In this "no barracks" case, U.C.L.A. could keep $30,000, so the university would be equally well off under the two schemes, and allocate the remaining

$20,000 among *all* veterans, of whom there are, let us say, 2,500. Each veteran receives $8 per month. How would the veterans fare now compared with the other schemes?

When subleasing of the barracks was not allowed, 1,000 veterans chose to live in the barracks at a rent of $30, and the remaining 1,500 received nothing from the university. Now, under the "no barracks" plan, with $20,000 being distributed among all veterans, clearly the 1,500 who would not have been in the barracks are better off: $8 is better than nothing. However, we cannot generalize about the other 1,000, for some of them will prefer $8 and no barracks apartment, while some would have preferred the barracks apartment and no $8.

Other Possibilities

When subleasing is allowed, it is again the case that 1,500 veterans do not benefit, for they cannot obtain an apartment. But the 1,000 with apartments can either keep the apartment at $30 or sublease at $40 and net $10 cash. In the "no barracks" case, with each veteran receiving $8 from U.C.L.A., those 1,000 who would have had a barracks apartment are worse off. However, if there were only 1,600 veterans, so that each receives $12.50 from the university, those who were willing to sublease (and perhaps even some of those who preferred to keep a barracks apartment when the alternative was to gain only $10 through subleasing) are better off.

And, of course, the greater the amount of money to split among a given number of veterans, the greater the share of each. If the market value of the land is $80,000, then $50,000 could be divided among the 2,500 veterans, giving each $20. That is, the better the alternative use U.C.L.A. has for its land, the greater and more widespread will be the benefits of utilizing the alternative and disbursing cash.

The Market Maximizes Alternatives for All Concerned

Let us summarize the conclusions from this array of possibilities. We began with veterans obtaining barracks apartments at the market-clearing rent of $30, without the right of subleasing. The university is discriminating not only in favor of veterans, but also in favor of those particular veterans who prefer a $30 barracks apartment to a $60 town apartment.

Now, if subleasing is allowed, another alternative is made available to both veterans and non-veterans. Those veterans who prefer to stay in the barracks have not lost, and those who prefer to sublease have gained. Similarly, some non-veteran students will not be interested in subleasing, but others are. Financially, U.C.L.A. is not affected. The introduction of subleasing rights has not hurt anyone, and some are benefited.

However, if subleasing is allowed, the apartments become more valuable. Even though a particular veteran might not demand an apartment at $30 for his own use, he is happy to rent at the pegged price of $30 in order to sublease at $40. The veterans' market is no longer cleared: all 2,500 veterans seek an apartment, and there are only 1,000 apartments. With a pegged rent of $30 and no prohibition on subleasing, the university is discriminating among veterans in a new way, viz., in favor of those 1,000 veterans who happen to acquire apartments when all 2,500 want apartments.

Suppose that U.C.L.A. decides to get out of the veteran-housing business and sell the land or lease it in its most profitable use. Then receipts are available to disburse among all veterans. It may well be that some of the veterans who would have acquired barracks apartments will not be pleased by giving up the apartment and receiving cash. However, the more the cash, i.e., the better is the alternative use to which the land is now devoted, the fewer and the less insistent will be the complaints. In any case, those veterans who did not have apartments will be benefited by distribution of the cash. No longer is there discrimination among the veterans, for the resources made available to the favored group are evenly disbursed among all members of the group.

THE ECONOMIC AND SOCIAL IMPACT
OF FREE TUITION

Rarely do educational issues provoke as much passion as the proposal to raise tuition fees in California colleges. Unfortunately, the passion has not been matched by reason—it is hard to find a clear statement of the consequences of or reasons for a zero tuition or a high tuition fee. It is hard to determine from the public comments whether the antagonists differ about what the consequences of alternative tuition arrangements would be or have different preferences with respect to well perceived consequences. Some defenders of zero tuition have asserted that zero tuition is necessary for aid to poorer students, for the maintenance of our great system of higher education, for the preservation of free and prosperous society, for achievement of great social benefits, for educational opportunity for all, that it is a hallowed century-old tradition, and that tuition is a tax on education. Some proponents of tuition fees have argued, for example, that the university and colleges are harboring delinquents who would not be there with full tuition, the poor are aiding the rich, students should pay tuition in order to appreciate their education, taxes are excessive, and low tuition requires exploitation of an underpaid faculty, to cite a few. Most of these arguments are so patently fallacious or nonsensical or irrelevant that they do disservice to the more intelligent arguments. But there are some propositions that merit closer examination. To evaluate them it is first necessary to identify at some length the issues that are involved in analyzing and thereby choosing among the alternatives—and in the process make clear my own preferences. If I overlook significant objectives or consequences, perhaps others will be stimulated to fill the gaps.

The issues represent a classic topic for applied economics—the effects of

Reprinted from Armen A. Alchian, *Economic Forces at Work* (Indianapolis: Liberty Fund, 1977), 203–26. This article was previously published in *New Individualist Review* (Winter 1968): 42–52.

Acknowledgment is made to the Lilly Endowment, Inc., for a research grant to UCLA during which the present article was written. The opinions expressed here in no way reflect any conditions of that research grant.

different means of allocating scarce resources among competing claimants. A rational analysis of the consequences of tuition systems requires separation of two questions: (1) Who should bear the costs of education? (2) If someone other than the student should pay for his education, in what form should the aid be given?

Unless the distinction between these two issues is grasped, confusion is inevitable. The case for zero tuition is *not* established by demonstrating that aid to students is desirable. Full tuition may still be desirable, with the desired aid taking the form of explicit grants-in-aid or scholarships from which the student pays the tuition fee of his chosen school.

The issue of the most desirable form of aid should be separated from still another closely related question: What is the desired method of financing and controlling *colleges*—as distinct from financing *students?* For example, aid to students in the form of zero tuition means also that the state finances the colleges' activities directly by legislative appropriations, with the students and their parents having less influence on financing and controlling the activities of colleges. Where student aid is in the form of grants-in-aid or scholarships, students and parents paying full tuition to their chosen colleges have a greater role in determining which colleges shall be financed and rewarded for superior performances. Recognition of these differences, in effect, explains why some people have asserted that the administrators and members of state universities and colleges, which are currently financed by direct legislative appropriation, have sought from self-interest, rather than educational interest, to maintain the impression that zero tuition is the only feasible or sensible means of aid to students—in order to repress student influence and control over the colleges while retaining the influence of politicians.

Advocates of subsidization of college students (regardless of the method) assume that if each student bore the full cost there would be too little college education as well as a decrease of educational opportunity. What makes it more desirable to have more education than if students pay full costs? Several arguments are advanced. Let us discuss these in ascending order of sophistication.

(1) Although the costs of education are less than the gains to the students themselves, some are unable to finance their education now. A subsidy would provide educational opportunity to the poor. (2) Cultural education, though not profitable in market earnings, and hence not capable of being paid for out of enhanced earnings, is nevertheless desirable. (3) Even if every student acquires as much education as is worthwhile to him, he would take too little, because the individual ignores the beneficial social gains indirectly conferred on

other members of society—giving what some people call "external social effects." Therefore, society at large should induce students to take more education than indicated by their private interests.

The argument that the poor cannot afford to pay for a profitable college education is deceptive. What is meant by a "poor" person? Is he a college-caliber student? All college-caliber students are rich in both a monetary and nonmonetary sense. Their inherited superior mental talent—human capital—is great wealth. For example, the college-caliber student is worth on the average about $200,000, and on the average, approximately $20,000–$50,000 of that has been estimated as the enhanced value derived from college training, depending upon his major field and profession.

Failure to perceive this inherent wealth of college-caliber students reflects ignorance of two economic facts. One is the enormous human wealth in our society. Every good educator recognizes that inanimate capital goods are not the only forms of wealth. The second fact is the difference between current earnings and wealth. For example, a man with a million dollars' worth of growing trees or untapped oil is a rich man—though he is not *now* marketing any of his wealth or services. So it is with the college-caliber student. Though his *current* market earnings are small, his wealth—the present wealth value of his future earnings—is larger than for the average person. This is true no matter what the current earnings or wealth of his parents. It is *wealth*, not current earnings nor parents' wealth, that is the measure of a student's richness. College-caliber students with low current earnings are not poor. Subsidized higher education, whether by zero tuition, scholarships, or zero-interest loans, grants the college student a second windfall—a subsidy to exploit his initial windfall inheritance of talent. This is equivalent to subsidizing drilling costs for owners of oil-bearing lands in Texas.

There remains an even more seriously deceptive ambiguity—that between the subsidization of college education and provision of educational *opportunity*. Educational *opportunity* is provided if any person who can benefit from attending college is enabled to do so despite smallness of *current* earnings. Nothing in the provision of full educational *opportunity* implies that students who are financed during college should not later repay out of their enhanced earnings those who financed that education. Not to ask for repayment is to grant students a gift of wealth at the expense of those who do not attend college or who attend tuition colleges and pay for themselves. This is true because, for one reason, our tax bills do not distinguish between those directly benefited by having obtained a zero-tuition educational subsidy and those not so benefited.

Alumni with higher incomes pay more taxes, but they do not pay more than people with equal incomes who financed their own education or never went to college.

Many discussions about educational opportunity refer to proportions of students from poorer and richer families at tuition-free colleges. However strong the emotional appeal, the proportion of rich- and poor-family students is relevant only to the separate issue of wealth redistribution per se, consequent to state-operated zero-tuition education. It has nothing to do with the extent of educational opportunity. Though data for California colleges and taxes suggest that lower-income groups provide a smaller proportion of students than of taxes to support education, such comparisons are irrelevant, so far as provision of educational opportunity is concerned. These data tell how much wealth redistribution there is among the less educated, the poor, the educated, and the rich. That wealth redistribution is good or bad depending upon whether one believes the educational system should be used as a device to redistribute wealth as well as to enhance wealth, knowledge, and educational opportunity. No matter how zero tuition in tax-supported schools may redistribute wealth, the provision of full educational opportunity does not require redistributions of wealth. Yet, it seems to me, many people confuse these two entirely separate issues or think the latter is necessary for the former. To think that college-caliber students should be given zero tuition is to think that smart people should be given wealth at the expense of the less smart.

When some zero-tuition university alumni say that without zero tuition they could not have attended college, they should have a modest concern for the implications of that statement. One poor, "uneducated" resident of Watts, upon hearing Ralph Bunche say that he could not have had a college education unless tuition were free, opined, "Perhaps it's time he repay out of his higher income for that privilege granted him by taxes on us Negroes who never went to college." That reply spots the difference between educational opportunity and a redistribution of wealth.

Full educational opportunity would be provided if college-caliber students could borrow against their future enhanced earnings. Students could repay out of their enhanced future earnings. Although, currently, loans are available from private lenders and also from publicly supported loans, a subsidy could provide a state guarantee of repayment of educational loans exactly as housing loans are guaranteed for veterans. Students could select among optional repayment methods. Some could contract to repay in full with interest; others could opt for a sort of insurance system, whereby the amount repaid was related to their income, with upper and lower limits to amounts repaid being specified. A host of possibilities are available. In fact today with income taxes, the college alumni are repaying part of the educational costs via taxes (but so are others who did not attend college).

Some people are impressed by the size of the debt that a college graduate would have to repay, but they should be impressed with the fact that the debt is *less* than the enhanced earnings he has thereby obtained and is an indication of the wealth bonanza given the student who is subsidized by society.

There remains one more facet of the educational opportunity argument. Even if a college education may be a very profitable investment for some person, he may, because of inexperience or lack of confidence, not appreciate his situation or be willing to borrow at available rates of interest. This presumably is an argument for subsidizing those students who lack confidence or understanding of their possibilities, and it may be a meaningful argument on its own ground, but it is not an argument for subsidizing "poor" students.

Pleas are made for subsidizing *cultural* education which, though it may add nothing to the student's future market earnings, will enhance his general welfare. But a person's welfare is increased if he gets more food, housing, recreation, beer drinking, and fancier cars. It would seem therefore that the relevant argument for helping students is one of helping them regardless of whether they wish their welfare increased via cultural education or better food. A grant of money to be spent as the recipient deems appropriate is an efficient form of aid—as judged by the recipient. Subsidized cultural education rather than money gifts could be justified if the giver knows better than the recipient what is good for the recipient. I cannot make that leap of faith for the collegiate student, although other people do it easily and confidently.

A case can be made for subsidizing the poor *and* the rich to take more education—more than a person would take when motivated by his own interests alone. It is often said there are privately unheeded net social benefits, so each person will underinvest in education from the social point of view, regardless of whether he is rich or poor; but we must separate the illusory from the real external available gains.

Education makes a person more productive, as, for example, a doctor, lawyer, merchant, or engineer. Other people benefit from his greater productivity, because more engineers enable lower costs of engineering services for the rest of society. Engineers, looking only to their private gain, would, it is said, undervalue the total benefit of having more engineers; too few people would seek sufficient engineering education. If this sounds persuasive, economics can teach you something. The increased supply of engineers reduces the prices of engineering services—even if by only a trivial amount—and thereby reduces the income of *other* engineers. Their income loss is the gain to the rest of society. This is a *transfer* of income from existing engineers to nonengineers; it is *not* a net social gain. The benefited parties gain at the expense of existing members of the engineering profession, who lose some of their scarcity value as more educated people are created. This is a transfer from the more educated to the less educated. A striking awareness of this effect is evident in the advocacy by labor groups of immigration restriction. Restricting the inflow of laborers of particular skills prevents reductions in wages of incumbent workers with similar skills and prevents a transfer of wealth from them to the rest of American society. An immigrant or a more educated person would have provided an increased product and he would have obtained that value by the sale of his services, but the lower wages to that *type* of services would have transferred some of the incomes of similar workers to the rest of society. This external *transfer* effect is not a net contribution to social output. It is not a reason for subsidizing education.

For external effects to serve as a valid basis for more education two conditions must be satisfied: (1) There must be a net social *gain* (not transfer) unheeded by the student. The ability to read reduces dangers and inconvenience to other people; ability to be sanitary enhances health of other people; or economic education may—but probably will not—prevent passage of socially detrimental, special-interest legislation. These are examples of education with external social gains, which we shall assume are not heeded by the student in his private actions because they do not affect the marketable value of his services. Professional education of doctors, engineers, lawyers, economists, mathematicians, etc., has not been shown to fit in that category. Perhaps education at the undergraduate collegiate level in the elements of law, psychology, political science, mathematics, and economics may make for better *nonmarket* decisions or actions.

I confess to a strong suspicion that such education is most significant at the grade school level, diminishes at higher levels, disappears for professional or cultural, artistic, personal satisfaction courses, and is possibly *reversed* at graduate levels (by overtraining and insistence on excessively high standards of training for granting of licenses to practice in some professions—though this is a point the validity of which is not crucial to the main issue here).

(2) The second condition is that there must be *further* external gains unheeded by students at the college level. The fact of having *achieved* net external

gains is not sufficient to warrant subsidization. The crucial condition is the failure to achieve still further available *incremental* net social gain from *further* education. Before concluding that they exist because of a tendency for people to ignore them, we should note that people attend college for reasons other than financial marketable gain. College attendance for personal reasons includes cultural, artistic education and attendance to find mates. All these tend to extend education beyond maximizing one's market wealth and possibly even beyond that yielding unheeded social gains. But the facts are not conclusive in *either* direction.

Incidentally, an especially common but erroneous contention, presumably relying on the external effect, is that the growth, prosperity, and unusual position of California depend upon the free-tuition higher education system. What does this mean? If this means that free tuition has contributed to higher wealth for the educated, then this is no argument for either free tuition or more education. If it means the prosperity and growth of aircraft, electronics, motion picture, or agricultural industries in California are dependent upon free tuition, the contention remains unsupported by any analytic or factual evidence, and in fact can be falsified by comparisons with other states. Even if it could be demonstrated that *subsidized* higher education was responsible, the issue of *free* tuition would still not be touched. If this means that free tuition did attract some people to seek their education in California, they proceeded to reap the gain in their own higher income. If they provided a real net social benefit, it should have exceeded the extent of their subsidization to be justifiable. The same proposition holds for residents of California. If this argument is accepted, it is difficult to justify charging newcomers a full tuition while permitting existing residents a "free tuition." Yet we have seen no proponent of zero tuition advocate zero tuition for all newcomers from all other states. If this means that the higher incomes for more people increase tax receipts, then the relevance of that completely escapes me. If this means California has a larger population, then this means higher land prices. But insofar as benefits to California have any relevance, I believe they should be reviewed as benefits to people in California rather than as benefits to owners of a geographically identified piece of land, unless by "California" one means "landowners or politicians," who indeed do prefer larger populations as a source of political power and higher land values.

To induce students to take more education than is privately worth their while—in order to obtain the otherwise unheeded external gains—does call for payments to students. If a student were paid for doing what he would have done anyway, or if his education were subsidized to increase his wealth, he would be receiving a gift. But a payment (whether as zero tuition or a money payment) to the student to *extend* his education, for the sake of achieving *real* external benefits that he otherwise would not have produced, is a payment for services, much as if he were to build houses for the benefit of the rest of society. Such payments may well be independent of the income or future income of the student as well as of his parents. Though there is nothing that says the rich would provide less real external effects from more education, my conjecture is that the rich would in any event take more education than the poor for cultural reasons and would therefore require a smaller inducement to take the "optimal" extra amount of education for external social benefits. This can form a basis for advocating more educational inducements to the poor than to the rich, but not necessarily by a zero-tuition inducement to rich and poor alike.

It should be noted however that there is already subsidization of higher education by private philanthropy on a scale that staggers the imagination. The endowment funds of colleges and philanthropic foundations aiding education run into the scores of billions. Even if only half of that were used to subsidize education (and the rest for research), the amount cannot be regarded as minor on any standard.

No matter what your beliefs about the validity or relevance of the preceding consideration, let us accept them, for the sake of analysis of alternative *means* of providing aid, for full educational opportunity, cultural aid, or extra inducements to education. (Of course, those who think the preceding arguments are too weak to warrant taxpayers' giving aid to college students can ignore all that follows, for to them there is no case for any state action nor for zero tuition.) The rest will want to ask, What is the best form of aid or inducement?

We can enable or induce students to take more education with the following offer: On the condition that you take certain kinds of education, we shall bear enough of the costs to induce you to do so. The costs he would have borne are the income forsaken and the tuition costs. (Food and living costs can be ignored, for he would be incurring them no matter what he did.) Which of the following is the preferred way of extending that aid to potential students? (1) We pay directly the costs of extra education by operating the school to provide the extra education; this is the zero-tuition system. (2) We pay him an equal amount on the condition he take the additional specified type of education, but he decides which school to attend, and he pays the tuition to the school. This is an educational voucher or G.I.-type educational bill of rights (used after World War II for veterans).

The first requires *also* that the state directly finance and operate the school providing the education; the second permits the student to choose from competing schools and to direct payment to the school he chooses. These two alternatives are sufficient to illustrate the major implications of zero- versus high-tuition modes of subsidy. The wealth effect for the student is superficially the same in either case, and the financial cost to the subscriber can be the same in each case, once it is decided how much education to subsidize for whom. The costs to the subscriber may be the same, but the results are not.

In the California state system of higher education, the tuition fee is zero for *all* state schools and for *all* kinds of training, regardless of whether it contributes to a net social gain and regardless of how rich the student is.

Zero tuition implies that the appropriate aid or subsidy for every student of a state school is exactly equal to the tuition cost no matter what subject he takes. No basis for zero tuitions as being the proper amount has ever been presented; maybe the aid should be even larger, to compensate for forsaken earnings.

Because low- or zero-tuition schools are believed to have a larger proportion of less wealthy students than high-tuition colleges, zero-tuition schools are believed to do a better job of providing educational opportunity for less wealthy students. But this entails the earlier confusion between provision of *opportunity* and provision of a wealth *bonanza*; zero-tuition schools give bigger wealth gifts to the mentally able students than do the high-tuition schools.

Of course, higher tuition will, *other things left unchanged*, reduce the number of financially insecure students attending tuition colleges. The case for raising tuition is not that aid should be denied but instead that "zero tuition" is a less desirable means of providing aid to students; it entails undesirable controls and political interference with education and lowers the quality of education. Yet there is another method of providing full educational opportunity *and* at the same time improving the quality and quantity of education and reducing political controls. The alternative is a system of full tuition supplemented by grants-in-aid to those who qualify as financially insecure and deserving students.

It is important to note that the financing of *colleges* to provide education is different from subsidizing *students*. The zero tuition is a subsidy to the *college* as well as to the student. Subsidies to *students* alone can be provided with a full-tuition system: in fact they are now being so provided by many private schools that do charge full tuition.

The alternative to the zero-tuition method of providing educational opportunity or giving aid is tuition *with* loans or with grants of money. The critical difference, in my opinion, between no tuition and tuition, under these circumstances, is that the former lets the state politician and college administrator and faculty directly exert more control over education whereas the latter enables the student to exercise more power by his choice of college.

Subsidies to whatever extent desired could be provided by a system of grants-in-aid via scholarships. That would appear to be more expensive *administratively* (but only administratively) than zero tuition precisely because an effort is made to eliminate the haphazard bonanzas in the zero-tuition system. The presumption is that the cost of selecting the students to be subsidized is less than the savings from the avoidance of subsidies to all students.

Tuition with grants-in-aid to students is not visionary. It is proven, practical, economical, and currently used. New York State already has a large system of Regents scholarships. California has a smaller-scale system with about 2,000 scholarships. After World War II, the federal government granted millions of veterans educational vouchers for tuition, books, and incidental expenses under an enormously successful act known as the G.I. Bill. All these granted aid regardless of the student's current financial status. In California the university and state colleges now receive about $500 million annually directly from the legislature. That would finance 250,000 scholarships of $2,000 each. The university's budget would finance 125,000 students, more than the number now attending.

At present many arrangements exist whereby private colleges take into account the financial status of students in deciding how much tuition to charge each student. Even more efficient would be a system of loans, with interest to be repaid after graduation out of the student's enhanced earnings. Under a loan system, the problem of filtering rich students from the financially distressed would be reduced to trivial dimensions, since the rich would have little, if anything, to gain by borrowing. This would provide full educational opportunity with little need for a means test.

Full tuition does not in any way restrict the achievability of full education opportunity. That can be achieved explicitly and openly by the scope of grants and subsidized loans. Just as social security and welfare payments are made in money, with the recipient choosing his purchases from competing producers, so a full-tuition system with grants-in-aid or loans would enable separation of the issue of the amount, if any, of the subsidy from that of the best means of providing and controlling education.

Under a system of full-tuition fees, with whatever loans and scholarship voucher grants are deemed desirable, students could choose their education from the whole world. Any accredited college or educational institution, whether it be for barbers, television technicians, beauty operators, mechanics, butchers, doctors, lawyers, or historians, could serve. Ours would then really be the best educational system in the world; no longer would Californians be confined to California state-operated schools. Whatever one's beliefs about the desirable degree of subsidy for more education, and whatever his beliefs about who should get it, the full-tuition voucher coupled with scholarships and loans would magically open a new, larger world of choice.

An alternative form of aid to students is a tax-credit allowance whereby parents or students could later receive a tax offset to their payments for tuition. This would put private college students on a more equal basis with low-tuition public colleges. In my opinion, this would be equality at the wrong level of equality. Rather than give tax credits as a means of maintaining zero tuition, I would prefer placing a tax liability on students attending public colleges with low or zero tuition. Whereas the tax credit provides subsidies and aid to all students at the expense of nonstudents, the tax-liability assessment places the costs of providing the education more squarely on those who benefit from the education. A tax credit gives equal treatment to private and public college students—at the expense of nonstudents. A tax liability gives equality to private and public college students and to college and noncollege people, with each bearing only the costs of service provided for their benefit. If tax-liability assessments are out of the question politically, the tax credit would be the next best; but it would not achieve one of the major purposes of a full-tuition system.

With full-cost tuition, competition among California colleges, and even among academic departments, would change. Instead of competition for funds being negotiated among university committees, deans, regents, state college boards, and legislators, competition would rely more on classroom behavior of instructors who would be more dependent on student attendance vis-à-vis other departments and other colleges. This would enormously enhance the power of the student in the former zero-tuition colleges. Giving students more attention and influence in the university would indeed occur, exactly as the customer exercises more power at the grocery—by his purchases and choice among competing products and stores, but not by leaping over the counter and insisting on power to run the store, as occurs with current protest. Currently at the grade school level many parents are turning to private schools precisely because the parents can choose more fully the kind of education given their children—via the power of the purse. The poorer people do not have that option, but they would with a tuition-grant system.

Since the producer usually knows more about what he is producing than does the consumer, the producer illogically tends to conclude that he is a better judge about the appropriate quality and quantity for the consumer. This tendency is especially rewarding if the producer can thereby obtain a sheltered competitive position in the production of the good. He would tend to produce a quality and quantity in a style related more to that which enhances his welfare and less to what students and parents prefer.

It is easy to see that with zero tuition the university faculty benefits from research and graduate activity that builds an impressive publication record and research status, with the currently less rewarding teaching of undergraduates being relegated to the less "distinguished," lower-ranking faculty or graduate students. The "publish or perish" rule would be less powerful under full tuition, because teaching would become a more important source of student-directed funds. Survival of the better teachers who are weak in publication would be enhanced. It is interesting and amusing to note, incidentally, that students at the University of California are now attempting to protect some members of the faculty from being dropped because of inadequate research and publication. The protection comes by the students "donating" funds to hire the man to give classes; this is a voluntary, spontaneous full-tuition system. If allowed to expand, students would determine who was on the staff and who got the bigger incomes, just as they now decide which restaurants shall survive and prosper.

This is a simple application of the old, powerful, fundamental principle of behavior. The lower the price at which goods are distributed, relative to the market value, the greater the degree of discrimination and arbitrary criteria that the "seller" will display. Its corollary is that the lower the seller's right to the monetary proceeds, the greater his gain from underpricing the goods. The gains to the university administration and faculty from low tuition are classic examples, first expounded in Adam Smith's *Wealth of Nations*. The greater the portion of a college's funds coming from tuition fees, the greater the power of the students and the greater the role teaching will play in the survival and prosperity of the members of the faculty. The less will the faculty choose which students shall attend, how they shall behave, etc. The lower is the ratio of tuition payments, the greater the power of the faculty over the students, because the students are less able to exert significant effects on the financing of schools or departments as a reward for "good" performance—as they can with restaurants. The faculty says "education is different," and students are poor judges of good education; students are swayed by popular, theatrical teachers and do not appreciate the more valuable scholarly teachers. One wonders how students happen to go to the better, and possibly tougher, schools in the first place. The faculty of any college prefers lower tuition—until the budget expenditures cannot be met from nontuition sources. And even then there is conflict of interest within the college between those who are threatened by the budget cut and those with tenure who are not. If the cut, or loss of income, would mean merely fewer undergraduates and fewer *new* teachers, clearly the least difficult resolution from the current faculty's interest is the reduction in new students rather than an increase in tuition.

With zero tuition the state schools have expanded relative to higher-tuition private colleges, and the state university, with its higher-salaried teachers and more expensive education, is more attractive to students than the state colleges and junior colleges. The ex-president and the administrators of zero-tuition institutions correctly insist that *zero* tuition is the great principle underlying the *growth* of the university, but it is not a source of better education for California students. We should not confuse the *amount* of money with the *way* the money is obtained. More and better education, as judged by students, could be obtained at the same, or less, cost with the full-tuition control of colleges coupled to loans and whatever grants-in-aid are desirable.

With full-cost tuition, the less expensive junior colleges would attract students and income from the university and colleges. Predictably, the few administrative voices heard in favor of higher tuition seem, from my observation, to come from junior college administrators who believe they would outperform the university if put on a quality-cost basis of competition for students.

A counterargument to the preceding propositions is that junior college education is "inferior" to university education. Although the quality of the university as a research institution is high, not as much can be established for its quality as a teaching institution to educate college students. The move to junior colleges with full tuition would occur if the more expensive university education were not matched by the higher quality as judged by students and parents. The university would have to improve its teaching to hold students at its higher costs. If it could not, the results would constitute evidence that the high-cost and high-quality combination was not a superior combination of quality, cost, and quantity. A Rolls-Royce gives higher-quality transportation than a Ford, but it does not follow that more Rolls-Royce autos should be produced than Fords. Education must be judged by the quality, quantity, and costs rather than in terms of only those who are educated at the highest, most expensive levels.

Yet, despite this patent fact of life, when faced with a budget cut, the administrators of the state university plump foursquare for "quality at all costs"—for maintenance of quality education for a selected few regardless of how many must be turned away and given instead an "inferior" education. On what criterion is it established that it is better to maintain the level of quality of education for fewer students at the cost of sacrificing education for others? Would one argue that in the event of a social security reduction, we should reduce the number of recipients in order to maintain the quality of those lucky enough to keep getting social security payments? But analogies aside, the elite, authoritarian arguments by university administrators and faculty for a given level of quality, regardless of the sacrifices imposed on excluded students or on taxpayers, are sobering evidence of the seductiveness of self-interest pleading.

The faculty and administration of higher education in California have evolved in the zero-tuition environment, with appropriately adapted behavioral traits. They have learned to use that political structure; they have learned how to appeal to the political processes and to legislators and governors for more financing. They have been almost exclusively reliant on the political process. They praise politicians for statesmanlike, responsible behavior when the university budget is increased; but if it is decreased, they cry of political interference. Having accepted almost exclusive dependence on financing directly from the political and legislative processes, they should not complain of "political interference" when that same political process examines more intently the budget and the operations of the university. Are they really surprised that the venerable law "He who pays, controls" still is effective?

Legislators generally tend to favor direct state legislative financing of education coupled with no tuition rather than full tuition with grants-in-aid. The closer the tuition approaches full cost, the less the power of the legislators over the educational institutions. It is not entirely accidental that Congress used a grant-in-aid system for veterans; there was no federal college system.

We must constantly remember the difference between paternalism and independence. Independence from the competition of political processes and politicians' interests can be enhanced by full tuition, but it will bring greater dependence on competition among educators in satisfying students' whims and interest. Either the students pay and control, or the political processes and politicians do. Yet some of the faculty seem to think they can avoid both. For educators there is no free lunch nor "free" tuition.

The situation reminds one of the Russian plight. Dissatisfaction with the quality of goods produced by Russian firms is sparking attempts to restore market prices as reflections of consumers' interests. While the Russian economists and consumers advocate more control via the market, producers and politicians show far less interest in weakening their power by moving away from socialism.

There remains a subtle, but effective means whereby full tuition would lead to *more* education than if directly provided by government at zero tuition. As matters stand now, an education at a tuition school may be worth $2,000, or, say, $500 *more* than the education at zero-tuition state schools. For that superior education worth $500 *more*, the student would have to pay the full-tuition cost of $2,000. He gets no relief for not using state schools. If education were on a full-tuition basis, this obstacle to more and higher-quality education would be removed. We should not assume that more spending by government for *direct* provision of education necessarily yields more education. This phenomenon, I conjecture, is powerful at all levels of education.

A preference for full tuition implies nothing whatsoever about the desirable extent of aid or subsidy to students. Unfortunately much of the debate has erroneously assumed that zero tuition is a necessary or preferred method of aid while full tuition is a device to avoid aid to students. No matter how much aid, if any, should be given to students, the case for full tuition does not rest on a denial of aid. It rests on the premise that whether or not aid is given to students the financing of schools should be controlled more directly by students and their parents because the kind of education thereby made available is deemed to be better by those who advocate full tuition.

Full tuition, plus grants-in-aid to whatever extent one believes is justified, directs educational activities more to the interest of students and less to that of the university staff. And after all, is it not the students whose interests are fundamental rather than the university's as an institution? Is it the students' interests as reckoned by students and parents rather than the convenience to the educators that is a better guide? My choice of answers is obvious. I suspect that these are the crucial issues on which advocates of zero tuition will differ with me.

My opposition to zero tuition arises because I do not like the way it redistributes wealth, nor do I like the totality of the effects of the kinds of competition it induces relative to that which would prevail under full tuition supplemented by grants and loans. The latter yields more variety of educational opportunities and just as much educational opportunity and, presumptively, greater detectability and survival of superior education. It reduces the producers' control over the products that the customers can have. The influence of selecting their colleges and controlling payments is a trait with high survival in the world outside of academia and which should be cultivated. The decreased role of the state and political activity in administering education is also a consequence I find congenial. Higher tuition would improve the quality of education rather than reduce it. The quantity would be affected not by either a zero or a high tuition, but by how much is spent for education. Zero tuition does not mean more is spent for education, nor that more poor people can attend. To believe it does is to think zero tuition is the only or best way to subsidize or aid students—and that contention raises the fundamental question of what is the best way.

All these consequences seem to work against my interests as a member of a zero-tuition college. If I thought this one exposition of economic analysis and one man's preferences really were capable of converting our system of educational subsidies from the zero-tuition to a full-tuition system with scholarships, loans, and vouchers, I might be less willing to expose it, for the price may be high enough to make me join with those who, whatever may be their reason, prefer the Holy Zero (excuse me, the *free*) tuition system.

WHAT PRICE ZERO TUITION?

ARMEN A. ALCHIAN AND WILLIAM R. ALLEN

Since the fiasco in the Garden of Eden, mankind has suffered from scarcity: there cannot be enough goods and services to satisfy completely all the wants of all the people all the time. Consequently, man has had to learn the hard way that in order to obtain more of this good he must forego some of that: most goods carry a price, and obtaining them involves the bearing of a cost.

Poets assure us that the best things in life are free. If so, education is a second-best good, for it decidedly is not free. But if education is not free, if a price must be paid, who is to pay it? By developed instinct, the economist initially presumes it to be appropriate that payment of the price should be made by those who receive the good. "Those who get should pay" is a strong rule of thumb; the economist will deviate from it only for profoundly compelling reasons.

But general economic theory does not assert that we must charge tuition to allocate resources and distribute educational goods, nor does economic theory tell us that zero tuition is best. And, of course, there is an infinitude of alternatives between all or nothing.

Zero tuition means a public subsidy—a system of individually non-voluntary gifts from the community at large to the recipients. And, as with any system of subsidy, we may ask why this particular group is to be subsidized, what members of the group, to what extent, and in what manner, and what, precisely, is the substance of the gift.

In the California system of zero tuition[1] in the university and state colleges, the particularized gifts go to a small portion of a select group. The community

Reprinted, by permission of the author, from *Michigan Quarterly Review* (Fall 1968): 269–72.

1. Our discussion stems most immediately from the continuing controversy in California over proposed tuition in the state university and the several state colleges. In those institutions, no tuition has been charged state residents, but various "fees" total nearly $250 per year for the university and about $130 for the colleges (non-residents are now charged a tuition of $1200 by the university and some $770 by the colleges). In January 1967, newly elected Governor Ronald Reagan suggested tuition charges of $400 and $200 for the university and the colleges, respectively; shortly thereafter, he proposed the more modest charges of $250–$280 and $150–$160 (in addition to existing fees). In late sum-

has singled out a few of its members as eligible for the gift of some expenses paid at certain schools. Not everyone can receive the gift, and those who do receive it must take it only as zero tuition in a public college in California. Now, such selective and closely specified subsidization may be the very best use we can devise for these resources of the community. But the mere fact of its selectivity, which is not uniform everywhere and at all times, creates some small doubt that zero tuition is certainly the optimal scheme.

Are we sure—indeed, has there been general and appreciable concern—that subsidization of college students is the best use of these resources? The amount of resources involved is very substantial, and they have many alternative uses. There are ways and ways of enhancing the welfare of persons individually and in the aggregate. We would be naïve simply to assume, on paternalistic faith, that this *particular* group should be subsidized and should receive this *particular* subsidy in this *particular* form. And is it perfectly apparent that *all* students in the select group of eligibles should receive subsidization and to the *same* degree, regardless of college performance (above some unimpressive minimum), field of specialization, and personal financial circumstance?

And *how much* should the subsidy be? Defense of zero tuition implies that the appropriate subsidy for every student in a state school is exactly equal to the cost of full tuition. In fact, no basis for this proposition of proper amount of aid has ever been presented. Might the amount not be less—or more? If tuition should be zero, why not include books and fees in the gift? And any living expenses unique to attending college? And compensation for foregone earned income? For are not some frustrated but "deserving" young scholars denied college by these other costs as well as by tuition? And yet, though many speak passionately and confidently in support of zero tuition, few advocate these apparently obvious extensions of the subsidy.

Finally, is it truly self-evident that the *form* of the gift should be waived tui-

---

mer 1967, the university Board of Regents rejected the tuition proposal but agreed to raise "fees" by an amount to be determined later.

A survey by the University of Oregon in November 1966 (many have since been raised) includes the following data for fees-plus-tuition for undergraduate state-residents in state universities:

New York	$500	Indiana	$330
Ohio	459	Oregon	330
Minnesota	375	North Carolina	303
Michigan	348	Texas	156

tion? How about charging tuition and putting at least some of the money thus collected into a scholarship fund? Or perhaps charge tuition and put the proceeds into a loan fund? Or, still again, charge tuition and then subsidize by making grants or loans to eligible students to apply to their expenses in attending *any* college in the world?

The supporters of zero tuition contend that, although the costs of education are less than the gains to the students themselves, some are now unable to finance their education, and a subsidy is required to provide educational opportunity to the poor. But this argument can be deceptive: college-calibre persons are, in fact, rich in their inherited mental talent. Such "human capital" is wealth, and, for the talented, this wealth is of great magnitude. Further, slighting such human wealth is to ignore the difference between wealth and current earnings. A man with a pool of untapped oil is rich, although he is not now marketing his resource. Similarly, the current earnings of an intelligent young student may be small, but his wealth—the present value of his future earnings—is large. College students, even those with little present income, are not poor. Subsidized higher education gives the student a *second* windfall, a subsidy to exploit his inherited windfall of talent. This is like subsidizing drilling costs for owners of oil-bearing lands.

The distinction between current earnings and wealth provides the basis for a second distinction, viz., between subsidizing through zero tuition and providing educational opportunity. Educational opportunity is provided if any person who can benefit from attending college is enabled to do so despite smallness of current earnings. To be sure, one way to provide educational opportunity is by charging zero tuition. But that is *not* the only way and *not* necessarily the best way. Providing educational opportunity does *not* imply that students who are financed through college should be excused from later repaying out of their enhanced earnings those who financed that education.

Educational opportunity can be provided by allowing students to borrow against their future income, which presumably will be enlarged by their present training. (Under a loan system, as contrasted to one of grants, the problem of filtering rich students from the financially distressed would be reduced to trivial dimensions, for the rich would have little, if anything, to gain by borrowing: no inquiries into parental incomes would be necessary.) Even now, both public and private loans are available, but a subsidy by the state would guarantee repayment of educational loans, as housing loans are guaranteed for veterans. Further, students could select from several methods of repayment: some could contract to repay in full with interest; others might choose a sort of insurance system, whereby repayments are related to income, with specified upper and lower limits. Indeed, with today's income taxes, college alumni are repaying part of their educational subsidy, but others are making similar payments without having received such subsidy.

Some are impressed by the size of the debt a college graduate would have to repay. They should be impressed, rather, with the fact that the debt is *less* than the enhanced earnings he has been equipped to receive and is, in fact, an indication of the huge bonanza given the subsidized student by society. Some may not realize that a college education is a very profitable investment, or may lack confidence, or underestimate their possibilities, and hence are unwilling to borrow. But this is no argument for subsidizing moneyless students in the aggregate.

Some people support zero tuition because it redistributes wealth. And indeed it does, but not as they suppose. The present system of zero tuition actually redistributes wealth *from the poor to the rich*. Lower-income groups provide the state schools with a smaller proportion of students than of taxes; the value of college benefits received over state taxes paid is much smaller for the poor than for the rich. The residents of Watts, in short, subsidize the residents of Beverly Hills to attend UCLA. To advance a subsidy to students and not require repayment is to grant students a gift of wealth at the expense of those who do not attend college or who attend tuition colleges and pay for themselves.

Some have advocated plans of education financing to redistribute wealth in the opposite direction: charge every student tuition, but use *all* of the proceeds to reimburse the poorest students for their tuition payments. Channeling all of the tuition receipts into student grants desirably avoids, it has been said, subsidization of the community by the students, although presumably it is acceptable for buyers of other goods to "subsidize" sellers of those goods.

But, to revert to our earlier point, whether one believes it desirable or undesirable to use the educational program as a device—surely a relatively clumsy device—to redistribute, as well as to enhance, wealth, note that redistribution of wealth is *not* required in order to provide educational opportunity.

Another argument for subsidized education is the gain to society in educated people who might otherwise under-invest in education. To the extent that society does benefit from extending a person's education beyond limits determined on solely private criteria, there is a case for subsidization of rich as well as poor students.

But pursue this argument only with great care. For one thing, we must distinguish between *net social gains* and *mere transfers of income* within the community, as newly trained people enter an occupation and thus lower the prices of services sold by members of the group. Furthermore, we must ask if these social gains can be augmented by *additional* education in which individuals would *not* invest without subsidization. Defense of education subsidization, then, on grounds of "external" benefits to the community requires demonstration of *net social gains* from *additional education*, with such gains *unheeded by the student* in his private decisions because the social gains do not affect the marketable value of his services.

This case for subsidization seems perfectly valid at the grade-school level. At least the criterion of social gain versus income transfer seems readily satisfied: the community experiences a net gain (rather than a transfer of wealth) in having its members early taught to read, write, comprehend elementary arithmetic, and follow basic practices of hygiene. That this case for subsidization is equally strong, or exists at all, for education at higher levels through graduate school is much less obvious.

The large question of the *mode* of subsidization (if any) remains. California provides zero tuition for all state schools, for all kinds of training, and for all eligible students, regardless of their income. But, as we have emphasized, providing educational opportunity need *not* require a bonanza through zero tuition. The case for positive tuition need *not* be based on the contention that aid to students should be denied; rather, the basic contention can be that zero tuition is a relatively undesirable *means* of providing aid.

Briefly consider two alternative modes of aiding students: (1) the community directly pays the costs of building and operating the school to provide the education, the aid being reflected in zero tuition, and (2) the community pays students the equivalent of tuition and allows them to buy their education at any school, as the federal government has done with veterans and, in a limited fashion, as New York has done with students in general. The immediate grant of wealth to the student and the financial cost to the subsidizer can be approximately the same in either case, but the results are not. The second scheme directly subsidizes *students*, opening for them the widest possible world of choice and thereby providing them with the best possible educational system; the existing scheme of zero tuition only indirectly subsidizes students through financing *particular schools*, which curtails the student's range of choice and centers control over education in the state politician and college administrator (and faculty member) rather than in the consumer of the product.

Of course, we are not confined to a single alternative to the present arrangement of zero tuition. The general point, let it be remembered, is that charging tuition does not restrict the attainability of educational opportunity. A system of full tuition supplemented by grants to those who qualify—or even better, by ready loans—is not only consistent with but would tend to promote the quality and even the quantity of education.

The financing of higher education poses a classic topic for applied economics: the effects of different means of allocating scarce resources among competing claimants. In general, the economist prefers the efficient use of scarce resources usually induced when receivers pay for what they receive.

The community of California has been extraordinarily generous to the public colleges and university. The investment has been conspicuous, although no more real than the transfer of wealth from those who immediately subsidized the schools to those who have been direct beneficiaries. We are now being told that the great and growing costs of the university are to be shared more equitably: those who get should pay. Even if some type of subsidized higher education is desirable, zero tuition is not necessarily desirable. And if tuition is charged, the university can still survive as a first-rate institution. For budgetary reasons (which we have not stressed), the university may not thus survive without it.

Perhaps state residents in the aggregate have received a positive payoff from subsidizing the university. But to the extent that there has been a net social gain, students are twice-blessed—first, as students receiving a training costing some ten times what they pay in fees and ultimately returning to them a stream of income perhaps another ten times the cost, and second, as members of the community at large. When we consider additionally that the students come from socio-economic strata well above the lowest, we may understandably wonder why it is so often deemed beastly to require these favored few to bear their share of the burden. Those who are blessed only once (and then but indirectly and impersonally as members of the general community) can be excused for insisting that the twice-blessed should make two payments.

Note what can be involved in students putting aside the role of parasites. It need involve, not a curtailment of consumption now by students, but only a reduction of consumption out of tomorrow's income through borrowing. This mode of financing the university replaces subsidization of the privileged students with investment by the students in their own behalf. The beneficiaries of the resource expenditure then make the payment; those who get, pay.

THE PURE ECONOMICS OF GIVING

ARMEN A. ALCHIAN AND WILLIAM R. ALLEN

1. The Utility of Giving

Charity or philanthropy totals to billions of dollars annually. Charitable foundations and colleges are two prime examples—not to mention religious groups and individual gifts. Musical concerts, museums, libraries, and art galleries are open to the public at prices far below those that would clear the market, precisely because the sponsor wants to be charitable. The Ford, Gulbenkian, Mellon, and Rockefeller Foundations, to name but a few of the largest, are supposed to give wealth—not sell it. Almost every university provides services at less than costs because they are supported by people who want to give educational opportunities to (smart) young people. In all these cases of charity, because the price is zero, a long list of applicants must be screened on some other competitive, discriminatory basis. How do the results differ from those of market-price competition? Economic analysis will shed light on that question—perhaps with some surprises.

The *economics* of charity or gifts may seem contradictory. If, according to economic theory, people seek to increase their utility, how then can they give gifts? Are these acts to be set aside from economics as unexplainable behaviour? Not at all. I may believe that other people should consume certain goods, and I may so value their doing that I am prepared to pay. Thus I pay to have milk and food for my children. I may so value other people's reading of good literature that I am willing to pay to make it available to them. For this kind of situation, we see people engaging in charity or philanthropy.

The postulates of economic theory do not say that man is concerned only about himself. He can be concerned about other people's situations also.

From my point of view, I would rather you were richer than poorer, even if it cost me something. It is even possible that a £1 decrease in my wealth could reduce my utility by *less* than a £1 increase in *your* wealth would increase *my* utility. Then I would contribute wealth to you. The likelihood of this happening is

Reprinted from *The Economics of Charity* (London: Institute of Economic Affairs, 1973), by permission of the Institute of Economic Affairs.

stronger if my wealth is large and yours is small. And that is a refutable proposition. As my wealth increases relative to yours, my willingness to contribute to you will increase just as an increasing amount of sweets increases my willingness to give up sweets for ice cream. Furthermore, a *matching grant* would induce me to give still more, because now I know that each pound I give up gets you more than £1. This implies that matching grants should be commonly observed in charity. And they are.[1]

II. The Economic Analysis of Giving

Who Gains What from a Gift?

A gift (unintentional or intentional) can be defined as an allocation at a price below the open-market price by those "giving away" the goods. Suppose I own a house that would rent for £100 monthly in the open market; however, I offer it to you for only £40 as a favour. Suppose you would have been prepared to pay £80 for this house. We now have three valuations: A—the market rent of the house (£100), B—the price at which you *would* have been willing to rent the house (£80), and D—the price of the house to you (£40). We want one more item of information: How much would you have spent on housing if I had not made you this special offer? Your answer we shall suppose to be £65, denoted by C; that is, you would have chosen a smaller or inferior house if I had not offered you the £100 one for £40. The following new concepts can now be specified. The difference between A and D (i.e., A − D) is the total wealth transferred *from* me, the donor. The house is worth £100, and I get only £40 for it. In this transfer of £60 of wealth from me, what did you get?

First, compare what you did pay, £40, with what you would have paid for some house (£65) had I not provided you with this unusual opportunity. This difference (C − D) is (£65 − £40) £25, a measure of how much *money* you can henceforth release every month from housing purchases and use in any way you like. Call this an increase in your "money" wealth, a gift of £25 to you. The quantity (C − D) *could* be negative, indicating that the recipient would spend less on this kind of good if the subsidy had not been offered.

Second, compare the housing expenditure you would have made had this special offer not been available with what the house I made available is worth to *you*. This difference (B − C) is, in our example, £80 − £65 = £15. You now have

1. Income-tax reductions for gifts are another way to reduce the donor's costs of giving money to other people—by making other taxpayers pay more to offset my reduced tax payments.

£15 more of wealth in the *specific* form of housing than you otherwise would have had.

Of my £60 wealth transfer, we have accounted for £40: £25 (C − D) as a *general* (money) wealth increase to you and £15 (B − C) more to you of a *specific* resource, housing; that leaves £20 (A − B) unaccounted for. As far as *you* are concerned, that extra £20 is simply wasted: You have acquired for £40 a £100 house that you value at only £80. Although I have borne a cost of £60, the gift is worth only £40 to you. From your point of view, if I had given you £60 in money to spend as you wished, you would have been better off by £20. This "waste" (from your point of view) of £20 is the third component of the £60 gift.

Do not forget *my* (the donor's) point of view. Is there a waste of £20? If I am fully aware of these implications, and nevertheless choose to make the particular gift that I do, then from my point of view it is worth £60 to me to give you the gain of £25 in cash and £15 in superior housing. It is worth more than £20 to *me* to induce you to live in a house that costs £100 (but which you think is worth only £80). I have put you in an environment that I prefer for you.

For *every* instance in which goods are transferred (from me to you) at less than the free-market exchange-equilibrium price, we can summarise the analysis succinctly if we let

A be the market value of the transferred goods;
B the hypothetical price which, if existing, would have induced you to buy the goods;
C the money you would have paid for whatever amount of the transferred good you otherwise would have purchased;
D the amount actually paid by you.

Then,

(A − D) is the net total cost to me of the resources transferred to you which can be subdivided into the following three components:

(A − B) is the waste, from your (the receiver's) point of view, but not necessarily from mine (the giver's);

(B − C) is the value to you of the extra specific resources made available to you;

(C − D) is the general-purchasing-power wealth transfer to you.

But there is more to consider. We must not ignore the impact that opportunities to capture subsidies or gifts will have on the behaviour of potential receivers in their attempts to qualify for the subsidies. Prospects of competitive applicants can be improved if they spend money or revise their activities so as to reach a more advantageous position, as determined by the allocative criteria used by the donor. Each applicant will be induced to spend an amount, at the most, equal to the expected value of the subsidy (as valued by the potential recipient). This is an extra cost not included in the prior concepts—and sometimes an important source of livelihood for those who can help applicants qualify for these gifts. Examples are lawyers, public relations experts, and politicians.

III. Applications of the Analysis

Business Dinner Dance for Employees

To illustrate the consequences of a gift, let us apply the analysis to an employees' dinner dance sponsored by a business firm. Suppose the cost of the dinner is £14 per person, but the company sells tickets to employees for only £6. Question: Who gets what by this company gift? The quantity A is £14, the market value or cost of the service being sold for £6, which is denoted D (using the letters in the earlier example). We now consider several alternatively circumstanced employees.

Employee I would have spent £14 on a dinner dance anyway, even without this subsidy. His C is £14. If he were willing to buy this particular dinner-dance ticket even if the price had been the full £14, his B is also £14. Now we can carry through the computations. The company spends £8 per ticket as a subsidy $(A - D) = (£14 - £6) = £8$. Employee I gets a cash gain of £8, $(C - D) = (£14 - £6)$ = £8. His gain in *specific kind* of goods is zero, for $(B - C) = £14 - £14 = 0$. From his point of view there is no waste, for $(A - C) = £14 - £14 = 0$. The subsidy has given him simply a cash release of the full amount of the £8 subsidy, to spend however he wishes.

Consider employee II, who does less dinner dancing and would have spent only £7 for dinner dancing in the absence of this particular party. His C is £7. Suppose further that he would have been willing to pay £9 for this particularly elaborate party if the price had been that high, but he would have refused this particular party if the price were higher. His B is £9. For him, $C - D = (£7 - £6)$ = £1; he gets £1 cash gain. His $(B - C) = (£9 - £7) = £2$, which means he gets £2 more of dinner dancing (as he values it) than he otherwise would. And the component $(A - B) = £14 - £9 = £5$ is a measure of the waste of company money. The company spent £14 for something worth only £9 to him. Of the total £8 net cost to the company, £5 was a waste and £2 gave employee II more dinner dancing than he otherwise would have had, and £1 was his cash gain.

And then there is employee III, who does not think the dinner dance is worth even £6. He buys no ticket and gets no gain of any kind.

Question: If you were the owner of the company, what would you think of partially subsidised dinner dances as a scheme to aid the employees to have a good time? Which employees?

Reconsider employee II, who would have paid £9 for a dinner-dance ticket. Why does he not play it smart? Why does he not buy a ticket for £6 and sell it to some outsider for £14, thereby gaining £8? This is better for him than the alternative gain of £1 in money and £2 more of dinner-dance activity. But the company prohibits him from doing so, probably because the managers do not want outsiders at the dance. Then why does not our employee resell the ticket to some other employee? There are two cases to consider. On the one hand, the supply of tickets at £6 may be large enough to provide all that the employees want at that price. But if the supply of tickets is not large enough to accommodate all demanders at £6, the lucky employees who first get tickets could resell them at a higher price and take their gift entirely as generalised money gains, rather than as less-valued dinner-dance activity. Permitting resale is to break the connection between dinner dancing and gifts, allowing some gift to those who do not dinner dance.

To make this analysis strike home, inquire if at your place of employment some have special parking rights not granted to others. If so, apply the above analysis to discern who gains what as compared with selling the parking rights.

Foreign Aid

The United States government grants aid (gifts) to some foreign governments, ostensibly for specific purposes. If the United States government gives $10 million to the Egyptian government to build a dam, what has Egypt gained? What would the Egyptians have done without the gift of aid? Suppose they intended to build the dam anyway, financing it by domestic saving. To that extent, a gift for the dam releases wealth of the Egyptian government for other things. The gift purportedly "for a dam" is actually for general purposes—the Egyptian government now simply has $10 million more than it otherwise would have. Conceivably it could lower taxes—thus giving the Egyptians that much more income for general consumption—or the government itself will spend the extra funds.

Why, then, give the money "for a dam"? One possible answer is that otherwise they would not have built the dam, so the gift does provide one more dam.

The embarrassing implication of this answer is that this use of the money for the dam is so unproductive that the Egyptian government itself would not have paid for the dam. Or, if they were too poor to have done so, a simple gift of $10 million to the Egyptians with no strings on its use would have enabled the Egyptians themselves to decide what were the most valuable uses of the extra wealth made available. Of course, government officials of both the United States and Egypt understand all this, and the "conditional" form of the grant is employed primarily to try to induce the Egyptian government to behave more in accord with the United States government's view of Egypt's interest.

Free School Transportation

Children in state schools are given free bus rides to school. From this gift (subsidy) of bus rides to schoolchildren, who gains what? The answer should now be easy. The parents of the children must be classed according to those who would have provided transportation for their children and those who would have made their children walk. The first group receive all the subsidy as a general increase in their wealth. They can buy more of all things with the wealth which otherwise would have paid for their children's transportation. The other parents get no gain in general wealth, but take it all in the specific form of better transportation for the children. "Free bus rides" for schoolchildren turn out then to be composites of gifts of wealth to parents and of better transportation for children, with some families getting all of it in general wealth, some in mixtures, and some exclusively in more transportation.

The corollary of our general proposition is that gifts might as well be resaleable or given as money by the donors to the extent that the recipients already possess or use the services or resources given to them. If I am given a case of beer each month by some kind-hearted person who thinks he is inducing me to drink more beer, he should note that my family already consumes a case a month. Therefore, I shall temporarily stop buying beer and use the released wealth for other purposes. Whether he gives beer (whether or not he lets me sell it) or money is essentially irrelevant.

iv. Unintentional Charity

Intentional and unintentional gifts cannot always be distinguished. Nor, as we shall see, can we conclude that every allocation of resources made at less than a market-clearing price, even at a price as low as zero, involves a gain to the recipient.

TV Station Franchises

Currently, anyone wanting to operate a new television station in the United States must first obtain permission of the Federal Communications Commission (FCC). Rights to operate a station are valuable, and many applicants appeal to the FCC for authorisation.[2] Each will try to show why he is the proper person. How? In sales of government-owned forests and oil lands, the "right" person is the one who will bid the most, with the proceeds going to the public treasuries. But the law creating the FCC forbids it to allocate channels on the basis of competitive money bids. Nor is "first come, first served" the rule (although it was for radio in the early 1920s). Instead, the commission in some unspecified manner chooses among applicants.

The applicant is asked to show why the community "needs" another station—over protestations of the existing station owner, whose television station's value would fall. Because there is no money-price competition of the open-market-place variety, other competition in terms of applicants' attributes takes on more significance. Money that would have been paid to the government under price competition for that right or "property" will instead be devoted, at least in part, to competition for the commissioners' support. Since something worth millions is at stake, millions are spent seeking the licence.

Criteria of Selection

On what criteria do commissioners select the winner? That is what the various applicants would like to know. They do know that the applicant should be a man of respectability, good moral standing, public service, and high education. A newspaper publisher or a radio-station operator has an advantage, for he is experienced in news collecting and dissemination. If he does not put on religious programmes, if he plays only jazz and Western shows and intends to present few if any "cultural" programmes, he will lose competitive rank. He must detect the preferences, tastes, and kinds of shows that commissioners think the public ought to be shown; then he must suggest that he will present those programmes. He must be careful not to offer explicit, detectable bribes to the commissioners. On the other hand, if in the past he hired some of the

---

2. The number of channels that could be used at one time is not a technologically fixed constant. It depends upon the kind of receiving and transmitting equipment. With more expensive and sensitive receivers and transmitters, the number of available channels could be increased considerably. And the possibilities with cable are enormous.

FCC technical staff to operate his other radio or television stations, of if he is an ex-Congressman, or if he employs an ex-Congressman as a legal counsel to advocate his case to the FCC, this indicates that he recognises able people, and he therefore could successfully operate a television station. All the value of the rights to broadcast accrues neither to the federal taxpayers nor to the winning applicant; instead, part is consumed in legal fees, costs of publicity, production of kinds of programmes the FCC prefers, and other expenses to win the licence. Thus, even though the nominal price of the licence is zero, the costs of getting it are substantial—not to mention the costs of the losers' efforts.

The magnitude of the gift is revealed by the jump in the stock prices of companies that receive licences. Fortunately for the station owners, this wealth gain is transferable: They can sell that station to other people instead of keeping the gift in the form of a television station. Was it the intention of the government to make a gift? The *motivation* of this rationing procedure is to "safeguard" the public and to provide the public with what is "good." The preceding illustration does not imply that the Federal Communications Commission acts irresponsibly. The commissioners act just as anyone else would in the same situation.

More examples could be presented. Competitive prices are not used initially in the United States to allocate licences to operate (a) scheduled passenger airplanes, (b) liquor stores (in many states), (c) taxis (in most cities), (d) banks (in most states), and (e) sugar beet and tobacco farms.[3] But these rights are saleable once they have been awarded. For example, the right to operate a taxi in New York City sells for about $25,000.

Non-transferable Gifts

There is a class of possibly unintended gifts where the allocated goods cannot be reallocated or resold after they are initially allocated. Rights to enter university, obtain a medical training, enter the United States or the UK, join some unions, adopt a child, play golf on a publicly owned golf course, camp in a national park—these rights are often allocated at zero prices or at prices below those that would clear the market. (Consequently, there are "shortages" and allocation by methods discussed in the earlier examples.) Whether or not the allocated item is subsequently resaleable does not destroy the fact of gift. However, that affects the extent to which the gift can be realised as an increase in the recipient's general wealth, instead of only as a gain in a particular kind of good.

3. Similar examples, including (a), (b), and (c), could be given for the UK.

For example, when a municipally owned golf course underprices its services and has a waiting list and "shortage" of playing space, those "lucky" enough to get access receive a particularised gain—if they have not had to pay other costs to get on the reservation list.

Nothing in economic analysis warrants a judgement about which allocative procedures are good or bad. That judgement must be based on criteria derived from other sources.

AUTHORS CITED

Alchian, Armen A., 134n4, 208n49, 215n1, 228n16, 229n19, 272n2, 274n6, 278n9, 282n16, 287n1, 288nn3–5, 293n8, 296n10, 337nn4, 5, 413n13, 444n3, 557n9, 632n13, 664n18, 665n20, 685n91

Allen, William R., 664n18

Ashenfelter, Orley, 201n37

Atwood, Jane, 196–97n31

Averch, Harvey A., 442–43n2

Axelrad, Sidney, 587n9

Azariadis, Costas, 202–3n39

Baker, Tyler, 248n29, 255n45

Barovick, Richard L., 222

Baumol, William J., 442n1

Becker, Gary S., 7nn5–6, 187n16, 187–88n17, 377n3, 404n4, 405n5, 406n6, 442–43n2

Berle, Adolf A., 76n4, 616n3, 618n7, 620n8, 621n10

Bernstein, David, 679n73

Beste, G. W., 521n6

Birch, David, 124n33

Blackstone, William, 33n17

Blank, David M., 522n8

Bork, Robert, 182n5, 240n8, 242n15, 244n20, 245n23

Bradley, Michael, 283n17

Buchanan, James M., 141n6, 667n25, 691n101

Canes, Michael E., 195–96n30

Carnevale, M. L., 360n3

Coase, Ronald H., 126n1, 142n8, 179n1, 207n47, 229n19, 287n2, 663n8

Coleman, Jules L., 661n1, 667n26, 681n82

Counts, S., 580n5

Crain, W. Mark, 282n16

Crawford, Robert G., 215n1, 228n16, 229n19, 272n2, 278n9, 296n10, 665n20, 685n91

Cyert, Richard M., 442–43n2

Darby, Michael R., 189n20

Daum, Arnold R., 198n32

Davis, Joseph S., 565n2

Debreu, Gerard, 539n1, 540n2

De Chazeau, Melvin G., 195–96n30

DeHaven, James C., 517n2

Demsetz, Harold, 134n4, 208n49, 229n19, 274n6, 287n1, 288n3, 293n8, 301n14, 332n2, 663n10, 667n24, 678n72, 681n80

Devons, Ely, 565n2

Director, Aaron, 410n10

Dodd, Peter R., 283n17

Downie, Jack, 442–43n2

Downs, Anthony, 4n2

Dukeminier, Jesse, 687n95

Eisenberg, Melvin A., 284n19

Ekelund, Robert L., Jr., 279n12

Epstein, Richard A., 663n12, 667n27, 681n83, 686n92, 687n94

Fabricant, Solomon, 455n1

Faith, Roger L., 215n1

Fama, Eugene F., 281nn14, 15, 283n17

Feller, David E., 200n35

Fischel, William A., 671n44

Frankel, P. H., 195–96n30

Viner, Jacob, 142n7

Warner, Jerold B., 304n17
Waterman, Alan T., 534n21
Weisbrod, Burton A., 635n15
Williams, Glanville, 33n17, 57n3
Williamson, Harold F., 198n32
Williamson, Oliver E., 179n2, 184n8,
215n1, 228nn15, 16, 244n20, 272n1,
273n4, 278n10, 288n4, 297n11,
442n2, 627n12
Wolfe, Dael, 584n7
Woodward, Susan, 279n11, 300n13,
302n16, 337nn4, 5

Zeller, Frederick, 235n25

SUBJECT INDEX

AAA (Associates for Antitrust Analysis), 238
absentee landlords, 174
academic freedom, 376, 392
acts of God, 18–19
"Agency Problems and the Theory of the Firm" (Fama), 641
agents: moral hazard and, 326; role in contracts, 236
agricultural industry structure, 198–205. *See also* sharecropping
agricultural land ownership vs. rental, 206
air pollution, 145–47
Alchian, Armen A.: colleagues, 258–60; dynamic shortage approach, 524; on nonpecuniary utility, 443–44; "Production, Information Costs, and Economic Organization," 260, 264, 274; work at RAND corporation, 259–60
alienable private property, 99–100
allocation of costs, 613–14
allocation of property rights, 77–78
allocation of resources and goods, 68–69; effects of different means of, 701; international and intertemporal comparisons of efficiency, 557–58; judgments about, 730; at less than market-clearing prices, 727–30; via market prices, 467. *See also* misallocation; optimal allocation of resources
antitrust law: Bell Telephone breakup, 357; development of economic theory and, 346–49; effect on communication among firms, 354; *Monsanto Company v. Spray-Rite Corporation*, 238–57; Oliver

Williamson's discussion of, 339; single entity criteria, 275–76; view of the firm, 267
appropriable quasi rents, 180–85; example, 191–211. *See also* expropriable specific quasi rents; opportunistic behavior
arbitration provisions in labor contracts, 200n35
Archimedian point, 684–85n90
Arizona v. Maricopa County Medical Society, 250–52
assets: financing, 332; intangible personal, 208–11; maintenance issues, 185nn11, 12; ownership integration, 296–97; plastic and implastic, 295–96; quasi-rent value, 180–81; specificity, 324. *See also* brand-name capital; goods; resources
Associates for Antitrust Analysis (AAA), 238
athletes, preferential treatment, 437–40. *See also* college football; professional athletes
Auster, Richard, 160n9, 178
authority vs. power, 600
automobile insurance: accident compensation plans, 611–14; compulsory uniform insurance, 607
automobile manufacturing: industry structure, 192–94; regulations, 610, 647–48
Averch, Harvey A., 442, 444

baby seal slaughter, 88
"bad" allocation, 549

undermining of, 140. *See also* police powers of the state

law of demand, 462–63

laws: limitations to, 54; violation of, 612

Lay Letter of Lay Commission of U.S. Catholic Church, 111–13

layoffs, 311; NLRB ruling, 223–37

leasing agreements. *See* rental and leasing agreements

legal monopoly, 96

legal rights, 12; history of law of property, 33; property rights and, 27–30

legislation: in a capitalist society, 604–8; public ownership and, 613

leisure, definition, 156n5

lexicographic type of utility function, 451

liability, meaning of term, 140–41

liability laws for manufacturers, 607

licensed professions, 77

light and sound rights, 22–23

limited liability of corporate shares, 99, 278–79, 331; impacts of, 300–301

limited profit ownership. *See* profit-restricted enterprises

locational specialization, 665

long-term contracts, 273–76; exclusive-dealing, 193–94; vs. short-term contracts, 183–84n6, 184n11; for teamwork with dependent resources, 297; tenure as, 396

loss, definition, 18

Lucas v. South Carolina Coastal Council: contract theory of common law applied to, 689–90; lower court opinions, 668–70; Supreme Court decision, 670–80; why damages compensable, 677

lumber rights, 630

Macaulay, Stewart, 153n2, 177

Mahon. See Pennsylvania Coal Co. v. Mahon

Malmgren, Henry B., 160n9, 177

management: of corporations, 167; definition, 280–81; in public and profit-restricted vs. privately owned enterprises, 484; relationship to stock ownership dispersion, 617–18; specialization of labor in, 280

managerial behavior: general theory of, 451; in government vs. corporate setting, 638–39; in public vs. privately owned enterprises, 471

managers: compensation, 621–23; competition among, 282–83; competition within firms by, 624–25; of condominiums, 212; conflicts with stockholders, 301–4, 305; in different types of firms, 450; efficiency from competition between, 618; and expropriable specific quasi rents, 306; extent to which they maximize value, 465–67; incentive to respond to market prices, 474–80; inefficient, 463–64; monitoring of, 641; of mutual associations, 634–35; nonpecuniary benefits, 449–50; own utility maximization vs. profit maximization of owners, 441–52; risk bearing by, 619–20; salaries and expenditures, 444, 445; shirking by, in corporations, 167; shirking by, in socialist firms, 166; stock market and performance of, 281; who also invest and own, 640. *See also* employee agents

Manne, Henry, 167–69n14, 178, 645

manufacturers' resale price maintenance, 313

March, James G., 442

marginal cost equalization, 346

Maricopa. See Arizona v. Maricopa County Medical Society

marketability, 74

market-clearing money prices: attenuations in, 88; in firms, 73; in firms compared with publicly owned agencies, 75. *See also* non-money-market-clearing prices

This book is set in Quadraat, a typeface designed by Fred Smeijers and released in various weights and forms in the 1990s. Quadraat is a modern interpretation of the old-style Dutch faces of the eighteenth century, which were noted for their readability and clarity. Early in his career, Smeijers learned the now nearly lost craft of cutting metal type punches by hand, giving him an understanding of how the process of making the physical type affects the individuality of the letters. Quadraat is a striking example of a digital face that unifies these distinctive features in a harmonious whole. Its narrow, upright italic is unusual but works well with the roman text.

TheSerif, designed by Luc de Groot and introduced in 1994, is used in its bold and plain variations for much of the display type.

This book is printed on paper that is acid-free and meets the requirements of the American National Standard for Permanence of Paper for Printed Library Materials, z39.48-1992. ∞

Book design by Richard Hendel, Chapel Hill, North Carolina
Typography by Graphic Composition, Inc., Athens, Georgia
Printed and bound by Edwards Brothers, Inc., Ann Arbor, Michigan